Why Do You Need This New Edition?

Why you should adopt this *new* edition of *Perspectives on Argument* for a more effective and up-to-date treatment of argument and contemporary controversies . . .

❶ Extensive Consideration of Visual Argument. Visual argument is now presented in parallel with written argument, beginning in Chapter 1 and continuing throughout.

❷ Generous Illustration Program. Now includes over 150 images with corresponding discussion questions and writing prompts. The image program is complemented with full-color production throughout.

❸ New Readings and Student Essays. One-third of the 51 essays for analysis in "The Rhetoric" are new, and three-fourths of the 69 essays in "The Reader" are new. Nearly two-thirds of the 120 essays throughout the book are new. Three of the 12 student essays are new. Two new issue areas in "The Reader" cover Environment and Immigration. Global perspectives on the seven issue areas in "The Reader" have been added to this edition. Each issue area is accompanied by a set of related issue questions and essays that provide different perspectives on the issue.

❹ New Examples. New examples, including visual examples, that clarify the types of claims and types of proofs appear in Chapters 6 and 7, and an extended example of how to use the rhetorical situation when viewing or creating visual argument appears in Chapter 3.

❺ Updated Web References. "Web Sites for Further Exploration and Research" have been added or updated for each issue area in "The Reader" to guide students to possible research sites.

❻ Argument Analysis Paper. The new assignment requires students to review and synthesize all they have learned about argument theory and apply it to an analysis of a classic argument in the Appendix to Chapter 10.

❼ Revised Toulmin Description. Emphasizes all six parts in Chapter 5, with increased attention to backing. Also shows how different parts are used, as needed, to make an argument more convincing to a particular audience.

❽ E-Book. A full, electronic version of *Perspectives on Argument* is housed in a book-specific version of MyCompLab®. Visit www.mycomplab.com for details.

❾ Prereading Questions. New "Questions to Answer Before You Read" have been added to each of the essays in "The Reader" so that all essays in the book now include this feature to help students engage with their reading.

❿ Ethical Argument. New coverage in Chapters 8–10 teaches students how to distinguish ethical from unethical argument.

⓫ Revised Worksheets. Ten boxed worksheets have been numbered, shortened, and simplified for easier use. They are listed in the Alternate Table of Contents.

⓬ Online Sources. New information on different types of online sources and Web address extensions has been added in Chapter 12.

Perspectives on Argument

Sixth Edition

 ## Nancy V. Wood

University of Texas at Arlington

PEARSON

Prentice
Hall

Upper Saddle River, New Jersey 07458

Library of Congress Cataloging-in-Publication Data
Wood, Nancy V.
   Perspectives on argument / Nancy V. Wood.—6th ed.
      p. cm.
   Includes bibliographical references and index.
   ISBN-13: 978-0-205-64897-9
   ISBN-10: 0-205-64897-5
   1. English language—Rhetoric.   2. Persuasion (Rhetoric)   3. College readers.
4. Report writing.   I. Title.
   PE1431.W66 2009
   808'.042—dc22   2008039131

VP/Editorial Director: Leah Jewell
Editor in Chief: Craig Campanella
Senior Editor: Brad Potthoff
Editorial Assistant: Gina Aloe
VP/Director of Marketing: Tim Stookesbury
Executive Marketing Manager: Megan Galvin-Fak
Senior Marketing Manager: Sandra McGuire
Marketing Assistant: Jean-Pierre Dufresne
Text Permissions Specialist: Kathleen Karcher
Development Editor in Chief: Rochelle Diogenes
Development Editor: Leslie Taggart
Permissions Assistant: Peggy Davis
Senior Operations Specialist: Sherry Lewis
Manager, Image Rights and Permissions: Zina Arabia

Manager, Visual Research: Beth Brenzel
Image Permissions Coordinator: Richard Rodrigues
Image Researcher: Kathy Ringrose
Senior Art Director: Nancy Wells
Interior and Cover Designer: Wanda Espana / weedesigns
Full-Service Project Management: Sarvesh Mehrotra, Aptara®, Inc.
Copyeditor: Diane Nesin
Composition: Aptara®, Inc.
Printer/Binder: Courier Companies, Inc.
Cover Printer: Phoenix Color Corporation
Text Font: Meridien Roman 10/12

Cover photos (clockwise from top left): Goran Tomasevic / Reuters American LLC / Corbis; Kim Lidbrook / epa / Corbis; Win McNamee / Reuters America LLC / Corbis; Ben Sklar/Stringer / Getty Images News / Getty Images; John W. McDonough / Sports Illustrated / Getty Images; Yannis Kontos / Polaris

Credits and acknowledgments for material borrowed from other sources and reproduced, with permission, in this book appear on pages 746–749.

Pearson Education Ltd, London
Pearson Education Singapore, Pte. Ltd.
Pearson Education Canada, Inc.
Pearson Education–Japan
Pearson Education Australia PTY, Limited

Pearson Education North Asia, Ltd., Hong Kong
Pearson Educación de Mexico, S.A. de C.V.
Pearson Education Malaysia, Pte. Ltd.
Pearson Education Upper Saddle River, New Jersey

Prentice Hall
is an imprint of

PEARSON

www.pearsonhighered.com

10 9 8 7 6 5 4 3 2
Student ISBN-13: 978-0-205-64897-9
         -10:   0-205-64897-5
   Exam ISBN-13: 978-0-205-64906-8
         -10:   0-205-64906-8

Brief Contents

Part IV   Further Applications: Argument and Literature 481

Part V   The Reader 525

Contents

Part II   Understanding the Nature of Argument for Reading, Writing, and Viewing Images   149

xi

Part III Writing a Research Paper That Presents an Argument   363

Part IV   Further Applications: Argument and Literature   481

Part V   The Reader   525

xix

Alternate Table of Contents

ALPHABETICAL LISTING OF ISSUES IN THE ESSAYS

MAJOR ASSIGNMENTS

(Other assignments, in addition to those listed here, appear in the Exercises and Activities sections at the ends of the chapters.)

Issue Proposal, 30, 31
Provides initial information about an issue and shows how to test it to see if it is arguable. Student example, 31–32.

Argument Style Paper, 51–52
Describes student's usual style of argument and analyzes the outside influences on this style.

CLASS PROJECTS

WORKSHEETS

EXAMPLES OF ARGUMENT STRATEGIES IN "READER" ARTICLES

Preface

Purpose

The most important purpose of *Perspectives on Argument* is to teach students strategies for critical reading, critical thinking, research, and writing that will help them participate in all types of argument, both inside and outside of the classroom. In this sixth edition, for the first time, visual argument is made available as another type of argument that students can analyze by using the same tools they use for analyzing written argument. A basic assumption is that argument exists everywhere and that students need to learn to participate productively in all forms of argument, both written and visual, including those they encounter in school, at home, on the job, and in the national and international spheres. Such participation is critical not only in a democratic society but also in a global society in which issues become more and more complex each year. Students who use this book will learn to identify controversial topics that are "at issue," to read texts and images and form reactions and opinions of their own, and to write argument papers that express their individual views and perspectives.

A central idea of this text is that modern argument is not always polarized as right or wrong; instead, it often invites or even imposes multiple perspectives on an issue. Another idea, equally important, is that not all argument results in the declaration of winners. The development of common ground and either consensus or compromise are sometimes as acceptable as declaring winners in argument. Students will learn to take a variety of approaches to argument, including taking a position and defending it, seeking common ground at times, withholding opinion at other times, negotiating when necessary, and even changing their original beliefs when they can no longer make a case for them. The perspectives and abilities taught here are those that an educated populace in a world community needs to coexist cooperatively and without constant destructive conflict.

Special Features

Both instructors and students who pick up *Perspectives on Argument* have the right to ask how it differs from some of the other argument texts that are presently available. They deserve to know why they might want to use this book instead of another. This text, which is targeted for first-year and second-year students enrolled in argument or argument and literature classes in two-year and four-year colleges, is both a reader and a rhetoric. Within this reader and rhetoric format are a number of special features that, when taken together, make the book unique.

▶ **Reading, critical thinking, and writing** are taught as integrated and interdependent processes. A chapter that combines instruction in reading and writing shows how they can be integrated to create better argument. Extensive instruction in critical reading, critical viewing, and critical thinking appear throughout. Assignments and questions that invite critical reading, critical viewing, critical thinking, and original argumentation writing appear at the end of every chapter in "The Rhetoric" and at the end of every section of "The Reader."

▶ **Visual argument analysis** is introduced in Chapter 1 and taught throughout the book. Students learn to apply the same ideas they have learned about written argument to visual argument as well. Images in the book are accompanied by questions for analysis and for writing, further reinforcing the concepts taught in the chapters. In Chapter 9 students learn to create their own visual arguments.

▶ **Cross-gender and cross-cultural communication styles** are presented in a unique chapter that provides for a classroom in which every student can find a voice. Students learn to identify and develop their own unique styles of argument and to recognize how their styles may have been influenced by family background, gender, ethnic background, or country of origin. Also included are international students' perspectives on the argument styles of their countries. Many readings in the book are by authors of varied cultural and ethnic backgrounds.

▶ **Audience analysis** includes the concepts of the discourse community, the familiar and the unfamiliar audience, and Chaim Perelman's concept of the universal audience. Students are also taught to anticipate the initial degree of resistance or agreement from a potential audience along with ways to modify or change audience opinion.

▶ **Explanations of the elements and structure of argument** include the **Toulmin model of argument,** the **classical modes of appeal,** the **traditional categories of claims** derived from classical stasis theory, and the **rhetorical situation.** Theory is integrated and translated into language that students can easily understand and apply. For example, students learn to apply theory to recognize and analyze the parts of an argument while reading text or viewing images and to develop and structure their own ideas in writing argument or in creating visual argument.

▶ **Productive invention strategies** help students develop ideas for papers.

▶ **Library and online research is presented as a creative activity** that students are invited to enjoy. Workable strategies for research and note taking are provided along with criteria for evaluating all types of sources, including those found online. Students are taught to document researched argument papers according to the most up-to-date **MLA** and **APA styles.**

▶ **Exercises, class projects, and writing assignments at the ends of the chapters invite individual, small group, and whole class participation.** Collaborative exercises encourage small groups of students to engage in critical thinking, and whole class projects invite students to participate in activities that require an understanding of argument. Classroom-tested **writing assignments** include the **exploratory paper,** which teaches students to explore an issue from several different perspectives; the **position paper based on "The Reader,"** which teaches students to incorporate readily available source material from "The Reader" in their first position paper; the **Rogerian argument paper,** which teaches students an alternative argumentation strategy that relies on establishing common ground with the audience; the **argument analysis paper,** new to this edition, which teaches students to demonstrate their understanding of argument theory by writing an analysis of the argument strategies in a classic argument; and the **researched position paper,** which teaches students to locate outside research, evaluate it, and use it to develop an issue of their own choosing. **Examples of student papers** are provided for each major type of paper. The writing assignments in this book are models for assignments that students are likely to encounter in their other classes.

▶ **Summary Charts at the end of "The Rhetoric" present the main points of argument** in a handy format. They also integrate the reading and writing processes for argument by placing strategies for both side by side and showing the interconnections.

▶ **WHERE IS IT? A Quick Reference to Major Writing Assignments and Sample Papers by Students** appears on the inside front cover of the book to help students quickly locate frequently visited pages.

▶ **WRITING A RESEARCH PAPER THAT MAKES AN ARGUMENT: Suggestions and Ideas** appears on the inside back cover of the book so that students can locate pertinent sections quickly.

▶ **A total of 120 different readings** in "The Rhetoric" and "The Reader" provide students with multiple perspectives on the many issues presented throughout the book. Twelve of these readings are argument papers written by students.

▶ **The readings provided in "The Reader" are clustered under 16 subissues** that are related to the seven major general issue areas that organize "The Reader." This helps students focus and narrow broad issues. Furthermore, the readings in each subissue group "talk" to each other by offering different perspectives on the issue, and accompanying questions invite students to join the conversation.

New to This Edition

▶ **New images.** More than 150 new images have been added throughout the book, and students are invited to view them from the perspective of argument. Students develop fresh critical and analytical understanding when they view images as possible arguments.

▶ **New image exercises.** Each image in this edition is accompanied by an explanation of the context in which it first appeared and by questions for discussion. Images in "The Reader" are also accompanied by questions for writing. Students learn to create their own visual arguments in Chapter 9. New examples of visual arguments created by students demonstrate some of the possibilities.

▶ **Ethical argument.** An expanded Chapter 8, "The Fallacies and Ethical Argument," teaches students not only how to recognize fallacies but also how to distinguish ethical from unethical argumentation. Criteria for judging the ethical and unethical qualities in argumentation are provided. In Chapters 9 and 10 these criteria are applied to visual and Rogerian argument.

▶ **The Argument Analysis Paper.** In this new assignment students review and synthesize the argumentation theory they have learned in earlier chapters and apply it as they analyze and respond to a well-known classic argument.

▶ **Extended discussion and new examples to further clarify the exploratory paper assignment** appear in Chapter 4. Students are also introduced to the idea of **exploring an issue through multiple visual perspectives.** A new assignment teaches them to explore an issue visually by collecting a set of images that express a variety of perspectives on an issue.

▶ **A revised description of the Toulmin model in Chapter 5 emphasizes the importance of all six parts, with special attention to backing.** This chapter also shows how different parts are used, as needed, to make an argument more convincing to a particular audience.

▶ **New examples, including visual examples, to clarify the types of claims and types of proofs** appear in Chapters 6 and 7, and **an extended example of how to use the rhetorical situation when viewing or creating visual argument** appears in Chapter 3.

▶ **New information on different types of online sources and Web address extensions** has been added in Chapter 12.

▶ **Ten boxed worksheets have been numbered, shortened, and simplified** for easier use. They are listed in the Alternate Table of Contents.

▶ **Oral argument has been moved to the end of Chapter 13** to help students adapt their written research papers for oral presentation in a class symposium.

▶ **One–third of the 51 essays for analysis in "The Rhetoric" are new, and three-fourths of the 69 essays in "The Reader" are new, which means nearly two-thirds of all the essays** in the book are new. **Three of the 12 student essays** are new as well.

▶ **New questions to answer "Before You Read" have been added to each of the essays in "The Reader"** so that all essays in the book now include this feature to help students engage with their reading.

▶ **Ninety-nine images in "The Rhetoric" and 53 images in "The Reader" are accompanied by questions for analysis and writing.** Some of these images support ideas in accompanying essays, and some of them are stand-alone visual arguments.

▶ **Two new issue areas in "The Reader" include Environment and Immigration. Global perspectives** on the seven issue areas in "The Reader" have been added to this edition. Each issue area is accompanied by a set of related issue questions and essays that provide different perspectives on the issue. The **new questions** include "What Is the Status of the Traditional American Family? How Is the Family Being Redefined?" "How Are Web 2.0 Technologies Changing the Way We Live and Our Knowledge of the World?" "What Are the Benefits and Dangers of Genetic Engineering both for Individuals and for Society? "How Important Is Race to American Identity? "To What Extent Does Individual Identity Depend on Ethnic Affiliation?" "Is Global Warming a Problem, and If It Is, What Can Be Done about It?" "How Can We Resolve the Economy versus Environment Debate?" "How Should We Respond to the Global Problem of Illegal Immigration?' "Do Good Fences Make Good Neighbors When Defining National Borders?" "What Is the Relationship Between Immigration and Nationality" and "Is War Inevitable? How Does War Become Integral to Society?"

▶ **"Web Sites for Further Exploration and Research" have been added or updated for each issue area in "The Reader"** to guide students to possible research sites.

Organization

The book is organized into five parts and, as much as possible, chapters have been written so that they stand alone. Thus instructors can assign them in sequence or in any order they prefer as a supplement to their own course organization.

    Part One: Engaging with Argument for Reading, Writing, and Viewing Images. This part introduces students to issues and the characteristics of argument, both written and visual, in Chapter 1; helps them recognize their preferred style of argument in Chapter 2; teaches them to analyze the rhetorical situation when reading, writing, and viewing arguments in Chapter 3; and provides specific strategies for integrating reading, viewing, critical thinking, and writing in Chapter 4. Writing assignments include the issue proposal, the argument style paper, the analysis of the rhetorical situation paper, the summary-response paper, the summary-analysis-response paper, and the exploratory paper.

    Part Two: Understanding the Nature of Argument for Reading, Writing, and Viewing Images. This part identifies and explains the parts of an argument according to Stephen Toulmin's model of argument in Chapter 5; explains the types of claims and purposes for argument in Chapter 6; presents the types of proofs along with clear examples and tests for validity in Chapter 7; identifies the fallacies, provides criteria for recognizing ethical argument, and teaches students to write ethical argument themselves in Chapter 8; teaches students to extend and apply in new ways what they have learned about argument to the analysis and creation of visual argument as they encounter it in all parts of their lives in Chapter 9; and explains Rogerian argument as an alternative to traditional argument and as an effective method for building common ground and resolving differences in Chapter 10. Writing assignments include the Toulmin analysis, the position paper based on "The Reader," Rogerian argument papers, and the argument analysis paper.

Part Three: Writing a Research Paper That Presents an Argument. This part teaches students to write a claim, clarify purpose, and analyze the audience in Chapter 11; to use various creative strategies for inventing ideas and gathering research materials in Chapter 12; and to organize, write, revise, and prepare the final manuscript for a researched position paper in Chapter 13. Oral argument is taught at the end of Chapter 13 to help students who are preparing their research papers for oral presentation to the class. Methods for locating and using resource materials in the library and online are presented in Chapters 12 and 13. An Appendix to Chapter 13 provides full instruction for documenting sources using both MLA and APA styles.

Part Four: Further Applications: Argument and Literature. Chapter 14 suggests ways to apply argument theory to reading and writing about literature. Assignments include writing papers about argument and literature and analyzing excerpts from a graphic novel.

Part Five: The Reader. This part is organized around the broad issues concerning families and personal relationships; modern technology; crime and the treatment of criminals; race, culture, and identity; the environment; immigration; and war and peace. Strategies and questions to help students explore issues and move from reading, viewing, and discussion to writing are also included.

Support for Instructors and Students

INSTRUCTOR'S MANUAL

My co-contributors and I have included six chapters in the *Instructor's Manual*, that provide syllabi, day-by-day teaching journals, and handouts to facilitate classroom management in six different types of argument classes that use *Perspectives on Argument* as the primary textbook. Since these six classes and syllabi have been classroom tested repeatedly, they may be followed or changed and adapted with confidence. One class follows the textbook closely, another employs a considerable amount of student discussion of issues, a third includes a number of effective ways for teaching visual argument, a fourth describes an argument class that can be taught in a computer classroom, the fifth describes a class that can be taught online as a distance education class, and the sixth describes a class that can be taught in a five-week summer session.

Other chapters in the manual provide descriptions of each chapter's contents and the exercises that accompany them, and also answers to the review questions at the end of each chapter in "The Rhetoric." Instructors can save themselves considerable time by reading these descriptions before they read the chapters themselves. A set of class handouts ready for photocopying is also provided. Copies of this manual may be obtained from your Pearson representative, who can also provide you with the address for the online version.

MYCOMPLAB®

The new MyCompLab® integrates the market-leading instruction, multimedia tutorials, and exercises for writing, grammar, and research that users have come to identify with the program with a new online composing space and new assessment tools. The result is a revolutionary application that offers a seamless and flexible teaching and learning environment built specifically for writers. Created after years of extensive research and in partnership with composition faculty and students across the country, the new MyCompLab provides help for writers in the context of their writing, with instructor and peer commenting functionality, proven tutorials and exercises for writing, grammar and research, an e-portfolio, an assignment-builder, a bibliography tool, tutoring services, and a gradebook and course management organization created specifically for writing classes. An e-book version of *Perspectives on Argument* is also available in MyCompLab. This online version integrates the many resources of MyCompLab into the text to create an enriched, interactive learning experience for writing students. Visit www.mycomplab.com for more information.

E-BOOK

As an added convenience, an electronic version of the full text of *Perspectives on Argument* resides in the book-specific version of MyCompLab.

Acknowledgments

My greatest debt is to my husband, James A. Wood, who has also taught and written about argument. He helped me work out my approach to argument by listening to me, by discussing my ideas, and by contributing ideas of his own. He was particularly generous in providing his expertise with communication theory as we discussed the ideas for Chapter 9 on visual argument. The process renewed my faith in peer groups and writing conferences. Most writers, I am convinced, profit from talking through their ideas with someone else. I have been lucky to work with someone so knowledgeable and generous with his time and insights.

For this sixth edition, I owe a special debt to Christy Desmet of the University of Georgia who located all of the new essays and images that appear in "The Reader" and updated and wrote the explanatory material and questions that accompany them. Her imaginative contributions will make this version of "The Reader" especially appealing to the students who rely on it for their reading and writing assignments.

I also owe a debt to the first-year English program at the University of Texas at Arlington. When I joined the department a number of years ago, I found myself caught up in the ideas and challenges of this program. It provided me with much of the interest and motivation to write this book.

For many years I participated in the training of graduate teaching assistants who teach argument. Many of these students, and some are now faculty members elsewhere, contributed recommendations for revisions in earlier editions that remain a part of this sixth edition. They include Bridgette Arnold, Nancy Rosenberg, Terriann Gaston, Martha Warren, Matt Carter, Nicole Siek, Christine Flynn Cavanaugh, Vera Csorvasi, Martha Villagomez, Barbara Saurer, Sara Latham, Vannetta Causey, Donna Brown, Kody Lightfoot, Beth Brunk, Chris Murray, Leslie Snow, Samantha Masterton, J. T. Martin, Brad McAdon, Kimberly Bessire, Cheryl Brown, Mathew Levy, Alan Taylor, Deborah Reese, Toni Manning, Kevin Pajak, Sandi Hubnik, Judy Donaldson, and Lynn Atkinson. Many other graduate teaching assistants in our program have also taught with this book and have made useful recommendations and suggestions. I am always grateful to them for their insights and enthusiasm.

I am also indebted to other colleagues and friends who have helped me with this book. The late James Kinneavy is the originator of the exploratory paper as it is taught in this book. Audrey Wick, a seasoned teacher of argument, has provided me with much counsel and advice. My colleague Tim Morris helped me think through some of the ideas in Chapter 14, and he provided me with many excellent examples of poems and other literary works that make arguments. Robert Leston provided examples for the MLA-APA section. Beth Brunk, Samantha Masterton, Sarah Arroyo, Robert Leston, and Nancy Rosenberg have all provided chapters in the *Instructor's Manual*. Ruth Gerik formatted and typed it. It has been a constant pleasure to work with these bright, energetic, and creative colleagues, and I am grateful to all of them for the contributions they have made to this sixth edition.

I wish I had the space to acknowledge by name the many undergraduate students from argument classes, including my own, who read earlier editions and made recommendations for this sixth edition. Some of them also contributed their own essays and visual arguments to be used as examples, and their names appear on their work. I paid particularly close attention to these students' comments, and I know their suggestions and contributions have made this a better book for other argument students throughout the country.

At Prentice Hall, my greatest debt is to Phil Miller, who got me started with this project, and to Yolanda de Rooy, president of Humanities and Social Sciences for Prentice Hall. I also thank Brad Potthoff, Senior Editor, who helped me plan positive changes for this sixth edition and then provided me with support and encouragement throughout the revision process. Thanks also to Tim Stookesbury, Director of Marketing, and to Sandra McGuire, Senior Marketing Manager, who have always encouraged me with their good cheer and positive outlook. Sarvesh Mehrotra did an excellent job of guiding this book through all phases of production. I owe a big debt to him and also to Diane Nesin who read the book twice, first as copy editor and then, again, as proofreader. She made suggestions and corrections that significantly improved the general appearance and readability of the book. I have felt fortunate to work with such conscientious, reliable, and capable professionals.

Colleagues around the country who have provided additional ideas and recommended changes that have helped improve all six editions of this book include Margaret W. Batschelet, University of Texas at San Antonio; Linda D. Bensel-Meyers, University of Tennessee; Mary Cantrell, Tulsa Community College; Gregory Clark, Brigham Young University; Dan Damesville, Tallahassee Community College; Thomas Dukes, University of Akron; Larnell Dunkley Jr.,

Benedictine University; Alexander Friedlander, Drexel University; William S. Hockman, University of Southern Colorado; James Kinneavy, University of Texas at Austin; Elizabeth Metzger, University of South Florida; Margaret Dietz Meyer, Ithaca College; Barry R. Nowlin, University of South Alabama; Susan Padgett, North Lake College; Randall L. Popken, Tarleton State University; William E. Sheidley, United States Air Force Academy; Heather Shippen, Duquesne University; Diane M. Thiel, Florida International University; Pat Tyrer, West Texas A&M University; Jennifer Welsh, University of Southern California; Shannon Martin, Elizabethtown Community College; Keith Rhodes, Northwest Missouri State University; Kim Donehower, University of Maryland; Lynce Lewis Gaillet, Georgia State University; Carol David, Iowa State University; Sue Preslar, University of North Carolina, Charlotte; John Schaffer, Blinn College; Bob Esch, University of Texas at El Paso; Richard Grande, Pennsylvania State University; Kim Stallings, University of North Carolina, Charlotte; Julie Wakeman Linn, Montgomery College; Raquel Scherr Salgado, University of California, Davis; Perry Cumbie, Durham Technical Community College; and Claudia Milstead, University of Tennessee. I am grateful to them for the time and care they took reviewing the manuscript.

The reviewers for this edition are Carrie Hoffman, University of Texas-Pan America; Joanna Johnson, University of Texas at Arlington; Lucinda Ligget, Ivy Tech Community College; Rene Martin; Miami Dade College; Barry Nowlin, University of South Alabama; Martha Payne, Ball State University; Andrea Powell, Ball State University; Wayne Robbins, Western Carolina University; Gail Rosen, Drexel University; Carol Schuck, Ivy Tech Community College; Rusty Spell, University of Texas-Pan America; Evert Villarreal, University of Texas-Pan America; Scott Warnock, Drexel University; Anna Wiley, Ivy Tech Community College.

I also want to acknowledge the many instructors and students around the country and the world who have e-mailed observations and suggestions for improvements. It is a special treat to receive e-mail from people who are using the book and have ideas for improving it. Indeed, I thank all of you who use this book. I like to hear about your experiences with it, and I am especially interested in your ideas for improving the chapters and readings. My e-mail address is woodnv@uta.edu.

This book has been a genuinely collaborative effort, and I expect that it will continue to be. I hope students will profit from the example and learn to draw on the expertise of their instructors and classmates to help them write their papers. Most writing is more fun and more successful when it is, at least partly, a social process.

N. V. W.

Engaging with Argument for Reading, Writing, and Viewing Images

The strategy in Part One is to introduce you to the nature of issues and the special characteristics of argument, both written and visual, in Chapter 1; to help you begin to develop a personal style of argument, in Chapter 2; to teach you to analyze the context and motivation for an argument, with special emphasis on analyzing your audience, in Chapter 3; and to teach you to develop an integrated process for reading and writing argument, in Chapter 4. The focus in these chapters is on you and how you will engage with argument as both a reader and a writer. When you finish reading Part One:

▶ You will understand what argument is and why it is important in a democratic society.

▶ You will have found some issues (topics) to read and write about or to interpret visually.

▶ You will have analyzed your present style of argument and considered ways to adapt it for special contexts.

▶ You will know how to analyze the rhetorical situation, including the audience, for arguments you read and write.

▶ You will have new strategies and ideas to help you read and view argument critically, think critically, and write argument papers.

▶ You will have experience with writing an issue proposal, a summary-response paper, a summary-analysis-response paper, and an exploratory argument paper.

CHAPTER 1

A Perspective on Argument

You are engaged in argument, whether you realize it or not, nearly every day. Argument deals with *issues,* ideas or topics that have not yet been settled, that invite two or more differing opinions, and that are consequently subject to question, debate, or negotiation. Pick up today's newspaper or a current newsmagazine and read the headlines to find current examples of societal issues such as these: What should be done to reduce global warming? Should the Internet be censored? Should gays and lesbians be allowed to marry? To what extent should one government participate in solving the problems of other governments? How should youthful offenders be punished? What is the best way to provide health care both to people in the United States and in developing countries? Should public officials be held to higher ethical standards than everyone else? Or, alternatively, think of examples of issues closer to your daily experience at school: Why are you going to college? What close relationships should you form, and how will they affect your life? Which is the more important consideration in selecting a major: finding a job or interest in the subject? How can one minimize the frustrations caused by limited campus facilities? Is it good or bad policy to go to school and work at the same time? How much educational debt should you undertake?

Whether they seem remote or close to you, all of these issues are related to larger issues that have engaged human thought for centuries. In fact, all of the really important issues—those that address life and death, the quality of life, ways and means, war and peace, the individual and society, the environment, and others like them—are discussed, debated, and negotiated everywhere in the world again and again. There are usually no simple or obvious positions to take on such important issues. Still, the positions we do take *on* them and, ultimately, the decisions and actions we take in regard *to* them can affect our lives in significant ways. In democratic societies individuals are expected to engage in effective argument on issues of broad concern. They are also expected to make moral judgments and to evaluate the decisions and ideas that emerge from argument. Equally, they are expected to take actions based on these judgments and evaluations—to vote, to serve on a jury, to assent to or protest a policy, and so on.

The purpose of this book is to help you participate in two types of activities: the evaluation of arguments you encounter and the formulation of arguments of your own. The book is organized in parts, and each part will help you become a more effective participant in the arguments that affect your life. Part One will help you engage with argument personally as you begin to identify the issues, argument styles, and processes for reading and writing that will work best for you; Part Two will help you understand the nature of argument, both written and visual, as you learn more about its essential parts and how certain strategies operate in argument to convince an audience; Part Three will provide you with a process for thinking critically and writing an argument paper that requires research, critical thought, and clear presentation; Part Four will teach you to analyze uses of argument in literature; and Part Five will provide you with many good examples of effective argument to analyze and draw on as you create original argument in different styles and formats.

What Is Your Current Perspective on Argument?

What do you think about when you see the word *argument*? It is best to begin the study of any new subject by thinking about what you already know. You can then use what you know to learn more, which is the way all of us acquire new knowledge. See the short list of five actual student responses describing some of their initial views about argument provided here. Check the responses that match your own, and add others if you like.

_____ 1. Argument attempts to resolve issues between two or more parties.
_____ 2. Argument is rational disagreement, but it can get emotional.
_____ 3. Argument can result in agreement or compromise.
_____ 4. Argument is angry people yelling at each other.
_____ 5. Argument is standing up for your ideas, defending them, and minimizing the opposition by being persuasive.

The responses in the list, with the exception of response 4, "angry people yelling at each other," are consistent with the approach to argument that appears in this book. We omit response 4 because no argument is effective if people stop listening, stop thinking, and engage in vocal fighting. "Yes, it is!"–"No, it isn't!" accompanied by a fist pounding on the table gets people nowhere.

Now answer this question: What would happen if a society were to outlaw all forms of argument? In effect, under the law all individuals are to share the same views, and there is to be no disagreement. Here are some student responses to the question. With which descriptions do you agree?

_____ 1. Everyone would think the same thing.
_____ 2. There would not be any progress.
_____ 3. There would be no new knowledge.
_____ 4. Life would be boring.

A key idea in this book is that argument is literally to be found everywhere[1] and that without it, we would have the stagnant society suggested in these student responses. You will become more aware of argument as it impacts your life if you consider the notion that argument can be found in virtually any context in which human beings interact and hold divergent views about topics that are at issue. Further, argument can appear in a variety of forms: it can be written, spoken, sung, or chanted, and it can be read, heard, or observed in pictures that are either still or moving. Argument can be explicit, with a clear purpose and position, as in an advertisement for a soft drink or a brand of blue jeans; or it can be implicit, communicating a more subtle position on an issue that the audience has to think about and figure out, as in some of the photographs taken in war zones. Most issues invite a spectrum of perspectives and views for individuals to hold. Few issues are black and white, nor can most issues be viewed in pro and con terms anymore. Keep these complexities in mind as we now attempt to define argument and describe why it is important to study it and learn to argue well.

A Definition of Argument

Since the classical era, argument theorists have defined and described argument in different ways. Some definitions focus on providing convincing evidence for a point of view on a controversial issue and persuading an audience to agree with it. In this argument situation, a judge or a vote sometimes declares a winner. Examples of this type of argument can be found in courts of law where lawyers argue about whether the defendant is guilty or not guilty or in legislative assemblies where legislators argue in favor of or against new legislation. Another group of definitions of argument emphasize the importance of multiple views and perspectives, learning about them and making comparisons, and reasoning and gaining insights toward reaching an agreement or consensus on a position or point of view that is acceptable to everyone, at least for the present time. Examples of this type of argument can be found in policy meetings in which participants must agree on courses of action and in classrooms where students and professors reason together to establish viable solutions to puzzling questions and problems.

---

[1]I am indebted to Wayne Brockriede for this observation and for some of the other ideas in this chapter. See his article "Where Is Argument?" *Journal of the American Forensic Association* 11 (1975): 179–82.

The definition of argument we shall use in this book is a broad one that includes both of these types of argument: *The goal of argument is to bring about a change in an audience's initial position on a controversial issue. Depending on the situation and audience, at times this goal is achieved by an arguer who presents a claim along with reasons and evidence to convince an audience to agree with the position taken; at other times, arguers create the possibility of agreement by acknowledging different points of view and working to identify one view or a combination of views that are acceptable to most or all audience members.* Both kinds of argument are taught in this book.

The basic method that argument of both kinds employs can be described as **making a claim** (expressing a point of view on an issue that is communicated by the arguer) and **supporting it with reasons and evidence** to convince an audience to change the way they think about the issue. All forms of productive argument include these components.

Recognizing Traditional and Consensual Argument

The definition of argument presented in this chapter allows for two basic approaches to argument, the traditional and the consensual. The traditional approach to argument has been dominant in Western culture. That approach is founded in Greek classical philosophy and rhetoric. Aristotle made it clear in his book *Rhetoric,* written sometime between 360 and 334 B.C., that a person making an argument should find all of the available means of persuasion to convince an audience to change positions and agree with the arguer. You are familiar with this model of argument. You observe it every day when you watch news programs and political discussion shows on television or when you read editorials and letters to the editor in magazines and newspapers. When you engage in argument, either orally or in writing, you probably quite naturally consider or turn to the traditional approach.

▶ **Examples of traditional argument.** One example of traditional argument is the ***public debate*** among candidates for public office or among other individuals who want to convince their audiences to side with them and accept their points of view. Public debates are often televised, allowing candidates to state and explain their views on many subjects; people also write about their views, explaining how their analyses or views are better than opposing positions or views. The judge or decider is the viewing public or a reader, who may or may not pick a winner. ***Courtroom argument,*** with lawyers pleading a case (opposed sets of alleged facts) before a judge and jury, is another example of traditional argument. As in debate, lawyers take opposing sides and argue to convince a judge and jury of the guilt or innocence of a defendant. The desired outcome is that one of them wins.

Another example of traditional argument, known as ***single-perspective argument,*** occurs when one person develops a perspective on an issue and argues to convince a mass audience to agree with this single view. You encounter this type of argument frequently on television and in newspapers, journals, books, and public speeches. The issue and the arguer's position are usually clear. Opposing views, if referred to at all, are refuted or otherwise dismissed. An example might be a politician who wants to convince the public that marriage should exist only between a man and a woman. This arguer provides reasons and evidence and refutes the views of another politician who favors gay marriage. It may not be clear whether anyone "wins" such an argument. Polls, letters to the editor, or a change in policy may present indications about how some members of the audience have reacted.

One-on-one, everyday argument, also a type of traditional argument, can be very different from convincing a judge or a large, unspecified audience. In the one-on-one situation, the person arguing needs to focus on and identify with the other person, think about what that person wants and values, and be conciliatory, if necessary. Each participant either wins, loses, or succeeds in part. Examples might be a salesperson who wants to sell a customer a car or a student who writes a letter to convince a professor to accept a late paper.

▶ **Examples of consensual argument.** In contrast to traditional argument with its emphasis on winning, consensual argument emphasizes agreement. You will probably encounter both of these types of argument in your college classes. In *dialectic,* one type of consensual argument, two or more people participate as equals in a dialogue to try to discover what seems to be the best position on an issue. A questioning strategy is often used to test the validity of differing views. The ancient Greek philosopher Plato used this form of argument in his *Dialogues* to examine such questions as *What is truth?* and *What is the ideal type of government?* You may have seen this type of exchange referred to as "the Socratic method" because Plato's teacher, the philosopher Socrates, asks many of the questions in the *Dialogues.*

Professors sometimes use dialectic to help students think about and finally arrive at positions that can be generally accepted by most of the class. In a philosophy class, for example, the professor may ask the question *How can one establish a personal hierarchy of values?* and then describe a situation in which an individual is faced with a conflict of values. For example, Can one remain loyal to a friend if one must break a law in the process? The professor first asks class members to describe the values that are in conflict in this situation, then to compare the relative strength and importance of these values, and finally to prioritize them in a way that is agreed to by the class. The objective is to discover, through questions and answers, a bedrock of ideas that most or all of the class can accept in common. There are no winners. There is instead a consensual discovery of a new way to look at a difficult issue. Students then may be asked to write papers in which they describe their understanding of this new consensus view.

Another type of consensual argument is *academic inquiry*. Its purpose is to discover, through reading, discussion, and writing, new views, new knowledge, and new truths about complex issues. For example, English majors engage in academic inquiry when they read, discuss, and write about their insights into the motivation of a character in a novel. Political science majors take part in academic inquiry when they find themselves contributing to a new understanding of the benefits of strong state governments. The participants in such inquiry find that there are few clear-cut pro and con positions; there is no judge; the emphasis is not on winning. Anyone can participate; there are potentially as many views as there are participants. The result of academic inquiry, ideally, is to reach well-founded consensus on academic and social issues. Consensus may take some time to emerge, and it may also be challenged later when someone proposes a whole new way of looking at a particular issue.

Negotiation and mediation are conducted in arenas where people must employ argument to reach consensus on plans of action that solve problems. The Palestinians and the Israelis, for example, cannot both claim ownership of the same land, so other solutions continue to be negotiated. Negotiation can take place between two people, one on one, or in a group meeting. A special characteristic of negotiation is that the negotiators usually represent an entire business, organization, or government, and, as a result, many people not present at the negotiating table must ultimately be as satisfied with the final agreements as the negotiators themselves. Often, negotiation involves both competition (for example, both parties claim rights to fish in the same waters) and cooperation (they have to figure out how to make that possible). For negotiation to be successful, all those involved must state their positions, including the views or claims of the groups or governments they represent, and support them with reasons and evidence both in writing and orally. Everyone must be willing to consider alternative views and reasons and to modify their original views in order to reach consensus and resolve the problem.

Mediation is becoming a frequent alternative to a court trial. A judge assigns trained mediators to help parties who are in conflict resolve a problem that would otherwise have to be solved by a judge and possibly a jury. The mediators act as go-betweens and help the individuals involved see their problems in new ways so that they can figure out how to solve them outside of the courtroom. You may be taught methods for negotiation or mediation in your business or other classes, in which case you will be able to draw on what you know about argument to help you understand and use these practices.

A final type of consensual argument you may use frequently is known as *internal argument.* Most of us argue with ourselves when we experience internal conflict because we need to increase personal motivation, make a decision, or solve a problem. New Year's resolutions, to-do lists, and time management charts are examples of internal argument and decision making. As in other forms of consensual argument, different possibilities are identified, reasons for and against are considered, and a satisfactory resolution is finally reached.

Recognizing Visual Argument

At the beginning of this chapter, you were advised to look at the headlines of a current newspaper or newsmagazine to identify some current issues. Did you notice also that many of the headlines and stories are accompanied by photographs and other kinds of visual images? Their purpose is often to reinforce or examine an idea in the written stories, making them more immediate, compelling, and convincing to audiences. Such images function as parallel visual arguments or as the visual extension of the ideas in the written argument. Other images may stand alone, making an argument themselves, without an accompanying story or essay. Stand-alone visual arguments of this type are usually accompanied by a few words to explain their significance as arguments.

Let's take a look at two examples of images that have been used either to further develop and enhance the ideas in a written argument or to make an independent argument with only a few words of explanation to highlight the argumentative significance. As you look at these images, view them from the perspective of argument; that is, determine whether or not each image is about an issue that has not been resolved or settled and that potentially inspires two or more different perspectives or views. Describe the issue and the position the image appears to take. You will often have to infer this information because it will not always be directly stated in words either on or near the visual itself.

Figure 1.1 ■ comes from a daily newspaper and reinforces the ideas developed in an accompanying article about violence in Pakistan on the day former Prime Minister Benazir Bhutto returned to that country after eight years in exile. Her return in the fall of 2007 was controversial because it was resisted by radical jihadists who also harbored negative feelings for the United States as well as by various political opponents. Bhuto favored a democratic government, was supported by the United States, and was a long-time rival of General Pervez Musharraf, the president of Pakistan at that time. Suicide bombers attacked her motorcade as she made her way through Karachi, Pakistan. Later in the year, she was assassinated. This story, which may seem remote to many people in the United States and other countries, takes on much more force

Figure 1.1 *Shroud-wrapped bodies were brought to a morgue from around Karachi, and families went there to identify the dead yesterday.*

A photograph of the aftermath of suicide bombings in Karachi, Pakistan, which took the lives of more than a hundred people and wounded many more. This image serves as support to reinforce the ideas in a newspaper article about these suicide bombings and the effect they have had on citizens. View this image as an argument. What issue does it address? What position does it take? What effect does it have on you as a viewer of this visual argument? What makes it effective?

when accompanied by the photograph in Figure 1.1. It shows some of the results of the violence on individual Pakistanis the day after the first suicide bombings.

Figure 1.2 ■ is a stand-alone visual argument that makes an argument about global warming. It is an illustration from a book titled *Global Warming: The Causes, The Perils, The Solutions, The Actions: What You Can Do* and published by Time Books in 2007. Notice that it is accompanied by a few words of text that explain some of its significance as argumentation. Look at these two images, read the captions, and answer the questions that accompany them to help you think about them as arguments.

Chapter 9 will go into much more detail about visual argument by explaining how it works and how it is different from both written and oral argument. In the eight chapters that lead up to Chapter 9, however, you will discover that much of the same instruction that will help you read and write arguments will also help you analyze the visual argument that is present everywhere in our society. Visual argument provides further evidence for the idea introduced earlier in this chapter that argument can be found everywhere. Look for visual argument on television, in newspapers and magazines, on billboards, signs, packaging and marketing materials, on the Internet, in movies, Web sites, video games, and books. You will

Like a polar bear clinging to a shrinking ice floe in the Arctic Ocean, many of us have held on to the dwindling hope that global warming is a vague concern for the future. But as extreme weather patterns disrupt lives everywhere, it is clear that climate change is an immediate threat to our planet that must be addressed now.

Figure 1.2

9

A photograph of a polar bear trying to get its bearings in a place where most of the ice pack in its native environment has melted. This is a stand-alone visual argument that is accompanied by a few words of explanation. View it as an argument, and read the caption. What issue does it address? What position does it take? What effect does it have on you as a viewer of this visual argument? How effective is it as a visual argument?

also be provided with information throughout this book to help you analyze and produce visual argument yourself.

These examples and explanations of types of traditional argument, consensual argument, and visual argument demonstrate that effective argument takes many forms. Also, it does not take place automatically. Special conditions are necessary if argument is to be effective. Let's look at some of these conditions to expand our perspective on argument even further.

Under What Conditions Does Argument Work Best?

To work best, a productive and potentially successful argument, whether presented in writing, in speech, or in images, requires the following elements:

▶ **An issue.** An argument needs as its central focus an issue that has not yet been settled or has become unsettled. In addition, there must be the potential for the issue to generate at least two or more views. For example, the handgun issue has more than the two extreme views often expressed that people should either be allowed or not allowed to own them. Between these extremes, people take a variety of positions, including the view that owning and using handguns may be acceptable for certain purposes, such as hunting, or that handguns themselves can be modified to limit their use.

▶ **An arguer.** Ideally, every argument requires a person who is motivated to initiate the argument, to take a position on the issue, to obtain and consider information, and to communicate a position to others. This person needs to develop expertise on an issue and be willing to take a risk to express his or her own ideas about it. Furthermore, the arguer should seek to go beyond the "current wisdom" about an issue and find fresh perspectives and approaches that will suggest original insights to the audience. For example, an individual arguing for tougher handgun laws needs to present fresh reasons and evidence to get people's attention and agreement. Michael Moore did this in his persuasive Oscar-winning film documentary about handguns, *Bowling for Columbine* (2002).

▶ **An audience.** An audience for an argument, whether friendly or hostile, should ideally be willing to listen to or read and consider new views or perspectives. The audience should also be capable of understanding, thinking, questioning, discussing, and answering. The arguer may be familiar with the audience's background and values or, in the case of a totally unknown audience, the arguer may have to imagine their background, motives, and values. The arguer should respect the audience and want to communicate with them. It is a compliment to draw someone into discussion on an issue, so the arguer should try to show that he or she cares about the audience, their interests and their context or state of mind. This approach will ensure an audience who reads and listens and does not shut the arguer out or otherwise try to escape. Receptive audiences are potentially willing to change their minds, a desirable outcome of argument.[2] Consider, for example, an audience member who favors handgun ownership, who is a parent of schoolchildren, and who is willing to think about an opposing view because a respectful fellow parent has written a letter to the editor describing the problem of children carrying handguns to school.

▶ **Common ground.** Effective argument requires the establishment of some common ground between the audience and the arguer that is relevant to the issue. If two parties are too far apart and share no common ground, they usually do not understand one another well enough to engage in dialogue. For example, people who disagree on the abortion issue often find themselves at a standoff, they fight rather than argue, and their disagreement sometimes results in violence. At the other extreme, if two parties are already in complete agreement, there is usually no need to argue. For example, two parents who agree that their child should go to college do not argue about that part of the child's future. Common ground may be established between an arguer and an audience through the discovery of common interests—common ideas, experiences, motives, or values—or even through recognizing common friends or enemies. As soon as two parties realize they have something in common, they can more easily achieve identification, even if it is minimal, and engage in constructive argument. Imagine, once again, two parties who disagree on handgun ownership. One party believes handgun ownership should be forbidden in order to stop random killing. The other party believes people should own handguns to protect themselves from random killers. Both agree that such killing is bad and must be stopped, and this basic agreement provides the common ground they need to begin to engage in constructive argument about handgun ownership. Figure 1.3 ■ (on page 12) diagrams these possible situations.

▶ **A forum.** People need forums for argument so they can feel creative and know they will be heard. Available forums include public places for argument, such as the courtroom or legislative assembly; much more widely available forums include various media, such as magazines, journals, newspapers and other print sources, television and radio programs of all sorts, motion pictures, the arts, and photographs and other graphic materials. College is a forum for argument. Professors and students argue in class, at meals, and in dorms and apartments. Outside speakers present argument. The argument class, with its discussions, papers, and other assignments, can be an excellent forum for practicing argument, particularly if both the students and the instructor work to create an environment in which all students participate and respect one another.

▶ **Audience outcomes.** Successful arguments should produce changes in the audience. At times, the arguer convinces the audience, and the members of the audience change their minds. Sometimes a successful negotiation is achieved: people find themselves in consensus, a decision is reached, and a plan of action is started. Other arguments may not have such clear-cut results. A hostile audience may be brought to a neutral point of view. A neutral audience may decide it is

[2]Some of the observations in this chapter about the special conditions for argument, especially for the audience, are derived from Chaim Perelman and Lucie Olbrechts-Tyteca, *The New Rhetoric: A Treatise on Argumentation* (Notre Dame, IN: University of Notre Dame Press, 1969), pt. 1.

11

Figure 1.3 Establishing Common Ground.

THE ISSUE: SHOULD LIMITS BE PLACED ON HANDGUN OWNERSHIP?

Possibility 1: *Complete agreement and no argument.*
Two individuals believe that all private citizens should be allowed to own one or more handguns to protect themselves from random shooters. They agree totally and share the same common ground. They have nothing to argue about.

Possibility 2: *Total disagreement, no common ground, and no argument.*
One individual believes private citizens should have the right to own handguns to protect themselves from random shooters, and another believes that no private citizen should own handguns for any purpose. They disagree totally, and there is no common ground. Productive argument is nearly impossible.

Possibility 3: *Two parties discover something in common, and there is a possibility of argument.*
The two parties discover they each hold their positions because of their fear of random shooters. One wants to own a handgun to kill a random shooter in self-defense. The other wants to banish handguns so that random shooters will have trouble obtaining them. They have an important point in common: they both want to stop random shootings. They share common ground on that point, even though they may disagree on other points. The common ground creates the possibility for productive argument about what can be done to stop random shooting, the ultimate goal.

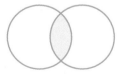

important to take a stand. There are times when it is a significant accomplishment just to get the audience's attention and raise the level of consciousness of those engaged. This success can lay the groundwork for a possible future change of minds.

How much can you expect to change people's thinking as you discuss and write about issues that are important to you or that you think are important to

12

examine? For students in argument class, this can be an urgent question. They wonder whether they must convince their teachers as well as their classmates of their point of view in every paper or presentation if they are to achieve good grades. Such a demand is too great, however, since audiences and the outcomes of argument vary too much. Convincing the teacher and your fellow students that the argument paper is effective with a particular audience is a good—and probably the best possible—outcome in argument class. As one professor put it, "My ambition is to return a paper and say that I disagreed with it completely—but the writing was excellent—A!"[3]

Under What Conditions Does Argument Fail?

We have just examined the optimal conditions for argument. Now, let's look at the conditions that can cause it to flounder or fail.

▶ **No disagreement or reason to argue.** We have already seen that no argument can take place when there is no real disagreement, no uncertainty, or no possibility for two or more views. Also, neutral people who do not have enough interest in an issue to form an opinion do not argue. For example, people who do not use computers may be neutral about the issues surrounding spam e-mail. Argument also cannot take place unless people perceive an issue as a subject for argument. Orientation leaders who try to persuade students to consider one major over another will not succeed with students who have already decided on their majors.

▶ **Risky or trivial issues.** Big or risky problems are difficult for some people to argue about because they can call for radical or sizable change. Finding a new career or dissolving a longtime relationship may fit into this category, and many people, wisely or not, tend to leave such difficult issues alone rather than argue about them. Religious issues or issues that threaten global disaster are also sometimes too big, too emotional, or too scary for many people to argue about them. At the other extreme, some issues may be perceived as low risk, trivial, boring, or even ridiculous. Some family arguments fall into this category, such as what to eat for dinner or who should take out the trash. One person may care, but the rest do not.

▶ **Difficulty in establishing common ground.** We have pointed out that arguments that lack common ground among participants are not effective. You may encounter difficulties when trying to establish common ground with those who have made up their minds on certain issues and who no longer want to listen or consider a change. Those individuals who hold fast to prejudiced beliefs about various groups of people, for example, may dismiss information that defies their favorite stereotypes. It is also difficult to argue with some religious people who take certain issues on faith and do not perceive them as subjects for argument. Finally,

---

[3]Hilton Obenzinger, "The Israeli–Palestinian Conflict: Teaching a Theme-Based Course," *Notes in the Margins* (Winter 1994), 12.

Figure 1.4 *When Argument Fails.*

Cartoons and comic strips often make visual arguments

argument cannot take place when one party is not motivated to argue. "Don't bring that up again" or "I don't want to discuss that" puts an end to most argument.

◗ **Standoffs or fights that result in negative outcomes.** When argument is not working, as in some of the situations just described, the outcomes are negative also. For example, a standoff occurs, the parties assert or retreat to their original views, and then refuse to be moved. In another instance, emotions may be strong, verbal fighting breaks out, and extreme views are expressed. No one agrees with anyone else. People shake their heads and walk away, or they become hurt and upset. Some individuals may become strident, wanting to debate everyone to demonstrate that they are right. When classroom argument results in such negative outcomes, some students drop the class, others fall silent and refuse to participate, and everyone becomes anxious.

One important aim of this book is to provide you with the insight and skill to manage these negative situations so that more constructive argument can take place. Students are in an excellent position to overcome much of the fear, resistance, and aversion associated with difficult issues and, by using evidence and good sense, get down to work and face some of them. Understanding audience members, especially their attitudes, needs, and values, is an important first step. Another useful idea to keep in mind is that most arguers have more success with certain audiences than with others, depending on the amount of common ground. Even in the most difficult situations, some common ground can be found among people who seem to disagree on almost everything. Recent research suggests that one vehicle for establishing common ground is through narratives, with each side relating personal experiences and stories. Even the most hostile adversaries can usually relate to one another's personal experiences and find unity in the common villains, heroes, or themes in their stories. In establishing common ground through stories, participants often find that the issues themselves change or are transformed in ways that make them easier for both parties to argue.[4]

[4]Linda Putnam, in the keynote speech to the Texas Speech Communication Association Conference, Corpus Christi, TX, October 1993, reported these results from her study of negotiations between teachers and labor union leaders.

14

Arguing effectively in difficult situations requires a conscious effort to avoid both stereotypical reactions and entrenched behavioral patterns. Past habits must be replaced with new strategies that work better. It is sometimes difficult to make such changes because habits can be strong, but it is possible to do so, and the stakes are often high, especially when the choice is constructive argument or verbal fighting and standoffs.

Distinguish between Ethical and Unethical Argument

Throughout this book you will be given information to help you distinguish between *ethical argument*, which approaches issues in insightful, useful, and beneficial ways, and *unethical argument*, which manipulates an audience and may even harm it. An example of an ethical argument might be a plan for an effective and economical way to rebuild an area that has been destroyed by hurricanes, floods, or fire. An example of unethical argument might be an invitation to acquire a new credit card that tempts the user to incur a huge debt with high interest that will be either difficult or impossible to pay back. This second example of an unethical argument may also be accompanied by a photograph of people who have acquired new clothes, new cars, and exciting new lifestyles by using their new credit cards. You may recognize this image as dishonest, manipulative, and unethical, but it can still be persuasive if the viewer longs for the particular benefits promised by the new card.

To help you distinguish ethical from unethical argument, consider the arguer's general approach (whether it is traditional or consensual and whether it is accompanied by visuals or not), the specific purpose of the argument (to restore a community or to make money at others' expense), the general competency and reliability of the arguers (a government bureau with access to funds or a company that makes its money by charging high interest rates), and the quantity, quality, and reliability of the information presented. Learn to detect misleading and biased information as well as information that is untrue. Chapters 7, 8, and 9 will provide you with additional information to help you do this, but you can use your common sense as well as your moral sense now to help you evaluate argument and make such judgments.

Part of evaluating argument requires that you read, listen, look, and analyze objectively, without making negative prejudgments. This can be difficult when you encounter opinions and values different from your own. To help you maintain your objectivity, think of yourself as a fair, unbiased person who needs to gain information and an understanding of it before you respond. When you do respond, think of yourself as a capable and ethical arguer who is willing to evaluate and participate in argument because it is important to you and to the society in which you live.

It is time now to think about issues that you might want to write about as you practice argument method, change past habits, and perhaps experiment with new strategies to help you argue more effectively.

Engaging with Issues

To summarize, the most easily arguable issues are those that invite two or more views, that are perceived by all parties as issues, that are interesting and motivating to all participants, and that inspire research and original thought. They also promise common ground among participants, and they do not appear too big, too risky, too trivial, too confusing, too scary, or too specialized to discuss profitably. You may, however, find yourself drawn to some of the more difficult issues that do not meet all of these criteria, and you should not necessarily shun them because they are difficult. You will need to work with your audience in creative ways and consider the entire context for argument, regardless of the nature of the issues you select. Most important at this point is that you identify several issues that are arguable and important to you and to your classroom audience. Identifying issues will help you keep a high level of motivation and receive the maximum instructional benefits from argument class. Finding arguable issues yourself is much better than accepting assigned issues as writing topics.

So, now the search begins. What will help you search out and select arguable issues? Issues exist in contexts, and the issues most engaging to you will probably emerge from the parts of your life that demand your greatest attention and energy. For example, people who are compellingly engaged with their professions think about work issues; new parents think about child-rearing issues; dedicated students think about issues raised in class; and many teenagers think about peer-group issues. To begin the search for your issues, examine those parts of your life that demand your most concentrated time and attention right now. Also, think about the special characteristics of issues in general. Here are a few of them.

▶ **Issues are compelling.** People get excited about issues, and they usually identify with a few in particular. Most people can quickly name one or more issues that are so important and so interesting to them that they think about them often, sometimes daily. If you live in the Northwest, for example, the preservation of old-growth forests may be an issue for you. If you are preparing for a career in education, creating equal access to quality education may be an issue you care about. Can you think of particular issues that are compelling to you?

▶ **Issues often originate in dramatic life situations.** Things happen all around us—global terrorism seems out of control, people find they can download music from the Internet, but whether to pay or how to pay for it becomes an issue, Congress proposes legislation that would provide health care for poor children, and the president vetoes it, the number of illegal immigrants entering the United States increases. As the issues around us change, we inevitably respond with questions: What should be done to stop global terrorism? How much is a song that is available on the Internet worth? Who should be responsible for paying for children's health care, the government or the parents of the children? Should U.S. borders be patrolled, or should immigrants be offered work permits? Pay attention to the stories that are newsworthy this week, and identify the issues associated with them. Select the ones that interest you the most.

▶ **Current issues can be linked to enduring issues that have engaged people for ages.** For example, the controversy about genetically engineering new plant and animal life is related to age-old issues associated with the preservation of life as it has evolved on this planet: Will genetic engineering help cure human disease? Or will genetic engineering be profoundly destructive to existing life forms? Affirmative action issues are linked to the enduring issue of whether or not all people are created equal: Will affirmative action contribute to racial profiling? Or will it actually decrease discrimination? Look at Box 1.1 ■ for additional examples of contemporary public issues we have linked with enduring issues to demonstrate the timeless quality of many of them. See if you can add examples as you read through those in the "Current" column.

Box 1.1	Examples of Current and Enduring Public Issues.

▶▶▶ **What Are Some Public Issues?**

CURRENT ISSUES	ENDURING ISSUES
Ways and Means Issues	
Should everyone pay taxes? In what proportion to their income?	From what sources should a government obtain money, and how should it spend it?
Should free trade be limited?	
How much business profit can be sacrificed to keep the environment clean and safe?	
Should scholarships and fellowships be taxed?	
How can we reduce our dependence on foreign oil?	
How should we finance health care?	
Is the national debt too high, and if so, what should be done about it?	
Quality of Life Issues	
Should more resources be directed to protecting the environment?	What is a minimum quality of life, and how do we achieve it?
Are inner cities or rural areas better places to live?	
How can we improve the quality of life for children and senior citizens?	
What effect will global climate change have on our lives?	

17

continued

Box 1.1	*continued*

CURRENT ISSUES	ENDURING ISSUES
Personal Rights versus Social Rights Issues	
Should individuals, the government, or private business be responsible for the unemployed? Health care? Day care? The homeless? Senior citizens? Drug addicts? People with AIDS? Race problems? Minority problems? Dealing with criminals? Worker safety? Deciding who should buy guns?	Can individuals be responsible for their own destinies, or should social institutions be responsible? Can individuals be trusted to do what is best for society?
War and Peace Issues	
How much should the government spend on the military? Should the United States remain prepared for a major world war? Should you, your friends, or your family be required to register for the draft? To what extent should a government pursue negotiation as an alternative to war?	Is war ever justified, and should countries stay prepared for war?
Self-Development Issues	
What opportunities for education and training should be available to everyone? How well are job-training programs helping people get off welfare and find employment? Should undocumented workers be allowed the same opportunities to participate in society as citizens?	What opportunities for self-development should societies make available to individuals?
Human Life Issues	
Should abortions be permitted? Should capital punishment be permitted? Is mercy killing ever justifiable? Should stem cell research be allowed?	Should human life be protected under any conditions? What or who will define the limits of a person's control of their own life? And what or who limits a government's interest or control?

continued

Box 1.1 *continued*

Foreign Affairs Issues

Which is wiser, to support an American economy or a global economy?

How much foreign aid should we provide, and to which countries?

Should college graduates be encouraged to participate in some type of foreign service like the Peace Corps?

Should the United States defend foreign countries from aggressors?

In world politics, how do we balance the rights of smaller countries and different ethnic groups against the needs of larger countries and international organizations?

Law and Order Issues

Is the judicial system effective?

Does the punishment always fit the crime?

How serious a problem is racial profiling?

How can global terrorism be eradicated?

To what degree have we sacrificed our privacy for national security?

What is an appropriate balance between the welfare and protection of society as a whole and the rights of the individual?

▶ **Issues go underground and then resurface.** Public concern with particular issues is not constant. Experts may think about their issues continuously, but the public usually thinks about an issue only when something happens that brings it to public attention. How to deal with increasing population is an example of such an issue. Experts think about that issue almost daily, but the general public may note it or think about it only when new information is released. For example, in 1999 the world's population reached six billion people. It had doubled in only forty years, a fact that prompted a considerable amount of argument in the media, particularly about future population growth and the ability of the planet to sustain it. As one commentator stated, the media often make arguments out of the news. Persistent issues are, of course, always alive in the background and always important, but we do not think about all of them all of the time. Think back. Are there some issues that used to concern you that you have neither thought about nor read about for a long time? What are they?

▶ **Issues sometimes are solved, but then new ones emerge.** Some issues command so much public attention that the people who can do something about them finally perceive them as problems and pass laws or take other measures to solve them. As soon as an issue is solved, however, other, related issues spring up in its place. For example, for many years, people argued about what to do about health care. As soon as health maintenance organizations (HMOs) became widely accessible, new issues emerged about the quality of care that patients received in these organizations and how physicians could profit economically from these changes in the delivery of health care. The present-day health care debate is motivated by the millions of uninsured individuals. Are there other issues of this type that might interest you? Think of problems that now seem solved but probably are not fully solved for all people or for all times.

▶ **Issues seem to be getting more complex.** Issues seem to become more and more complex as the world becomes more complex. In an interview, the actress Susan Sarandon, who has always been engaged with social issues, stated that in the mid-to-late 1960s, when she was in college, the issues seemed simpler, more black and white. The issues at that time, for example, centered on civil rights and the Vietnam War. "We were blessed with clear-cut issues," she says. "We were blessed with clear-cut grievances. Things were not as gray as they are now."[5]

Because issues are now more complex, people need to learn to engage with them in more complex ways. The word *perspectives,* as used in this book, refers not only to a broader perspective on issues and argument itself, including viewing images and reading essays as though they were arguments when that is appropriate, but also to the variety of perspectives that individuals can take or must accommodate others taking on particular issues. Few issues are black and white, and not many can be viewed in pro or con terms anymore. Most invite several different ways of looking at them and require language that reflects their complexity.

As you develop your own perspectives on the complex issues that engage you, keep in mind that it takes many years to become an expert. You will want to look at what experts say and write, though you will not have the background and information to write as comprehensively as they do. When you write your argument, you will want to research and write on a limited aspect of the issue you engage, one that you can learn enough about. Limiting your topic will permit you to get the information and gain the perspective to be convincing. Suggestions that can help you limit your approach to a complex issue will be made in future chapters.

How Should You Engage with Issues?

Remember that *issues are everywhere.* Listen for issues in lectures and look for them in your textbooks. Ask your professors to identify the major issues in their fields. Box 1.2 ▪ page 21 illustrates some of the issues you are likely to encounter in your other college classes. These are examples of issues that your professors argue about, the subjects for academic inquiry. You may be expected to take positions and develop arguments yourself on these or similar issues if you take classes in some of these fields.

---

[5]Ovid Demaris, "Most of All, the Children Matter." *Parade,* March 1, 1992, 4–5.

Box 1.2   Examples of Academic Issues across the Disciplines.

▶▶▶ What Are Some Academic Issues?

In Physics—Is there a unifying force in the universe? Is there enough matter in the universe to cause it eventually to stop expanding and then to collapse? What is the nature of this matter?

In Astronomy—What elements can be found in interstellar gas? What is the nature of the asteroids? What criteria should be used to identify a new planet?

In Biology—What limits, if any, should be placed on genetic engineering?

In Chemistry—How can toxic wastes best be managed?

In Sociology—Is the cause of crime social or individual? Does television have a significant negative effect on society? What effects do computers have on their users?

In Psychology—Which is the better approach for understanding human behavior, nature or nurture? Can artificial intelligence ever duplicate human thought?

In Anthropology—Which is more reliable in dating evolutionary stages, DNA or fossils?

In Business—Can small, privately owned businesses still compete with giant conglomerate companies? Are chief executive officers paid too much?

In Mathematics—Are boys naturally better than girls at learning math? Should the use of calculators be encouraged? Should calculators be allowed in testing situations?

In Engineering—How important should environmental concerns be in determining engineering processes? To what extent, if any, are engineers responsible for the social use of what they produce? How aggressive should we be in seeking and implementing alternative sources of energy? Should the government fund the development of consumer-oriented technology to the same extent that it funds military-oriented technology?

In History—Have historians been too restrictive in their perspective? Does history need to be retold, and if so, how? Is the course of history influenced more by unusual individuals or by socioeconomic forces?

In Political Science—Where should ultimate authority to govern reside: with the individual, the church, the state, or social institutions? Is power properly divided among the three branches of government in the United States?

In Communication—How can the best balance be struck between the needs of society and freedom of expression in the mass media? How much impact, if any, do the mass media have on the behavior of individuals in society?

In English Literature—Is the concept of literature too narrowly focused in English departments? If yes, what else should be considered literature?

As you read, try to add examples from your other courses. Read newspapers and newsmagazines, look at images to get ideas (see Figure 1.5 ■ on page 22), listen to public radio, and watch television programs that hold discussions of issues. Browse through some of the newly acquired books in the library and look for issues. Listen for issues in conversations and discussions with friends and family.

Figure 1.5 *This ramshackle, overcrowded school near Kindu on the Congo River exemplifies the problems Congo faces in building a functioning government.*

Develop the habit of looking at images to help you find issues you may want to write about. This image reinforces some of the ideas in a newspaper article about the problems that exist in Congo, Africa. What issues does it raise for you? For five minutes, quickly write what comes into your mind as you look at this picture. Read what you have written. What emerges that might be a possible future paper topic?

22

Identify campus issues. If you attend a house of worship or belong to organizations, listen to the issues that surface there.

As you watch for and think about the issues that might engage you, start making a list of those you particularly want to learn more about. Make a corresponding list of some of the other groups or individuals who may also be interested in these topics and jot down the views they may hold. Such lists will come in handy when it is time to select topics for your argument papers and begin analyses of your potential audiences.

Review Questions

1. What did you think of when you encountered the word *argument* as you began to read this chapter? What do you think now?
2. Provide three examples of your own to illustrate the statement "Argument is everywhere." One of your examples should be a visual argument.
3. Describe traditional and consensual argument. Give two examples of each.
4. What are some of the conditions necessary for argument to work best?
5. What are some of the conditions that may cause argument to fail?

Exercises and Activities

A. Class Project: Understanding Common Ground

1. *Build common ground with your classmates.* Create pairs of students, appoint one in each pair as the scribe, and have each pair take five minutes to discuss and record ideas, experiences, and so on that they have in common. Now create groups of four students by teaming two pairs, appoint a scribe for this group, and have the groups take five minutes to discuss and record what all four members have in common. The scribes then give one-minute reports about what each group has in common. As you listen to these reports, a sense of what the whole class has in common will emerge.

2. *Discover common ground about argument.* Return to your groups of four for five minutes and have the scribes record answers to these questions: (1) What do you think of when you hear the word *argument*? (2) What effect might finding common ground have on your ideas about argument? Finally, have the scribes take two minutes to report to the class on these findings.

3. *Write about common ground.* Write for five minutes about the common ground you think already exists in your classroom. What do you and your classmates have in common? How do you differ? How are your ideas about argument and common ground similar to or different from those of your classmates? What effect will common ground in your class have on the argument that takes place there? Discuss what you have written with the class.

B. Class Project: "Argument Is Everywhere"

1. Test the idea that argument can be found everywhere. Each member of the class should bring in an example of an argument and explain why it can be defined as argument. Each example should focus on an issue that people are still arguing about and on which there is no general agreement. Each student should also define a position on the issue, and the position should be supported with reasons and evidence. Look for examples in a variety of contexts: newspapers, magazines, the Internet, television, motion pictures, music, sermons, other college classes, conversations, and printed material you find at work, at school, and at home.

   Bring in actual examples of articles, images, letters to the editor, bumper stickers, advertisements, or other easily transportable argument formats, or provide clear and complete descriptions and explanations of argument sources you cannot bring to class, such as lectures, television shows, or billboards. Students should give two- to three-minute oral reports on the example of argument they have selected, including a description of the issue and some of the reasons and evidence offered. This is most easily achieved by completing the statement "This arguer wants us to believe . . . , because. . . ." The class should decide whether all examples described in this activity are indeed examples of argument.

23

2. State whether you think the argument you have provided is ethical or unethical, and say why.[6]

C. Reading, Group Work, and Class Discussion: What Makes a Good Written Argument?

Read the following two argument essays. Then, in small groups, answer the questions listed below for each of them.

1. What is the issue?

2. What is the author's position on the issue?

3. What reasons and evidence are given to support the author's position?

4. What makes each of these arguments successful?

5. What are the weaknesses in the arguments, if any?

Finally, in class discussion, compile a list of the best as well as the weakest features of argumentation in each essay. Keep a copy of this list. It is a starting point. You will add to it as you learn more about what it takes to make a good argument.

BEFORE YOU READ: Who pays for your college education? How do you feel about this arrangement?

ESSAY #1   **PAY YOUR OWN WAY! (THEN THANK MOM)**[*]
Audrey Rock-Richardson

The author, who lives in Utah, wrote this essay in 2000 after she had completed her college education. She wonders why more students do not do what she did.

1   Is it me, or are students these days lazy? I'm not talking about tweens who don't want to do their homework or make their bed. I'm referring to people in legal adulthood who are in the process of making hugely consequential life decisions. And collectively, their attitude is that they simply cannot pay for college.

2   Don't get me wrong. I realize that there are people out there who pay their own tuition. I know that some cannot put themselves through school because of disabilities or extenuating circumstances. But I have to say: the notion that parents must finance their children's education is ridiculous.

---

[6]I am indebted to Cedrick May for the basic idea for this project.

*From *Newsweek,* September 11, 2000, 12. All rights reserved. Reprinted by permission.

3   During college I consistently endured comments from peers with scholarships and loans, peers who had new Jeeps and expensive apartments, all who would say to me, eyes bulging, "You mean your parents didn't help you at *all*?"

4   I resented my fellow students for asking this, first because they made it sound like my parents were demons, and second because they were insinuating that I wasn't capable of paying my own way. "How did you pay tuition?" they'd ask. My response was simple: "I worked." They would look at me blankly, as though I had told them I'd gone to the moon.

5   As an undergrad (University of Utah, 1998), I put myself through two solid years of full-tuition college by working as a day-care provider for $4.75 an hour. I then married and finished out seven more quarters by working as an interpreter for the deaf and a tutor in a private school.

6   I didn't work during high school or save for years. I simply got a job the summer following graduation and worked 40 hours a week. I didn't eat out every weekend, shop a lot or own a car. I sacrificed. I was striving for something bigger and longer-lasting than the next kegger.

7   Looking at the numbers now, I'm not sure how I managed to cover all the costs of my education. But I did. And I bought every single textbook and pencil myself, too.

8   I remember sitting in a classroom one afternoon during my senior year, listening to everyone introduce themselves. Many students mentioned their part-time jobs. There were several members of a sorority in the class. When it came to the first girl, she told us her name and that she was a sophomore. "Oh," she added, "I major in communications." After an awkward silence, the teacher asked, "Do you work?"

9   "Oh, no," she said emphatically, "I go to school full time." (As if those of us who were employed weren't really serious about our classes.)

10   The girl went on to explain that her parents were paying tuition and for her to live in a sorority house (complete with a cook, I later found out). She was taking roughly 13 credit hours. And she was too busy to work.

11   I, on the other hand, was taking 18, count 'em, 18 credit hours so I could graduate within four years. I worked 25 hours a week so my husband and I could pay tuition without future loan debt. And here's the kicker: I pulled straight A's.

12   I caught a glimpse of that same girl's report card at the end of the quarter, and she pulled C's and a few B's, which didn't surprise me. Having to juggle tasks forces you to prioritize, a skill she hadn't learned.

13   I'm weary of hearing kids talk about getting financial help from their parents as though they're entitled to it. I am equally tired of hearing stressed-out parents groaning, "How are we going to pay for his/her college?" Why do they feel obligated?

14   I do not feel responsible for my daughter's education. She'll find a way to put herself through if she wants to go badly enough. And (I'm risking sounding like my mom here), she'll thank me later. I can say this because I honestly, wholeheartedly thank my parents for giving me that experience.

15   I'm not saying that it's fun. It's not. I spent the first two years of school cleaning up after 4-year-olds for the aforementioned $4.75 an hour and taking a public bus to campus. My husband and I spent the second two struggling to pay out our tuition. We lived in a cinder-block apartment with little privacy and no dishwasher.

16   Lest I sound like a hypocrite, yes, I would have taken free college money had the opportunity presented itself. However, because my parents put themselves through school they expected me to do the same. And, frankly, I'm proud of myself. I feel a sense of accomplishment that I believe I couldn't have gained from 50 college degrees all paid for by someone else.

17   Getting through school on our own paid off in every way. My husband runs his own business, a demanding but profitable job. I write part time and work as a mother full time. I

believe the fact that we are happy and financially stable is a direct result of our learning how to manage time and money in college.

18   So, kids, give your parents a break. Contrary to popular belief, you can pay tuition by yourself. And you might just thank your mother for it, too.

For Discussion:

What are your opinions about who should pay the bills for a college education? What are the advantages of doing it yourself? What are the disadvantages? If your parents had saved money and were intent on paying for your education, what would you say to them?

BEFORE YOU READ: Are there any annoying distractions in any of your classes? What are they? What could be done to eliminate them?

ESSAY #2   THE LAPTOP ATE MY ATTENTION SPAN*
Abby Ellin

The author lives in New York and writes a regular column, "Preludes," for the *New York Times* about starting out in business.

1   [What is] the latest issue on business school campuses? It's not whether to start your own dot-com before graduation, but whether you should be allowed to use your laptop in the classroom as you please.

2   While more and more schools—especially business schools—provide Internet access in class and require students to lug their laptops with them, some are imposing rules on what their students can and cannot do with them in class.

3   But why, in the sedate hallways of graduate schools, is there need for debate on rules of discipline? It seems that some students, although smart enough to earn M.B.A.'s, have not figured out how the old, generally unwritten rules of conduct apply to the wired classroom. More and more students are sending instant messages to one another (chatting and note-passing, 21st century–style), day trading (as opposed to daydreaming) and even starting their own companies, all in class.

4   The resulting commotion has annoyed many students. Jen McEnry, 28, a second-year M.B.A. student at the University of Virginia's Darden Graduate School of Business Administration, recalled that a classmate once downloaded an e-mail attachment during a finance lecture. The attachment automatically turned on the sound on the student's computer, which then delivered a booming message: "Oh my God, I'm watching porn!" Everyone roared at the practical joke, but the problem was clear.

5   "It's distracting when people are day trading, checking their e-mails or surfing the Web," Ms. McEnry said. All the more distracting because Darden relies heavily on classroom participation.

6   At Columbia University, the business school's newspaper reported that a student-run "chat room" ended up on the overhead projector in the middle of class. University officials denied the report. But by January, cyberspace had so intruded on classroom

New York Times, April 16, 2000, B15.

26

space at Columbia that a committee of professors and students came up with a code of professional conduct. "We're trying to find ways professors and students can use technology effectively and appropriately to create leaders," said Jeff Derman, a second-year M.B.A. student who heads the panel.

7   Yet how can M.B.A. students, whose average age is about 28 nationally, not know that it's rude to click away in class? After all, they presumably know not to walk out in the middle of a lecture, however boring. The rules of etiquette shouldn't change just because of technology.

8   Still, some business schools have gone beyond issuing rules. Two years ago, Darden officials installed a switch in each classroom; a professor can program it to shut down the students' Net-surfing at fixed times. The students, however, found that they could override the teacher's decision by sneaking over before class and flicking the switch back on. It became a kind of game, the Battle of the Button.

9   The students spent hours arguing the broader issues. Should computers be banned from class? (No, we're adults! We pay to be here!) Should networks be shut off? (Of course not! Web access is an inalienable right!) Should professors be able to turn off the systems? (That's, like, so 1984!)

10   Blood started to boil: Students got mad at professors, professors got mad at students, students got mad at each other and everyone cursed technology. Why should they have to deal with all this when all they really wanted to do was learn how to be a millionaire?

11   Ms. McEnry proposes a standard of reasonable necessity. "If I'm expecting something important, like news about a job or something, then it's O.K. to go online," she said. "There are really pressing issues in people's lives, and they need to have access."

12   She's not kidding. Ms. McEnry found out that she had been elected president of the Student Association after her friends found the news on the school's Web site and told her. In class. [. . .]

13   At the Columbia business school, Safwan Masri, vice dean of students and the M.B.A. program, takes a temperate tone. "These kids have grown up with computers; they can multitask," he said, explaining why Columbia decided against a Web shutdown switch. "We don't want to act as police. They're adults. We'd like to think they can control themselves."

14   I agree. Let them control themselves. And if they can't, here's my suggestion to them: Take a computer to the Metropolitan Opera. Log on. Write e-mail. Check your portfolio. At the end of the night, you'll be lucky to still have a computer.

For Discussion:

Does this article describe a problem that you have experienced in your classes or labs? What do you think instructors should do? Do you think that students ever talk on cell phones or answer their beepers at inappropriate times? Elaborate. How do you think instructors should respond to that?

D. Group Work and Class Discussion: Analyzing Visual Argument

Look at the two images reprinted in this section. They are both stand-alone visual arguments, accompanied by titles or small amounts of text. The first is a painting, and the second is a photograph. You could analyze these as works of art, but you are not being asked to do that here. Instead, you will analyze them as visual arguments. Many images are subtly and deliberately persuasive, and you can learn to recognize, analyze, and evaluate them as arguments, just as you would print materials.

27

Organize into small groups, read the written commentary that accompanies each image, and answer these questions.

1. What is the issue?
2. How would you state the claim (the point of view on the issue that is communicated by the arguer)?
3. What reasons and evidence are given to support the position?
4. What makes the image interesting and effective as a visual argument?

Image 1:

This painting, titled *Blessed Art Thou,* is by the artist Kate Kretz. It features the actress Angelina Jolie and three of her children floating in the heavens above the check-out counters at a Wal-Mart. It has been distributed on the Internet and has also been written about in newspapers.

The artist has said that even though she has made many paintings, this is the first painting that has made her famous.

For Discussion: Why were people so taken with this painting when it first appeared? What is the significance of the title of the painting? What is the final effect of depicting the actress in this way, while, at the same time, including people checking out at a Wal-Mart store in the lower part of the painting? How would you explain the meaning of this painting? Can you think of other examples of the public holding celebrities in what has seemed to be an exaggerated high regard? Describe some of the visual argument associated with these celebrities and their activities.

Image 2:

This photograph is titled *The Tide Is High*. It presents an abandoned home in Nags Head on North Carolina's Outerbanks and shows the erosion from rising sea levels surrounding it. In 2000, beach erosion in the area also forced the relocation of the nearby Cape Hatteras lighthouse approximately 2,900 feet inland from its previous oceanside location.

For Discussion: What did you first think when you looked at this photograph? How did the description of it change your perception? Do you find this photo convincing as a visual argument? What do you conclude about the alleged situation depicted here?

SOURCE: © Gary Braasch

E. Before You Write: Finding Compelling Issues for Future Argument Papers

The objective is to make a list of the issues that interest you so that you can draw possible topics from this list for future argument papers. You will need topics for the exploratory paper on pages 144–145, the position paper based on "The Reader" on page 276, the Rogerian argument paper on pages 328–329, and the researched position paper on pages 425–426.

1. *Become acquainted with the issues in "The Reader."* Turn to the table of contents for "The Reader." Sixteen issue questions organize the essays in the seven issue sections. Check all of the issue questions that interest you.

2. *Report on the issues in "The Reader."* This exercise provides class members with a preview of the issues and the articles and images in "The Reader." Individuals or pairs of students should select from the sixteen issue questions in the table of contents until they have all been assigned. Then follow these instructions to prepare a report for the class.

   a. To understand the content, read "The Issues" at the beginning of each issue section.
   b. Also read "The Rhetorical Situation" for the issue section.
   c. Read the questions at the end of the issue section.
   d. Read the issue question you have selected and the articles that accompany it. Study the images as well.
   e. Give a two-minute oral report in which you identify the issue question, briefly describe the articles and images, and identify at least two issues that these articles and images have raised for you.

3. *Find "your" issues.* Most students have issues that they really care about. What are yours? Think about what has affected you in the past. Think about your pet peeves. Think about recent news items on television or in the newspaper that have raised issues for you. Make a class list of the issues that concern you and the other students in your class.

4. *Identify campus issues.* What issues on campus concern you? What could be changed at your college to improve student life and learning? Make a class list.

F. Before You Write: Applying the Twelve Tests

Before you write about an issue, apply the twelve tests of an arguable issue that appear in Box 1.3 ■ on the next page to make certain that it is arguable. If all of your answers are yes, you will be able to work with your issue productively. If any of your answers are no, you may want to modify your issue or switch to another one.

G. Writing Assignment: Writing a Short Argument on a Campus Issue

Select the campus issue that interests you the most, apply the twelve tests in Box 1.3, and write a 250- to 300-word argument about it. Use the two

Box 1.3	Twelve Tests of an Arguable Issue.

▶▶▶ Do You Have an Arguable Issue?

If you cannot answer yes to all of these questions, change or modify your issue.

Your issue (phrased as a question): _____

Yes _____ No _____ 1. Is this an issue that has not been resolved or settled?

Yes _____ No _____ 2. Does this issue potentially inspire two or more views?

Yes _____ No _____ 3. Are you willing to consider a position different from your own and, perhaps, even modify your views on this issue?

Yes _____ No _____ 4. Are you sufficiently interested and engaged with this issue to inspire your audience also to become interested?

Yes _____ No _____ 5. Do other people perceive this as an issue?

Yes _____ No _____ 6. Is this issue significant enough to be worth your time?

Yes _____ No _____ 7. Is this a safe issue for you? Not too risky? Scary? Will you be willing to express your ideas?

Yes _____ No _____ 8. Can you establish common ground with your audience on this issue—common terms, common background, and related values?

Yes _____ No _____ 9. Will you be able to get information and come up with convincing insights on this issue?

Yes _____ No _____ 10. Can you eventually get a clear and limited focus on this issue, even if it is a complicated one?

Yes _____ No _____ 11. Is it an enduring issue, or can you build perspective by linking it to an enduring issue?

Yes _____ No _____ 12. Can you predict one or more audience outcomes? (Think of your classmates as the audience. Will they be convinced? Hostile? Neutral? Attentive? Remember that any outcomes at all can be regarded as significant in argument.)

short arguments on pages 24–26 and 26–27 as models. Write a title that identifies your issue. Then make a statement (a claim) that explains your position on the issue, followed by reasons and supportive evidence to convince a college official to accept your views and perhaps take action to improve the situation.

H. Writing Assignment: Writing a One-Page Issue Proposal

Issue proposals help you organize and develop your thoughts for longer argument papers. Once you have selected an issue, test it with the twelve tests, do some background reading as necessary, and write a proposal that responds to the following four items:

1. Introduce the issue, and then present it in question form.

2. Explain why it is compelling to you.

3. Describe what you already know about it.

4. Explain what more you need to learn.

The following is an example of an issue proposal that was written by a student.*

STUDENT PAPER #1   Prisna Virasin
Issue Proposal
Professor Wood
English 1302
2 February 2008

The Barbie Controversy

Introduce the issue.

1   It is interesting that a small, blond, blue eyed, plastic doll could cause an uproar. Barbie has succeeded (intentionally or not) in inciting heated opinion on whether she is fit to be the image of the perfect woman for millions of impressionable young girls. Some people have stated that Barbie's proportions are humanly impossible, with her exaggerated bustline and minuscule waist. They claim that these impossible proportions could lead girls to develop a poor body image. Barbie doll

Present it in question form.

defenders state that Barbie is a part of most girls' lives while they are growing up. Is Barbie bad? Does she have the power to affect girls psychologically all over the country or perhaps the world?

Explain why it is compelling to you.

2   I am interested in the Barbie controversy because, like many girls growing up in America, I was obsessed with Barbie when I was a child. Now, as a college student, I am very interested in female icons and their role in self-image development. I also have to fight the voices in my head telling me that I am too short and too fat, and I am not sure exactly where these voices have come from.

Describe what you already know about it.

3   I know that the Barbie doll product is pervasive in American society. I have never met a woman or girl who has not played with at least one Barbie. Barbie's image has appeared in McDonald's Happy Meals, in

*The format shown in this paper (and similar student papers throughout this book) reflects an MLA documentation style that is modified to accommodate space limitations. For example, all MLA-style student papers are double-spaced throughout. For actual MLA guidelines and a sample student paper showing the correct, more complete MLA format, see the Appendix to Chapter 13, pages 429–456.

computer programs, on her own clothing line, on school supplies, and in every major American store with a toy section.

Explain what more you need to learn.

4   I need to do more research on the validity of the claim that Barbie affects girls' self-images either detrimentally or positively. I would like to explore the pervasiveness of Barbie internationally and compare the domestic sales figures to the international sales figures. Also, if Barbie proves to be a detriment to girls' self-images, I would like to seek out some proposed solutions and discuss their feasibility.

chapter 2

Identifying Your Preferred Argument Style

S ometimes students resist the idea of engaging with issues and participating in argument because they think they will be required to hold an opposing view, to debate, or to be contentious or aggressive in class, and they feel that they do not do these things well. This chapter will develop the important idea that even though everyone can and should participate in argument, everyone may not participate in the same way. You already have a preferred style of argument, developed by several influences in your background. Many students who read and commented on this chapter in earlier editions of this book identified family and cultural backgrounds as particularly potent forces influencing the ways in which they argue. In addition, some researchers think that men tend to argue differently from women, that some Asians argue differently from Europeans and Americans, and that African Americans and Hispanic Americans may have distinctive styles that are influenced by their cultures. We will look at some of these causes for differences in this chapter, and you may want to argue about them. They are controversial. This chapter invites differing views on the issues it raises.

Another purpose of this chapter is to encourage you and your classmates at the outset to become aware of how each of you argues best. Thus you will learn to recognize, rely on, and perhaps even improve your existing style of argument. You will also learn from others how to modify or change to another style in certain situations when your preferred style may not be working well. This process will help you learn flexibility. Finally, you will learn to recognize and adapt to other people's styles, and you will therefore become a more sensitive and persuasive arguer, more likely to establish the common ground essential for the give-and-take of argument.

Individual tendencies and preferences in argument are present in many but not all situations that invite argument. If you discover, for example, that in most instances, you prefer reaching consensus over winning the argument, this discovery does not mean that you should always argue for consensus. Furthermore, if you discover that you are reluctant to participate in argument, your reluctance does not mean that you cannot find a way to participate. An awareness of individuals' predominant styles should reduce the dissonance and discomfort experienced by the participants in argument classes in which a single argument style or perspective may seem to dominate. The goal is to create and maintain an inclusive classroom where everyone has a voice and where every approach and style is tolerated and understood. This is a worthy real-life goal as well for a world in which cultural, racial, and gender diversity often influences the nature and special characteristics of the ongoing conversations about issues.

The Adversarial and Consensual Styles of Argument

Most argument classes contain a mix of students who favor either the adversarial or the consensual style of argument. Some students exhibit a combination of these styles. The adversarial approach to argument is usually associated with the traditional approach. The arguer is intent on changing the other person's mind. Further, the arguer usually tries to refute the opponent by showing what is wrong or invalid with the opponent's view. The views of the person doing the arguing are supposed to prevail. You are familiar with this form of argument. You observe it, for example, when political candidates debate public issues to impress voters with their analysis and ability to win, or when lawyers defend a client in court. Figure 2.1 ■ provides an example of adversarial argumentation.

Some modern authors now amend this view of argument. In *The Argument Culture: Moving from Debate to Dialogue,* sociologist Deborah Tannen states that all topics and all occasions do not call for the same approach to argument.[1] She claims that in our culture, we typically approach issues as though there were only one approach: we present them as a fight between two opposing sides. We look at many issues in an adversarial frame of mind since our assumption is that succeeding against opposition provides an answer and therefore is the best way to solve problems or to get anything done.

The three groups in our society who are most likely to engage with issues as conflicts are politicians, lawyers, and journalists. When an issue comes to public attention, journalists, for example, often set up a debate between politicians and then jump in themselves to keep the debate going. Journalists look for politicians who are willing to express the most extreme, polarized views on an issue with the ostensible objective of presenting both sides.

Our culture also likes to settle issues with litigation that pits one party against the other. We have frequent opportunities to watch trial argument on television

---

[1]Deborah Tannen, *The Argument Culture: Moving from Debate to Dialogue* (New York: Random House, 1998).

Figure 2.1 *Example of Adversarial Argumentation.*

Pointing to convicted sniper John Allen Muhammad, Attorney Paul S. Ebert delivers his closing remarks during the penalty phase of Muhammad's trial. Can you imagine yourself in the role of an attorney arguing in a courtroom?

and to read about it in a journal or newspaper. The objective is always to declare a winner. The argument culture as exhibited in the media, in the courts, and in the political arena carries over to the classroom, according to Tannen. Often students learn to start essays with opposition, and some students are quick to criticize and attack most of what they read. These approaches are sometimes necessary, as in courtroom argument or in public and collegiate debate. Such forums for argument frequently require rebuttal and a declaration of winners. However, if this is regarded as the only approach to controversial issues, we can create new problems as we try to solve others.

Tannen claims that, as a society, we have to find constructive and creative ways of resolving disputes and differences. It is better, she says, to make an argument for a point of view than to have an argument, as in having a fight. She also notes the value of studying argument in other cultures because some cultures work for agreement more than others. Tannen's subtitle, *Moving from Debate to Dialogue,* suggests an alternative to the win-lose model of argument. As she points out, other ways exist for dealing with issues: negotiating disagreement, mediating conflicts in an effort to find agreement, and resolving differences to clear the way to get things done. The old culture of conflict has the potential of becoming destructive to families, workplaces, communities, or even the world. The culture of conflict can be replaced in some situations with other possibilities, including working for consensus. Figure 2.2 ■ (on page 36) shows a group of businesspeople collaborating in a meeting in order to reach a consensus.

Which style is more typical of you, the adversarial, as shown in Figure 2.1, or the consensual, as shown in Figure 2.2? You probably use both at times, but which are you more likely to turn to first in argument? With which style are you more comfortable? The checklist in Box 2.2 on page 51 will help you find out. Now consider the influences in your life that may have caused you to prefer one style over the other.

Figure 2.2
Example of Consensual Argumentation.

This group of businesspeople is working together to find common ground on a problem along with solutions acceptable to everyone. Can you imagine yourself in such a situation, making contributions that others would be willing to listen to and accept?

Individual Styles of Argument

When students are asked to describe their styles of argument—that is, what they do when they have to be convincing—individual differences in style and strategy surface right away. Some of these differences seem to be related to home training and role models, others may be related to gender, and others seem to be attributable to the background and experience provided by different cultures or nationalities. Modern research indicates that men and women describe different approaches to argument often enough to suggest that gender may contribute in some way to differences in argument style. African American, Asian American, Hispanic American, and Native American cultures may also produce recognizably distinct styles and approaches. Students from non-Western cultures commonly describe approaches to argument that may strike Americans as distinctive and even unique.

These differences among styles are usually neither consistent nor strong enough for typecasting. In fact, in some studies, a sizable minority of men indicate they prefer the styles that the researchers have identified as predominantly female.[2] Also, a particular style may be more convincing in some contexts than in others, so that students who have a preferred style find that they vary it at times to meet the demands of particular argumentation situations. Thus no single style emerges as best for all occasions for anyone. For example, one student in the

---

[2]Carol S. Pearson, "Women as Learners: Diversity and Educational Quality," *Journal of Developmental Education* 16 (1992): 10.

group that test-read this book reported that when he argues with close friends about baseball players, he always wants to be right, he is very contentious and argumentative, and he expects to win. On the job, however, where he has low status in an office of four women, he never argues to win but rather tries to achieve agreement or consensus. Another student said she argues most aggressively when she is secure in her knowledge about the subject. She is tentative or even silent when she is not sure of her facts. Students also point out that there is a difference between home or "kitchen" argument and argument that takes place in school or on the job. Home argument may be more emotional and less controlled, especially in some cultures, than the reasoned discourse that one associates with school or work. Now let us look at some of the factors that can influence the ways in which you prefer to argue.

Influence of Background, Experience, and Role Models

Students frequently identify their upbringing or early experience as an influence on their argument style. Many students from military families, for example, say that argument was not encouraged at home. Orders were given in military fashion, and opposing views were not encouraged. These students, out of habit, may spend more time listening than talking in an argument class. Other students, such as those whose parents are teachers, lawyers, or politicians, have reported that arguing about issues occurred frequently in their households. These students may be the ones who speak the most in class. Nevertheless, whether they speak easily and often or prefer to listen, students will and do participate in the critical thinking that enables them to write productively about issues.

U.S. Supreme Court justices as a body are brilliantly skilled in argument. Yet, as individuals, they do not participate in argument in exactly the same way. To take one example, when Justice Clarence Thomas was asked by high school students in a televised session why he did not ask more questions that would initiate oral argument in cases being presented before the Court, he described aspects of his background and experience that have influenced the ways in which he typically participates in argument.

> There's no reason to add to the volume. I also believe strongly, unless I want an answer, I don't ask things. I don't ask for entertainment, I don't ask to give people a hard time. I have some very active colleagues who like to ask questions. Usually, if you wait long enough, someone will ask your question. The other thing, I was on that other side of the podium before, in my earlier life, and it's hard to stand up by yourself and to have judges who are going to rule on your case ask you tough questions. I don't want to give them a hard time. But I'm going to give you a more personal reason, and I think this is probably the first time I ever even told anybody about it. How old are you? You're 16. When I was 16, I was sitting as the only black kid in my class, and I had grown up speaking a kind of a dialect. It's called Geechee. Some people call it Gullah now, and people praise it now. But they used to make fun of us back then. It's not standard English. When I transferred to an all-white school at your age, I was self-conscious, like we all are. It's

like if we get pimples at 16, or we grow six inches and we're taller than everybody else, or our feet grow or something; we get self-conscious. And the problem was that I would correct myself midsentence. I was trying to speak standard English. I was thinking in standard English but speaking another language. So I learned that—I just started developing the habit of listening. And it just got to be—I didn't ask questions in college or law school. And I found that I could learn better just listening. And if I have a question I could ask it later. For all those reasons, and a few others, I just think that it's more in my nature to listen rather than to ask a bunch of questions. And they get asked anyway. The only reason I could see for asking the questions is to let people know I've got something to ask. That's not a legitimate reason in the Supreme Court of the United States.[3]

Students also sometimes account for their argument styles by identifying the well-known arguers who are most like themselves as the role models they would like to imitate as they develop their styles. Those students watch such model individuals on television or in the movies, and when the students find themselves in argument situations, they tend to imitate the people and styles they admire. If you find it difficult to initiate argument in class or to talk as much as some of the other students, Justice Thomas may be one role model who will appeal to you.

Influence of Gender

Many people think there are differences in the ways that men and women argue and that the basis for these differences lies in the power relationships that exist between the sexes in certain situations. Advocates of this view point out that men are often able to dominate an argument, while women tend to remain silent. Deborah Tannen, in *You Just Don't Understand: Women and Men in Conversation,* provides detailed descriptions of some differences between the argument styles of men and women.[4] Tannen asserts that many men make connections with one another primarily through conflict. (She qualifies this assertion because she realizes that she cannot generalize about *all* men.)

Tannen quotes Walter Ong, a scholar of cultural linguistics, who claims that men see the world as competitive, and the competition can be either friendly and involved or unfriendly. Men, furthermore, like self-display and achieve it often by reporting what they see and what they know. According to Ong, typical male behavior is centered on "the idea of contest, including combat, struggle, conflict, competition, and contention."[5] Ong reminds us, too, that many men enjoy ritual combat such as rough play and sports. Friendship among men frequently takes the form of friendly aggression. Ong also asserts, according to Tannen, that in daily argument, men expect the discussion to stick to the rules of logic. In sum, they expect argument to be adversarial, to include clashes, to take the form of debate, and to rely primarily on logic.

---

[3]Justice Clarence Thomas, "In His Own Words," *New York Times,* December 14, 2000, A17.
[4]Deborah Tannen, *You Just Don't Understand: Women and Men in Conversation* (New York: Ballantine Books, 1990), esp. ch. 6, "Community and Context."
[5]Ibid., 150.

Here is what one young man in an argument class wrote about his argument style.

> My head is as hard as a rock, and if I choose to disagree with you, I have the capability of tuning you out without you ever knowing it. I see things my way and tend to disagree with most people, even if they're right. Being wrong is a hard pill for me to swallow, and if I can avoid it, I will.[6]

For the checklist on page 52, this young man marked as being most typical of him every item in the adversarial column and no items in the consensual column.

Tannen says that most women do not like ritualized combat. They do not like conflict, either, and will often try to avoid it at all costs. Women tend to be the peacemakers and to want to work for the general good. They are as interested in making connections with other people as men are in competing. Making connections and keeping the peace are such strong tendencies in women's argument that even when women are being competitive and critical, they often mask their actual intentions with apparent cooperation and affiliation. Women, in fact, are often less direct than men in argumentation situations, and their indirect style sometimes causes men to think that women are trying to be devious and to manipulate them.

To summarize Tannen, men's power comes from acting in opposition to others and to natural forces. Women's power comes from their place in a community. For women, in fact, life is often a struggle to keep from being cut off from the group and to stay connected with the community.

The requirements of a particular situation, however, may be more influential than gender in determining the argument style that an individual or a group prefers at a particular time. In some cases, males find they prefer connection and consensus over contention and winning, and many females like the excitement and energy associated with winning debates. In fact, generalizations about male and female styles of argument do not always hold up. If you feel you are an exception, you will find many other students who are also.

Here is the way one young woman in an argument class characterized her style of argument.

> My parents have played a major role in influencing my argument style. Both of my parents have always been very opinionated and vocal in regard to issues that they feel strongly about. I am also very aware of the lack of respect that females receive while they are speaking. Females are often not taken as seriously [as men], and much of what they have to say is disregarded. I refuse to be ignored. I make it a point to express my feelings on issues that are of importance to me.[7]

This young woman has a distinct style, and she can describe it. She tends toward the adversarial. Her boyfriend, who attended class with her, described himself as a consensual arguer. He was influenced, he said, by his mother, who also favored the consensual approach.

---

[6]From a student paper by Tucker Norris; used with permission.
[7]From a student paper by Jennifer M. Hart; used with permission.

A young male student in an argument class, when asked to describe his style of argument, said that it was important to him to keep the peace, to negotiate, to work things out, and to gain consensus in argument. When he discovered that some of these qualities may be associated with female styles of argument, he quickly changed his description of himself, saying instead that he liked to win at any cost. Apparently, this young man did not want his classmates to question his masculinity, so he switched his description of himself to something less accurate. Actually, however, when questioned, a number of the male students in class admitted they preferred negotiation over winning at any cost. The women in the class, even those who preferred to think of themselves as winners, still strongly supported the idea of men as negotiators rather than aggressive winners.

As you analyze your own argument style and the styles of your classmates, you may discover that the people who break the hypothetical male-female stereotypes are some of the most effective arguers in class. In a recent discussion about argument, one woman commented that she disagreed so totally with an anti–gay rights group in her part of the country that she absolutely did not want to cooperate with it in any way or try to reach consensus. Instead, she wanted to argue and win. In another discussion, a businessman made the point that if he did not work for consensus in his business, he would not get anywhere with his fellow workers, and nothing would ever be accomplished.

Deborah Tannen makes a plea for the flexibility that can come from adapting features of both adversarial and consensual styles. Both men and women, she says, could benefit from being flexible enough to borrow one another's best qualities: "Women who avoid conflict at all costs," she suggests, "would be better off if they learned that a little conflict won't kill them. And men who habitually take oppositional stances would be better off if they broke their addiction to conflict."[8] It is also useful to realize that what may sometimes seem like an unfair or irrational approach to argument may simply be a manifestation of a particular individual's style. Such a realization makes it less frustrating, usually, to argue with such an individual.

Influence of Culture

Now consider the possibility that members of different cultural groups in America may exhibit distinct styles of argument and that individuals learn these styles through affiliation with their groups. Here are some differences that may be influenced by cultural identity as well as by experience.

It is widely recognized that many African Americans tend to focus strongly on issues and that even though they make effective use of logical and ethical appeal in argument they sometimes also make superior use of emotional

---

[8]Tannen, *You Just Don't Understand*, 187.

appeal. African American students report that much of their experience with argument styles comes from family interactions and also from the broad American cultural backdrop for the African American culture. The number and variety of African American magazines and publications on modern bookstore shelves attest to this group's strong interest in the issues that affect African American culture. Two other distinctly black forums for argument are available to many African Americans: rap music, which is relatively new, and the black church, which is an older, traditional, and more extensive institution. Both provide African Americans with the opportunity to observe and imitate distinctive black styles of argument.

Contemporary issues, presented forcefully and emotionally, form the main content of much rap music, as Sister Souljah, the New York rapper, recognized in 1992. "I think it would be a good idea," she said, "for members of Congress and the Senate and all people who consider themselves policy makers to listen to the call of help that is generated by rap artists."[9] At that time she saw rap music as a deliberate effort to organize black people to think about issues and to engage in social action. She and other rap artists, in fact, organized a ten-point program to engage African Americans in such issues as African life, economics, education, spirituality, defense, and how not to support racism. Nearly ten years later, at a "Hip-Hop Summit" held in 2001 in New York City, the attendees, including artists, politicians, music executives, and civil rights and religious leaders, identified a number of new initiatives and agreements regarding the future of rap music. One of these initiatives echoes the remarks made by Sister Souljah ten years earlier. An important goal for the hip-hop community in the future will be to work with civil rights organizations "to educate and address issues such as freedom of speech and racial profiling."[10]

The black church is regarded as another potent forum for argument. In an article describing a protest against a questionable court decision, the author observes that the African American church was at the forefront of the protest, "stepping into its time-honored role in politics and advocacy for social change."[11] Some of the most influential African American leaders who have addressed black issues have also been preachers in black churches. Included in this group are Martin Luther King Jr., Malcolm X, and Jesse Jackson.

The following description of his argument style was provided by a black student in an argument class. As you can see, he attributes some of his preferences and characteristics as an arguer to the fact that he is young, black, and male.

> What influences my style of argument the most is the fact that I am a young black male. The fact that I am young makes me want to be fair and direct with my opponent. That is, I attempt to be free of vagueness, ambiguity, and fallacies. Also, the fact that I am black affects the way I approach my audience. For instance, I tend to

---

[9]Sheila Rule, "Rappers' Words Foretold Depth of Blacks' Anger," *New York Times,* May 26, 1992, B1.
[10]Kevin Chappell, "Hip-Hop at the Crossroads," *Ebony,* September 2001, 110.
[11]Gracie Bonds Staples and Anjetta McQueen, "Ministers Lead Prayers in Call for Awakening," *Fort Worth Star-Telegram,* March 27, 1993, 1.

use emotional language, and my language is sometimes racially manipulative. I think that blacks tend to see people's race before they see people's attitudes and feelings. Finally, the fact that I am a male probably influences my argument. I think that males tend to be a bit more harsh in their argument. They tend to want to "rock the boat" and stir some emotions. I think that this is a strong tendency in my argument style. The use of facts, emotions, fairness, and strong language is very typical of black argument.[12]

Some Asian American students, according to recent research, may be more reluctant than other students to participate in argument because of their particular cultural background. Students who have spent a portion of their school years in Japan, China, or other Far Eastern countries or whose parents or grandparents come from these countries are quite likely to regard argument class as an odd environment that has little to do with them. This statement is particularly true if they view the class as a place where pro and con issues are debated and winners are declared. Such argumentation and debate are not traditionally practiced in many countries in the Far East. Carl Becker, a professor of Asian curriculum research and development, explains some of the reasons for this lack of formal argumentation practiced there. For these Asians, sympathetic understanding and intuition are more important means of communication than logic and debate. Furthermore, many Asians do not like to take opposite sides in an argument because they do not like becoming personal rivals of those who represent the other side. They value harmony and peace, and argument, as they perceive it, has the potential to disturb the peace.[13]

Here is the self-reported argument style of a young Asian American student in an argument class. This account was written at the beginning of the semester.

> My style of argument is to avoid argument as much as possible. I think that I argue more with other men than I do with women. I think the reason I don't argue a lot is because I analyze the situation a bit too much, and I can pretty much tell what the outcome is going to be. During argument I usually blank out what the other person is saying and think about when they are going to stop talking.[14]

He was more comfortable and skilled with argument at semester's end. He credited argument class, finally, with teaching him to listen more, argue more, and be less self-centered.

The Asian students who test-read this book warned that not all Asian cultures are the same and that the reluctance to argue may be stronger in some Asian cultures than others. For example, a Sri Lankan student pointed out that in her country, as well as in India and Bangladesh, argument is encouraged. Students also observed that there is a tradition of lively, contentious, and even

---

[12]From a student paper by Kelvin Jenkins; used with permission.
[13]Carl B. Becker, "Reasons for the Lack of Argumentation and Debate in the Far East," *International Journal of Intercultural Relations* 10 (1986): 75–92.
[14]From a student paper by Jim Lui; used with permission.

combative kitchen argument among close family members in some Asian cultures. This, they say, is typical of the Korean culture. Amy Tan, in her books about her childhood in a Chinese immigrant household, gives examples of the lively home argument in that culture as well. Outside of the home, however, many Asians tend to be reluctant to enter into argument. For students reluctant to speak out, argument class is a safe place for developing and practicing that special ability.

Since Hispanic cultures promote strong family ties and group values, many Hispanic students seem to favor connection over contention and negotiation over winning. Female Hispanic students describe their styles of argument variously. One student says she tries to listen and understand others' points of view. Another says she likes the fact that she can express her feelings without hurting other people, while yet another says she likes a negotiated solution even though she would at times like to be more assertive.

A Study of the Influence of Students' Gender and Culture on Their Argument Style

The descriptions of argument style you have read in this chapter were written by students enrolled in argument classes in response to an assignment that asked them to describe their current argument styles. These students, along with more than six hundred others, also completed a questionnaire about their argument styles and were asked to reveal their gender and their cultural background. The idea was to see whether the links between style and gender and background characteristics already discussed in this chapter seemed to have any validity.

The students were questioned in three areas. First, they were asked how they viewed the outcomes of argument. Second, they were asked to report on their personal participation in argument. Finally, they were asked about their present style of argument. Several possible answers were provided for each of the three items, and students were asked to identify one item under each question that best described them and then to identify two others that also described them, but perhaps not quite so forcefully. The questions appear in Box 2.1 ■ on page 44. As you read them, answer them yourself. Under each question, identify the item you agree with most as number 1. Then number the additional items that also describe your opinions and practices as 2 and 3.

You may now want to compare your own answers to the questions with those reported by other students. Of the 647 argument class students who completed this questionnaire one week after classes started, 69 percent were second-semester first-year students, 19 percent were sophomores, and 12 percent were juniors and seniors. Also, 53 percent were male and 47 percent female. Of the males, 69 percent were white, 9 percent were black, 12 percent were Asian, and

---

| **Box 2.1** | **Student Questionnaire on Attitudes and Style in Arguments.** |

▷▷▷ What Is Your Argument Style?

How would you answer these questions? Identify as number 1 the item with which you agree most. Then identify as 2 and 3 the additional items that also describe you.

1. How would you describe the usual outcomes of argument?
_____ Argument helps people understand each other's points of view.
_____ Argument separates and alienates people.
_____ Argument causes conflict and hard feelings.
_____ Argument resolves conflict and solves problems.
_____ Argument can change people's minds.
_____ Argument rarely changes other people's minds.

2. How would you describe your personal participation in argument?
_____ Argument makes me feel energized, and I like to participate.
_____ Argument makes me uncomfortable, and I dislike participating.
_____ I participate a lot.
_____ I participate sometimes.
_____ I never participate.
_____ I think it is fun to argue.
_____ I think it is rude to argue.

3. What is your style of argument at present?
_____ I am contentious and enjoy conflict.
_____ I am a peacekeeper, and I value conflict resolution.
_____ I try to win and show people I am right.
_____ I try to listen, understand, make connections, and negotiate solutions.
_____ I tend to use reason and facts more than emotion.
_____ I tend to use emotion more than reason and facts.

10 percent were Hispanic. Of the females, 64 percent were white, 15 percent were black, 13 percent were Asian, and 8 percent were Hispanic. The percentages were weighted to indicate the relative strength of preference for each group in order to make more accurate comparisons.

One of the most interesting results of this study was that no items on the questionnaire were rejected by all students. Every item on the questionnaire was marked by at least a few students as being typical or somewhat typical of themselves. These students' responses suggest the wide diversity of attitudes and preferences among them.

In answer to the first question, about argument outcomes, both male and female students overwhelmingly favored the response that the usual outcome of argument is to help them "understand others." Scoring highest in this area, however, were Asian men. "Changing minds" and "resolving conflict" were in second and third places among the preferences of the entire group. Clearly, more students thought argument resolves conflict than thought argument causes it. Only a few students indicated that argument separates and alienates people. There was essentially no difference between male and female responses to this first question.

Male and female students were also very similar in their assessment of their participation in argument. Most students reported that they "participated some-times" instead of "never" or "a lot." Both women and men reported that they are energized by argument, they like it, and they find it "fun to argue." Asian women were the largest identifiable group among students who said they found argument "uncomfortable" so that they disliked participating. Not all of them, however, responded in this way. African American men and women ranked themselves slightly higher than the other groups in perceiving argument as ener-gizing and enjoyable. Only a few students, and about the same number of males as females, thought it was "rude to argue" and said they "never participated."

Male and female students differed more in their responses to question 3, "What is your style of argument at present?" than they did in their responses to the other two questions. "Listening and connecting" was the style favored over the others by both men and women of all groups, but more women than men identified themselves with this style. More females than males also reported that they use emotion in argument more than reason, and more males than females favored reason and facts over emotion. White males said they "try to win" more than the other groups. Asian males and females identified themselves as "peace-keepers" somewhat more than the other groups, even though a significant num-ber of the students in the other groups saw themselves this way as well. Finally, only a few of the men and even fewer of the women said they were "contentious" and that they "enjoyed conflict."

Although no Native American students participated in this study, research on Native American culture and values suggests that Native American students value community and cooperation more than rivalry and competition. Also, in traditional Native American culture, young people are expected to agree with authority figures, especially with those seen as older and wiser. Thus Native American students are often reluctant to debate, particularly with the teacher.[15]

We concluded that the differences among these groups of students are cer-tainly not great enough to create stereotypes. College students, in fact, often break stereotypes for two basic reasons: because of their close association with one

---

[15]B. C. Howard, *Learning to Persist/Persisting to Learn* (Washington, DC: Mid-Atlantic Center for Race Equity, American University, 1987).

another, leading directly to greater flexibility, adaptability, and increased tolerance, and because of their common goal to become educated. Among the students who answered the questionaire, the strongest tendencies that seem to confirm the notion that gender and cultural background influence them as arguers were that Asian students were less enthusiastic about argument than the others, that white males liked to win more than any of the other groups, and that more females than males said they typically try to listen and connect.

Some of our findings, however, are not typical of the tendencies described by recent researchers. For instance, listening, understanding, making connections, and negotiating solutions was a preferred style for nearly as many men as for women, and the contentious, conflictive style was less popular with both groups. Also, it seems clear that these students as a group value knowing the facts; are suspicious of too much emotion, particularly if it results in anger and loss of control; and have positive opinions about the outcomes and uses of argument.

The study mainly emphasizes the many differences in argument style that can be found in argument classrooms. The study confirms the importance of the goals for argument class listed at the beginning of this chapter: students need to learn to value one another's styles, to develop flexibility by extending their own styles and learning to borrow from others, and to adapt to styles other than their own.

Influence of Nationality

Argument class can be thought of as a microcosm of the larger world, particularly when the students in it represent a variety of countries and cultures. Cultural backgrounds outside of the United States can sometimes exert a powerful influence over the way in which individuals view and practice argument. Studying argument across cultures is a complicated field, and most of its findings are tentative because of the vast individual differences in people from culture to culture. Still, even tentative findings are important for the argument classroom. Hypothesizing about how argument differs according to nationality helps students focus on the preferences in argument styles that may be typical of certain groups and cultures. Developing an awareness of these characteristics and preferences and learning to adapt to them not only helps students achieve the goals of the inclusive argument classroom but also helps prepare students for lifelong communicating and negotiating with people from other countries and cultures. For example, diversity among workers and an inclusive work environment are increasingly valued in many workplaces. Figure 2.3 ■ is an ad for a company that consults with other companies to help them meet these objectives.

Here are some examples of some possible differences in argument style associated with nationality. Deborah Tannen claims that argument in some societies is a way of coming together, a pleasurable sign of intimacy, a kind of game that people play together. This observation is particularly true of Italy, Greece, and Eastern

Diversity is the mix. Inclusion is making the mix work.

Hewitt

Hewitt Associates is a global human resources outsourcing and consulting firm delivering a complete range of integrated services to help companies manage their total HR and employee costs, enhance HR services, and improve their workforces.

Making the world a better place to work.

www.Hewitt.com

Figure 2.3 *An Advertisement for Hewitt Associates.*

This consulting firm meets its purpose, "making the world a better place to work," by helping companies with employees all over the world respond to diversity and create inclusive work environments where everyone can get along and contribute to company goals. How might your experiences in your argument class help prepare you for working in such a global environment?

47

Europe. To outsiders, the argument in these countries may seem to be conflictual rather than a reasoned inquiry into issues. Italian *discussione* strikes outsiders as loud, contentious arguing, but to Italians it is a friendly game. Greeks and Eastern Europeans may appear bossy and overbearing. In their view, however, they are showing friendly caring.[16]

In the following account, a student from Vietnam describes a different attitude and style of argument in his country.

> The Vietnamese are taught not to argue with their elders. When I was a little child, my parents always told me that it is bad to argue with your parents and elders. Since the first grade, my teachers told us that it is bad to argue, even among friends. That is why I did not like to argue. I did not want to be disrespectful to another person. When I came to the United States and attended school, I learned that in this society you are encouraged to argue for your opinion.[17]

Here is another example of a student, this time from Israel, who attributes his predominant style of argument to his country of origin.

> I am an Arab and a Palestinian, and my argument style is different from other styles used here in the United States. In my country children are taught not to argue with what their elders tell them. This is not only taught at home, but at school too. In school teachers come second to parents when it comes to advice. Parents are considered to be wiser and more experienced in life, and it is considered disrespectful to argue with them. Arguing, in fact, can lead to certain punishment.[18]

Finally, a Taiwanese student says that his argument style is influenced by both personal and cultural factors.

> My argument style is more like the consensual than the adversarial. I think there are two reasons for this. One is personal, and the other is cultural. Personally, I don't like to argue with people over issues. I want to be in harmony with people. Therefore, I always try to avoid the situation of confrontation with other people because I find confrontation embarrassing. Secondly, argumentation is not encouraged in my culture, which always puts harmony as the ultimate goal. In fact, the word "argue" has a negative connotation in my culture. In my culture, if you argue with someone, it is regarded as a kind of quarrel, or a kind of verbal fight. However, I do believe that it is necessary to argue with people occasionally. We don't need to quarrel with them, but at least we have to defend our ideas and perspectives. I just want my perspectives to be heard and understood. I think in the future I will be more aggressive in defending my perspectives.[19]

International students in your class may be able to provide additional examples that represent predominant styles of argument in their countries and cultures, along with an analysis of what causes them.

---

[16]Tannen, *You Just Don't Understand*, 160–62.
[17]From a student paper by Lan Mai; used with permission.
[18]From a student paper by Edward Stephan; used with permission.
[19]From a student paper by Scott Hsu; used with permission.

Some researchers have speculated about the reasons for the differences in argument styles in different cultures. *Preferred cultural values* and *preferred patterns of thinking* may be the two major factors that differentiate argument styles across cultures.[20] Differences in value systems from culture to culture are often particularly obvious. For example, Americans who relocate to Saudi Arabia are sometimes surprised when they receive copies of newspapers from outside the country. Before the newspapers are delivered, the Saudi censors use wide felt-tipped ink pens to obliterate visual material that is offensive to their cultural values. Pictures of a ballerina's legs and arms may be colored over, as well as other parts of the female anatomy usually kept covered in Arab countries.

You may want to discuss with your classmates, particularly if some of them come from other countries or have lived in another country for a while, what values and patterns of thinking are preferred in their cultures (or in other cultures they know) since these are believed to have an effect on the common ground that is established in cross-cultural argument.[21] For example, according to some researchers, Americans value individual achievement, hard work, and independence, and in their patterns of thinking, they tend to prefer generalizations backed by examples and experience to pure reasoning unaccompanied by examples. The Japanese, like Americans, value achievement, but they also value serenity and self-confidence. Characteristic of their thinking patterns are the preferences to make suggestions, to give hints, and to communicate indirectly. Researchers who have studied Japanese argument claim that the Japanese like ambiguity, or saying one thing and meaning something else. They often use understatement. Their communication can seem incomplete to outsiders because they often omit logical links, expecting others to infer them. The Japanese dislike contention and debate.[22]

You see that understanding the value systems and preferred patterns of reasoning of other cultures can be very important in establishing the common ground necessary for productive argument across cultures. As you read newspaper accounts of intercultural communication and argument, watch for the problems and misunderstandings that can arise from an absence of shared values and shared ways of thinking.

Argument is fundamental to democracy, and it flourishes in democratic societies. In totalitarian societies, however, if it exists at all, it must usually go

---

[20]Gregg B. Walker, "Assessing Multicultural Argument in the Law of the Sea Negotiations: A Rationale and Analytical Framework," in *Spheres of Argument: Proceedings of the Sixth SCA/AFA Conference on Argumentation*, ed. Bruce E. Gronbeck (Annandale, VA: Speech Communication Association, 1989), 600–603.

[21]Ibid. Walker summarizes the results of considerable cross-cultural research into the values and patterns of thought preferred by different cultures. See his article for additional sources and information. Pearson, "Women as Learners," also summarizes some of the cultural values included here.

[22]Michael David Hazen, "The Role of Argument, Reasoning and Logic in Tacit, Incomplete and Indirect Communication: The Case of Japan," in *Spheres of Argument: Proceedings of the Sixth SCA/AFA Conference on Argumentation*, ed. Bruce E. Gronbeck (Annandale, VA: Speech Communication Association, 1989), 497–503.

underground. Thus argument in such countries may be heard only in the secret meetings of opposition political groups or in private meetings of citizens. Written argument may appear in underground newspapers or in material written by dissidents or political exiles. Forums for argument in such societies are severely limited compared with those in democratic societies. Students from such countries may at first find it difficult to participate in argument.

All participants in argument, whether they come from democratic or totalitarian societies, need to work to establish common ground if argument across cultures and gender boundaries is to be successful. This effort can be difficult and time-consuming. An issue that has been argued and debated through the ages is the fishing, navigation, and territorial rights to the oceans of the world. In the 1970s, the United Nations Conference on the Law of the Sea was charged with the task of reaching agreement among nations on access to and use of the seas. This group spent nine years engaged in intercultural argument and negotiation, finally reaching agreement on some, but not all, of the issues.[23]

When Boris Yeltsin was president of Russia, he made an effective attempt to achieve common ground on his visit to Japan, in late 1993, when there was considerable tension between the two countries. Unlike some of his predecessors, Yeltsin was accomplished in building common ground. Soon after arriving in Japan, he apologized for Russia's treatment of thousands of Japanese prisoners of war who were sent to Siberia after World War II. More than sixty thousand of them died, and many Japanese believed an apology was long overdue. Later, Yeltsin repeated this apology to the Japanese prime minister and bowed deeply to express his remorse, a gesture that is valued in the Japanese culture.[24] His efforts, according to reports, relieved a considerable amount of tension between the two countries because of the common ground he established. When common ground is not established, the consequences can be devastating. Wars are a frequent alternative to productive argument and negotiation, especially when the differences between the arguing parties are extreme.

The concept of all people knowing how to argue effectively to resolve differences in personal, national, and international relationships is potentially a very powerful idea. Think of a country and a world where major problems are resolved through profitable argument instead of through confrontation, shouting, fighting, or war. You will often fervently disagree with other people; in fact, life would be boring if you never disagreed. Yet, even when you disagree, even when you decide to enter an ongoing argument, you can learn to use a style that is comfortable and natural for you and also ethical and effective. This is preferable to the alternatives: either remaining silent or becoming involved in destructive arguments that solve nothing and may even cause harm.

---

[23]Walker, "Assessing Multicultural Argument," 599–600.
[24]David E. Sanger, "Yeltsin, in Tokyo, Avoids Islands Issue," *New York Times,* October 14, 1993, A5.

Review Questions

1. Describe the adversarial style of argument. What three groups in American society are associated with adversarial argument?

2. Describe the consensual style of argument. Under what circumstances might it be more effective than adversarial argument?

3. What are some of the possible influences on individual preferred styles of argument? Which would you say have had an effect on your preferred style of argument?

4. What are some of the possible differences researchers have identified between men's and women's styles of argument? Do you agree or disagree? What in your own experience has influenced your answer to this question?

5. Why might it be important to be aware of different argument styles in international or cross-cultural argument? Give an example of a problem that could arise and a few of your ideas of how to deal with it.

Exercises and Activities

A. Self-Evaluation: Is Your Preferred Argument Style Consensual or Adversarial?

Do you visualize yourself as a lawyer writing briefs and arguing in the court-room, as a politician writing on public issues and arguing for votes, or as a journalist writing an argument in favor of a controversial new policy? Or, for you, is it easier to imagine yourself as a professor conducting a class discussion that helps students reach consensus on an issue and write about what they have discovered, or as a negotiator working with a group to resolve a conflict? Look back at Figures 2.1 and 2.2 on pages 35 and 36. With which situation do you most easily identify and imagine yourself as a participant? Box 2.2 ■ provides a summary of some of the characteristics of consensual and adversarial styles of argument. If you have not already done so, check the items that are most typical of you. Does one list describe your style of argument better than the other? Or, can your style be described best by items taken from both lists? Given this analysis, how would you say you typically prefer to argue?

B. Writing Assignment: The Argument-Style Paper

Think about the last time you had to argue convincingly for a certain point of view. Write a 300- to 500-word paper in which you describe your predominant argument style. Include the following information.

1. In your argument, what was the issue, what were you trying to achieve, and what did you do to achieve it?

2. Was that typical of your usual style of argument? If yes, explain why; if no, explain why and describe your usual style.

Box 2.2	Two Styles of Argument.

▷▷ Which Style Best Describes You?

Check all statements that apply in both columns. Does one style tend to predominate, or do you have a mixed style?

CONSENSUAL STYLE

_____ I prefer to be indirect.
_____ I like to give reasons.
_____ I prefer cooperation.
_____ I favor group consensus.
_____ I like affiliation.
_____ I hate to fight.
_____ I prefer to avoid confrontation.
_____ I dislike contentious argument.
_____ I am nonaggressive.
_____ I solicit many views on an issue.
_____ I am both logical and emotional.
_____ I try to make connections.
_____ I prefer negotiating.
_____ I favor the personal example, story, or anecdote.
_____ I want to keep the community strong.

ADVERSARIAL STYLE

_____ I am direct and open.
_____ I like to reach conclusions.
_____ I prefer competition.
_____ I favor individual opinions.
_____ I like conflict.
_____ I like to fight.
_____ I like confrontation.
_____ I like contentious argument.
_____ I am aggressive.
_____ I tend to see issues as two-sided, pro and con, right or wrong.
_____ I am primarily logical.
_____ I tend to be adversarial.
_____ I prefer winning.
_____ I favor abstract ideas.
_____ I want to keep the individual strong.

3. What has influenced your style of argument? Consider home training, role models, gender, culture, nationality, national heritage, or any other life experiences that have influenced you.

4. How would you describe your ideal arguer, and how would you like to be more like this person in your own arguing?

5. What do you like best about your current style of argument? What would you like to change? How can you become more flexible in your style?

C. **Class Project: Creating a Classroom Environment for Argument and Analyzing Your Class as an Audience**

1. Read aloud the argument-style papers written by class members for Exercise B. Discuss the different styles described in these papers and some of the influences that have helped create them.

2. Discuss creating a classroom environment that can accommodate all of these styles. Jürgen Habermas, a modern European philosopher and

rhetorician, described an ideal environment for argument.[25] Read each statement of Habermas's ideal situation, and indicate by raising your hand whether you agree or disagree. Be able to explain why. What would you eliminate? Why? What would you add? Why?

a. Each person should have the freedom to express ideas and critique others' ideas directly, openly, and honestly.

b. The use of force and personal power that tend to inhibit some participants should be eliminated.

c. Arguments based on an appeal to the past and tradition are to be exposed. These arguments superimpose the past on the present, and everyone does not share the same past.

d. The aim of argument is to arrive at truth through consensus and an adherence of minds.

What are the implications of accepting or rejecting these statements for your classroom?

3. Characterize your class as an audience after reading all their argument style papers. Write for five minutes about the characteristics your class holds in common and also about the types of diversity that are evident in your class. What generalizations can you finally make about your class as an audience? Discuss the results.

D. Group Work and Class Discussion: Using Gender, Nationality, and Cultural Background to Strengthen Written Argument

The following six essays are written by authors who have drawn on their own or others' unique experiences as members of a particular culture or gender. When you have read the essays, discuss them in small groups of four or five students. Appoint a scribe to record your findings and report them to the class. The following questions will help organize your discussion.

1. What experiences associated with culture, gender, or nationality do these authors draw on to strengthen their arguments?

2. What is effective in their arguments as a result? Be specific.

3. What can you conclude about drawing on experiences associated with a culture, gender, or nationality to strengthen an argument?

4. Would drawing on personal experiences of your own, as these authors have done, be consistent with your personal argument style? If your answer is yes, what experiences associated with your culture, gender, or nationality might you use to develop an issue that is important to you?

5. Describe the audience each of these authors seems to be addressing. To whom will each of these essays appeal? Who will resist them?

53

---

[25]Habermas's ideas are summarized by James L. Golden, Goodwin F. Berquist, and William E. Coleman in *The Rhetoric of Western Thought,* 4th ed. (Dubuque, IA: Kendall Hunt, 1989), 438.

> **BEFORE YOU READ:** What childhood memories do you recall with pleasure?

ESSAY #1   WE KNEW WHAT GLORY WAS*
Shirlee Taylor Haizlip

Shirlee Taylor Haizlip is also the author of *The Sweeter the Juice: A Family Memoir in Black and White.*

1   When I was growing up in the 40's and 50's, my father would pack up the car every August and squeeze in my mother, four children, several dolls and a picnic lunch. It was the time before air-conditioning, and the drive was hot, dusty and, after New York, without bathrooms.

2   We left long before dawn, because for a dark-skinned man driving a large shiny sedan holding a white-looking wife, the journey from Connecticut to the South was not without peril. It was essential that each leg of the trip be made before nightfall. We knew that safety lay within the homes and the churches of my father's friends and colleagues, the black ministers we would visit. They were our underground railroad.

3   My father was a Baptist pastor who ministered to a medium-sized black church in a Connecticut mill town. His father was a minister who had founded a major black Baptist church in Washington. At the beginnings of their careers, both had led small country churches in North Carolina, Virginia and West Virginia. Later, as popular officers of the National Baptist Convention and known for their dramatic oratory, the two were frequent guest preachers at rural churches throughout the South.

4   Traditionally, my father and his father before him preached a week of revival services at these houses of worship. After my grandfather died, my father continued to return to the South each year. For him, the churches were touchstones of faith, of culture, of triumph over slavery. For him, they were living, breathing links to the past and an indestructible foundation for the future.

5   There was more than a spiritual connection. When they were in college, my four uncles, all of whom played musical instruments and had glorious voices, would sometimes join my father and present musical programs of spirituals and the light classics to appreciative Southern congregations, all too often deprived of other cultural experiences.

6   At other times, my dad, resplendent in a white suit, would offer solo recitals. When he crooned "Danny Boy" or "When I Grow Too Old to Dream" in his high tenor vibrato and with exquisite diction, the fans moved a little faster, the backs sat up a little straighter and the shouts of "Sing it, Rev!" were as heartfelt as they were for his renditions of "Amazing Grace" or "His Eye Is on the Sparrow."

7   I cannot hear the Three Tenors sing without thinking of my father standing in the pulpit of a spare little church, singing like a melancholy angel.

8   To reach many of the churches, we drove up deserted dirt roads covered by gracefully arching kudzu-fringed trees. Just when we thought we would never get there, a clearing materialized. There at its edge stood the church, often the only building for miles

---

*New York Times, June 23, 1996, A13.

around, plain as a line drawing in a children's coloring book, more often than not in need of a fresh coat of paint. Never lonely looking, it seemed instead a natural part of the landscape, splendid in its simplicity.

9   Before the service, with admonitions of keeping our "best" clothes clean fading in our ears, my siblings and I would play with other children, running and jumping, catching fireflies, hiding and seeking in the darkening silver twilight. Each night, the revival crowd would get bigger and livelier. By the end of the week, the church was full, the room was hot and the penitents were saved.

10   During every service, I watched as my father, in high Baptist style, "picture painted" the stories of Moses and Job, Ruth and Esther. I listened as he moaned and hummed and sang the tales of W. E. B. Du Bois and Frederick Douglass, the Scottsboro Boys and Emmett Till. I clapped for joy as he brought the worshipers to their feet with promises of survival now and salvation later. In that place, at that time, we knew what glory was.

11   After the service, in the pitch blackness of a muggy summer night, we would drive back to our host's house, listening to parish gossip and ghost stories, accept offers of freshly made iced tea and every once in a while homemade ice cream. Sweetly, another church night had ended.

12   The best was yet to come. At the close of the week, we celebrated the homecoming, the end of the weeklong revival, behind the church, where picnic benches were felicitously placed among sweet-smelling pines. We ate miles of delicious food and drank lakes of sweet punch.

13   Usually there was a modest graveyard somewhere near the picnic grounds. We did not play there. Our parents had taught us better than that. Mold-covered gravestones barely hinted at the life stories they marked. The bones of slaves lay side by side with the bones of their emancipated children. All of their spirits were free to be free, at last.

14   As I grew older, I would learn about the lives of the church members from the comfort of my mother's side. I would grow to understand that there, in that place, every single church member was *somebody*.

15   In God's house, if nowhere else, they were C.E.O.'s and presidents, directors and chairmen, counselors and managers. In God's house, if nowhere else, they were women of infinite grace and men of profound dignity. Forever, amen.

16   With traditions that began in slavery, the parishioners carried forward, bit by precious bit, the dreams of their forebears. In their roles as deacons, trustees, missionaries and choir members, those domestics, handymen, cotton and tobacco farmers and teachers sang and prayed on hard, scrabbly benches, validating and celebrating themselves and one another, warmly and well, week after week, year after year, generation after generation.

17   Surely their oils and essences seeped into the well-worn pews. Surely the whorls of their fingertips left lovely striations in the wood, at which their grandbabies would stare before they fell off to sleep.

18   Not only did they tend to the church's business, they looked after the elderly and the infirm, encouraged the young to learn, learn, learn and rallied their communities in times of economic stress, natural disaster or social crisis. It did not escape my understanding that the church encompassed all. Seldom were there outcasts.

19   For me as a child, those beautiful little structures were places beyond enchantment. As an adult, I understood that the churches were indeed the collective soul of black folks.

20   I never thought that this particular reality could end. Although I have visited the South as an adult and know that some of those churches have been abandoned, enlarged or modernized, in my mind's eye all of them remain storybook sanctuaries, testament to

my own faith, the faith of my father, his father and the larger black community. [. . .]

21 Heartsick now, my soul's light has been dimmed. Church after church in the South has been destroyed by fire, torched by arsonists. I watch the television images as long as I can. Then I hide my eyes behind my fingers, peeking at the screen as if it were a horror film, while hellish flames consume the heavenly places of my youth.

22 I ask my father across the void, Who will put out the flames, Dad? Where can we go now to be safe?

For Discussion:

What makes this an effective argument? What do you visualize as you read? How do you participate in this essay and identify with its characters?

BEFORE YOU READ: What freedoms do you value? Which freedoms seem to have been most curtailed since 9/11? Have you been affected personally?

ESSAY #2   **WE'RE FIGHTING TERROR, BUT KILLING FREEDOM**[*]
Randall Hamud

56

Randall Hamud is a lawyer who lives in San Diego. He wrote this essay twenty-three months after September 11, 2001.

1 In the last 23 months I've received countless threats accusing me of being a terrorist, but this one caught my attention because it was in Spanish. *"Te vas a morir!"* the voice on my answering machine said. "You're going to die!" The caller, a Hispanic man who had probably experienced racial discrimination at some point in his life, should have known better.

2 I'm an Arab-American lawyer. Shortly after September 11, the families of three young Arab Muslim men asked me to represent them. The men had been arrested in San Diego as material witnesses and taken to New York to testify in front of the grand jury investigating the attack. They were acquainted with Nawaf Alhamzi and Khalid Almihdhar,

two of the terrorist hijackers who crashed the plane into the Pentagon. Alhamzi and Almihdhar had visited San Diego the year before the attack and befriended my clients.

3 Though my clients knew nothing about the hijackers' plans, the Bush administration wasn't taking any chances. Immediately after September 11, approximately 1,200 Arab and Muslim men were arrested. Many of them are still in secret custody.

4 My clients appeared before the grand jury, and none of them was ever charged with terrorism. Despite this, most people perceived them to be terrorist suspects. As soon as I became associated with their cases, I began receiving death threats.

---

[*]*Newsweek,* September 1, 2003, 11.

5   Matters worsened in May 2002 when I received a telephone call from Zacarias Moussaoui's mother. He's the alleged "20th hijacker" who is on trial for his life in Virginia. His mother retained me to try to persuade him to cooperate with his defense lawyers. Though I represented her, not her son, more death threats rained down on me. I, too, was now considered a terrorist. Nothing could be farther from the truth.

6   I was born in Los Angeles to Lebanese-American parents. They taught me to go to school and make something of myself. I graduated from UCLA School of Law and started a private practice. I speak Spanish, not Arabic, because if you do business in southern California, knowing Spanish is a good idea. I own a quarter horse, love football and am a member of the NRA. I am a mainstream American.

7   I'm also a secularized Muslim. While I was growing up, my family attended the local mosque once a week. Back then, Islam in America was "Westernized." The imam didn't have a beard, men and women weren't segregated except during prayers and the services were in English.

8   Today, Islam in America is much more fundamentalist. The imams wear tunics and conduct services in Arabic. Men and women are completely segregated, and the women are strongly encouraged to wear *higab* (head scarves) or burqas.

9   I attend mosque only on special holidays, so most local Muslims know I'm not a devout practitioner of Islam. They didn't trust me at first, but that changed when they saw me vehemently defending my clients in court and protesting the government's treatment of Arabs and Muslims in the media.

10   Even so, I didn't join the fight to protect my own kind; I simply believe the rule of law has been the first victim of the war on terrorism. For example, a material witness can be arrested only if he or she is not cooperating with the government. My clients had been fully cooperating, but investigators claimed they were not in order to arrest them and spirit them away to New York.

11   On April 30, 2002, New York federal district court Judge Shira Scheindlin ruled that the material-witness statute couldn't be used to arrest grand-jury witnesses. She released one of my clients and declared that the testimony of four FBI agents was "not credible" or "misleading."

12   My clients were lucky—many of those now in custody may never see a courtroom. The government arrested Jose Padilla—an American citizen—in Chicago, labeled him an "enemy combatant" and contends that he can be held in military prison indefinitely without access to an attorney. Since when does the Constitution allow citizens arrested on U.S. soil to be held beyond the reach of the courts?

13   The Bush administration is playing fast and loose with our rights. We are only beginning to understand the full impact of the Patriot Act—which was shoved through Congress in the aftermath of September 11—on our civil liberties. Federal agents can now search your home and office without your knowledge, and force your bank, your doctor and even your library to turn over their records about you.

14   Are Americans willing to sacrifice their freedoms in order to combat terrorism? I hope not. As Ben Franklin said, those who would trade liberty for security deserve neither. I'm not fighting for Arabs and Muslims; I'm fighting for all of us.

For Discussion:

What is the issue in this essay, and what position does the author take on it? What does the author mean by "the rule of law" in paragraph 10? What is your position on this issue? Give reasons for your views.

57

> **BEFORE YOU READ:** What is affirmative action? Have you or anyone you know ever been affected by affirmative action policies? How?

ESSAY #3   **A VIEW FROM BERKELEY***

Chang-Lin Tien

The late Chang-Lin Tien was chancellor of the University of California at Berkeley when he wrote this article.

1   When the debate over affirmative action in higher education started to simmer, the stance I took as the chancellor of the University of California at Berkeley seemed to surprise many people.

2   To be sure, my view—that we *should* consider race, ethnicity and gender along with many other factors in admissions—has put me at odds with some constituencies, including the majority of the Regents of the University of California. Last July, these officials voted to end affirmative action admission policies.

3   And with California voters to decide later this year whether to end all state affirmative action programs, silence might seem a more prudent course for the head of a major public university. We already have enough battles to fight, my staff sometimes reminds me: declining public funding, for example.

4   A few students and friends have hinted that it might make more sense for me, as an Asian-American, to oppose affirmative action.

5   Asian-Americans, who are not considered underrepresented minorities under affirmative action, have divergent views. Some are disturbed by the "model minority" stereotype; they say it pits them against other minorities and hides the discrimination they still face. Others—including the two Asian-American Regents who voted to end affirmative action—believe the only fair approach is to base admissions on academic qualifications. That also opens the door to more Asians.

6   So why do I strongly support affirmative action? My belief has been shaped by my role in higher education. And by my experience as a Chinese immigrant. I know first-hand that America can be a land of opportunity. When I came here, I was a penniless 21-year-old with a limited grasp of the language and culture. Yet I was permitted to accomplish a great deal. My research in heat transfer contributed to better nuclear reactor safety and space shuttle design. My former students are professors and researchers at some of America's best schools and business concerns.

7   But as I struggled to finish my education here, I also encountered the ugly realities of racial discrimination. This, too, is part of America's legacy and it is inextricably connected to the need for affirmative action.

8   When I first arrived in this country in 1956 as a graduate student, for example, I lived in Louisville, Ky. One day I got on a bus and saw that all the black people were in the back, the white people in the front. I didn't know where I belonged, so for a long time I stood near the driver. Finally, he told me to sit down in the front, and I did. I didn't take another bus ride for a whole year. I would walk an hour to avoid that.

9   I served as a teaching fellow at Louisville for a professor who refused to pronounce my name. He addressed me as "Chinaman." One day he directed me to adjust some valves in a large laboratory apparatus. Climbing a ladder,

---

New York Times, March 31, 1996, Special Education Section, 30.

I lost my balance and instinctively grabbed a nearby steam pipe. It was scorchingly hot and produced a jolt of pain that nearly caused me to faint. Yet I did not scream. Instead, I stuffed my throbbing hand into my coat pocket and waited until the class ended. Then I ran to the hospital emergency room, where I was treated for a burn that had singed all the skin off my palm.

10   Outwardly, my response fit the stereotype of the model-minority Asian: I said nothing and went about my business. But my silence had nothing to do with stoicism. I simply did not want to endure the humiliation of having the professor scold me in front of the class.

11   Of course, four decades later, there have been major civil rights advances in America. But serious racial divisions remain. That's why colleges and universities created affirmative admissions programs. The idea was to open the doors to promising minority students who lacked educational and social opportunities.

12   As Berkeley's chancellor, I have seen the promise of affirmative action come true. No racial or ethnic group constitutes a majority among our 21,000 undergraduates. And Berkeley students enter with higher grades and test scores than their predecessors. They graduate at the highest rate in our history.

13   I think that affirmative action should be a temporary measure, but the time has not yet come to eliminate it. Educational opportunities for inner-city minority students, for example, still contrast dramatically with those of affluent students in the suburbs, where many white families live.

14   And as a public institution, the university needs to look at broader societal needs, including greater leadership training of California's African-American and Hispanic population.

15   I try to explain this when, as occasionally happens, Asian-American or white friends complain to me that their child, a straight-A student, didn't get into Berkeley because we give spaces to others. I also say that we use admission criteria other than test scores, grades and ethnicity, including a genius for computers, musical talent, geographical diversity.

16   Besides, a straight-A average wouldn't guarantee admission to Berkeley even if there were no affirmative action. For a freshman class with 3,500 places, we get about 25,000 applicants. This year, 10,784 of them had a 4.0 high school record.

17   What's more, helping minority students may not be the most compelling reason for preserving affirmative action.

18   Every time I walk across campus, I am impressed by the vibrant spirit of this diverse community. In teeming Sproul Plaza, the dozens of student groups who set up tables represent every kind of social, political, ethnic and religious interest. In the dorms, students from barrios, suburbs, farm towns and the inner city come together.

19   When there are diverse students, staff and faculty (among whom there are still too few minorities), everybody stands to gain.

20   Of course, interactions between students of different backgrounds can bring misunderstanding. Some white students tell me they feel squeezed out by black and Latino students they believe are less deserving, as well as by overachieving Asian-American students. Some African-American and Latino students confide they sometimes feel their professors and white classmates consider them academically inferior, a view that's slow to change even when they excel.

21   Still, the overall message I get time and again from students and recent graduates is that they have valued the chance to challenge stereotypes.

22   So I was stunned by the Regents' decision to end affirmative action admissions policies, which goes into effect by 1998. I even debated whether to resign.

23   In Chinese, however, the character for "crisis" is actually two characters: one stands for danger and the other for opportunity. And I took the Chinese approach. Noting that the Regents had reaffirmed their commitment to

diversity when they discarded affirmative action, I decided to stay to try to make a difference.

24   Recently, I joined the superintendents of the major urban school districts of the San Francisco Bay area to announce a campaign: The Berkeley Pledge.

25   Under this program, Berkeley is deepening its support for disadvantaged youth trying to qualify for admission. One way will be to provide educational expertise for teachers; another will be to create incentives for pupils at selected school "pipelines" that begin in kindergarten. We also are stepping up our recruitment of exceptional minority students.

26   America has come a long way since the days of Jim Crow segregation. It would be a tragedy if our nation's colleges and universities slipped backward now, denying access to talented but disadvantaged youth and eroding the diversity that helps to prepare leaders.

For Discussion:

What are the major reasons Chancellor Tien provides for retaining affirmative action in higher education? Do you share his views? Give reasons for your answer, and use some of your own experiences to support your reasons, just as he does.

BEFORE YOU READ: How do you think ex-convicts should be treated when they reenter society?

ESSAY #4   GIVING PEOPLE A SECOND CHANCE*
Ernest Martinez

Ernest Martinez writes about his experience as an instructor in inmate vocational education at Wasco State Prison in Wasco, California.

1   I am very proud of being Mexican American and am both privileged and honored to have been blessed with a career as an educator. Yet, I sometimes think that when discussing the many Hispanic issues that we often attribute to a fractured American society, I believe we often do to ourselves what we don't want others to do to us: ostracize ourselves. On the one hand, we rally together as Hispanics to seek out equal opportunity and revel in the triumphs of our unity. But on the other hand, when we hear of our many Hispanic brethren who are ex-convicts who need employment avenues for reentry into society, we close our eyes and ears to their cry for assistance. We blame society for their plight and thrust the burden of our people on the very government we condemn for lack of opportunity.

2   For the past several years, I have been part of the lives of inmates by teaching them vocational studies. These inmates are an example to us all that it is only by the grace of God that we are not in their place. We can all attest to the fact that we have done something for which we have simply not been caught— for example, drinking alcoholic beverages as minors, or driving without a license, or hanging around with the wrong people and being at the wrong place at the wrong time, or telling little "white lies" while filing our taxes. These are all examples of "crimes" that we've gotten away with. And instead of being imprisoned, we are known as law abiding citizens. The inmates of Wasco State Prison have not been so lucky, graced or blessed.

---

*Hispanic, June 1996, 64.

3   I believe many of the inmates with whom I work are persons like you and me. Unfortunately, they took "the road less traveled," and found themselves in a situation that was beyond their ability to handle or solve. This is not only "man as the problem," but the "problems of man." There are many parallels that we can draw between ourselves—those of us in the professional and business communities in need of not only able but willing people—and the backgrounds, personalities, character traits, abilities, needs, and yes, even aspirations, of the many prison inmates wanting and asking for a "Chapter Two" in their lives.

4   The business environment today is not solely based on equipment, products, or services. It's dependent on the skills, talents, and savvy of people. We're not only in an information age today; we are in an Age of Man, whereby sales can only be made and increased through the interpersonal relationships that we create between provider and consumer, between our companies and our customers. The world respected organization, business, and management guru Dr. Peter Drucker has said, "Show me an organization or business that does not believe people are their greatest resource and I'll show you an organization with built-in limits to its success, and perhaps one destined for certain failure." Remember the old saying, "El ojo del amo engorda el caballo." [The literal meaning is, "The eye of love fattens the horse"; the metaphorical meaning is that "anything seen through the eyes of love seems better."] Only if we can secure our fiscally solvent present can we launch into a more expansive tomorrow. And, again, we can only do this if we focus on people as our greatest asset today.

5   I am of the ardent belief that many prison inmates are highly functional, tremendously skilled, fabulously talented, and often technically gifted. Some are inordinately intelligent, while others are blessed simply with the extraordinary ability to work diligently. I've learned over the years working as educator of vocational studies with inmates that their crime was more a matter of poor judgment rather than of faulty character. And while not so naive as to believe that all inmates are worthy of a "Chapter Two," I can empathize with how hard it is to take a breath when one is in a whirlwind. The momentum of the moment is a tremendous force in this "survival of the fittest" society.

6   This is not to mean that we are to be guilt-driven, but rather people-motivated. This is not to promote philanthropy, but to be responsible in not overlooking a pool of prospective employees that is often not considered in the equation. This is not to say that every prison inmate is right for our companies, but to instead entertain the financial and accessible feasibility of hiring persons (both men and women) who want to work hard and need the opportunity to do so. And, this is not about hiring the "lessor among us," but to seek the "gold hidden behind and beneath a bushel."

7   Yes, many among the prison population are the very best of people, both in skill and desire, and in character and spirit. These people represent a select group who did the crime and served their time. They possess abilities, skills, and talents that range from refined artistic propensities, technical adeptness, and computer literacy, to management skills, professional polish, and interpersonal qualities. And, while they may need the power of your push or the compassion of your pull, they are people who can and will show a watching world that it is possible to "turn a large ship in a harbor."

8   If they can turn their lives around from the dungeons of prison to the epic of hope, they can also be a tremendous testimony to what is possible in the world of Hispanic business and to society at large.

For Discussion:

Do you think this article might persuade business owners and managers to hire ex-convicts? Would you be persuaded if you could hire? Why or why not? Give a detailed explanation of your views about hiring individuals who have been through a vocational training program in prison.

61

> **BEFORE YOU READ:** How alike or how different from you were your grade-school teachers? Did you prefer to be taught by someone who was a member of your culture or nationality? Or did that not matter? Why?

ESSAY #5 ## ONE OF OUR OWN: TRAINING NATIVE TEACHERS FOR THE 21ST CENTURY*

Suzette Brewer

The author, a Cherokee, explains how Native American children can benefit from being taught by native teachers.

1   As a first-grader in Farmington, New Mexico in 1980, Regine Brown was excited about the traditional Navajo dress her grandmother had made for her and couldn't wait to wear it to school. That day, she also wore a beaded necklace that had been given to her by her great-great-great grandmother.

2   When she got to school, rather than admiring her attire, a non-Indian teacher with no evident cultural understanding of the dress or the necklace derided her for not wearing "normal clothes." The teacher tore off the beaded necklace in front of Brown's classmates as the little girl stood in embarrassed silence, watching all 150 beads of the necklace sprinkle to the floor.

3   "I got down on my hands and knees and picked up each and every bead, because I knew how many there were," remembers Brown, now 27. "When I picked them up, I gave myself 150 reasons why I was a good person. It showed me not to treat kids that way because it ruins them mentally."

4   It was an incident that she would never forget, a scene that seared itself permanently into her heart and mind—and one that would ultimately serve to motivate Brown as an educator to change the world in her own way: teaching Navajo children the importance and pride of their heritage while preparing them with a solid base of academics.

5   She is not alone. It is the kind of experience that Indian children have faced since the beginning of European colonization: the destruction of their culture and sense of self in the very school systems that had been set up to educate them. As a result, many Indian adults have bad memories of school and are not motivated to let their own children be subjected to the same treatment. This, say experts, contributes to the low educational attainment and retention rates among the nation's K–12 Native students.

6   Today, however, Brown and many like her are attending tribal colleges to become teachers in their own home communities, filling a critical need in local tribal K–12 schools where Indian children have very few role models to look to in their education. Brown, who wants to teach bilingual elementary education on the Navajo reservation, will graduate from Diné College in Tsaile, Arizona in May.

7   Diné College's teacher training program— unofficially referred to as "grow your own"— is one of the few in the country that is geared specifically toward tribal culture, and Diné is one of a handful of tribal colleges that are now offering teaching degrees. Others, like Sinte Gleska University in South Dakota and Salish-Kootenai Community College in Montana, are also offering four-year teaching degrees. Some of the two-year tribal colleges, like Ft. Berthold in New Town, North Dakota and Lac Courte Oreilles Ojibwa Community College in Hayward, Wisconsin, have matriculation

Native Peoples, March–April 2002, 52–53.

agreements with state colleges so students may finish their degrees and become teachers.

8   It is a trend that many involved in Indian education feel is necessary, not only for the role modeling, but also for improving student retention rates and test scores. And in areas of the country where the Native language is spoken as a first language, experts say that bilingual, bicultural education is the key to success in preserving unique Indian cultures that may be endangered while giving Indian children the tools to navigate mainstream society.

9   "We know that dealing with two languages is a lot easier in a school setting, teaching both at the same time," says Ben Barney, a professor and cultural specialist at Diné College. "Cognitive thought and language in terms of reading, writing and comprehension are more sophisticated when a person is proficient in multiple languages, because it forces the person to think on a number of different levels at the same time."

10 Therefore, says Barney, bilingual instruction enhances a person's education because it increases their ability to think, read and write in two languages, which is a significant focus of Diné's teacher training program. It is a teaching method that is just as valid and important, he says, as for those children who attend private schools with language programs that focus on Western European languages, such as French and German.

11 Bilingual Navajo-English teaching is why he believes the Diné program is so successful, with nearly all of the students being recruited for teaching positions prior to graduation. It is clearly filling a sorely needed gap in tribal education. "We didn't want the standard teacher education program at Diné," Barney says. "The mainstream program does not fit here."

12 Many times, he says, teachers who have been trained at mainstream universities come to the reservation and have to be retrained to suit the needs, culture and atmosphere of the Indian population. By using teaching methods that have been proven to work among Indian students, Barney says the success rates for both students and teachers increase.

13 "The teacher education program here is a core-language program that can be fitted to suit any tribe—not just the Navajo," Barney says. "But the language element and culture are both very important because they work in tandem with who these children are as Native people and how they view the world."

14 Many Indian people believe, in fact, that the survival of their Native languages is crucial because much of their culture lies within their language and loses some of its meaning when translated into English.

15 "English is the dominant language of the United States, and as soon as you put a Native person in their traditional dress they become a toy to mainstream culture, which is diminishing to them," says Barney. "But in our program, you don't have to take off your 'Navajo-ness' at the door to be a teacher—self-identity and acceptance of oneself are an important part of our mission in training teachers for elementary education."

16 For students like Regine Brown, being able to reverse the trend of centuries of governmental policies and to give children on the Navajo reservation a sense of pride and self-esteem in their education is the happy outcome of a childhood incident that might have turned her away from education for good.

17 "This was something I promised myself," she says. "The kids on the rez need someone of their own to teach—someone who understands them, their backgrounds and where they're coming from culturally. And it's something that I'm looking forward to when I graduate."

For Discussion:

In your opinion, should teachers serve as role models for the students they teach? Why or why not? Do you favor bilingual education for children who speak a language other than English when they start school? Why or why not? Would you like to be taught by teachers who represent your culture or gender? Why or why not?

ESSAY #6   WHY I WANT A WIFE*

Judy Brady

Judy Brady's famous essay first appeared in *Ms.* magazine in 1971.

1 I belong to that classification of people known as wives. I am A Wife. And, not altogether incidentally, I am a mother.

2 Not too long ago a male friend of mine appeared on the scene fresh from a recent divorce. He had one child, who is, of course, with his ex-wife. He is looking for another wife. As I thought about him while I was ironing one evening, it suddenly occurred to me that I, too, would like to have a wife. Why do I want a wife?

3 I would like to go back to school so that I can become economically independent, support myself, and, if need be, support those dependent upon me. I want a wife who will work and send me to school. And while I am going to school I want a wife to take care of my children. I want a wife to keep track of the children's doctor and dentist appointments. And to keep track of mine, too. I want a wife to make sure my children eat properly and are kept clean. I want a wife who will wash the children's clothes and keep them mended. I want a wife who is a good nurturant attendant to my children, who arranges for their schooling, makes sure that they have an adequate social life with their peers, takes them to the park, the zoo, etc. I want a wife who takes care of the children when they are sick, a wife who arranges to be around when the children need special care, because, of course, I cannot miss classes at school. My wife must arrange to lose time at work and not lose the job. It may mean a small cut in my wife's income from time to time, but I

guess I can tolerate that. Needless to say, my wife will arrange and pay for the care of the children while my wife is working.

4 I want a wife who will take care of *my* physical needs. I want a wife who will keep my house clean. A wife who will pick up after my children, a wife who will pick up after me. I want a wife who will keep my clothes clean, ironed, mended, replaced when need be, and who will see to it that my personal things are kept in their proper place so that I can find what I need the minute I need it. I want a wife who cooks the meals, a wife who is a *good* cook. I want a wife who will plan the menus, do the necessary grocery shopping, prepare the meals, serve them pleasantly, and then do the cleaning up while I do my studying. I want a wife who will care for me when I am sick and sympathize with my pain and loss of time from school. I want a wife to go along when our family takes a vacation so that someone can continue to care for me and my children when I need a rest and change of scene.

5 I want a wife who will not bother me with rambling complaints about a wife's duties. But I want a wife who will listen to me when I feel the need to explain a rather difficult point I have come across in my course of studies. And I want a wife who will type my papers for me when I have written them.

6 I want a wife who will take care of the details of my social life. When my wife and I are invited out by my friends, I want a wife who will take care of the babysitting arrangements. When I meet people at school

---

*Reprinted by permission of the author.

that I like and want to entertain, I want a wife who will have the house clean, will prepare a special meal, serve it to me and my friends, and not interrupt when I talk about things that interest me and my friends. I want a wife who will have arranged that the children are fed and ready for bed before my guests arrive so that the children do not bother us. I want a wife who takes care of the needs of my guests so that they feel comfortable, who makes sure that they have an ashtray, that they are passed the hors d'oeuvres, that they are offered a second helping of the food, that their wine glasses are replenished when necessary, that their coffee is served to them as they like it. And I want a wife who knows that sometimes I need a night out by myself.

7   I want a wife who is sensitive to my sexual needs, a wife who makes love passionately and eagerly when I feel like it, a wife who makes sure that I am satisfied. And, of course, I want a wife who will not demand sexual attention when I am not in the mood for it. I want a wife who assumes the complete responsibility for birth control, because I do not want more children. I want a wife who

will remain sexually faithful to me so that I do not have to clutter up my intellectual life with jealousies. And I want a wife who understands that *my* sexual needs may entail more than strict adherence to monogamy. I must, after all, be able to relate to people as fully as possible.

8   If, by chance, I find another person more suitable as a wife than the wife I already have, I want the liberty to replace my present wife with another one. Naturally, I will expect a fresh, new life; my wife will take the children and be solely responsible for them so that I am left free.

9   When I am through with school and have a job, I want my wife to quit working and remain at home so that my wife can more fully and completely take care of a wife's duties.

10   My God, who *wouldn't* want a wife?

For Discussion:

What is Brady really saying when she says she wants a wife? What solutions would you propose for the problem of who should be responsible for all of the tasks and duties described in this essay?

E. Group Work and Class Discussion: Using Gender, Nationality, and Cultural Background to Strengthen Visual Argument

The five advertisements reprinted here were created by advertisers who have drawn on other people's experiences as members of a particular culture, gender, or nationality. When you have studied these ads, discuss them in small groups of four or five students. Appoint a scribe to record your findings and report them to the class. The following questions will help organize your discussion.

1. What is the purpose of each advertisement? What is being advertised?

2. What experiences with culture, gender, or nationality do these advertisers draw on to strengthen their arguments?

3. What is effective in their arguments as a result? Be specific.

4. What can you conclude about drawing on experiences with culture, gender, or nationality to strengthen a visual argument?

5. Describe the audience each of these advertisers seems to be addressing. To whom will each of these advertisements appeal? Who will resist them?

Image 1: Mary J. Blige and Her New Car.

Blige is an award-winning artist. But she is also a mother and wife. If you want it all too, the obvious, vehicle choice is the Chevy Tahoe Hybrid.

For Discussion: What qualities does the individual in this advertisement possess that make her a good subject for advertising this car?

66

Image 2: Young Man Doing His Banking.

For Discussion: How would you describe the cultural identity of the individual in this ad? Describe some of his apparent attitudes, talents, and values. Do you identify with him? What characteristics do you share with him that makes this ad convincing to you? What do you resist in this ad, if anything, that makes the ad less convincing to you?

CROW RESERVATION,
HOME OF LITTLE BIGHORN COLLEGE

IF I STAY ON THE REZ

I CAN LEARN BIOLOGY
IN MY NATIVE LANGUAGE.

TRIBAL COLLEGES PROVIDE CURRICULUM SUPPORTING INDIAN IDENTITY AND DEVELOPMENT.
SOMETIMES THEY'RE THE ONLY PLACE INDIANS CAN LEARN THEIR NATIVE LANGUAGE AND CULTURE.

LEARN HOW THE TRIBAL COLLEGES PROVIDE QUALITY EDUCATION TO NATIVE AMERICANS. 1-800-776-FUND | COLLEGEFUND.ORG

AMERICAN INDIAN COLLEGE FUND ◗ EDUCATING THE MIND AND SPIRIT

Image 3: If I Stay on the Rez.

For Discussion: What is "the Rez"? What do you find striking about this ad, if anything? Why? What is your reaction to the ideas and values in the ad? Do you accept or resist them? How would the general effectiveness of this ad change if a 25-year-old Caucasian man were pictured giving his views about attending a nearby community college?

67

**Image 4:
Blood Donor.**

For Discussion:
Why do you think the advertisers feature this particular young man in this ad? What does his nationality contribute to the ad, if anything? Would the ad be as effective with a middle-aged Caucasian woman pictured in it? Why or why not? Consider the words in the upper left corner. What is their purpose? What do they contribute to the overall message and general effectiveness of the ad?

68

You wouldn't recognize me in an elevator, but if you ever needed it, I would give you my blood.

When you help the American Red Cross, you help America. **American Red Cross**

America is a place where we look out for each other.
And with someone in America needing blood every two seconds,
there's someone who needs you to roll up your sleeve today.

Call 1-800-GIVE LIFE or visit givelife.org

**Image 5:
Cell Phones in
Africa.**

For Discussion:
What countries
and nationalities
are depicted in
this ad? How is
this ad different
from other cell
phone ads you
may have seen?
What are the
main ideas and
values that are
expressed in this
ad? Guess about
its appeal for its
target audience.
How effective is
it? Who would
embrace it? Who
would resist it?

F. Class Discussion and Writing Assignment: International Argument

Read the following article, in which the author explains what "yes" (*hai*) means in Japanese. Are there other examples of words, gestures, customs, beliefs, or values like this one that could create confusion or distrust among people from different cultures? Draw on the experiences of international students both in and outside of class and on international news reports. Write a paper in which you explain one of the differences you have identified, along with what would be required to achieve common ground and better understanding.

> **BEFORE YOU READ:** Has anyone from another culture or nationality ever said or done something that confused you? What was it? How were you confused?

ESSAY #7   A SIMPLE "HAI" WON'T DO*

Reiko Hatsumi

Reiko Hatsumi writes novels as well as essays.

70

1   Having spent my life between East and West, I can sympathize with those who find the Japanese *yes* unfathomable. However, the fact that it sometimes fails to correspond precisely with the Occidental *yes* does not necessarily signal intended deception. . . . It marks a cultural gap that can have serious repercussions.

2   I once knew an American who worked in Tokyo. He was a very nice man, but he suffered a nervous breakdown and went back to the U.S. tearing his hair and exclaiming, "All Japanese businessmen are liars." I hope this is not true. If it were, all Japanese businessmen would be driving each other mad, which does not seem to be the case. Nevertheless, since tragedies often arise from misunderstandings, an attempt at some explanation might not be amiss.

3   A Japanese *yes* in its primary context simply means the other has heard you and is contemplating a reply. This is because it would be rude to keep someone waiting for an answer without supplying him with an immediate response.

4   For example: a feudal warlord marries his sister to another warlord. . . . Then he decides to destroy his newly acquired brother-in-law and besieges his castle. Being human, though, the attacking warlord worries about his sister and sends a spy to look around. The spy returns and the lord inquires eagerly, "Well, is she safe?" The spy bows and answers *"Hai,"* which means "yes." We sigh with relief thinking, "Ah, the fair lady is still alive!" But then the spy continues, "To my regret she has fallen on her sword together with her husband."

5   *Hai* is also an expression of our willingness to comply with your intent even if your request is worded in the negative. This can cause complications. When I was at school, our English teacher, a British nun, would say, "Now children, you won't forget to do your homework, will you?" And we would all dutifully chorus, "Yes, mother," much to her consternation.

---

*New York Times, April 15, 1992, A12.

6   A variation of *hai* may mean, "I understand your wish and would like to make you happy but unfortunately . . ." Japanese being a language of implication, the latter part of this estimable thought is often left unsaid.

7   Is there, then, a Japanese *yes* that corresponds to the Western one? I think so, particularly when it is accompanied by phrases such as *sodesu* (It is so) and *soshimasu* (I will do so). A word of caution against the statement, "I will think about it." Though in Tokyo this can mean a willingness to give one's proposal serious thought, in Osaka, another business center, it means a definite *no*. This attitude probably stems from the belief that a straight-forward *no* would sound too brusque.

8   When talking to a Japanese person it is perhaps best to remember that although he may be speaking English, he is reasoning in Japanese. And if he says "I will think about it," you should inquire as to which district of Japan he hails from before going on with your negotiations.

For Discussion:

Give some examples of what Japanese persons may really mean when they say yes as described in this article. Do you ever say one thing and mean something else? Give an example. What effect does this have in your communication with others?

CHAPTER 3

The Rhetorical Situation: Understanding Audience and Context

Y ou are probably beginning to realize by now that argument does not take place in a vacuum. Instead, a situation occurs that raises questions in people's minds and motivates them to discuss and argue in an attempt to resolve the issues and problems that emerge. For example, the price per barrel of crude oil goes up and issues emerge: How can the United States become less dependent on foreign oil? What are viable alternate energy sources? Or, How effective are hybrid cars? Professor Lloyd Bitzer calls a situation that motivates issues and argument a *rhetorical situation,* because it stimulates discussion and encourages change. Rhetorical situations existed for the Declaration of Independence in 1776 when the issue was independence and its authors declared that the North American colonies should be independent from Great Britain, and for Abraham Lincoln's Gettysburg Address that he delivered in 1863 at the site of a famous Civil War battle. The issue was national unity. The time, place, and existing circumstances of these rhetorical situations provided the motivation for the authors of these documents to write them.[1] Five elements, according to Bitzer, are present in every rhetorical situation, and they can be analyzed.

In this chapter we focus on the rhetorical situation as readers, creators of visual argument, and writers employ it. Analyzing the rhetorical situation is an important critical reading strategy: it can be used as a tool for analysis throughout the reading process; it can be employed in a similar way to gain a fuller understanding of visual argument; and it is a potent critical thinking strategy that can help the writer plan and write a better argument.

---

[1]Lloyd Bitzer, "The Rhetorical Situation," *Philosophy and Rhetoric* 1 (January 1968): 1–14.

Analyze the Rhetorical Situation When You Read an Argument

According to Bitzer, a rhetorical situation has five elements. We rearrange the elements in order to form the acronym TRACE, from the initial letters of these five elements, to help you remember them: the *Text*, the *Reader* or audience, the *Author*, the *Constraints*, and the *Exigence* or cause. Now look at each of them to see how they can help you read, understand, and evaluate writing that presents an argument.

Text. The text is the argument. Whether it is written, visual, or spoken, the text will have characteristics you can analyze. These include the type of text (essay, letter, book, image, debate, etc.), the content of the text, and the format, organization, argumentation strategies, language, and style that are employed by the author.

Reader. The potential reader or audience for the text ideally must care enough to read or otherwise take in the text and pay attention. An audience might change their perceptions as a result and, perhaps, will mediate change or act in a new way. A rhetorical situation invites such audience responses and outcomes. Most authors have a targeted or intended reading audience in mind. You may identify with the targeted audience, or you may not, particularly if you belong to a different culture or live in a different time. As you read, compare your reactions to the text with the reactions you imagine the targeted or intended reading audience might have had.

Author. The author writes or develops an argument to convince a particular audience. You can analyze the author's position, motives, values, and degree of expertise. If you do not have direct information about the author, you will need to infer or guess at much of this information as you consider the argument text.

Constraints. Constraints include the people, events, circumstances, and traditions that are part of the situation that constrain or limit a targeted audience and cause them to analyze and react to the situation in a particular way. Constraints also include the beliefs, attitudes, prejudices, interests, and habits that influence the audience's perceptions of the situation. The author brings another set of constraints to the situation. These include the author's character, background, available resources, and style. The limits inherent in the type of text being produced, whether written, spoken, or visual, can also provide constraints. Constraints may draw the author and audience together, or they may drive them apart. They influence the amount of common ground that will be established between an author and an audience. Look at the cartoon in Figure 3.1 ■ (on page 74) for an example of constraints that are driving people apart. The constraints in this example are the basic assumptions about who governs in this family. What would you say are the father's constraints in this situation, and how do they differ from those of the rest of the family?

73

Figure 3.1 *Constraints in the Form of Basic Assumptions Driving People Apart.*

"Because this family isn't ready to hold democratic elections—that's why!"

Here are some additional examples of constraints: (1) An audience feels constrained to mistrust the media because it thinks reporters exaggerate or lie. This constraint may cause this audience to be cynical and suspicious of an essay written by an editor that praises reporters for always writing the truth. (2) Another essay, by a famous biologist, presents the global environmental and overpopulation crisis in such catastrophic and frightening terms that a particular audience is constrained, through fear, to shut out the argument and refuse to consider it. (3) Some voters have lost their faith in political leaders. When they are mailed brochures that argue in favor of particular candidates and that ask them to support these candidates with donations, their constraints cause them to throw these materials away without looking at them.

Here are two more examples of constraints that may be closer to you: (1) You parked your car in a no-parking zone because you were late to class, and the police feel constrained by law to give you a ticket. You have different constraints, and you write to the hearings board that more and closer parking should be available to students to help them get to class on time. The hearings board has its own constraints and will probably turn down your plea. (2) You believe everyone should share the household chores equally, and the person you live with disagrees. Both of you are constrained by your past experiences in living with other people, possibly by traditions that influence your ideas about gender roles in this type of division of labor, and also by perceptions about who has the most time to spend on the chores. Both parties may have to work hard to create the common ground necessary to resolve this issue. Notice how the constraints present on both sides in these examples influence the way the audience and the arguer react to the rhetorical situation and to the issues it generates.

Exigence. Exigence is the part of the situation which signals that something controversial has occurred or is present and that a problem needs to be resolved by some response from an audience. Here are some examples of exigence for argument: people become suspicious of genetically engineered foods because of negative newspaper reports; a third-world country threatens to resume nuclear testing; a football player is badly injured in a game and the fans of the opposing team cheer in delight. In all cases, something is wrong, imperfect, defective, or in conflict. Exigence invites analysis and discussion, and sometimes also a written response to encourage both individual public awareness and discourse about problematic situations.

Study the following set of questions. They will help you analyze the rhetorical situation and gain insight into its component parts when you are the reader.

Text. What kind of text is it? What are its special qualities and features? What is it about?

Reader or audience. Who is the *targeted audience*? What is the nature of this group? Can they be convinced? What are the anticipated outcomes? If you are reading a historical document—for example, the Declaration of Independence—you might ask further, How did the readers at the time the text was written differ from other readers of the time or from modern readers? Were they convinced? Did they act on their convictions?

Now consider how *you as a reader* compare with the targeted audience and ask, Am I typical of one of the readers the writer anticipated? What is my initial position? What are my constraints? Do I share common ground with the author and other audience members? Am I open to change? Does this argument convince me? Am I motivated to change my mind or modify the situation? How?

Author. Who is the author? Consider background, experience, education, affiliations, and values. What is motivating the author to write?

Constraints. What special constraining circumstances will influence the reader's and the author's responses to the subject? Think about the people, events, circumstances, and traditions that are already in place along with the beliefs, attitudes, prejudices, interests, habits, and motives held by both the author and the reader that may limit or constrain their perceptions. Do the constraints create common ground, or do they drive the reader and author apart?

Exigence. What happened to cause this argument? Why is it perceived as a defect or problem? Is it new or recurring?

The student editorial from a college newspaper reprinted below addresses grading policies. Read the essay first and then read the analysis of the rhetorical situation that follows it. This analysis provides an example of how readers can use the rhetorical situation to help them understand argument.

75

> **BEFORE YOU READ:** What are your opinions about the grading policies in your classes?

ESSAY #1   "A" IS FOR "ABSENT"*

Chris Piper

Chris Piper was a broadcast journalism major at the University of Texas at Arlington when he wrote this essay for the student newspaper, for which he also worked as a proofreader.

1 Last semester, I enrolled in one of the most dreaded courses in any communication degree plan. Most save it until the very end of their college career, but I took it as a sophomore.

2 Remarkably, I did very well on all of the tests. Also, the professor gave me high marks on almost every project. But when final grades came out, I ended up with a "C." My absences dropped my average more than 10 points. Admittedly, I earned the grade given to me. The syllabus clearly stated what would occur if I missed more than my allotted "freebies."

3 But my refusal to attend class does not excuse policies that subvert the value of learning and education, emphasizing attendance instead.

4 Professors who implement attendance policies often argue, "If this were a job, and you failed to show up, you would be fired." There is, however, one big difference between going to work versus going to class.

5 A job pays for my service, but I pay my professors for their services. I spend plenty of money on my education, and my choice to fully take advantage of the expense is exactly that—my choice.

6 When evaluating superior standardized test scores, such as what one might make on the SAT and ACT, admissions officers don't ask whether students attended prep courses before the exam. Obviously, a high score denotes that a test taker knows the material.

7 I truly believe most professors want their students to score well, which is why they implement attendance policies. I am touched by the sentiment. But if missing class leads to poor results by traditional grading methods—tests, quizzes, projects, etc.—then so be it. The student body could use some winnowing out.

8 I imagine a few instructors adopt attendance policies to stroke their own egos—to ensure a crowd is present when they enlighten the eager masses. But I'm arguing the validity of such rules regardless of any questionable motives. If a student can earn good grades on required work without attending class, then instructors should grade that student accordingly.

9 I encourage professors to give pop quizzes in place of attendance policies. At the very least, a quiz measures comprehension of pertinent material. Of course, such a change would mean more work for professors.

10 But that's what students are paying for.

For Discussion:

What is the issue? What is the author's position on the issue? What reasons and evidence are given to support the author's position? What is your position on this issue? How much common ground do you share with your instructors on this issue?

*Chris Piper. "'A' is for 'Absent,'" *Shorthorn*, October 21, 2003, 3.

Here is an analysis of the rhetorical situation for "'A' Is for 'Absent.'"

▶ Example of an Analysis of a Rhetorical Situation from the Reader's Point of View

Text. This is an argumentative editorial in the student newspaper that provides reasons and personal experience to prove that professors should not have attendance policies that lower students' grades for excessive absences.

Reader or audience. The targeted readers are other students who have had or could have similar experiences. The author expects the students to identify with him and agree that such policies should be abolished. Other readers might include professors and administrators who would probably be less likely to agree with the author.

Author. The author is a sophomore majoring in communications who had good grades on tests and projects but who lost ten points and ended up with a C for missing more classes than the syllabus allowed. The author also is a proofreader for the college newspaper.

Constraints. The author is constrained by the belief that students are customers who pay professors for their services and should be able to take advantage of those services on their own terms. He is also constrained by the idea that students can learn enough material to merit good grades without going to class. He expects his readers to hold the same beliefs. Another constraint he recognizes is the right of the professors to determine grading policy.

Exigence. The student received a C grade in a course in which he thought he should have had a higher grade.

Now consider how an understanding of the rhetorical situation can help you analyze images.

Analyze the Rhetorical Situation When You View a Visual Argument

It has been said that the twenty-first century wars in Afghanistan and Iraq are more photographed than any wars in history. It has also been said that the preponderance of the images photographers have sent back from both war zones have been negative in effect because they often show the worst side of these wars. Figure 3.2 ■ (on page 78) is an exception. Look at the image, read the caption that accompanies it, and consider the questions in the margin. Then read the following analysis of the rhetorical situation of the image and notice how much more you learn about this photo and its possible effect on an audience.

Figure 3.2
Photograph from an Iraqi War Zone.

This image appeared as a stand-alone image in a national United States newspaper. View this photograph as an argument. How is it different from many of the images of war you have seen on television or in newspapers? How does it affect you as a viewer?

A Gruesome Discovery, and a Helping Hand
Staff Sgt. Osman Koroma of Maryland yesterday with Ahmed, one of 24 disabled children rescued from an orphanage in Baghdad by American and Iraqi soldiers in June. The children, who were near death from starvation and neglect, are recovering at another orphanage in the capital. The soldiers who made the discovery were recognized at a ceremony yesterday.

▶ Example of an Analysis of the Rhetorical Situation from the Viewer's Point of View

Text. This is a photograph from a war zone in Iraq. It is printed in an American newspaper. It depicts a U.S. soldier and a disabled Iraqi child.

Viewer or audience. The targeted viewers are people in the United States, but also in other parts of the world, who read this newspaper either online or in print. The photographer expects the audience to be interested in what is going on in Iraq in general, but also to show an interest in this particular incident that might strike them as unusual when compared with other war images. The photographer would expect a sympathetic audience who shares his humanitarian values.

Photographer or artist. Photographer Spencer Platt is an award-winning photojournalist who works for Getty Images, a major source of digital images used by the news media. He is known for photographs that sometimes exhibit unexpected contradictions as they are found in real life.

Constraints. The artist is constrained by the idea that war does not always result in killing and destruction of property. At times, good and generous acts as well as unexpected cooperation can occur in the midst of war. He expects viewers to accept these constraints when they view his photograph, which will result in common ground with his audience.

Exigence. An American soldier rescues a disabled Iraqi child who was starving and near death in an orphanage and moves him to another orphanage where he will receive better care. Iraqi soldiers cooperate in this effort.

Next, consider how an understanding of the rhetorical situation of written arguments also helps you as a writer.

Use the Rhetorical Situation When You Write an Argument

As a writer, you can use the rhetorical situation to help you think critically and make decisions about your own writing. All five elements of the rhetorical situation are important considerations for writers. Three elements are in place before you begin to write. They are the *exigence,* the *reader or audience,* and the *constraints.* When you begin to write, the other two elements are added: you, the *author,* and the *text* that you create. Figure 3.3 ■ provides a diagram of these five elements that depicts some of the relationships among them.

Now consider each of the five elements from the writer's point of view. Use TRACE to help you remember the elements. As a writer, however, you will think

Figure 3.3 *The Five Elements of the Rhetorical Situation That the Writer Considers While Planning and Writing Argument.*

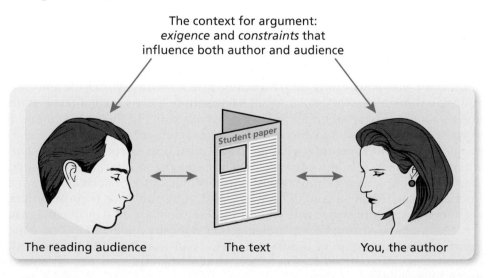

The context for argument:
exigence and *constraints* that
influence both author and audience

The reading audience   The text   You, the author

about them not in the order presented in the mnemonic but in the order suggested in the previous paragraph.

What Is the Exigence?

The exigence of a situation will provide an author with the motivation to write about an issue. Issues often emerge from real-life events that signal something is wrong. One student found a topic when a relative who had spent time in jail could not get employment after he was released. Another student from a country outside of the United States became interested in intercultural differences and decided to write about the relative value of retaining her own culture or assimilating with a new one. Yet another student discovered an exigence when she read a negative article about Barbie dolls and remembered her positive experiences with them when she was younger.

Such occurrences can cause the writer to ask the questions associated with exigence: *What issues, including problems or defects, are revealed? Are these new issues or recurring issues? How severe is the problem or defect?*

Who Is the Reader or Audience?

According to the definition of argument established in Chapter 1, productive argument must create common ground and achieve some definable audience outcomes. To do this, a writer needs to analyze the audience's present opinions, values, and motives, and show as often as possible that the author shares them. Both audience and author must cooperate to a certain degree for argument to achieve any outcomes at all. To help you analyze the values and motives you hold in common with your audience, refer to Box 3.1 ■ for a list of the needs and values that motivate most audiences.

To help you understand your audience, ask: *Who are my readers? Where do they stand on my issue? How can I establish common ground with them? If they disagree with me, will they be willing to change or modify their views, or not?*

What Are Some of the Constraints?

Remember that constraints influence the ways in which both you and your audience think about the issues. What background, events, experiences, traditions, values, or associations are influencing both you and them? If you decide to write to convince an audience that has no experience with criminals to hire people with criminal records, what are their constraints likely to be? How hard will it be for them to adopt your views? Or if you are an international student who is comparing your culture with the American culture to decide how much to change and adapt to American ways, and your audience is only familiar with its own culture, what will you do to help them see this problem as you see it? If you are writing for an audience that is mostly male and has no experience with or memories of Barbie dolls, what constraints would you run into if you tried to convince them that Barbie dolls are an important part of children's experience?

| Box 3.1 | Needs and Values That Motivate Most Audiences. |

▶▶▶ What Motivates an Audience?[2]

1. **Survival needs:** food, warmth, and shelter; physical safety
2. **Health:** physical well-being, strength, endurance, energy; mental stability, optimism
3. **Financial well-being:** accumulation of wealth; increased earning capacity; lower costs and expenses; financial security
4. **Affection and friendship:** identification in a group; being accepted, liked, loved; being attractive to others; having others as friends or objects of affection
5. **Respect and esteem of others:** having the approval of others; having status in a group; being admired; having fame
6. **Self-esteem:** meeting one's own standards in such virtues as courage, fairness, honesty, generosity, good judgment, and compassion; meeting self-accepted obligations of one's role as employee, child or parent, citizen, member of an organization
7. **New experience:** travel; change in employment or location; new hobbies or leisure activities; new food or consumer products; variety in friends and acquaintances
8. **Self-actualization:** developing one's potential in skills and abilities; achieving ambitions; being creative; gaining the power to influence events and other people
9. **Convenience:** conserving time or energy; satisfying the other motives with considerable ease

To help you understand the constraints held by both you and your audience, ask: *How are our training, background, affiliations, and values either in harmony or in conflict? Will constraints drive us apart or help us build common ground? If they drive us apart, what additional information can I provide to build common ground and bring us closer together? Where will my argument appear? Will it be a paper for an instructor, a letter to a supervisor, a letter to an editor, or a posting in an online chat room? Each medium has its own requirements.*

You are in a position now to think about the remaining two elements of the rhetorical situation: you, the *author,* and the *text* you will write.

Who Is the Author?

You will now need to think of yourself as an author of argument. You may have selected one or more issues to write about at this point. Before beginning your research, reflect on what you already know about your issue and what you still need to learn. Draw on your own experience, if you have some that applies. For instance, one student might think about her relative's experiences in prison and

---

[2]The list in Box 3.1 is based on Abraham Maslow's hierarchy of needs and motives from his book *Motion and Personality,* expanded by James A. Wood in *Speaking Effectively* (New York: Random House, 1988), 203–204. Used with permission.

imagine a better life for him, another might feel out of place in America and wonder how much he should change, and yet another student recalls her Barbie dolls and looks back with pleasure on the many hours she spent playing with them. Make brief notes on this experience to use later in your paper. If you have no direct experience to draw on, research, reading, and critical thinking will provide the material for your paper.

To better consider your role as the author, ask these questions: *Why am I interested in this issue? Why do I perceive it as a defect or problem? Is it a new or old issue for me? What is my personal background or experience with this issue? What makes me qualified to write about it? Which of my personal values are involved? How can I get more information? What is my purpose and perspective? How can I make my paper convincing?*

How Should the Text Be Developed to Fit the Situation?

Your text (paper) may be written in response to an assignment in your argument class, in which case it should meticulously follow the assignment requirements. You might also, however, write a paper for another class, a proposal at work, or a letter to the editor of a newspaper, to name a few possibilities.

Questions such as the following will help you decide what your completed argument text might look like: *What is the assignment? What final form should this paper take? Should I use an adversarial or a consensual style? How can I build common ground? Should I state the issue and my position on it right away, or should I lead up to it? How can I make my position original and interesting? What types of support should I use? How will I conclude my argument?*

▶ Example of an Analysis of a Rhetorical Situation When You Are the Writer

Exigence: What is motivating you to write on this issue? You neglected to turn in two early assignments in a course, and you suddenly realize that the zeroes you received then will lower your final grade from a B to a C. If you get a C, you will lose your scholarship. You decide to write to your instructor to find a way to raise your grade.

Reader or Audience: Who is going to read this? Your instructor (the audience) has already announced a policy of no late work. Nothing has been said about extra-credit work, however. You will try to establish common ground with the instructor by proposing an extra-credit project that will benefit not just you, but the entire class. You will describe in detail a successful experience you had with online research on your paper topic. The class is struggling with online research, the teacher wants the students to learn it, she does not have much time to teach it, and you can help fill the gap.

Constraints: Will your values and attitudes drive you and your instructor apart, or will they help you develop common ground? The instructor will have time constraints in class and may be unwilling to give you class time for your project. To address that constraint, you decide to ask for only five minutes, and you offer to prepare handouts that describe your online research in a way that will benefit your classmates.

The instructor may also have constraints about replacing missed assignments with extra-credit work. If one student is allowed to do this, she reasons, will all the others want to also? You point out that the project you are proposing is more difficult than the early assignments you missed and probably few, if any, students will want to follow your example.

You create common ground with your instructor by showing you are serious about the course and its standards. You decide to admit to your bad judgment when you failed to complete assignments, to point out that you have done well since then, and to commit to completing the remaining assignments carefully and on time. You also explain the importance of the extra-credit work to your future as a student. Without your scholarship, you will have to drop out of school. You know that you and your teacher share a desire to keep students in school. You and your instructor have common ground on that matter as well.

Author: What do you know? What do you need to learn? You are the author. You have read the class policies in the syllabus and know you have to work with them. You know you have computer expertise that many others in the class lack. You need to learn how to present what you know both orally and in written handouts to help the rest of the class.

Text: What should your argument look like? You will write a one-page proposal to your instructor in which you describe in detail what you would like to present to the class about online research. You ask that this assignment be used to raise the zero grades you received earlier in the course. You attach a second page that shows a sample of the handouts you will prepare for the class.

83

The class activities and writing assignments at the end of this chapter will help you use the information about the rhetorical situation that you have learned in this chapter. For example, one of the activities instructs you to analyze the rhetorical situation for each issue you select to write about in future papers, and another asks you to conduct an audience analysis of your class members who will read the various drafts of your papers. Before you turn to the activities and writing assignments, however, you will need additional information to help you think about and analyze an audience for an argument paper.

Conducting an Audience Analysis

The purpose of argument is to bring about some change in an audience. Here are several additional considerations to help you understand your audience and plan your argument strategies to bring about change.

Determine the Audience's Initial Position and Consider How It Might Change

As part of your planning, project what you would regard as acceptable audience outcomes for your argument. Think particularly about the degree of common ground you initially share with your audience because it is then easier to plan for audience change. There are several possibilities for initial audience positions and possible changes or outcomes.

▶ *A friendly audience.* You may be writing for a friendly audience, one that is in *near or total agreement with you* from the outset. The planned outcome is to *confirm this audience's beliefs and strengthen their commitment.* You can be straightforward with such an audience, addressing them directly and openly with your claim at the beginning, supported with evidence that they can accept. Political rallies, religious sermons, and public demonstrations by special-interest groups, such as civil rights or environmental groups, all serve to make members more strongly committed to their original beliefs. When you write for a friendly audience, you will achieve the same effect.

▶ *An undecided audience.* This audience either mildly agrees with you or mildly opposes you. They *may possess no clear reasons* for their tendencies or beliefs. Possible outcomes in this case usually include (1) *final agreement* with you, (2) *a new interest* in the issue and a commitment to work out a position on it, or (3) *a tentative decision* to accept what seems to be true for now. To establish common ground with this kind of audience, get to the point quickly and use support that will establish connections. Types of support that establish connections with an audience are described in Chapter 7.

▶ *A neutral audience.* Other audiences may be *neutral on your issue, uncommitted and uninterested in how it is resolved.* Your aim will be to *change the level of their indifference* and encourage them to take a position. You may only be able to get their attention or raise their level of consciousness. As with other audiences, you will establish common ground with a neutral audience by analyzing their needs and by appealing to those needs.

▶ *A hostile, resistant audience.* A hostile audience, which may fully disagree with you, may also be closed to the idea of change at all, at least at first. Anticipated outcomes for such audiences might include *avoiding more hostility* and *getting people to listen and consider possible alternative views.* You will learn strategies in Chapter 11 to help you appeal to such audiences. It is always possible that a hostile audience might have their minds *changed* or at least *compromise.* If all else fails, sometimes you can get a hostile audience to *agree to disagree,* which is much better than increasing their hostility.

▶ *An unfamiliar audience.* When you do not know your audience's position, it is best to *imagine them as neutral to mildly opposed* to your views and direct your argument with that in mind. Imagining an unfamiliar audience as either hostile or friendly can lead to extreme positions that may cause the argument to fail. Imagining the audience as neutral or mildly opposed ensures *an even tone* to the argument that *promotes audience interest and receptivity.*

Think of your relationship with your audience as if it were plotted on a sliding scale. At one end are the people who agree with you, and at the other end are those who disagree. In the middle are the neutral audience and the unknown audience. Other mildly hostile or mildly favorable audiences are positioned at various points in between. Your knowledge of human nature and argument theory will help you plan strategies of argument that will address all these audience types and perhaps cause them to change their initial position on the sliding scale.

Analyze the Audience's Discourse Community

Besides analyzing your audience's initial position and how it might change, it is also useful to identify the audience's *discourse community*. An audience's affiliations can help define the nature of the audience itself. Specialized groups who share subject matter, background, experience, values, and a common language (including specialized and technical vocabulary, jargon, or slang) are known as discourse communities.

Consider discourse communities composed of all scientists, all engineers, or all mathematicians. Their common background, training, language, and knowledge make it easier for them to connect, achieve common ground, and work toward conclusions. The discourse community itself creates some of the common ground necessary for successful academic inquiry or for other types of argument.

You are a member of the university or college discourse community where you attend classes. This community is characterized by reasonable and educated people who share common backgrounds and interests that enable them to inquire into matters that are still at issue. You are also a member of the discourse community in your argument class, which has a common vocabulary and common tasks and assignments. Outsiders visiting your class would not be members of this community in the same way that you and your classmates are. To what other discourse communities do you belong?

Compare argument in your class with argument at home, at work, or with your friends. The strategies for connecting with others, building common ground, and arguing within the context of each of your discourse communities can vary considerably. With some reflection, you will be able to think of examples of the ways you have analyzed and adapted to each of them already. You can improve your natural ability to work with audiences by learning several conscious strategies for analyzing and adapting to both familiar and unfamiliar audiences.

Analyze and Adapt to a Familiar Audience

In working with a familiar audience, ask questions such as the following to learn more about them:

▶ Who are the members of your audience and what do you have in common with them?

▶ What are some of the demographic characteristics of this audience? Consider number, age, organizational affiliations, interests, and college majors.

▶ What is the present position of audience members on your issue, and what audience outcomes can you anticipate?

▶ What experience do audience members have with your issue? Ask about their knowledge and background, including both positive and negative experiences and obstacles.

▶ What beliefs, values, motives, goals, or aims about your issue do you share?

Construct an Unfamiliar Audience

Sometimes you will not be able to gather direct information about your audience because these readers will be unfamiliar to you and unavailable for study. In this case, you will need to draw on your past experience for audience analysis. To do so, imagine a particular kind of audience, a *universal audience,* and write for them when you cannot collect direct audience information.

Chaim Perelman, who has written extensively about the difficulty of identifying the qualities of audiences with certainty, developed the concept of the universal audience.[3] He suggests planning an argument for a *composite audience,* one with distinct individual differences but also important common qualities. This universal audience is educated, reasonable, normal, adult, and willing to listen. Every arguer constructs the universal audience from his or her own past experiences, and consequently the concept of the universal audience varies somewhat from individual to individual and culture to culture.

The construct of the universal audience can be useful when you write papers for your other college classes. It is especially useful when the audience is largely unknown and you cannot obtain much information about them. Imagine writing for a universal audience on those occasions. Your professors and classmates as a group possess the general qualities of this audience.

When you complete the analysis of your audience, go back through the information you have gathered and consciously decide which audience characteristics to appeal to in your paper. You will then be in a position to gather materials for your paper that will be convincing to this particular audience. You will develop reasoning and support that audience members can link to their personal values, motives, beliefs, knowledge, and experience. Similarly, you need to show the same care in adapting to the needs of a universal audience. Since this audience is reasonable, educated, and adult, reasoning and support must be on their level and should also have broad applicability and acceptance. The universal audience inspires a high level of argumentation. *Careful research, intelligent reasoning, and clear writing style are requirements for this audience.*

Use your understanding of the rhetorical situation to help you read and also to help you get ideas and plan your own argument writing. It can be useful at every stage when you are reading, thinking, and writing about issues. The Summary Chart of the Rhetorical Situation (page 512) provides a brief version of the elements of the rhetorical situation as it applies to both reading and writing. Use it as a quick reference worksheet as you read or plan and write argument.

Review Questions

1. What are the five elements in the rhetorical situation? Use TRACE to help you remember.

2. How can a reader use the rhetorical situation to analyze an argument essay? How can a viewer use the rhetorical situation to analyze an image? How can

---

[3]See Perelman and Olbrechts-Tyteca, *The New Rhetoric,* for additional details on the universal audience.

a writer use the rhetorical situation during the planning phase of writing a paper?

3. Why is the audience important in argument? What types of positions might an audience initially hold? What possible outcomes are associated with arguments directed to each of these audiences?

4. What is a discourse community? To what discourse communities do you belong? How does a discourse community help establish common ground for its members?

5. What is the universal audience? What are the special qualities of this audience? Why is it a useful idea?

Exercises and Activities

A. Class Discussion: Analyzing the Rhetorical Situation for an Essay

Read the following essay by Brent Staples. Then answer the questions for discussion that follow the essay.

BEFORE YOU READ: Do you listen to the radio when you are driving in the car? Which stations? What is your opinion of them?

ESSAY #2   DRIVING DOWN THE HIGHWAY, MOURNING THE DEATH OF AMERICAN RADIO*

Brent Staples

The author, who holds a Ph.D. in psychology from the University of Chicago, is an editorial writer for the *New York Times*. He is also the author of an award-winning memoir. *Parallel Time: Growing Up in Black and White.*

1 Brooklynites who park their cars on the streets sometimes post signs—"nothing of value" and my favorite, "no radio, no nothing"—pleading with thieves not to break in. The smash and grabs are less frequent than they once were. But those of us who live here are no longer surprised by the pools of shattered glass—known as "sidewalk diamonds"—left by the thieves who make off with air bags, radios and anything else they can carry.

2 My aging Volvo will be parked safely in a garage after getting the new compact disc player that I hope to install by summer's end. Burglar magnet that it is, the CD player symbolizes my despair that commercial radio in New York—and most other major markets—has become so bad as to be unlistenable and is unlikely to improve anytime soon. I listen religiously to the public radio station WBGO in Newark, the best jazz station in the country. Man does not live by jazz alone. If you

*New York Times, June 8, 2003, A12.

want decent pop, rock or country, you pretty much have to spin it yourself.

3   Commercial stations in New York are too expensive to be anything but bland, repetitive and laden with ads and promotions. A station that could be had for a pittance 30 years ago can go for more than $100 million in a big market like New York. Congress increased the value of the stations in 1996, when it raised the cap on the number of stations that a single company could own; now, three corporate entities control nearly half of the radio listenership in the country.

4   I grew up glued to radio and was present at the creation of legendary album format stations like WMMR in Philadelphia and WXRT in Chicago. These stations played rich blends of rock, pop and jazz, and sometimes featured local bands. (This wide-ranging format enriched the collective musical taste and paid dividends by producing ever more varied strains of popular music.) Commercials were typically kept to between 8 and 12 minutes per hour, and 20 minutes or more could pass before the announcer broke in to give the station's call letters.

5   This format was profitable, but not on the money-raining scale required since Wall Street got wise to the radio game. Faced with pressure from investors and more corporate debt than some nations, the megacompanies that acquire a hundred stations each must squeeze every cent out of every link in the chain. They do this by dismissing the local staff and loading up squalling commercials and promotional spots that can take up as much as 30 minutes per hour during morning "drive time."

6   The corporate owners then put pressure on their remaining rivals—and often force them to sell out—by promoting national advertising packages that allow commercials to be broadcast on several stations, or all over the country, at once. Disc jockeys are often declared expendable and let go. Where they remain in place, they are figureheads who spin a narrow and mind-numbing list of songs that have been market-tested to death, leaving stations that sound the same from coast to coast.

7   Critics have focused on the way corporatized radio fails to cover local news and on free-speech issues, like the one that emerged when a country band, the Dixie Chicks, was booted from corporate air for criticizing the president over the war in Iraq. If the stations find the Dixie Chicks too challenging to tolerate, it's easy to imagine them marginalizing genuinely controversial news and programming.

8   Corporate radio's treatment of the Dixie Chicks argues against those who wish to remove all remaining federal limits on corporate ownership—not just of radio, but of television as well. The dangers posed by concentrated ownership go beyond news and censorship issues, to the heart of popular culture itself. By standardizing music and voices around the country, radio is slowly killing off local musical cultures, along with the diverse bodies of music that enriched the national popular culture.

9   Independent radio even 25 years ago was as important to a civic landscape as city hall or the local sports star who made good. The disc jockeys (or "on-air personalities," as they came to be called) embodied local radio to the public. You could hear their distinctive influences when you drove into Philadelphia, Chicago, Minneapolis or Wheeling, W.Va.; radio stations could be identified not just by the call letters but from the unique blend of music that was played in each place.

10   Pre-corporate radio commonly played established, nationally known musicians along with unknown locals and traveling bands. In town for a show, a young, unknown Elvis could swivel-hip down to the local station for airplay and some chat. This sort of thing was still possible in the early 1980's, when an unclassifiable band out of Athens, Ga., called R.E.M. became hugely popular while barnstorming the country in a truck. R.E.M. forced itself onto the air without conceding its weirdness and became one of the most influential bands of the late 20th century.

11   Radio stations where unknown bands might once have come knocking at the door

no longer even have doors. They have become drone stations, where a once multifarious body of music has been pared down and segmented in bland formats, overlaid with commercials. As record companies scramble to replicate the music that gets airplay, pop music is turning in on itself and flattening out.

12   Those of us who are breaking with radio are saddened to leave the community of listeners to which we have belonged for most of our lives. But we realize as well that the vitality of the medium, like youth, is lost and forever behind us.

For Discussion:

Use TRACE to analyze this essay. How would you describe the text itself? How would you characterize the reader or audience that the author may have had in mind when writing this essay? What do you learn about the author? What are some of the possible constraints that might have influenced the author? What constraints influenced you as you read this essay? What is the exigence for this essay? How much common ground do you share with this author? Do you find this argument convincing or not? Why?

B. Writing Assignment: Analyzing the Rhetorical Situation in Written Argumentation

Read one of the seven articles that appear at the end of Chapter 2 (Haizlip, page 54; Hamud, page 56; Tien, page 58; Martinez, page 60; Brewer, page 62; Brady, page 64; or Hatsumi, page 70). Then write a 300- to 400-word paper in which you explain the rhetorical situation for this essay. Answer the following questions using TRACE.

1. How would you describe the text itself?
2. How would you characterize the reader or audience that the author may have had in mind while writing the essay? To what degree do you identify with this audience?
3. What do you learn about the author?
4. What are some of the possible constraints that might have influenced the author? What constraints influence you as you read this essay?
5. What is the exigence for this essay?

C. Group Work: Analyzing the Rhetorical Situation in Visual Argument

The three images reprinted here are visual arguments that memorialize historic events. They may not appear at first to be visual arguments until you learn something about the history and original rhetorical situations in which they were situated. All three are photographs, and they are accompanied by enough explanation to help you understand the rhetorical situations in which they occurred. This will allow you to evaluate their effectiveness as visual arguments, both now and when they first appeared.

Form small groups, view each image, read the written commentary and essays that provide information about the photos, and answer the "For Discussion" questions that follow them. Then answer the following questions about their rhetorical situations. Refer back to the example of the analysis of the rhetorical situation from the viewer's point of view on pages 77–79, if you need to recall its details.

1. *Image.* What type of image is it? What are its qualities and features? What is it about?

2. *Viewer or audience:* Who do you think was targeted as the most appropriate audience at the time each photo was taken? Who might still regard each of these photos as a compelling visual argument?

3. *Photographer:* What do you know about the photographer, and what may have motivated that individual to take the photo? What might have been the intended result?

4. *Constraints:* What constraints influenced the photographer? Consider the influential events, circumstances, and traditions already in place at the time each photo was taken. Consider, also, the possible beliefs, attitudes, motives, and prejudices of the photographer. How about your constraints? Do any of your beliefs, attitudes, or prejudices seem to match those of the photographer, or are they different? Do the possible constraints you have identified create common ground between you and the photographer, or do they drive you apart?

5. *Exigence:* What motivated the photographer to take each of these photos? What happened? Was it perceived as a defect or problem? If yes, why? Was it new or recurring?

Image 1: This photograph was taken in 1956 early in the civil rights movement in Alabama when the issue was segregation in public facilities. Until this time, African American people were required to sit only at the back of public buses. A new national ruling gave them the right to sit wherever they wanted to sit. In the photograph, Rosa Parks, an African American civil rights activist, tests this new ruling by taking a seat in the front of the bus with a white man seated behind her. This is a famous photograph. It appears on the walls of buses in New York City and has come to symbolize change brought about by the movement for civil rights that continued into the next decades.

Image 1:
Rosa Parks Rides in the Front of the Bus.

Look at the image and read the essay that follows. It explains the history of this photograph and will provide you with the information you need to analyze the rhetorical situation.

Rosa Parks riding a Montgomery, Ala., bus in December 1956, after the Supreme Court outlawed segregation on buses.

> **BEFORE YOU READ:** What more would you like to know about the individuals and the situation depicted in the Rosa Parks photograph?

ESSAY #3   **THE MAN BEHIND ROSA PARKS***

Peter Applebome

The author has been a reporter and editor at the *New York Times* newspaper since 1987 where he is now the deputy metropolitan editor. His work has appeared in many other publications as well. He often writes about education and culture.

1   Almost everyone has seen the famous study in black and white, one of those rare photographs that enters the collective memory as a snapshot not of a moment but of an era and maybe something more. It's now on almost any bus in New York City and many of its suburbs, an invitation not just to remember but to reflect.

2   At the front of a bus, previously reserved for white riders, is Rosa Parks, head slightly bowed, face turned to the window to her left, seemingly lost in thought as she rides through Montgomery, Ala. In the seat behind her, is a young white man looking to his right, his face hard, almost expressionless. The two, the only figures visible on the bus, seem a few inches and a universe apart, each seemingly looking at and for something utterly different.

3   Everyone knows her. No one knows him.

4   Except for Catherine Chriss, his daughter. And, like his identity, hidden in plan sight, unknown even to the veterans of that era still living, what's most telling about the real story of the black woman and the white man is how much of what we think we know is what we read into the picture, not what's there.

5   The man on the bus, Nicholas C. Chriss, was not some irritated Alabama segregationist preserved for history but a reporter working at the time for United Press International out of Atlanta. . . .

6   Mr. Chriss, who also worked for *The Los Angeles Times* and *The Houston Chronicle*, publicly disclosed his role in the picture just once. It was three paragraphs in the middle of a 2,183-word article he wrote for *The Chronicle* in 1986 about his experiences covering the civil rights movement.

7   He explained that the picture was taken on Dec. 21, 1956, the day after the United States Supreme Court ruled Montgomery's segregated bus system illegal. (Actually, the ruling had come a month earlier, but it was not until Dec. 20 that the district court entered the order putting it into effect.) He said that he boarded the bus in downtown Montgomery and that he and Mrs. Parks were the only riders up front.

8   He wrote: "It was a historic occasion. I was then with the United Press International wire service. A UPI photographer took a picture of Mrs. Parks on the bus. It shows a somber Mrs. Parks seated on the bus looking calmly out the window. Seated just behind her is a hard-eyed white man.

9   "Each anniversary of that day, this photo-graph is brought out of musty files and used in various publications around the world. But to this day no one has ever made clear that it was a reporter, I, covering this event and sitting behind Mrs. Parks, not some sullen white segregationist! It was a great scoop for me, but Mrs. Parks had little to say. She seemed to want to savor the event alone." . . .

10   Still, if little known, the history of the picture is explored in at least one source, the biography of Rosa Parks by Douglas Brinkley,

New York Times, December 7, 2005, A1 and A33.

first published in 2000 as part of the Penguin Lives series of biographies.

11   Mr. Brinkley said Mrs. Parks, in interviews with him, said she left her home at the Cleveland Courts housing project specifically for a picture of her on a bus and that the idea was for her to be seated in the front of the bus with a white man behind. Similar photo opportunities were arranged for the Rev. Dr. Martin Luther King Jr. and others during the day, he said.

12   Mr. Chriss then agreed to sit behind her for the purpose of the picture. Mr. Brinkley does not identify Mr. Chriss in the book and says that a reporter and two photographers from *Look* magazine arranged for the picture. He said Mrs. Parks told his she was reluctant to take part in the picture, but both the journalists and members of the civil rights community wanted an image that would dramatize what had occurred.

13   "It was completely a 100 percent staged event," Mr. Brinkley said. "There was nothing random about it." . . .

14   None of that diminishes the achievement or her life, just as, perhaps, the true story of the picture need not detract from its power. It's just a reminder that history is almost always more complicated and surprising than the images that most effectively tell its story.

For Discussion:

If you had no knowledge about the rhetorical situation in which the Rosa Parks photograph is situated, how likely would you have been to interpret it as a visual argument? How does an analysis of the rhetorical situation help you understand it as an argument? Why do you think a copy of this picture is posted in New York City buses? Were you surprised to learn that this photo was staged? What difference, if any, does that make in its effect as a visual argument? What other visual arguments can you think of that have been staged?

Images 2 and 3: The next two images are Holocaust photographs taken in the early 1940s during the Second World War at the Auschwitz concentration and death camp in Poland. The issues were anti-Semitism, genocide, and the desire on the part

Image 2:
Auschwitz Victims of Medical Experiments.

This is a photograph of an Israeli soldier in Jerusalem, Israel, who is viewing historical photographs at the Yad Vashem Holocaust Memorial Museum of Jewish victims from Auschwitz. Photojournalist David Silverman, who works for Getty Images and has been based in Israel and the West Bank since 1991, took this photo the week before the 60th anniversary of the liberation of Auschwitz.

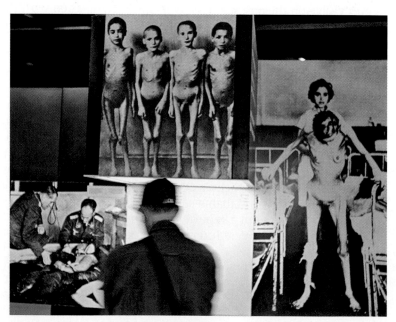

Auschwitz Exhibit at Jerusalem's Yad Vashem Holocaust Memorial

An SS Officer's Auschwitz Photo Album
SS officers and death camp staff at leisure near Auschwitz, one of 116 newly discovered snapshots from a Nazi officer's scrapbook donated to the Holocaust museum in Washington.

Image 3: Camp Officials at Leisure.

This is a photograph of some of the Nazi SS who ran the Auschwitz concentration and death camp in the 1940s in Poland. Approximately 6,000 individuals worked at Auschwitz. Look at the image, read the following essay, and analyze the rhetorical situation.

of the Nazis, who ran this camp, to create a so-called master race. More than a million Jews died in the gas chambers at Auschwitz, were the victims of deadly medical experiments, or died of other causes such as starvation. Answer the "For Discussion" questions that follow Essay 4 and then analyze the rhetorical situation for images 2 and 3 separately.

BEFORE YOU READ: How would you imagine the lives of the thousands of SS officers who lived and worked at Auschwitz during the Second World War?

ESSAY #4 IN THE SHADOW OF HORROR, SS GUARDIANS RELAX AND FROLIC*

Neil A. Lewis

The author is a freelance journalist and contractor who writes for the *New York Times*.

1   Last December, Rebecca Erbelding, a young archivist at the United States Holocaust Memorial Museum, opened a letter from a former United States Army Intelligence officer who said he wanted to donate photographs of Auschwitz he had found more than 60 years ago in Germany.

2   Ms. Erbelding was intrigued: Although Auschwitz may be the most notorious of the Nazi death camps, there are only a small

New York Times, September 19, 2007, B1 and B6.

number of known photos of the place before its liberation in 1945. Some time the next month, the museum received a package containing in 16 cardboard pages, with photos pasted on both sides, and their significance quickly became apparent.

3   As Ms. Erbelding and other archivists reviewed the album, they realized they had a scrapbook of sorts of the lives of Aushwitz's senior SS officers that was maintained by Karl Höcker, the adjutant to the camp commandant. Rather than showing the men performing their death camp duties, the photos depicted, among other things, a horde of SS men singing cheerily to the accompaniment of an accordionist, Höcker lighting the camp's Christmas tree, a cadre of young SS women frolicking and officers relaxing, some with tunics shed, for a smoking break.

4   In all there are 116 pictures, beginning with a photo from June 21, 1944, of Höcker and the commandant of the camp, Richard Baer, both in full SS regalia. The album also contains eight photos of Josef Mengele, the camp doctor notorious for participating in the selections of arriving prisoners and bizarre and cruel medical experiments. These are the first authenticated pictures of Mengele at Auschwitz, officials at the Holocaust museum said.

5   The photos provide a stunning counterpoint to what up until now has been the only major source of preliberation Auschwitz photos, the so-called Auschwitz Album, a compilation of pictures taken by SS photographers in the spring of 1944 and discovered by a survivor in another camp. Those photos depict the arrival at the camp of a transport of Hungarian Jews, who at the time made up the last remaining sizable Jewish community in Europe. The Auschwitz Album, owned by Yad Vashem, the Israeli Holocaust museum, depicts the railside selection process at Birkenau, the area where trains arrived at the camp, as SS men herded new prisoners into lines.

6   The comparisons between the albums are both poignant and obvious, as they juxtapose the comfortable daily lives of the guards with the horrific reality within the camp, where thousands were starving and 1.1 million died.

7   For example, one of the Höcker pictures, shot on July 22, 1944, shows a group of cheerful young women who worked as SS communications specialists eating bowls of fresh blueberries. One turns her bowl upside down and makes a mock frown because she has finished her portion.

8   On that day, said Judith Cohen, a historian at the Holocaust museum in Washington, 150 new prisoners arrived at the Birkenau site. Of that group, 21 men and 12 women were selected for work, the rest transported immediately to the gas chambers.

9   Those killings were part of the final frenetic efforts of the Nazis to eliminate the Jews of Europe and others deemed undesirable as the war neared its end. That summer the crematoriums broke down from overuse and some bodies had to be burned in open pits. A separate but small group of known preliberation photos were taken clandestinely of those burnings.

10   Auschwitz was abandoned and evacuated on Jan, 18, 1945, and liberated by Soviet forces on Jan. 27. Many of the Höcker photos were taken at Solahütte, an Alpine-style recreation lodge the SS used on the far reaches of the camp complex alongside the Sola River.

11   Though they as yet have no plans to exhibit the Höcker album photos, curators at the Holocaust Memorial Museum have created an online display of them on the museum's Web site (ushmm.org).

For Discussion:

How does an analysis of the rhetorical situations for images 2 and 3 help you perceive them as visual arguments? What is the effect of viewing these two photos together? What conclusions can you draw from these photos about the Holocaust, the Nazi death camps, the individuals imprisoned there, and the Nazi SS officers who worked there?

D. **Before You Write on Your Issue: Applying the Rhetorical Situation**

The following worksheet will help you understand the rhetorical situation for any issue you have selected to write about and have already tested to see whether it is arguable (page 30). Complete the worksheet by yourself. You are working with limited information, so you may need to guess at some of the answers.

Worksheet 1	Rhetorical Situation

1. **Exigence**
   What is motivating you to write on this issue? What happened? Why is it compelling to you?

2. **Reader or Audience**
   Who is going to read this? Where do you think they might stand on your issue right now? What are the chances of establishing common ground? What is the best approach to change their minds?

3. **Constraints**
   How do you think your training, background, affiliations, values, and attitudes about your issue are either in harmony or in conflict with those of your audience? What constraints can you use to build common ground?

4. **Author**
   What is your position or perspective on your issue? What do you already know? What do you need to learn? How can you be convincing?

5. **Text**
   What are you writing? What should it look like? What specifications do you need to follow? Review the assignment for your paper.

E. **Writing Assignment: Writing a Letter to a Specific Audience**

Read the following rhetorical situation and write a letter in response to one of the four individuals in the prompts that appear immediately after it. Do not confer with other members of the class. Make sure at least some students write in response to each of the four prompts.

The Rhetorical Situation

You are enrolled in a freshman English class and your teacher allows you to be absent five times before she gives you an F for the course. If you are tardy to class three times, it counts as an absence. You have been absent five times and tardy to class twice. Your parents are angry at you for missing class so much, and they say that if you fail English you will have to get a job and start paying rent to live at home. Your teacher has explained that if you are tardy or absent from class one more time, she is going to fail you. You really want to do better; you are determined to change your ways.

On the way to class you have a blowout on the freeway. You pull over to change the tire and when you get the spare from the trunk, it is flat. This is not your fault, as you have just had your car serviced and the tires checked. A fel-

95

low motorist pulls over and helps you, but by the time you get a good tire on your car and drive to class, you are forty-five minutes late. You enter the classroom as quietly as you can. Your best friend raises her eyebrows. Your teacher gives you a stern look. You feel terrible.

The Writing Prompts

1. You are too embarrassed to talk to your teacher. Write her a letter to explain what happened and ask her for another chance.

2. Your parents are too angry to talk to you. Write them a letter to explain what happened and to ask their forgiveness.

3. You are very upset with the tire company. Write them a letter to explain what happened and ask for a reimbursement.

4. You don't have time to talk to your best friend after class. Write her a note to explain what happened and tell her what you intend to do about it.[4]

You and your classmates should now read some of these letters aloud. When you read them, do not divulge who the intended audience is. Ask the other students to guess who the intended reader of the letter is. Continue doing this until you have a sampling of all four letters and the class has guessed to whom each has been written.

Discuss the Results

What clues helped you surmise the audience for each letter? How are the letters different from each other? In your discussion, consider how each audience influenced the purpose for writing each letter, the tone of each letter, and the type and level of vocabulary used in each letter.

F. **Class Discussion and Writing Assignment: Analyzing Your Class as an Audience**

In Chapter 1 you began to learn about what you and other members of your class have in common (Exercise A1 on page 23), and in Chapter 2 you characterized your class as an audience in terms of the various argument styles preferred by class members (Exercise C3 on page 53). Now, learn more about your class as an audience by answering the questions listed here.

1. How many students are in your class? What are some of the qualities and features you have in common?

2. Consider some of the demographics of your class (ask for a show of hands to answer some of these): How many are traditional college-age students (18–22 years old); and how many are older, new, or returning students? Count the number of men and the number of women. How many are international students, and what countries do they represent? How would you describe the cultural diversity in the class? How many in the class agree that their heritage or native culture influences their personal life? How many are first-years and sophomores? How many are juniors and seniors?

---

[4]I am indebted to Samantha Masterton for this assignment.

How many work part-time? How many work full-time? What are some of the types of work represented in class?

3. What college majors are represented in your class?

4. What are some of the groups class members belong to that are important to them? Consider political, religious, social, and living groups. Ask for students to volunteer this information.

5. What are some of the special interests and hobbies of class members? Make a list.

Using this class survey data, write as full a description of your classroom audience as you can. Which of the issues that you have considered writing about would immediately interest them? Why? Which would they find less interesting? Why? What could you provide in your paper to increase their interest?

CHAPTER 4

Reading, Thinking, and Writing about Issues

This chapter teaches strategies to help you complete assignments that require reading, thinking, and writing about issues. Though you may now regard reading, thinking, and writing as quite separate activities, you will discover that in combining them you will produce better papers. You can practice doing so as you use the strategies taught here in writing three types of argument papers, explained later in this chapter: (1) the summary-response paper; (2) the summary-analysis-response paper; and (3) the exploratory paper. Assignments for these papers require you to interweave reading, thinking, and writing about issues.

At the outset it is useful to sharpen your awareness of how you read and write now so that you will have a solid place to start as you consider and add new strategies. Most people like their current reading and writing processes and are able to describe them. Try it. First, imagine that your professor has given you a fairly difficult scholarly article to read. You must understand it, think about it, and remember the main ideas. How do you proceed with such an assignment? What do you typically do *before you read, while you are reading, when you encounter difficult passages,* and *after you finish reading*?

Now imagine writing a college paper on a subject that requires some research but also a considerable amount of critical thinking on your part. How would you *get started, write the first draft, break through writer's block* (if that occurs), and *rewrite and revise your paper*?

Look at the possible descriptions of the reading and writing processes as they are modified for argument in the Summary Charts on pages 511–523. Many of the specific strategies described there will be taught in more detail below. As you read through the strategies in this chapter, notice particularly that *readers are often actively thinking and writing as they read,* and that *writers, in turn, are often reading and thinking as they write.*

Getting Started on a Writing Assignment

Before you begin work on a writing assignment for an argument paper, take some time to organize a work space equipped with the materials you will need. Then take a few minutes to understand the assignment and schedule sufficient time to complete it. Begin by dividing the assignment into small, manageable parts: assign a sufficient amount of time for each part and set deadlines for completing each part. Here is an example.

ANALYZE THE ASSIGNMENT AND ALLOCATE TIME

Assignment

Write a five- to six-page, typed, double-spaced argument paper in which you identify an issue from "The Reader," take a position on the issue, make a claim, and support it so that it is convincing to an audience of your peers. Do as much reading as you need to do, but plan to draw material from three to five sources in writing your paper. Use MLA style (explained in the Appendix to Chapter 13, pages 429–456) to document your sources and prepare your bibliography.

Analysis of Assignment

Week 1

Select one of the seven issue areas from "The Reader" and read the introductory information about it. Select an issue question and write down your initial ideas.	2 hours Tuesday
Read the articles on your issue question in "The Reader," and write summaries and responses.	3 hours Wednesday
Take a position yourself and write a tentative outline or list of ideas.	2 hours Thursday
Explain your outline or list to a peer group in class. Get ideas for improvement and write them down.	Friday's class
Write a first draft.	2 hours Saturday

Week 2

Read the first draft to your peer group and gather ideas for improvement.	Monday's class
Do more thinking and writing. If necessary, read more to fill in the needs of the first draft.	2 hours Wednesday

| Write the second draft. | 2 hours Thursday |
| Read the second draft to your peer group. Plan final revisions. | Friday's class |

Week 3

| Rewrite, revise, and prepare final copy. | 2 hours Tuesday. Hand in Wednesday |

Notice that the work on this paper has been spread out over three weeks and is divided into manageable units. If this schedule were followed, a student would be able to complete this paper successfully, on time, and without panic and discomfort. A total of fifteen hours have been set aside for the various stages. The student's focus should be, however, on finishing the paper as quickly as possible, not on using all of this time.

Here is a professional writer who cautions about the importance of working to finish rather than working to put in time: "Don't set your goal as minutes or hours spent working; it's too easy to waste that time looking up one last fact, changing your margins, or, when desperate, searching for a new pen." Instead, she advises, set a realistic writing goal for each day and work until you complete it.[1] Another author advises that you avoid creating units of work that are so large or unmanageable that you won't want to—or will have trouble—completing them, such as writing an entire paper in one day. It may sound doable on the surface to write a whole paper in one day or one night, "but you'll soon feel overwhelmed," and "you'll start avoiding the work and won't get *anything* done." Remember, she says, "it's persistence that counts" in completing writing projects.[2]

IDENTIFY AN ISSUE, NARROW IT, AND TEST IT

The assignment just described directs you to identify an issue on which to write. You may start with a broad issue area such as crime, technology, immigration, or the environment, but you will need to find a more narrow and specific issue to write about within this broad area. The map in Figure 4.1 ■ on page 101 shows one technique for generating more specific issues related to a broad issue area. A group of students created this map to help them find specific issues about race. Reading about your issue can also uncover a particular aspect or interpretation that you want to explore. When you have an issue you think you can work with, write it as a question and apply the twelve tests of an arguable issue (page 30) to it. You may also take a position on the issue and write a tentative claim. Add reasons for your position on the claim, if you can at this point. Keep your audience in mind as you do so. Additional information on how to write claims appears in Chapters 6 and 11.

---

[1]Peggy Rynk, "Waiting for Inspiration," *Writer,* September 1992, 10.
[2]Sue Grafton, "How to Find Time to Write When You Don't Have Time to Write." *The Writer's Handbook,* ed. Sylvia K. Burack (Boston: Writer, 1991), 22.

ISSUES RELATED TO RACE

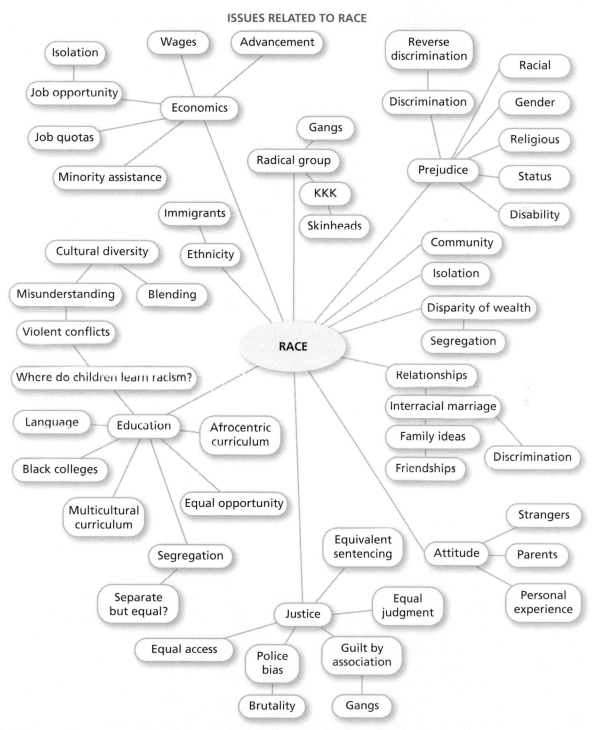

Figure 4.1 *A Map Can Help You Discover Specific Related Issues for Paper Topics.*

DO SOME INITIAL WRITING, READING, AND THINKING

Get off to a strong start by using some of these suggestions.

Write Down Everything You Now Know about Your Issue

As soon as you have an issue in mind, begin to make notes. You are often at your most creative when an idea for a paper first occurs to you, so write insights and ideas immediately to use later in your paper. This practice guarantees that some of the material in your paper will be your original ideas. Do you have an idea right now about the position you think you may take on your issue? Can you list some reasons for it? Can you think of some examples? Write out as much as possible now and enter it in your computer file or notebook.

A professional writer describes this type of writing as a tool that helps one think. This author sets out a number of suggestions that could be particularly useful for the writer of argument.

Write quickly, so you don't know what's coming next.
Turn off the censor in your head.
Write from different points of view to broaden your sympathies.
Collect quotations that inspire you and jot down a few notes on why they do.
Write with a nonjudgmental friend in mind to listen to your angry or confused thoughts.
When words won't come, draw something—anything.
Don't worry about being nice, fair, or objective. Be selfish and biased; give your side of the story from the heart.
Write even what frightens you, *especially* what frightens you. It is the thought denied that is dangerous.
Don't worry about being consistent. You are large; you contain multitudes.[3]

Read to Improve Your Background Information

Start with broad reading to find out who else is interested in your issue and what positions they take. Try the encyclopedia, books, or the Internet. Use a search engine such as *Google* or *Yahoo!* and enter a keyword in the search box that is related to your issue to begin to find basic information online. Detailed information on how to conduct more thorough and reliable online and print research appears in Chapter 12 (pages 380–407). At this point, write notes on the ideas that strike you, and write your original reactions to these ideas as they occur to you. If you find material you want to read and note further, record where you found it so that you can go back and read it more thoroughly later.

[3]Marjorie Pellegrino, "Keeping a Writer's Journal," *Writer*, June 1992, 27.

Clip or Copy Images to Add to Your File

Make your issue more vivid and memorable in your own mind by collecting some related visual materials. Don't limit yourself to photographs, prints, or drawings. Create flowcharts of ideas, include tables and graphs, or make concept maps like that shown in Figure 4.1. Fully notate the sources of these materials in case you decide later to use some of them in your paper. If you are a visual learner, this practice will be especially useful in helping you understand your issue. Even if you do not use any images in your paper, your collection will help you write better descriptions of the visual aspects of your issue and that, in turn, will help the reader visualize what you are writing. It is also possible that you will decide to include an image or two in your paper to support some of your key ideas.

Use Critical Thinking Prompts

Get additional insights and ideas about your issue by using some well-established lines of thought that stimulate critical thinking. The "Critical Thinking Prompts" in Box 4.1 ■ (page 104) will help you think about your issue in some new ways. First, write what you now think you want to prove about your issue, and then write your responses to each of the prompts. You will be pleased by the quantity of new information these questions generate for your paper. Here is an example to get you started.

▶ Example of How to Use Critical Thinking Prompts

What is your issue? My issue is old-growth forests. I want to preserve those on the western coast of the United States.

Associate it. This is an enduring environmental issue. It is associated with other environmental issues, including reducing greenhouse gases that cause global warming and saving wildlife like the spotted owl, deer, and the other animals that live in these forests. It is also associated with preserving natural beauty and the history of these areas.

Describe it. These trees are as much as 3200 years old. The giant sequoias in California, for example, are huge, majestic trees that can reach heights of 325 feet. People standing among them appear to be very small, and when they look up, they can barely see the tops. Even the sky seems farther away than usual. It is awe-inspiring to walk among these trees because of their size, their age, and their beauty.

Compare it. Saving these forests from logging is similar to preserving natural lakes, national parks and forests, and other wilderness areas from commercial interests.

These responses will give you the idea. As you work through all the prompts, you will find that some are more productive than others for a particular issue. Use as many as you can. If you do not yet know enough to respond to some prompts, add information later when you have done more reading.

Box 4.1	Use These Prompts to Help You Think Critically about Your Issue.

▶▶▶ Critical Thinking Prompts

What is your issue? _____

Use some, but not all, of these prompts to help you think about it.

1. *Associate it.* Consider other related issues, broader issues, or enduring issues. Also associate your issue with familiar subjects and ideas.

2. *Describe it.* Use detail. Make the description visual if you can by forming pictures in your mind or by looking at the visual materials you have collected in your file and then describing them.

3. *Compare it.* Think about items in the same or different categories. Compare your issue with topics you know or understand well. Compare what you used to think about the issue with what you think now. Give reasons for your change of mind.

4. *Apply it.* Show practical uses or applications. Show how it can be used in a specific setting.

5. *Divide it.* Illuminate your issue by dividing it into related issues or into parts of the issue.

6. *Agree and disagree with it.* Identify the extreme pro and con positions and reasons for holding them. List other approaches and perspectives. Say why each position, including your own, might be plausible and in what circumstances.

7. *Consider it as it is, right now.* Think about your issue as it exists, right now, in present time. What is its nature? What are its special, contemporary characteristics?

8. *Consider it over a period of time.* Think about your issue in the past as well as how it might present itself in the future. Does the issue change? How? Why?

9. *Decide whether it is a part of something bigger.* Put it in a larger category, and consider the insights you gain as a result.

10. *Analyze it.* Consider its parts and assess how the parts are related.

11. *Synthesize it.* Put it back together in new ways so that the new whole is different. Ask if it is clearer and better than the old whole.

12. *Evaluate it.* Decide whether it is good or bad, valuable or not valuable, moral or immoral, ethical or unethical. Give evidence to support your evaluation.

13. *Elaborate on it.* Add and continue to add explanation until you can understand the issue more easily. Give some examples to provide further elaboration.

14. *Project and predict.* Answer the question, "What would happen if . . . ?" Extend its frame outward and its meanings and possibilities forward.

15. *Ask why, and keep on asking why.* Examine every aspect of your issue by asking why.

TALK IT THROUGH

It is often valuable to talk with others to clarify your ideas when you are in the early stages of a writing project. Many people find it easier to speak the first words than to write them. Typical audiences for an initial talk-through may include other students in your argument class. Your instructor, in conference, may also ask a few questions and then listen to you explore your ideas. A writing center tutor can do the same for you, as can friends or family members. After such sessions, do rapid freewriting (writing without paying attention to sentence structure, grammar, or punctuation), listing, or outlining to preserve the good ideas that have surfaced.

Read to Develop Arguments for Your Paper

As you start reading in more detail, you will need to learn to recognize written argument.

RECOGNIZING ARGUMENTATION PURPOSE IN WRITTEN ARGUMENT

Some texts are obviously intended as argument, and others conceal their argumentation purpose, making it more difficult to recognize. You can learn to recognize argument purposes if you think of a continuum of six types of purpose, ranging from obvious argument at one extreme to objective writing at the other. Each of the six types exhibits not only a different authorial intention but also a different relationship between the author and the audience. These descriptions can also help you establish your own purpose when you are the writer.

1. *Obvious argument.* The author's purpose is to take a position and to change minds or convince others. The author's point of view and purpose are clearly expressed along with reasons and supporting details that appeal to a wide audience.

2. *Extremist argument.* Authors who hold fast to prejudiced beliefs and stereotypes about various people, causes, or special projects sometimes rely on strongly expressed values and emotional language to appeal to specific audiences who may already share their views. The aim is to strengthen these views and prompt people to act. Think of an animal rights activist writing to convince others to join the cause and take action to protect animals.

3. *Hidden argument.* Some texts seem to be written to inform but, on closer reading, actually favor one position over another. Supporting material may be

carefully selected to favor a particular view. Also, emotional language, vivid description, or emotional examples can be signs that the author has strong opinions and intends not only to inform but also to convince. For example, in an article about college financial aid, all of the examples are about students who failed to pay their loans, and none are about responsible students who did pay. The author has a position that manifests itself in biased reporting. The intention, even though concealed, is to convince people to question current financial aid practices.

4. *Unconscious argument.* Some authors who try to write objectively are influenced unconsciously by strong personal opinions, and the result is an unconscious intent to change people's minds. Imagine a journalist who strongly opposes war being sent to write an objective article about an active war zone. Negative perceptions creep in even as this writer presents the facts. Stacked or selected evidence, emotional language, quotations from authorities who agree with the author, or even pictures with a clear point of view may attest to an argumentative purpose though the author is unaware of it.

5. *Exploratory argument.* In exploratory essays, the author lays out and explains three or more of the major positions on a controversial issue. The reader is invited to view an issue from several perspectives and to understand all of them better. If the author has a position, it may or may not be revealed.

6. *Objective reporting.* The author may report facts and ideas that everyone can accept. The author's own point of view, opinions, or interpretations are deliberately omitted. You might find writing like this in almanacs, data lists, weather reports, some news stories, and government, business, science, and technical reports. The audience reads such material for information. Read this material carefully, however, because sometimes the author's opinion slips in even in this type of writing.

APPLYING THE SIX TYPES OF ARGUMENTATION PURPOSE TO VISUAL ARGUMENT

Even though the descriptions in the previous section apply mainly to written argument, you can easily modify them to help you analyze visual argument as well. Refer to the same six categories to help you recognize the possible intention of the person who created an image. Here are some examples. An image may take an obvious argumentation position on an issue, as in the photograph of the derelict beach house on page 28. Or images may support extremist positions that the viewers already accept. Look back at the photograph of the Israeli soldier on page 92 who is viewing the victims of the death camp experiments at Auschwitz. You can assume that the soldier sympathizes with the victims. These images may motivate him to want to continue to protect Israel. Emotional images that appear on anti-abortion, anti-war, or anti-gay marriage Web sites provide further examples. They will be persuasive to you only if you already agree with the positions they depict.

Figure 4.2 *The President Arguing for War Funds without Strings.*

Is this photograph an example of objective reporting, or is it hidden argument? Notice what is included in the photo and also what is left out. How are the individuals in the photo positioned? What are they looking at? What do you conclude about the implied personal interactions in this photograph?

War of Words President Bush, with Dick Cheney, said Democrats "undercut the troops" by tying war funds to timelines to leave.

Some images may at first appear to be recording facts without creating issues or controversy, but as you look more closely, you discover unconscious or hidden bias in favor of a particular position, and you find you are looking at an argument. Take another look at the photograph on page 93 of the SS officers of the Auschwitz death camps spending leisure time. As soon as you understand the rhetorical situation for this photograph, it no longer seems merely an objective record of a few people having a good time.

Look at the photograph in Figure 4.2 ■ as another example. This photo originally appeared in a newspaper as an objective report that the president had made a speech. The subject of the speech the need for additional funds to continue the war in Iraq—is explained in the caption. Take another look, however, and see if you can detect some signs of hidden or unconscious argument in this picture. Who would you say the president is looking at in this photo? How about the vice president? Who is missing from this photo? As you answer the questions posed in the margin note to the right of the photograph, you might begin to wonder where the audience is. By not showing it, what is the photographer suggesting? This photo appeared in a newspaper that was often critical of this president's policy on continuing the Iraq war, and the Congress at the time was not always cooperative. Images of political figures and images in ads are good places to look for additional examples of unconscious or hidden argument.

Visual argument can also take the form of exploratory argument. In such cases, several images illustrate different visual perspectives on an issue in a way that is similar to an exploratory essay, which in writing identifies and explains several different perspectives on an issue. Examples of visual exploratory argument appear later in this chapter on pages 132 and 146 where, in each case, an issue is explored visually. An exercise at the end of this chapter invites you to create a visual exploratory argument yourself.

107

Finally, some images may be mainly objective. Tables of figures, graphs, and other presentations of numbers and additional data qualify as visual argument and may be objective in that they present information and facts everyone would accept. Scientific drawings or photos of procedures that are designed to teach fit into this category as well. Remember, however, that someone selects and presents—essentially edits out as much as includes—visual information, and even in the most ostensibly objective formats, it is always possible for bias and opinion to find its way in just as it does in written material.

ACADEMIC ARGUMENT

Much of what you read in college will be academic writing assigned by your professors and found in textbooks or scholarly journals or books. Any of the types of argumentation just described may appear in academic writing. The ideas in academic writing are often controversial, with authors taking positions on issues and presenting their ideas as either explicit or hidden argument. Academic writing may seem complex and unfamiliar, especially at the beginning of a class: it is new to you, it contains specialized vocabulary, it is dense with many new ideas, and, compared with easier material, it will often contain fewer examples and transitions. Its sentences and paragraphs are often longer as well. Your purpose in reading such material is to understand it, analyze it, evaluate it, and, frequently, to take a position and write about it.

Your instructor will expect you to use academic style in your college papers. You will engage with complicated issues that invite varying perspectives that seldom take shape as simple pro and con positions. You will learn to take positions on these kinds of issues and to support your ideas with your own reasons and examples and also with paraphrased, summarized, or quoted material from other writers. Your readers will expect you to document these outside sources so that they can trace the materials you relied on to their origins. The student-written argument essays at the end of each chapter in this book and in the Appendix to Chapter 13 serve as models for the academic writing you will be expected to do in college. All of the sample student papers are listed in the "Where Is It?" section on the inside front cover of this book. The essays in "The Reader" are examples of the various types of outside sources you will read to help you think and write on topics. Not all of them are written in academic style. Now let's turn to some strategies–things you can do—to help you complete projects that require reading about issues.

READ WHILE CONTINUING TO THINK AND WRITE

Begin to read about the issue on which you intend to focus. Combine thinking and writing with your reading to help you gather ideas for your paper: summarize the big ideas, write your responses, and record your thoughts on paper or in an open computer file.

Reading and writing together helps with two types of thinking. First, you will think about the material you read and perhaps even rephrase or summarize it to understand it better. Second, you will think beyond the material you read to generate your own ideas. Your reading, in other words, becomes a springboard for original thoughts and ideas. The strategies offered next will help you read, think, and write about the essays in "The Reader" as well as in books and articles you locate in the library or online. These strategies will also help you create a written record of what you have read and thought so that you can use it later in your paper.

SURVEY AND SKIM TO SAVE TIME

A stack of books and a collection of articles can seem daunting if you are not sure where to start. A good way to begin is to survey and skim. Survey a book or an article before you read it for information about the type of work it is, and skim parts of it to discover what the major ideas along with a few of the supporting details are. Surveying accompanied by skimming will also help you decide which parts of specific articles or books you will want to read more carefully later. This strategy saves you time and helps you confidently plan your reading. Box 4.2, ■ on page 110, lists the steps for surveying books and chapters or articles.

When you finish surveying, you can begin to read the passages you have identified for closer reading. The strategies that follow will help you with close reading and creative thinking.

IDENTIFY AND READ THE INFORMATION IN THE INTRODUCTION, BODY, AND CONCLUSION

The organization of ideas in argument texts is not very different from other kinds of texts. Much of what you read, for example, follows the easily recognizable introduction, main body, and conclusion format. The introduction may provide background information about the issue and the author, inspire attention, state the main point, define important terms, or forecast some of the ideas to be developed in the main body. The text body will explain and develop the author's main point by giving reasons and support to prove it. The end or conclusion either summarizes by restating important points or concludes by emphasizing the most important point, whatever it is that the author wants you to accept, remember, or believe. Not all texts follow this pattern exactly, but enough of them do to justify your checking what you read against it.

LOOK FOR CLAIMS, SUBCLAIMS, SUPPORT, AND TRANSITIONS

All arguments have the structural components you are familiar with from other kinds of reading and writing. The main difference is their names. The special characteristics of the components of argument will be described when the Toulmin model is discussed in Chapter 5. We start using Toulmin's terms here, however, to

Box 4.2	How to Survey.

▶▶▶ Steps for Surveying Books, Articles, and Chapters

Survey a book or an article before you read it to become acquainted with its structure and general qualities, and skim certain parts for the major ideas and a few of the supporting details.

Books. To survey a book (not a novel), follow these six steps in the order given.

1. Read the *title* and focus on what it tells you about the contents of the book.
2. Read the *table of contents.* Notice how the content has been divided and organized into chapters.
3. Skim the *introduction.* Look for background information about the subject and author and for any other information that will help you read the book.
4. Examine the special *features* of the book. Are there headings and subheadings in boldface type that highlight major ideas? Is there a glossary? An index? A bibliography? Are there charts? Other visuals?
5. Read the title and first paragraph of the *first* and *last chapters* to see how the book begins and ends.
6. Read the title and first paragraph of the *other chapters* to get a sense of the flow of ideas.

This procedure should take about half an hour. It will introduce you to the main issue and approaches in a book, and your reading will then be easier and more focused.

Articles and Chapters. To survey an article or a chapter in a book, follow these six steps in this order.

1. Read the *title* and focus on the information in it.
2. Read the *introduction*, which is usually the first paragraph but can be several paragraphs long. Skim for a claim and any forecasts of what is to come.
3. Read the *last paragraph* and look for the claim.
4. Read the *headings* and *subheadings*, if there are any, to get a sense of the ideas and their sequence. If there are no headings, read the first sentence of each paragraph to accomplish the same goal.
5. Study the *visuals:* pictures, charts, graphs. Read their captions. They often illustrate major ideas or key details.
6. Identify the *key words* that represent the main concepts.

Surveying an article or chapter takes ten to fifteen minutes. It introduces you to the issue, the claim, and some of the support.

help you become familiar with them. The thesis of an argument, which shapes the thinking of the entire text and states what the author finally expects you to accept or believe, is called the *claim.* The main ideas or *subclaims* are assertions, reasons, or supporting arguments that develop the claim. They usually require *support* in the form of facts, opinions, evidence, visual images, and examples. Support makes the claim and subclaims clear, vivid, memorable, and believable. *Transitions* lead the reader from one idea to another and sometimes state the relationships among ideas. There is a constant movement between general and specific material in all texts, including argument texts, and this movement becomes apparent when the ideas are presented in various types of outline form.

READ WITH AN OPEN MIND AND ANALYZE THE COMMON GROUND BETWEEN YOU AND THE AUTHOR

At times you will agree with an author and at other times you will disagree. Try to avoid letting your biases and opinions interfere with your comprehension of what the author is saying.

Suppose you begin to read the article on affirmative action, "A View from Berkeley" by Chang-Lin Tien (pages 58–60). Consider some responses that readers of argument might make at this point. If you happen to agree with this author's ideas, you are more likely to read carefully, marking the best passages and insisting on reading them aloud to someone else. However, if you believe that affirmative action provides unfair and unnecessary advantages to minorities, you may be tempted not to read the essay at all or to read it hastily and carelessly, dismissing the author as wrongheaded or mistaken. If you are neutral on this issue, with opinions on neither side, you might read with less interest and even permit your mind to wander. These responses distract you and interfere in negative ways with your understanding of the article.

Once you become aware of such unproductive responses, you can compensate for them by analyzing the common ground between you and the author. Finding common ground obligates the reader to fairness. Thus you can use this information to help you read more receptively and nonjudgmentally. What common ground do you have with Tien? For example, could you identify with Tien's worries about being scolded and humiliated by his professor when he was in college himself? You may have common ground with Tien on that score. When you have established common ground, try to generate interest, read with an open mind, and suspend judgment until you have finished reading his article. Finally, reassess your original position to determine whether you now have reason to modify or change your perspective.

UNDERSTAND THE KEY WORDS

Sometimes figuring out the meaning of one word in a difficult passage will suddenly make the whole passage easier to understand. For example, if you read the title of "A Simple 'Hai' Won't Do" (pages 70–71), you may be baffled by it until you learn that *hai* means "yes" in Japanese. Once you have that information, the article makes much more sense.

When reading material suddenly seems difficult, go back and look for words you do not understand. Always identify the key terms, those that represent major concepts. In this book so far, *rhetorical situation, survey, claim,* and *subclaim* are examples of key terms. To find the meaning of difficult words and key terms, first

111

read the context in which you find the word or key term. A word may be defined in a sentence, a paragraph, or several paragraphs. Major concepts in argument are often defined at length, and understanding their meaning will be essential to an understanding of the entire argument. If the context does not give you enough information, then try the glossary, the dictionary, or another book on the subject. Remember that major concepts require longer explanations than a single synonym.

UNDERLINE, ANNOTATE, AND SUMMARIZE IDEAS

As you begin to read, underline with a pen or pencil and write notes in the margin to help you concentrate and understand. These notes will also help you review and find information later. The key to marking a text is to do it selectively. Do not color an entire paragraph with a highlighter. Instead, underline only the words and phrases that you can later reread and still get a sense of the whole. Bon key words. Jot the major ideas in the margins, or summarize them at the ends of sections. Write the big ideas along with your personal reactions on the flyleaves of a book or at the ends of chapters or articles. If you do not own the book, write on self-stick notes and attach them to the book pages. You can also write on paper organized in a folder or in an open computer file you are maintaining for your research.

Here is an example. This essay about polar bears and climate change has been underlined and annotated as recommended. A brief summary has been added at the end to capture the main point. Note that this material is now very easy to understand.

ESSAY #1   ## THE RACE FOR SURVIVAL*

Jerry Adler

Adler writes for newsmagazines and appears on television news shows.

Needed a symbol of global warming

1 Ten years ago, when environmental lawyer Kassie Siegel went in search of an animal to save the world, the polar bear wasn't at all an obvious choice. Siegel and Brendan Cummings of the Center for Biological Diversity in Joshua Tree, Calif., were looking for a species whose habitat was disappearing due to climate change, which could serve as a symbol of the dangers of global warming. Her first candidate met the scientific criteria—it lived in ice caves in Alaska's Glacier Bay, which were melting away—but unfortunately it was a spider. You can't sell a lot of T shirts with pictures of an animal most people would happily step on.

Newsweek, June 9, 2008, 42.

Spider, seabird, coral not dramatic enough.

2   Next, Siegel turned to the Kittlitz's murrelet, a small Arctic seabird whose nesting sites in glaciers were disappearing. In 2001, she petitioned the Department of the Interior to add it to the Endangered Species list, but Interior Secretary Gale Norton turned her down. (Siegel's organization is suing to get the decision reversed.) Elkhorn and staghorn coral, which are threatened by rising water temperatures in the Caribbean, did make it onto the list, but as iconic species they fell short insofar as many people don't realize they're alive in the first place. The polar bear, by contrast, is vehemently alive and carries the undeniable charisma of a top predator. And its dependence on ice was intuitively obvious; it lives on it most of the year, lurking near breathing holes to occasionally snatch a 150-pound seal from the water with one bone-crunching bite. But it took until 2004 for researchers to demonstrate, with empirically derived climate and population models, that shrinking sea ice was a serious threat to the bears' population. On Feb. 16, 2005—the day the Kyoto Protocol to curb greenhouse-gas emissions took effect, without the participation of the United State—Siegel petitioned to list polar bears as endangered. Three years later her efforts met with equivocal success, as Interior Secretary Dirk Kempthorne—under court order to make a decision—designated the bears as "threatened," a significant concession from an administration that has stood almost alone in the world in its reluctance to acknowledge the dangers of climate change. The Endangered Species Act (ESA), whose quaint lists of snails and bladderworts sometimes seemed stuck in the age of Darwin, had been thrust into the mainstream of 21st-century environmental politics. Break out the T shirts!

Polar bear is dramatic— an iconic species

Polar bear now on endangered species list

113

Summary:
With much time and effort, polar bear has finally become the icon of global warming. Now central to environmental politics.

WRITE OUTLINES OR MAPS

If you have read, annotated, and summarized a reading selection and still feel you should understand it better, try writing an outline or a map of the key ideas in it. Both outlines and maps lay out ideas in a visual form and show how they are related to each other. Seeing the organization of ideas improves your understanding and ability to critically evaluate the selection.

Make an Outline

To make an outline, write the claim, the most general idea, at the left-hand margin; indent the subclaims under the claim; and indent the support—the specific facts, opinions, examples, illustrations, other data, and statistics—even further. You may not always need to write an outline. Sometimes you can make a simple

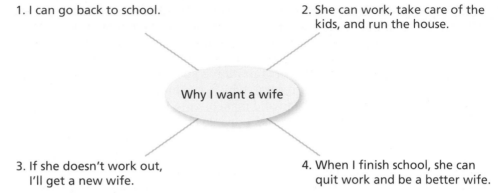

Figure 4.3 *Map of Ideas for "Why I Want a Wife".*

1. I can go back to school.

2. She can work, take care of the kids, and run the house.

Why I want a wife

3. If she doesn't work out, I'll get a new wife.

4. When I finish school, she can quit work and be a better wife.

mental outline to help you remember the claim and some of the ideas that support and develop it. Here is an outline of the essay "Why I Want a Wife" (pages 63–64).

OUTLINE OF *"WHY I WANT A WIFE"*
    Claim: I would like to have a wife.
        Subclaim: I could go back to school.
            My wife would work and run the household.
            Support (examples): She would take care of the children,
                keep the house clean,
                put my things away,
                fix good meals, listen to me,
                take care of my social life, and
                be sensitive to my sexual needs.
        Subclaim: If she didn't work out, my wife could be replaced.
            Support: If so, she gets the children and I start a new life.
        Subclaim: When I finish school, my wife quits her job, stays home,
                and becomes a better wife.
    Conclusion: "Who *wouldn't* want a wife?"

Make a Map

As an alternative to summaries or outlines, make a map of the ideas in a text. For many students, maps are the preferred way to reduce and reorganize the material they read. To make a map, write the most important idea, the claim, in a circle or on a line, and then attach major subclaims and support to it. Make your map in very brief form. Figure 4.3 ■ is a possible map of the essay "Why I Want a Wife" (see pages 64–65). You can be creative with map formats. Use whatever layout will give you a quick picture of the major ideas.

Take Notes and Avoid Plagiarism

From the start, record the information from your reading that you may want to quote, paraphrase, or summarize later when you write your paper. If you have an outline or list of ideas in your computer, type in such material at appropriate spots. If you are keeping paper notes in a folder, write out the passages in full and fully identify the author and publisher information for later detailed documenting of the source. Write out or type in your own ideas as they occur to you as well.

Copy quoted material exactly as it is written and place it in quotation marks immediately, with the author's name and brief source information at the end. You must add the author's name and the location of the original material (page or paragraph number, title or site, etc.) to paraphrased or summarized material as well. Label your own ideas as "mine," or put them in square brackets [ ]. Here are examples drawn from "The Race for Survival" (pages 112–113).

❱ Example of a Quote

"The polar bear, by contrast, is vehemently alive and carries the undeniable charisma of a top predator" (Adler, "The Race for Survival" 113).

❱ Example of a Paraphrase

Adler describes the difficulty of selecting an iconic animal that everyone would associate with global warming. ("The Race for Survival" 112).

❱ Example of a Summary

According to Jerry Adler, it took ten years to select an animal to symbolize the dangers of global warming. After rejecting less dramatic species, environmentalists selected the polar bear because it depends on ice to survive, and it is familiar. ("The Race for Survival" 112–113).

❱ Example of Your Idea

The polar bear is also photogenic when it appears in images that present strong visual arguments in favor of the reality of global warming.

If you follow this advice on taking notes, you will have no problem with plagiarism. Just in case you are still unclear about what plagiarism is exactly, here is a recent statement made by the Council of Writing Program Administrators that will help you.

> In an instructional setting, plagiarism occurs when a writer deliberately uses someone else's language, ideas, or other original (not common-knowledge) material without acknowledging its source. This definition applies to texts published in print or online, to manuscripts, and to the work of other student writers.[4]

Plagiarism is regarded as an extremely serious personal and academic violation because it negates the purpose of education, which is to encourage original and analytical thinking in a community in which expression of thought is both respected and protected.

[4]From "Defining and Avoiding Plagiarism: The WPA Statement on Best Practices" (2003). The full statement can be accessed at www.wpacouncil.org/positions/plagiarism.html.

Online research seems to have increased the incidence of plagiarism in student work. Some students find it tempting to copy and paste information from online articles into their own papers without using quotation marks and without documenting the source. Sometimes a student will mix their own words with the words of the quoted author and neglect to put the source's words in quotation marks. The result is a strange mix of styles and voices that creates a problem for the reader, who cannot easily sort out the student's words from those of the person being quoted. This, too, is plagiarism.

Lynne McTaggart, a professional writer whose work was plagiarized by a well-known author and commentator, explains plagiarism in this way.

> Plagiarism is the dishonorable act of passing someone else's words off as your own, whether or not the material is published. . . . Writers don't own facts. Writers don't own ideas. All that we own is the way we express our thoughts. Plagiarism pillages unique expressions, specific turns of phrase, the unusual colors a writer chooses to use from a personal literary palette. . . . In this age of clever electronic tools, writing can easily turn into a process of pressing the cut-and-paste buttons, . . . rather than the long and lonely slog of placing one word after another in a new and arresting way.[5]

McTaggart was shocked to read a book by a best-selling author that included material from her book, exactly as she had worded it, in passage after passage throughout the work without proper acknowledgment.

Here is another example of this error. The late Stephen E. Ambrose, an author of popular history books, was accused of plagiarism when his book *The Wild Blue* was published in 2001.[6] Both professional historians and the media criticized him publicly, and he suffered considerable embarrassment. Figure 4.4 ■ reproduces two of several illustrations of the plagiarized passages along with the original passages as they were presented in the *New York Times*. Compare the passages in the two columns until you understand why those in the right-hand column present a problem. This will help you avoid making the same mistake yourself.

Notice that Ambrose added footnotes in his book to show in general where the material came from, but he did not place quotation marks around the material that he copied directly. Kirkpatrick, the *New York Times* critic, reflects the opinions of several professional historians when he explains, "Mr. Ambrose should have marked direct quotations in the text, or at the very least noted the closeness of his paraphrase in his footnotes, historians say. College students caught employing the same practices would be in trouble."[7] When criticized, Ambrose admitted his mistake, and he was quoted as saying, "I wish I had put the quotation marks in, but I didn't."[8] He said he would do things differently in future books: "I am sure going to put quotes around anything that comes out of a secondary work, always."[9]

---

[5]Lynne McTaggart, "Fame Can't Excuse a Plagiarist," *New York Times*, March 16, 2002, A27.
[6]David D. Kirkpatrick, "As Historian's Fame Grows, So Do Questions on Methods," *New York Times*, January 11, 2002, A1, A19.
[7]Ibid, A19.
[8]Ibid, A1.
[9]Ibid, A19.

EXCERPTS

ECHOES IN PRINT

Stephen E. Ambrose, the author of historical best-sellers, appears to have reused words and phrases from other works, though passages are attributed in footnotes to original authors.

| From *The Rise of American Air Power,* 1987, by Michael S. Sherry | From *The Wild Blue,* 2001, by Stephen E. Ambrose |

ON JOHN STEINBECK'S WORK WRITING PROPAGANDA ABOUT AIRMEN

"Crewmen supposedly sprang from the frontier tradition of the 'Kentucky hunter and the Western Indian fighter.'. . . Like Lindbergh 15 years earlier, the airman was presented as both individualist and joiner, relic of the past and harbinger of the new era, free spirit and disciplined technician, democrat and superman, 'Dan'l Boone and Henry Ford.'"

"Steinbeck wrote that the men of the AAF sprang from the frontier tradition of the 'Kentucky hunter and the Western Indian fighter.' He presented the airman as both individualist and a joiner, a relic of the past and a harbinger of a new era, a free spirit and a disciplined technician, a democrat and a superman, 'Dan'l Boone and Henry Ford.'"

ON THE DANGERS OF ANOXIA (DEPRIVATION OF OXYGEN)

"Anoxia from shortages of oxygen both compounded the perils of frostbite and posed a serious danger in and of itself."

"Anoxia from shortages of oxygen compounded the threat of frostbite and posed a serious danger in and of itself."

Figure 4.4 *Examples of Plagiarism.*

Source: David D. Kirkpatrick, "As Historian's Fame Grows, So Do Questions on Methods," *New York Times,* January 11, 2002, A19.

You can avoid plagiarism by differentiating between your ideas and those of others at all stages of the writing process. This is why you are advised to enclose all direct quotations in quotation marks in your notes, to introduce paraphrases and summaries drawn from other people's works with the names of the authors in your notes, and to keep your own ideas separate from those of others by labeling them or placing them in brackets or a different font. You may safely and responsibly use other people's ideas and words in your paper, but you must always acknowledge that they are theirs. More instruction on how to separate your words from those of others when you incorporate source material into your paper occurs on pages 418–421. More detailed information on how to cite many different types of sources appears in the Appendix to Chapter 13 (pages 429–479).

If the passages you have drawn from outside sources are reasonably short, support your own ideas, and you clearly indicate where you found them, then you have done the right thing. If the passages are copied into your paper as though you had written them yourself, then you could receive a poor grade in the course or even be expelled from college. Understand too that you fail to link reading to thinking when you are reading to copy. It is a theft from someone else, but also from yourself. And, of course, you don't learn to improve your own writing when you copy other people's words instead of writing your own.

Write Your Paper, Read It, Think about It, and Revise It

At some point you will feel that you are ready to read through the material you have gathered and put it in some kind of order so that you can write your paper. Here are some strategies to help you accomplish that.

REFOCUS YOUR ISSUE AND RECONSIDER YOUR AUDIENCE

Read through the materials you have gathered and see if your issue has changed or shifted focus during your reading, thinking, and writing. Select the aspect of your issue that now interests you the most and that you have sufficient materials and ideas to develop. Keep in mind your time constraints and word limitations. Rewrite or refine your claim at this point to make your focus clear and convincing to your audience. You will probably want to adjust or rewrite it once again as you do your final read-through and finish your paper.

Consider whether you can strengthen your argument by doing more reading, probably in sources you have already located. You may also rethink your evaluation of some of the sources you have used. Information on how to evaluate sources appears on pages 387–390.

As you reconsider your audience, think about what they already know and what they still need to learn. Review your areas of agreement and disagreement and the amount of common ground you share. What will you need to include in your paper to convince them to consider your point of view. The way you organize your ideas may influence the way they receive them. For more help, review the specific kinds of audiences and how to appeal to each of them on pages 83–85.

MAKE AN EXTENDED OUTLINE TO GUIDE YOUR WRITING

A written outline helps many people see the organization of ideas before they begin to write. Other people seem to be able to make a list or even work from a mental outline. Still others "just write" and move ideas around later to create order. There is, however, an implicit outline in most good writing. The outline is often referred to metaphorically as the skeleton or bare bones of the paper because it provides the internal structure that holds the paper together. An outline can be simple—a list of words written on a piece of scrap paper—or it can be elaborate, with essentially all major ideas, supporting details, major transitions, and even some of the sections written out in full. Some outlines actually end up looking like partial, sketchy manuscripts.

If you have never made outlines, try making one. Outlining requires intensive thinking and decision making. When it is finished, however, you will be able to turn your full attention to writing, and you will never have to stop to figure out what to write about next. Your outline will tell you what to do, and it will ultimately save you time and reduce much of the difficulty and frustration you would experience without it.

WRITE THE FIRST DRAFT

The objective of writing the first draft is to get your ideas in some kind of written form so that you can see them and work with them. Include quoted, paraphrased, and summarized material in your draft as you write. Here is how a professional writer explains the drafting process.

> Writing a first draft should be easy because, in a sense, you can't get it wrong. You are bringing something completely new and strange into the world, something that did not exist before. You have nothing to prove in the first draft, nothing to defend, everything to imagine. And the first draft is yours alone, no one else sees it. You are not writing for an audience. Not yet. You write the draft in order to read what you have written and to determine what you still have to say.[10]

This author advises further that you "not even consider technical problems at this early stage." Nor should you "let your critical self sit at your desk with your creative self. The critic will stifle the writer within." The purpose, he says, is "not to get it right, but to get it written."[11]

Here is another writer, Stephen King, who advises putting aside reference books and dictionaries when concentrating on writing the first draft.

> Put away your dictionary. . . . You think you might have misspelled a word? O.K., so here is your choice: either look it up in the dictionary, thereby making sure you have it right—and breaking your train of thought and the writer's trance in the bargain—or just spell it phonetically and correct it later. Why not? Did you think it was going to go somewhere? And if you need to know the largest city in Brazil and you find you don't have it in your head, why not write in Miami or Cleveland? You can check it . . . but *later*. When you sit down to write, *write*. Don't do anything else except go to the bathroom, and only do that if it absolutely cannot be put off.[12]

You will be able to follow this advice if the materials you have gathered before drafting are available to guide you and keep you on track. If you occasionally get stuck, you can write some phrases, freewrite, or even skip a section that you cannot easily put into words. You will have another chance at your draft later. Right now, work only to capture the flow of ideas, either as they are written on an outline or as they are organized in your mind. You will discover, as you write, that many of the ideas that were only half formed before you began to write will now become clear and complete as you get insight from writing.

119

---

[10]John Dufresne, "That Crucial First Draft," *Writer*, October 1992, 9.
[11]Ibid., 10–11.
[12]Stephen King, "Everything You Need to Know about Writing Successfully—in Ten Minutes," *The Writer's Handbook*, ed. Sylvia K. Burack (Boston: Writer, 1991), 33.

BREAK THROUGH WRITER'S BLOCK

Most writers suffer from writer's block from time to time, and there are a number of ways to get going again if you find that you are stuck while writing your first draft.

▶ *Read what you have written so far.* Concentrate on the ideas, think about what you need to write next, and jot down a few notes to remind yourself what you want to do. Then get back to writing.

▶ *Read more about your issue.* If you don't have enough material, take notes on additional sources. Place limits by doing directed reading to meet specific needs.

▶ *Reread your outline, lists, and other idea notes.* Add new ideas that occur to you as you read, and rearrange ideas into new combinations.

▶ *Freewrite, read some more, and freewrite again.* Write fast, in phrases or sentences, on your topic without imposing any structure or order. Go through it later, crossing out what you can't use, changing phrases to sentences, adding material in places, and soon you will find that you are started again.

▶ *Use critical thinking prompts.* Revisit Box 4.1(page 104). These prompts will help you think in new ways about your topic and generate new ideas and information as well.

▶ *Talk about your ideas with someone else.* Either talk with someone or ask someone to read the draft as it now is and write their comments on it.

▶ *Give yourself permission to write a less than perfect first draft.* You can paralyze yourself by trying to produce a finished draft on the first try. Lower your expectations for the first draft. Remind yourself that you will need to return later and fine-tune it as well as fix any flaws or omissions.

REVISE THE DRAFT

Resist the temptation to put your paper aside when you have finished drafting and declare it finished. Now is your opportunity to become its first careful reader and to improve it in significant ways. Working with a rough draft is easier than outlining or drafting. It is, in fact, creative and fun to revise because you begin to see your work take shape and become more readable and convincing. It is worthwhile to finish your draft early enough so that you will have several hours to read and revise before you submit it in its final form to a reader.

Look at Your Draft as a Whole

When you have a draft, print it and lay it out in front of you so that you can see it as a whole. Look at organization first. How does your paper begin? Have you written an introduction that informs your audience about the subject of your paper? What are your main points? Where does each of them begin and end? Have you used enough transitional material to make your ideas stand out? Do you have enough support to make each of your main points believable to your audience? Think about your audience and decide whether you need to add information to make your paper more persuasive. How do you conclude your paper? Is your ending strong and memorable?

If you cannot answer these questions about your paper, try making a list or an outline of the most important ideas in it. Apply this test: Can you state the claim or the main point of your paper and list the parts that develop it? Take a good look at these parts, rearrange them if necessary and make them clearer and more complete.

Now, read paragraph by paragraph. Do you make links between the end of one paragraph and the beginning of another so that the ideas in them flow and appear to be clearly related to each other? Is most of each paragraph about one idea? Is that idea developed with sufficient supporting detail?

Check your sentences. Is each a complete thought? Do they all make sense? Rewrite problem sentences or sentence fragments. As a final check, read your entire paper aloud and listen for problems. Correct with pencil as you go along. You can enter corrections into the computer later.

Ask Revision Questions to Help You Locate Other Problems

Ask these seven questions about your draft, which direct your attention both to global revisions for improved clarity and organization and to surface revisions for errors in grammer and usage.

1. *Is it clear?* If you cannot understand your own writing, other people won't be able to either. Be critical of your own understanding as you read your draft. If you encounter confusing passages, stop and analyze why they are confusing and then rewrite them until the words represent what you mean or want to say.

2. *What should I add?* Sometimes in writing the first draft you will write such a sketchy version of an idea that it does not explain your thinking or fully state what you want to say. Add fuller explanations and examples, or do extra research to improve the skimpy or unsubstantiated parts of your paper.

3. *What should I cut?* Extra words, repeated ideas, and unnecessary material often crowd into the first draft. Every writer cuts during revision. Stephen King, who earns millions of dollars each year as a professional writer, describes how he learned to cut the extra words. His teacher was the newspaper editor John Gould, who dealt with King's first feature article, as he describes in this excerpt.

He started in on the feature piece with a large black pen and taught me all I ever needed to know about my craft. I wish I still had the piece—it deserves to be framed, editorial corrections and all—but I can remember pretty well how it looked when he had finished with it. Here's an example:

Last night, in the ~~well-loved~~
(gymnasium ~~of~~) Lisbon High School, partisans
and Jay Hills fans alike were stunned by
an athletic performance unequalled in school
history: Bob Ransom, ~~known as "Bullet" Bob~~
~~for both his size and accuracy,~~ scored

> thirty-seven points. He did it with grace
>
> and speed . . . and he did it with an odd courtesy
>
> as well, committing only two personal fouls
>
> in his ~~knight-like~~ quest for a record which
>
> has eluded Lisbon's ~~thinclads~~ basketball team since 1953 . . .

When Gould finished marking up my copy in the manner I have indicated above, he looked up and must have seen something on my face. I think he must have thought it was horror, but it was not: it was revelation.

"I only took out the bad parts, you know," he said. "Most of it's pretty good."

"I know," I said, meaning both things: yes, most of it was good, and yes, he had only taken out the bad parts. "I won't do it again."

"If that's true," he said, "you'll never have to work again. You can do *this* for a living." Then he threw back his head and laughed.

And he was right: I *am* doing this for a living, and as long as 1 can keep on, I don't expect ever to have to work again.[13]

4. ***Are the language and style consistent and appropriate throughout?*** Edit out words that create a conversational or informal tone in your paper. For example:

Change: And as for target shooting, well go purchase a BB gun or a set of darts.[14]

To read: For target shooting, a BB gun or a set of darts serves just as well as a handgun.

Also, edit out cheerleading, slogans, clichés, needless repetition, and exhortations. You are not writing a political speech.

You will learn more about language and style in Chapter 7. In general, use a formal, rational style in an argument paper unless you have a good reason to do otherwise. Use emotional language and examples that arouse feelings only where appropriate with a particular audience to back up logical argument.

5. ***Is there enough variety?*** Use some variety in the way you write sentences by beginning some with clauses and others with a subject or a verb. Vary the length of your sentences as well. Write not only simple sentences but also compound and complex sentences. You can also vary the length of your paragraphs. The general rule is to begin a new paragraph every time you change the subject. Variety in sentences and paragraphs makes your writing more interesting to read. Do not sacrifice clarity for variety, however, by writing odd or unclear sentences.

6. ***Have I used the active voice most of the time?*** The active voice is more direct, energetic, and interesting than the passive voice. Try to use it most of the time. Here is a sentence written in the active voice; it starts with the subject.

Robotics is an exciting new technology that could enhance nearly every aspect of our lives.

---

[13]King, 30–31.
[14]From a student paper by Blake Decker: used with permission.

Notice how it loses its directness and punch when it is written in the passive voice.

Nearly every aspect of our lives could be enhanced by robotics, an exciting new technology.

7. *Have I avoided sexist language?* Avoid referring to people in your paper as though they were either all male or all female. However, using such expressions as "he or she" or "himself or herself" sounds inclusive but comes across as awkward. Solve this problem by using plural nouns (*students* instead of *student*) and pronouns (*they* instead of *he or she*) Occasionally, you may need to rewrite a sentence in the passive voice. It is better to write, "The U.S. Constitution is often used as the guide when making new laws," than to write, "He or she often uses the U.S. Constitution as a guide when making new laws."

Avoid the Seven Most Common Errors Students Make

1. Write three or more similar items in a *series,* separated by commas, with the final item connected by *and* or *or*.

   Example: The National Rifle Association, firearms manufacturers, and common citizens are all interested in gun control.[15]

2. Use *parallel construction* for longer, more complicated elements that have a similar function in the sentence.

   Example: Parents who fear for their children's safety at school, passengers who ride on urban public transit systems, clerks who work at convenience stores and gas stations, and police officers who try to carry out their jobs safely are all affected by national policy on gun control.

3. Keep everything in the same *tense* throughout. Use the present tense to introduce quotations.

   Example. As Sherrill *states*, "The United States is said to be the greatest gun-toting nation in the world." Millions of guns create problems in this country.

4. Observe *sentence boundaries*. Start sentences with a capital letter, and end them with a period or question mark. Make certain they express complete thoughts. Do not punctuate a clause as a sentence. In the following sentence, the "because" clause is incorrectly punctuated as a sentence.

   Example (incorrect): Because criminals, including terrorists, can buy guns easily in this country. There should be a system for checking the background of everyone who purchases a gun.

   The clause is actually a part of the rest of the sentence. Change the period to a comma to correct this common error.

   Example (correct): Because criminals, including terrorists, can buy guns easily in this country, there should be a system for checking the background of everyone who purchases a gun.

123

---

[15]The examples presented here are drawn from a student paper by Blake Decker. I have revised his sentences for the sake of illustration.

5. Make *subjects agree* with *verbs.*

Example: Restrictions on gun control *interfere* [not *interferes*] with people's rights.

6. Use *clear and appropriate pronoun referents.*

Example: The *group* [one whole] is strongly in favor of gun control, and little is needed to convince *it* [not *them*] of the importance of this issue.

7. Use *commas* to set off long initial clauses, to separate two independent clauses, and to separate words in a series.

Example: When one realizes that the authors of the Constitution could not look into the future and imagine current events, one can see how irrational and irresponsible it is to believe that the right to bear arms should in these times still be considered a constitutional right, and according to Smith, the groups that do so "are shortsighted, mistaken, and ignorant."

Check for Final Errors, Add or Adjust the Title, and Type or Print Your Paper

Just before you submit your paper, check the spelling of every word you are not absolutely sure you know. If spelling is a problem for you, buy a small spelling dictionary that contains only words and no meanings. Also use the spell-checker on the computer. If you use a spell-checker, you should still read your paper one last time since a computer cannot find every kind of error. At this point you should format your paper and correct all the typographical errors that remain. Add a title or adjust your existing title, if necessary. Be sure that the final title provides information that will help the reader understand what your paper is about.

Complete the revision process by reading your paper aloud one more time. Read slowly and listen. You will be surprised by the number of problems that bother your ears but were not noticeable to your eyes. Your paper should be ready now to submit for evaluation. Print out the paper so that it is easy to read.

Organize Your Own Process for Reading, Thinking, and Writing about Issues

As you consider how you can adapt and use the ideas on reading, thinking, and writing about issues presented in this chapter, remember to keep the process flexible. You are not likely to use all of the strategies examined here for reading, thinking, and writing each time you write a paper.

Though these strategies have been explained in an apparent order, you will not necessarily follow them in this order. You might survey several sources and write an entire section of a paper during the prewriting stage, or you might stop to read and then do some rewriting and revising while you are working on the initial draft. The strategies are not steps: they are suggestions to help you complete a specific research task and write an argument paper. By integrating them with your present reading and writing processes, you will develop an effective way of researching and writing argument papers that is uniquely yours. The bare bones of the process can be stated simply.

- Select an issue, narrow it, take a tentative position, and write a claim.
- Do some reading, some thinking, and take some notes.
- Create a structure.
- Write a draft.
- Revise and edit it.

Practice Your Process by Writing These Papers

You can practice reading, thinking, and writing about issues by understanding and learning to write the three types of papers that will be described next in this chapter: the summary-response paper, the summary-analysis-response paper, and the exploratory paper. These papers can help you think about and develop ideas for papers described in future chapters.

THE SUMMARY-RESPONSE PAPER

A summary-response paper is composed of two parts: (1) the summary shows that you understand what an argument says, and (2) the response shows your reaction to it, including the ideas it generates in your mind.

A summary answers these questions: *What is this about? What did the author say about it?* To write a summary, follow these steps:

a. Survey first. (See instructions on page 110.) Identify the issue, the claim, and some of subclaims, or ideas that support the claim. This will help you answer the question, *What is this about?*

b. Write a brief list of words or phrases that represent the subclaims or the main points the author makes about the claim. You may be able to do this when you finish surveying. If you cannot, go back and read section by section or paragraph by paragraph and make notes on what appear to be the main points. This will help you answer the question, *What did the author say about the claim?*

c. Write a summary in your own words and in complete sentences that includes the author's claim and the main points that support it. Use the words and phrases you have written to guide you.

Here is an example of a summary of "Driving Down the Highway, Mourning the Death of American Radio," which appears on pages 87–89.

▶ Example of a Summary

Summary of "Driving Down the Highway, Mourning the Death of American Radio"

The author likes to listen to the radio play certain types of music when he drives, and he misses the variety of types of music he used to listen to before commercial companies took over the ownership of many independent radio stations. He complains that some of the large radio corporations control more than one hundred stations and their main objective is to make a profit. Consequently, they play the same music on stations across the country, play too many commercials every hour, fail to cover local news, take bland positions on important issues, and no longer feature unknown bands to help them get started. Only three corporations control nearly half of the radio stations in the country. The author intends to install a CD player, even though he realizes it could get stolen, to play his favorite music without interruption.

A response answers these questions: *What are your personal reactions to this essay? How much common ground do you have with the author? What in the essay is new to you? What else does it make you think about? What do you like or dislike about it?*

▶ Example of a Response

Response to "Driving Down the Highway, Mourning the Death of American Radio"

I have noticed the same changes on the stations I listen to when driving. Sometimes it seems there are nearly as many commercials as songs, and I hear the same songs over and over again. Like radio, television now seems to interrupt programming with more advertisements than in the past. This practice makes money for the station owners, but the quality of both radio and television is suffering as a result. No wonder iPods and TiVos are so popular. They provide one answer to the problem.

THE SUMMARY-ANALYSIS-RESPONSE PAPER

Add an analysis to a summary-response paper* to demonstrate that you understand why a particular argument is effective. Insert the analysis between the summary and your response.

An analysis answers these questions: *How is the essay organized? What and where is the claim? What supports the claim? Is the support adequate and relevant? How does the author establish personal authority? What audience does the author assume? How does the author make the argument, including the support, effective for that audience? What overall qualities in this essay make it an effective (or ineffective) argument?*

---

*Thanks to Beth Brunk-Chavez for this assignment.

▶ Example of an Analysis

Analysis of "Riding Down the Highway, Mourning the Death of American Radio"

The essay opens with a description of the danger of installing CD players in cars and makes the claim at the end of the second paragraph that people now have to install and listen to CDs in their cars because modern commercial radio has deteriorated in quality. The rest of the essay is organized by comparing and contrasting corporate and precorporate radio. Paragraphs 3 and 5–8 describe the problems with modern corporate radio, and paragraphs 4 and 9–12 describe the comparative strengths of independent, precorporate radio.

The support includes statistics, which establish the extent and power of corporate radio, and examples and descriptions of the music one could expect to hear both on corporate and precorporate radio. The support is adequate and also relevant to the author's claim.

The author establishes his authority by giving specific examples of early radio that he remembers and thus demonstrates his experience and devotion to music. He assumes an audience who likes to listen to a variety of types of music, uninterrupted by commercials, when traveling by car. He makes his argument appeal to this audience by using language associated with popular music, like "spin it" and "pop, rock, or country." He establishes immediate common ground with this audience in the introduction in which he refers to his experiences with car CD-player thieves and, later, when he refers to famous musicians most people recognize who could be heard on radio in earlier times but would not be heard now.

This is an effective argument because the author establishes common ground with all people who like to drive and listen to music and convinces them with comparisons and examples that radio has deteriorated in recent years and is not likely to improve. Thus he establishes the need to "spin it yourself."

Summary-response and summary-analysis-response papers preserve ideas from your reading, including your own ideas, and often provide original material and even phrasing for future papers that you write on the same subject, such as the Rogerian paper in Chapter 10 and the researched position paper in Chapters 11–13.

THE EXPLORATORY PAPER

In the exploratory paper,[16] the arguer identifies not just one position but as many of the major positions on an issue as possible, both past and present, and explains them through summaries and an analysis of the overall rhetorical situation for the issue. The analysis of the rhetorical situation in these papers explains what caused the issue and what prompted past and present interest and concern with it, identifies who is interested in it and why, and examines the constraints of the inquiry and the various views in the ongoing conversation associated with it. The summaries of the positions not only explain each of the different perspectives on the issue but also provide the

---

[16] I am indebted to the late Professor James Kinneavy of the University of Texas at Austin for the basic notion of the exploratory paper.

Box 4.3	Examples of Issues and Perspectives That Emerged from the Iraq War.

Issue 1: Why did the United States and its allies start a war in Iraq?

Perspectives: 1. To abolish weapons of mass destruction.
2. To encourage freedom and democracy in Iraq.
3. To destroy international terrorists.
4. To protect foreign oil supplies.
5. To remove a dictator who was perceived as a dangerous threat to the stability in the Middle East.
6. To showcase U.S. military capabilities.

Issue 2: What did the United States and its allies need to do to succeed in this war?

Perspectives: 1. Send more troops.
2. Supply the existing troops with better equipment.
3. Keep a few troops in Iraq indefinitely.
4. Withdraw all troops.
5. Rebuild the parts of Iraq destroyed by the war.
6. Work with the Iraqi government to establish democracy there.

usual reasons cited to establish the validity of each perspective. The writer's own opinions are not expressed at all or are withheld until later in the paper.

The war in Iraq created a rhetorical situation because it raised many issues that motivated people all over the world to discuss and argue in an attempt to resolve what were perceived as problems associated with this war. Box 4.3 ■ shows two of the many issues that emerged from this war. Several different perspectives held by individuals and groups who often disagreed with each other are also listed. Notice that the issues that emerged from the Iraq war did not invite simple pro and con positions. This is true of most rhetorical situations that motivate people to argue about issues. In between the either-or, people can and do take a variety of other positions that are not absolute or extreme.

Here are some additional examples. The issue of what to do with convicted criminals invites more perspectives than either putting criminals in jail or putting them to death. Intermediate positions might include sending them to various types of rehabilitation programs, releasing elderly inmates to their families when they are too old or too feeble to be a threat to society, or segregating different types of offenders in correctional institutions. The immigration issue in the United States invites more perspectives than either letting all foreigners in or keeping them all out. Other possibilities include issuing green cards to certain categories of immigrants or providing work permits for immigrant workers for a limited period of time.

There are a number of advantages to writing and reading exploratory papers. When writers and readers view an issue from many perspectives, they acquire a greater depth of understanding of it and the various views taken. Exploratory papers also help establish common ground between writers and readers. Writers, by restating several opposing positions along with the usual reasons for accepting them, are forced to understand that opposing views have commonalities that permit not only qualified but also multiple perspectives. The reader is interested because the exploratory paper explains several views, which usually include the reader's. The reader is consequently more willing to learn about the other positions on the issue. Exploratory papers can provide mutual understanding and common ground for the next stage in argument, the presentation of the writer's position and reasons for holding it.

Exploratory papers are a common genre in argument writing. You will encounter them in newspapers, newsmagazines, other popular magazines of opinion, and scholarly journals. They are easy to recognize because they take a broad view of an issue, and they explain multiple perspectives instead of just one. You will find examples of the exploratory paper at the end of this chapter (pages 139 and 142).

HOW TO WRITE AN EXPLORATORY PAPER

Your challenge now is to write an exploratory paper of your own. Look at your issue from several angles to decide which position you prefer. If you are later given the assignment to write a position paper on your issue, you will have discovered your own position, and you will also understand some of the other views that you may want to refute. The exploratory paper assignment appears on page 144 and the worksheet on pages 144–145. To complete it successfully, follow these general suggestions.

1. *Select an issue, and do some research and reading.* You will need an issue to write about that invites several different perspectives. You may have identified several issues already. If you do not have an issue, either read a set of related articles in "The Reader" or read about a topic that interests you on the Internet or in the library. Refer to "How Should You Engage with Issues?" (Chapter 1, page 20), and then refer to "Locating Sources for Research" (Chapter 12, pages 382–387). Take notes on the different perspectives you identify in this material. You might also make copies of the material you locate so that you can quote it later in your paper. (In both cases, document the sources for correct citation later.)

   An example of an issue that invites several perspectives is handgun control: some people believe there should be no restrictions on personal handgun ownership; other people believe possession of handguns should be banned for everyone except police officers and military personnel; a third group believes people have a right to own handguns, but with restrictions, including background checks, special training, and licensing. Notice these are three different positions on this issue, not merely three separate ideas about the issue.

   As you plan the perspectives for your exploratory paper, you can think about perspectives that are for, against, or somewhere else on the spectrum of possibilities; perspectives that represent three (or more) possible approaches or "takes" on an issue; perspectives that describe three (or more) possible ways to solve an issue; perspectives that provide three (or more) ways of interpreting an issue;

and so on. These perspectives may be yours or other people's. You may actually find four or five different approaches that different groups of people hold.

2. ***Analyze the rhetorical situation.*** Sketch out answers to the three parts of the rhetorical situation for your issue that are already in place before you begin to write: the exigence, the reading audience, and the constraints. To establish exigence ask, *What happened to arouse interest in this issue in the first place?* To establish audience ask, *Who shares my position on the issue, and who takes other positions?* To establish constraints ask, *What are some of the values, beliefs, and constraining circumstances that cause these groups and individuals to hold their positions?* Or, ask, *What do each of these groups or individuals value, want, and believe in regard to the issue?*

3. ***Write a draft, and include transitions.*** Draw on the ideas for drafting a paper discussed in this chapter (page 119). As you write your draft, include transitions to separate and emphasize the different perspectives on your issue. You might use transitions such as "some people believe," "others believe," and "still others believe"; "one perspective on this issue is," "another perspective is," and "a final perspective is"; or "one way to look at this issue is," "another way is," and "a third way is."

4. ***Work summarized ideas and quotes from your research into your draft.*** In an exploratory paper, you mainly summarize or paraphrase, in your own words, the positions you describe. If you decide to add direct quotations to make these summaries clearer or more interesting, work the quotations smoothly into your draft so that they make sense in context and are easy to read. Tell your reader where the summarized, paraphrased, and quoted material came from by citing original sources fully.

   If you refer to an article from "The Reader," show where it was originally published and also where it is published in this book. Find original publication information for each article in this book at the bottom of the first page of the article. To create such a citation, follow example 21 on page 442.

   For further information on how to incorporate source material into your draft, see pages 418–420. For further advice on how to cite these sources in the text itself, see the Appendix to Chapter 13, pages 432–436.

5. ***Revise your paper, and check your citations of source material.*** Follow the suggestions for revision that appear in this chapter (pages 120–124). At the end of your paper, list the works quoted in your text by creating a Works Cited page, if you are following MLA style, or a References page, if you are following APA style. To help further, look at the student example of an exploratory paper at the end of this chapter, on pages 142–144.

Submit Your Paper for Peer Review

If you can, put the draft of your exploratory paper aside for twenty-four hours, then read it critically and make changes to improve it. It helps to read the paper aloud at this point to get an even better idea about what can be improved. Then seek the opinion of other students in a class peer review session. Peer review sessions may include only three or four of your fellow students. You may be asked to provide each member of the review group with a photocopy of your paper so that, as you read your paper aloud to them, they can follow along and begin to mark problem areas to discuss later. Or you may participate in a round-robin reading session, in which group members read all of the papers silently and make brief notes before they discuss the papers one by one. In some cases, your instructor may join the group as an equal member and participate with students in asking questions that call your attention to areas that could be improved. Still another way of conducting peer reviews is for pairs of students to exchange papers to take home and read before the next class. This provides each student with time to read another student's paper more than once, if necessary, to locate areas for improvement.

There are several advantages to submitting your paper for review. No matter how well you write, revise, and edit a paper, another reader is almost always likely to have suggestions that can make your final paper better. Peer groups also make the writing task less isolating and provide immediate feedback from a real audience. They help you become a more sensitive critic of your own and others' work. Most professional writers rely heavily on other people's opinions at various stages of writing. Look at the prefaces of some of the books you are using this semester. Most authors acknowledge the help of several people who have read their manuscript and made suggestions for improvement.

If peer review groups are not conducted in your writing class, try to find someone else, like a writing center tutor or another student, to read your draft. Most writers need someone to read their work as they continue to refine it.

Expressing Multiple Perspectives through Visual Argument

Another way to express multiple perspectives on an issue besides an exploratory paper is through a collection of images that express different perspectives on it. An example of such an exploratory visual essay created with images as the central content appears on page 132. Most images need a few words of explanation for them to make their point. In this case, the title at the top and the five brief captions below the photographs explain the issue—walling off enemies—and various perspectives on how this has been done in four different countries. In the United States, walls are now in place on some parts of the border with Mexico, and more are being planned. Like the walls in China, Berlin, Israel, and Baghdad depicted in Images 1–4, this wall aims to separate people or keep people, such as illegal or undocumented Mexican immigrants and others who are perceived as enemies of a kind by many people, out.

Walling Off Your Enemies: The Long View

Image 1: **The Chinese Perspective.**

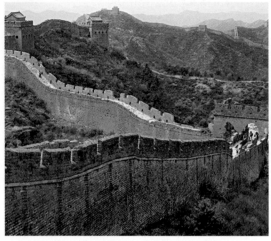

The Great Wall of China, was first built between the fifth and third centuries B.C., to protect the northern borders of China. It is about 4,000 miles long at present.

Image 2: **The German Perspective.**

The Berlin Wall, which separated East Berlin from West Berlin for 28 years, fell in 1989, an event that led to the reunification of Germany in 1990.

Image 3: **The Israeli Perspective.**

This wall separates Israelis from Palestinians in the West Bank at the present time.

Image 4: **The Iraqi Perspective.**

In Baghdad, Americans are putting up walls to secure neighborhoods.

These four photographs of walls provide four different perspectives on how governments have coped with perceived enemies by building walls. What do you think about the idea of building walls for protection from enemies? How effective is this solution? What other solutions can you think of that might also work or that might even work better?

Review Questions

1. Briefly describe a process for producing an argument paper that employs reading, thinking, and writing.

2. What are the advantages of outlining your ideas before you write a draft?

3. Name at least three specific suggestions for revision made in this chapter and describe in detail how you could use each of them.

4. Describe the exploratory paper along with some of the benefits for writing it. Then, describe exploring a topic visually along with some of the benefits of this form of communicating.

5. What is plagiarism, and what can you do to avoid it?

Exercises and Activities

A. **Class Project: Creating Composite Lists of the Reading, Thinking, and Writing Processes of Class Members**

This exercise gives you an opportunity to share with your classmates what you presently do when you read, think about, and write argument. When all class members contribute their strategies to composite class lists, the result is usually a very complete description of possible reading and writing processes. Include information, as you go along, about how you think as you read and write.

First, focus on describing what you do when you read and think about argument. Write the title "Reading Argument," and under it write the four headings "Prereading Strategies," "Reading Strategies," "Strategies for Reading Difficult Material," and "Postreading Strategies." Write five minutes to describe your current strategies in each area. Include thinking strategies in your description. Share these strategies with the class, creating master lists on the board.

Second, repeat this activity for writing argument. Write the title "Writing Argument," and under it write the four headings "Prewriting Strategies," "Drafting Strategies," "Strategies to Use When You Get Stuck," and "Postwriting Strategies." Write five minutes to describe your current strategies in each area and include thinking strategies in your description. Class members then contribute to composite lists on the board.

When you have written these lists, complete the following activities and discuss the results with the class.

1. Study the strategies for reading, thinking, and writing that your class has identified. Then,

   a. Discuss the ways in which writing is used as a part of the reading process.
   b. Discuss the ways in which reading is used as part of the writing process.
   c. Discuss how thinking is used as a part of both processes.

2. Turn to the Summary Charts on pages 511–523 and read the descriptions of possible strategies that you could employ at various stages to help you read, think about, and write argument. Discuss strategies you would consider adding to your present reading, thinking, and writing processes.

B. Class Discussion: Recognizing Written Argument

This reprinted article by Gina Kolata was published as a news article. Answer the following questions to help you figure out what type of argument is present, if any, here. Refer back to the description of six types of argumentation purpose on pages 105–106 to help you make your analysis.

1. What is the main issue in this article? It is not directly stated.

2. What are the author's attitudes toward the subject at issue?

3. What supporting material favors the author's point of view? Notice emotional language, vivid description, emotional examples, and the drawing that provide clues to the author's personal point of view.

4. What is the author's intention in this article? To explain? To convince? Or both?

5. What does the author hope you will conclude when you finish reading? Justify your answer with evidence from the article.

BEFORE YOU READ: What do you know about sperm banks, and what is your present opinion of them?

---

134 ESSAY #2 **PSST! ASK FOR DONOR 1913***

Gina Kolata

The author is a well-known science journalist for the *New York Times.* She has also published her work in *Science* magazine.

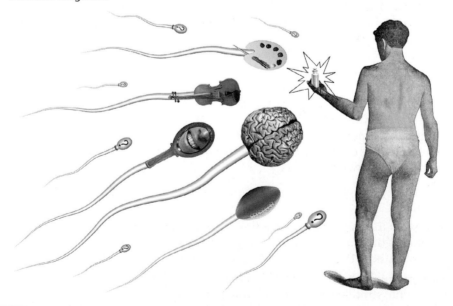

New York Times, February 18, 2007, 5.

1   In the old days, nearly two decades ago, when Jeffrey Harrison was selling his sperm to California Cryobank, sperm banks did not tell clients much. Women learned that Donor 150 (Mr. Harrison, who was one of the bank's most-requested donors) was six feet tall, had blue eyes and was interested in philosophy, music and drama.

2   But they did not learn, for instance, that despite those interests, Mr. Harrison was also "sort of a free spirit," as Danielle, one of his donor-conceived daughters, said after finding him last week.

3   Mr. Harrison, 50, lives in a recreational vehicle near Los Angeles, eking out a living doing odd jobs and taking care of dogs.

4   While the women who used his sperm may be perfectly satisfied, women today seem to be looking for a more unquestionably accomplished sort of man. Handsome and brilliant. Talented and charming. Loving and kind. A match one might only dream of finding in the flesh.

5   "Many women see this as another way to give their child a head start in life," says Lori Andrews, a professor at Chicago-Kent College of Law who has studied the sperm bank industry, of the high stakes of sperm selection.

6   And increasingly, say the banks, women want proof of perfection before buying a dream donor's sperm.

7   They ask for SAT scores and personality test results. They want baby pictures, pictures of the donor as a teenager, and photos of him as an adult. They want to hear his voice on audio files and they want to read his answers to written questions.

8   As more and more is added to the profile, its compilation becomes almost a striptease as the veil of anonymity falls away, eventually revealing all but name and address.

9   The reason for offering clients previously unimaginable degrees of access to information is competition.

10   "It's kind of an arms race," explains William Jaeger, director of Fairfax Cryobank, in Fairfax, Va., which, along with California Cryobank, based in Los Angeles, is among the largest sperm banks in the country.

11   "One year someone adds a personality profile, the next year someone adds something else," Mr. Jaeger says. "If one of your competitors adds a service, you add a service."

12   Supplying donors who will be saleable is quite a burden for the banks, which say they accept only about 1 to 2 percent of donor applicants. Often a man's sperm is not good enough, reproductively, or his medical history is problematic. Others are now rejected because their looks or education or even their demeanor is wrong.

13   "We're somewhat in the position of someone who is arranging a blind date," says Dr. Charles Sims, medical director and a founder of California Cryobank.

14   So who is Mr. Right for today's woman?

15   He can't be fat.

16   "We look for a height-weight ratio that is within the norm," Dr. Sims explains.

17   Being short is negotiable.

18   "If you have a 5-foot-7 or -8 donor who is a medical student or Ph.D. scientist, that outweigh the height issue in many situations, Dr. Sims says.

19   Education matters. California Cryobank only takes men who are in college or who graduated from a four-year college. At the Fairfax bank, "there is a preference for guys with medical and law degrees," Mr. Jaeger says.

20   Some sperm banks reveal more about their depositors than others.

21   The Fairfax bank, for example, provides adult photos if the donor agrees. The California bank does not, fearing that they could identify the donor years later and cause real problems. The Fairfax bank asks donors if their offspring can contact them when they are 18. The California bank will not do that but will try to discreetly contact a donor and ask if he wants to be identified to an adult child.

22   "We have felt we have some obligation to anticipate issues that a young man of 21 or 22

135

or 23 may not anticipate," Dr. Sims says. "To take an extreme example, let's say we had Bill Clinton as a donor when he was in college. Later he becomes president."

23 The Fairfax bank also includes "staff impressions" of donors in its dossiers. The staff seems to have favorable impressions of everyone, but, some are more favorable than others.

24 Among the most favorable of all is a man who appears to also be the most-requested donor.

25 "Women sort of fall in love with him," says Joy Bader, director of client services.

26 The most-requested donor is of Colombian-Italian and Spanish ancestry, is "very attractive, with hazel eyes and dark hair," and, Ms. Bader adds, is "pursuing a Ph.D."

27 The bank's files have one man, Donor 1913, who fits this description.

28 Donor 1913, the staff notes in his file, is "extremely attractive," adding in a kind of clinical swoon, "He has a strong modelesque jaw line and sparking hazel eyes. When he smiles, it makes you want to smile as well."

29 Donor 1913 is an all-around nice guy, they say. "He has a shy, boyish charm," the staff reports, "genuine, outgoing and adventurous."

30 He also answers questions, including, "What is the funniest thing that ever happened to you?"

31 Donor 1913 relates an incident that occurred when he asked his girlfriend's mother to step on his stomach to demonstrate his strong abdominal muscles.

32 "As she stepped on top of my stomach, I passed gas," he writes,

33 Is Don Juan the gas-passer also the most popular donor at Fairfax Cryobank?

34 Mr. Jaeger, the director, says he'll never tell. He cautions that discussing the most popular donor, whoever it is, might pose a problem—there is already a waiting list for his sperm, and publicity can only make it worse.

35 "We just can't keep enough of his units on hand, "Mr. Jaeger says.

For Discussion:

Does this essay qualify as an argument? Why? Provide evidence for your answer. What does the drawing contribute? If the author had to express her opinion on the subject she writes about, what would it be? What is your opinion?

C. Writing Assignment: The Summary-Response Paper

1. Select the issue area in "The Reader" that interests you the most. Read the "Rhetorical Situation" section for that issue. Then select one of the issue questions and read the set of essays related to the question. Using your own words, write a one-page summary-response paper for each of these essays: divide a piece of paper horizontally in half and write a summary on the top half and your response on the bottom half. Refer to the instructions and sample summary on pages 125–126 and the sample response on page 126 to help you.

2. Find an article related to your issue, and write a one-page summary-response paper about it.

D. Class Discussion and Writing Assignment: The Summary-Analysis-Response Paper

The following essay, "The Year That Changed Everything" by Lance Morrow, is an example of the type of academic argument you might find in a history class. Historians often make claims that argue for their interpretations of historical facts and provide evidence for their interpretations. Read, underline, and annotate the essay. Then briefly discuss answers to the following questions as a class.

1. Who is the author? What are his qualifications? What may have motivated him to write about this subject?

2. What do you know about the year 1948? Who in your family would remember this year well? What do you know about the three presidents mentioned in this essay?

3. Finally, write a summary-analysis-response paper. Drawing on the notes you have taken on your reading and discussion of the essay, write a 300- to 500-word paper in which you first summarize the essay, then analyze the essay, and last, respond to the essay. Use the following prompts labeled "Summary," "Analysis," and "Response" to guide your writing.

   ▶ *Summary:* What is this about? What did the author say about it?

   ▶ *Analysis:* Describe the organization of the essay. Include a description of the claim. Describe and evaluate the support. Consider types, quantity, quality, and relevance of the support. Then answer these questions: How does the author establish his authority? What audience does the author assume? How does the author make his writing, including the support, effective for the audience? What overall qualities in this essay make it an effective (or ineffective) argument?

   ▶ *Response:* What are your personal reactions to this essay? How much common ground do you have with the author? What in the essay is new to you? What else does it make you think about? What do you like or dislike about it?

> **BEFORE YOU READ:** Do you have any associations with the year 1948? What do you know about Presidents Nixon, Kennedy, and Johnson?

ESSAY #3   THE YEAR THAT CHANGED EVERYTHING*
Lance Morrow

> Morrow is an author and columnist for *Time* magazine. This essay appeared in the magazine and comes from Morrow's book *The Best Year of Their Lives: Kennedy, Johnson, and Nixon in 1948: Learning the Secrets of Power* (2005).

1   People who lived through tumultuous years like 1914 or 1941 or 1968 recognized them at the time for what they were: pivotal and world changing. But sometimes it is only after the passage of a generation or two, as a phase of history rolls on and its direction

Time, March 18, 2005, 90.

becomes clearer, that its point of origin emerges. 1948 was one of those years.

2   The nation turned away from depression and world war to what became America's vast peacetime imperial consumerism—the automobile-and-suburb culture. The baby boom was in utero, or in diapers. George W. Bush and Bill Clinton were approaching the terrible twos. In LIFE, an ad for Mutual Life Insurance showed a drawing of a man just about Richard Nixon's age (35)—hair Brylcreemed straight back like Nixon's—bending over a child about 2 years old sleeping in a crib. The father in the ad says, "Goodnight, Mr. President . . . and big dreams."

3   That summer, Nixon, a freshman member of the House Un-American Activities Committee, presided over the Alger Hiss case—a gaudy, sensational, two-year-long pageant of congressional hearings and court trials that would bring the cold war home, divide Americans and launch the young Nixon on a trajectory toward the White House.

4   Congressman Lyndon Johnson was locked in a fight for his political life in Texas—an epic run for the U.S. Senate against the popular conservative former Governor, Coke Stevenson. Johnson beat Stevenson, in a runoff primary election, by 87 suspect, late-counted votes from south Texas.

5   Freshman Congressman John Kennedy, recovering from his first onset of Addison's disease, learned that his sister Kathleen—the third of the golden trio of Joe Jr., Jack and "Kick"—had been killed in a plane crash while flying with her married lover for a holiday on the Riviera. Joe Jr. had died toward the end of the war in another plane, which blew up over the English Channel. Jack fell into a period of morbidity. The Kennedy family concealed the truth about Kathleen's aristocratic lover. Kennedy ever after concealed the truth about his Addison's

disease; if voters had known that Kennedy suffered from a debilitating illness, his future political career, and his election as President, would have been impossible.

6   If there had been no Hiss case, if Johnson had lost, if Kennedy had told the truth about his disease—history would have been different. The dramas turned on secrets. Nixon probed the hidden communist lives of Hiss and Whittaker Chambers. Kennedy locked the truth of his medical condition in a secret compartment. Johnson went to desperate lengths to prevent the disputed ballot box from being opened.

7   It was an era of secrets—political, personal, atomic. The cold war, just beginning, took form upon a battlefield of deadly concealed knowledge, of espionage and counterespionage, the terrible prize of which was the secret of the power to destroy the world. The *Saturday Evening Post* still gave Americans a Norman Rockwell version of themselves as an essentially lovable and virtuous people. The first programs in the new medium of television worked the same vein. But the war—as war always is—had been a violent exploration of the possibilities of human nature. Technology had expanded the possibilities in the direction of apocalypse. Americans asked what they always ask about themselves: Are we a good people or a bad people?

8   In 1948 Alfred Kinsey published his report on Americans' previously concealed sex lives. The Nobel Prize in Medicine went to the Swiss chemist Paul Hermann Muller, for his work in developing the "miracle" compound DDT. Fourteen years later, during the Kennedy Administration, the *New Yorker* would begin serializing Rachel Carson's *Silent Spring*. George Orwell transposed two numbers to get *1984*.

9   Gandhi was assassinated by a Hindu militant from an organization called Mahasabha (the Great Society). The Marshall Plan began. The state of Israel was born. In the summer of

the Berlin airlift, Lyndon Johnson clattered across Texas in history's first campaign-by-helicopter—Lyndon swooping down ex machina to meet and greet the astonished farmers.

10   1948 was the year when three future U.S. Presidents passed through formative ordeals and emerged reborn—launched toward their destinies. All three of those destinies would be literally or politically fatal years later, in the Vietnam-Watergate era, which, in turn, formed the U.S.'s present leaders. The year 1948 was the seedbed.

For Discussion:

How does the author characterize the year 1948? What "formative ordeals" occurred in the lives of Presidents Nixon, Johnson, and Kennedy that made 1948 a momentous year for them? What events followed as a result? Has there been a comparable year in your life? What were the "formative ordeals" for the president serving in that year, if you know of any? Do you think the concept of "formative ordeals" applies to you? To everyone? Give an example and explain why.

E. Group Work: Analyzing an Exploratory Paper

    1. For practice, analyze this exploratory paper together.

BEFORE YOU READ: Have you been paid to do chores at home? What is your present position on paying children to do family chores?

ESSAY #4   **KIDS AND CHORES: ALL WORK AND NO PAY?***
    Jeff D. Opdyke

        Opdyke covers personal finance for the *Wall Street Journal* and writes the column "Love and Money."

What is the rhetorical situation?

1   A few nights ago I asked my seven-year-old son to help set the table for dinner. His reply: "Can I have two dollars?"

2   Several weeks earlier, he wanted a quarter for helping fold some clothes. And when my wife, Amy, asked him to complete a chore he had already agreed to do, he tried to renegotiate so he could get a dollar for it.

What is the issue?

3   We didn't pay him for any of it, and generally don't for most chores. As I've told him, he has reached an age where he has no choice but to pitch in and contribute to the family's upkeep.

4   Still, Amy and I are trying to formulate a philosophy on what we will and won't pay for when it comes to housework. It isn't easy. On one hand, there's no reason he should be paid for chores like setting the table or cleaning his room. Then again, some chores do deserve extra rewards—and paying for them also can help us encourage our son's entrepreneurial spirit.

Wall Street Journal. Reprinted in *Fort Worth Star-Telegram,* February 1, 2004, 4F.

What are the three perspectives?

Describe the common ground.

What is Grace's perspective?

What was the author's grandfather's perspective?

What is the perspective of the friend at the office?

5   But the distinction between paying and nonpaying chores is both hard for us to make and hard for him to understand.

6   If you pay for too much, kids begin to assume you should pay for everything—and they'll figure they have the power to reject the work if they think the price is too low. But if you don't pay for anything, you get nothing but resentment.

7   Thus, we're learning that when it comes to kids and their chores, managing expectations is as important as the chore itself.

8   Just as there is a wide disparity in allowance programs among parents, moms and dads tackle this issue in numerous ways.

9   Some get in the habit early on of paying for just about any chore, and the pattern sticks as the kids grow older. Others pay for no chores, expecting that as a member of the family a kid is required to perform certain tasks. And many parents, like me and Amy, are somewhere in between, trying to navigate a fuzzy line between expectation and encouragement.

10   The common denominator is that all parents face this at some point, usually around first or second grade—roughly the stage when kids begin to understand the significance of money and the frustrations of not having enough to buy what Mom and Dad won't.

11   My friend Grace went through this with her seven-year-old not long ago.

12   He went through a phase, she says, "when he was asking to get paid to do anything around the house." Grace generally told him "no."

13   One day, Grace told her son to pick up his toys. When he asked what the assignment was worth, Grace realized she'd had enough with the constant request for money for simple chores around the house.

14   "I put a stop to that impertinence right then and there," Grace says. "I told him that if I paid him to pick up his toys, then he needs to pay me for his food, his clothes, his toys, rent, etc." The message sunk in; he stowed his toys without seeking remuneration.

15   Now, when I was a kid I didn't get paid for many things. My grandfather would tell me to cut the grass, so I cut the grass. My grandmother would ask me to straighten up the disaster in my bedroom, so I cleaned my room. They didn't offer money as an enticement; the work was simply expected.

16   My friend at the office grew up similarly, responsible for working outside after school every day. He had to cut the grass and weed in the spring and summer, rake leaves in the fall and shovel snow in the winter. Thirty minutes pretty much every day—after which he could play with his friends.

17   In retrospect, he says, he learned a lot about outdoor work—about planting shrubs, for instance, and building walks—that has served him well as an adult with his own house. But what stuck with him even more was how much he disliked it.

18   "It was part of my job in the house and I pretty much hated most of it," my friend says. "It was torture because all I wanted to do was play baseball. But I had to get the chores done first."

19   So my friend did what many people do: He went the other direction when he had his own kids, and rarely asked them to do anything. And he looks back on raising his son and daughter, now in their late teens, and says, "I think I made a mistake."

20   The problem, he says, is that he "set the bar too low on the required things. We expected them to do stuff like clear the table. But anything above and beyond, I offered to pay."

21   In the end, he says, "that backfired. When they got older, they didn't really want to do the work, even for money. That was partly because they had outside jobs. But it was mainly because I had undermined the expectation that they *must* work in the house. I had set it up so these jobs were optional—they could turn them down if they wanted to. So I ended up having to do all the stuff as an adult that I hated as a kid because my kids didn't want to do it."

What is the author's perspective?

22   Basically, my friend says he learned, as I'm learning now, "that I should have set a much higher minimum expectation for being a family member."

23   He's now applying that lesson to his preteen daughter. "She's expected to do much more around the house, like cleaning or helping cook or keeping her room straight," he says. "She's too young still, but I won't be paying for folding clothes or cutting the grass or raking leaves."

24   Speaking of leaves . . . over the fall I was raking the blanket of foliage that covers our yard every year when my son came wandering up from the tool shed with a kid-sized rake I had bought him last year at Home Depot.

25   "If I help you rake, Dad, can I have a dollar?"

26   Now, I knew his efforts would be short-lived and that, more than likely, I'd have to rake over his tracks. But to have your son willingly volunteer to help is a heartwarming feeling and a bonding experience.

27   "Sure, buddy."

28   I was right; he lasted about 10 minutes before he decided to play in the leaves instead of rake them. Still, I paid him his dollar and thanked him for taking the initiative to help around the house.

29   Then, I took the opportunity to lay some groundwork: "You know, one day you're going to be old enough where Mommy and I are going to expect you to rake the leaves without getting paid—and that day is getting closer."

30   "OK," he replied. "Maybe we can start when I'm your age."

For Discussion:

What is the issue? Describe the rhetorical situation that motivated the author to write this essay. How do you think this author imagines his audience? What are the different perspectives on the issue? Locate some transitional words and phrases that separate and emphasize the different perspectives. What is the author's perspective? What common ground, if any, exists between you and this author? What is your perspective, and is it mentioned in this article?

141

F. Paired Student Activity: Analyzing a Student Exploratory Paper

The following is an example of an exploratory paper written by Prisna Virasin, a student in an argument class. Her issue proposal on this subject appears on pages 31–32, and her position paper on pages 446–455. Take a few minutes to read Prisna's paper. Then work in pairs to answer the following questions. Report your answers to the class.

1. What is the issue?

2. Describe the parts of the rhetorical situation that were in place when Prisna started to write. What is the exigence? Who are the groups of people interested in this issue? What are their positions? What are some of the constraints of these groups?

3. What are the perspectives on the issue that the author identifies? Make a list.

4. What transitions does the author use? Underline them.

5. What is the author's perspective? Why does she hold it?

You may want to use Prisna's paper as a model for your own exploratory paper.*

BEFORE YOU READ: What do you know about Barbie dolls?

142

STUDENT PAPER #1   Prisna Virasin
Exploratory Paper
Prof. Wood
English 1302
1 March 2008

The Controversy behind Barbie

Explain the issue.

1   The Barbie doll was created in 1959 by Ruth Handler, the cofounder of Mattel. Handler created the doll after seeing her daughter, whose nickname was Barbie, and her daughter's friends play with their paper dolls. According to Gaby Wood and Frances Stonor Saunders, Handler realized that little girls wanted a doll "they could aspire to be like, not aspire to look after" (38). This was a revolutionary idea because before the creation of Barbie, the toy store doll selection mainly consisted of baby dolls, which encouraged girls to pretend to be mothers. For Handler, according to Wood and Saunders, Barbie "has always represented the fact that a woman has choices" (39). The "Barbie Dolls" entry on the *History Channel* Web site states, "ninety percent of all American girls in the last forty years have owned at least one Barbie. . . . Each week Mattel sells over 1.5 million dolls—that's two dolls per second."

Describe the rhetorical situation.
▶ Exigence
▶ Interested parties
▶ Constraints

---

*See the Appendix to Chapter 13 for the actual MLA format guidelines for student papers.

What is the first
perspective?

2   The fact that Handler created Barbie as a challenge to the ideology
that the proper role for women was that of a mother has become ironic
in light of the present feminist protest against the Barbie doll. The Barbie
protesters have stated that Barbie is responsible for the development of
poor body image in girls. They believe that the Barbie's proportions
create impossible images of beauty that girls will strive toward. If Barbie
were a human she would be seven feet tall with a thirty-nine-inch chest
measurement, twenty-two-inch waist measurement, and thirty-three-
inch hip measurement ("Barbie Dolls").

3   In addition to protests of the Barbie's physical appearance, there is
also the issue of the doll's intellectual image. Barbie detractors have
criticized the Barbie lifestyle, which seems to center around clothes,
cars, dream homes, and other material possessions. Protests followed
the release of the talking Barbie that localized such expressions as
"Math is hard" and "Let's go shopping." Parents feared that the first
sentence would reinforce the stereotype that girls were less skilled
at math than boys. The second sentence seemed to reinforce the
importance of clothes, physical appearance, and material goods. In her
article, "Giga-What? Barbie Gets Her Own Computer," Ophira Edut
criticizes educational materials based on Barbie for the image they
reinforce. Edut states that the Barbie computer is bundled with typing
tutor software while the boys' Hot Wheels computer is bundled with
adventure games. Also, the Barbie Rapunzel CD-ROM is touted by
Mattel to expose girls to fine art and creativity when the only creative
function of the program is changing Barbie's clothes and hairstyle
interactively on the computer screen.

What is the second
perspective?

4   Supporters of the Barbie doll state that the toy is a fun part of
growing up. They refer to the simple fun of playing with Barbie
dolls. They believe that Barbie as a figure is a tool in building girls'
imaginations. They also maintain that Barbie as a figure is a positive
role model because she is able to do almost anything. Barbie was an
astronaut before the first woman went into space. Barbie has been
a veterinarian, a doctor, a businesswoman, and to top it all off, a
presidential candidate.

What is the third
perspective?

5   Between the anti-Barbie camp and the pro-Barbie camp, there are
the Barbie moderates. The Barbie moderates do not completely agree
with how Mattel chooses to portray the "ideal American woman," nor
do they view the doll as all evil. They see the positive aspects of the
Barbie (the many professions, the ability to foster imaginative play,
and the message that girls can choose to be whomever they want)
and the negative aspects of the Barbie as a figure (a materialistic
nature, a focus on outward appearance, and the vapid blond stereotype).
The moderates state that by banning Barbie dolls, we will not be
solving the problem of poor body image. They believe that Barbie is a
scapegoat—the figure (or doll) to blame for all the negative feelings
that children develop about themselves. Although the moderates do

143

What is the author's perspective? Why does she hold it?

not agree with the image of women that Barbie seems to sustain, they also do not believe that this doll (or figure) is the source of the problem.

6   As a twenty-something female who grew up in America, I am very interested in the Barbie debate. I played with Barbie dolls almost obsessively from first to third grade. I designed clothes for them out of handkerchiefs and tissues and dreamed about becoming a fashion designer. I remember envying the girls who had Barbie Ferraris and dream houses. I looked on in horror as my little sister cut Barbie's hair short and colored it hot pink with a marker. In college, when I was introduced to feminism, I tried to deny any past connection to Barbie. I was ashamed to have ever associated with this figure. I felt sorry for the girls who looked like walking Barbie dolls, always worried about looking perfect. I realize now that I cannot blame thoughts of being fat, short, or out of style on a doll or girls that look like dolls. I agree with the Barbie moderates. As simple as the Barbie looks, it seems that the Barbie issue is more complicated than "Barbie good" or "Barbie bad." The debate encompasses many interesting and controversial issues concerning how we view beauty and how we view ourselves. In my eyes, Barbie is a scapegoat. We, as an entire culture, need to look at our ideas about beauty and what we are teaching children about themselves.

Works Cited

"History of Toys: Barbie Dolls." *History.com*. A&E Television Networks, 2008. Web. 15 Feb. 2008.

Edut, Ophira. "Giga-What? Barbie Gets Her Own Computer." *AdiosBarbie.com*, n.d. Web. 17 Feb. 2008 <http://www.adiosbarbie.com/bology/bology_computer.html>.

Wood, Gaby, and Frances Stonor Saunders. "Dream Doll." *New Statesman* 15 Apr. 2002: 38–40. *Academic Search Complete*. Web. 18 Feb. 2008.

For Discussion:

Did you ever play with a Barbie or G.I. Joe? If not those, what were your favorite childhood toys? How did they affect your imagination and self-image? Have they had any lasting effects on you?

G. Writing Assignment: Write an Exploratory Paper

Review "How to Write an Exploratory Paper" (pages 129–130) to help you complete this assignment. Then write a 750- to 900-word exploratory paper. Use the worksheet on page 145 to help you plan your exploratory paper. Follow MLA style (see the Appendix to Chapter 13), unless you are advised otherwise.

Worksheet 2   Exploratory Paper

1. Write your issue in a complete sentence. Explain it, and include the information that provides background and makes the issue interesting to your readers.

2. Explain the parts of the rhetorical situation that are already in place as you begin to write. Describe the exigence or context for your issue, including what happened to make people interested in it. Identify the individuals or groups of people interested in this issue, with a brief introduction to their positions. Mention some of the constraints of these groups: for example, What do they think, value, and believe?

3. Describe at least three different positions on your issue, state who holds them, and give some of their reasons for holding them. You may explain more than three positions, if you want or need to do so. Jot down the positions.

   a. Position 1:_____

   b. Position 2:_____

   c. Position 3:_____

   _____

4. Explain your personal interest in the issue and the position you favor.

II. Group Work: Analyzing an Argument Essay That Employs Visual Perspectives on the Issue as Support

The following essay was written at a time when some members of Congress were advocating the addition of a flag burning amendment to the United States Constitution. Read the essay, study the images, and answer the "For Discussion" questions that follow.

> **BEFORE YOU READ:** Is flag burning an issue you feel strongly about? Why or why not?

ESSAY #5   FORGET FLAG BURNING*

Major General Robert Scales (Ret.)

The author, a retired major general, commanded two units in Vietnam and was awarded a Silver Star. He served thi years in the Army.

1 Some in congress appear to be taking a sabbatical from the long war on terrorism to introduce a constitutional amendment banning the burning of the flag. The debate over such an amendment may or may not be worth having, but one thing is clear at a time

Time, July 3, 2006, 100.

Joe Rosenthal, *Marines Raising the American Flag at Iwo Jima.*

Leonard Detrick, *Anti-Vietnam War Protesters.*

Andrew Lichtenstein, *Memorial with People Holding Folded Flag.*

when the country is at war, now is not the time for such tertiary considerations.

2   I understand reverence for the flag. It comes naturally to soldiers. We commit our lives to serving intangibles, swearing oaths to a piece of parchment or saluting an expanse of cloth decorated with stars and stripes. We understand symbolism because symbolism is what in large measure compels us to do a job that might result in our demise.

3   The American flag symbolizes freedom. The Constitution we soldiers are pledged to defend guarantees freedom of expression even when freedom of expression includes the right to deface the flag, however obnoxious that act may be. Of course, I'm old enough to remember flag burning when flag burning was "cool." I was in Hawaii, on R. and R., halfway through my tour in Vietnam. My wife and I were watching television when student war protesters in California—none of whom had the slightest chance of facing violent death in combat— illuminated their campus by torching Old Glory. I was appalled by the sight. A short time later, Walter Cronkite informed the world that my unit, the 101st Airborne, was beginning an offensive in the A Shau Valley. I left for Vietnam the next day to confront an enemy that undoubtedly would have

punished those protesters had they burned the North Vietnamese flag in Hanoi.

4   But that was then. The image of the flag that soldiers see today is different. Instead of flags aflame, we see flags covering coffins of soldiers and Marines returning the hard way from Iraq and Afghanistan. Pushing forward a constitutional amendment is labor-intensive work. I'm concerned how such a diversion during wartime might appear to those who are still serving in harm's way.

5   Please don't get me wrong. I have many friends in Congress, patriots all. Each one of them has been to Iraq and Afghanistan many times. Although he refuses to advertise the fact, one was wounded there during an inspection tour last year. My concern relates not to the sincerity of Congress but to the perceptions among our young men and women that their overseers are suddenly distracted at a time when attention to their needs has never been more necessary.

6   Our soldiers want to be assured that Congress is doing all it can to reduce losses in what Lincoln ruefully termed the "terrible arithmetic" of war. They want to know that Congress is doing all it can to give them the weapons they need to maintain the fighting advantage over the enemy.

They are concerned that their equipment is wearing out under constant use. They and their families are worried that not enough soldiers are in the pipeline to replace them.

7   We know from letters and conversations that our young soldiers returning from combat are concerned about the future of their institutions. They want to know who is focused on reshaping our Army and Marine Corps so that both services will be better able to fight the long fight against radical Islam. How will Congress fund the future? Where will the new weapons and equipment come from? They are also worried about more personal issues like housing and health care for themselves and their families.

8   Dan Brown was my First Sergeant in Vietnam. I was new to war. He had served in two. He gave me a piece of advice then that Congressmen intent on changing the subject should heed: "In combat the main thing is to keep the main thing the main thing. Otherwise, you die." The main thing today for Congress and the nation should be the war in Iraq. Soldiers are sworn to defend the right to free speech with their lives even if "speech" is expressed in despicable ways. What they want in return is the assurance that our lawmakers will hold their interests dear.

9   So the message from most of us soldiers is clear: Debate a flag-burning amendment if you wish. But don't create the perception among our young men and women in combat that there are more important issues than their welfare at the moment. Wait a while. At least for their sake, wait until the last flag-draped coffin comes home.

For Discussion:

What three perspectives on the flag of the United States are expressed in the three photographs? What three wars do they represent? State the claim made in the essay. Which photograph best illustrates the claim? What effect is created by placing photographs next to each other in this order?

I. Creative Assignment: Exploring an Issue Visually

Select an issue and create a visual exploratory essay by gathering three or more images that express different perspectives on the issue. Use the photographs of the walls on page 132, the hands on pages 304–305, the flags on page 146, the "bad lovers" on page 540, and the ways of reading on page 571 as examples to get you started. As a class, brainstorm together to generate some ideas that will work for this assignment. Here are a few ideas to get you started: modifying your personal image, embracing new media, selecting a major, planning your career, making a major purchase such as a car or computer. Search for images on the Internet or in magazines or newspapers.

Understanding the Nature of Argument for Reading, Writing, and Viewing Images

The purpose of the next six chapters is to explain the essential component parts of an argument and show how they operate together to convince an audience. Chapter 5 identifies the parts of an argument as explained by Stephen Toulmin in what has come to be known as the Toulmin model. Chapter 6 describes the types of claims and purposes in argument. Chapter 7 describes how support, warrant, and backing combine to provide proof for argument and also discusses language and style. Chapter 8 alerts you to fallacies or false proofs and provides criteria for judging ethical argument. Chapter 9 teaches the unique characteristics of visual argument and reviews ideas from earlier chapters that apply to visual argument, and Chapter 10 presents Rogerian argument as an alternative strategy to traditional argument. When you finish reading Part Two:

▶ You will understand and be able to identify the essential parts of an argument.

▶ You will know the key questions that arguments attempt to answer.

▶ You will be able to identify types of claims and purposes in argument.

▶ You will understand how argument employs proof, language, and style to appeal to your reason, your emotions, and your sense of values about people's character.

▶ You will understand fallacies and the differences between ethical and unethical argument.

▶ You will know how to analyze and create visual arguments.

▶ You will know how to write a traditional position paper, a Rogerian argument paper, and an argument analysis paper.

CHAPTER 5

The Essential Parts of an Argument: The Toulmin Model

T he purpose of the chapters in Part Two is to present ideas from argument theory that will help you add strategies for reading, writing, and viewing argument with confidence and expertise. Because people have been analyzing argument and writing theories of argument for twenty-five hundred years, there is a considerable tradition of theory to draw on to help with this task. This theoretical background is especially useful because theory describes argument, and once you possess good descriptions, argument will be more familiar and consequently easier for you to read, write, or view yourself.

In acquiring new understandings of argument, you will be adding to what you already know as you gradually build a stronger and larger body of knowledge and comprehension. Eventually, you will achieve "all-at-onceness," a quality Ann E. Berthoff utilizes in her book *The Sense of Learning* to describe the use of many ideas, bits of information, and strategies about reading, writing, and viewing that finally come together so that you are able to practice them unconsciously, simultaneously, and automatically.[1]

For now, however, you are still expanding your knowledge. Your goals in this chapter will be to gain a better understanding of the anticipated outcomes of argument and to identify the component parts as they are identified by Stephen Toulmin in his model for argument.

The Outcomes of Argument: Probability versus Certainty

In Chapter 1 you learned that arguable issues require the possibility of at least two different views. It is the nature of argument to invite differing views and perspectives on issues. Outcomes can include achieving a

[1]Ann E. Berthoff, *The Sense of Learning* (Portsmouth, NH: Boynton/Cook, 1990), 86-91.

closer agreement with a friendly audience or getting the attention of and even perhaps some consensus from a neutral or hostile audience. Notice that these outcomes of argument are usually not described as establishing "certainty" or "truth" in the same sense that mathematics and science seek to establish certainty and truth. We do not argue about the fact that $2 + 3 = 5$ or that the area of a circle is πr^2. Mathematical proofs seek to establish such truths. Argument seeks to establish what is *probably* true as well as what might be expedient or desirable on balance for the future. Arguers tell you what they think for now along with what they think should be done, given their present information. On that basis, you decide what you think for now, given your present information.

Throughout history, some thinkers have been drawn more to the idea of establishing truth and some have been drawn more to the idea of establishing probabilities. Among the ancient Greek philosophers, Plato was interested in establishing truth. He employed dialectic, the question-and-answer method used in his dialogues, to help participants discover the Platonic ideals or forms of truth. Aristotle, on the other hand, was interested in probabilities. The *Rhetoric*, written somewhere between 360 and 334 B.C., is a key book in the history of argument theory, and its purpose is to train persuasive speakers to be convincing to audiences. Aristotle observes the orators of his time and, in the *Rhetoric*, describes what they do. He notes that they are involved with matters and views concerning both the present and the future that are probably true rather than certainly true. The reason for the orators' perspective lay in the audience. The ancient audience, like modern audiences, would disagree with many views that were stated as absolutely true. Those audiences could think of exceptions and reasons why certain views might not be true. Responsible persuaders, to communicate effectively, had to modify and qualify their views to make them acceptable to their audiences. They had to present probabilities instead of absolute truths. Thus views that are probably true comprise the realm of argument. To understand that realm better, it is useful to understand the parts that contribute to the whole argument.

The Parts of an Argument according to the Toulmin Model

Stephen Toulmin, a modern English philosopher, developed a six-part model of argument in his book *The Uses of Argument*, and this model has been useful to many people for explaining the essential parts of an argument.[2] Like Aristotle, Toulmin was interested in describing how to establish probability. At the time Toulmin wrote his book, his colleagues were logicians who were interested in discovering truth rather than probabilities. Toulmin tells us that his book had a chilly welcome among them. His graduate adviser at Cambridge, he explains, "was

---

[2]Stephen Toulmin, *The Uses of Argument* (Cambridge; UK: Cambridge University Press, 1958). I have adapted and added applications of the model to make it more useful for reading and writing.

deeply pained by the book, and barely spoke to me for twenty years." Another colleague described it as "Toulmin's *anti*-logic book."[3] Amid this, Toulmin expected his book to be a failure. His editors, however, assured him that people were buying it, and Toulmin found out who many of these people were when he visited the United States some time later. Professors in speech departments and departments of communication all over the United States were using his book to teach students to become better speakers and arguers. If you have ever taken a speech class, you may have already encountered the Toulmin model of argument. As time went by, the model was picked up by English departments to help students improve their reading and writing of argument. The Toulmin model has also been used in schools of law to help students learn to present legal argument. You will find that you can employ the model to help you write essays, reports, letters of application, proposals, legal memos, or any other document intended to convince others. The Toulmin model is also useful in designing or interpreting visual argument, such as photographs, television, or motion pictures, and in writing or analyzing persuasive speeches. The Toulmin model is a very natural and practical model because it follows normal human thought processes. You have had experience with all its parts either in the everyday arguments you carry on with your friends and family or in the arguments that you see on television.

The Toulmin model has six parts. The first three parts are present in every argument, including both traditional and consensual argument. They are (1) the *claim;* (2) the *data*, encompassing subclaims and specific supporting details, which we are calling *support,* and (3) the *warrant*. The other three parts are used as needed to strengthen an argument and adapt it to the needs and beliefs of a particular audience. These parts are (4) the *backing*, (5) the *rebuttal*, and (6) the *qualifier.* Figure 5.1 ■ shows Toulmin's diagram of these six parts of the model.

To illustrate how these parts work together, let us examine an actual argument. For example, the narrator of a television program makes the *claim* that critical thinking is more important now than it was seventy-five years ago. This is followed by *support* that includes pictures of modern scientists launching space shuttles and air traffic controllers directing airplanes to land. These individuals seem intent and busy. It appears to be clear that if they do not think critically, there will be trouble. Then the camera switches to children riding on an old-fashioned school bus of seventy-five years ago. One boy is saying that he wants to grow up and be a farmer like his dad. This youngster is relaxed and bouncing along on the bus. He does not look like he is thinking critically or that he will ever need to do so. The unspoken part of this argument—the assumption that the author of this program hopes the audience will share—is the *warrant*. The author hopes the audience will agree, even though it is not explicitly stated, that farmers of seventy-five years ago did not have to think critically, that modern scientists and engineers do have to think critically, and that critical thinking was not so important then as now. The author wants the audience to look at the two bits of support, the scientist and the farmer's son, and make the leap necessary to accept

---

[3]"Logic and the Criticism of Arguments," in James L. Golden, Goodwin F. Berquist, and William E. Coleman, *The Rhetoric of Western Thought,* 4th ed. (Dubuque, IA: Kendall Hunt, 1989), 375.

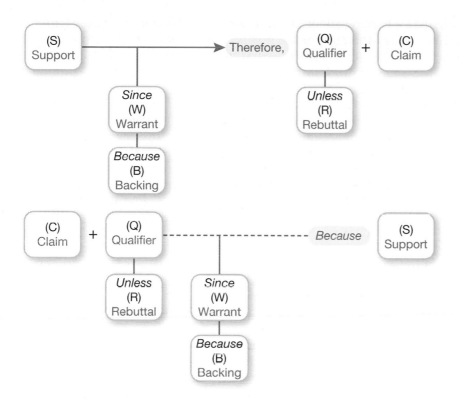

Figure 5.1 *A Diagram of the Toulmin Model of Argument Showing the Six Parts: Claim, Support, Warrant, Backing, Rebuttal, and Qualifier.*

Note that an argument can be configured either as "support therefore claim" or as "claim because support."

the claim. The author hopes the audience will think, "That's right, those scientists and that young boy don't seem to share the same demands for critical thinking. Times have changed. Critical thinking is more important now than it was seventy-five years ago." Those three parts, the *claim*, the *support*, and the *warrant*, are the three parts you will find present in any argument.

Suppose, at this point, however, that some members of the audience do not accept the claim. An additional three parts of the model are available to make the argument stronger. Here is how these parts could be incorporated into the argument. It might be presented like this: The camera then shifts to an elderly man, who says, "Wait a minute. What makes you assume farmers didn't think? My daddy was a farmer, and he was the best critical thinker I ever knew. He had to think about weather, crops, growing seasons, fertilizer, finances, harvesting, and selling the crops. The thinking he had to do was as sophisticated as that of any modern scientist." This audience member is indicating that he does not share the unstated warrant that farmers of seventy-five years ago had fewer demands on their thinking processes than modern scientists. In response to this rejoinder, the author, to make the argument convincing, provides *backing for the warrant*. This backing takes the form of additional support. The camera cuts to the narrator of the program: "At least two out of three of the farmers of seventy-five years ago had small farms. They grew food for their families and traded or sold the rest for whatever else they needed. The thinking and decision making required of them was not as complicated and demanding as that required by modern scientists. Your father was an exception."

Even though this backing allows for exceptions that should make the argument more convincing to the older man, it still relies on the belief, assumed to be acceptable to the rest of the audience, that the majority of old-time farmers did not have the same critical thinking demands placed on them as modern scientists do.

Notice that this backing takes the form of a smaller unit of argument within the argument. It is linked to the main argument, and it is used to back up the weakest part of the main argument. Furthermore, this smaller argument has a claim-support-warrant structure of its own: (1) the *claim* is that most farmers did not have to think like modern scientists; (2) the *support* is that two out of three did not have to think like modern scientists, and that this man's father was an exception; and (3) the *warrant*, again unstated, is that the old man will believe the statistics and accept the idea that his father was an exception. If he resists this backing for the new warrant by asking, "Hey, where did you get those statistics? They're not like any I ever heard," then another argument would need to be developed to cite the source of the figures and to convince the man of their reliability. As you can see, the requests for backing, for more information to serve as further proof, can go on and on. Let's leave the man defending his father and the narrator, though, and look at what else might appear in this argument.

Suppose the camera now shifts to a modern science professor who wants to take exception to the claim itself by making a *rebuttal*. She makes her own claim: "The critical thinking required seventy-five years ago was demanding and sophisticated. Critical thinkers of that time had to figure out how to get the country out of a severe recession, and they had to develop the technology to win World War II." These opinions are then supported with factual evidence that includes pictures of individuals thinking.

After all of these challenges, exceptions, and requests for more information, the author at this point finds it necessary to *qualify* the original claim in order to make it acceptable to more of the audience members. Qualifying involves adding words and phrases to the claim like *sometimes, seems to be, may be*, or *possibly* to make it more acceptable to the audience. In this case, the narrator now restates the qualified claim: "Critical thinking, because of modern science, seems to some people to be more important now than it was seventy-five years ago." Compare this with the original claim that critical thinking *is* more important now than it was seventy-five years ago. Figure 5.2 ■ diagrams this argument according to the Toulmin model. You have probably never systematically used this or any other model to read or write argument. The model can serve as a kind of guide for reading and analyzing arguments, both written and visual, and also for writing or composing them. Authors do not usually use the model as an exact formula, however. Rather, it describes what can be, but is not necessarily always, present in an argument. Consequently, when you read or view argument, you will at times easily recognize parts of the model and at other times you will not. Some arguments, in fact, may not contain one or more of the parts at all, such as a rebuttal, for example. You are not getting it wrong if you read and do not find all of the parts. When you write (or create an argument visually), you do not need to make all parts explicit either. The following sections provide some details about each of the six parts that will help you understand them better.

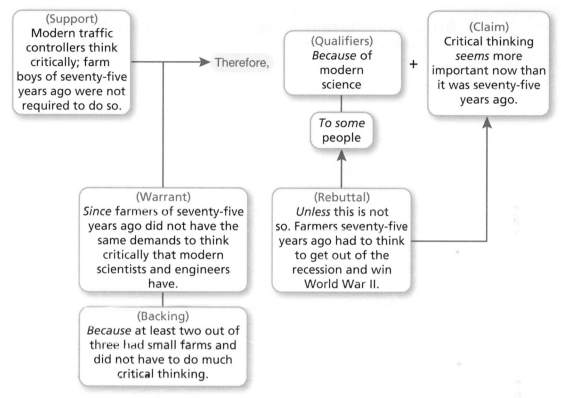

Figure 5.2 *An Example of the Six Elements in the Toulmin Model.*

CLAIM

Discover the claim of an argument by asking, "What is the author trying to prove?" Or plan a claim of your own by asking, "What do I want to prove?" The claim is the main point of the argument. Identifying the claim as soon as possible helps you focus on what the argument is all about.

Synonyms for *claim* are *thesis, proposition, conclusion,* and *main point.* Sometimes an author of an argument in a newspaper or magazine will refer to the "proposition," or an individual arguing on television will ask, "What is your point?" Both are referring to the claim. When someone refers to the claim as the conclusion, don't confuse it with the idea at the end of an argument. The claim can appear at the end, but it can also appear at other places in the argument. The claim is sometimes stated in a sentence or sentences called the *statement of claim.* This sentence can also be called the *thesis statement,* the *purpose sentence,* the *statement of focus,* or the *statement of proposition.*

The terms used in this text to describe the main elements in argument, along with some of their synonyms, appear in Box 5.1 ▪ on the next page. Become familiar with them so that you will understand other writers on the subject who may vary the terminology.

To locate the claim, what should you look for? The claim may be explicitly stated at the beginning of an argument, at the end, or somewhere in the middle.

Box 5.1	Argument Terminology: Terms Used in This Book and Some of Their Synonyms.

▶▶▶ What Terms Are Used in Argument?

TERMS	SYNONYMS	
Claim	thesis	main point
	proposition	macro-argument
	conclusion	controlling idea
Statement of claim	thesis statement	statement of focus
	purpose sentence	statement of proposition
Subclaims	reasons	lines of argument
	main ideas	supporting arguments
	micro-arguments	specific issues
	arguments	
Support	evidence	proof
	opinions	premise
	reasons	statistics
	examples	explanations
	facts	information
	data	personal narratives
	grounds	images
Warrants	assumptions	cultural values
	general principles	presuppositions
	widely held values	unstated premises
	commonly accepted beliefs	generally accepted truths
	appeals to human motives	

Alternatively, it may not be stated anywhere. It is sometimes *implied*, in which case you will be expected to *infer* it. To infer an implicit claim, use what you already know about the subject along with what you have just read to formulate your own statement of it. In this case, the author is paying you a kind of compliment in assuming that you are smart and will figure out the claim for yourself. You should probably make your own claims in your written arguments clear and explicit, however, at least at first.

Another interesting variation on the claim occurs in the case of irony. In using irony the author states one thing but means something else. Usually, the stated claim in ironic argument is exaggerated, outrageous, or a bit odd. An example is the claim in a written or visual satire or in an ironical essay like "Why I Want a Wife" (pages 64–65). In reading or viewing such argument you might think, "Surely the author doesn't *mean* this." What does the author really mean? Again, you use your background and judgment to figure that out.

Authors often make conscious decisions about where to place a claim and whether to make it explicit or implicit. Their decisions are related to their notions about the audience. A claim at the beginning is straightforward and draws the reader in right away, such as the claim in "A View from Berkeley" (pages 58–60) in paragraph 2: "We *should* consider race, ethnicity and gender along with many other factors in [college] admissions." Both parties are thinking along the same lines, together, from the outset. Or an author may decide to lead up to the claim, in which case it may appear either in the middle or at the end. For example, the claim in "The Laptop Ate My Attention Span" (pages 26–27) appears at the end, in the final paragraph: "I agree. Let them control themselves," the author says, agreeing with college officials, but then she qualifies her claim with what ought to happen to students who log on to their laptops at inappropriate times.

Delaying the claim pulls the audience in and increases interest and attention. "What is this author after?" the audience wonders, and reads to find out. The end of an essay is the most emphatic and memorable place for a claim. Many authors prefer to put the claim there to give it as much force as possible. There is some risk involved in putting the claim at the end. Students who use this strategy must be careful to insert cues along the way so that readers understand where the argument is headed and do not feel they are being led through a random chain of topics. Both the unstated claim and the ironic claim require that the reader pay special attention because it is the reader's responsibility to make the inference that the author expects. As a result of this effort, the reader may find an inferred claim especially convincing and memorable.

The claim, whether implied or explicitly stated, organizes the entire argument, and everything else in the argument is related to it. The best way to identify it, if it is not obvious or easy to locate, is to complete the following statement as soon as you have finished reading: "This author wants me to believe that . . ." When you have finished that statement, you have the claim. As a writer, you can check your own claim during revision by completing this statement: "I want my audience to agree that . . ." If you can do this, you understand the concept of the claim, and you will be able to recognize the main point in the arguments you read and to use a claim to articulate the main point in any argument you write. These open statements can be completed as well to access the claim in a visual argument you view or produce.

SUPPORT

Discover the support in an argument by asking, "What additional information does the author supply to convince me of this claim?" Or, if you are the author, ask, "What information do I need to supply to convince my audience?" You can summarize the most essential elements of an argument as a *claim with support.* Aristotle wrote in the *Rhetoric* that the only necessary parts of an argument are the statement of proposition (the claim) and the proof (the support). There has been general agreement about those two essential parts of an argument for more than twenty-three hundred years.

The synonyms that Toulmin uses for *support* are *data* and *grounds,* the British equivalents. In the United States you will often read arguments in which the author claims to be "grounding" a claim with particular support, and *data* is sometimes used as a synonym for *facts and figures.* Other synonyms for support are *proof, evidence,* and *reasons.* Authors also refer to major evidence as *premises.* When you encounter that term in your reading, remember that premises lead to and support a conclusion (a claim). Do not confuse premises with the claim.

Subclaims

At the first level of support are the *subclaims,* which are the supporting arguments or reasons for the claim. Here is an example that illustrates the relationships among an issue area, at the most general level in the example, a specific related issue that represents an idea about the general issue area, a claim that is made in response to the specific related issue, and four subclaims that are used to support the claim. The subclaims are at the most specific level in this example because they represent ideas about the claim.

▶ Issue Area: The Environment

Specific related issue: How serious are the world's environmental problems?

> *Claim:* The environment is the single-most serious problem the world faces today.
>
> *Subclaims:* 1. The rain forests are being destroyed, causing global warming.
> 2. Increasing population is depleting resources in some parts of the world.
> 3. Many important water sources are being polluted by industry.
> 4. The ozone layer, which protects us from harmful sun rays, is being destroyed by chemicals.

Specific Support

The second level of support is the *specific support.* Specific support provides the evidence, opinions, reasoning, examples, and factual information about a claim or subclaim that make it possible for us to accept it. Look back at the claims and subclaims in the example above. If you are to take this claim seriously, you will want some additional specific support to make it convincing.

To locate such support, what should you look for in the argument? One bit of good news: support is always explicitly stated, so you will not have to infer it as you sometimes have to infer the claim. Thus an understanding of the types of specific support is all you really need to help you recognize it. Let us look at some of the most common types.

Facts

In a court of law, *factual support* (the murder weapon, for example) is laid out on the table. In written argument, it must be described. Factual support can include detailed reports of *observed events* or *places;* specific *examples* of real happenings; references to *events,* either *historical* or *recent;* and *statistical reports.* Factual support is vivid, real, and verifiable. Two people looking at it together would agree on its existence and on what it looks like. They might not agree on what it *means* to each of them—that is, they might interpret it differently. Nevertheless, essentially, they would agree on the facts themselves.

Opinions

When people start interpreting facts and events, opinion enters the picture. Opinions may be the personal opinions of the author or the opinions of experts the author selects to quote. The author can use direct quotations, set off in quotation marks, or summaries or paraphrases of what someone else thinks or reports. Furthermore, opinions may be informed, based on considerable knowledge and excellent judgment, or they may be ill-founded, based on hearsay and gossip. The most convincing opinions are those of experts, whether they are those of the author or of another person. Experts possess superior background, education, and experience on an issue. Contrast in your own mind the opinions of experts with the uninformed opinions of people who are surprised in the streets by reporters and asked to give their opinions. Ill-founded, baseless opinion is boring and rarely convincing. In contrast, informed personal opinions and the opinions of experts can be more interesting and convincing than the facts themselves.

Examples

Examples can be real or made up, long or short. They are used to clarify, to make material more memorable and interesting, and, in argument particularly, to prove. Examples that are real, such as instances of actual events or references to particular individuals or places, function in the same way that fact does in an argument. They are convincing because they are grounded in reality. Made-up or hypothetical examples are invented by the writer and, like opinions, can only demonstrate what may be the case. Personal experience is one type of example that is frequently used in argument. Writers often go into considerable detail about the experiences that have influenced them to think and behave as they do. Combining personal experience with the opinions and reasoning derived from it is a common way to develop a claim.

Images

Images are also used to support claims and subclaims and make them more vivid and believable to the audience. You have already encountered several examples of images used in this way. Look back at the three images of American flags associated with World War II, the Vietnam War, and the war in Iraq on page 146, and the sperm donor on page 134. Images used as support make abstract ideas more concrete and easier to grasp. They also make them more memorable.

Different authors manage support in different ways, depending on the requirements of the subject, their purpose, and their audience. When the issue is an abstract idea and the audience is informed, the author may present mainly opinions and few, if any, facts or examples. Such arguments include a claim and blocks of logical reasoning organized around subclaims to develop and prove the claim. If you were to outline the argument, you might not need more than two levels, as in the claim and subclaim example on page 158. When the subject requires more specific support or the audience needs more information to be convinced, specific materials at lower levels are required to ground the subclaims in facts, figures, quotations from others, visual images, or author opinions.

The next example expands on the example on page 158 by adding specific support.[4]

▶ Issue Area: The Environment

Specific related issue: How serious are the world's environmental problems?

    Claim: The environment is the single-most serious problem the world faces today.

        Subclaim: The rain forests are being destroyed, causing global warming.

            Support: Global warming could cause the oceans to rise, the number of storms to increase, and more droughts. *(opinion)*

            Support: Look back at the photographs of the polar bear clinging to the dwindling piece of ice on page 9 and the home abandoned by rising sea levels on page 28. Both illustrate current examples of global warming. *(images)*

        Subclaim: Increasing population is depleting resources in some parts of the world.

            Support: One-third of the world does not have enough food and is in danger of starvation. *(fact)*

        Subclaim: Many important water sources are being polluted by industry.

            Support: By 2025, two-thirds of the world's population may live in areas where there is a serious water shortage. *(opinion)*

        Subclaim: The ozone layer, which protects us from harmful sun rays, is being destroyed by chemicals.

            Support: It was widely reported in the fall of 2003 that the hole in the ozone layer was significantly larger than it had been the previous year. *(fact)*

Quality support helps build common ground between the arguer and the audience. Rantings, unfounded personal opinions that no one else accepts, or feeble reasons like "because I said so" or "because everyone does it" are not effective support. Audiences usually do not believe such statements, they do not share

---

[4]The support in the example is drawn from Jeffrey Kluger and Andrea Dorfman, "The Challenges We Face," *Time*, August 26, 2002, A7+.

experiences or ideas suggested by them, and they lose common ground with the arguer when they read or hear them.

When reading argument, to help you focus on and recognize the support, complete this sentence as soon as you finish: "The author wants me to believe that . . . [the claim] because . . . [list the support]." When you read to revise your own writing, you can complete this statement: "I have convinced my audience to believe [the claim] because [list your support]."

WARRANTS

Warrants are the assumptions, general principles, conventions of specific disciplines, widely held values, commonly accepted beliefs, and appeals to human motives that are an important part of any argument.[5] Even though they can be spelled out as part of the written argument, usually they are not. In many instances it would be redundant and boring if they were. For example, an argument might go as follows:

Claim: The president of the United States is doing a poor job.
Support: The economy is the worst it has been in ten years.

The unstated *warrants* in this argument might include the following *generally accepted beliefs:* the president is responsible for the economy; when the economy is weak, it is a sign that the president is doing a poor job; or, even though the president may be doing well in other areas, a robust economy is the main index to overall performance. You may think of other ways of expressing the warrants in this argument. Since individual audience members vary in their backgrounds and perspectives, not everyone will state the warrants in exactly the same way.

Here is another example, and this one relies on a *value warrant*.

Claim: Business profits are adversely affected by environmental protection laws.
Support: Obeying environmental protection laws that call for clean air, for example, costs industry money that could otherwise be realized as profit.

The unstated *warrants* in this argument involve the relative value individuals place on the environment and on business profit and might be stated in this way: profit is more important than clean air; businesses must make a profit to survive; or environmental protection laws are threatening the capitalistic system.

Finally, here is an example of a warrant that relies on a *commonly accepted convention* of a specific discipline, which in this case is the discipline of writing.

Claim: You have received a failing grade on this paper.
Support: You have many sentence fragments and subject-verb agreement errors in your paper.

---

[5]Toulmin's warrants are somewhat similar to Bitzer's constraints in the rhetorical situation. Bitzer, however, extends the concept of constraints to also include the resources available to the writer or producer and the type of text being created, whether written, spoken, or visual. Thus *constraints* is a broader concept than *warrants.*

The unstated *warrants* could be stated as follows: these kinds of errors result in a poor or failing grade in college papers, or the conventions of writing college papers do not allow fragments and subject-verb agreement problems.

When you encounter argument in your other college courses, try to identify the warrants that are implicit in them and that are also part of the generally accepted knowledge or conventions that inform these particular disciplines. Such warrants could include laws in physics, equations in mathematics, or theories in philosophy. This underlying or foundational information is not always spelled out in every argument, particularly if the people who are arguing share the same background information about these conventions, laws, equations, or theories.

Warrants originate with the arguer. Note, however, that the warrants also exist in the minds of the audience. They can be *shared* by the arguer and the audience, or they can be *in conflict*. Furthermore, if the audience shares the warrants with the arguer, the audience will accept them and the argument is convincing. If the warrants are in conflict and the audience does not accept them (they believe private enterprise, not the president, is responsible for improving the economy, or they believe sentence fragments are acceptable in academic writing because many widely admired writers have used them), the argument is not convincing to them.

Warrants provide critical links in argument. For instance, they link the support to the claim by enabling an audience to accept particular support *as* proof of or justification for a particular claim. Without the linking warrant, the support may not be convincing. Here is an example.

Claim:	The appeal process for criminals should be shortened . . .
Support:	because the appeals for criminals on death row can cost more than $2 million per criminal.
Expected warrant:	Spending more than $2 million to keep a convicted criminal alive a little longer is a waste of money. *(This individual shares the author's warrant, the link is made, and the argument is convincing.)*
Alternative warrant:	We are dealing with human life here, and we should spend whatever is necessary to make certain we have a fair conviction. *(This individual supplies an opposing warrant, the link between claim and support is not made, and the argument is not convincing.)*

Supply your own warrant in the following argument.

Claim:	The government should abolish loan funds for college students . . .
Support:	because many students default on their loans, and the government cannot tolerate these bad debts.
Warrant:	*(Do you believe that evidence supports that claim? If yes, why? If no, why? Your answer provides the warrant. Is the argument convincing for you?)*

These examples demonstrate that the warrant links the evidence and the claim by justifying particular evidence as support for a particular claim. Notice also, however, that the warrant attempts to establish a link between the author and the audience as well. Shared warrants result in successful arguments. When the warrant is not shared or when there are conflicting warrants, the audience will question or disagree with the claim.

Besides being related to what people commonly believe, value, want, or accept as background knowledge in a discipline, warrants are also culture-bound. Since values, beliefs, and training vary from culture to culture, the warrants associated with them also differ from culture to culture. Tension between Japan and the United States was caused by a Japanese official's claim that American workers are lazy and do not work hard enough. American workers were angry and countered with a rebuttal about how hard they think they work. Japanese and American workers have different work schedules, attitudes, and experience with leisure and work time. Consequently, the part of both arguments that was unstated, the warrant, described hard work in different ways for each culture. The lack of a shared warrant caused the tension. Furthermore, neither side was convinced by the other's argument.

Japanese claim:	American workers are lazy . . .
Support:	because they work only 40 hours a week.
Japanese warrant:	People who work only 40 hours a week are lazy.
American rebuttal:	American workers are hardworking . . .
Support:	because they work 40 hours a week.
American warrant:	People who put in 40 hours a week are industrious and hardworking.

Perhaps now you have begun to appreciate the importance of shared warrants in argument. Shared warrants are crucial to the success of an argument because they are the most significant way to establish common ground between reader and writer in argument. Shared warrants and common ground, as you can imagine, are particularly important in international negotiations. Skillful negotiators analyze warrants to determine whether or not both parties are on common ground. If they are not, communication breaks down and argument fails.

At this point, you may wonder why authors do not spell out the warrants, since they are so essential to the success of the argument. There are two reasons for leaving warrants unstated so that the audience has to supply them. First, an audience who supplies the warrant is more likely to accede to the argument through a sense of participation. If there is potential for agreement and common ground, it will be strengthened by the audience's supplying the warrant. Second, remember that audiences differ and that their views of the warrant also vary, depending on their past experiences and present perceptions. A stated warrant negates the rich and varied perceptions and responses of the audience by providing only the author's interpretation and articulation of the warrant. Less active participation is then required from the audience, and the argument is less powerful and convincing to them.

To help you discover warrants, ask questions such as the following:

What is left out here?
What does this author value? Do I share those values?
What is causing this author to say these things?
Do I believe that this evidence supports this claim? Why or why not?

163

As the author of argument, you should consider your audience and whether or not they will accept your warrants. Let's turn now to the other three parts of the Toulmin model that an arguer can use to adapt an argument to a particular audience. All or none might appear in a written argument.

BACKING

You should have a sense by now that warrants themselves may require their own support to make them more acceptable to an audience, particularly if the audience does not happen to share them with the author. An author may provide backing, or additional evidence and ideas to "back up" a warrant, whenever the audience is in danger of rejecting it. When you are the author, you should provide backing also.

Backing sometimes appears as appeals to generally accepted knowledge and beliefs that are held by most individuals or groups of people who belong to a specific discipline or culture. These beliefs are sometimes spelled out explicitly as backing for a warrant, and at other times they are implied and the audience has to supply them by examining the logic of the argument and making inferences.

Here is an example of backing for a warrant.

Claim: Immigrants should be allowed to come into the United States . . .
Support: because immigration has benefited the U.S. economy in the past.
Warrant: Current economic conditions are similar to past conditions.
Backing: Now, as in the past, immigrants are willing to perform necessary low-paying jobs that American citizens do not want, particularly in the service areas. Furthermore, immigrants perform these jobs better than citizens and for less pay.

Look for backing in an argument by identifying the warrant and then by asking whether or not you accept it. If you do not, try to anticipate additional information that would make it more acceptable. Then examine whether the author supplied that or similar additional support. When you are the writer, consider your audience. Will they accept your warrant, or can you strengthen it by supplying additional information or by appealing to common values and beliefs that will help justify your claim?

REBUTTAL

A rebuttal establishes what is wrong, invalid, or unacceptable about an argument and may also present counterarguments or new arguments that represent entirely different perspectives or points of view on the issue. To attack the validity of the claim, an author may demonstrate that the support is faulty or that the warrants are faulty or unbelievable. Counterarguments start all over again, with a new set of claims, support, and warrants.

Here is an example of a rebuttal for the argument about immigration.

Rebuttal 1: Immigrants actually drain more resources in schooling, medical care, and other social services than they contribute in taxes and productivity.

Rebuttal 2:   Modern immigrants are not so willing to perform menial, low-skilled jobs as they were in past generations.

Here is an example of a counterargument for the immigration argument.

Claim: Laws should be passed to limit immigration . . .
Support: because we have our own unskilled laborers who need those jobs.
Warrant: These laborers are willing to hold these jobs.

Rebuttals can appear as answers to arguments that have already been stated, or the author may anticipate the reader's rebuttal and include answers to possible objections that might be raised. Thus an author might write a rebuttal to the claim that we should censor television by saying such a practice would violate the First Amendment. Or, if no claim has been made, the arguer could anticipate what the objections to television violence might be (violence breeds violence, children who see violence become frightened, etc.) and refute them, usually early in the essay, before spelling out the reasons for leaving television alone.

Look for a rebuttal or plan for it in your own writing by asking, "What are the other possible views on this issue?" When reading ask, "Are other views represented here along with reasons?" Or, when writing ask, "How can I answer other views?" Phrases that might introduce refutation include *some may disagree, others may think,* or *other commonly held opinions are,* followed by the opposing ideas and your reasons and evidence for rejecting them.

165

QUALIFIERS

Remember that argument is not expected to demonstrate certainties. Instead, it establishes probabilities. Consequently, the language of certainty (*always, never, the best, the worst,* and so on) promises too much when used in claims or in other parts of the argument. It is not uncommon for an author to make a claim and, still writing, begin revising and qualifying it to meet the anticipated objections of an audience. Thus words such as *always* and *never* change to *sometimes; is* or *are* change to *may be* or *might; all* changes to *many* or *some; none* changes to *a few;* and *absolutely* changes to *probably* or *possibly.* Qualified language is better for demonstrating probability in argument. Look to see whether the author has stated the claim in other parts of the argument in probable or absolute terms, and then read the entire argument to figure out why or why not. For example, the following is a qualified version of the first claim that all immigrants should be allowed to enter the United States. These qualifications would make the original claim more acceptable to the people who offered the rebuttals and counterargument.

Immigrants should be allowed to enter the United States only if they can prove that they already have jobs yielding sufficient income to offset social services and that no American citizens are currently available to perform these jobs.

Value of the Toulmin Model for Reading, Writing, and Viewing Argument

The Toulmin model has some advantages that make it an excellent model for reading, writing, and viewing argument. Its most essential advantage is that it invites common ground and audience participation in the form of shared warrants, increasing the possibility of interaction between author and audience. Backing, rebuttals, and qualifiers also encourage an exchange of views and common ground because they require an arguer both to anticipate other perspectives and views and, at times, to acknowledge and answer them directly. The backing, for instance, requires additional evidence and references to common cultural values and beliefs to satisfy audience concerns. The rebuttal requires answers to different or opposing views. The qualifier requires a modification of the claim to gain audience acceptance. The backing, rebuttal, and qualifier in the Toulmin model invite the audience to participate. They encourage dialogue, understanding, and agreement as argument outcomes. These features make the model valuable for examining the multiple perspectives likely to be expressed in response to complex modern issues.

The model works for reading or writing not only in debate and single-perspective argument but also in academic inquiry, negotiation, dialectic, Rogerian argument (explained in Chapter 10), or any other form of argument that requires exchange and attempts to reach agreement. It can even be a useful tool for one-on-one argument or personal decision making.

Writers of argument find the Toulmin model useful as both an invention strategy and a revision strategy. It can be used to help an author come up with the essential parts of an argument in the first place, and later it can be used to check and evaluate the parts of a newly written argument. See page 173 for a writing assignment that uses the Toulmin model as a tool to help the writer think about the parts of a position paper. See page 172 for an example of a student-written position paper with its Toulmin elements labeled in the margins.

Readers of argument find the model useful for analyzing and describing the essential parts of a written argument. Listeners find it just as useful for analyzing and describing the essential parts of an argumentative speech. Viewers find they can use the model to analyze visual argument, whether it appears alone as an argument, independent of text with only a few words of explanation, such as in some paintings, cartoons, or photographs; or as support for ideas in a written text, such as photographs, drawings, graphs, and charts that illustrate and explain; or as in moving images that support ideas being explained orally on television, in motion pictures, or on the Internet. Figure 5.3 provides an example of a Toulmin analysis of a cartoon that makes an argument.

The Toulmin model can be used to write or to analyze both consensual and adversarial arguments. It accommodates all of the various forms of arguments. The model is summarized in a handy chart for quick reference for the use of both readers and writers in the Summary Charts (page 515).

This cartoon will be convincing to you if you share the warrant and the backing. If you place a different value on standardized tests than this cartoonist, it will not convince you.

Figure 5.3 *A Toulmin Analysis of a Cartoon That Makes an Argument.*

Claim: This job applicant is not prepared for any job . . .

Support: because he has taken tests in high school that rely on answer sheets, like those used with standardized tests, and he cannot communicate effectively.

Warrant: The knowledge learned and tested in standardized tests is irrelevant to jobs in the real world; this hampers students' communication skills.

Backing: Many people believe that standardized tests fail to measure the critical thinking skills and communication skills, especially writing, that are required for success in the workplace

Rebuttal: A rebuttal is implied against the position that standardized testing is an adequate test of students' knowledge and job skills.

Qualifier: There is none.

167

Review Questions

1. Name and describe the six parts of the Toulmin model. Which parts, stated or inferred, can be found in any argument? Which parts are used, as needed, to make an argument more convincing to a particular audience?

2. What are some synonyms for the claim, the support, and the warrant? Consult Box 5.1 (page 156).

3. What are subclaims? What are some types of specific support?

4. Define warrants. Why does argument work better when warrants are shared by the arguer and the audience? How does backing strengthen a warrant?

5. Give some examples of qualifiers.

Exercises and Activities

A. Group Work and Class Discussion: Truth versus Probability

This activity invites you to compare topics that are true and therefore not arguable with topics that are probable and thus open to argument. Think about one other course you are taking this semester and write down one example of something you have learned in that course that is absolutely true or untrue about which you would not or could not argue. Then write one example of something you have learned in that course that is only probably true or untrue and that you therefore see as arguable. Make a class list of these examples. Think carefully about everything you put in the true and untrue columns. These must be topics that no one would argue about because they have been proved to be true or untrue. Here are some key words to help you think about these two types of information.

True: certain, fact, exact statement, right, correct, valid; wrong, incorrect, invalid

Probable: possible, opinion, qualified, reasonable, sound; unreasonable, unsound

You will be learning both types of information in college. Which topics on the probable list might be good topics for argument papers?

B. Group Work and Class Discussion: Using the Toulmin Model to Analyze an Advertisement

Study the advertisement that appears on the next page. Answer the following questions.

1. *What is the claim?* Complete the sentence, "The author wants me to believe that . . ." Is the claim stated or implied?

2. *What is the support?* Complete the sentence, "The author wants me to believe that . . . [the claim] because . . . [support]." Look for subclaims (*reasons*) and specific support (e.g., *facts, opinions, examples*).

3. *What are the warrants?* Ask, "What does this author value or believe regarding the claim? Are these values or beliefs stated or implied? Do I agree or disagree with them?" Recall, also, that the warrants supply a link between support and claim. Ask, "Can I accept this evidence as support for this claim? Why or why not?" If you do not see how the evidence supports the claim, the argument will not be convincing to you.

4. *Is there backing for any of the warrants?* Ask, "Does the author supply any additional information or rely on any commonly accepted cultural beliefs and attitudes that would make it easier for me to accept the warrants, whether they are stated or implied? What are they?"

5. *Is there a rebuttal?* Ask, "Are other views on the issue represented here along with reasons? What are they?"

6. *Is there a qualifier?* Ask, "Is the claim stated in absolute terms (e.g., *always, never, the best, the worst*) or in probable terms (e.g., *sometimes, probably, possibly*)?"

7. *Do you find this ad convincing?* Why or why not?

C. Group Work and Class Discussion: Using the Toulmin Model to Analyze a Cartoon

Analyze the cartoon on page 170 and discuss the answers to the following questions:

a. What is the claim?

b. What is the support?

Dr. Jay Grossman is featured here in a Department of Defense awareness campaign highlighting the community involvement and contributions of those who have served in the US Military. Dr. Grossman is currently featured in a number of high-profile publications, including *Time*, *People*, *Sports Illustrated*, *Scientific American*, *Better Homes and Gardens*, and *The New Yorker*.

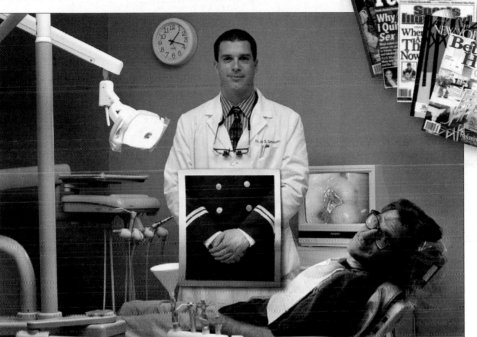

Dr. Jay Grossman is proud of his multidisciplined approach to dentistry — several specialties in one office to help patients avoid the complicated referral process. Dr. Grossman is also proud of his wife and three children.

SENSE OF COMMUNITY

– DR. JAY GROSSMAN
UNITED STATES NAVY 1990-1991

But what Dr. Grossman finds especially rewarding is the few hours he spends each month in a program called "Homeless not Toothless." A program he created to invite Los Angeles' homeless citizens into the practice for free dental care. This passion was not part of the curriculum in dental school. It came from an organization that emphasizes respect for people and commitment to a cause larger than one's self: The United States Navy.

The qualities you acquire while in the Military are qualities that stay with you forever.℠

TODAY'S MILITARY
See it for what it really is.℠
1.866.VIEW NOW
www.todaysmilitary.com
Active • Guard • Reserve

Call Dr. Jay Grossman at (310) 820 0123

SOURCE: Jeff Staler: © Columbus Dispatch/Dist. by Newspaper Enterprise Association, Inc.

      c. What are the warrants?

      d. What is the backing?

      e. Are rebuttals or qualifiers present? If so, describe them.

D. Group Work and Class Discussion: Using the Toulmin Model to Read and Analyze a Short Essay

Read the article on page 171. Then answer the questions and discuss your answers with the class. You can expect some disagreement because of your differing backgrounds and experiences. If you disagree on some of these answers, try to figure out what is causing your differences.

      a. What is the claim? Is it explicitly stated, or did you have to infer it?

      b. What are some examples of support?

      c. What are the author's warrants? Does the author supply backing for the warrants? If yes, how?

      d. Do you share the author's warrants, or do you have conflicting warrants? If you have conflicting warrants, what are they?

      e. Is there a rebuttal in the article? If yes, what is it?

      f. Is the claim qualified? How?

      g. Do you find this argument convincing? Why or why not?

BEFORE YOU READ: When you were a child, did you learn the names of farm animals and the sounds they make? If yes, has this been useful information to you?

ESSAY #1   **CALLING BLUE: AND ON THAT FARM HE HAD A CELLPHONE***

Virginia Heffernan

The author writes television reviews for newspapers. This one appeared in the *New York Times*. The subject is the first episode of a new show entitled *Blue's Room*, a spin-off of the popular children's series *Blue's Clues* that features some of the same puppets and characters.

1 If any minority lifestyle is overrepresented in the early education of children in the United States, it's farm life.

2 Long since agribusiness made working family farms scarcer than hen's teeth, little Americans still sing and learn far too much about chickens, eggs, sheep, wool, dells, troughs, pigs and goats. Not exactly news they can use. Better that kids of today be taught about ring tones, A.T.M.'s cubicles, Best Buys and cup holders.

3 But then look at "Blue's Room," the first episode of the big new spinoff of the blockbuster "Blue's Clues," fresh out on Nick Jr. There are the puppets in overalls: Blue, and her little brother Sprinkles. And here are their tasks: shucking corn, gathering eggs, milking a cow.

4 That's right: milking a cow. A full-dress demo has the puppets showing the audience how to squeeze the udders to fill a tin pail. This archaism is meant to be part of a progressive, cutting-edge educational television series. It's shocking.

5 "Blue's Room" is styled by the channel as "the ultimate play date" and a chance for viewers to enter Blue's world: a dreamy playroom with everything fun in it, including an oafish guy named Joe (Donovan Patton, a stage actor, who also appears on "Blue's

Clues"). It must be said that Joe's a little bit creepy, in the way of grown men who superintend children's shows. This effect is not lessened by his Old McDonald uniform. On the first episode he's mostly absent and the puppets are left to do tasks he assigns them. When he comes home, they all celebrate their obsolete achievements while Joe pretends to play the banjo.

6 The farm theme, blessedly, is around for only episode one. After that the puppets get all fancy with themes that include music, art and transportation. But the ambition is not restricted to the content of the show. Nick Jr. is also going all out to saturate children's media with "Blue's Room" as it plans for the "spinoff series"—in the words of the press release—"to roll out on multiple platforms including wireless carriers, video on demand, Nick Jr. video and DVD release."

7 Brave new world. And we're still teaching our children about milking cows?

For Discussion:

Do you agree with the author that children do not need to be taught about farm animals and farm life? Why or why not? What subjects would you include in a new, progressive television series aimed at preschool children?

*New York Times, January 26, 2007, B33.

E. Writing Assignment and Class Project: Writing a Toulmin Analysis and Reporting on It in Class

a. Clip a short article, an advertisement, a cartoon, or a letter to the editor and use the Toulmin model to analyze it.

b. Write a 250- to 300-word paper in which you identify and explain the claim, support, warrants, and backing in your example. Provide further information about rebuttals or qualifiers, if they are present.

c. In class, circulate the item you clipped among your classmates. Either read your paper or give a two- to three-minute oral report in which you describe the parts of the argument to the class.

A student-written analysis of the cartoon about the price of oranges (page 170) is included below. Reading this student paper should help you write your Toulmin analysis paper. Also, discuss whether you and your classmates agree with this analysis. The Toulmin model is usually not applied in exactly the same way by everyone. There are no absolutely correct answers because different readers' interpretations vary.*

STUDENT PAPER #1

Mohamed T. Diaby Jr.
Toulmin Analysis
Prof. Wood
English 1302
February 12, 2008

Toulmin Analysis of the "Price of Oranges" Cartoon†

Identifies claim and support

1   The reader has to infer the claim of this cartoon since it is not directly stated. The claim is that the price of oranges will go way up in the United States if they are picked by legal U.S. workers. The support is provided by the shopper, who is considering buying the oranges, and the sign that says they are handpicked by U.S. workers but their price is 3 for $20 dollars, a prohibitively high price for oranges.

Analyzes warrant

2   The implied warrant is that illegal immigrants will work for lower wages than legal workers, which keeps the price of oranges low.

Identifies backing

3   The backing is also implied and reinforced by the picture. It suggests that oranges are a staple and are purchased frequently by family shoppers. It also reinforces the common belief that many people will not be able to buy oranges that are handpicked by U.S. workers because they will be too expensive.

Infers rebuttal

4   No direct rebuttal or qualifier appears in this cartoon. I think, however, that this cartoon could be considered as a rebuttal to those who think illegal immigrants should be sent home and no longer allowed to work in the United States. As a rebuttal, this cartoon suggests the consequences of that popular position if it were enforced.

---

*See Appendix 1 for the actual format guidelines for student papers.
†This paper is modeled on a paper done by Mohamed Diaby Jr. in an argument class.

F. **Prewriting: Using the Toulmin Model to Get Ideas for a Position Paper**

You have used the Toulmin model in Exercises B through E to read and analyze other people's argument. Now use it to identify the main parts of an argument you will write. You may use the model to help you plan any argument paper. If, however, you have written an exploratory paper based on an issue in "The Reader" for Exercise G in Chapter 4, you may have already identified the position you favor for a position paper. This will help you write your claim. Use the Toulmin model as a prewriting exercise to help you develop ideas for a position paper. (The assignment for the "Position Paper Based on 'The Reader'" appears as Exercise F in Chapter 8.)

1. Write the claim. All of the rest of your paper will support this claim.

2. Write the support. Write two or three subclaims you will develop in the paper. To help you do this, write the word *because* after the claim, and list reasons that support it. Also jot down ideas for specific support for these subclaims, such as examples, facts, opinions, or visual images that come from your reading of the essays or from your own experience.

3. Write the warrants. Decide whether to spell out the warrants in your paper or to leave them implicit so that the reading audience will have to infer them.

4. Decide on the backing. Assume that your classmates are your audience. They may be reading drafts of your paper. In your judgment, will some of them require backing for any of your warrants because they will not agree with them otherwise? If so, how can you back these warrants? Write out your ideas.

5. Plan rebuttal. Think about the positions others may hold on this issue. You identified some of these positions in your exploratory paper. Write out your strategies for weakening these arguments.

6. Decide whether to qualify the claim to make it more convincing to more people. Write one or more qualifiers that might work.

Read what you have written, and make a note about additional information you will need to find for your paper. Save what you have written in a folder or in your open computer file. You will use it later when you complete your planning and write your position paper.

G. **Group Discussion: Understanding Value Warrants**

Often, both the warrants and the backing for warrants come from the systems of values that people hold. The values will not be spelled out in an argument, yet they will still influence the arguer and make an argument more convincing to an audience member who happens to share them. The following essay describes six American value systems. These systems are somewhat oversimplified, and they do not identify all American value systems nor suggest their relative power. They are useful, however, to help you understand some of the values people may hold. Read the essay and answer the questions for discussion at the end.

173

> **BEFORE YOU READ:** What values are important to you? How would you describe core American values?

ESSAY #2   AMERICAN VALUE SYSTEMS*

Richard D. Rieke and Malcolm O. Sillars

> Rieke and Sillars are speech communication professors whose most recent book is *Argumentation and Critical Decision Making.*

1   By careful analysis individual values can be discovered in the arguments of ourselves and others. There is a difficulty, however, in attempting to define a whole system of values for a person or a group. And as difficult as that is, each of us, as a participant in argumentation, should have some concept of the broad systems that most frequently bring together certain values. For this purpose, it is useful for you to have an idea of some of the most commonly acknowledged value systems.

2   You must approach this study with a great deal of care, however, because even though the six basic value systems we are about to define provide a fair view of the standard American value systems, they do not provide convenient pigeonholes into which individuals can be placed. They represent broad social categories. Some individuals (even groups) will be found outside these systems. Many individuals and groups will cross over value systems, picking and choosing from several. Note how certain words appear as value terms in more than one value system. The purpose of this survey is to provide a beginning understanding of standard American values, not a complete catalog.[1]

The Puritan-Pioneer-Peasant Value System

3   This value system has been identified frequently as the *puritan morality* or the *Protestant ethic.* It also has been miscast frequently because of the excessive emphasis placed, by some of its adherents, on restrictions of personal acts such as smoking and consuming alcohol.[2] Consequently, over the years, this value system has come to stand for a narrow-minded attempt to interfere in other people's business, particularly if those people are having fun. However, large numbers of people who do not share such beliefs follow this value system.

4   We have taken the liberty of expanding beyond the strong and perhaps too obvious religious implications of the terms *puritan* and *Protestant.* This value system is what most Americans refer to when they speak of the "pioneer spirit," which was not necessarily religious. It also extends, we are convinced, to a strain of values brought to this country by Southern and Eastern European Catholics, Greek Orthodox, and Jews who could hardly be held responsible for John Calvin's theory or even the term *Protestant ethic.* Thus, we have the added word *peasant,* which may not be particularly accurate. Despite the great friction that existed between these foreign-speaking immigrants from other religions and their native Protestant counterparts, they had a great deal in common as do their ideological descendants today. On many occasions after describing the puritan morality we have heard a Jewish student say, "That's the way my father thinks," or had a student of Italian

---

or Polish descent say, "My grandmother talks that way all the time."

5   The Puritan-Pioneer-Peasant value system is rooted in the idea that persons have an obligation to themselves and those around them, and in some cases to their God, to work hard at whatever they do. In this system, people are limited in their abilities and must be prepared to fail. The great benefit is in the striving against an unknowable and frequently hostile universe. They have an obligation to others, must be selfless, and must not waste. Some believe this is the only way to gain happiness and success. Others see it as a means to salvation. In all cases it takes on a moral orientation. Obviously, one might work hard for a summer in order to buy a new car and not be labeled a "puritan." Frequently, in this value system, the instrumental values of selflessness, thrift, and hard work become terminal values where the work has value beyond the other benefits it can bring one. People who come from this value system often have difficulty with retirement, because their meaning in life, indeed their pleasure, came from work.

6   Likewise, because work, selflessness, and thrift are positive value terms in this value system, laziness, selfishness, and waste are negative value terms. One can see how some adherents to this value system object to smoking, drinking, dancing, or cardplaying. These activities are frivolous; they take one's mind off more serious matters and waste time.

7   Some of the words that are associated with the Puritan-Pioneer-Peasant value system are:

Positive: activity, work, thrift, morality, dedication, selflessness, virtue, righteousness, duty, dependability, temperance, sobriety, savings, dignity

Negative: waste, immorality, dereliction, dissipation, infidelity, theft, vandalism, hunger, poverty, disgrace, vanity

The Enlightenment Value System

8   America became a nation in the period of the Enlightenment. It happened when a new intellectual era based on the scientific findings of men like Sir Isaac Newton and the philo- sophical systems of men like John Locke were dominant. The founders of our nation were particularly influenced by such men. The Declaration of Independence is the epitome of an Enlightenment document. In many ways America is an Enlightenment nation, and if Enlightenment is not the predominant value system, it is surely first among equals.

9   The Enlightenment position stems from the belief that we live in an ordered world in which all activity is governed by laws similar to the laws of physics. These "natural laws" may or may not come from God, depending on the particular orientation of the person examining them; but unlike many adherents to the Puritan value system just discussed, Enlightenment persons theorized that people could discover these laws by themselves. Thus, they may worship God for God's greatness, even acknowledge that God created the universe and natural laws, but they find out about the universe because they have the power of reason. The laws of nature are harmonious, and one can use reason to discover them all. They can also be used to provide for a better life.

10   Because humans are basically good and capable of finding answers, restraints on them must be limited. Occasionally, people do fool- ish things and must be restrained by society. However, a person should never be restrained in matters of the mind. Reason must be free. Thus, government is an agreement among individuals to assist the society to protect rights. That government is a democracy. Certain rights are inalienable, and they may not be abridged; "among these are life, liberty and the pursuit of happiness." Arguments for academic freedom, against wiretaps, and for scientific inquiry come from this value system.

11   Some of the words associated with the Enlightenment value system are:

Positive: freedom, science, nature, rationality, democracy, fact, liberty, individualism, knowledge, intelligence, reason, natural rights, natural laws, progress

Negative: ignorance, inattention, thoughtlessness, error, indecision, irrationality, dictatorship, fascism, bookburning, falsehood, regression

The Progressive Value System

12 Progress was a natural handmaiden of the Enlightenment. If these laws were available and if humans had the tool, reason, to discover them and use them to advantage, then progress would result. Things would continually get better. But although progress is probably a historical spin-off of the Enlightenment, it has become so important on its own that it deserves at times to be seen quite separate from the Enlightenment.

13 Richard Weaver, in 1953, found that "one would not go far wrong in naming progress" the "god term" of that age. It is, he said, the "expression about which all other expressions are ranked as subordinate. . . . Its force imparts to the others their lesser degrees of force, and fixes the scale by which degrees of comparison are understood."[3]

14 Today, the unmediated use of the progressive value system is questioned, but progress is still a fundamental value in America. Most arguments against progress are usually arguments about the definition of progress. They are about what "true progress is."

15 Some of the key words of the Progressive value system are:

Positive: practicality, efficiency, change, improvement, science, future, modern, progress, evolution

Negative: old-fashioned,[4] regressive, impossible, backward

The Transcendental Value System

16 Another historical spin-off of the Enlightenment system was the development of the transcendental movement of the early nineteenth century. It took from the Enlightenment all its optimism about people, freedom, and democracy, but rejected the emphasis on reason. It argued idealistically that there was a faculty higher than reason; let us call it, as many transcendentalists did, intuition. Thus, for the transcendentalist, there is a way of knowing that is better than reason, a way which *transcends* reason. Consequently, what might seem like the obvious solution to problems is not necessarily so. One must look, on important matters at least, to the intuition, to the feelings. Like the Enlightenment thinker, the transcendentalist believes in a unified universe governed by natural laws. Thus, all persons, by following their intuition, will discover these laws, and universal harmony will take place. And, of course, little or no government will be necessary. The original American transcendentalists of the early nineteenth century drew their inspiration from Platonism, German idealism, and Oriental mysticism. The idea was also fairly well limited to the intellectuals. By and large, transcendentalism has been the view of a rather small group of people throughout our history, but at times it has been very important. It has always been somewhat more influential among younger people. James Truslow Adams once wrote that everyone should read Ralph Waldo Emerson at sixteen because his writings were a marvel for the buoyantly optimistic person of that age but that his transcendental writings did not have the same luster at twenty-one.[5] In the late 1960s and early 1970s, Henry David Thoreau's *Walden* was the popular reading of campus rebels. The emphasis of anti-establishment youth on Oriental mysticism, like Zen, should not be ignored either. The rejection of contemporary society and mores symbolized by what others considered "outlandish dress" and "hippie behavior" with its emphasis on emotional response and "do your own thing" indicated the adoption of a transcendental value system. Communal living is reminiscent of

the transcendental "Brook Farm" experiments that were attempted in the early nineteenth century and described by Nathaniel Hawthorne in his novel *The Blithedale Romance*.

17   In all of these movements the emphasis on humanitarian values, the centrality of love for others, and the preference for quiet contemplation over activity has been important. Transcendentalism, however, rejects the common idea of progress. Inner light and knowledge of one's self is more important than material well-being. There is also some tendency to reject physical well-being because it takes one away from intuitive truth.

18   It should be noted that not everyone who argues for change is a transcendentalist. The transcendental white campus agitators of the late 1960s discovered that, despite all their concern for replacing racism and war with love and peace, their black counterparts were highly pragmatic and rationalistic about objectives and means. Black agitators and demonstrators were never "doing their thing" in the intuitive way of many whites.

19   It should also be noted that while a full adherence to transcendentalism has been limited to small groups, particularly among intellectuals and youth, many of the ideas are not limited to such persons. One can surely find strains of what we have labeled, for convenience, transcendentalism in the mysticism of some very devout older Roman Catholics, for instance. And perhaps many Americans become transcendental on particular issues, about the value to be derived from hiking in the mountains, for example.

20   Here are some of the terms that are characteristic of the Transcendental value system:

Positive: humanitarian, individualism, respect, intuition, truth, equality, sympathetic, affection, feeling, love, sensitivity, emotion, personal kindness, compassion, brotherhood, friendship, mysticism

Negative: science,[6] reason, mechanical, hate, war, anger, insensitive, coldness, unemotional

The Personal Success Value System

21   The least social of the major American value systems is the one that moves people toward personal achievement and success. It can be related as a part of the Enlightenment value system, but it is more than that because it involves a highly pragmatic concern for the material happiness of the individual. To call it selfish would be to load the terms against it, although there would be some who accept this value system who would say, "Yes, I'm selfish." "The Lord helps those who help themselves" has always been an acceptable adage by some of the most devout in our nation.

22   You might note that the Gallup poll . . . is very heavily weighted toward personal values. Even "good family life" rated as the top value can be seen as an item of personal success. This survey includes only a few social values like "helping needy people" and "helping better America," and even those are phrased in personal terms. That is, the respondents were asked "how important you feel each of these is to you." The personal orientation of the survey may represent a bias of the Gallup poll, but we suspect it reflects much of American society. We are personal success–oriented in an individual way which would not be found in some other cultures (e.g., in the Japanese culture).

23   Here are some of the terms that tend to be characteristic of the Personal Success value system:

Positive: career, family, friends, recreation, economic security, identity, health, individualism, affection, respect, enjoyment, dignity, consideration, fair play, personal

Negative: dullness, routine, hunger, poverty, disgrace, coercion, disease

177

The Collectivist Value System

24 Although there are few actual members of various socialist and communist groups in the United States, one cannot ignore the strong attachment among some people for collective action. This is, in part, a product of the influx of social theories from Europe in the nineteenth century. It is also a natural outgrowth of a perceived need to control the excesses of freedom in a mass society. Its legitimacy is not limited to current history, however. There has always been a value placed on cooperative action. The same people today who would condemn welfare payments to unwed mothers would undoubtedly praise their ancestors for barnraising and taking care of the widow in a frontier community. Much rhetoric about our "pioneer ancestors" has to do with their cooperative action. And anticollectivist presidents and evangelists talk about "the team." At the same time many fervent advocates of collective action in the society argue vehemently for their freedom and independence. Certainly the civil rights movement constituted a collective action for freedom. Remember the link in Martin Luther King, Jr.'s speech between "freedom" and "brotherhood"?

25 But whether the Collectivist value system is used to defend socialist proposals or promote "law and order," there is no doubt that collectivism is a strong value system in this nation. Like transcendentalism, however, it is probably a value system that, at least in this day, cannot work alone.

26 Here are some of the terms that tend to characterize the Collectivist value system:

Positive: cooperation, joint action, unity, brotherhood, together, social good, order, humanitarian aid and comfort, equality

Negative: disorganization, selfishness, personal greed, inequality

27 Clearly, these six do not constitute a complete catalog of all American value systems.

Combinations and reorderings produce different systems. Two values deserve special attention because they are common in these systems and sometimes operate alone: *nature* and *patriotism*. Since the beginning of our nation the idea has prevailed that the natural is good and there for our use and preservation. Also, since John Winthrop first proclaimed that the New England Puritans would build "a city on the hill" for all the world to see and emulate, the idea has endured that America is a fundamentally great nation, perhaps God-chosen, to lead the world to a better life. This idea may be somewhat tarnished in some quarters today, but there is no doubt that it will revive as it has in the past. Linked to other value systems we have discussed, it will once more be a theme that will draw the adherence of others to arguments.

Notes

1. The following material draws from a wide variety of sources. The following is an illustrative cross-section of sources from a variety of disciplines: Virgil I. Baker and Ralph T. Eubanks, *Speech in Personal and Public Affairs* (New York: David McKay, 1965), pp. 95–102; Clyde Kluckhohn, "An Anthropologist Looks at the United States," *Mirror for Man* (New York: McGraw-Hill, 1949), pp. 228–261; Stow Persons, *American Minds* (New York: Holt, Rinehart and Winston, 1958); Jurgen Ruesch, "Communication and American Values; A Psychological Approach," in *Communication: The Social Matrix of Psychiatry,* eds. Jurgen Ruesch and Gregory Bateson (New York: W. W. Norton, 1951), pp. 94–134; Edward D. Steele and W. Charles Redding, "The American Value System: Premises for Persuasion," *Western Speech,* 26 (Spring 1962), pp. 83–91; Richard Weaver, "Ultimate Terms in Contemporary Rhetoric," in *The Ethics of Rhetoric* (Chicago: Henry Regnery, 1953), pp. 211–232; Robin M. Williams, Jr., *American Society,* 3rd ed. (New York: Alfred A. Knopf, 1970), pp. 438–504.

2. It is ironic that the original American Puritans did not have clear injunctions against such activity.

3. Weaver, p. 212.

4. Note that "old-fashioned" is frequently positive when we speak of morality and charm but not when we speak of our taste in music.

5. James Truslow Adams, "Emerson Re-read," in *The Transcendental Revolt*, ed. George F. Whicher (Boston: D. C. Heath, 1949), pp. 31–39.

6. It is interesting to note, however, that one of the major organizations in the United States with transcendental origins, the Christian Science Church, combines transcendentalism with science.

For Discussion:

1. Can you find your own system of values in this article? Of the six value systems described, with which of them do you most closely identify?

2. Look back at the positive words associated with each system of values. Describe a visual image that could be used to depict each system. Use your imagination and describe what you see in your mind that would help readers visualize and understand each of these systems of values.

3. Which value systems do you find operating in the selections listed below that you have analyzed in this and earlier chapters? What value warrants are implicit in each of these selections? Provide reasons for your answers. There are no correct answers. Use your imagination and have some fun with this exercise.

"Sense of Community" ad (page 169)
"Pay Your Own Way! (Then Thank Mom)" (pages 24–26)
"We Knew What Glory Was" (pages 54–56)
"A View from Berkeley" (pages 58–60)
"Giving People a Second Chance" (pages 60–61)
"One of Our Own: Training Native Teachers for the 21st Century" (pages 62–63)
"We're Fighting Terror, But Killing Freedom" (pages 56–57)

4. When your system of values does not match the system of values implicit in an argument essay, what happens? How does a difference in value systems influence your acceptance of the author's argument?

179

Types of Claims

T his chapter and the one that follows it expand on and develop some of the ideas in Chapter 5. In Chapter 5, the claim, the support, and the warrants were identified as three parts present in every argument. This chapter, along with Chapter 7, provides additional information about these three parts. Claims are the subject of this chapter. Support and warrants, which constitute the proofs of an argument, are the subject of the next chapter.

Argument theorists categorize claims according to types, and these types suggest the fundamental purposes of given arguments. Becoming aware of these categories and the special characteristics associated with each of them helps you understand more fully the purposes and special features of the arguments you read and improves your writing of them. When reading, as soon as you identify the type or category of claim in an argument, you can predict and anticipate certain features of that type of argument. This technique also helps you follow the author's line of thought more easily. When writing, knowing the types of claims can provide you with frameworks for developing your purpose and strategy.

When you begin to read argument with the idea of locating the claim and identifying it by type, your ability to identify and understand all the parts of an argument will increase. An understanding of proofs, the subject of Chapter 7, will improve your understanding further. Chapters 6 and 7, taken together, will teach you how to recognize and use both claims and proofs, the major components of argument. First, however, learn the strategy described next for analyzing an argument to get a preliminary sense of its purpose and to identify its parts.

Getting a Sense of the Purpose and Parts of an Argument

Survey

Follow the procedures for surveying a book or an article on page 110. Your objective is to find the claim and some of the main subclaims or parts.

Divide the Argument into Its Parts

Draw a line across the page (or make a light mark in the margin) each time the subject changes. This physical division of a written argument into its parts is called *chunking*. For example, in a policy paper that proposes a solution to a problem, the explanation of the problem would be a major chunk, as would be the explanation of the solution.

Ask Why the Parts Have Been Placed in That Particular Order

Try to determine whether the parts have been placed in a logical order to facilitate understanding, for instance, or whether they have been placed in a psychological order that leads up to the conclusion or action step at the end. There are other possibilities as well. Try to get a sense of how the author thought about and organized the parts.

Analyze the Relationships among the Parts

When you have speculated about why the author put the parts in a particular order, go a step further and think about the relationships among these parts. Do the parts all contribute to a central idea, such as a specialized definition? Or are other relationships apparent, such as causes for effects or solutions for problems?

When you begin to write argument, write a claim, list a few supporting reasons that represent the tentative parts, and then think about the best sequence for these parts. The relationships among them will become clearer to you as you rearrange them in an order that is logical to you.

Once you have a sense of the overall purpose and shape of an argument, you can then identify the type of claim that predominates in it.

Five Types of Claims

Virtually all arguments can be categorized according to one of five types of claims. You can identify each argument type by identifying the questions the argument answers. In general, certain types of organization and proof are associated with certain types of claims, as you will see in the following discussion. There are no hard-and-fast rules about using specific organizational strategies or types of proof to develop specific types of claims. Knowing common patterns and tendencies,

181

however, helps readers make predictions about the course of an argument and helps writers plan and write their own arguments.

Here are the five categories of claims, along with the main questions that they answer.

1. *Claims of fact:* Did it happen? Does it exist?
2. *Claims of definition:* What is it? How should we define it?
3. *Claims of cause:* What caused it? Or, What are its effects?
4. *Claims of value:* Is it good or bad? What criteria will help us decide?
5. *Claims of policy:* What should we do about it? What should be our future course of action?

The sections that follow provide additional explanations of the five types of claims, along with the general questions they answer, some examples of actual claims, a list of the types of proof (explained more fully in the next chapter) that are most typically associated with each type of claim, the organizational strategies that one might expect for each type, and a short written argument that illustrates each type as it appears in practice.

CLAIMS OF FACT

When you claim that you turned a paper in on time even though the professor cannot find it, or that you were not exceeding the speed limit when a police officer claims that you were, you are making claims of fact.

Questions answered by claims of fact. Did it happen? Is it true? Does it exist? Is it a fact?

Examples of claims of fact. (Note that all of the "facts" in these claims need to be proved as either absolutely or probably true in order to be acceptable to an audience. All of these claims, also, are controversial.) The ozone layer is becoming depleted. Increasing population threatens the environment. American drivers are becoming more responsible. America's military is prepared for any likely crisis. The abominable snowman exists in certain remote areas. Women are not as effective as men in combat. A mass murderer is evil, not insane. The American judicial system operates successfully.

Types of support associated with claims of fact. Factual support, as you might guess, is especially appropriate for claims of fact. Such support includes both past and present *facts, statistics, real examples,* and *quotations from reliable authorities. Inductive reasoning,* which cites several examples and then draws a probable conclusion from them, is also a common type of argument for claims of fact. *Analogies* that establish comparisons and similarities between the subject and something else that is commonly accepted as true are useful. *Signs* that present evidence of a past or present state of affairs are also useful to establish claims of fact. *Expert opinion,* when used to support claims of fact, is usually based on fact.

Possible organizational strategies. *Chronological order,* which traces what has occurred over a period of time, usually in the order in which it occurred, can be used to develop claims of fact. For example, the history of the increase in population might be provided to show how it has happened in time, from then to now. Or *topical order* may be used. In topical order reasons to support a fact are identified and then developed topic by topic. Thus reasons might be given for the existence of the abominable snowman, with each one developed at length. This chapter is organized according to topics: the five types of claims.

The claim of fact itself is often stated at or near the beginning of the argument unless there is a psychological advantage for stating it at the end. Most authors make claims of fact clear from the outset, revealing early what they seek to establish.

An example of an argument that contains a claim of fact. This essay argues that fewer Americans identified themselves as multiracial in a 2005 Census Bureau survey when compared with Bureau surveys taken in 2000 because many individuals prefer to think of themselves as members of one race rather than two or more, even when they are in fact multiracial. The article seeks to establish the fact that the Census, usually considered an accurate measure, is inaccurate in counting this group of people.

> **BEFORE YOU READ:** Think of some of the celebrities you know about, including sports figures, politicians, and film stars, who are multiracial. Do they usually identify themselves as multiracial or as a member of only one of the races they represent?

183

ESSAY #1   FEWER CALL THEMSELVES MULTIRACIAL*
Haya El Nasser

The author is a journalist who writes articles about immigration and other subjects for the newspaper *USA Today.*

Facts

1   The share of Americans who identify themselves as multiracial has shrunk this decade, an unexpected trend in an increasingly diverse nation.

Statistics

2   About 1.9% of the people checked off more than one race in a 2005 Census Bureau survey of 3 million households, a meaningful decline from two surveys in 2000.

Quotation from authority

3   There's no overall explanation for the drop, says Reynolds Farley, a research scientist at the University of Michigan's Institute for Social Research who analyzed the trend.

Claim of fact

4   The data show that the nation continues to wrestle with racial identity even in the face of growing diversity, he says. "We're a society where we still basically assume everyone is in one race," he says.

*USA Today, May 4–6, 2007, 1.

Facts and statistics presented visually

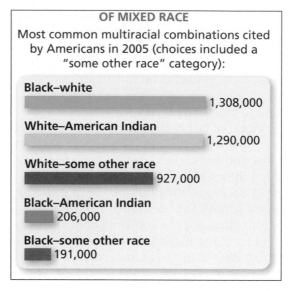

OF MIXED RACE

Most common multiracial combinations cited by Americans in 2005 (choices included a "some other race" category):

Black–white
1,308,000

White–American Indian
1,290,000

White–some other race
927,000

Black–American Indian
206,000

Black–some other race
191,000

Examples

Facts

Statistics
Inductive reasoning leading to unexpected conclusion

Quotations From authorities

Could also serve as <u>claim of fact</u>

5   Multiracial groups fought that concept in the 1990s. The small but vocal movement gained momentum in 1997 after golfer Tiger Woods proclaimed his race "Cablinasian"—for Caucasian, black, American Indian and Asian. The spotlight hit other multiracial celebrities, including singer Mariah Carey, actress Halle Berry and Yankees shortstop Derek Jeter.

6   Mixed-race Americans lobbied the government to stop requiring people to choose one race category on Census and other federal forms. The 2000 Census for the first time allowed people to check more than one race. About 2.4%, or 6.8 million people, did so in the full Census.

7   The numbers were expected to rise as more children were born to mixed-race parents and multiracial organizations sprouted on college campuses. The opposite happened.

8   The Census Bureau's American Community Survey of 3 million households a year shows a clear trend, Farley says. In the 2000 ACS survey, 2.1% checked more than one race. The drop to 1.9% in 2005 is "a slight decrease but statistically significant," Farley says.

9   Jungmiwha Bullock, president of the Association of MultiEthnic Americans, is not surprised. Some believe that identifying more than one race negates racial identity, she say. "To say you're black and Asian doesn't mean you're not black" she says. "I don't say I'm half black and half Korean. I'm 100% black, and I'm 100% Korean."

10   The Census numbers "clearly underestimate how many people are mixed race," says Daniel Lichter, a professor at Cornell University who has studied intermarriages. "People aren't willing to define themselves as such."

11   Many multiracial people identify themselves as black if they grew up in a black neighborhood, he says.

12   "There's a lot of pressure from society to choose one race," says Sara Ferry, 28, a school psychologist in Philadelphia who has a black father and a Chinese-American mother. "That's unfortunate."

For Discussion:

Why do you think fewer people identified themselves as multiracial on the 2005 American Community Survey compared with the 2000 data, the year this category was available for the first time? What does the author seem to think is the reason for this change? Do you agree or disagree? Do you know any multiracial people? Do they tend to identify themselves as members of two or more races, or do they identify themselves primarily as a member of one race? Why? Can you give examples?

CLAIMS OF DEFINITION

When you claim that an athlete who receives compensation for playing a sport is "professional," and therefore loses "amateur" status, or when you argue with a friend whether or not any war can ever be considered a "just" war, you are making a claim of definition.

> ***Questions answered by claims of definition.*** What is it? What is it like? How should it be classified? How should it be interpreted? How does its usual meaning change in a particular context?
>
> ***Examples of claims of definition.*** (Note that here we are looking at definition claims that dominate the argument in the essay as a whole. Definition is also used as a type of support, often at the beginning, to establish the meaning of one or more key terms.) We need to define what constitutes a family before we talk about family values. To determine whether an art exhibition is not art, but pornography, we need to define what we mean by pornography in this context. To determine whether the police were doing their job or were engaging in brutality, we need to establish what we mean by police brutality. To determine whether a person is mentally competent, we need to define what we mean by that designation. If we have established the fact that a young man killed his wife, shall we define this killing as self-defense, a crime of passion, or premeditated murder?
>
> ***Types of support associated with claims of definition.*** The main types of support used to prove claims of definition are *references to reliable authorities and accepted sources* that can be used to establish clear definitions and meanings, such as the dictionary or a well-known work. Also useful are *analogies and other comparisons*, especially to other words or situations that are clearly understood and that can consequently be used to shed some light on what is being defined. *Examples, both real and hypothetical,* and *signs* can also be used to clarify or develop definitions.
>
> ***Possible organizational strategies.*** *Compare-and-contrast organization* can dominate the development of a claim of definition and serve as the main structure. In this structure two or more objects are compared and contrasted throughout. For example, in an essay that expands the notion of crime to include white-collar crime, conventional crime would be compared with white-collar crime to prove that they are similar.
>
> *Topical organization* may also be used. Several special qualities, characteristics, or features of the word or concept are identified and explained as discrete topics. Thus in an essay defining a criminal as mentally competent,

185

the characteristics of mental competence would be explained as separate topics and applied to the criminal. Another strategy is to *explain the controversy* over the term and *give reasons* for accepting one view over another.

An example of an argument that contains a claim of definition. This editorial complains about the substitution of the phrase "very low food security" for the common term *hunger* in the government's annual hunger report. The author argues that the common word is more powerful and will stir more people to action than the longer, vaguer phrase. Decide whether or not you agree. (Note the sources of the definitions used.)

BEFORE YOU READ: How many people do you think are hungry on a daily basis in America?

ESSAY #2   BROTHER, CAN YOU SPARE A WORD?*
Editorial

Authority: The report

1   First the good news: the government's annual hunger report shows a slight decline last year in the number of citizens in need of food. Now the bad news: the annual hunger report has dropped the word "hunger."

Definitions

Statistics

2   Instead, there were 35 million Americans last year suffering from "low food security," meaning they chronically lacked the resources to be able to eat enough food. Of these, 10.8 million lived with "very low food security," meaning they were the hungriest among the hungry, so to speak.

Definition

3   Bureaucratic terminology about food security has always been a part of the hunger report, but so was the plain word "hunger." The Agriculture Department decided that variations of "hungry" are not scientifically accurate, following the advice of the Committee on National Statistics of the National Academies. The specialists advised that being hungry was too amorphous a way to refer to "a potential consequence of food insecurity that, because of prolonged, involuntary lack of food, results in discomfort, illness, weakness or pain that goes beyond the usual uneasy sensation."

Statistics

4   The government insists that no Orwellian plot is in the works to mask a national blight. The goal has been to cut what we'll call the hungry households to no more than 6 percent of the population. But hungry people persist at nearly twice that rate, despite the slight drop last year.

Claim based on definition

To the extent that more public empathy is needed to prod a stronger attack on low food security, we opt for "hunger" as a most stirring word.

---

*New York Times, November 20, 2006, A26.

For Discussion:

Why is this author arguing that the word *hunger* should be used in the government's annual hunger report instead of the term "very low food security"? Why do you think government writers made this substitution? Which of these choices do you think best describes the condition of the millions of Americans who never have enough food to eat?

CLAIMS OF CAUSE

When you claim that staying up late at a party caused you to fail your exam the next day or that your paper is late because the library closed too early, you are making claims of cause.

Questions answered by claims of cause. What caused it? Where or what is its source? Why did it happen? What are the effects? What will probably be the results over the short term? Over the long term?

Examples of claims of cause. The United States champions human rights in foreign countries to further its own economic self-interests. Clear-cutting is the main cause of the destruction of ancient forests. Legalizing marijuana could have beneficial effects for medicine. DNA testing is causing courts to review some of their death penalty decisions. The long-term effect of inadequate funding for AIDS research will be a disastrous worldwide epidemic. A lack of family values can lead to crime. Censorship can have good results by protecting children.

Types of support associated with claims of cause. The argument must establish the probability of a cause-and-effect relationship. The best type of support for this purpose is *factual data,* including *statistics* that are used to prove a cause or an effect. *Analogies,* including *both literal and historical* analogies that parallel cases in past history, are also used to show that the cause of one event could also be the cause of another similar event. Another type of support is based on the use of *signs* to establish certain causes or effects. *Induction,* which entails citing several examples as a cause, may be used to invite the inductive leap to a possible effect as the end result. *Deduction* is also used to develop claims of cause. Premises about effects are proposed, as in the Sherlock Holmes example in Chapter 7 (page 228), and a conclusion about the possible cause is drawn.

Possible organizational strategies. One strategy is to describe *causes and then effects.* Thus clear-cutting would be described as a cause that would lead to the ultimate destruction of the forests, which would be the effect. Or *effects* may be described and *then the cause or causes.* The effects of censorship may be described before the public efforts that resulted in that censorship. You may also encounter *refutation* of other actual or possible causes or effects.

An example of an argument that contains a claim of cause. The following article reports on a study that claims cigarette smoking causes quick and powerful nicotine addiction in young smokers. In other words, the cause, smoking, is shown to produce almost immediate effects, addiction. Prior to this study, people generally assumed that young smokers could try a few cigarettes without becoming addicted. The author quotes the authors of the study as well as an outside authority on addiction, provides statistics, and concludes with a new explanation of the cause–effect relationship between smoking and addiction. The conclusions of this study, according to the author, may be challenged because of the nature of some of the data. Consequently, it is possible that not everyone will agree with this cause-and-effect argument. What do you think?

BEFORE YOU READ: How long and how much do you think a teen-aged person can experiment with smoking cigarettes before becoming addicted to them?

ESSAY #3   ## NICOTINE ADDICTION IS QUICK IN YOUTHS, RESEARCH FINDS*

Nicholas Bakalar

The author is a writer and editor who has written on medicine, health and wellness, animals, and science for the *New York Times* and other magazines and newspapers.

188

Claim of cause

1   A young cigarette smoker can begin to feel powerful desires for nicotine within two days of first inhaling, a new study has found, and about half of children who become addicted report symptoms of dependence by the time they are smoking only seven cigarettes a month.

Authority

2   "The importance of this study is that it contradicts what has been the accepted wisdom for many decades," said Dr. Joseph R. DiFranza, the lead author, "which is that people had to smoke at least five cigarettes a day over a long period of time to risk becoming addicted to nicotine. Now, we know that children can be addicted very quickly." Dr. DiFranza is a professor of family medicine at the University of Massachusetts.

Statistics

3   The researchers recruited 1,246 sixth-grade volunteers in public schools in Massachusetts, interviewing them 11 times over a four-year period. They also took saliva samples to determine blood levels of nicotine and link them to addictive behavior. At some time during the four years almost a third of the children puffed on a cigarette, more than 17 percent inhaled, and about 7.5 percent used tobacco daily.

Statistics

4   Since inhaling is required for sufficient drug delivery to cause dependence, the researchers limited their analysis, published in the July issue of *The Archives of Pediatrics and Adolescent Medicine,* to the 217 inhalers in the group. Their average age when they first inhaled was 12.8 years. Of these, almost 60 percent had lost some control over their smoking, and 38 percent developed tobacco dependence as defined by the widely used diagnostic manual published by the World Health Organization.

New York Times, July 31, 2007, D8.

Source of definition 5   In the 10 percent of children who were most susceptible, cravings began within two days of the first inhalation, and saliva analysis showed that being dependent did not require high blood levels of nicotine throughout the day. In some cases dependence could be diagnosed as early as 13 days after the first smoking episode.

Statistics 6   For most inhalers, daily smoking was not required to cause withdrawal symptoms. More than 70 percent had cravings that were difficult to control before they were smoking every day. The biochemical analyses confirmed this: the symptoms of dependence began mostly at the lowest levels of nicotine intake.

Authority 7   "We know very little about the natural history of dependence," said Denise B. Kandel, a professor of socio-medical sciences at Columbia and a widely published addiction researcher who was not involved in the study. "This is really the first study that addresses the issue. Its strength is that DiFranza has followed a community sample of adolescents and interviewed them every three months, which is very difficult to do.

8   "On the other hand," she continued, "his definition of dependence is based on single symptoms, which may be open to question."

Definition 9   The definition of tobacco addiction is controversial, but the scientists used widely accepted criteria to diagnose dependence and a well-validated questionnaire to determine the extent to which smokers had allowed the habit to dictate their behavior.

10   The researchers write that it may seem implausible that intermittent smoking could provide relief from withdrawal symptoms. But in fact a single dose of nicotine has effects on the brain that can last as long as a month, and the nicotine obtained from just one or two puffs on a cigarette will occupy half of the brain's nicotinic receptors, the molecules specifically sought by nicotine in tobacco addiction.

Data 11   The authors acknowledge that some of their data is retrospective and comes from self-reports, which can be unreliable, and that it is not possible to draw conclusions about other populations from their sample. In addition, they did not consider the roles of puberty, alcohol and other drug use. But the study has considerable strengths in measuring frequency and duration of smoking and in collecting exposure data by biochemical analysis as well as by repeated interviews.

Cause and effect 12   "People used to think that long-term heavy use caused addiction," Dr. DiFranza said. "Now, we know it's the other way around: addiction is what causes long-term heavy use."

For Discussion:

How is the usually accepted cause–effect relationship between smoking and tobacco dependence in young people modified by this study? Why is a definition of tobacco dependence important in the study? Why do individuals who evaluate this study need to agree with the definition of tobacco dependence used by the researchers? Is the study itself well-grounded? What are some of the possible problems with the reliability and soundness of the study? What are some of its strengths? Based on

189

your experience and on the experience of people you know, how would you evaluate the reliability of this study?

CLAIMS OF VALUE

When you claim that sororities and fraternities are the best extracurricular organizations for college students to join or that one college major is better than another, you are making a claim of value.

Questions answered by claims of value. Is it good or bad? How bad? How good? Of what worth is it? Is it moral or immoral? Who thinks so? What do those people value? What values or criteria should I use to determine its goodness or badness? Are my values different from other people's values or from the author's values?

Examples of claims of value. Computers are a valuable addition to modern society. Prayer has a moral function in the public schools. Viewing television is a wasteful activity. Mercy killing is immoral. The contributions of homemakers are as valuable as those of professional women. Animal rights are as important as human rights.

Types of support associated with claims of value. *Appeals to values* are important in developing claims of value. The arguer thus appeals to what the audience is expected to value. A sense of a common, shared system of values between the arguer and the audience is important for the argument to be convincing. These shared values must be established either explicitly or implicitly in the argument. (Recall the essay "American Value Systems" in Chapter 5, pages 174–178, here.) *Motivational appeals* that suggest what the audience wants are also important in establishing claims of value. People place value on the things that they work to achieve.

Other types of support used to establish claims of value include *analogies, both literal and figurative,* that establish links with other good or bad objects or qualities. Also, quotations from *authorities* who are admired help establish both expert criteria and judgments of good or bad, right or wrong. *Induction* is also used by presenting examples to demonstrate that something is good or bad. *Signs* that something is good or bad are sometimes cited. *Definitions* are used to clarify criteria for evaluation.

Possible organizational strategies. *Applied criteria* can develop a claim of value. Criteria for evaluation are established and then applied to the subject that is at issue. For example, in arguing that a particular television series is the best on television, criteria for what makes a superior series are identified and then applied to the series to defend it as best. The audience would have to agree with the criteria to make the argument effective. Or suppose the claim is made that toxic waste is the worst threat to the environment. A list of criteria for evaluating threats to the environment is established and applied to toxic waste to show that it is the worst of all. Another possibility would be to use *topical organization* by first developing a list of reasons why something is good or bad. Then each of the reasons is examined as a separate topic.

You may also expect that *narrative* structure will sometimes be used to develop a claim of value. Narratives are real or made-up stories that can illustrate values in action, with morals or generalizations noted explicitly or implicitly along the way. An example of a narrative used to support a claim of value is the New Testament parable of the Good Samaritan who helped a fellow traveler. The claim is that helping one another in such circumstances is valued and desirable behavior.

An example of an argument that contains a claim of value. The following article describes some of the negative American values that are communicated through the movies and the Iraq war to other parts of the world. The author describes another set of values that, in his opinion, more accurately represent the true nature of America. Notice how the author appeals to values that the audience is also expected to accept.

BEFORE YOU READ: How do you think America is regarded by other countries around the world? How should it be regarded?

ESSAY #4   WHAT SETS US APART*

Mortimer B. Zuckerman

The author is the chairman and editor-in-chief of *U.S. News & World Report* and is the publisher of the *New York Daily News*.

191

Quotations from authorities	1 The only things that "every community in the world from Zanzibar to Hamburg recognizes in common" are American cultural artifacts—the jeans and the colas, the movies and the TV sitcoms, the music, and the rhetoric of freedom. That observation was made 65 years ago by Henry Luce in his essay "The American Century," but—to paraphrase President Reagan—Luce hadn't seen anything yet. We have lived through an astounding acceleration in the dissemination of American cultural values with profound implications for the rest of the world. As Plato is widely quoted as having said, "Those who tell the stories rule society."
Examples	2 Our storytellers—encapsulated in the one word *Hollywood*—make up a significant piece of America's "soft power." Through the media's projection of the American narrative, the world gets some pretty good insight into America's ideals. Most of the time, since World War II, we have reflected the rule of law, individual freedom, defense of human rights, and the just use of American power against fascism and communism. The American narrative, as portrayed, say, by Jimmy ("aw shucks") Stewart in the Frank Capra classic *It's a Wonderful Life,* enchanted the world.
Narrative	3 The message from American pop culture has long been antiauthoritarian, challenging power in ways unthinkable in many countries. The hero,

---

*U.S. News and World Report, July 3/July 10, 2006, 72.

going up against the odds, projected a populist narrative that celebrated the common decencies against the wicked authorities or the excesses of capitalism. Millions who saw such films around the globe derived a sense of phantom citizenship in America, an appetite for the life that only liberty can bring.

Statistics
Examples

4   The universality of the commercial appeal was due in part to Hollywood's munificent creative and marketing skills, but also fundamentally in the fact that we are such a richly heterogeneous society that our exports had been pretested at home. Hollywood supplies over 70 percent of the European film markets and 90 percent of those of the rest of the world, with the possible exception of India. To reach the younger populations under the age of 25, who constitute the bulk of the moviegoing audience, Hollywood has been offering more dumbed-down blockbusters based on action, violence, sex, and special effects like *Jurassic Park*. Such films travel more easily than movies with subtle dialogue or predominantly American references, like *Forrest Gump*. For similar reasons, comedy was structured to hinge on crude slapstick rather than situational wit and wordplay.

New narrative
Comparison
Definition

5   The underside of this commercial success is the cultural deficit of associating America with crime, vacuity, moral decay, promiscuity, and pornography—a trend that also worries American parents; Asian and Muslim worlds are already in revolt against it, but also against the libertarian and secular messages of American media. Our media project defiance and ridicule not just of illegitimate authority but of any authority at all—parents, teachers, and political leaders. Even in the West this elicits as much loathing as love. Abroad, it may make dictatorship more difficult, but it also makes democracy less attractive. These images have contributed to make *Americanization* a dirty word, with the American lifestyle and American capitalism widely viewed as an anarchic revolutionary force. It is perceived as trampling social order in the ruthless pursuit of profits, creating a new class system, based on money, combined with an uninhibited pursuit of pleasure and a disordered sense of priorities in which the needs of the less successful are neglected. What's more, America is increasingly seen as certain of its own righteousness, justifying the use of force to impose American views and values.

Opinion poll

6   So America's narrative, which has waxed for so long, is now waning in its universal appeal. Witness the decline of America's image abroad. In the most recent Pew Research Center poll, favorable opinion of the United States has fallen in most of the 14 countries surveyed, dropping dramatically in Europe, India, and Indonesia, but especially in the Middle East. The main provocation is the war in Iraq. It made anti-Americanism respectable again and crystallized long-standing grievances over American environmental policy and perceived support for globalization, multinational corporations, the death penalty, and friendly authoritarian governments around the world.

Appeal to values
New definition

7   These perceptions are badly skewed. They fail to do justice to what is so wonderful about the United States: its individualism, its embrace of diversity, its opportunities for freedom, the welcome it extends to new-comers, and the uniqueness of an entrepreneurial, pragmatic society

that is dramatically open to energy and talent. No other country provides the environment for self-help, self-improvement, and self-renovation. No other country possesses our unique mood of buoyancy, optimism, and confidence for the future.

Claim of value

8   How we portray ourselves positively (while not ignoring the warts) is a challenge to our creative talents—and to all of us.

For Discussion:

According to this author, what American values were projected to other parts of the world during most of the time since World War II? What values are currently projected to other countries by the entertainment industry and by America's participation in the Iraq war? What effect has this had on perceptions of American values in other countries? Why does the author refer to these perceptions as "America's narrative"? How does he think this narrative should change? Describe the changes. How much common ground do you share with this author? Give some examples of how you either agree or disagree with him.

CLAIMS OF POLICY

When you claim that all new students should attend orientation or that all students who graduate should participate in graduation ceremonies, you are making claims of policy.

Questions answered by claims of policy. What should we do? How should we act? What should future policy be? How can we solve this problem? What concrete course of action should we pursue to solve the problem? (Notice that policy claims focus on the future more than the other types of claims, which tend to deal with the past or present.)

Examples of claims of policy. The criminal should be sent to prison rather than to a mental institution. Everyone should be taught to recognize and report sexual harassment in the workplace. Every person in the United States should have access to health care. Small business loans must be made available to help people reestablish their businesses after a natural disaster. Both filmmakers and recording groups should make objectionable language and subject matter known to prospective consumers. Battered women who take revenge should not be placed in jail. Genetic engineering should be monitored and controlled. Parents should have the right to choose the schools their children attend.

Types of support associated with claims of policy. Data and *statistics* are used to support a policy claim, but so are *moral and commonsense appeals* to what people value and want. *Motivational appeals* are especially important for policy claims. The audience needs to become sufficiently motivated to think or even act in a different way. To accomplish this degree of motivation, the arguer must convince the audience that they want to change. *Appeals to values* are also used for motivation. The audience becomes convinced they should follow a policy to achieve important values.

Literal analogies sometimes support policy claims. The arguer establishes what other similar people or groups have done and suggests the same thing can work in this case also. Or a successful effort is described, and the claim is made that it could work even better on a broader scale. This is another type of literal analogy, because it compares a small-scale effort to a large-scale, expanded effort.

Argument from authority is also often used to establish claims of policy. The authorities quoted, however, must be trusted and must have good credibility. Effort is usually made to establish their credentials. *Cause* can be used to establish the origin of the problem, and *definition* can be used to clarify it. Finally, *deduction* can be used to reach a conclusion based on a general principle.

Possible organizational strategies. The *problem–solution* structure is typical of policy claims. The problem is first described in sufficient detail so that the audience will want a solution. Then the solution is spelled out. In addition, the solution suggested is usually shown to be superior to other solutions by anticipating and showing what is wrong with each of the others. In some arguments the problem and solution sections are followed by a *visualization* of how matters will be improved if the proposed solution is accepted and followed. Problem–solution arguments often end with an *action* step that directs the audience to take a particular course of action (vote, buy, etc.).

An example of an argument that contains a claim of policy. The following article addresses the problem caused by a small number of students who ask professors to raise their grades at the end of the semester when they have actually earned their lower grades. The author, who is a physics professor, describes this problem from his point of view, establishes why accurate grades are important to society, and establishes a new policy that he will follow to deal with this problem at the end of each semester. Notice how he describes the problem and then his solution.

BEFORE YOU READ: Are you ever tempted to ask a professor for a higher grade at the end of the semester, even when you are not certain you have earned it?

ESSAY #5   **MAKING THE GRADE***

Kurt Wiesenfeld

The author is a professor of physics at Georgia Tech in Atlanta. He wrote this article for the "My Turn" column in *Newsweek* magazine more than ten years ago. The problem he describes persists today in the experience of many college faculty.

Problem with examples   1   It was a rookie error. After 10 years I should have known better, but I went to my office the day after final grades were posted. There was a tentative knock on the door. "Professor Wiesenfeld? I took

*Newsweek, June 17, 1996, 16.

your Physics 2121 class? I flunked it? I wonder if there's anything I can do to improve my grade?" I thought: "Why are you asking me? Isn't it too late to worry about it? Do you dislike making declarative statements?"

2   After the student gave his tale of woe and left, the phone rang. "I got a D in your class. Is there any way you can change it to 'Incomplete'?" Then the e-mail assault began: "I'm shy about coming in to talk to you, but I'm not shy about asking for a better grade. Anyway, it's worth a try." The next day I had three phone messages from students asking *me* to call *them*. I didn't.

Comparison   3   Time was, when you received a grade, that was it. You might groan and moan, but you accepted it as the outcome of your efforts or lack thereof (and, yes, sometimes a tough grader). In the last few years, however, some students have developed a disgruntled-consumer approach. If they don't like their grade, they go to the "return" counter to trade it in for something better.

Grades as signs   4   What alarms me is their indifference toward grades as an indication of personal effort and performance. Many, when pressed about why they think they deserve a better grade, admit they don't deserve one but would like one anyway. Having been raised on gold stars for effort and smiley faces for self-esteem, they've learned that they can get by without hard work and real talent if they can talk the professor into giving them a break. This attitude is beyond cynicism. There's a weird innocence to the assumption that one expects (even deserves) a better grade simply by begging for it. With that outlook, I guess I shouldn't be as flabbergasted as I was that 12 students asked me to change their grades *after* final grades were posted.

Definition
Comparisons   5   That's 10 percent of my class who let three months of midterms, quizzes and lab reports slide until long past remedy. My graduate student calls it hyperrational thinking: if effort and intelligence don't matter, why should deadlines? What matters is getting a better grade through an unearned bonus, the academic equivalent of a freebie T shirt or toaster giveaway. Rewards are disconnected from the quality of one's work. An act and its consequences are unrelated, random events.

Faulty deductive
reasoning
Values   6   Their arguments for wheedling better grades often ignore academic performance. Perhaps they feel it's not relevant. "If my grade isn't raised to a D I'll lose my scholarship." "If you don't give me a C, I'll flunk out." One sincerely overwrought student pleaded, "If I don't pass, my life is over." This is tough stuff to deal with. Apparently, I'm responsible for someone's losing a scholarship, flunking out or deciding whether life has meaning. Perhaps these students see me as a commodities broker with something they want—a grade. Though intrinsically worthless, grades, if properly manipulated, can be traded for what has value: a degree, which means a job, which means money. The one thing college actually offers—a chance to learn—is considered irrelevant, even less than worthless, because of the long hours and hard work required.

7   In a society saturated with surface values, love of knowledge for its own sake does sound eccentric. The benefits of fame and wealth are more obvious. So is it right to blame students for reflecting the superficial values saturating our society?

8   Yes, of course it's right. These guys had better take themselves seriously now, because our country will be forced to take them seriously later, when the stakes are much higher. They must recognize that their attitude is not only self-destructive, but socially destructive.

Problem

The erosion of quality control—giving appropriate grades for actual accomplishments—is a major concern in my department. One colleague noted that a physics major could obtain a degree without ever answering a written exam question completely. How? By pulling in enough partial credit and extra credit. And by getting breaks on grades.

Comparison

9   But what happens once she or he graduates and gets a job? That's when the misfortunes of eroding academic standards multiply. We lament that schoolchildren get "kicked upstairs" until they graduate from high school despite being illiterate and mathematically inept, but we seem unconcerned with college graduates whose less blatant deficiencies are far more harmful if their accreditation exceeds their qualifications.

Effects
Causes

10   Most of my students are science and engineering majors. If they're good at getting partial credit but not at getting the answer right, then the new bridge breaks or the new drug doesn't work. One finds examples here in Atlanta. Last year a light tower in the Olympic Stadium collapsed, killing a worker. It collapsed because an engineer miscalculated how much weight it could hold. A new 12-story dormitory could develop dangerous cracks due to a foundation that's uneven by more than six inches. The error resulted from incorrect data being fed into a computer. I drive past that dorm daily on my way to work, wondering if a foundation crushed under kilotons of weight is repairable or if this structure will have to be demolished. Two 10,000-pound steel beams at the new natatorium collapsed in March, crashing into the student athletic complex. (Should we give partial credit since no one was hurt?) Those are real-world consequences of errors and lack of expertise.

11   But the lesson is lost on the grade-grousing 10 percent. Say that you won't (not can't, but won't) change the grade they deserve to what they want, and they're frequently bewildered or angry. They don't think it's fair that they're judged according to their perform-ance, not their desires or "potential." They don't think it's fair that they should jeopardize their scholarships or be in danger of flunking out simply because they could not or did not do their work. But it's more than fair; it's necessary to help preserve a minimum standard of quality that our society needs to maintain safety and integrity. I don't know if the 13th-hour students will learn that lesson, but I've learned mine. From now on, after final grades are posted, I'll lie low until the next quarter starts.

Claim
The solution

For Discussion:

What do you think of the reasons the author's students have used to try to get him to raise their grades after final grades have been posted? What reasons does he give for not raising their grades? Why is accurate grading important to students in the long run and also to society? How is the author going to solve this problem with his students in the future? Is it a solution for the student or for the professor?

Claims and Argument in Real Life

In argument, one type of claim may predominate, but other types are usually present as supporting arguments or subclaims. Thus it is not always easy to establish the predominant claim in an argument or to establish its type. You may find, for example, some disagreement in your class discussions when you try to categorize a claim according to type. The reason for this disagreement is that two or more types of claims will be present in almost any argument. Close reading will usually reveal a predominant type, however, with the other types serving as subclaims. For example, a value claim that the popular press does harm by prying into the private lives of public figures may establish the fact that this is a pervasive practice, may define what should be public and what should not be public information, may examine the causes or, more likely, the effects of this type of reporting, and may suggest future policy for dealing with this problem. All can occur in the same article. Still, the dominant claim is one of value, namely, that this practice of newswriters is bad.

It is useful when reading argument to identify the predominant claim because doing so helps you identify (1) the main purpose of the argument, (2) the types of support used, and (3) the organizational strategies that structure it. It is also useful to identify other types of subclaims and to analyze why they are used and how they contribute to the argument purpose. When planning and writing argument, identify a predominant claim and its type as well as the types of the subclaims, support, and organization early in the process. This awareness gives you more control of the writing and the argument itself. The types of support and the organizational patterns that are particularly appropriate for developing different types of claims are explained and illustrated in this chapter. For quick reference, a chart of the types of support that can best be used for each type of claim appears in Table 13.1 (page 414). A second chart that shows the organizational patterns that can best be used to develop each type of claim appears in Table 13.2 (page 415). Refer to these tables for a quick summary of the suggestions to help you develop your claim and purpose for argument papers you write.

As you read and write argument, you will also notice that claims follow a predictable sequence when they originate in real-life situations. In fact, argument appears most vigorous in dramatic, life-and-death situations or when a person's character is called into question. We see claims and rebuttals, many kinds of support, and every conceivable organizational strategy in these instances. For example, as juvenile crime in this country increased in recent years, the issues that emerged included these: What is causing young people to commit crimes? What can be done to protect the family unit? Is the educational system adequate? Should the criminal justice system treat young offenders differently from older criminals? Does racial discrimination contribute to juvenile crime? How can we make inner cities more livable? How can we improve social programs?

Such real-life situations, particularly when they are life-threatening, as juvenile crime often is, not only generate issues but also many arguments. Interestingly, the types of arguments usually appear in a fairly predictable order. The first arguments made in response to a new issue-generating situation usually involve claims of fact and definition. People first have to come to terms with the fact that something significant has happened. Then they need to define what happened so that they can understand it better.

The next group of arguments that appear after fact and definition typically are inquiries into cause. People often need to figure out why the event happened. Multiple causes are considered and debated. Following cause, people begin to evaluate the goodness or badness of what has happened. It is usually after all of these other matters have been dealt with that people turn their attention to future policy and how to solve problems.

The issues and claims that emerged from the September 11, 2001, terrorist attacks on the World Trade Center in New York City follow this pattern. Again, people were caught off guard, and the first questions that emerged as people watched their television sets were questions of fact: "What is happening? Is this a bomb? Are we being attacked?" Definition arguments followed. The issue was how to define what had happened, which would help determine the country's response. The president and his advisers defined the situation as an act of terrorism and then declared a "war on terrorism."

Causal arguments engaged people for a long time after the initial event. Possible causes of the attacks included the presence of evil in the world, the terrorists' desire for power, religious conflicts, the uneven opportunities between developed and developing nations, hatred of America, even biblical prophecy. At the same time, many value arguments appeared in the media. The questions were, "How bad is this?" and "Can any good be discovered?" Pictures of grieving survivors and of the excavation work at Ground Zero, along with obituaries of the dead, forcefully demonstrated the bad effects. Some good was found in the heroic efforts of passengers on one of the hijacked flights, who had attacked the terrorists by trying to retake the plane and died with them, as well as in the selfless efforts of New York police officers and firefighters, many of whom died in the rescue effort in the buildings.

Deliberations about policy followed. Many American citizens, on their own initiative, decided to fly the American flag and to donate money to the survivors. Government officials set policy on how to conduct a war on terrorism. Many additional arguments about policy followed: how to get the donated money to the deserving victims, how to identify the terrorists and then how to find and kill them, how to know when the war was over, and how best to protect the country from future attack.

You may be able to think of other issues that have inspired a variety of arguments and claims in this same roughly predictable order. It is useful to pay attention to the issues that come out of dramatic events, the types of claims that are generated by them, and the order in which these claims appear. Such analysis will help you anticipate the course an issue will take. It will also help you determine at what point in the ongoing conversation about an issue you happen to be at a given moment. You can then speculate about the aspects of the issue that have already been argued and that are likely to be argued in the future.

Value of the Claim Types and the Claim Questions for Reading, Viewing, and Writing Argument

Readers and viewers of argument find the list of the five types of claims and the questions that accompany them useful for identifying the claim and the main purpose in an argument: to establish fact, to define, to establish cause, to assign value, or to propose a solution. Claims and claim questions can also help readers identify minor purposes in an argument, those that are developed as subclaims. When a reader is able to discover the overall purpose of an argument, it is much easier to make predictions and to follow the argument.

Viewers of visual argument will discover that images express the same types of purposes as those found in written argument: some images primarily establish facts, others define a term or a problem, still others establish cause–effect relationships, assign value to a subject, or propose a solution to a problem. Look at the images in Exercise D on pages 213–217 and see if you can identify the types of claims made in each of these cases.

Writers of argument find the list of the five types of claims and the questions that accompany them useful for analyzing an issue, writing a claim about it, and identifying both the controlling purpose for a paper and additional ideas that can be developed in the paper. Here is an example of how this can work. The author writes the issue in the form of a question, as in the example "Should high schools be safer places?" Then the author asks the claim questions about this issue and writes a paragraph in response to each of them: Is it a fact that high schools are unsafe places? How should we define *unsafe*? What causes a lack of safety in high schools, and what are the effects? Is a lack of safety good or bad? What criteria could be established to judge the goodness or badness of safety in high schools? What can be done to make high schools safer places? Finally, the author reads the paragraphs and selects the one that is most promising to form the major claim and purpose in the paper. For example, suppose the author decides to write a policy paper, and the claim becomes "Parents, students, teachers, and administrators all need to cooperate to make high schools safer places." To show how that can be done becomes the main purpose of the paper. The information generated by asking the other claim questions, however, can also be used in the paper to provide reasons and evidence. The claim questions, used in this way as part of the prewriting process, can generate considerable information and ideas for a paper.

Review Questions

1. What are the five types of claims?
2. What are the questions associated with each type?
3. What is a predictable sequence that claims follow when they originate in a dramatic, real-life situation?
4. How do claims typically appear in written argument? That is, do writers usually limit themselves to a single purpose and claim or not? Discuss.
5. What events have occurred in the past few months either on campus or on the national or international level that have generated issues? What are some of these issues?

Exercises and Activities

A. **Class Discussion: Predicting Types of Claims**

Bring in the front page of a current newspaper. Discuss headlines that suggest controversial topics. Predict from each headline the type of claim that will be made.

B. **Group Work: Reading and Analyzing Types of Claims**

The class is divided into five groups, and each group is assigned one of the five articles that follow. Prepare for group work by reading the article assigned to your group. Then, with your group, apply the new reading strategies described in this chapter by answering the following questions. Assign a person to report your answers to the class.

1. Which sentence is the claim? Remember that it can appear at the beginning, in the middle, or at the end of the essay. Underline it.
2. What type of claim is it? Decide which of the five types of claims this claim represents.
3. What are one or two examples of support used in the essay? To help you identify support, review the margin labels that identify the support in the five sample readings in the chapter.
4. How would you summarize the argument in the essay in two or three sentences?
5. What is your reaction to the author's position?
6. Where might you position this argument in an ongoing conversation about the issue? At the beginning, the middle, or the end? Why?

> **BEFORE YOU READ:** What dangers and threats do you worry about?

ESSAY #6   **LET'S STOP SCARING OURSELVES***

Michael Crichton

The author has a degree in medicine but has spent his career as a writer. He is the author of best-selling novels *The Andromeda Strain* and *Jurassic Park.*

1 This year I turned 62, and I find I have acquired—along with aches and pains—a perspective on the world that I lacked as a younger person. I now recognize that for most of my life I have felt burdened by highly publicized fears that decades later did not turn out to be true.

2 I was reminded of this when I came across this 1972 statement about climate: "We simply cannot afford to gamble . . . We cannot risk inaction. Those scientists who [disagree] are acting irresponsibly. The indications that our climate can soon change for the worse are too strong to be reasonably ignored." This author wasn't concerned about global warming. He was worried about global cooling and the coming ice age.

We're all going to freeze! Or is it sizzle?

3 It may be mostly forgotten now, but back then many climate scientists shared his concern: Temperatures around the world had fallen steadily for 30 years, dropping half a degree in the Northern Hemisphere between 1945 and 1968. Pack ice was increasing. Glaciers were advancing. Growing seasons had shortened by two weeks in only a few years.

4 In 1975, *Newsweek* noted "ominous signs that weather patterns have begun to change . . . with serious political implications for just about every nation." Scientists were predicting that "the resulting famines could be catastrophic."

5 But it is now clear that even as *Newsweek* was printing its fears, temperatures already had begun to rise. Within a decade, scientists would be decrying a global warming trend that threatened to raise temperatures as much as 30 degrees in the 21st century. Such predictions implied palm trees in Montana, and they have since been revised downward. By 1995, the UN midrange estimates were about 4 degrees over the next 100 years. Although concern about warming remains, the prospect of catastrophic change seems increasingly unlikely.

Oh no, it's a population explosion!

6 Similarly, for all of my adult life, informed people have lived in continual anxiety about an exploding world population and the inevitable resulting mass starvation and environmental degradation.

7 In the 1960s, experts like Paul Ehrlich spoke with conviction: "In the 1970s the world will undergo famines—hundreds of millions of people are going to starve to death." Ehrlich argued for compulsory population control if voluntary methods failed. In the 1970s, The Club of Rome (a global think tank) predicted a world population of 14 billion in the year 2030, with no end in sight.

8 Instead, fertility rates fell steadily. By the end of the century, they were about half what they were in 1950, with the result that many now expect world population to peak at 9 billion or so and then to decline. (It's estimated to be about 6 billion today.)

9 And mass starvation never occurred either. Instead, per capita food production increased through the end of the century because of the "green revolution" resulting from increased agricultural efficiency and better seeds. Grain produc-

Parade, December 5, 2004, 6–7.

201

tion increased as much as 600% per acre, bringing unprecedented crop yields around the world.

10 These changes were exemplified by the rise of India, which in the 1960s was widely acknowledged to be a symbol of the over-population disaster. Western children were chided to finish their food because of the starving children in India. By 2000, however, India had become a net exporter of grain, and Americans were worried about outsourced jobs to that nation's highly educated work-force. Almost no one concerned about population spoke of an explosion anymore. Instead, they discussed the new problems: an aging population and a declining population.

We're running out . . . of everything!

11 The 1970s saw the use of computers to predict future world trends. In 1972, The Club of Rome used its computers to warn us that raw materials were fast running out. By 1993 we would have exhausted our supplies of gold, mercury, tin, zinc, oil, copper, lead and natural gas. Yet 1993 came and went. We still have all these things, at prices that fluctuate but over the long term have generally declined.

12 What seems to be more accurate is that there is a perennial market for dire predictions of resource depletion. Human beings never tire of discussing the latest report that tells us the end is near. But, at some point, we might start regarding each breathless new claim with skepticism. I have learned to do so.

The machines are taking over!

13 Any catalog of false fears and counterfeit crises must include examples of the ever-present threat posed by technology. Nobody of my generation will ever forget the looming crisis of too much leisure time, an issue much discussed in the 1960s. Since machines would soon be doing all our work, we needed to learn watercolor painting and macramé to pass the time. Yet, by the end of the century, Americans were regarded as overworked, overstressed and sleepless. The crisis of leisure time had gone the way of the paperless office.

14 More sinister were the health threats posed by technology, such as the fears about cancer from power lines. The great power-line scare lasted more than a decade and, according to one expert, cost the nation $25 billion before many studies determined it to be false. Ironically, 10 years later, the same magnetic fields that were formerly feared as carcinogenic now were welcomed as healthful. People attached magnets (the best ones were imported from Japan) to their legs and backs, or put magnetic pads on their mattresses, in order to experience the benefits of the same magnetic fields they previously had avoided. Magnet therapy even became a new treatment for depression.

Be very afraid!

15 Along with all the big fears have been dozens of lesser ones: saccharin, swine flu, cyclamates, endocrine disrupters, deodorants, electric razors, fluorescent lights, computer terminals, road rage, killer bees—the list goes on and on.

16 In this tradition, the association of cell phones and brain cancer has emerged as a contemporary concern, flourishing despite a lack of conclusive evidence of any direct link. I was drawn to one British study which suggested that cellular radiation actually improved brain function, but it got little publicity. And, of course, the best-documented hazard from cell phones—their use while driving—is largely ignored. (Handheld cell phones are only marginally more dangerous than speaker phones. The real danger comes from using a phone at all while driving.)

17 Fittingly, the century ended with one final, magnificent false fear: Y2K. For years, computer experts predicted a smorgasbord of horrors, ranging from the collapse of the stock market to the crash of airplanes. Some people withdrew their savings, sold their houses and moved to higher ground. In the end, nobody seemed to notice much of anything at all.

18 "I've seen a heap of trouble in my life, and most of it never came to pass," Mark Twain is supposed to have said. At this point in my life, I can only agree. So many fears have turned out

to be untrue or wildly exaggerated that I no longer get so excited about the latest one. Keeping fears in perspective leads me to ignore most of the frightening things I read and hear—or at least to take them with a pillar of salt.

19   For a time I wondered how it would feel to be without these fears and the frantic nagging concerns at the back of my mind. Actually, it feels just fine.

20   I recommend it.

For Discussion:

In your own experience, can you think of any predicted events or problems that were presented as facts that are about to occur but that did not actually occur? What were they? What is your opinion about worrying about such matters? Do you agree with the author, or do you have other ideas about how such scares should be dealt with?

BEFORE YOU READ: What do you know about the evolution-creation debate?

ESSAY #7   **UNINTELLIGENT DESIGN***
Jim Holt

The author writes for a number of print and online magazines, including the *New York Times Magazine.*

1   Recently a school district in rural Pennsylvania officially recognized a supposed alternative to Darwinism. In a one-minute statement read by an administrator, ninth-grade biology students were told that evolution was not a fact and were encouraged to explore a different explanation of life called intelligent design. What is intelligent design? Its proponents maintain that living creatures are just too intricate to have arisen by evolution. Throughout the natural world, they say, there is evidence of deliberate design. Is it not reasonable, then, to infer the existence of an intelligent designer? To evade the charge that intelligent design is a religious theory—creationism dressed up as science—its advocates make no explicit claims about who or what this designer might be. But students will presumably get the desired point. As one Pennsylvania teacher observed: "The first question they will ask is: 'Well, who's the designer? Do you mean God?'"

2   From a scientific perspective, one of the most frustrating things about intelligent design is that (unlike Darwinism) it is virtually impossible to test. Old-fashioned biblical creationism at least risked making some hard factual claims—that the earth was created before the sun, for example. Intelligent design, by contrast, leaves the purposes of the designer wholly mysterious. Presumably any pattern of data in the natural world is consistent with his/her/its existence.

3   But if we can't infer anything about the design from the designer, maybe we can go the other way. What can we tell about the designer from the design? While there is much that is marvelous in nature, there is also much that is flawed, sloppy and downright bizarre. Some nonfunctional oddities, like the peacock's tail or the human male's nipples, might be attributed to a sense of whimsy on the part of the designer. Others just seem grossly inefficient. In mammals, for instance, the recurrent laryngeal nerve does not go directly from the cranium to the larynx, the way any competent engineer would have arranged it. Instead, it extends down the neck to the chest, loops around a lung ligament and then runs back up the neck to the larynx. In a giraffe, that means a 20-foot length of

New York Times Magazine, February 20, 2005, 15–16.

nerve where 1 foot would have done. If this is evidence of design, it would seem to be of the unintelligent variety.

4   Such disregard for economy can be found throughout the natural order. Perhaps 99 percent of the species that have existed have died out. Darwinism has no problem with this, because random variation will inevitably produce both fit and unfit individuals. But what sort of designer would have fashioned creatures so out of sync with their environments that they were doomed to extinction?

5   The gravest imperfections in nature, though, are moral ones. Consider how humans and other animals are intermittently tortured by pain throughout their lives, especially near the end. Our pain mechanism may have been designed to serve as a warning signal to protect our bodies from damage, but in the majority of diseases—cancer, for instance, or coronary thrombosis—the signal comes too late to do much good, and the horrible suffering that ensues is completely useless.

6   And why should the human reproductive system be so shoddily designed? Fewer than one-third of conceptions culminate in live births. The rest end prematurely, either in early gestation or by miscarriage. Nature appears to be an avid abortionist, which ought to trouble Christians who believe in both original sin and the doctrine that a human being equipped with a soul comes into existence at conception. Souls bearing the stain of original sin, we are told, do not merit salvation. That is why, according to traditional theology, unbaptized babies have to languish in limbo for all eternity. Owing to faulty reproductive design, it would seem that the population of limbo must be at least twice that of heaven and hell combined.

7   It is hard to avoid the inference that a designer responsible for such imperfections must have been lacking some divine trait— benevolence or omnipotence or omniscience, or perhaps all three. But what if the designer did not style each species individually? What

if he/she/it merely fashioned the primal cell and then let evolution produce the rest, kinks and all? That is what the biologist and intelligent-design proponent Michael J. Behe has suggested. Behe says that the little protein machines in the cell are too sophisticated to have arisen by mutation—an opinion that his scientific peers overwhelmingly do not share. Whether or not he is correct, his version of intelligent design implies a curious sort of designer, one who seeded the earth with elaborately contrived protein structures and then absconded, leaving the rest to blind chance.

8   One beauty of Darwinism is the intellectual freedom it allows. As the arch-evolutionist Richard Dawkins has observed, "Darwin made it possible to be an intellectually fulfilled atheist." But Darwinism permits you to be an intellectually fulfilled theist, too. That is why Pope John Paul II was comfortable declaring that evolution has been "proven true" and that "truth cannot contradict truth." If God created the universe wholesale rather than retail— endowing it from the start with an evolutionary algorithm that progressively teased complexity out of chaos—then imperfections in nature would be a necessary part of a beautiful process.

9   Of course proponents of intelligent design are careful not to use the G-word, because, as they claim, theirs is not a religiously based theory. So biology students can be forgiven for wondering whether the mysterious designer they're told about might not be the biblical God after all, but rather some very advanced yet mischievous or blundering intelligence—extraterrestrial scientists, say. The important thing, as the Pennsylvania school administrator reminded them, is "to keep an open mind."

For Discussion:

What have you been taught about the cause of life on earth? What options does this author discuss? Which do you think he favors?

> **BEFORE YOU READ:** What do you think: Does an abundance of material possessions contribute more to personal happiness or to unhappiness?

ESSAY #8   WHEN IT'S ALL TOO MUCH
Barry Schwartz

The author teaches psychology at Swarthmore College. This article is adapted from his book *The Paradox of Choice: Why More Is Less,* published in 2004.

1   One day I went to the GAP to buy a pair of jeans. A salesperson asked if she could help. "I want a pair of jeans—32–28," I said. "Do you want them slim fit, easy fit, relaxed fit, baggy or extra-baggy?" she replied. "Do you want them stonewashed, acid-washed or distressed? Do you want them button-fly or zipper-fly? Do you want them faded or regular?"

2   I was stunned. A moment or two later, I sputtered out something like, "I just want regular jeans. You know, the kind that used to be the only kind."

3   She pointed me in the right direction. The trouble was that with all these options available to me now, I was no longer sure that "regular" jeans were what I wanted. Perhaps the easy fit or the relaxed fit would be more comfortable. So I tried on all the pants and scrutinized myself in a mirror. Whereas very little was riding on my decision, I was now convinced that one of these options had to be right for me, and I was determined to figure it out.

4   The jeans I chose turned out to be just fine, but it occurred to me that buying a pair of pants should not be a daylong project. Purchasing jeans was once a five minute affair, now it was a complex decision.

5   Buying jeans is a trivial matter, but it is an example of a much larger issue. When people have no choice, life can be almost unbearable. As the number of choices increases, the autonomy, control and liberation this variety brings can be powerful and positive.

6   But if the number of choices keeps growing, negative effects start to appear. As choices grow further, the negatives can escalate until we become overloaded. At this point, choice no longer liberates us; it might even be said to tyrannize.

The Explosion of Choices

7   Modern life has provided a huge array of products to choose from. Just walk into any large supermarket or drugstore looking for hair-care products, and you'll likely be confronted with more than 360 types of shampoo, conditioner and mousse. Need a painkiller? There are 80 options. How about toothpaste? You have 40 types to pick from.

8   In addition, we now have to make choices in areas of life in which we used to have few or no options. We have to decide which telephone service providers and retirement pension plans are the best for us. Modern cosmetic surgery allows us to change virtually any aspect of our appearance. An explosion of tolerance for "alternative" lifestyles has given us real choices about whether to be monogamous, whether (and when) to marry, whether

Parade, January 4, 2005, 4–5.

(and when) to have kids and even whether to have intimate relations with partners of the same or the opposite sex (or both).

More Choices . . . More Happiness?

9 It seems a simple matter of logic that increased choice improves well-being. But, in fact, the opposite is true. Respected social scientists such as psychologist David G. Myers and political scientist Robert E. Lane tell us that increased choice and increased affluence have, in fact, been accompanied by decreased well-being.

10 The American "happiness quotient" has been going gently but consistently downhill for more than a generation. In the last 30 years—a time of great prosperity—the proportion of the population describing itself as "very happy" has declined. The decline was about 5%. This might not seem like much, but 5% translates into about 14 million Americans.

11 Not only that, but today, as a society, more Americans than ever are clinically depressed. By some estimates (for example, those of psychologist Martin Seligman in his book *Learned Optimism*), depression in the year 2000 was about 10 times as likely as it was in 1900.

12 Of course, no one believes that a single factor explains this. But accumulating evidence from psychological research indicates that the explosion of choice plays an important role. It seems that as we become freer to pursue and do whatever we want, we get less and less happy.

The More We Have, the More We Want

13 Increases in our expectations are partly to blame. The more we are allowed to be the masters of our fates, the more we expect to be. We believe we should be able to find work that is exciting, socially valuable and remunerative. We expect spouses who are sexually, emotionally and intellectually stimulating. Our children should be beautiful, smart, affectionate,

obedient and independent. And everything we buy is supposed to be the best of its kind.

14 With all the choices available, we may believe we should never have to settle for things that are just "good enough." Those who accept only the best, I call maximizers. In my research, I've found that maximizers are less happy, less optimistic and more depressed. At the very least, maximizing behavior can lead to dissatisfaction—and, sometimes, paralysis.

15 I have a friend who makes going out to dinner a nightmare. He struggles to select a dish and changes his mind repeatedly as his companions sit and stew. And I see my students agonize about which of many paths to follow when they graduate. Many of them are looking for jobs that will give them everything, and they expect to find them.

Only Ourselves to Blame

16 We are told we are now in the driver's seat when it comes to what happens in our lives. If we fail, it's our own fault. This might sound only fair, but the pressure we are put under can be enormous—especially in crucial areas of our lives such as medical care.

17 For example, people in one study were asked whether, if they got cancer, they would want to be in charge of their treatment decisions; 65% said yes. Unless, however, they actually had cancer. Then only 12% said yes. People with cancer have experienced the awesome psychological consequences of being responsible for a life-and-death decision, and they don't want that responsibility.

18 Unattainable expectations, plus a tendency to blame ourselves for our failures, make a lethal combination.

19 This is the paradox: Here we are, living at the pinnacle of human possibility, awash in material abundance. We get what we say we want, only to discover that it doesn't satisfy us. The success of 21st-century life turns out to be bittersweet. And I believe that a significant contributing factor is the overabundance of choice.

For Discussion:

Are you easily satisfied with what you have, or are you always thinking about trying to accomplish or get more? What would you need in material possessions to make you happy? Has this article changed your opinions on this subject of choice in any way?

BEFORE YOU READ: How would you define "war casualties" in the context of the wars in Iraq and Afganistan?

ESSAY #9   WAR CASUALTY TOTAL JUMPS, BUT IS REVISED AFTER ARTICLE*

Denise Grady

The author is a reporter for the science news department of the *New York Times*. She writes articles about medicine and biology.

1   For the last few months, anyone who consulted the veterans Affairs Department's Web site to learn how many American troops had been wounded in Iraq and Afghanistan would have found this number: 50,508.

2   But on Jan. 10, without explanation, the figure plummeted to 21,649.†

3   Which number is correct? The answer depends on a larger question, the definition of *wounded*. If the term includes combat or "hostile" injuries inflicted by the enemy, the definition the Pentagon uses, the smaller number would be right.

4   But if it also applies to injuries from accidents like vehicle crashes and to mental and physical illnesses that developed in the war zone, the meaning that veterans' groups favor, 50,508 would be accurate.

5   A spokesman for the veterans' department, Matt Burns, said the change in the count was made simply to correct an error. Mr. Burns said the department posted the higher figure by mistake in November, when an employee who was updating the site inadvertently added noncombat injuries listed by the Defense Department.

6   The previous total on the Web site was 18,586, strictly for combat injuries. Apparently, no one noticed the sudden leap.

7   The 50,508 figure caught the attention of the Pentagon when Linda Bilmes of Harvard mentioned it in an opinion article on Jan. 5 in *The Los Angeles Times*. A few days later, said Ms. Bilmes, who teaches public finance, she had a call from Dr. William Winkenwerder Jr., assistant secretary of defense for health affairs, challenging the number.

8   Ms. Bilmes explained that she had used the government tally, the one on the "America's Wars" page of the veterans' department Web site. She faxed him a copy.

9   A few days later, the number on the Web site was changed.

10   A spokeswoman for Dr. Winkenwerder confirmed that he had called the veterans' department to have the figure corrected, that the worker had misunderstood the Defense Department figures.

New York Times, January 30, 2007, A17.

†A year after this article was written, the official figure of individuals categorized as hostile casualties was 28,870.

11   For her purposes, Ms. Bilmes said, the higher figure was the relevant one because she was writing about the future demands that wounded veterans would place on the veterans' health care system. Many of the veterans would be treated in the system regardless of whether they had been injured in combat or in vehicle crashes.

12   About 1.4 million troops have served in Iraq or Afghanistan, and more than 205,000 have sought care from the veterans' agency, according to the government. Of those, more than 73,000 sought treatment for mental problems like post-traumatic stress disorder.

13   No one disputes that more than 50,000 troops have been injured in Iraq and Afghanistan or that nonhostile injuries can be serious. Of the more than 3,000 deaths that have occurred, 600 have been listed as nonhostile.*

14   The Pentagon generally directs reporters to www.defenselink.mil, which lists counts of the wounded and dead. The deaths are divided into hostile and nonhostile, but the injuries include just those "wounded in action."

15   Another site on the Web, http:// siadapp.dior.whs.mil/personnel/CASUALTY/ castop.htm, shows diseases and nonhostile injuries. It is the source of the higher counts.

16   "The government keeps two sets of books," said Paul Sullivan, director of research and analysis for Veterans of America. Until last March, Mr. Sullivan was a project manager in the Veterans Affairs Department who monitored the use of disability benefits by Afghanistan, gulf war and Iraq veterans.

17   He suggested that the differing numbers might be cleared up by a bill that has been introduced in the Senate to improve the collection of health information on Afghanistan and Iraq veterans.

For Discussion:

What is the issue in this article? How does definition change the issue? How do you think war injuries from the wars in Afganistan and Iraq should be defined, counted, and correctly reported? Who would be benefited by your solution? Who would be burdened?

*A year after this article was written, the official figure for hostile war deaths was more than 4,000.

BEFORE YOU READ: What are some of the little things that annoy you? Do you ever try to do anything about them?

ESSAY #10   **NO NEED TO STEW: A FEW TIPS TO COPE WITH LIFE'S ANNOYANCES***

Ian Urbina

The author is an editor at *Middle East Report,* which is based at the Middle East Research and Information Project (MERIP) in Washington, DC.

1   When Seth Shepsle goes to Starbucks, he orders a "medium" because "grande"— as the coffee company calls the size, the one between big and small—annoys him.

New York Times, March 15, 2005, A1, A24.

2   Meg Daniel presses zero whenever she hears a computerized operator on the telephone so that she can talk to a real person. "Just because they want a computer to handle me doesn't mean I have to play along," she said.

3   When subscription cards fall from magazines Andrew Kirk is reading, he stacks them in a pile at the corner of his desk. At the end of each month, he puts them in the mail but leaves them blank so that the advertiser is forced to pay the business reply postage without gaining a new subscriber.

4   Life can involve big hardships, like being fired or smashing up your car. There is only so much you can do about them. But far more prevalent—and perhaps in the long run just as insidious—are life's many little annoyances.

5   These, you can do something about.

6   To examine the little weapons people use for everyday survival is to be given a free guidebook on getting by, created by the millions who feel that they must. It is a case study in human inventiveness, with occasional juvenile and petty passages, but tons of tips for others who have struggled with the grande-versus-medium conundrum. And the originators of these tips are happy to share them.

7   "They're an integral part of how people cope," said Prof. James C. Scott, who teaches anthropology and political science at Yale University, and the author of *Weapons of the Weak,* about the feigned ignorance, foot-dragging and other techniques Malaysian peasants used to avoid cooperating with the arrival of new technology in the 1970's. "All societies have them, but they're successful only to the extent that they avoid open confrontation."

8   The slow driver in fast traffic, the shopper with 50 coupons at the front of the check-out line and the telemarketer calling at dinner all inflict life's thousand little lashes. But some see these infractions as precious opportunities, rare chances for retribution in the face of forces beyond our control.

9   Wesley A. Williams spent more than a year exacting his revenge against junk mailers. When signing up for a no-junk-mail list failed to stem the flow, he resorted to writing at the top of each unwanted item: "Not at this address. Return to sender." But the mail kept coming because the envelopes had "or current resident" on them, obligating mail carriers to deliver it, he said.

10   Next, he began stuffing the mail back into the "business reply" envelope and sending it back so that the mailer would have to pay the postage. "That wasn't exacting a heavy enough cost from them for bothering me," said Mr. Williams, 35, a middle school science teacher who lives in Melrose, N.Y., near Albany.

11   After checking with a postal clerk about the legality of stepping up his efforts, he began cutting up magazines, heavy bond paper, and small strips of sheet metal and stuffing them into the business reply envelopes that came with the junk packages.

12   "You wouldn't believe how heavy I got some of these envelopes to weigh," said Mr. Williams, who added that he saw an immediate drop in the amount of arriving junk mail. A spokesman for the United States Postal Service, Gerald McKiernan, said that Mr. Williams's actions sounded legal, as long as the envelope was properly sealed.

13   Sometimes, small acts of rebellion offer big doses of relief.

14   "I've come to realize that I'm almost addicted to the sick little pleasure I get from lashing out at these things," said Mr. Kirk, 24, a freelance writer from Brooklyn who collects and returns magazine inserts. When ordering a pizza from Domino's, Mr. Kirk says he always requests a "small," knowing that he will be corrected and told that medium is the smallest available size. "It makes me feel better to point out that

their word games aren't fooling anyone," he said.

15   The Internet offers a booming trade to help with this type of annoyance-fighting behavior. For example, shared passwords to free Web sites are available at www.bugmenot.com to help people avoid dealing with long registration forms. To coexist with loud cellphone talkers, the Web offers handheld jammers that, although illegal in the United States, can block all signals within a 45-foot radius.

16   Mitch Altman, a 48-year-old inventor living in San Francisco, said that in the last three months he has sold about 30,000 of his key-chain-size zappers called TV-B-Gone, which can be used discreetly to switch off televisions in public places. "When you go to a restaurant to talk with friends, why should you have to deal with the distraction of a ceiling-mounted television?" Mr. Altman said.

17   Some Web sites specialize in arming people against online annoyances. The site www.slashdot.org posted the name and the mailing address of one of the worst known spammers, encouraging people to sign the spammer up for catalogs and other junk mail to be sent to the spammer's home. Mr. McKiernan of the Postal Service said that this tactic also appeared to be legal, but might constitute harassment.

18   Some groups are more frustrated than others. In 2002, Harris Interactive, a market research group based in Rochester, conducted a phone survey called the Daily Hassle Scale that asked 1,010 people to rank the aggravations they faced in a typical day. The survey found that poor people and African-Americans suffer the most stress from the everyday annoyances such as noisy neighbors, telemarketers and pressure at work, but it did not explain why.

19   Professor Scott said that his own habit was to write "England" rather than "United Kingdom" on letters he sends to his British friends. He described this as his way of disregarding British claims to Wales and Scotland.

20   "As a tactic, it doesn't amount to much except a way to provide a tiny and private sense of satisfaction," he said. "But that's something."

For Discussion:

What do you remember most vividly from this essay? Why do you think it struck you? What is the final effect of reading so many examples? What is the main point that they exemplify?

C. Group Work: Reading and Analyzing Claims and Subclaims

The following essay uses several types of claims and associated purposes. One type of claim, however, predominates in the essay, and the other claims support and develop it. First, divide the essay into "chunks" by drawing a line across the page each time the author changes the type of claim and purpose. Label the type of claim and predominant purpose of each chunk (*example:* fact, to establish the facts). Then underline the predominant claim and describe the purpose of the essay. Speculate about the reasons the author had for placing the parts of this essay in this particular order. Discuss the relationship between the parts.

Much argument writing combines claims in this way, and you may want to study the pattern of claims used here as a possible model for one of your own argument papers.

> **BEFORE YOU READ:** Do you know any individuals who have returned home to live with their parents after they had been gone for a time? What were the circumstances?

ESSAY #11   BRINGING UP ADULTOLESCENTS*

Peg Tyre

Tyre, a former CNN reporter, now writes freelance articles about various public issues.

1   When Silvia Geraci goes out to dinner with friends, she has a flash of anxiety when the check comes. She can pay her share—her parents give her enough money to cover all her expenses. It's just that others in her circle make their own money now. "I know I haven't earned what I have. It's been given to me," says Geraci, 22, who returned to her childhood home in suburban New York after graduating from college last year. "It's like I'm stuck in an in-between spot. Sometimes I wonder if I'm getting left behind." Poised on the brink of what should be a bright future, Geraci and millions like her face a thoroughly modern truth: it's hard to feel like a Master of the Universe when you're sleeping in your old twin bed.

2   Whether it's reconverting the guest room back into a bedroom, paying for graduate school, writing a blizzard of small checks to cover rent and health-insurance premiums or acting as career counselors, parents across the country are trying to provide their twentysomethings with the tools they'll need to be self-sufficient—someday. In the process, they have created a whole new breed of child—the adultolescent.

3   For their part, these overgrown kids seem content to enjoy the protection of their parents as they drift from adolescence to early adulthood. Relying on your folks to light the shadowy path to the future has become so accepted that even the ultimate loser move—returning home to live with your parents—has lost its stigma. According to the 2000 Census, nearly 4 million people between the ages of 25 and 34 live with their parents. And there are signs that even more moms and dads will be welcoming their not-so-little-ones back home. Last week, in an online survey by MonsterTRAK.com, a job-search firm, 60 percent of college students reported that they planned to live at home after graduation—and 21 percent said they planned to remain there for more than a year.

4   Unlike their counterparts in the early '90s, adultolescents aren't demoralized slackers lining up for the bathroom with their longing-to-be-empty-nester parents. Iris and Andrew Aronson, two doctors in Chicago, were happy when their daughter, Elena, 24, a Smith graduate, got a modest-paying job and moved back home last year. It seemed a natural extension of their parenting philosophy—make the children feel secure enough and they'll eventually strike out on their own. "When she was an infant, the so-called experts said letting babies cry themselves to sleep was the only way to teach them to sleep independent of their mother," says Iris. "But I never did that either." Come fall,

*_Newsweek_, March 25, 2002, 38–40.

211

Elena is heading off to graduate school. Her sister, who will graduate from Stanford University this spring, is moving in. Living at home works, Elena explains, because she knows she's leaving. "Otherwise, it'll feel too much like high school," says Elena. "As it is, sometimes I look around and think, 'OK, now it's time to start my homework.'"

5   Most adultolescents no longer hope, or even desire, to hit the traditional benchmarks of independence—marriage, kids, owning a home, financial autonomy—in the years following college. The average age for a first marriage is now 26, four years later than it was in 1970, and childbearing is often postponed for a decade or more after that. Jobs are scarce, and increasingly, high-paying careers require a graduate degree. The decades-long run-up in the housing market has made a starter home a pipe dream for most people under 30. "The conveyor belt that transported adolescents into adulthood has broken down," says Dr. Frank Furstenberg, who heads up a $3.4 million project by the MacArthur Foundation studying the adultolescent phenomenon.

6   Beyond the economic realities, there are some complicated psychological bonds that keep able-bodied college graduates on their parents' payroll. Unlike the Woodstock generation, this current crop of twentysomethings aren't building their adult identity in reaction to their parents' way of life. In the 1960's, kids crowed about not trusting anyone over 30; these days, they can't live without them. "We are seeing a closer relationship between generations than we have seen since World War II," says University of Maryland psychologist Jeffrey Jensen Arnett. "These young people genuinely like and respect their parents."

7   To some, all this support and protection—known as "scaffolding" among the experts—looks like an insidious form of codependence. Psychiatrist Alvin Rosenfeld says these are the same hyperinvolved parents who got minivan fatigue from ferrying their kids to extracurricular activities and turned college admission into a competitive sport. "They've convinced themselves they know how to lead a good life, and they want to get that for their kids, no matter what," says Rosenfeld.

8   By the time those children reach their 20s, says market researcher Neil Howe, their desires for the future are often indistinguishable from the desires of their parents. "The Me Generation," says Howe, "has simply turned into the Mini-Me Generation."

9   Trying to guarantee your children the Good Life, though, can sometimes backfire. A few years ago, Janice Charlton of Philadelphia pressured her daughter, Mary, then 26, to get a master's degree, even agreeing to cosign two $17,000 school loans if she did. Mary dropped out, Janice says, and the loans went into default. "I'm sorry I ever suggested it," says Janice. "We're still close but it's a sticky issue between us."

10   Many parents say they're simply ensuring that their kids have an edge in an increasingly competitive world. When Tom D'Agnes's daughter, Heather, 26, told him she was thinking about graduate school, D'Agnes, 52, flew from their home in Hawaii to San Francisco to help her find one. He edited the essay section of her application and vetted her letters of recommendation, too. While Tom's wife, Leona, worried about creating a "dependency mentality," Tom was adamant about giving his daughter a leg up.

11   Parents aren't waiting to get involved. Campus career counselors report being flooded with calls from parents anxious to participate in their college senior's job search. Last fall the U.S. Navy began

sending letters describing their programs to potential recruits—and their parents. "Parents are becoming actively involved in the career decisions of their children," says Cmdr. Steven Lowry, public-affairs officer for Navy recruiting. "We don't recruit the individual anymore. We recruit the whole family."

12   The steady flow of cash from one generation of active consumers to another has marketers salivating. These twenty-somethings are adventuresome, will try new products and have a hefty amount of discretionary money. "They're willing to spend it on computers and big-screen TVs, travel and sports cars, things that other generations would consider frivolous," says David Morrison, whose firm, Twentysomething Inc., probes adultolescents for companies like Coca-Cola and Nokia.

13   Jimmy Finn, 24, a paralegal at the Manhattan-based law firm of Sullivan & Cromwell, made the most of his $66,000 annual income by moving back to his childhood home in nearby Staten Island. While his other friends paid exorbitant rents, Finn bought a new car and plane tickets to Florida so he could see his girl-friend on the weekends. He had ample spending money for restaurants and cabs, and began paying down his student loans. "New York is a great young person's city but you can't beat home for the meals," says Finn.

14   With adultolescents all but begging for years of support after college, many parents admit they're not sure when a safety net becomes a suffocating blanket. "I've seen parents willing to destroy themselves financially," says financial planner Bill Mahoney of Oxford, Mass. "They're giving their college graduates $20,000, $30,000, even $40,000—money they should be plowing into retirement." And it might only buy them added years of frustration. Psychiatrists say it's tough to convince a parent that self-sufficiency is the one thing they can't give their children.

15   No matter how loving the parent-child bond, parents inevitably heave a sigh of relief when their adult kids finally start paying their own way. Seven months ago, when Finn's paralegal job moved to Washington, D.C., he left home and got an apartment there. The transition, he said, was hard on his mother, Margie. Mom, though, reports that she's doing just fine. She's stopped making plates of ziti and meatballs for her boy and has more time for her friends. "The idea all along was that he should be self-sufficient," she says. It just took a little while.

For Discussion:

This article will raise most of the claim questions in your mind: What are adultolescents? Do they really exist? What has caused this situation? How good or bad is it? What should we do about it? The author deals with all these questions. Which of these questions, however, seems to dominate the article? What are your experiences with the trend described in this article? Compare your experiences with those of your classmates.

D. Group Work and Class Discussion: Analyzing Types of Claims in Visual Argument

Create five groups, as you did for Exercise A, except with this assignment have each group look at all of the five images that follow, read the remarks that accompany them, and then assign each of them to one of the five claim categories listed here. The images themselves follow a different order from the list of categories, so your objective is to match each visual with one of the categories. Discuss the results as a class.

a. This visual primarily establishes fact. What is the fact? How convinced are you by this image?

b. This visual shows cause and effect. What is the cause? What is the effect? Do you accept the cause–effect relationship depicted here? Why or why not?

c. This visual is mainly about establishing value. What is being evaluated? Is the value assigned to it positive or negative? Do you agree or disagree? Why or why not?

d. This visual helps define a concept in the essay that appears on pages 207–208 of this chapter. In fact, it accompanied the essay originally and served as part of the proof. What does this photo define, and how is it related to the definition problem described in the essay?

e. This visual provides a possible solution for a problem. What is the problem, and what is the solution?

**Image 1:
War Casualties.**

This image originally accompanied the essay on pages 207–208. Consider it in the context of the essay. Here is the information that accompanies the opening of a new rehabilitation center in San Antonio, Texas. It is "designed to treat the growing number of severely wounded veterans of the Iraq war, some of whom attended the ceremony."

Image 2:
Lunch at the United States–Mexico Border Fence.

Mireya Leal shares a picnic lunch through the U.S.–Mexico border fence with her husband Raymundo Orozco, near Tijuana, Mexico. (AP)

This photograph appears in an Associated Press online article in the *Banderas News*, a Puerto Vallarta, Mexico, Web site. The title of the article is "Mexican, U.S. Mayors Blast Border Fence." The idea of a border fence, as this article makes clear, is unpopular in Mexico. A section of the fence already in place in California is depicted in this photograph. Consider the caption and decide what type of claim it makes. This image adds a Mexican perspective to the exploratory visual essay "Walling Off Your Enemies: The Long View," on page 132.

Image 3:
The Rhône Glacier.

Retreat *A drawing on an 1870 postcard shows the Rhône Glacier sweeping into Gletsch, Switzerland; in 2005 the glacier could hardly be seen.*

The small postcard that is superimposed on the larger photograph in this image are both pictures of the same place in Switzerland, only the pictures are taken at different times. What is the issue? Consider the caption above and decide what type of claim is being made?

**Image 4:
Liberate Your
Cool.**

What type of claim
is established by this
advertisement for a
scanner? What is the
claim? How effective
is this claim, in your
opinion?

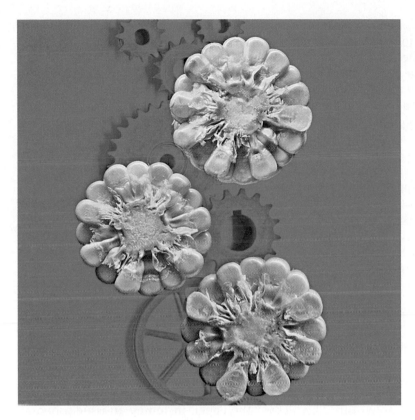

Image 5:
Corn Power.

Only two words accompany this image (Corn Power), but they should be enough to help you decide what type of claim is being made. What is the issue? What is the claim? What type of claim is it?

E. Writing Assignment: Types of Claims

Write a 250- to 300-word paper that is organized around a single type of claim. Use the following claims about campus issues as starter sentences for your paper. Before you write, spend a few minutes with classmates to brainstorm some ideas for each of the papers. If you need more information, go to the Financial Aid Office for topic *a*, the Office of Student Affairs for topics *b* or *d*, to the Registrar's Office for topic *e*, and the Office of Institutional Studies or the Registrar for topic *c*. You might also interview students and faculty or consult the Internet. Use some of the ideas about organizational patterns and support described in this chapter to help you think about and develop your ideas.

a. Is it true? Does it exist? *Claim of fact:* <u>Financial aid for students (is or is not) readily available on our campus</u>.

   Hint: Try a claim with reasons (or topical order) pattern of organization. Add facts, statistics, and real examples.

b. How should we define it? *Claim of definition:* <u>A dangerous level of alcohol consumption is not defined by everyone in exactly the same way</u>.
   Hint: Explain the controversy over what is considered a dangerous level. Quote an authoritative source that defines the term "dangerous level." Compare definitions of dangerous and not-dangerous levels and use examples and statistics as support.

c. What caused it? What are the effects? *Claim of cause:* <u>Various causes contribute to the student dropout problem in colleges</u>.
Hint: Describe the major causes for students leaving college before they graduate. Use factual data, including statistics and examples as support. Describe the effects on the students themselves.

d. Is it good or bad? *Claim of value:* <u>Student organizations (do or do not) contribute significant positive value to the college experience</u>.
Hint: Make a list of the positive values that student organizations provide students, or make a list of negative values that show students should not join these organizations. Apply them to one or more student organizations. Appeal to what most students would value or want.

e. What is the problem and what should we do to solve it? *Claim of policy:* <u>Students do not always know their academic standing in all of their courses during a semester, and measures should (or should not) be taken to correct this lack of information</u>.
Hint: Try a problem–solution pattern of organization. Use examples, comparisons, quotes from authorities, and appeals to values and motives.

F. Prewriting: Using the Claim Questions to Generate Ideas for a Position Paper

The claim questions can be used to invent ideas for any argument paper. If, however, you are gathering ideas for the assignment for the "Position Paper Based on 'The Reader'" (Exercise F in Chapter 8), you may want to use the claim questions to generate additional material for the paper. (You may have already completed other prewriting activities for the paper, including an issue proposal, Chapter 1, Exercise H; summary-response papers, Chapter 4, Exercise C; an exploratory paper, Chapter 4, Exercise G; and a Toulmin analysis, Chapter 5, Exercise E.) Now, write a tentative claim based on the position you favored in your exploratory paper and use the claim questions to refine or revise this claim.

1. Write your issue in the form of an issue question. *Example:* Is parking a problem on campus?

2. Apply the claim questions to the issue question and write a paragraph in response to each question.

   a. ***Fact:*** Did it happen? Does it exist?
   b. ***Definition:*** What is it? How can we define it?
   c. ***Cause:*** What caused it? What are the effects?
   d. ***Value:*** Is it good or bad? What criteria will help us decide?
   e. ***Policy:*** What should we do about it? What should be our future course of action?

3. Read the paragraphs you have written, and select the one that interests you the most and that also seems most promising as the focus for your paper. Now look at your tentative claim and revise it, if necessary, to bring it in line with your new purpose and focus. You may also, of course, use information from the other paragraphs you have written to develop subclaims and support for your paper. Save what you have written in a folder or in your open computer file. You will use it later when you plan and write your position paper.

CHAPTER 7

Types of Proof

Y ou learned in Chapter 5 that the claim, the support, and the warrants are the three parts that are present in any argument. Chapter 6 helped you understand claims. This chapter will help you understand the support and warrants that provide proofs for a claim. You will be introduced first to the different types of proof, then to the language and style associated with each of them. Chapter 8 will alert you to some of the fallacies or pseudoproofs that can occur in argument.

As you understand and begin to work with the proofs, you will discover that they are not uniform patterns that are obvious and easy to recognize. Indeed, slippery and imperfect as they are, they simply represent an attempt to describe what goes on in the real world of argument and in the minds of writers and readers of argument. Understanding them can put you closer to an author, permitting you better to understand how that individual thought about, interpreted, and developed a particular subject. When you switch roles and become the author yourself, your knowledge of what can happen in argument helps you develop your own thoughts and effective arguments.

The Traditional Categories of Proof

The traditional categories of proof, like much of our most fundamental argument theory, were first articulated by classical theorists, and they are still useful for describing what goes on in real-world argument today. Recall from Chapter 5 that, in the *Rhetoric,* Aristotle said that an arguer must state a claim (or a proposition) and prove it. He also went into detail about the broad categories of proof that can be employed to establish the probability of a claim. Aristotle's categories of proof remain useful because they accurately describe what classical arguers did then and what modern arguers still do and because they have become such an accepted part of our intellectual heritage that, like generations before us, we learn these methods and use them to observe, think about, and interpret reality. Aristotle's ideas and observations still provide accurate descriptions of what goes on in argument.

Aristotle distinguishes between proofs that can be produced and laid on the table, so to speak, like a murder weapon, fingerprints, or a written contract, and proofs that are invented and represent the creative thinking and insights of clever and intelligent people.

Aristotle divides this second category of proof into three subcategories: proofs that appeal to logic and reason, proofs that establish the credibility of the source, and proofs that appeal to the emotions. The Greek words used to refer to the proofs are *logos* (logic), *ethos* (credibility), and *pathos* (emotion).

Logical proof appeals to the audience's reason, understanding, and common sense. It is consistent with what people know and believe, and it gives fresh insight and ideas about issues. As proof, it relies mainly on such support as reasoned opinion and factual data as well as on warrants that suggest the soundness and truth of such support. Aristotle declared that logical proof is the most important kind of proof in argument, and most modern theorists agree with him. Richard M. Weaver, a well-known modern rhetorician, for example, says that argument has its primary basis in reasoning and that it appeals primarily to the rational part of humans. Logical proof, he says, provides the "plot" of argument.[1] The other two types of proof are also present and important, however.

Proof that establishes ethos appeals to the audience's impressions, opinions, and judgments about the individual stating the argument. An arguer who demonstrates competence, good character, fair-mindedness, and goodwill toward the audience is more convincing than the arguer who lacks these qualities. Those who project such favorable qualities to an audience have established good *ethos.* Audiences are more likely to trust and believe individuals with good *ethos* than those without it. At times, arguers also need to establish the *ethos* of the experts whom they quote in their arguments. They usually accomplish this purpose by providing information about these authorities so that audiences will appreciate their mastery or expertise and consequently be more willing to accept what they say.

Emotional proof is used to appeal to and arouse the feelings of the audience. The audience's feelings are aroused primarily through emotional language, examples, personal narratives, and vivid descriptions of events that contain emotional elements and that provoke strong feelings in other people. Emotional proof is appropriate in an argument when it is used to develop the claim and when it contributes to the sense of logical conviction and agreement that are argument's intended outcomes. A well-reasoned set of logical proofs contributes to such outcomes. Emotion contributes as well to the strength of the acceptance of a logical conclusion. Imagine, for example, an argument in favor of increasing taxes to build housing for homeless people. The logical argument would describe reasons for these taxes, methods for levying them, and recommendations for spending them. The argument would be strengthened, however, by one or more vivid and emotional examples of homeless people who lead miserable lives.

---

[1]Richard M. Weaver, "Language Is Sermonic," in Richard L. Johannesen, ed., *Contemporary Theories of Rhetoric: Selected Readings* (New York: Harper & Row, 1971), 163–79.

Visual argument also relies on these same proofs to strengthen its claims; however, visuals are often more powerful than words because they communicate so quickly. Take a look at the Dow Chemical Company advertisement in Figure 7.1 ■ below. This ad relies on all three types of proof to make the audience believe the claim that this company is more interested in people all over the world than it is in mere chemistry and chemicals. Examine the ad, read the next paragraph, and answer the questions in the margin next to the ad for yourself.

The producers and authors of the ad expect you to link three elements: the *logical* chemical symbol in the ad; the *emotionally appealing* young Tibetan boy whom they describe as having "one of the best minds on the planet"; and the *value statements* that help create the company's *ethos*—"When you look at the world through the eyes of the Human Element, anything is possible" and "Our bond with the Human Element. It is the chemistry of life on Earth. And that's what the Dow Chemical Company is all about." Now think about the *warrant*. When you have considered all of the proof, you might state the warrant this way: of course this boy can learn chemistry and become a successful chemist, if he is given the opportunity and the support. The ad also suggests that because the company values people, Dow Chemical will encourage and possibly provide that support. The *backing* for the warrant assumes that many viewers first looking at the picture of this boy would think that because of his dress and where he lives, he is unlikely to receive a good science education and become a scientist. The proofs and the warrant challenge that initial assumption. The producers and

Figure 7.1

Analyze the proofs used in this Dow Chemical Company advertisement. First, look at the ad itself and then, since the words in the ad are too small to read here, read instead the explanation and analysis of this ad in the accompanying paragraphs on this page and the next. Now comment on the use of *logos, ethos,* and *pathos* in this ad. How do they work together to make the claim? How convincing is this ad? Why do you think so?

authors of the ad expect the audience to conclude that the company has humanitarian goals and is supportive of disadvantaged people in the world.

The next three sections will introduce you to seven types of logical proof, one type of proof that builds *ethos,* and two types of emotional proof. All are commonly used in argument. The number and variety of logical proofs is greater because logical thinking dominates and provides the "plot" for most argument. However, most arguments rely on a variety of proofs because offering several types of proof usually makes a stronger argument than relying on only one.

Each type of proof will be explained according to the following format so that you can understand each kind as quickly and easily as possible.[2]

> ***Examples:*** Examples follow a brief general description of each proof.
>
> ***Claim and support:*** Describes what to look for on the printed page, that is, what types of support you can expect to find, and how to find the claim.
>
> ***Warrant:*** Identifies what you are expected to assume to make logical connections between the support and the claim. The warrants associated with types of proof suggest specific ways of thinking about support and its function in an argument.
>
> ***Tests of validity:*** *Validity* in argument is measured by using your knowledge of the structure of argument and its components and by what you might term a "questioning receptivity" to argumentation. This is another way of describing the critical reading or listening method that requires that you probe whether or not a proof (analogy, statistic, etc.) or argument itself is sound, genuine, effective, authoritative, and believable. You are provided with questions to ask to help you test the reliability and validity of the proof. These questions focus your attention on the support and on the warrant and on how they do or do not function together as effective proof. The questions can also help you locate the weaknesses in an argument, which will help you plan rebuttal and formulate argument of your own.

In Exercise B at the end of the chapter, you will have the opportunity to identify and analyze the proofs in a short essay so that you can see how they operate in written argument. Other exercises show you how to use the proofs in your own writing.

Types of Logical Proof: *Logos*

Logical proofs (also called substantive proofs) include facts, reasons, and opinions that are based on reality. Such proofs rely on factual information, statistics, and accounts of actual events, past and present. The support used in logical proof is real and drawn from experience. Logical (or substantive) warrants guarantee the

---

[2]In this chapter I have drawn on some of Wayne Brockriede and Douglas Ehninger's ideas in "Toulmin on Argument: An Interpretation and Application," *Quarterly Journal of Speech* 46 (1969): 44–53. I have expanded and adapted these authors' analysis of proofs to make it apply to the reading and writing of argument as explained in this book.

reliability and relevance of this support. Logical proofs represent common ways of thinking about and perceiving relationships among the events and data of the real world and offer those ideas and relationships as support for a line of argument.

A MNEMONIC DEVICE

It is helpful to be able to recall easily the full range of logical proofs either when you are reading argument or when you are developing an argument so that you can use them to your advantage. Figure 7.2 ■ provides a mnemonic device that will help you remember them. It shows the first letter of each proof arranged to make a nonsense word, SICDADS, and a picture to help you remember it. You can run through this mnemonic mentally when you are thinking about ways to develop the ideas in a paper or other format for your argument.

Sign
Induction
Cause
Deduction
Analogies (historical, literal, figurative)
Definition
Statistics

"SICDADS" refuted by logical proof.

Figure 7.2 *The Seven Logical Proofs: Their Initials Spell Out SICDADS.*

223

Let us now consider the seven logical proofs in the order provided by the mnemonic SICDADS.

ARGUMENT FROM SIGN

A *specific visible sign* is sometimes used to prove a claim. A sign can be used to prove with certainty: someone breaks out in chickenpox, and the claim, based on that certain sign, is that the person has chickenpox. A sign also can be used to prove the probability of a claim: a race riot, someone argues, is probably a sign of the claim that people think they are treated unfairly. On the other hand, the sign may turn out to be a pseudoproof, the "proof" of a false claim: a child asks, "Why should I believe in Santa Claus?" and the parent answers, "Look at all the toys under the tree that weren't there yesterday." That support is used as a sign for the claim that Santa Claus exists.

Example of Sign

An example of an argument from sign used in the essay "Undocumented, Indispensable" by Anna Quindlen (page 247) appears on the next page. Would you say that the claim based on this sign is a certain or a probable claim?

> *Claim:* The rumbling sounds caused by thousands of people marching and carrying signs that describe why they march is a sign of public unrest.
> *Support (sign):* There is rumbling in San Francisco caused by thousands of people who are marching and carrying signs.
> *Warrant:* This march indicates that there is public unrest in San Francisco.

Claim and Support

Look for visible clues, symptoms, and occurrences that are explained as obvious and clear signs of a certain belief or state of affairs. Look for the conclusion or claim that is made on the basis of these signs.

Sign Warrants

You are expected to assume that the sign is actually a sign of what the author claims it to be.

Tests of Validity

Is this really a sign of what the author claims it to be? Is there another explanation for the sign?

ARGUMENT FROM INDUCTION

Inductive argument provides a number of examples and draws a claim, in the form of a conclusion, from them. The audience is expected to accept the group of examples as adequate and accurate enough to make the inductive leap to the claim. Inductive argument is also called argument from generalization or argument from example because the claim is a generalization made on the basis of the examples. To help you remember the special features of inductive argument, learn its prefix *in-*, which means "in" or "into," and the root *duc,* which means "lead." *An inductive argument uses examples to lead into a claim or generalization about the examples.*

Examples of Induction

Here is an example of induction. Four different people take their cars to the same car repair shop and are overcharged. The claim is then made that anyone who takes a car to that repair shop will probably be overcharged.

　　Inductive reasoning is the basis of the scientific method. Most scientific conclusions are reached inductively. When a sufficient number of phenomena are observed repeatedly, a generalization is made to explain them. Here is an example.

> *Claim (generalization):*　The sun always comes up.
> *Support:*　For example, the sun has come up every day of recorded history.
> *Warrant:*　Every day provides a sufficient number of days to make the claim that the sun always comes up.

Here is a third example. This inductive reasoning appears in the article "Nicotine Addiction Is Quick in Youths, Research Finds" (pages 188–189).

Examples: One-third of the 1,246 sixth graders who volunteered for the study of cigarette addiction developed tobacco dependence quickly, some within two days, and before they were daily smokers.

Claim (generalization made on the basis of examples): A young cigarette smoker can begin to feel powerful desires for nicotine within two days of first inhaling, and about half of children who become addicted report symptoms of dependence by the time they are smoking only seven cigarettes a month.

Warrant: The examples are enough to make us accept the claim.

Consider this fourth and final example of argument from induction. In the Declaration of Independence (pages 254–256), Thomas Jefferson listed several examples of "repeated injuries" that the king of England was guilty of in dealing with the United States. From these examples, Jefferson drew the conclusion that the United States was justified in declaring the United States free and independent of Great Britain. The warrant is that the repeated injuries gave sufficient reason for the United States to take action and declare independence.

Induction demonstrates probability rather than truth whenever there is the possibility of an example that would prove an exception. For instance, a child is discovered who smokes off and on in sixth grade and never develops cigarette addiction. Yet, an apple always falls from a tree, thereby demonstrating gravity, and the sun always comes up, demonstrating that law of nature. No one has been able to find exceptions to disprove these last two generalizations.

To be effective, inductive argument requires a sufficient number of examples. When a generalization is made on the basis of only one or a few examples, it is called a *hasty generalization*. To claim, for instance, that an office worker should always be able to enter a certain amount of data because he did it once may not be accurate. To make a broad generalization, such as *all* office workers ought to be able to enter a certain amount of data because *one* employee was able to, is called a *sweeping generalization*. An inadequate sample of cases weakens or invalidates an inductive argument.

Claim and Support

Look for a group of examples followed by a generalization (claim) based on the examples; or the generalization (claim) may be stated first and then be followed by several examples.

Inductive Warrants

You are expected to assume that the list of examples is representative and that it shows a definite trend. You are also expected to assume that if you added more examples of the same general type, the conclusion would not change.

Tests of Validity

Is the sample adequate? Would more examples continue to show the trend? Are there examples that show an opposite trend or that provide an exception? (Is a child who smokes without developing an addiction a single exception?) Can we make the inductive leap from the examples to the generalization to demonstrate that it is probably true?

ARGUMENT FROM CAUSE

Argument from cause places the subject in a *cause-and-effect relationship* to show that it is either the cause of an effect or the effect of a cause. It is very common in argument to explain or to justify a claim with cause-and-effect reasoning. In the article "Nicotine Addiction Is Quick in Youths, Research Finds" (pages 188–189), the author uses inductive reasoning to gather and report a sufficient number of examples to allow him to make the cause–effect claim that small amounts of nicotine can produce nicotine dependence in young people.

Historians frequently use argument from cause. When they ask why a certain historical event occurred, they are seeking the cause, though they do not always agree on the same causes. For example, several causes have been given for the most recent war on Iraq, including the existence of weapons of mass destruction, threatened U.S. oil interests, and the need to liberate the Iraqi people (see Box 4.3, page 128). There has been considerable disagreement about which of these are the actual causes for that war. There has also been disagreement about the immediate and long-term effects that each of these causes may eventually have on the history of that country.

Visual arguments also can make claims of cause. This is particularly true for advertisements. Buying a certain product is often shown to cause beneficial results. Look back at the advertisement for scanners on page 216 for an example.

Example of Cause

The argument used in "Bringing Up Adultolescents" (pages 211–213) provides another example of argument from cause.

> *Warrant:* Adultolescents are postponing the responsibilities of adulthood.
> *Support:* Many college graduates in their twenties and thirties return home to be supported by their parents.
> *Claim:* Parents are turning many of their adult children into adultolescents in an effort to ensure that they get good jobs and become as successful as they are.

Claim and Support

Look for examples, events, trends, or people who have caused certain things to happen. Look for the effects. For example, "Video games cause children to become violent." Or turn it around and look for the effects first and then the causes: "Many children are violent as a result of playing too many violent video games." Look also for clue words such as *cause, effect, resulted in, as a result, as a consequence,* and *because* to indicate that cause-and-effect reasoning is being used. Finally, the claim states what you are expected to conclude as a result of this cause-and-effect reasoning: "Too much time on the Internet may cause depression," or "Fewer job opportunities and overly indulgent parents together are causing the phenomenon of adultolescents."

Causal Warrants

You are expected to assume that the causes really do create the identified effects or that the effects really are the results of the named causes.

Tests of Validity

Are these causes alone sufficient to create these effects? Could these effects result from other causes? Can I think of exceptions to the cause-and-effect outcome that is claimed here?

ARGUMENT FROM DEDUCTION

Deductive argument is also called argument from principle because its warrant is a general principle. Remember that the warrant may or may not be stated explicitly in an argument. Etymology can help you remember the special features of deductive argument. The prefix *de-* means "from" and the root *duc* means "lead." *A deductive argument leads from a general principle,* which is the warrant, applies it to an example or specific case, which is described in the support, and draws a *conclusion,* which is the claim.

Examples of Deduction

In Chapter 5 you learned that argument deals with matters that are probably rather than certainly true. People do not argue about matters that are certainly true because they already agree about them. Here is an example of a deductive argument based on a general principle that people would agree with and accept as true. Thus they would not argue about it.

General warrant:	Every person has a unique DNA sequence.
Support (specific case):	The accused is a person.
Claim:	The accused has a unique DNA sequence.

This example might be used as a minor argument to support a claim that someone is guilty of a crime. It would never be the main issue in an argument, however, because it is not arguable.

Most of the deduction you will encounter in argument is arguable because it deals with probabilities rather than with certainties. Consider this example: The author of "'A' Is for 'Absent'" (page 76) states the general principle for his argument as follows: Students with high test scores and excessive absences should receive grades based only on the test scores and not the absences. The specific case is the author himself, who has good test scores but also excessive absences. The conclusion is that the author should receive grades based only on the test scores and not the absences. Not everyone would accept this conclusion and would therefore argue with the author.

227

Here is another example of deductive reasoning. Fictional sleuth Sherlock Holmes used deduction to reach his sometimes astonishing conclusions. Holmes examined the supporting evidences—footprints in this example—and deduced that the man who left them walked with a limp. The general principle, that most uneven footprints are left by people who limp, is an assumption that is important in Holmes's deductive thinking even though it is not stated in the argument. It does not need to be spelled out for readers who are able to supply that warrant themselves as they accept Holmes's conclusion. The Holmes deduction can be summarized as follows: the purpose of this argument is to establish the type of person who left these footprints.

> *Unstated warrant:*   Most uneven footprints are left by people who limp.
> *Support (specific case):* These footprints are uneven.
> *Claim:*   The person who left these footprints walks with a limp.

Is there any part of that argument that you might challenge as only possibly or probably rather than as certainly true? If so, you can argue about it.

Claim and Support

Identify the claim by answering this question: "On the basis of a general principle (warrant), implied or stated, what does the author expect me to conclude about this specific example or case?"

Deductive Warrants

You are expected to assume that a general principle about a whole category of phenomena (people, places, events, and so forth) has been stated or implied in the argument and that it is accurate and acceptable. You are expected to decide that since the general principle, or warrant, and the support for the specific case are both accurate and acceptable, the conclusion is also acceptable and probably true.

Tests of Validity

Is the warrant sound and believable? Does the warrant apply to the example or case? Is the support for the case accurate? How reliable, then, is the conclusion?

If the reader has a problem with either the warrant or the example in a deductive argument, the conclusion will not be acceptable. Consider Holmes's warrant that uneven footprints are left by people who limp. That may be convincing to some readers but not others. For instance, a reader might reflect that a person who is pretending to limp or is carrying a heavy valise in one hand could also leave uneven footprints. This reader would then question the warrant and decide that the proof is not even probably true.

Here is another example of a deductive argument that would not be equally successful with all audiences.

> *Unstated warrant:*   Families cannot be happy when the mother works
>   outside the home.
> *Support (specific case):* The mother in this family works outside the home.
> *Claim:*   This is an unhappy family.

For readers who come from happy homes with working mothers, the warrant in this example would seem faulty.

In the next example of a deductive argument, the support could be a problem for some readers who might have trouble accepting it because they think children's stories are not literary and do not have deep symbolic levels of meaning. Another reader might disagree and argue for the opposite point of view, providing examples of children's stories that have such literary qualities and thus refute the other readers' claim. Whether or not a reader accepts the conclusion depends entirely on whether the reader also accepts the warrant and support.

Warrant:	All literary stories have deep symbolic levels of meaning.
Support (specific case):	This children's story has deep symbolic levels of meaning.
Claim:	Children's stories are literary stories.

All parts of a deductive argument need to be well-grounded, accurate, and acceptable to an audience for it to be convincing.

Induction and Deduction Sometimes Work Together

A number of examples are cited and a generalization is made based on those examples—this is the inductive part of the argument. The generalization can then be utilized as the starting point for a deductive argument, one in which it serves as the warrant, that part of the argument that the audience needs to accept. This generalization is combined with a specific case, and a claim is made that is based on applying the generalization to the specific case. Here is how this can be structured. (We will use the essay "'A' Is for 'Absent'" on page 76 again as the example.)

Induction: Recall that the warrants are implied by the arguer and assumed by the audience.

Examples:	Suppose the author interviewed other students in his class and found 7 people who believe that students with high test scores on exams and excessive absences should be graded only on their test scores and not on their absences.
Claim (generalization):	Grading policies should be based on test scores and not penalize for absences.
Warrants:	The opinions of those 7 students is a sufficient number for the instructor to change the grading policy. Student opinion can change an instructor's grading policy.

Deduction: Now the claim of the inductive argument becomes the warrant or general principle that is the starting place for the deductive argument.

General warrant:	Grading policies should be based on test scores and not penalize for absences.
Specific case:	The author has high test scores and many absences.
Claim:	Therefore, the author should receive a high grade.

Tests of Validity

Examine the two inductive warrants: Are those seven students enough to create a change in an instructor's grading policy? Can student opinion change an instructor's grading policy in a class? If you answer no to both those questions, then you will not accept the general warrant in the deductive argument either because it is based on the unacceptable warrants in the inductive argument: students don't set grading policy, and even if they did, seven students would not be a large enough number to make this change. Both the inductive and the deductive arguments can be shown to be invalid because they are based on faulty warrants.

ARGUMENT FROM HISTORICAL, LITERAL, OR FIGURATIVE ANALOGY

Historical and literal analogies explore similarities and differences between items in the same general category, and *figurative analogies* do the same, only with items in very different categories. In drawing analogies, we show how something we may not know much about is like something we know in greater detail. *In other words, we interpret what we do not know in the light of what we do know.* We then supply the warrant that what happened in one case will happen in the other, we draw conclusions, and we make a claim based on the comparisons in the analogy.

Historical Analogies

These explain what is going on *now* in terms of what went on in similar cases *in the past.* Future outcomes are also often projected from past cases. The idea is that what happened in the past will probably repeat itself in the present. Also, the two events are so similar that the results of the former will surely be the end result of the latter.

Example of a Historical Analogy

The following example compares a present event with a past event.

Claim:	People will lose faith in the war in Iraq.
Support:	People lost faith in the Vietnam War.
Warrant:	The two wars are similar.

Literal Analogies

These compare two items in the same category: two school systems, two governments, two religions, two individuals. Outcomes are described as in historical analogies—that is, what happened in one case will happen in the other because of the similarities or the differences.

Example of a Literal Analogy

Two similar items (spending policies) are compared in this example.

Claim: The state should spend more money on education.
Support: Another state spent more money with good results.
Warrant: The two states are similar, and the results of one will be the results of the other.

Figurative Analogies

These compare items from two different categories, as in metaphor, but the points of comparison in a figurative analogy are usually spelled out in more detail than they are in a metaphor. Many figurative analogies appeal to emotion rather than to reason. Figurative analogies are effective as logical proof only when they are used to identify *real qualities* that are shared by both items and that can then be applied to help prove the claim logically. When the items in a figurative analogy are compared either to add ornament or to stir up an emotional response, the analogy functions as emotional proof. It engages the emotions rather than reason.

Examples of Figurative Analogies

Here are some examples of figurative analogies used as logical proof. To prove that reading a difficult book should take time, Francis Bacon compares that activity with taking the time to chew and digest a large meal. The qualities of the two activities, rather than the activities themselves, are compared. Since these qualities are not spelled out, the audience must infer that both take time and that understanding, like digestion, benefits and becomes a permanent part of the individual. Here is this argument laid out so that you can see how it works.

Claim: Reading a difficult book should take time.
Support: Digesting a large meal takes time.
Warrant: Reading and eating are sufficiently alike that they can be compared.

In another example of a figurative analogy used as logical proof, the human fossil record is compared to an apple tree in early winter that has only a few apples on it. The quality that the fossil record and the tree have in common, which the reader must infer, is that both tree and fossil record have a complicated system of branches and limbs. Also, the few apples on the tree are like the few available fossils. At one time there were many of both. The qualities compared in these two instances improve a rational understanding of the fossil record.

Here is a third example of a figurative analogy. This analogy comes from an ad sponsored by the Sierra Club, a group that works to protect the environment. Two pictures are placed side by side. The first is of the Statue of Liberty, which is 305 feet high, and the second is of a giant sequoia tree, which is 275 feet high. A question is posed: "Would you destroy the Statue of Liberty for scrap metal?" We are expected to reason by analogy and compare destroying the Statue of Liberty for scrap metal with destroying the tree for lumber or sawdust. The individual who created this ad hopes this analogy will encourage people to want to protect the trees as much as they want to protect the Statue of Liberty. Would you say that this figurative analogy appeals mainly to emotion or to reason?

Let's look at a second visual example of a figurative analogy. Turn back to Chapter 1, Figure 1.2, on page 9. Look at the picture and read the words that accompany it. The author is comparing the polar bear clinging to the shrinking ice with individuals who are clinging to the idea that global warming does not or will not affect them. Neither will come out well. Does this figurative analogy appeal more to emotion or to reason? Why do you think so?

Claim and Support

Look for examples of items, events, people, and periods of time that are being compared. Whether these items are drawn from the past or the present, as in the case of historical or literal analogies, they must be drawn from the same category: two types of disease, two types of school systems, two types of government, and so on. Look for the clue words *compare, contrast, like, similar to,* and *different from* to signal that comparisons are being made.

In the case of figurative analogies, look for two items being compared that are from totally different categories. Identify the qualities that they have in common. Look for the clue words *like, as, parallel, similar to,* or *compare.* Discover claims that are made as a result of comparing similarities or differences.

Comparison Warrants

You are expected to assume that the items being compared are similar as described and that what happens in one case will probably occur in the other. For figurative analogies you are expected to assume that the qualities of the two items are similar and significant enough so that reference to one will help explain the other and will serve as convincing proof.

Tests of Validity

Are the two items similar as claimed? Can I think of ways they are not similar or of other qualities they share that would change the claim? Are the outcomes really likely to be the same in both cases? Why or why not?

For figurative analogies: Are the qualities of these two items similar, significant, and real enough to help prove a logical argument? Or are they so dissimilar, so far-fetched, or so trivial that the comparison does not prove anything? Does the analogy serve as an ornament, an emotional appeal, or a logical proof?

ARGUMENT FROM DEFINITION

Definition is extremely important in argument. It is difficult to argue about any subject unless there is general agreement about the meanings of the *key terms,* especially when they are part of the claim. Sometimes an entire argument is based on the audience's acceptance of a certain meaning of a key term, which is often in the form of an if-then statement. If the audience accepts the definition, the arguer says, then the claim should be accepted "by definition."

Examples of Definition

An argument against gay marriage can be laid out as deduction, in the manner shown in the example below. Notice that *if* marriage is defined as a union between a man and a woman, *then* by definition two men or two women cannot marry.

Warrant:	Marriage is defined as the union of a man and a woman.
Support (specific case):	Two people of the same sex are not a man and a woman.
Claim:	Two people of the same sex cannot marry.

For the audience to accept gay marriage, they would have to change their definition of marriage to include a marriage between two men or two women. If that were done, there would no longer be an argument on this subject.

Here is a second example, from "Brother, Can You Spare a Word?" (page 186). It also can be laid out as a deductive argument.

Warrant:	"Low food security" and "very low food security" are bland terms that weaken and minimize the concept "hunger."
Support (specific case):	The government's annual report uses the terms "low food security" and "very low food security" in place of the word *hunger.*
Claim:	The government's annual report weakens and minimizes the *idea* of hunger by using the blander terms.

We will accept the claim that the concept of hunger is minimized in the annual report only if we accept the warrant that the word *hunger* is a more stirring term with stronger emotional connotations than the blander terms "low food security" and "very low food security."

Even though *argument by definition takes the form of deductive argument,* it is listed separately here to emphasize the important function of definition in arguments that depend on it as major proof.

Claim and Support

Look for all definitions or explanations of words or concepts. These may be a sentence, several paragraphs, or an entire essay in length. Notice if the definition is used simply to define a word or if it is used as part of the proof in the argument, as in the case of "Brother, Can You Spare a Word?" Look for a claim that you are expected to accept as a result of the definition.

Definition Warrants

You are expected to assume that the definition describes the fundamental properties and qualities of the term accurately so that it can be used to prove the claim.

Tests of Validity

Is this an accurate and complete definition? Is it convincing in this context? Are there exceptions or other definitions for this term that would make the final claim less reliable?

ARGUMENT FROM STATISTICS

Like other forms of logical proof, statistics describe relationships among data, people, occurrences, and events in the real world, only they do so in quantitative terms. An example of statistics used as proof appears in paragraph 3 on page 211 of the essay "Bringing Up Adultolescents." Here numbers and percentages are given to demonstrate the extent of the problem of adult children living with their parents, which is the subject of the essay.

Modern readers have considerable faith in numbers and statistics. They seem more "true" than other types of support to many people. It is more convincing to some, for example, to make the claim that we should end draft registration because it costs $27.5 million per year than simply to claim that we should end it because we no longer need it.

Read statistical proofs carefully to determine where they come from and how reliable, accurate, and relevant they are. Always note whether the original figures have been altered or interpreted in some way. Figures are often rounded off or stated in different terms, such as percentages or plots on a graph. They are also sometimes compared to other material that is familiar to the audience to make them more interesting or memorable.[3] In addition, the use of various types of graphs or charts make data and statistics visual and easier to grasp and remember.

Example of Statistics

Here is an example of a use of misleading statistics in an article titled "Can a 15-Year-Old Be a 'Woman without a Spouse'?"[4]

> ***Claim:*** A majority of American women now live without a spouse.
> ***Support:*** It is reported that 51% of American women live without a spouse.
> ***Warrant:*** This 51% represents a majority.

This article critiques a previous article in a newspaper that reports, "For what experts say is probably the first time, more American women [in 2005] are living without a husband than with one." This was such a striking statistic that the original article appeared on the front page of the newspaper. The subsequent critique of the article pointed out that teenagers, ages 15 to 17, were included in the report, and that 90% of that group (6 million) were still living with their parents. One reader pointed out that it was dishonest to include 15-year-old women as

---

[3]James Wood, *Speaking Effectively* (New York: Random House, 1988), 121–27.
[4]*New York Times*, February 11, 2007, Op-Ed, 12. Byron Calame, the author of the article, is a public editor, that is, the in-house editor who serves as the readers' representative. He receives complaints about writing or interpretations in articles, checks facts, and critiques accounts in the *New York Times* for fairness and accuracy.

"women living without a spouse" in the survey because some states do not even permit people to marry at age 15. By removing high school age women (ages 15–17) from this group, the figure dropped, leaving 48% of American women living without a spouse. By eliminating all teenagers and counting only women 20 years or older, the figure dropped to 47%, and neither adjusted figure could be presented as a "new majority." Sources for the statistics were the Census Bureau data and the Census Bureau's 2005 American Community Survey. Both are reliable sources. The problem with the report was the inclusion of individuals in it who did not belong, which falsely elevated the figures.

Claim and Support

Look for numbers and data, in both their original and their converted form, graphs and charts of figures, and interpretations of them, including comparisons. Look for a claim based on the data.

Statistical Warrants

You are expected to assume that the data have been gathered and reported accurately by competent people, that they are representative and complete unless stated otherwise, and that they have been interpreted fairly and truthfully.

Tests of Validity

Where did these statistics come from? To what dates do the statistics apply? How reliable is the source? How accurate are they? How are they presented? Have they been rounded off, changed, or converted? How has the change affected their accuracy? Do they prove what they are supposed to prove? Have they been interpreted fairly, or are they exaggerated or skewed? Has enough backing been provided to prove their reliability? With what are they compared, and how does this comparison contribute to their final significance? Is any significant information left out?

Tests of Validity for Statistics Presented as Graphs

Statistics are sometimes presented in graph form. The tests of validity in this case include these: Where did the information come from? What information is included in the sample? How was it gathered? Is anything significant left out or ignored because it didn't fit? Are the charts and graphs labeled accurately? Are there any exaggerations?

Proof That Builds Credibility: *Ethos*

The materials provided in argument that help the audience gain a favorable impression of the arguer, the group the arguer represents, or the authorities and experts the arguer cites or quotes help create *ethos*, or the credibility of the author.

The author may build credibility by referring to experience and credentials that establish his or her own expertise. Note how James Gilligan provides his own credentials in the first paragraph of his essay "Reflections from a Life Behind Bars: Build Colleges, Not Prisons" on pages 592–596. He has been a prison psychiatrist for twenty-five years. Another way is to quote others or to use arguments from authority.

ARGUMENT FROM AUTHORITY

We are usually inclined to accept the opinions and factual evidence of people who are authorities and experts in their fields.

Examples of Authority

In an article that claims California will have another earthquake, the author describes and provides the credentials for several professors of geology from the major universities in Southern California as well as scientists from the U.S. Geological Survey Office before quoting their opinions as support.

Claim: California will have an earthquake.
Support: Professors and scientists say so.
Warrant: These experts are reliable.

Authors themselves sometimes establish their own credentials by making references to various types of past experience that qualify them to write about their subject. They also sometimes assert the *ethos* of the group they represent, in statements like "the great Republican Party," or they establish the group's *ethos* by citing their accomplishments.

Claim and Support

Look for all references to the author's credentials, whether made by the author or by an editor. Look for references to the author's training, education, professional position, background, and experience. Notice, also, references to the audience's concerns, beliefs, and values that demonstrate the author's effort to establish common ground and to show fairness and goodwill toward the audience. Look for references to groups the author may represent, and notice how they are described. Look for direct or paraphrased quotations from experts. Differentiate between facts and statements of opinion. Look for credential statements about these experts. Look for claims that are made more valid as a consequence of this expert opinion.

Authoritative Warrants

You are expected to assume that the information provided about the author, the group, or the expert is accurate, that these authorities are honorable, fair, reliable, knowledgeable, and experienced, and that they also exhibit goodwill toward the audience.

Tests of Validity

Is there enough information to establish the true character and experience of the author? Is this information complete and accurate? Is there enough information about the group to believe what the author says about it? Are the credentials of the experts good enough to make their contributions reliable? Also, are the credentials relevant to the issue? (A star athlete may not be the best judge of soft drinks or fast food.) If a source is quoted, is the source reliable? Argument based on authority is as good as the authorities themselves.

Types of Emotional Proof: *Pathos*

Some argument theorists would say that there should be no appeals to emotion or attempts to arouse the emotions of the audience in argument. The idea is that an argument should appeal only to reason. Emotion, they claim, clouds reasoning and judgment and gets the argument off course. Richard M. Weaver, quoted earlier in this chapter, would disagree. Weaver points out that people are not just austerely unemotional logic machines who are interested only in deduction, induction, and cause-and-effect reasoning. People also use language to communicate feelings, values, and motives.[5]

Furthermore, when we consider that the source of much argument lies in the dramatic, emotionally laden occurrences of everyday life, we realize how impossible it is to eliminate all emotion from argument. As you read the many argument essays in this book, study the emotional material that professional writers use. Try to develop a sense of when emotion contributes to argument in effective and appropriate ways and when it does not. In general, emotional proofs are appropriate in argument when the subject itself is emotional and when it creates strong feelings in both the writer and the reader. For writers of argument, emotion leads to positions on issues, influences the tone of the writing, and informs some of the interpretations. For readers, emotion leads to a stronger engagement with the issue and influences the final outcomes. Emotional proof is appropriate when the occasion justifies it and when it strengthens logical conviction. It is inappropriate when it merely ventilates feelings, serves as an ornament, or distracts the audience from the logical conclusion of the argument. Types of emotional proof focus on *motivation*, or what all people want, and on *values*, or what we consider good or bad, favorable or unfavorable, acceptable or unacceptable.

MOTIVATIONAL PROOFS

Some proofs appeal explicitly to what all audiences are supposed to want, such as food, drink, warmth and shelter, sex, security, belongingness, self-esteem, creativity, or self-expression. Authors also sometimes appeal to (or through) the opposites of these needs and values, relying on hunger, cold, fear, self-doubt,

237

---

[5]Weaver elaborates on some of the distinctions between logic and emotion in "Language Is Sermonic."

boredom, or other types of dissatisfaction to motivate people to change their behavior and restore themselves to a more positive state of being. Advertisements aimed at convincing young people that they should avoid taking illegal drugs often show the negative effects of drugs to appeal to people's sense of fear. The purpose of motivational proof is to urge the audience to take prescribed steps to meet an identified need.

Examples of Motivational Proofs

Advertisements and speeches by political candidates provide obvious examples of motivational proof. Drink a certain beer or buy a brand of blue jeans, and you will be irresistible to others. Similarly, support a particular candidate, and you will personally gain job security and safe neighborhoods.

> *Claim:* You should support this candidate.
> *Support:* This candidate can help you get job security and safe neighborhoods.
> *Warrant:* You want job security and safe neighborhoods.

Here is another example: Brent Staples, in "Driving Down the Highway, Mourning the Death of American Radio" (pages 87–89), appeals to what car owners want when they listen to music while they are driving.

Claim and Support

To find the claim, look for what you are asked to believe or do to get what you want.

Motivational Warrants

Look for references to items or qualities that you might need, want, or fear.

Tests of Validity

What am I supposed to need or fear? Do I really need it or fear it? What am I supposed to do? Will doing what is recommended satisfy the need in the ways described?

VALUE PROOFS

Some proofs appeal to what all audiences are expected to value, such as fairness, reliability, honesty, loyalty, industry, patriotism, courage, integrity, conviction, faithfulness, dependability, creativity, freedom, equality, and devotion to duty.

Examples of Value Proofs

Here is an example that claims that a school curriculum can contribute to the values of equality and acceptance if it is multicultural.

Claim:	The curriculum should be multicultural.
Support:	A multicultural curriculum will contribute to equality and acceptance.
Warrant:	You value equality and acceptance.

Here is a second example: John Opdyke, in his essay "Kids and Chores: All Work and No Pay?" (pages 139–141), appeals to the values that influence parents when they are training their children to do chores, which in this case include fairness, reliability, and industry. (A sometimes competing, sometimes supporting value—recognizing that your children are individuals and need to learn and exercise choice—is also discussed and, for some readers, may be a value of stronger appeal.)

Claim and Support

Look for value statements that are generally accepted by everyone because they have been proved elsewhere many times. Examples include "Freedom of speech is our constitutional right," "There should be no freedom without responsibility," and "Individuals who have the courage of conviction are to be trusted." Look for slogans that display such values as "Honest Abe," "The home of the free and the brave," and "Honesty is the best policy." Or look for narratives and examples that display values, such as the story of an industrious, thrifty, and ambitious mother who is on welfare. When the values are not directly stated, ask, "What values or beliefs are causing the author to say this?" Look for a claim that shows what will result if the recommended values are accepted.

Value Warrants

You are expected to assume that you share the author's values and that they are as important as the author says they are.

Tests of Validity

What are the values expressed or implicit in this argument? Do I share these values with the author? If not, how do we differ? What effect do these differences have on my final acceptance of the claim?

A MNEMONIC DEVICE

The mnemonic VAM (for *value, authority,* and *motivation*) may help you remember and use the proofs involving *ethos* and *pathos.*

Logos, Ethos, and *Pathos* Communicated through Language and Style

You can learn to recognize logic, *ethos,* and emotion in argument not only by the use of proofs but also by the language and style associated with each of these types of appeal. Actually, you will not often encounter pure examples of one of these styles, but instead you will encounter a mix, with one of the styles predominating. The same is true of writing. You may plan to write in a logical style, but emotion and *ethos* seep in and actually help you create a richer and more varied style for your argument.

LANGUAGE THAT APPEALS TO LOGIC

The language of logical argument, which is the language associated with reason, is sometimes called rational style. Words that carry mainly denotative meaning are favored in rational style over connotative and emotionally loaded language. The denotative meaning of a word is the commonly held meaning found in the dictionary. It is the meaning most people would agree on because to denote is to name or indicate specifically. Examples of words that have predominantly denotative meanings and that are emotionally neutral include *introduction, fact, information, question*, and *literal meaning*. Most people would agree on the meanings of those words and could produce synonyms. Words with strong connotative meaning may have many extra, unique, symbolic, or personal meanings and associations attached to them that vary from person to person. Examples of words with connotative meaning include *rock star, politician, mugger, family values*, and *human rights*. Asked to define such words, different people would provide meanings and examples that would not be exactly alike or match the denotative meanings of these words in a dictionary.

For support, rational style relies on opinion in the form of reasons, literal or historical analogies, explanations, and definitions and also on factual data, quotations, and citations from experts and authorities. Furthermore, the reader is usually not required to make as many inferences as for other, less formal styles of writing. Most parts of the argument are spelled out explicitly for the sake of agreement and better adherence of minds.

Slogans that elicit emotional responses, such as "America is the greatest country," "The American people want change," or "Now is the time for healing," are generally omitted in rational style. Slogans of this type substitute for logical thinking. Readers think better and draw better conclusions when provided with well-reasoned opinion, quotations from authorities, and facts.

For example, in the opening paragraph of an essay titled "The Lost Art of Political Argument," Christopher Lasch uses rational style to argue in favor of argument and debate.

> Let us begin with a simple proposition: What democracy requires is public debate, not information. Of course it needs information too, but the kind of information it needs can be generated only by vigorous popular debate. We do not know what we need to know until we ask the right questions, and we can identify the right questions only by subjecting our own ideas about the world to the test of public controversy. Information, usually seen as the precondition of debate, is better understood as its by-product. When we get into arguments that focus and fully engage our attention, we become avid seekers of relevant information. Otherwise, we take in information passively—if we take it in at all.[6]

---

[6]Christopher Lasch, "The Lost Art of Political Argument," *Harper's*, September 1990, 17.

Rational style, as you can see in this excerpt, evokes mainly a cognitive, rational response from its readers.

LANGUAGE THAT DEVELOPS *ETHOS*

Authors who seek to establish their own credentials and good character use language to provide a fair-minded view of reality that is restrained and accurate rather than exaggerated or overly opinionated. When language is used to create positive *ethos,* an audience will trust the author as a credible source of information and opinion.

Language that develops *ethos* has several specific characteristics. To begin with, the writer exhibits a consistent awareness of the audience's background and values by adopting a vocabulary level that is appropriate for the topic and the audience. The writer does not either talk down to or overwhelm the audience, use technical jargon for an audience unfamiliar with it, or use slang or colloquial language unless the context specifically calls for that. Rap music, for example, invites a different vocabulary level than a scholarly paper does.

Writers intent on establishing *ethos* are sensitive to different audiences and what they will admire, trust, and accept. They try to use language precisely and to say exactly what they mean. They project an honest desire to communicate by avoiding ranting, filler material that gets off the subject, or anything that the audience would perceive as offensive or repugnant.

As you have probably already realized, an author can destroy *ethos* and alter an audience's favorable impression by changing the language. A student who uses colloquial, everyday expressions in a formal essay written for a professor, a commencement speaker who shouts obscenities at the audience, a father who uses formal, abstract language to talk to his five-year-old—all have made inappropriate language choices for their particular audiences, thereby damaging their *ethos* with those audiences.

When you read argument, notice how an author uses language to build connections and trust as well as to establish reliability with the audience. When you write argument, use language that will help the audience regard you as sincere and trustworthy. Appropriate language is essential when you write a college paper. The use of slang, slogans, and street language and expressions in otherwise formal writing damages your credibility as a serious thinker. Writing errors, including mistakes in spelling, punctuation, and grammar, also destroy *ethos* because they indicate a lack of concern and goodwill for your readers.

Here is an example of language that builds effective *ethos* with an audience. These excerpts come from Martin Luther King Jr.'s "Letter from Birmingham Jail." An explanation of the rhetorical situation for this letter and the full text of the letter appear in the Appendix to Chapter 10. Briefly, however, King was jailed because of his involvement in the civil rights movement in Birmingham, Alabama, and he had been criticized publicly for his participation by eight fellow clergymen of that city. He wrote this letter to those clergymen. Notice that he deliberately uses language that is sincere and honest and that establishes his credibility as a trustworthy and responsible human being with values his audience is likely to share. He does not come across as a troublemaker or a man who is angry at the system, as one might find with someone who has been jailed for participating in civil rights demonstrations. Rather, he comes across as thoughtfully conscious of his actions and ethically bound to participate as he is.

My Dear Fellow Clergymen:

While confined here in the Birmingham city jail, I came across your recent statement calling my present activities "unwise and untimely." . . . Since I feel that you are men of genuine good will and that your criticisms are sincerely set forth, I want to try to answer your statement in what I hope will be patient and reasonable terms.

I think I should indicate why I am here in Birmingham, since you have been influenced by the view which argues against "outsiders coming in." . . . I, along with several members of my staff, am here because I was invited here. I am here because I have organizational ties here.

But more basically, I am in Birmingham because injustice is here. Just as the prophets of the eighth century B.C. left their villages and carried their "thus saith the Lord" far beyond the boundaries of their home towns, and just as the Apostle Paul left his village of Tarsus and carried the gospel of Jesus Christ to the far corners of the Greco-Roman world, so am I compelled to carry the gospel of freedom beyond my own home town. Like Paul, I must constantly respond to the Macedonian call for aid.

Moreover, I am cognizant of the interrelatedness of all communities and states. I cannot sit idly by in Atlanta and not be concerned about what happens in Birmingham. Injustice anywhere is a threat to justice everywhere. We are caught in an inescapable network of mutuality, tied in a single garment of destiny. Whatever affects one directly, affects all indirectly. Never again can we afford to live with the narrow, provincial "outside agitator" idea. Anyone who lives inside the United States can never be considered an outsider anywhere within its bounds.

Highlight the language in these passages that you think King used to establish good *ethos* with the eight clergymen. Notice how King deliberately uses language to project sincerity and goodwill toward this audience. He also selects examples and appeals to values that are compatible with their interests and values. King's letter is a classic example of argument that establishes effective *ethos* with a particular audience.

Now look back at "'A' Is for 'Absent'" (page 76) and notice the language, values, and examples that this author uses to build *ethos* with a certain type of student audience. He describes a "dreaded" course, refers to the class absence policy as "allotted 'freebies,'" says that attendance policies "subvert the value of learning and education," and suggests that, since tuition pays for the professor, students should be able to make their own rules about attending class. The same language could destroy his *ethos* with readers who disagree with him.

LANGUAGE THAT APPEALS TO EMOTION

References to values and motives summon feelings about what people regard as good and bad and about what they want, and authors use the language associated with emotional style in a variety of ways to express and evoke feelings about these matters. The following paragraphs describe a few special techniques that are characteristic of emotional style. Examples of each are drawn from "Bringing Up Adultolescents" (pages 211–213).

Emotionally loaded language evokes connotative meanings and causes the audience to experience feelings and associations at a personal level that are not described in dictionaries. Here is an example: "It's hard to feel like a Master of the Universe when you're sleeping in your old twin bed." Underline the words and phrases in the sentence that draw forth your emotions.

Emotional examples engage the emotions, as in this example: "When Silvia Geraci goes out to dinner with friends, she has a flash of anxiety when the check comes. She can pay her share—her parents give her enough money to cover all her expenses. It's just that others in her circle make their own money now." Most readers can share this type of anxiety.

Vivid description of an emotional scene creates an emotional reader response, as in this example: "Jimmy Finn, 24, a paralegal at the Manhattan-based law firm of Sullivan & Cromwell, made the most of his $66,000 annual income by moving back to his childhood home in nearby Staten Island. While his other friends paid exorbitant rents, Finn bought a new car and plane tickets to Florida so he could see his girlfriend on the weekends. He had ample spending money for restaurants and cabs, and began paying down his student loans." Notice how this description brings you into the scene, causing you to imagine the daily life of Jimmy Finn.

Narratives of emotional events draw readers into a scene just as vivid description does. Here is a story about a mother and her daughter: "A few years ago, Janice Charlton of Philadelphia pressured her daughter, Mary, then 26, to get a master's degree, even agreeing to cosign two $17,000 school loans if she did. Mary dropped out, Janice says, and the loans went into default. 'I'm sorry I ever suggested it,' says Janice. 'We're still close but it's a sticky issue between us.'" By describing the emotions of the mother, the author invites the reader to share them.

Emotional tone, created by emotional language and examples, indicates that the author has a strong feeling about the subject and wants the audience to share that feeling. Here is an example: "No matter how loving the parent-child bond, parents inevitably heave a sigh of relief when their adult kids finally start paying their own way. Seven months ago, when Finn's paralegal job moved to Washington, DC, he left home and got an apartment there. The transition, he said, was hard on his mother, Margie. Mom, though, reports that she's doing just fine." Also, irony and sarcasm should always be viewed as examples of emotional tone. They indicate strong feeling and a desire for change.

Figurative analogies contribute to emotion in an argument, particularly when two emotional subjects are compared and the resulting effect appeals more to emotion than to reason. For example, a researcher who is studying the adultolescent phenomenon states, "The conveyor belt that transported adolescents into adulthood has broken down." The comparison of an operational and a broken conveyor belt, particularly in their relationship to moving students toward adulthood, is supposed to have an emotional effect on the reader.

Emotional style is the easiest of all the styles to recognize because it uses charged language and is often close to our own experiences. Do not become distracted by emotional material or use it excessively in your own arguments. Remember, in argument, logic is the plot and emotion and *ethos* add support. Box 7.1 ■ on page 244 provides a summary of the characteristics of language used to appeal to reason, to establish *ethos*, and to appeal to emotion.

243

Box 7.1	A Summary of Language and Style in Argument.

▶▶▶ How Do You Make Appeals in Argument?

TO APPEAL TO LOGIC	TO DEVELOP *ETHOS*	TO APPEAL TO EMOTION
Style		
Theoretical abstract language	Language appropriate to audience and subject	Vivid, concrete language
Denotative meanings		Emotionally loaded language
Reasons	Restrained, sincere, fair-minded presentation	Connotative meanings
Literal and historical analogies		Emotional examples
Explanations	Appropriate level of vocabulary	Vivid descriptions
Definitions	Correct grammar	Narratives of emotional events
Factual data and statistics		Emotional tone
Quotations		Figurative analogies
Citations from experts and authorities		
Informed opinion		
Effect		
Evokes a cognitive, rational response	Demonstrates author's reliability, competence, and respect for the audience's ideas and values through reliable and appropriate use of support and general accuracy	Evokes an emotional response

Value of the Proofs for Reading, Viewing, and Writing Argument

Analyzing the proofs in an argument focuses a reader's attention on the author's reasoning, use of supporting detail, and warrants. These are the elements in an argument that convince an audience. Applying the tests of validity to the proofs can also help a reader recognize faulty reasoning, which can implicate and sometimes reveal a manipulative or immoral purpose in the argument. You will learn more about faulty reasoning in the next chapter. It is not convincing once you figure out how it works.

Viewers of argument, just like readers, should first establish whether a visual image presents a position on a subject that is open to different interpretations and vantages or serves restrictively as support for a particular position, and then make an attempt to state the claim and analyze the proofs that support it. Look for the ways in which the creator of the image appeals to your reason, to your sense of fairness and good will, and to your emotions. Warrants and backing will also be present in visual arguments. Analyze them to gain further insight into the image as argument. You can also apply the tests of validity to visual argument, just as you would with written argument.

Writers of argument can use the proofs to help them think of ways to develop a claim. By running through the list of proofs and asking relevant questions—What do I need to define? Should I use statistics? Can I generalize from some examples? What caused this? To what can I compare this? Whom should I quote? To what audience values and motives can I appeal?—authors invent and structure ideas and locate material to be used at the concrete, specific level in a paper. The specific material is what makes a paper convincing. Also, thinking about the proofs makes authors more consciously aware of their own warrants and helps them decide whether to make the warrants explicit in the argument or whether to leave them implicit so that the audience has to supply them. Finally, an awareness of proofs can help writers avoid inadequate or irrelevant proof and faulty reasoning in their writing.

The exercises and activities for this chapter will provide you with practice in using the proofs to invent support and warrants for a position paper. The proofs and the tests for validity are summarized for both readers, viewers, and writers in the Summary Charts on pages 511–523.

Review Questions

1. Describe logical proofs. Name the seven types of logical proof. (Use the mnemonic SICDADS to help you remember them.)

2. Describe proofs that build *ethos*, or credibility. Name one type of proof that builds *ethos*.

3. Describe emotional proofs. Name two types of emotional support and explain why they appeal to the emotions.

4. Describe some of the features of the language and style associated with the three types of proof.

5. How does visual argument employ the proofs? Give an example.

Exercises and Activities

A. Class Discussion: Analyzing *Logos*, *Pathos*, and *Ethos* in an Advertisement

Study the advertisement on the next page (Image 1. Meet the Philip Morris Generation), and identify the logical proofs, the emotional proofs, and the proofs that establish *ethos*. Use the mnemonics SICDADS and VAM to help you remember the proofs. Which type of proof is strongest in this ad, in your opinion? How effective is the ad? Why do you think so?

245

Image 1:
Meet the Philip Morris Generation

Meet the Philip Morris Generation

A **record** to be **ashamed** of.

Philip Morris claims it doesn't want kids to smoke. But a major study shows that Marlboro, the Philip Morris flagship brand, is by far the best-selling cigarette among young smokers. On average, 60 percent of 8th, 10th and 12th graders — boys and girls — prefer Marlboro. Among white high school seniors it's even higher, at 70 percent.

This means that of the 3,000 kids who become regular smokers every day, about 1,800 head for Marlboro Country. A third of these kids will die early from tobacco-caused disease.

Once again, Philip Morris says one thing but does another.

Tobacco vs. Kids. Where America draws the line.®

American Cancer Society • American Medical Association • American Academy of Child & Adolescent Psychiatry • American Academy of Pediatrics • American Association for Respiratory Care • American College of Preventive Medicine • American Medical Women's Association • American Public Health Association • Association of Schools of Public Health • Girls Incorporated • INFACT • Interreligious Coalition on Smoking or Health • Latino Council on Alcohol and Tobacco • National Association of School Nurses • National Association of Secondary School Principals • National Hispanic Medical Association • Summit Health Coalition

CAMPAIGN for TOBACCO-FREE Kids®

To learn more, call 800-284-KIDS or visit our web site at www.tobaccofreekids.org.
The National Center for Tobacco-Free Kids, 1707 L Street NW, Suite 800, Washington, DC 20036

B. Class Discussion: Analyzing the Proofs in an Essay

Underline the material in each paragraph that helps you answer the questions in the margin.

BEFORE YOU READ: What are your present opinions about illegal immigration and undocumented workers in the United States?

ESSAY #1   UNDOCUMENTED, INDISPENSABLE*
Anna Quindlen

Anna Quindlen is a best-selling author of novels, nonfiction books, and children's books. She wrote the column "Public and Private" for the *New York Times* for many years. The column won a Pulitzer Prize in 1992. She now writes another regular column called "The Last Word," which appears every other week in *Newsweek* magazine and one of which is reprinted here.

What is taking place?

What is it a *sign* of?

1 On May Day a persistent rumble came from Market Street in San Francisco, but it was not the oft-predicted earthquake, or at least not in the geologic sense. Thousands of people were marching down the thoroughfare, from the Embarcadero to city hall, holding signs. No HUMAN BEING IS ILLEGAL. I AM A WORKER, NOT A CRIMINAL. TODAY I MARCH, TOMORROW I VOTE. I PAY TAXES.

What *historical analogy* is made?

What result from the past will be repeated in the present?

2 The polyglot city by the bay is so familiar with the protest march that longtime citizens say it handles the inconveniences better than anyplace else. Some of them remember the Vietnam War marches, the feminist rallies. The May Day demonstration bore some resemblance to both, which was not surprising. Immigration is the leading edge of a deep and wide sea change in the United States today, just as those issues were in their own time.

What is the *effect* of new residents on established residents?

What *causes* this effect?

3 Of course, this is not a new issue. The Founding Fathers started out with a glut of land and a deficit of warm bodies. But over its history America's more-established residents have always found ways to demonize the newcomers to the nation needed to fill it and till it. It was only human, the contempt for the different, the shock of the new.

How does "conventional wisdom" *define* immigrants? What *definition* is more accurate?

What are these *statistics* used to prove?

4 Today, because so many immigrants have entered the country illegally or are living here on visas that expired long ago, the demagoguery has been amped up full throttle. Although the conventional wisdom is that immigrants are civic freeloaders, the woman with a sign that said I PAY TAXES was reflecting the truth. Millions of undocumented immigrants pay income taxes using a special identification number the IRS provides. They pay into the Social Security system, too, even though they're not eligible to collect benefits. In fact, they may be helping to keep the system afloat, with $7 billion currently in a designated suspense file, much of which is believed to have come from undocumented workers.

*Newsweek, May 15, 2006, 78.

247

What are these *statistics* used to prove?

What *general principles* are stated here?

What is the *example*?

What is the *counterargument*?

What do some members of Congress say *causes* low wages? What does the author say is the real *cause*?

What *historical analogy* is drawn here? What does the author say the result would be?

What are the author's unique *credentials* for writing on this subject? How does this effect her *ethos*?

What *motives* and *values* are appealed to in this paragraph?

Underline examples of *emotionally loaded language*.

5 A man carrying a sign saying I AM A WORKER, NOT A CRIMINAL said he pays taxes, too, through his construction job. All three of his children were born in the United States. Although he said he had a hard time deciphering government forms—and don't we all?—he had applied for a green card and had been waiting for four years. In 2004 there was a backlog of more than 6 million unprocessed immigration petitions, a record high. So much for suggestions that immigrants are lax about regularizing their status. Clearly the laxity is at least partly federal.

6 It's true that immigrants use government services: schools, public hospitals. It's also true that many pay their way through income and sales taxes. Despite the rhetoric, no one really knows whether they wind up being a loss or a gain for the economy. Certainly lots of them work. A state like Arizona, for instance, could not keep pace with the demand for new homes at reasonable cost without immigrant workers, many of them undocumented.

7 The counterargument is that that drives down the wages of American citizens. It's galling to hear that argument from members of Congress, who have not raised the federal minimum wage for almost a decade. Most of those politicians blame the workers for their willingness to accept low wages. Don't hold your breath waiting for significant sanctions against those companies that shut their eyes to the immigration status of their employees—and that also make large political contributions.

8 Americans who are really incensed by millions of undocumented immigrants can take action, just as those marching in the streets did. They can refuse to eat fruits and vegetables picked by those immigrants. They can refuse to buy homes on which they worked. After all, if a migrant worker like Cesar Chavez could organize a national boycott of grapes, then opponents of immigration could surely organize something similar. But they won't. We like our cheap houses and our fresh fruit. And our government likes the bait-and-switch, taking taxes from workers whose existence it will not recognize. The borders are most porous in Washington, D.C.

9 Full disclosure: I'm the granddaughter of immigrants, and I know how much of the melting pot is a myth. My grandparents always referred to my father as "an American boy," which meant he was not from Italy. It was not a compliment. They didn't melt; their daughter did, although one of the only times I ever saw her bitter was when she explained what the word "dago" meant.

10 There are big decisions to be made about the vast wave of undocumented workers in this country, issues that go beyond slogans and placards. But there's no premium in discussing those issues in xenophobic half-truths, in talking about what undocumented immigrants cost the country without talking about what they contribute, in talking about them as illegals when they are nannies, waiters, roofers and the parents of American citizens. One fact is indisputable: the essence of America is

free enterprise and human rights. It's why people come here in the first place. WE ARE ALL IMMIGRANTS, read signs on Market Street. Some of us just got here sooner.

For Discussion:

What is the issue? What is the author's position on the issue? Read the title and the final paragraph of the essay. Then state the claim of this essay: This author wants me to believe . . . What logical proofs does the author use to prove her claim? Which are most effective and why? How does she engage your emotions? What values and motives are present in this argument? Do you share them? How does she build *ethos*? Describe an audience who might be sympathetic to her *ethos* and her claim. Is this essay convincing to you? Why or why not?

C. **Group Work and Discussion: Analyzing Motivational and Value Proofs and Style**

Read the essay, "Sharing the Wealth," reprinted here. Focus on the emotional proofs and style in the essay, including appeals to the audience's feelings, motives (what they are expected to want), and values (what they are expected to value). Then answer the following questions and report your answers to the class.

1. What is the author's claim?

2. What motivational proofs are present in the essay? How does the author appeal to what people are expected to want? Review the list of what people are likely to want that appears on pages 237–238. It is not a complete list, and you may add to it. As you read the essay, notice what people in poor and developing countries are expected to want. Then consider what philanthropists are expected to want. How do the motivational appeals help support the claim?

3. What value proofs are present in the essay? Review the description of values that audiences are expected to hold on page 238 and add to the list, if you wish. As you read the essay, notice what the author expects the audience, the philanthropists, and the individuals who need help will value. How do the appeals to values help support the claim?

4. How does this essay appeal to your feelings?

5. Even though emotional support is used in this essay, it also contains logical support and support that establishes the *ethos* of certain individuals. Identify and analyze these other types of support in the essay. How do they support the claim?

6. How do the photograph at the beginning of the article and the graph at the end support the claim? What types of support predominate in each of these visual proofs?

> **BEFORE YOU READ:** If you had several billion dollars, what would you do with it?

ESSAY #2   **SHARING THE WEALTH***
Jeffrey Sachs

Sachs is an economist who currently heads Columbia University's Earth Institute. From 2002 to 2006, he was the director of the United Nations Millennium Project , which aims to reduce extreme poverty, disease, and hunger in the world by the year 2015. He is president and co-founder of the Millennium Promise Alliance, a nonprofit organization also aimed at ending extreme global poverty.

**Image 2:
Helping Out.**

How does this photograph support the ideas presented in the essay that follows it? What type of proof would you say predominates in it: *logos, pathos,* or *ethos*? Give reasons for your answer.

250

Helping Out. Bill and Melinda Gates and Warren Buffett address a press conference regarding a 31 billion dollar gift Buffett has made to the Gates Foundation to help developing countries.

1   What is the power of one when that one happens to be a John D. Rockefeller or a Bill Gates? If history is a guide, the answer is, quite a lot. I'm speaking not only about the power to reshape an industry like oil or personal computers but also about the ability to improve the world through philanthropy. Rockefeller proved that giving away money is much more than charity. It can be transformative. And if today's billionaires were to pool their resources, they could outflank the world's governments in ending poverty and pandemic disease.

2   A century ago, Rockefeller decided to put his vast fortune to public use, offering to endow a federal institution to fight disease, poverty and ignorance. Hotheads attacked him, claiming that he was just trying to buy a good name, and Congress demurred. So, instead, in 1913, Rockefeller set up the Rockefeller Foundation with two initial gifts totaling $100 million. No institution did more in the 20th century to further the cause of international development. It led the way in the eradication of hookworm in the U.S. South, helping pave the way for the region's economic development. It supported the Nobel-prizewinning work that created the yellow-fever vaccine. It helped Brazil eliminate a malaria-transmitting strain of mosquito. And perhaps most stunningly, it

Image 3:
Who Has the Money?

How does this chart support the ideas in the essay? What type of proof would you say predominates in it: *logos, pathos,* or *ethos*? Give reasons for your answer.

WHO HAS THE MONEY

The top five on the *Forbes* list of the world's wealthiest people come from all over the globe.

RANK	NAME	CITIZENSHIP	AGE	NET WORTH[*]	RESIDENCE
1	William Gates III	U.S.	51	56.0	U.S.
2	Carlos Slim Helú	Mexico	67	53.1	Mexico
3	Warren Buffett	U.S.	76	52.4	U.S.
4	Ingvar Kamprad	Sweden	81	33.0	Switzerland
5	Lakshmi Mittal	India	56	32.0	Britain

[*]In billions of dollars

funded the Asian Green Revolution, the transformative agricultural success that enabled India and other countries to escape endless cycles of famine and poverty.

3   Now Bill and Melinda Gates, backed by more than $30 billion of their own funds and an additional $31 billion of Warren Buffett's can do the same. Like the Rockefeller Foundation, the Gates Foundation rightly looks to technology for the breakthroughs that can end extreme poverty on a global basis. Its original focus has been on health technologies, but now the foundation is expanding to agriculture, water and other areas that are also critical in the fight against poverty.

4   Of course, Bill and Melinda Gates are not alone in contemporary transformative philanthropy. George Soros' support for brave truth tellers in Central Europe and the former Soviet Union helped catalyze the peaceful end of communism. The Google guys, Larry Page and Sergey Brin, are out to prove how information technologies can bring about major change. They have recently posted satellite imagery of Darfur, Sudan, in order to raise awareness and technical support for solutions in that violence-ravaged region. The dynamism of social entrepreneurship makes a mockery, alas, of

our political leadership. The Gateses, Buffett, Soros, Page and Brin have left George W. Bush and the rest of Washington in the dust. U.S. international aid is at a pitiful 0.17% of national income (just 17¢ per $100), with much of that squandered as failed " reconstruction aid" in Iraq.

5   According to *Forbes* magazine, there are some 950 billionaires in the world, with an estimated combined wealth of $3.5 trillion. Even after all the yachts, mansions and luxury living that money can buy have been funded many times over, these billionaires will still have nearly $3.5 trillion to change the world. Suppose they pooled their wealth, as Buffett has done with Bill and Melinda Gates. By standard principles of foundation management, a $3.5 trillion endowment would have a 5% payout of about $175 billion a year, an amount sufficient to extend basic health care to all in the poorest world; end massive pandemics of AIDS, TB and malaria; jump-start an African Green Revolution; end the digital divide; and address the crying need for safe drinking water for 1 billion people. In short, this billionaires' foundation would be enough to end extreme poverty itself. All in all, it's not a bad gig for men and women who have transcended the daily economic struggle

251

faced by the rest of humanity. They might also take note of the admonition of America's first megaphilanthropist, Andrew Carnegie, who wrote in 1889 that "the day is not far distant when the man who dies leaving behind him millions of available wealth, which was free for him to administer during life, will pass away unwept, unhonored, and unsung." Fortunately, plenty of new heroes seem ready for a different legacy.

For Discussion: What historical analogies are used in this essay? How do they contribute to the argument the author is making? What other comparisons are made? How do the visual proofs (the photo and the chart) work in the argument? What do you find most convincing in this essay? What do you find least convincing? Do you think the plan proposed would work? Why or why not? If you had billions of dollars, would you want to contribute some of your money to eradicate poverty in the world, as Bill and Melinda Gates and Warren Buffett have done? If yes, how would you go about it? If no, what would you do with your money instead?

D. Class Discussion: Adding Appropriate Visual Proof

Images 4 and 5 are relevant to the essay you just read by Jeffrey Sachs. Photographs like these, which portray extreme hunger and desperation in Africa, frequently appear as visual support when foundations or other groups seek money to help ease misery in the world, which is also the purpose of Sachs's essay. Yet in the Sachs essay another type of visual proof is used. In adding visual proof to support an essay, an author needs to make an appropriate choice. With that in mind, look at the images and answer these questions.

1. What type of visual proof predominates in Images 4 and 5?
2. Compare the photograph that accompanies the Sachs article with Images 4 and 5. Which type of visual proof do you think provides the most appropriate support for the Sachs article: Image 2, Image 3, Image 4, or Image 5? Consider the context of the essay and the proofs it relies on to provide reasons for your answer.

Image 4:
Malnutrition in Sudan.

Child famine viction in a feeding center in Sudan.

Why does this photograph qualify as a visual argument? What claim does it make? Do you think it would be a more appropriate addition to the Sachs article (page 250) than the original image that appears with it? Or if not, why?

Image 5:
Kenyan Refugees.

This photograph was designated by the *New York Times* as the "Picture of the Day" for January 15, 2008. Accompanying the photograph was the following explanation: "Kenyan refugees reached for bread during a food handout in Nairobi. As Parliament met for the first time since Kenya's election crisis erupted last month [December 2007], thousands of Kenyan refugees still struggled to get food and water after being forced from their homes in the ethnic violence that followed the disputed election. The photographer is Kim Ludbrook of the European Pressphoto Agency."

Does this photograph qualify as a visual argument? Why? What is its claim? What special qualities helped it earn the distinction of "picture of the day" in January 2008? Do you think it would be a more appropriate addition to the Sachs article (page 250) than the original image that appears with it? Why or why not?

E. Class Discussion and Writing Assignment: Proofs and Style in the Declaration of Independence

The Declaration of Independence, a classic argument, was written by Thomas Jefferson in 1776 to explain why the American colonies wanted to separate from Great Britain. It established America as independent states, and thus it is a revolutionary document with a revolutionary purpose.

1. Read the Declaration of Independence. To understand it better, divide it into its three major component parts. Draw a line at the end of part 1, which explains the general principles behind the revolutionary action. Then draw a line at the end of part 2, which lists the reasons for the action. Finally, identify the purpose of the third and last brief part of the document.

2. The document presents an argument with the value warrants stated in part 1, the support in part 2, and the conclusion in part 3. Summarize the ideas in each part of the argument.

3. Test the argument by questioning the warrants and the support. Do you agree with them? If you accept them, you accept the conclusion.

4. Identify some of the proofs in the document, and comment on their soundness and effectiveness.

5. Describe the predominant style in the document, and give examples that support your answer.

6. Write a 250-word paper in which you explain the insights you now have about the structure, proofs, and style of the Declaration of Independence.

253

> **BEFORE YOU READ:** What do you remember about the writing of the Declaration of Independence?

ESSAY #3   **THE DECLARATION OF INDEPENDENCE**

Thomas Jefferson

The Declaration of Independence was approved by Congress on July 2, 1776, and published two days later.

1 When in the course of human events, it becomes necessary for one people to dissolve the political bands which have connected them with another, and to assume among the Powers of the earth, the separate and equal station to which the Laws of Nature and of Nature's God entitle them, a decent respect to the opinions of mankind requires that they should declare the causes which impel them to the separation.

2 We hold these truths to be self-evident, that all men are created equal, that they are endowed by their Creator with certain unalienable Rights, that among these are Life, Liberty and the pursuit of Happiness.

3 That to secure these rights, Governments are instituted among Men, deriving their just powers from the consent of the governed.

4 That whenever any Form of Government becomes destructive of these ends, it is the Right of the People to alter or to abolish it, and to institute a new Government, laying its foundation on such principles and organizing its powers in such form, as to them shall seem most likely to effect their Safety and Happiness. Prudence, indeed, will dictate that Governments long established should not be changed for light and transient causes; and accordingly all experience hath shown that mankind are more disposed to suffer, while evils are sufferable, than to right themselves by abolishing the forms to which they are accustomed. But when a long train of abuses and usurpations pursuing invariably the same Object evinces a design to reduce them under absolute Despotism, it is their right, it is their duty, to throw off such government, and to provide new Guards for their future security.

5 Such has been the patient sufferance of these Colonies, and such is now the necessity which constrains them to alter their former Systems of Government. The history of the present King of Great Britain is a history of repeated injuries and usurpations, all having in direct object the establishment of an absolute Tyranny over these States. To prove this, let Facts be submitted to a candid world.

6 He has refused his Assent to Laws, the most wholesome and necessary for the public good.

7 He has forbidden his Governors to pass Laws of immediate and pressing importance, unless suspended in their operation till his Assent should be obtained; and when so suspended, he has utterly neglected to attend to them.

8 He has refused to pass over Laws for the accommodation of large districts of people, unless those people would relinquish the right of Representation in the Legislature, a right inestimable to them and formidable to tyrants only.

9 He has called together legislative bodies at places unusual, uncomfortable, and distant from the depository of their Public Records, for the sole purpose of fatiguing them into compliance with his measures.

10 He has dissolved Representative Houses repeatedly, for opposing with manly firmness his invasions on the rights of the people.

11   He has refused for a long time, after such dissolutions, to cause others to be elected; whereby the Legislative Powers, incapable of Annihilation, have returned to the People at large for their exercise; the State remaining in the meantime exposed to all the dangers of invasion from without, and convulsions within.

12   He has endeavored to prevent the population of these States; for that purpose obstructing the Laws for Naturalization of Foreigners; refusing to pass others to encourage their migration hither, and raising the conditions of new Appropriations of Lands.

13   He has obstructed the Administration of Justice, by refusing his Assent to Laws for establishing Judiciary Powers.

14   He has made Judges dependent on his Will alone, for the tenure of their offices, and the amount and payment of their salaries.

15   He has erected a multitude of New Offices, and sent hither swarms of Officers to harass our People, and eat out their substance.

16   He has kept among us, in time of peace, Standing Armies without the consent of our legislatures.

17   He has affected to render the Military independent of and superior to the Civil Power.

18   He has combined with others to subject us to jurisdictions foreign to our constitution, and unacknowledged by our laws; giving his Assent to their acts of pretended Legislation:

19   For quartering large bodies of armed troops among us:

20   For protecting them, by a mock Trial, from Punishment for any Murders which they should commit on the inhabitants of these States:

21   For cutting off our Trade with all parts of the world:

22   For imposing Taxes on us without our Consent:

23   For depriving us in many cases of the benefits of Trial by Jury:

24   For transporting us beyond Seas to be tried for pretended offenses:

25   For abolishing the free System of English Laws in a neighboring Province, establishing therein an Arbitrary government, and enlarging its Boundaries so as to render it at once an example and fit instrument for introducing the same absolute rule into these Colonies:

26   For taking away our Charters, abolishing our most valuable Laws, and altering fundamentally the Forms of our Governments:

27   For suspending our own Legislatures, and declaring themselves invested with Power to legislate for us in all cases whatsoever.

28   He has abdicated Government here, by declaring us out of his Protection and waging War against us.

29   He has plundered our seas, ravaged our Coasts, burnt our towns, and destroyed the Lives of our people.

30   He is at this time transporting large Armies of foreign Mercenaries to compleat the works of death, desolation and tyranny, already begun with circumstances of Cruelty & perfidy scarcely paralleled in the most barbarous ages, and totally unworthy the Head of a civilized nation.

31   He has constrained our fellow Citizens taken Captive on the high Seas to bear Arms against their Country, to become the executioners of their friends and Brethren, or to fall themselves by their Hands.

32   He has excited domestic insurrections amongst us, and has endeavored to bring on the inhabitants of our frontiers, the merciless Indian Savages, whose known rule of warfare, is an undistinguished destruction of all ages, sexes and conditions.

33   In every stage of these Oppressions We have Petitioned for Redress in the most humble terms: Our repeated Petitions have been answered only by repeated injury. A Prince, whose character is thus marked by every act which may define a Tyrant, is unfit to be the ruler of a free people.

34   Nor have We been wanting in attention to our British brethren. We have warned them from time to time of attempts by their legislature to extend an unwarrantable jurisdiction over us. We have reminded

them of the circumstances of our emigration and settlement here. We have appealed to their native justice and magnanimity, and we have conjured them by the ties of our common kindred to disavow these usurpations, which would inevitably interrupt our connections and correspondence. They too have been deaf to the voice of justice and of consanguinity. We must, therefore, acquiesce in the necessity, which denounces our Separation, and hold them, as we hold the rest of mankind, Enemies in War, in Peace Friends.

35 We, therefore, the Representatives of the *United States of America,* in General Congress, Assembled, appealing to the Supreme Judge of the world for the rectitude of our intentions, do, in the Name, and by authority of the good People of these Colonies, solemnly publish and declare, That these United Colonies are, and of Right ought to be Free and Independent States; that they are Absolved from all Allegiance to the British Crown, and that all political connection between them and the State of Great Britain,

is and ought to be totally dissolved; and that as Free and Independent States, they have full power to levy War, conclude Peace, contract Alliances, establish Commerce, and to do all other Acts and Things which independent States may of right do. And for the support of this Declaration, with a firm reliance on the protection of Divine Providence, we mutually pledge to each other our Lives, our Fortunes and our sacred Honor.

For Discussion:

Describe the rhetorical situation for the Declaration of Independence. Why is it usually described as a "revolutionary document"? What are the four "self-evident" truths or human rights mentioned in this document? Do all people have equal claim to these rights, or can you think of constraining circumstances when certain individuals might be denied these rights? Do individuals pursue these rights, or do governments guarantee them? What is the difference? Discuss.

F. Prewriting: Using the Proofs to Generate Ideas for a Position Paper

You have analyzed other authors' use of proofs in the preceding exercises. Now think about how you can use the proofs in your own writing. If you are working on a "Position Paper Based on 'The Reader'" (Exercise F in Chapter 8), you will already have a claim, and you may have already used the Toulmin model (page 173) and the claim questions (page 218) to help you develop the structure and some of the ideas for your paper. Use the mnemonics SIC-DADS and VAM to help you consider the proofs and ask the following questions. Write out answers for those that are most promising.

1. *Signs:* What symptoms or signs will demonstrate that this is so?

2. *Induction:* What examples can I use and what conclusions can I draw from them? Are they convincing enough to help the reader make the "inductive leap"?

3. *Cause:* What has caused this? Why is this happening? Think of explanations and examples of both cause and effect.

4. *Deduction:* What concluding statements do I want to make? What general principles and examples (or cases) are they based on?

5. *Analogies:* How can I show that what happened in one case will probably happen again in another case? Can I use a literal analogy to compare

items in the same general category? Can I use a figurative analogy to compare items from different categories? Can I demonstrate that history repeats itself by citing a historical analogy?

6. *Definition:* What words or concepts will I need to define?

7. *Statistics:* What statistics can I use? Would they be more convincing in graph form?

8. *Values:* To what values can I appeal? Should I spell them out or leave them implicit? Will narratives and emotional language make my appeals to values stronger?

9. *Authority:* Whom should I quote? What can I use from my own background and experience to establish my own expertise? How can I use language to create common ground and establish *ethos*?

10. *Motives:* What does my audience need and want in regard to this topic? How can I appeal to those needs? Will emotional language help?

11. *Visual proof:* Could I strengthen my paper with visual proof, if that is part of the assignment? What could I use?

CHAPTER
8

The Fallacies and Ethical Argument

I n an advertisement for a health club, an attractive, muscular man is embracing a beautiful, slim woman. Both are dressed in exercise clothing. The caption reads, "Studies show diets don't work. This picture shows exercise does." No further evidence is provided. You do not have to be an expert in argument theory to sense that something is wrong with this proof.

Responsible and honest proof relies on skillful use of support and acceptable warrants to prove a claim. Since argument deals with probability instead of certainty, an argument may be perceived as very convincing, somewhat convincing, or not convincing at all. The success of the argument depends on the proofs. Weak support or a faulty or unacceptable warrant weakens an argument, but it is still an argument. The reader must ask the test of validity questions identified in Chapter 7 to evaluate the reliability and strength of the proofs. Ultimately, the reader must assess the validity of the entire argument itself and decide whether it is well developed or underdeveloped, acceptable or unacceptable, moral or immoral.

There are encounters in arguments, as in the case of the advertisement just described, in which a reader will find material that may appear at first to be a proof but really is not a proof at all—it is a *pseudoproof*, or what is commonly called a *fallacy*. Fallacies lead an audience astray, they distort and distract, they represent inadequate reasoning or nonreasoning, and they either exaggerate or oversimplify a claim instead of proving it.

The author of the advertisement in the opening example expects the reader to accept a number of unstated warrants that most people would reject were they explicitly stated: (1) The studies about dieting are a reasonable sample to show that dieting does not change the shape of your body; (2) the best way to take up effective exercise and develop a well-shaped body is to join an exercise club; and (3) if you improve the shape of your body, you will find romance on the floor of the exercise club. The visual support is the picture of the two attractive people who are embracing in their exercise clothes. The final claim, based on those warrants and that support, of course, is that you should join the exercise club.

Suppose you encounter the exercise club advertisement at a time when you feel overweight, out of shape, and unloved. You might be tempted to believe the argument because the warrants and the support reflect what you would wish to believe or want to be so. Fallacies can seem convincing when they appear to support what an audience already believes or wants to believe.

Warrants that few people would find convincing can create the common ground necessary for successful argument if they hold an emotional appeal to someone's deep prejudices, unreasonable biases, or irrational beliefs or wishes. You may have encountered Web sites on the Internet, like those supported by hate groups, for example, that present support and warrants that you would never find acceptable. As you analyze the reasoning on these sites, you discover that much of it is extremist and that it supports only one narrow view. The support is often distorted, insufficient, unreliable, exaggerated, or oversimplified. Furthermore, the warrants are untrue, and emotional material is used to stir up excessive feelings rather than to prove a rational point. You can also often identify a number of specific fallacies on such sites.

When you are tempted to believe an argument that does not seem logical to you or seems to have something wrong with it, consider why you are tempted to believe it. If fallacies and unacceptable reasoning are weakening the claim or proving the argument false, analyze it and expose these problems. This will be comparatively easy to do if you already strongly disagree with the ideas and harder to do if, for some reason, you are tempted to accept them.

You will encounter fallacies in advertisements or other visual media, letters to the editor, some forms of journalism such as Web logs (known as blogs), and other argument writing that you find both in print and online. Avoid quoting sources that contain fallacies, and avoid fallacies in your own writing. Fallacies in your writing, whether created by you or by the authors you choose to quote, weaken your argument and damage your *ethos*. Recognize fallacies by asking, "Is this material even relevant? Is it adequate? Do I agree? Does it support the claim?" Learning the common types of fallacies will also help you recognize and avoid them. Described here are the most common ones, in the same categories we have used for genuine proofs: logic, character (*ethos*), and emotion.

259

Fallacies in Logic

Fallacies pose as logical proof, but you will see that they are really pseudoproofs that prove nothing at all. You may have trouble remembering all of their names; many people do. Concentrate instead on the fallacious thinking characterized by each of them, such as introducing irrelevant material; exaggerating; providing wrong, unfair, inadequate, or even no support; harboring unacceptable warrants; drawing inappropriate conclusions; and oversimplifying the choices.

Begging the Question

No support is provided by the arguer who begs the question, and the claim is simply restated, over and over again, in one form or another. For example, "Capital punishment deters crime because it keeps criminals from committing murder" simply restates the same idea in other words. Have you ever encountered people who claim something is true because they say it is true? If the individual is a recognized authority on the issue, then such a claim may be accurate and relevant. Imagine, however, a politician who claims that a work of art is immoral because he thinks it is. No criteria for judging the morality or immorality of art are provided. We are simply asked to accept the subjective opinion of someone who may know very little about art. This individual is begging the question.

There are many examples one might document in political speech, but here are two familiar forms: "Everyone knows that the president of the United States has done his best for the environment because he said so," or, "Americans think the country is in a recession because they feel that it is." The name of this fallacy, begging the question, is easily remembered by imagining that the arguer, when asked for support, begs off and simply restates the claim in the same or different words.

Red Herring

A red herring provides irrelevant and misleading support that pulls the audience away from the real argument. For example, "I don't believe we should elect this candidate because she would have to put her kids in day care" is a red herring; qualifications to hold office have nothing to do with household arrangements. Whether or not the police were racist in the O. J. Simpson trial was a red herring in the sense that even though their alleged racism might have provided a motive for planting evidence, their racism was unrelated to whether Simpson was innocent or guilty of murder. Another red herring in the O. J. Simpson case that influenced some people was the idea that the accused was a great sports hero and we should not degrade great sports heroes by trying them for murder. Also, authors of detective fiction use red herrings in their plots as false clues to divert the reader's attention from the real murderer.

To remember the red herring fallacy, recall that the fish, the red herring, was at one time used to train hunting dogs to follow a scent. It was not a true scent, however. The herring scent was irrelevant to the real smells of the real hunt, and the fallacy, the red herring, is irrelevant to an argument when it introduces such unrelated support. To argue that a person's parental responsibilities is a factor in the person's qualifications for a job or that sports heroes should be treated differently from other people is to use this "fishy" fallacy.

Non Sequitur

Non sequitur is Latin for "it does not follow." In this type of fallacy, the conclusion does not follow from the evidence and the warrant. Here are some examples: the professor in the Hawaiian shirt and gold chains must be an easy grader; the self-consciously beautiful woman who has applied for a job as a secretary would not do the job well; that man with the powerful new computer must be highly skilled in the use of computer technology. The warrants for these three examples are that the professor's clothes indicate how he will grade, beautiful women cannot be good secretaries, and owning powerful equipment implies the ability to use it. You can probably sense the problems with these warrants. They are so difficult for most people to accept that none of these examples come across as convincing arguments. Here is another example of a *non sequitur:* Women should not be placed in executive positions because they cannot drive cars as well as men.

Straw Man

A straw man involves attributing an argument to an opponent that the opponent never made and then refuting it in a devastating way. The arguer sets up an idea, refutes it, and appears to win, even though the idea may be unrelated to the issue being discussed. For example, a political candidate might set up a straw man by claiming that his opponent has said he is too old to do the job, when in fact the opponent has never mentioned age as an issue. Then the candidate refutes the age issue by detailing the advantages of age and appears to win the argument, even though this is not an issue at all. In fact, by refuting this false issue, the candidate may give the impression that he could refute any other arguments put forth by the opposition as well. The use of a straw man suggests competence where it might not actually exist.

Stacked Evidence

Stacking evidence to represent only one side of an issue that clearly has two sides gives a distorted impression of the issue. For example, to prove that television is an inspiring and uplifting medium, the only evidence given is that PBS nature shows are educational, *Friends* promotes personal bonds, and news programs and documentaries keep audiences informed. The sex and violence programming and the commercials are never mentioned.

Manufactured Evidence

Using fake evidence to prove a claim will discredit an entire argument and ruin the reputation of the individual who makes it up. A famous example occurred in 2004 when a South Korean scientist announced he had created human embryos through cloning, a development which would enable him to extract embryonic stem cells from them for use in further research on therapeutic cloning. This research held great promise for curing certain diseases and injuries. The results were published in *Science*, widely accepted as the most credible scientific journal.

A few months later, the announced research results were exposed as intentional fabrications. Because he had used fake or false evidence, the scientist had to step down from his official positions and *Science* retracted his papers.

Unreliable or Insufficient Evidence

Evidence should be verifiable, which means you should be able to look it up in another source and find the same information. There should also be enough evidence, and major information that could change the way one interprets the evidence should not be omitted. DNA evidence is often used in criminal cases to prove guilt. However, it is also increasingly being used to exonerate criminals who were wrongly accused of crimes in the first place and who have been in prison for many years in spite of their innocence. In these cases, the evidence used to convict them was insufficient or unreliable, and new DNA evidence proves that it was unreliable.

Exaggerated or Oversimplified Evidence

Here is an example of what can happen when exaggerated evidence is used. In 2006 members of the Duke University lacrosse team were accused of rape and indicted by a county district attorney who was later exposed and disbarred for exaggerating evidence in the case. The athletes were excused of all charges. The district attorney not only lost his law license but was also found guilty of criminal contempt and served a day in jail. A different example offers a chance to study evidence for this problem. Al Gore has been accused of exaggerating the evidence for global warming. Some people agree with that assessment, and many others disagree and argue that his evidence is impeccable. Read the articles about the environment and climate change in "The Reader" (pages 648–655) and decide for yourself.

Oversimplifying evidence can also discredit an argument. For example, to argue that handguns should be sold to "good" people and not to criminals oversimplifies. It is difficult to accept a conclusion based on evidence of this sort because it has no actual content.

Distorted Statistics

Statistics can be manipulated or changed so that they appear to support a claim when, actually, they do not. For example, the owner of a company argues that salaries in the company are good since the average salary is $40,000. What is left out is that one individual makes $120,000, while four others make only $20,0000 each. Presenting the average salary to suggest an equitable pay scale distorts the truth.

Take a close look at the numerical data presented in graphs and tables of figures. For example, in one graph you may read that the average income in America is $35,500 and in another you read that it is $24,000. This is puzzling until you realize that the $35,500 figure represents household income, or the amount made by all members of a household. The figure has been established by adding all existing household incomes and dividing by the total number of households to obtain the average, whereas the $24,000 is a mean figure of individual incomes rather than an average. The mean is derived this way: if all of the incomes of individuals were listed in order of most to least, one of these would appear in the middle of the list, with an equal number of incomes above and below it. That is the mean income. Read all of the explanations and titles that accompany numerical date so that you will understand exactly what the data actually state.

In reading graphs, notice the range of figures on the horizontal and vertical axes. Do they range from 0 to 100, or do they represent a smaller range, say, 80 to 100? A recent published line graph indicates that a popular stock is "plummeting," but the graph plots a change from $117 to $103 (a difference of $14) per share on the vertical axis and shows how this has occurred over a period of several months on the horizontal axis. Visually the graph suggests a steep decline, greater than what really occurred.

With samples of information, ask whether the sample as shown in tables and charts is fair and accurate. Many tables that summarize trends—such as the information from opinion polls, a history of research results, or a report of common cultural practices—present only the data from a sample because all possible data would be too massive to gather and interpret. When you examine such materials, determine what the sample is supposed to represent and whether or not the sample is fair. Also, determine the source of the data, which should be reported along with it. Spend some time reading and pondering tables of figures, charts, and graphs. Try to understand what is really going on in them, and make some judgments about their accuracy and value.

Either-Or

Some arguments are oversimplified by the arguer and presented as black-or-white, either-or choices when there are other alternatives. Some examples are "This country can either have a strong defense program or a strong social welfare program," "We can develop either a strong space program or an urban development program," "A woman can either be a mother or have a career," and "A man can either go to graduate school or become a company man." No alternative, middle-ground, or compromise positions are acknowledged.

Post Hoc

This is short for *post hoc, ergo propter hoc*, a Latin phrase that translates as "after this, therefore because of this." To put it more simply, *post hoc* is the fallacy of faulty cause. For example, it is fallacious to claim in an advertisement that people will be more attractive and more popular if they drink a certain brand of cola. Look at other advertisements on television or in magazines, and you will easily find other examples of *post hoc*, the claim that one thing causes another when there is actually no causal relationship between them. Think about the outdoor healthy virility of the Marlboro man, for example, and the suggestion that he got that way by smoking cigarettes. Another example is the person who finds romance by serving a particular spaghetti sauce or using a specific cologne.

Hasty Generalization

Sometimes arguers "jump to conclusions" by basing a conclusion on too few examples. For example, someone may conclude that the U.S. government is hopelessly flawed because the president and the Congress cannot reach agreement on a particular piece of legislation, or that since some students in urban schools belong to gangs, most students in those schools belong to gangs. Hasty generalizations often contribute to stereotyping.

Fallacies That Affect Character or *Ethos*

Fallacies that are aimed at attacking character or at using character instead of evidence for proof are misleading and can damage *ethos*.

Ad Hominem

Ad hominem means "to the man" in Latin. An *ad hominem* argument attacks a person's character rather than a person's ideas or policies. The press is notorious for such attacks during political campaigns, and so are some of the candidates themselves. The "character issue," for example, may receive more attention than more serious, substantive issues. Such *ad hominem* discussion scrutinizes negative information that is provided about the candidates' personal lives rather than about their ideas or the issues that concern them. The purpose of *ad hominem* argument is to discredit. Take another example of an *ad hominem* dispute, but in this case the beliefs or ethical qualities of a person are exposed to negative attack. For example, piety is said to have no validity because of the careless personal and financial habits of a television evangelist. This *ad hominem* argument directs attention away from the issue (here, bad actions) and toward the person as bad. Thus we become prejudiced and biased against an individual personally or an institution generally instead of evaluating facts or ideas when *ad hominem* exchange predominates.

Guilt by Association

The fallacy of guilt by association suggests that people's character can be judged by examining the character of their associates. For example, an employee in a company that defrauds the government is declared dishonest because of his employment with the company, even though he may have known nothing of the fraud. Or an observer is thrown into jail along with some political protesters simply because she was in the wrong place at the wrong time. Political figures are often judged as morally defective if they associate with people with questionable values and reputations. It is assumed that these individuals are members of these groups and guilty by association.

Using Authority Instead of Evidence

This is a variation of begging the question. The arguer relies on personal authority to prove a point rather than on evidence. For example, a salesman tells you to buy the used car because he is honest and trustworthy and he knows your neighbor.

Emotional Fallacies

Irrelevant, unrelated, and distracting emotional materials are often introduced into argument to try to convince the audience. Here are some examples.

Bandwagon Appeal

The argument is that everyone is doing something, so you should too. For example, everyone is watching reality TV, so you should jump on the bandwagon and watch it also. Political and other public opinion polls are sometimes used to promote the bandwagon appeal. The suggestion is that since a majority of the people polled hold a certain opinion, you should adopt it also.

When you feel yourself being influenced by what everyone else seems to be doing, decide whether basing your action on the bandwagon appeal is what you really want to do. Maybe you are about to jump on the bandwagon and eat more vegetables, which would be okay, but if you are about to drink too much alcohol because everyone else is doing it, then maybe you need to get off that bandwagon.

Slippery Slope

The slippery-slope fallacy is a scare tactic that suggests that if we allow one thing to happen, we will immediately be sliding down a slippery slope to disaster. This fallacy is sometimes introduced into environmental and abortion issues. If we allow loggers to cut a few trees, we will soon lose all the forests. Or if a woman is required to wait twenty-four hours to reconsider her decision to have an abortion, soon there will be so many restrictions that no one will be able to have an abortion. This fallacy is similar to the saying about the camel that gets its nose into the tent. If we permit the nose today, we have the whole camel to deal with tomorrow. It is better not to start because disaster may result.

Creating False Needs

Emotional proofs, as you have learned, appeal to what people value and think they need. Sometimes an arguer will create a false sense of need where none exists or will unrealistically heighten an existing need. The intent is to make the argument more convincing. Advertising provides excellent examples. The housewife is told she needs a shining kitchen floor with a high gloss that only a certain wax can provide. Parents are reminded that they want smart, successful children, so they should buy a computer for each of them. The ad for the health club described at the beginning of this chapter that promises both weight loss and romance creates a false need for people who may be only vaguely concerned about their weight and the possibilities of romance before reading this ad.

Distorted Emotional Appeal

Irrelevant and unrelated emotional examples or stories that are unrelated to the subject are sometimes used to try to prove a point. For example, providing horrible details about the suffering of a terminally ill patient to prove that assisted suicide should be legal can be irrelevant and unrelated to the claim. This is particularly true when the patient's suffering can be relieved in other ways, such as with meditation techniques or with drug therapies. Faulty analogies, like comparing governments to hungry wolves, distorted visuals, like showing how happy people can become by doing abdominal exercises, extreme slogans, like those printed on placards in public demonstrations, and hate language aimed at particular groups of people represent misuse and distortion of emotional appeal and, on close scrutiny, they can be exposed as ineffective proof.

These examples of fallacies provide you with a good sense of what constitutes fallacious reasoning. Armed with this list and with the tests of validity for genuine proofs listed under "Tests of Validity" in the Summary Charts (pages 511–523), you now have what you need to evaluate the strength and validity of the proofs in an argument. This information will help you make evaluations, form rebuttals to challenge weak arguments, and create arguments of your own that rely on genuine proofs instead of fallacies. We now leave unethical argument with its fallacies and faulty evidence and turn to the subject of ethics and morality in argument.

Ethics and Morality in Argument

A person's ability to argue persuasively has been recognized as a potentially powerful influence over other people for centuries. Thus the classical argument theorists, Aristotle, Cicero, and Quintilian, all recognized that citizens should be schooled in argumentation so that they could argue for the causes that would benefit society. They also argued that society needed moral arguers because, without them, immoral arguers would gain too much power. Plato criticized arguers who used their persuasive powers to manipulate people to achieve their own selfish ends. Basic standards that include skill in argumentation coupled with good judgment and common honesty have always been critical to ethical argument, both in classical times and in the present.

Ethical arguers must have the courage and willingness to argue logically and honestly from a strong sense of personal integrity and values. They should also have a strong sense of responsibility and feel obliged to come forward and advocate for what they believe is right. Emotional and motivational appeals should be consistent with positive value systems that will benefit not just one individual but all of society. Using emotions that cloud judgment or persuade individuals to accept ideas that the arguer does not really believe is clearly unethical.

Unethical individuals who argue mainly to manipulate public opinion often use unethical tactics to influence and gain adherence to their points of view. Such tactics include opinion polls that push for particular points of view, exaggerated or manipulated statistics, manufactured evidence, outright lies, and deliberately fallacious reasoning. Other tactics include recasting or redefining issues to make them easier to argue, as in some of the arguments about global warming that minimize its potential dangers to the planet. Language can also be manipulated to change audience perceptions. For example, the government's annual hunger report in 2006 was criticized for substituting the terms "low food security" and "very low food security" for the word *hunger*. It would seem that some people thought that changing the word *hunger*, with its strong negative connotations, to vague multiword terms with weaker connotations might subtly minimize the sting of the problems of poverty and starvation in the country (see page 186). All of these techniques can be very effective in changing audience opinion, even when they are based on false values and motives. For example, people were struck by letters discovered in Germany that were perfect examples of excellent argumentation but of subject matter that was totally immoral. These letters were the written orders for exterminating the Jews during World War II. Although Hitler was a convincing arguer in style, his values and his claims were immoral. In another example, a political consultant working for the president of the United States was exposed as a person who had no core values and who was more interested in manipulating public opinion than in determining what was the best course for the country. This individual was accused by many of believing in nothing.

It is important that you learn to recognize the differences between ethical and unethical argument. You can begin by asking the questions that follow and then searching for information that will help you answer them. Discussing these questions with others will help you achieve a sense of whether an argument is ethical or unethical. Also, gathering additional information about the issue and the arguer can help. Read reviews, editorials, commentaries, and look up biographical information about the author on the Internet. Inform yourself about the author's affiliations and background to help you discover his or her true purpose and motives, point of view, and values. Look for additional information on these matters, whether stated explicitly or implicitly, in the argument itself. Gather information on the rhetorical situation and understand some of the perspectives and positions held by others.

Ask These Questions to Help You Determine Whether an Argument Is Ethical or Unethical:

1. Has the arguer made an adequate effort to understand the issue and its consequences? Does the arguer also understand the positions held by other people?
2. Is the arguer just and fair-minded? Is the support fair, accurate, and convincing? Can I accept the warrants? Should the claim be qualified, if it is not already?
3. Does the arguer sincerely believe that the position he or she is proposing is in the best interests both of the audience and of the larger society?
4. Is the position being proposed actually in the best interests of the audience and the larger society? Ask, Who is benefited and who is burdened or hurt?
5. Does the arguer seem to be manipulating the audience by hiding the real purpose of the argument, by using inappropriate emotional appeals, by manufacturing evidence, by using inaccurate evidence, or by telling lies?
6. Is the arguer changing the definition of words or substituting unusual words for commonly used words to cloud people's perceptions of the issue?
7. Is the arguer recasting or rewording an issue to reduce its threat when it actually represents a significant threat?
8. Do the images distort or exaggerate, or do they present the individual or situation accurately? Do they function as reliable support that enhances the argument, or are they irrelevant, inaccurate, or insulting so that they weaken the argument?

Use this list of criteria to judge the ethical and moral qualities of the argumentation you read or view and let them also guide you when you write. You will be more convincing to your audience.

Review Questions

1. What are fallacies? Why are they also described as pseudoproofs? Under what circumstances might you be tempted to believe a fallacy?
2. What are some of the qualities that characterize fallacious thinking?
3. Name at least two fallacies in logic, two that affect *ethos*, and two emotional fallacies.
4. What is the difference between *ethos* and ethics in argument?
5. Describe some of the qualities of ethical argument.

Exercises and Activities

A. **Class Discussion: Analyzing Advertisements**

Look at the three reprinted advertisements on pages 269–271. The first comes from *Prevention*, a magazine that promotes healthful practices; the second comes from *Rolling Stone*, a biweekly magazine that focuses on music, liberal politics, and popular culture; and the third is from the *National Review,* a conservative magazine with a Right-leaning political and social viewpoint. All three of the ads are either selling products or promoting ideas. Study each one carefully and then answer the questions provided here.

1. What is advertised in each ad?
2. How would you state the claim communicated by each ad?
3. What reasons and evidence are used to support the claim?
4. Characterize the language used in each ad. For example, does any of the language establish the *ethos* of the advertiser, or appeal to logic, or to emotion? Provide some examples.
5. Describe the most obvious fallacies in each of these ads.
6. How does each ad fit the magazine in which it appears in terms of subject matter and values?

B. **Class Discussion: Bring a Fallacy to Class**

Review the fallacies in this chapter. Then find an example of a fallacy and either bring it to class or describe it to the class. Explain why it is a fallacy. Look at advertisements that appear in print, on television, or online; listen to political speeches and political commentary; visit Web sites, blogs, or simply listen to your friends and family.

C. **Group Work and Discussion: Analyzing Fallacies in Written Argument**

The argument on pages 271–273 is written by an author who holds strong opinions about the subject. As you read the essay, focus on those specific statements with which you cannot agree. Then try to figure out why you do not agree. Is the evidence weak or irrelevant? Are there fallacies in its structure? Expose the weaknesses in this argument. After making an assessment, discuss your findings with the class.

Looks like someone could use the right multivitamin.

Meetings, deadlines, and conference calls. And for a moment of peace, you head to the vending machine. Presenting Mega Men® from General Nutrition Centers. You see, it has thirty-nine premium vitamins, minerals, and herbs your body could really use. Including the things that are good for men, like saw palmetto, ginseng, and natural vitamin E. All of which must pass 150 quality checks before it gets to you. And, now is a great time to experience the benefits for yourself. Because when you pick up any GNC brand product, including Mega Men, we'll give you any other GNC brand product at half price.* It's just one more way we help you live your best life.

www.gnc.com

| 5,000 stores nationwide. | Nearly 70 years of expertise. | Backed by over 100 researchers & scientists. | A healthy 10 million customers each year. | GNC LiveWell. |

For the GNC location nearest you, call 1-800-477-4462. ©2002 General Nutrition Centers. May not be available outside the U.S. *See store for details.

Image 2:
A Body Spray Ad.

Before the ice caps melt, before the rainforests disappear, before it's too late!—strap on your bike helmet, take a left at Kyoto, and head straight to . . .

planet gore

. . . National Review Online's newest blog. At Planet Gore, expert analysts keep you abreast of all the tree-hugging, CO2-vilifying environmental cases being fought by America's leading Hollywood documentarian and Internet-inventor, and his holier-than-thou gang of greenpeacenik planet-savers.

planetgore.nationalreview.com

**Image 3:
An Ad for a Blog.**

271

BEFORE YOU READ: What do you associate with feminism?

ESSAY #1   **THE LATEST FROM THE FEMINIST "FRONT"***
Rush Limbaugh

The following is excerpted from the book *See, I Told You So*. The author is well known for his widely aired radio show.

1   Few of my "Thirty-five Undeniable Truths of Life" have stirred as much controversy and outrage as Number Twenty-four: "Feminism was established so that unattractive women could have easier access to the mainstream of society."

2   Many have suggested that this statement is too rough, insensitive, cruel, and unnecessarily provocative. However, there is one absolute defense of this statement. It's called truth. Sometimes the truth hurts. Sometimes the truth is jarring. Sometimes the truth is the most provocative thing you can tell someone. But the truth is still the truth. And it needs to be heard.

3   Likewise, for years I've been telling you that the feminist leadership is basically anti-male. I've said this in many different ways on many different occasions. But no matter how many times I have said it and no matter how cleverly I have rephrased this message, skeptics abound.

4   "Oh, Rush," people say, "aren't you going a little too far? Aren't you overstating your case?"

5   Well, folks, once again, I have to say it. The evidence that I was right all along about feminism—as with so many other things—is now overwhelming. [. . .]

6   The people who define modern feminism are saying that normal male deportment is

*Rush H. Limbaugh III, *See, I Told You So* (New York: Simon & Schuster, 1993), 221–23, 225–27.

harassment, near rape, abuse, and disrespect. These extremists, who make up the intellectual leadership of the modern feminist movement, are attempting to make the case that any expression of interest by a man in a woman is harassment. Inevitably, this is going to lead to several serious problems.

7   First among those is that men will become fearful about making any advances. This attitude will confuse men about what is right and what kind of behavior is acceptable. If no approach is welcome, then women will, by necessity, have to become the aggressors. Men will be afraid of crossing the line.

8   The second major problem with this trend is that it trivializes real sexual harassment, real rape. When people are labeling everyday, normal, male-female conduct as sexual harassment, we not only obliterate relations between the sexes, but we greatly trivialize true sexual harassment. Harassment is now being so broadly defined by some that it entails behavior that offends or annoys or interrupts your life.

9   The fact of the matter is that women have far more power than most of them realize. It's a biological fact that males are the aggressors. We all know this is true. That means that the ultimate power—the power to say yes or no—lies with women.

10   If consent is denied and the aggressive male physically forces himself on the woman to the point of penetration, then you have rape—real rape. But this is the exception. Most men are not rapists. But militant feminists seek to blur the distinctions. Let's look at date rape, for example. I have a problem with feminists seeking to expand the concept of rape by adding such adjectives as *date* and *acquaintance*. Words mean things. . . . Especially in these times of hypersensitivity, it is very important that we are clear in our word usage. This is even more the case when the word in question represents criminal behavior, in some cases punishable by life imprisonment. This is dead-serious, folks. Rape means rape. It either is, or it isn't. It matters

not whether it occurs on a date or on Mars. It is my belief that the date-rape concept has been promoted by those whose agenda it is to blur these distinctions. By calling it "date rape," the intent is to expand the scope of the very serious crime of rape, and to include within the category of "rape" behavior that certainly is not rape. Please don't misinterpret my meaning. As a firm believer that words have meaning, I'm very careful to use mine precisely. I condemn the act of rape as much as any other human being would. It is inexcusable. Confusing its definition by trying to expand its scope deceitfully will only redound to the detriment of real rape victims. That is unconscionable.

11   Some militant feminists apparently harbor such animosity for the opposite sex that they want to criminalize the process of courtship—the old-fashioned "chase." I have news for these people: It's normal for boys to pursue girls. It's natural for men to pursue women. This normal and natural process, once called the fine art of seduction, is being confused with harassment. What was once considered an important part of the process of finding a mate is being mischaracterized as rape.

12   How should you channel normal masculinity and the aggressive nature of the male? Would these women prefer men as husbands, or leaders of marauding gangs? That is basically the choice. Because women can be—and need to be—a great civilizing influence over men.

13   Do you realize that in some cities today men can be arrested for making a wolf whistle at a comely woman? Now, I'm not suggesting this is the kind of behavior we should encourage, but should it be criminalized? And what are the consequences of this sort of overreaction? The consequences are manifold. It's no wonder so many men and women have problems interacting. Rules and regulations like these are presumably meant to foster improved relations between men

and women, but their effect is just the opposite. What is being fostered is an adversarial relationship between the sexes.

14 Take, for instance, the young star of "The Wonder Years," Fred Savage. The then sixteen-year-old was hit with a sexual-harassment suit by a former staffer of the show, Monique Long, who claimed that Savage repeatedly asked her to have an affair with him and—egads!—touched her by holding her hand. The lawsuit also charged that Jason Hervey, another actor on the show, harassed Long during her two years on the show as a costume designer, at one point touching her "in a sexual way." Long, thirty-two, claimed she was asked not to return to the show because of her complaints about the actors.

15 Have things gotten to the point where a man, or boy, can't ask a woman out? Can't flirt? Is it a crime to hold somebody's hand? Wouldn't a more appropriate response to questionable behavior have been for this thirty-two-year-old woman to call the teenager's parents? Or even slap him in the face? Is our society so confused now about relations between men and women that a mature adult doesn't know how to deal with a flirtatious sixteen-year-old?

For Discussion:

What do you see that weakens this argument? How could the author have made it a stronger argument?

D. Class Discussion: Recognizing Ethical Argument

Read the historical material and look at the two photographs that accompany "The Gettysburg Address," read the text of the address, and be prepared to state your views on why the speech and the images are good examples of ethical argument. Review the questions for recognizing ethical argument on page 267 and answer them as they apply to this famous speech by President Abraham Lincoln. Answer question 8 to help you evaluate the two images.

Rhetorical Situation

Lincoln gave "The Gettysburg Address" during the Civil War when the issue facing the country was national unity. The following description and photograph are taken from the *The History Place™* Web site.

The Battle of Gettysburg occurred over three hot summer days, July 1 to July 3, 1863, around the small market town of Gettysburg, Pennsylvania. It began as a skirmish but by its end involved 160,000 Americans and effectively decided the fate of the Union.

On November 19, 1863, President Lincoln went to the Battlefield to dedicate it as a national cemetery. The main orator, Edward Everett of Massachusetts, delivered a two hour formal address. The president then had his turn. He spoke in his high, penetrating voice, and in a little over two minutes delivered this speech, surprising many in the audience by its shortness and leaving many others quite unimpressed.

Over time, however, his speech with its ending words—government of the People, by the People, for the People—have come to symbolize the definition of democracy itself.[1]

---

[1]"Abraham Lincoln: The Gettysburg Address," *The History Place: Great Speeches Collection*, July 4, 1996/2008. April 2008, http://www.historyplace.com/speeches/gettysburg.htm.

273

THE GETTYSBURG ADDRESS
Gettysburg, Pennsylvania, November 19, 1863

On June 1, 1865, Senator Charles Sumner commented on what is now considered the most famous speech by President Abraham Lincoln. In his eulogy on the slain president, he called it a "monumental act." He said Lincoln was mistaken that "the world will little note, nor long remember what we say here." Rather, the Bostonian remarked, "The world noted at once what he said, and will never cease to remember it. The battle itself was less important than the speech."

1   Four score and seven years ago our fathers brought forth on this continent, a new nation, conceived in Liberty, and dedicated to the proposition that all men are created equal.

2   Now we are engaged in a great civil war, testing whether that nation, or any nation so conceived and so dedicated, can long endure. We are met on a great battle-field of that war. We have come to dedicate a portion of that field, as a final resting place for those who here gave their lives that that nation might live. It is altogether fitting and proper that we should do this.

3   But, in a larger sense, we can not dedicate—we can not consecrate—we can not hallow—this ground. The brave men, living and dead, who struggled here, have consecrated it, far above our poor power to add or detract. The world will little note, nor long remember what we say here, but it can never forget what they did here. It is for us

Image 1:
President Lincoln among the crowd at Gettysburg.

Image 2:
The Soldiers' National Monument that stands in the center of the National Cemetery at Gettysburg, Pennsylvania.

the living, rather, to be dedicated here to the unfinished work which they who fought here have thus far so nobly advanced. It is rather for us to be here dedicated to the great task remaining before us—that from these honored dead we take increased devotion to that cause for which they gave the last full measure of devotion—that we here highly resolve that these dead shall not have died in vain—that this nation, under God, shall have a new birth of freedom—and the government of the people, by the people, for the people, shall not perish from the earth.[2]

For Discussion:

Lincoln was shot on April 14, 1865, and he died the next day. The Civil War ended May 26, 1865. What qualities make "The Gettysburg Address" an ethical argument? Describe the values in the address that help define it as an ethical argument. What are some of the most famous phrases in the address, and why are they still important? Describe how the address served the best interests of the audience and the larger society in 1863 and continues to serve in our society today. Comment on the images. How does Image 1 help establish the rhetorical situation for the address? What is the effect of including an old photograph instead of a modern one? Image 2 is a photograph of a monument. Describe the qualities of a monument that make it an effective visual argument.

E. **Prewriting: Questions to Evaluate Support and Eliminate Fallacies**

If you are working on a "Position Paper Based on 'The Reader' " (Exercise F in this chapter), you have already applied the Toulmin model to get a sense of the shape of your paper (page 173), and you have answered the claim questions (page 218) and the proof questions (pages 256–257) to generate subclaims and support for the paper as well. Now go back and evaluate your prewriting. Look at the subclaims and support to make certain all are complete and reliable. Look for fallacies. Correct or eliminate any items that might weaken your argument. Answering the following questions will help.

1. Do I have enough support to be convincing? What can I add?

2. Is my support reliable and convincing? How can I make it more so?

3. Is anything exaggerated or oversimplified? How can I be more accurate?

4. Do I rely too much on my own authority ("This is true because I say so") instead of giving support? Can I add support and the opinions of other authorities to be more convincing?

5. Am I weakening this argument with too much emotional appeal? Should any of it be eliminated?

6. Have I used any fallacies as proof? (Check especially for hasty generalizations and *post hoc* or faulty cause, probably the two most common fallacies. Look for other fallacies, and if you find any, either rewrite so that they are acceptable, or eliminate them.)

---

[2]*Abraham Lincoln Online. org,* 1995–2008. Speeches. April 2008, showcase.netins.net/web/creative/lincoln/gettysburg.htm.

F. Writing Assignment: A Position Paper Based on "The Reader"

For this assignment, you will write a position paper in which you make a claim and prove it. Your claim should be related to a topic you have selected from "The Reader." The paper should be about 1,000 words long, typed, and double-spaced.

Your purpose in this assignment is to use the argument theory you have learned in Chapters 5–8 to help you invent ideas and write. You will also draw on your own reasoning and information from the essays to help you argue.

Prewriting

If you have not already done so, complete some or all of the prewriting activities listed here so that you will have plenty of material to draw on when you draft your paper. They are explained on the pages cited.

1. Read the issue questions in "The Reader"; select the one that interests you the most; read the related essays; and write an issue proposal (page 31).

2. Write summary-response papers for each of the related essays (page 136).

3. Write an exploratory essay to help you understand the topic. (pages 144–145).

4. Use the Toulmin model (page 173) to help you find the elements for the paper; use the claim questions to refine and focus your claim and generate further ideas for subclaims (page 218); use the proof questions to develop convincing proofs for your claims (pages 256–257); and use the evaluation questions to improve your support and eliminate fallacies (page 275).

Writing a List or an Outline

Follow the instructions in Chapter 4, on pages 118–119, for making an extended list or outline. Consider possible organizational patterns you might use to organize your ideas (see pages 217–218). As an alternative, think about using one of the patterns listed here to organize your ideas and develop the claim.

▶ If you are writing a fact paper that answers the question "What happened?" consider using a chronological pattern. Use transitions such as *first, then,* and *next.* You can begin your paper with present events and use flashbacks to explain what occurred in the past, or you can simply explain things in the past to present order in which they occurred.

▶ If you are writing a definition paper that answers the question "What is it?" consider using comparison to establish meaning by showing what the item or idea you are defining is like and what it is not like. Or you can achieve a similar clarity by presenting examples of several meanings for the item or idea and then settle on the best of these meanings for your conclusion.

▶ If you are writing a cause paper that answers the question "What caused it?" consider using a cause-and-effect or effect-and-cause pattern of organization. Cause and effect explains how certain causes result in certain effects, and effect and cause describes the effects first and then explains what caused them.

▶ If you are writing a value paper that answers the question "Is it good or bad?" consider a claim-plus-reasons pattern. Complete the sentence "It is (good or bad) because . . . ," and add reasons and evidence.

▶ If you are writing a policy paper that answers the question "What should we do?" consider using the problem–solution pattern of organization. Describe the problem first, and then describe one or more solutions.

Drafting, Revising, and Final Editing

Use your extended list or outline to help you write a draft, revise the draft, and prepare the final copy. Follow the suggestions for drafting, revising, and editing in Chapter 4 (pages 119–124). Work quoted material into your draft as you write. Follow explanations and examples for integrating quoted material into your paper that appear in Chapter 13 (pages 418–421) and the Appendix to Chapter 13 (pages 429–479). Use MLA documentation to cite in-text references and to create a Works Cited page, unless you are advised otherwise. Follow the instructions and examples for MLA documentation in Chapter 4 and the Appendix to Chapter 13.

Read the example position paper based on an issue question in "The Reader" that is reproduced here. The question is "What should be done with young offenders?" This paper was written by Kelly Dickerson, a student in an argument class. The type of claim, the elements of the Toulmin model, and the proofs are identified in the margin.

Notice also how Kelly worked quoted material into her paper for ease of reading. Quotations flow with the rest of the text, and they are clear. Furthermore, the introductions for the quotations, along with the in-text citations, show the reader where to find the originals, if there is interest in locating them. Use this paper as a model to help you integrate quotations into your own paper and prepare a Works Cited page.*

STUDENT PAPER #1   Kelly Dickerson
Position Paper Based on "The Reader"
Professor Wood
English 1302
25 October 2008

Minor Problems?

Support: Definition

1   Every time Americans tune in to local news broadcasts or read daily papers, they are likely to be shocked at the increasing number of serious crimes committed by youths who are only sixteen or seventeen years old, or even younger. It is sometimes difficult to imagine these youngsters behaving like hardened criminals, but statistics continually prove that their crimes are often just as brutal as those committed by their adult counter-

Support: Authority

parts. Inevitably, people begin questioning how successful the juvenile justice system is in reforming these youths. Increasingly, violent juveniles

---

*See the Appendix to Chapter 13 for the actual MLA format guidelines for student papers.

are being tried and sentenced as adults in our legal system. Some of them, after the death sentence was reinstated in the United States in 1976, were even sentenced to death, at least until 2005 (Wallis, 609).

Warrant: The penalty was appropriate but is no longer an option.
Support: Facts

2   At that time the Supreme Court made it illegal to sentence anyone to death for crimes committed before the age of 18. Specifically, in 2005, the Supreme Court ruled that no one could be sentenced to death for crimes they had committed while they were 16 or 17 years old. A similar ruling in 1988 removed the death penalty as an option for individuals committing crimes when they were 15 years old or younger (Wallis, 609).

Support: Cause

3   What causes juveniles to commit serious crimes like murder, rape, robbery, physical assault, or illegal drug involvement? People hold different perspectives on this issue. Aristotle describes youths as "passionate, quick to anger, and apt to give way to it . . . their angry passions get the better of them" (608). Aristotle wrote 2,400 years ago, and modern descriptions of youth are not that different from his. Wallis quotes attorney Steven Presson who states, "We've been arguing for decades that kids don't have the same moral culpability that adults have" (609). Daniel Weinberger explains in "A Brain Too Young for Good Judgment" that the 15-year-old student who shot his fellow students at Santana High School has, because of his age, an immature brain. The prefrontal cortex, the part of the brain that is used for judgment and suppressing impulsive behavior, is not fully formed at that age (611). The difference between earlier times, including Aristotle's ancient Greece, and now, according to Weinberger, is that we live in a culture that romanticizes gunplay. In modern society, "if a gun is put in the control of the prefrontal cortex of a hurt and vengeful 15-year-old, and it is pointed at a human target, it will very likely go off" (612).

Support: Quotes from authorities

Support: Effect

Support: Example

4   Not all 15-year-olds commit such deadly crimes, but those who do should be held accountable. Examples of teen crime are vivid and terrifying. William Glaberson writes about Omar Ahmed Khadr, a 15-year-old Al Qaeda recruit who threw a grenade that killed a U.S. soldier in 2002. Khadr has been imprisoned in Guantánamo Bay, Cuba, for the past five years, and even though international law does not require special treatment for criminals under 18 years old, he is likely to be given less than a life term. Prosecutors in his case, however, claim that he was trained in terrorist activities by his family and should be held to adult standards (613). Other child fighters in Africa and other countries do not hesitate to kill when they have been trained to do so. Child killers are a more and more common occurrence around the world.

Warrant: The examples prove these individuals should be held accountable.

Subclaim: The punishment does not always fit the crime.

5   Despite the staggering increase in serious crimes committed by young offenders, the punishment that juveniles receive has traditionally almost never fit the severity of the crimes. Since the system views children as not being fully developed, physically or mentally, it has prevented them from being held accountable for their wrongdoing. With the recent lifting of the death penalty for juveniles, punishment may become even more lenient.

Warrant: The punishment should fit the crime.

6   When "children" commit horribly vicious crimes and are routinely treated as victims of society who are too delicate to receive the punishments

Warrant: Adult sentences are a deterrent to crime.

they deserve, they get the message that crime "pays" because there are no serious consequences for their actions. When the system lacks an element of fear, there is nothing to deter youthful offenders from committing future crimes. Assigning adult sentences to youths who commit serious crimes is absolutely just if the punishment is to fit the crime.

Rebuttal: Agree on minor crimes

7   Most pro-rehabilitation advocates argue that juvenile criminals are completely different from their adult counterparts and should therefore be treated differently in the justice system. I agree that rehabilitation efforts may be very important in decreasing the amount of juvenile crime, particularly repeat crime. However, I believe that these measures should be directed toward youths who have committed minor offenses. Nando, the young man Feuer describes in "Out of Jail, Into Temptation: A Day in a Life," would be a good candidate for a rehabilitation program. Sending him back to his former neighborhood without job training or money will almost certainly cause him to regress to his former way of life.

Support: Examples from authorities

Rebuttal, cont.: Disagree for serious crimes

8   Conversely, I feel that juveniles like the ones who shoot their classmates or indulge in terrorist activities, those who are convicted of serious crimes—including murder, rape, robbery, physical assault, and illegal drug involvement—should be tried as adults. Their actions are obviously more serious than those who commit misdemeanor offenses, and they almost always result in greater direct harm to society. A message has to be sent that we will no longer tolerate brutal crimes simply because of the age of the criminal. These youths must be held completely accountable for their crimes, suffering harsh consequences and ultimately realizing that they are no longer protected by the law. The cost to society is the same regardless of the age of the criminal. What comfort does it give to the family of a slain or injured victim that the person who killed or maimed their loved one was a minor? Parents of children shot and killed at school by teenage killers suffer no less because their child was shot by a young offender. Instead of treating the person who shot a fellow student like a victim of society, this person should be treated like any other person who victimizes society and causes pain to individuals and communities.

Warrant: Cost to society should determine punishment

Policy claim

279

Works Cited

Aristotle. *Rhetoric* II. 12. Trans. Lane Cooper. New York: Appleton-Century-Crofts, 1932. Wood 608–609.

Feuer, Alan. "Out of Jail, Into Temptation: A Day in a Life." *New York Times* 28 Feb. 2000. Wood 613–16.

Glaberson, William. "A Legal Debate in Guantanámo on Boy Fighters." *International Herald-Tribune* 2 June 2007. Wood 612–13.

Wallis, Claudia. "Too Young to Die." *Time* 14 Mar. 2005: 40. Wood. 609–610.

Weinberger, Daniel R. "A Brain Too Young for Good Judgment." *New York Times* 10 Mar. 2001: A27. Wood 610–12.

Wood, Nancy V. *Perspectives on Argument.* 6th ed. Upper Saddle River: Prentice, 2009. Print.

CHAPTER 9

Visual Argument

Y
ou may discover that you spend more time viewing argument than you do reading and writing it. In his article "Rise of the Visual Puts Words on the Defensive," David Carr claims, "In most magazines on today's newsstands, words are increasingly beside the point, mere graphic elements that are generally used to frame pictures."[1] Many of these pictures are used to express perspectives on argument. The same can be said of most advertisements you encounter. They usually contain pictures with comparatively few words of explanation. Textbooks now have more pictures, graphs, tables, maps, and other types of visuals than they did in the past. Add the Internet, movies, and television, and you will discover that much of the material you take in is visual and that it is often used to make or support an argument.

Images, in fact, when viewed from the perspective of argument, frequently take on additional meaning. That is, an image, on close scrutiny, can often be perceived as a visual argument in that it makes a claim about an issue and supports it, just as written argument does. The idea introduced in Chapter 1 that argument is everywhere takes on expanded meaning when you apply it to visual as well as to written argument.

You have been analyzing visuals from the perspective of argument in all of the preceding chapters. This chapter will reinforce the proposition put forward in earlier chapters that the same tools of analysis that you use to analyze written argument can be successfully applied to analyze visual argument. Visual argument, however, also has certain special characteristics that make it unique. Those characteristics are the subject of this chapter, which teaches you not only to analyze visual argument but also to create it yourself. Instruction and examples appear in the "Exercises and Activities" section at the end of the chapter.

---

[1] *New York Times*, April 1, 2002, C8.

Recognizing Visual Argument

You will need to discover, first, whether you are looking at an argument. Discover this by asking, *Is the visual about an issue that has not been resolved or settled?* and *Does this issue potentially inspire two or more different views?* If your answer to both of these questions is yes, then attempt to describe the issue and the perspective being developed. Next, use two types of information for further analysis. First, analyze the special features of visual argument that are explained later in this chapter to get a sense of how the argument works and how powerful it is. Second, apply argument theory to understand the material better as an argument. You already gained some experience with visual argument when you analyzed the advertisements on pages 169 and 246. You can extend that experience to analyze other types of visual argument as well.

Review the section "Apply the Six Types of Argumentation Purpose to Visual Argument" on pages 105–106 to help you recognize and classify types of visual argument. Just like written argument, visual argument can be straightforward, with an obvious purpose and claim; covert, with a hidden claim that you may need to infer; or even unconscious, with the artist advocating a point of view without being fully aware of it. Furthermore, argument expressed through pictures and speech can represent either commonly held or extreme points of view and can present one or several different views on an issue.

You will encounter visual argument both online and in print in a variety of forms, including advertisements, photographs, drawings, illustrations, paintings, sculptures, cartoons, diagrams, flowcharts, various types of graphs, visual demonstrations, tables of numbers, or even maps. Marketers use visual argument on billboards, on signs, and in packaging and other marketing materials such as brochures or various other types of promotional materials. All this visual material, whether in still or moving picture form, can be (and increasingly is) employed to further an argument and convince you of a particular point of view.

Notice how many of these venues for visual argument are a part of the modern media, a particularly potent context for visual argument. A recent study by the Kaiser Family Foundation found that young people ages 8–18 now spend up to six and a half hours a day listening, watching, reading, or interacting with materials that they access through modern media formats. Reflect on the amount of time you spend each day taking in or sending information via new media, and you may be surprised how much your life is impacted. Think also about the number and types of images you encounter in all media forms that can be characterized as visual arguments and that have been constructed to gain profit or power or both. This is a major characteristic of the modern media. Whenever you encounter visual argument in the media or anywhere else, make a point of identifying its purpose because it always has one.

Now let us look at some of the special features of visual argument that make it particularly effective for advancing arguments.

Why Visual Argument Is Convincing: Eight Special Features

The following special features of visual argument will demonstrate how it works and why it is convincing. However, not all visual argument demonstrates all of the special features described in this list, and sometimes these features combine or overlap with one another. They are separated and described here for purposes of instruction. Becoming aware of them will help you look at visuals as potential argument and also understand how images achieve their persuasive effect with an audience. The examples of visual argument in this chapter include classic photographs that illustrate issues associated with dramatic periods in U.S. history, such as World War II, the civil rights movement, and the Vietnam War. Others illustrate contemporary issues.

1. *Visual argument is immediate and tangible and pulls you into the picture.* Visual argument works on a different level of perception than written argument. To use a new media word, it has velocity. It communicates fast and evokes a rich, dense, and immediate response from a viewer. For example, if you are watching a moving picture, you may have the experience of either sharing or even taking part in the action yourself. At the least, you will react in some immediate way to what you are seeing. If the picture is still, you may experience its immediacy and timelessness. A moment has been captured and preserved forever on film. Look at the photograph in Figure 9.1. It has been characterized as the most famous picture from the Vietnam War.

Figure 9.1 Visual argument is immediate and tangible and pulls you into the picture.

In this photograph an officer in the South Vietnamese army is shooting a suspected member of the Vietcong, an armed rebel force supported by North Vietnam, and the photographer has captured the moment when the bullet enters this man's head and kills him. This picture provoked strong antiwar arguments in its time, and it continues to invite responses to issues associated with war. What pulls you into this picture? What issue does it raise for you? What position do you take on the issue?

Street Execution of a Vietcong Prisoner, 1968.

2. *Visual argument often establishes common ground and invites viewer identification through shared values and points of view.* You learned in Chapter 1 that common ground is a necessary ingredient of productive argument. Visual argument usually establishes common ground, including a sense of personal identification and shared values with the characters, the action, or the scene, and it does so more quickly than words in print. All viewers, however, may not experience the same degree of common ground or the same type of identification.

Look at the photograph in Figure 9.2 taken by American Douglas Martin. This is a picture of Dorothy Counts, an African American girl who enrolled in a newly desegregated high school in Charlotte, North Carolina, during the civil rights movement. Escorted by the individuals on either side of her, she makes her way to her first day of school. Dorothy is being taunted by white students in the background who wanted to keep their school segregated.

Dorothy Counts, now Dot Counts Scoggins, still lives in Charlotte, North Carolina. In 2007 the Charlotte-Mecklenburg Schools community celebrated both the 40th anniversary of the desegregation of the school system and the 50th anniversary of the difficult days that the young Dorothy Counts (she was 15 in 1957) spent in Harding High School in an effort to help desegregate public schools. The school district also invited a couple of the students who were screaming at her and making faces in this picture to the ceremony. They were present, and they apologized, after all these years.[2]

Dorothy Counts Entering a Newly Desegregated School, 1957.

Figure 9.2 Visual argument often establishes common ground and invites viewer identification through shared values and points of view.

This photograph won The Associated Press, World Press Photo of the Year Award in 1957 and remains one of the most famous pictures from the civil rights era. With whom do you identify and experience the greatest amount of common ground in this picture? Do you identify with Dorothy as she moves toward her first experiences in her new school? Do you identify with either of the individuals escorting her? Do you have anything in common with the white students in the background? What values are embedded in this image? What issue does the picture raise for you, and what position would you take on it?

[2]From information supplied by Professor Andy Brown and student Kristina Wolfe, of the University of North Carolina at Charlotte, and Dave Morris, long-time resident of Charlotte, NC.

Attitudes and values have changed radically in the years since this photograph was taken. The picture demonstrates the potential power and influence of visual argument. It memorializes an event that has now become a part of history and that vividly depicts the changed views on school segregation that are recognized now throughout the United States.

3. *Visual argument often evokes an emotional response.* Visual argument operates more directly on the emotions than written argument because images communicate more immediately than words. Visual argument is also less subject to conscious critical awareness and monitoring since most people think less critically about an image than they do a prose piece. You can test this yourself. Imagine reading an unillustrated account of a new car in the automotive section of the newspaper. Compare this with watching a hyped-up color television advertisement about the same car that includes pictures of interesting people driving to exotic locations. You will probably be more likely to think critically and rationally about the written account and more likely to respond emotionally to the visuals in the advertisement. Look for example at the photograph of the child in Figure 9.3. This image appeared in *Newsweek* magazine in 2003 and invoked a strong emotional response from many readers who wrote to the editor to express their profound sadness and concern for this child.

Figure 9.3 Visual argument often evokes an emotional response.

284

In the photograph the sacred shrine of Imam Ali has just been blown up, and the boy is crying in the midst of the rubble. Would you characterize your response to this picture as primarily rational or emotional? What in the image prompts your response? Describe your response.

A Young Boy Cries When One of Islam's Holiest Shrines Is Destroyed during the War in Iraq, 2003.

4. *Visual argument often relies on the juxtaposition of materials from very different categories, inviting the viewer to make new links and associations.* Use what you learned about figurative analogies in Chapter 7 (pages 231–232) to help you understand the strategy of juxtaposition in visual argument. In placing objects, people, or actions that are not usually associated with each other in a common context, a photographer invites the viewer to establish new associations and to reach new conclusions. Figure 9.4 is a well-known photograph of an

A Vietnam War Protester Placing Flowers in the Rifle Barrels of Troops Guarding the Pentagon during an Antiwar Demonstration, 1967.

Figure 9.4 Visual argument often relies on the juxtaposition of materials from very different categories, inviting the viewer to make new links and associations.

The juxtaposition of flowers and guns in the context of an antiwar demonstration invites the viewer to respond directly to how these different things appear together. What associations do you have with flowers and guns? Think of them separately and then together. How would you state the claim in this picture? Would you accept or argue against this claim?

anti–Vietnam War demonstrator at a march on the Pentagon in 1967. He is placing flowers that symbolize peace in the gun barrels of the troops that have been called in to protect the area.

5. *Visual argument often employs icons to prompt an immediate response from a viewer.* Icons are images that people have seen so often that they respond to them immediately and in predictable ways—or at least, it is on this that people who include iconic references in visual argument rely. The American eagle, for example, is more than a bird to most U.S. citizens. It symbolizes the nation and the values associated with a democratic form of government. Icons appear on computer screens and on the cash registers at McDonald's to prompt quicker responses than the words or numbers they replace. Examples of icons that might appear in visual argument include the villain and the good guy in western movies, the pert housewife and the cute baby in television commercials, the cross or the Star of David in religious imagery, or a picture of a starving child in an appeal for money. The photograph on the next page (see Figure 9.5) of Marines raising the U.S. flag on Iwo Jima toward the end of World War II has been printed so many times, including on postage stamps, that it has become a national icon. It has also inspired a famous statue in Arlington Cemetery in Washington D.C. This photograph, like the photograph of Rosa Parks on page 90, was staged. The first time these men raised the flag, they decided the flag was too small, so they got a bigger flag and raised it again. The photographer, Joe Rosenthal, took this picture of the second try, and he caught it just at the right time. He won a Pulitzer Prize for photography in 1945 for this image.

In the twenty-first century, the polar bear stranded on a small chunk of ice in a larger ocean of floating ice chunks has become the iconic visual argument for the movement to reduce global warming. See page 9 for one version of it.

Figure 9.5 Visual argument often employs icons to prompt an immediate response from a viewer.

What does this photograph, taken toward the end of World War II, communicate to you? What is its purpose? What is the effect of not seeing the faces of the men? Describe the composition, including the focal point of the picture and the arrangement of the different parts. What feelings does it evoke? Why has it become a national icon? Do you think the polar bear image (see page 9) will be as lasting or become as influential an icon (in this case, for global warming) as have these Marines raising the flag in commemoration of victory in World War II? Why or why not?

Marines Raising the Flag on Iwo Jima, 1945.

6. *Visual argument often employs symbols.* You have seen how icons invite viewers to respond with the commonly held, established meanings and feelings, or even to add to those that are usually associated with them. Icons are symbolic since most people look beyond their literal meaning and add the extra meanings they have come to represent. However, of the many symbols used in argument,

Figure 9.6 Visual argument often employs symbols.

This quotation by Graham Greene appears in the front of the book in which this picture appears: "How can life on the border be other than reckless? You are pulled by different ties of love and hate." Consider the location of this tree and that it was included in a book describing life on the United States–Mexico border. What symbolic meaning would you assign to it in this border context? How would you describe this meaning? What claim do you infer from looking at this picture? How might someone refute that claim? What type of proof is the tree in this context?

Tree Located on the Texas-Mexico Border.

few are so familiar that they can be classified as icons. Look at the color photograph of the split tree in Figure 9.6. This photograph appears in *The Border: Life on the Line* by Douglas Kent Hall. The caption under the picture is "Near El Paso, Texas." El Paso is located on the Texas-Mexico border. This particular tree is a symbol, but not an icon.

7. *Visual argument is selective.* Whenever you look at a visual argument, it is important to think not only about what is included in the picture but also about what is omitted from it. If you could stand back and see more of the entire scene, of which the picture itself is only a small part, your perception of the picture might change a great deal. In any such framed image, you are allowed to see only what the photographer sees or wants you to see. You can infer or imagine what else is there or what else is going on outside the frame of the picture. The power of images often resides in this "edited" quality, but it is also a limit that the viewer must keep in mind.

Look at the photograph in Figure 9.7 of a young girl in Afghanistan who is seeking an education. Notice the picture of the young girl provides emotional proof (*pathos*).

A Young Girl in Kabul, Afghanistan, Seeks an Education.

Figure 9.7 Visual argument is selective.

What is the main focus of this image? Who are the other figures in the background? The girl is looking up at someone or something. At what or whom do you think she is looking? How would this picture change had the photographer decided to photograph the entire scene in this room, with everyone in the room receiving equal attention? What is the effect of moving in on one individual and making everyone else in the room appear smaller than she? What claim is being made in this image?

287

8. *Visual argument invites unique interpretations from viewers.* Usually no two people looking at a visual argument will interpret it in exactly the same way since individual viewers bring information and associations from their own past experience and use it to fill in some of the meaning suggested by the picture. Readers do that too, of course, particularly when they infer a claim or supply the warrants in a written argument. When viewers, like readers, draw on their backgrounds to fill out the meaning of a visual argument, they become vested in its message since some of the meaning now belongs to them. As a result, these viewers are more likely to accept the argument.

Look, for example, at two images on pages 304 and 305. Image 1 shows a detail from Michelangelo's scenes of the Creation, which appear on the ceiling of the Sistine Chapel in Rome. Here God is passing life to human beings by stretching out His life-giving finger to the lifeless, limp finger of Adam. Now look at the close-up of the hands in Image 2 on the next page. In this postcard picture, God is passing a baseball along with the first impulses of human life. One viewer, looking at this picture, says the artist is claiming, "We have had baseball from the beginning of time." Another puts the claim this way: "God is giving baseball to the entire universe." A third viewer has a different idea: "God is playing games with human beings." How would you interpret the meaning of this picture? How would you argue in favor of your interpretation? Your answer, at least in part, will probably depend on your views about baseball.

Now look at Figure 9.8, which is a visual argument that invites individual interpretations. This is a photograph of two animal rights activists in Germany who have created a tableau with the girl sitting in the cage and the person dressed like a chicken sitting outside of the cage. Both are holding signs, written in Ger-

Figure 9.8 Visual argument invites unique interpretations from viewers.

The claim of this argument is clear from the writing on these activists' signs. Translated, the signs demand, "Free the hens. Get rid of all cages by 2012!" What is not clear, and therefore open to interpretation, is the significance of the support for the claim. Why do you think these individuals chose to stage their protest in this way? Why is the girl nearly nude, and why is she confined in a wire cage similar to a chicken's? Why is the individual outside of the cage in a chicken suit? What is the meaning of this support? What warrants are you expected to supply that will link this support to the claim? You are expected to make some inferences to understand this argument, and everyone may not make the same inferences.

Animal Rights Activist: Free Hens from Cage!
A nude animal rights activist holds a billboard on which is written "Free the hens. Get rid of all cages by 2012!" The activists protested raising hens in the cage, in Berlin, Jan. 16, 2008.

man, that state, when translated into English: "Free the hens. Get rid of all cages by 2012!" It is aimed at companies that keep chickens confined and crowded in small wire cages where they lay eggs and are fattened for the market. Many American students are also activists in the free-the-chickens movement, and, in some colleges and universities , they have persuaded their administrations to purchase only cage-free eggs for the student cafeterias. There is no correct interpretation of how the argument in Figure 9.8 is supposed to persuade a viewer to agree with the activists. Your guess may turn out to be as good as the next person's.

So far, the examples of the special features of visual argument have been applied to still images. All of these same features can be applied to motion pictures as well. Many documentaries and mainstream entertainment films take positions on controversial issues and argue for particular points of view. Examples of films that present arguments appear in the introductory material to each of the seven issue areas in "The Reader."

Motion picture directors and editors can create powerfully persuasive effects through the selection and juxtaposition of shots that lead the audience to see links and make associations that would not otherwise occur to them. Motion pictures also draw in the audience, engage their emotions, establish common ground, invite multiple interpretations, and rely on icons and symbols to create some of their meaning.

Let us turn now to a review of the argument theory you have learned in preceding chapters and consider how it can be used to analyze and critique visual argument.

Using Argument Theory to Critique Visual Argument

The Summary Charts on pages 511–523 provide a quick review of the argument theory you can use to analyze all types of visual argument in the same way that you would analyze written argument.

Consider the rhetorical situation to gain insight into the context for the argument, including the type of visual argument you are examining, the intended viewers, the artist's background and motivation, the possible constraints of all parties, and the exigence or outside motivation for the argument. Apply the Toulmin model to discover the claim, support, warrants, backing for the warrants, and the presense of a rebuttal or a qualifier.

Learn more about the claim and purpose for the argument by asking the claim questions. Establish which type of claim tends to predominate: a fact claim establishes what happened; a definition claim defines and clarifies what it is; a cause claim looks for causes and sometimes shows effects; a value claim looks at whether it is good or bad; and a policy claim establishes what we should do about it.

Then analyze the proofs. Which are present, *logos, ethos,* and/or *pathos,* and which type of proof predominates in the argument? What is the effect of the proofs? Then look at specific types of proof, including signs, induction, cause, deduction, analogies, definition, statistics, values, authority, and motives. How do those that are present further the argument? Refer to the tests of validity for each of the proofs you identify to judge their effectiveness.

Also, look for fallacies and consider the effect they have on the overall argument. Look for visual fallacies in particular. For example, ask if the image may have been selected or changed to represent a particular point of view. Ask whether a photo or film clip represents a unique or an exaggerated way of viewing a subject or whether it is an accurate picture of what really exists or happened. Consider the photographs taken of disasters, such as major floods or volcanic eruptions: they usually depict the worst, most extreme results of the disaster. You can at least wonder how representative these pictures are of what actually has happened.

Remember, too, that computers can be used to augment or change images. Tabloid newspapers sometimes create humorous composite images by placing one person's head on another person's body. Examine whether there is any evidence that a visual has been changed, doctored, or recreated in any way so that what you see as present in the image is a consequence of manipulation rather than insightful framing. Take time to look at visuals carefully. This helps you understand what is really going on in them and make some judgments about their accuracy and value.

Bias in Visual Argument

You will encounter bias in visual argument just as you do in written argument, except that, typically, it is more obvious in visual argument. All argument, by definition, shows bias for a particular point of view or a particular position. When you spot a visual argument that strikes you as biased, identify the source and type of bias being expressed. Here are two examples of biased images of Senator Hillary Clinton of New York when she was running for president of the United States. Figure 9.9 is a caricature of Clinton that appeared with an essay that criticized her idea for government-sponsored preschool for all four-year-old children. The article, which appeared in the conservative magazine *National Review*, opposed her idea as another government program that would be costly for taxpayers. Figure 9.10 is a more flattering photograph of Clinton addressing a large audience. It appeared in

Figure 9.9 *A caricature of Hillary Clinton*

How would you describe the biased point of view in this caricature of Hillary Clinton that appeared in the conservative magazine *National Review* during her campaign for her party's nomination for president?

Figure 9.10

How would you describe the biased point of view in this photograph of Hillary Clinton that appeared in a liberal newspaper that had also endorsed her nomination for president?

Worcester, Mass. *Senator Hillary Rodham Clinton at Clark University.*

the *New York Times,* a liberal newspaper that also had endorsed Clinton's 2008 candidacy for president.

Watching for fallacies, visual distortions, exaggerations, Photoshop changes in original images that have been applied to make them more persuasive, and outright or even less obvious bias in visual argument will help you make fair and objective critiques. In addition, ask these questions to make ethical evaluations of images: Does the arguer understand the issue and its consequences? Is the position proposed in the best interests of the audience? Is the arguer honest and fair-minded? Or, in contrast, is the arguer unethical and manipulative? Refer back to pages 266–267 for additional criteria to help you make an ethical evaluation of images. Try to put your own prejudices and favorite ideas aside while you make these objective judgments.

Sample Analysis of a Visual Argument

The following analysis of the political cartoon in Figure 9.11, page 292, draws on both the special features of visual argument and argument theory.[3]

Special Features of Visual Argument Employed in the Cartoon

Visual argument pulls the viewer in, creates common ground, evokes an emotional response, uses juxtaposition, employs icons, uses symbols, is selective, and invites a unique interpretation from the viewer.

1. I am pulled into this picture by the date on the large stocking and by the Christmas setting. Furthermore, common ground is established through the

---

[3]I am indebted to Sandi Hubnik for the cartoon and some of the analysis in this example.

Figure 9.11 *A political cartoon making a visual argument.*

Christmas tree and hearth, which I associate with goodwill toward others and also with giving.

2. The word *Charities,* the date September 11, and the Christmas tree and stockings evoke an emotional response. Also, the juxtaposition of these items causes me to associate Christmas with giving to the victims of September 11 and reminds me of other needy groups, including needy people who live in my area, whom I should remember at Christmastime.

3. The Christmas tree, the stockings, and the date September 11 have been seen so often that they can be considered icons. Thus they communicate quickly and forcefully.

4. The cartoonist, Doug Marlette, has selected what he wants to feature in this picture: the large and the small stockings, the date September 11, and the words *Charities* and *Others.* The fireplace and Christmas tree are only partially depicted, and no presents or people are included. As a result, the focus is on generous giving, as happens at Christmas, but to people outside our immediate families.

5. I interpret this picture by remembering all the people in New York who needed help after September 11, 2001, and I wonder which other charities were neglected as a result of funneling so much charitable giving to the 9/11 cause. I also remember the Salvation Army volunteers who solicit money for charity at Christmas. To me this picture means I should give more generously, like I would at Christmas, to all groups or persons outside my family that I consider needy and worthwhile.

Argument Theory Used for Analysis of the Cartoon

Useful theory includes applying the rhetorical situation (TRACE), the Toulmin model, the claim questions, and the types of proof, including *logos, ethos,* and *pathos*; identifying fallacies; bias; and determining whether or not the argument is convincing and ethical.

Rhetorical Situation:

Text: Political cartoon with an argumentation intent.

Reader/viewer: People who are able to give to charities.

Author/artist: Doug Marlette, a Pulitzer Prize–wining political cartoon-ist for Tribune Media Services.

Constraints: Some viewers may be wary of giving to charities because they are not sure the money reaches the people who need it; the artist is in favor of giving and thus makes us associate charitable giv-ing with the Christmas spirit of giving.

Exigence: The destruction of the World Trade Center twin towers by terrorists in New York on September 11, 2001.

Toulmin Model:

Claim: We should give to all charities, not just 9/11 charities.

Support: The big "September 11" stocking and the small "Other" stockings.

Warrant: There are "other" charities as important and deserving as the 9/11 charities.

Type of Claim: This is a policy claim. It suggests what we should do in the future.

Types of Proof: (*logos, ethos, pathos*):

Cause: The problem of uneven giving has been caused by the nature of 9/11.

Analogies: Stockings are like charities; giving to charities should be like stuffing stockings at Christmas.

Value: We value Christmas and giving to others. We value fairness.

Motivation: Christmas stockings should be equal in size because we all want the same amount of rewards or consideration.

Fallacies: We could test the validity of the analogy between Christmas stockings and charities. In this case the analogy works because a logical link can be made between Christmas giving and charitable giving, so there is no fallacy.

Bias: It is biased in favor of charitable giving.

Ethical Evaluation:

Best interests of sociey? Yes, because giving to 9/11 and other charities is positive and necessary.

Ethical? Yes, because charitable giving is an ethical activity, and the cartoon argues for equity and against inbalance.

We have described visual argument, explained why it is convincing, and illustrated how you can analyze it by examining its special features and applying argument theory. Let us change the focus now to present some ideas that will help you create visual arguments of your own. Visual argument can be used to provide support for a written argument, or it can stand alone as an independent argument. We will examine both possibilities.

Add Visual Argument to Support Written Argument

You may at times decide to add pictures, photographs, drawings, flowcharts, graphs, or other images to your papers as support for your claim. You can see from studying the images presented so far in this chapter that visual argument, when compared to written argument, is immediate and concrete, can appeal powerfully to the emotions, and can enhance an argument's message by making it convincing in ways that words alone cannot do. When an image is used as support, be certain that it functions as support for the specific claim or subclaim you are presenting. You will want your words and your visuals to work together to make your point, just as they do in Figure 9.7 on page 287.

Include images in your argument writing by adding clip art from the Internet or by using various types of printed visual material drawn from books, magazines, and newspapers. Downloaded images from the Internet can be pasted into your paper electronically. You can also use Photoshop to juxtapose or combine images that will invite your viewer to think about your claim in a new way. Printed images or drawings can be photocopied and pasted into your paper. Of course, if you prefer to, draw your own diagrams, flowcharts, or sketches to add visual support for the claim. Also, decide whether or not to add a line or two of explanation under each visual to explain its relationship to the written text. You will need to do that if the relationship between the ideas in the text and the visual support is not immediately clear to the reader. Document all visual sources to show where you obtained them. The MLA and APA sections in the Appendix to Chapter 13 show how to do that (see pages 429–479).

When you have quantities of numerical data, experimental results, or complex plans that are too cumbersome to describe in the written body of your paper, present it visually. Graphs, charts, tables, and flowcharts are valuable for condensing such material, often making it more easily accessible to the audience.

There are many different types of graphs, but the most commonly used are line, bar, and circle (or pie) graphs. These three kinds of graphs can be generated through common word processing packages such as Microsoft Word or WordPerfect for insertion in a paper. The examples that follow present graphs of data from *The World Almanac and Book of Facts*, an excellent source for up-to-date statistics on many subjects.

Bar graphs in particular are used when you want to compare measurements of some kind. The numbers used in the measurements are often large, and the bar graph offers a picture that makes the numbers easily understandable in relation to one another. Figure 9.12 provides an example of a bar graph that shows the most current number of AIDS cases reported in Africa as compared with other parts of the world. There are 24,500,000 cases in Africa compared with 38,600,000 in the world. The graph reports percentages. This graph appears in a paper that argues that AIDS education in Africa has been ineffective.

Line graphs are most often used to show a change in a measurement over time. Some of the different measurements associated with line graphs are temperature, height and weight, test scores, population changes, and profits or deficits. Figure 9.13

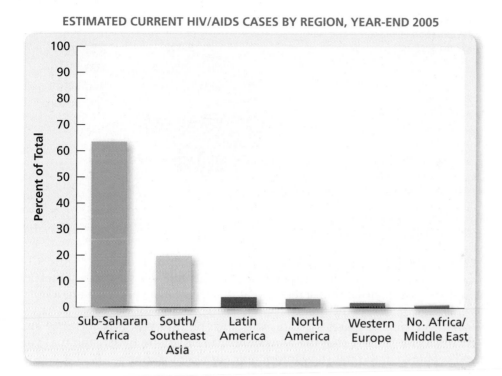

ESTIMATED CURRENT HIV/AIDS CASES BY REGION, YEAR-END 2005

Figure 9.12 *Bar Graph Comparing Large Numbers.*

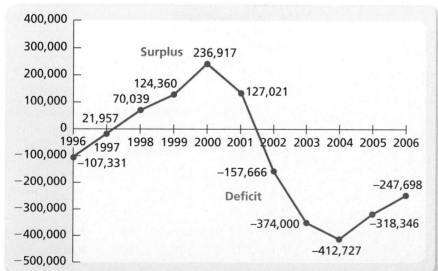

SUMMARY OF SURPLUSES AND DEFICITS
IN U.S. BUDGET, 1996–2006
(in millions of dollars)

Figure 9.13
Line Graph Showing Change Over Time.

Figure 9.14 *Circle Graph Showing How a Population or Market Is Divided into Sectors.*

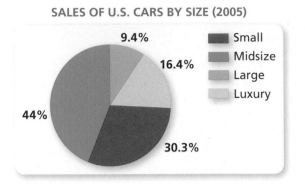

SALES OF U.S. CARS BY SIZE (2005)

9.4%
16.4%
44%
30.3%

Small
Midsize
Large
Luxury

shows the changes in the U.S. budget over time. It appears in a paper that argues that the United States needs to reduce its budget deficit.

Circle graphs are ordinarily used to show how something is divided. Figure 9.14 shows a circle graph that sums the percentage of the different sizes of automobiles sold in the United States during a recent year. It appears in a paper that argues that automobiles help deplete the ozone layer in the upper atmosphere.

Whatever kind of graph you use, you must be sure that it is correctly and clearly titled and labeled, that the units of measurement are noted, and that you report the source of the statistical information used in the graph.

When you find that the statistical information you want to include in a paper is too detailed and lengthy for a graph, a chart or a table is usually recommended. For example, Figure 9.15 provides the projected figures for population growth for ten major countries as well as for the world as a whole. It appears in a paper that argues in favor of zero population growth.

Figure 9.15 *Table Presenting Comparison Data.*

Population Projections for Selected Countries and World: 2006, 2025, And 2050

COUNTRY	2006	2025	2050
Bangladesh	147,365,352	204,538,715	279,955,405
Brazil	188,078,227	217,825,222	228,426,737
China	1,313,973,713	1,453,123,817	1,424,161,948
India	1,111,713,910	1,448,821,234	1,807,878,574
Iraq	26,783,383	40,418,381	56,360,779
Japan	127,463,611	120,001,048	99,886,568
Mexico	107,449,525	130,198,692	147,907,650
Nigeria	131,859,731	206,165,946	356,523,597
Russia	142,069,494	128,180,396	109,187,353
United States of America	298,444,215	349,666,199	420,080,587
World	6,528,089,562	7,963,750,137	n.a.

Create Visual Arguments That Stand Alone

We have suggested ways to use visual materials as illustrations that support ideas in written arguments. Many visual arguments are, however, quite independent of written text and stand alone as persuasive arguments themselves without the benefit of accompanying verbal explanations. Creating visual arguments of this type requires imagination, creativity, and critical thought. Like other types of argument, you will find visual arguments that stand alone all around you. Look at book covers, bulletin boards and displays, posters, tee shirts, and even your fellow students. Some of your classmates may dress and arrange their hair so that they are walking visual arguments. Figure 9.16 provides two examples.

You can use the same types of images and equipment for all visual argument. These include single or composite images, moving images, photographs, drawings, paintings, or even three-dimensional installations with objects placed in juxtaposition to make a claim. For example, a stack of books and a lightbulb could make the claim that reading helps people think and get ideas. Experiment with stock photography from the Internet, Photoshop or Paint Shop Pro, cameras and camcorders, posterboard and markers, scissors and paste.

For visual argument, as with other types of argument, you will need to make a claim about an issue that generates more than one perspective. Select an issue that is important to you and that you can make important to your audience. Reflect on all of the elements in the rhetorical situation as you would in creating a verbal argument. These include the materials and methods you will use; the characteristics and

(a)

(b)

Figure 9.16 *Clothing Can Make an Argument. (a) Singer, songwriter, and activist Bono, member of the rock group U2, makes a statement with his jacket. (b) Student Daniel Goergen and his message.*

interests of your viewers; your own resources and interests; the constraints, including values, that either pull you and your viewers together or push you apart; and your exigence or motivation for working with this issue in the first place. Use the Toulmin model to set up the main parts of your argument: you will need a claim, support, and warrants that you and your audience can share. Consider also how you can use *logos, ethos,* and *pathos* to create a persuasive and convincing argument.

Think through the **eight special features of visual argument** and how you will employ some of them to make your argument more convincing. You will want to create images that

▶ Communicate quickly and have immediate and tangible effects on viewers.

▶ Invite viewer identification and establish common ground through shared values.

▶ Engage the emotions of the viewers.

▶ Juxtapose materials from different categories so that the viewer will make new links and associations.

▶ Employ familiar icons that prompt immediate responses from viewers.

▶ Present visual symbols that viewers can easily interpret.

▶ Include only materials that viewers should focus on and omit everything else.

▶ Invite unique interpretations from viewers through visual subtleties that do not mean the same things to all people.

Consider adding a few words to your visual argument to enhance or extend its meaning. Pete Rearden, an artist who created the visual argument in Figure 9.17, suggests limiting word art, if it is used at all, to no more than two or three short sentences. Use minimum punctuation and make the words as immediate and concrete as possible.

Figure 9.17 *Visual Argument That Uses Words to Extend Its Meaning.*

In his visual argument, Rearden has photographed an area that a homeless person has established as an outdoor camp. Rearden is deeply concerned with homeless people and the fact that more than half of them are also mentally ill. These individuals have often told him that they are only camping out and will soon be returning to their homes. This rhetorical situation prompted Rearden to create the visual argument reproduced here. Notice that the words superimposed on the photograph add a dimension of meaning to the picture. They do not serve as a photoline that describes the picture. Instead, they create common ground by reminding viewers of going to camp without their parents; they juxtapose Dear Mom (with its immediate links to ideas of home) and the mess of the camp (which is less immediately readable) to invite associations; and they add emotional appeal with the words *mom, camp,* and *fun,* and the question, "Why don't you write me any more?" By adding these words, Rearden invites a more complex and personal interpretation from a viewer than the picture alone could provide. Notice, finally, what is left out of this picture. Consider that for many people, the homeless are the invisible members of society. Not all people would state the claim this picture makes in exactly the same way. How would you state it?

Practice applying the theory explained in this chapter by analyzing and creating visual arguments in the "Exercises and Activities" that follow.

Review Questions

1. Where are you likely to encounter visual argument? How do you recognize it?
2. What are the eight special features of visual argument that make it convincing?
3. What information about argument theory from earlier chapters in this book might you employ to help you analyze visual argument?
4. Describe some ways that you might use visual argument as support for a written argument.
5. What ideas from this chapter might help you create an effective visual argument that stands alone?

Exercises and Activities

A. Group Work and Class Discussion: Analyzing Visual Argument

In small groups, view the six photographs on the following pages from the perspective of argument, analyze them, and discuss them as a class. Here are some general questions to guide your discussion. Additional "For Discussion" questions accompany each image.

1. Is this a visual argument? Why do you think so?
2. What was occurring and in what context that prompted the photographer to take the photograph?
3. What is it about? What is the claim? What are the implied values or point of view?

4. Does it engage your emotions? What is your emotional reaction?

5. Does it establish common ground? Do you identify with anyone or anything in it?

6. What other special features of visual argument make it effective?

   ▶ Is it immediate and tangible? How does it pull you into the picture?
   ▶ What is included? Left out? Changed? Distorted? Exaggerated?
   ▶ Does it rely on juxtaposition? How? To what effect?
   ▶ Does it use icons? To what effect?
   ▶ Does it use symbols? To what effect?
   ▶ Would everyone interpret it in the same way? What is your interpretation?

7. What do you conclude about the purpose, meaning, and effectiveness of this image?

Image 1:

West Bank Barrier.

This photograph appeared on the front page of the *New York Times* in 2004 over the caption "Palestinians in ArRam, near Jerusalem, walked yesterday near part of the West Bank barrier built by Israel." This barrier, projected to be 436 miles long when completed, has been controversial since 2002 when the Israeli government decided to build a wall to protect its citizens from Palestinian suicide bombers.

For Discussion: Compare this photograph of the West Bank barrier with the photograph of it that appears on page 132. What is the main difference between the two photographs? What is the effect of this difference on the viewer? Read "The Mending Wall" by Robert Frost that appears on pages 492–493. Two men are repairing the rock wall between their farms. One of them makes the statement, "Something there is that doesn't love a wall." His neighbor has a conflicting view. He says, "Good fences make good neighbors." Apply each of these statements to the West Bank barrier. Which makes better sense in this context? What do you conclude about the final value of this barrier?

300

Image 2:
Crossing Over.

These two photos appeared together in *Newsweek* magazine, April 3, 2006, accompanied by the following caption: "Crossing Over: Mexicans traverse the U.S. border, protesters rally in D.C."

For Discussion: Each photo makes a different claim. Describe them along with the support provided for each. What warrants are implicit in each photo? What backing, in the form of pervasive cultural values in the United States and Mexico, enhance the persuasive strength of these photos? Compare the fence in this photo with the West Bank barrier (Image 1). Some people in the United States advocate building a strong barrier along the U.S.–Mexican border to keep Mexican workers and others from crossing over illegally; other people reject this idea. State your position on this issue along with your reasons for holding it.

Image 3
Coming Home to a Destroyed Neighborhood.

This photo is captioned, "Affluent Lebanese drive down the street to look at a destroyed neighborhood, August 15, 2006, in southern Beirut, Lebanon." During the summer of 2006, Hezbollah in Lebanon fired rockets into northern Israel, and Israel retaliated by bombing Hezbollah headquarters, airports, and major highways in Beirut, Lebanon. This photograph was taken the first day of the ceasefire. It shows four young women who have borrowed a car and a driver to return to their neighborhood. It is a candid shot, and the photographer, Spencer Platt, won the World Press Photo Award in 2007 for it.[4]

For Discussion: According to the photographer, many people look at this picture and ask if it is actually taken in the Middle East. What about it invites that reaction? Compare it with war zone photographs that you have seen of Iraq. What special characteristics of visual argument are present in this photo? Which predominate? State the claim. How would others in your class state the claim?

Image 4:
Mother and Child.

The caption for this photograph is, "Young mother and child awaiting evacuation from Sarajevo." Sarajevo is the capital city of the Federation of Bosnia and Herzegovina in Eastern Europe. The siege of Sarajevo took place during the Bosnian civil war fought in 1992–1995. A huge percentage of the people killed during this war were civilians. The photographer, Tom Stoddart, is a British photojournalist who spent four years photographing life in Sarajevo during the war.

For Discussion: What do you find compelling about this photograph? Describe its effect on you as a viewer. What emotions does it evoke? Do you experience a sense of common ground with anyone in the photograph? Describe it. The photographer took this picture in black and white instead of color. Discuss the advantages and disadvantages of black and white photography when compared with color. What other special features of visual argument are apparent in this photograph?

[4]Miki Johnson, "Spencer Platt Wins World Press Photo Award, *PopPhoto.com*, February 9, 2007, http://www.popphoto.com/photographynewswire/3794/spencer-platt-wins-world-press-photo-award.html.

Image 5:
LeBron James.

This photograph comes from the collection of the best sports photographs of 2007, compiled by *Sports Illustrated* magazine. LeBron James is the key figure in the photograph. He plays for the Cleveland Cavaliers, who were the champions in the National Basketball Association Eastern Conference in 2007 but who subsequently lost the national championship to the San Antonio Spurs in the NBA finals. James is 6 feet 8 inches tall, weighs 250 pounds, and has a 30.1 points per game average. The photograph was taken on February 18, 2007.

For Discussion: What pulls you into this picture? When viewed from the perspective of argument, what claim does this photograph make? Photographers sometimes say that they have to capture a particular moment to get a good picture. How does that observation apply to this picture? What other special features of visual argument are apparent here?

303

Image 6:
At Home Outdoors.

The individuals in this picture are aboriginal people of Balgo in the Great Sandy Desert of northwest Australia. Otherwise known as indigenous Australians, they are descended from the first known inhabitants of Australia. Traditionally, they spend their time outdoors. The house in this photograph is provided by the government, presumably to improve their lives, and it is used mostly for storage. This picture first appeared in *National Geographic* magazine in 1991.

For Discussion: What are the people in this photograph doing? Describe the cultural values shown in this photograph. Are there any conflicts in values? What does the photograph suggest about attempts by governments or organizations to impose new cultural customs or values on groups of people? How would you state the claim made by this picture? Comment on the use of juxtaposition here. What, if any, added content is related to the time of day indicated in the photograph?

B. **Group Work, Class Discussion, and Writing Assignment: Analyzing Multiple Perspectives on an Issue Expressed through a Collection of Visual Arguments**

1. Review "Expressing Multiple Perspectives through Visual Argument" along with the images on pages 132 and 146.

2. Look at the four images on this and the next page, understand the context for each of them, and answer the questions for discussion on page 306 that accompany them.

3. Write a title for the images that communicates what they have in common and what issue they address when viewed as a group of images that makes an argument.

4. Write an essay in which you describe the four different perspectives on the issue expressed by the photographs; write in detail about how each is related to and contributes to the development of the idea in your title. Draw a conclusion about this set of images that expresses your final assessment of them.

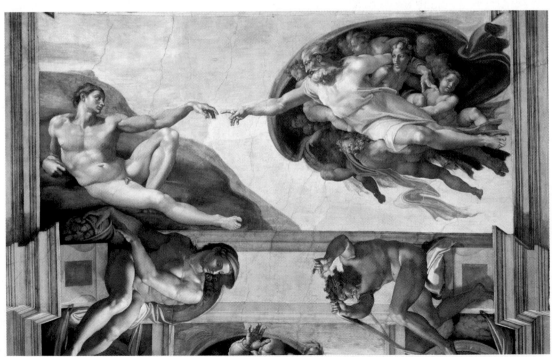

Image 1:
Adam and God.

This image is a reproduction of a work of art. It was painted on the ceiling of the Sistine Chapel in Rome by Michelangelo in 1511, where it can be viewed today; it depicts the creation of Adam.

Image 2: Play Ball.

This is a postcard collage, titled *Play Ball*, which adds a baseball to the hand of God reaching toward Adam.

Image 3: Robot with a Grappler.

This photo ran in the *New York Times* in 2002 over the caption, "A robot with a grappler holding a wounded Palestinian yesterday on a highway in Megiddo, Israel, 12 miles southeast of Haifa. Israeli Radio said the man was a suicide bomber whose explosives detonated prematurely."

Image 4: Missionary and Child.

This 1980 photograph is titled *Hands*. It shows the hands of a starving Ugandan child and a missionary.

For Discussion:

Compare the hands in each of the four photographs. How are they similar? How are they different? Discuss how juxtaposition is used in each of these photographs. What is the effect? What additional associations form in your mind as you look at each of these four photographs? What is your personal interpretation of each of them? That is, what does each communicate to you? How effective are each of these images as arguments? How effective are they as a collection of images that makes an argument?

C. **Individual Work and Class Discussion: Analyzing a Cartoon**

To help you with this exercise, follow the model for the analysis of a cartoon provided on pages 291–293 of this chapter, which employs both the special features of visual argument and argument theory as tools for analysis. Look at the cartoon, answer the questions that follow it on the next page, and discuss your answers with the class.

Questions about the Special Features of Visual Argument

1. What pulls you into this cartoon? What do you notice first? What can you say about the composition that draws you into it?

2. Do you experience common ground with anyone in the image? Are any values expressed that you share ?

3. Does this cartoon arouse your emotions? What is your emotional reaction?

4. Does the cartoon rely on juxtaposition? What is placed in juxtaposition, and what is the effect?

5. Do any icons appear in this cartoon? If yes, describe them. What do they contribute?

6. Do any symbols appear in this cartoon? If yes, describe them and consider what they contribute.

7. Is the image selective? That is, what is included, what is left out, and what is the effect?

8. How would you interpret this cartoon? What do you think the photographer's purpose is, what is the final effect, and what do you conclude about it?

Questions from Argument Theory

1. Describe the rhetorical situation: What type of text is this? Who are the intended viewers? Who is the cartoonist? What constraints of the viewers and the cartoonist can you infer? What is the exigence for this cartoon?

2. Apply the Toulmin model: What is the claim? What is the support? What is the warrant? What is the backing? Is there a rebuttal? Is there a qualifier?

3. What would you say is the type of claim made in this cartoon: fact, definition, cause, value, or policy?

4. What types of proof are employed? Comment on the use of *logos, ethos,* and *pathos*.

5. Are there any fallacies in this cartoon? If yes, describe them.

6. What is your ethical evaluation of this cartoon? Is its claim in the best interests of society? Why or why not?

D. **Individual Work: Locating a Visual Argument and Analyzing It in Class**

Find a visual argument. Look online or in printed magazines, newspapers, or books, and bring it to class. Why do you think the item you have selected is a visual argument? Identify the issue. Point out the special features of visual argument that make it convincing. State your interpretation of the claim, even if you have to infer it. Point out the support and the warrants and describe the backing. State why you do or do not find the argument convincing.

307

E. Creating a Stand-Alone Visual Argument and Writing an Analysis of It

This assignment requires you to create a visual argument, to write a paper in which you analyze it, and then to present and explain it to the class.

a. Identify an issue that you can make an argument about by using visual material. You may choose an issue either from one of the argument papers you have written or from one of the essays or visual arguments that appear in this book, or you may select a new issue.

b. Make a claim about the issue.

c. Create a visual argument. Draw on the suggestions made in this chapter (pages 297–299).

d. Include just enough writing on your visual argument to help viewers understand your claim.

e. Write a paper, about 250–350 words long, that explains and interprets your visual argument. Consider the following to include in your analysis or add other information. Your goal is to describe what you have expressed in your visual argument and explain to your viewers just how you created it to accomplish this goal.

1. Explain the rhetorical situation: What is the context for your issue and your visual argument?

2. Write a Toulmin analysis of your visual argument. Here is an example of a possible Toulmin analysis of the student-made collage on page 309 about artworks:

Issue:	Has art become too expensive?
Claim:	Art is too expensive.
Support:	The examples of art pasted on the dollar sign are expensive.
Warrant:	I cannot afford those artworks.
Backing:	Most people viewing this collage know how expensive these famous artworks are.
Inferred rebuttal:	I have money to buy less expensive artworks, and I think they are just as enjoyable to own.

3. Identify the type of claim, and describe how you have used *logos, ethos,* and *pathos.*

4. Describe your own interpretation of your argument. Why did you put it together as you did?

f. Share your visual argument with the class. Include the ideas in your written analysis. Ask for other interpretations from class members.

g. *Examples:* Three student-made visual arguments appear on pages 309 and 311–312. The first is a collage, the second is a sculpture, and the third is a graphic novel written for children that makes an argument through images and text. The second and third examples are accompanied by short analyses that explain what the students accomplished from their points of view.

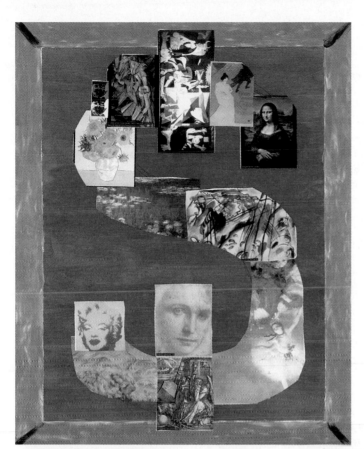

STUDENT VISUAL ARGUMENT 1

Untitled.

Elisabeth Elsberg, a student in a first-year writing class, created this collage from print images that were cut and pasted on to a painted background.

For Discussion: To work with audiences, icons must be immediately recognizable to most people. What parts of this artwork would you classify as iconic? Are they clearly iconic? How does this student use juxtaposition? Comment on the use of selectivity in this piece. What has been selected? What has been left out? How do you interpret this visual argument? How would you state its claim?

STUDENT VISUAL ARGUMENT 2

Never Again.

Karen Hernandez, the student who made this visual argument, created the figures out of clay. She then installed the clay figures on a platform that displays photographs from the Holocaust, with a title that expresses the claim: "Never Again".

ANALYTICAL ESSAY OF STUDENT VISUAL ARGUMENT 2

NEVER AGAIN
Karen Hernandez

The artist was a student attending the University of Texas at Arlington when she made the sculpture and wrote this essay about it. The graphic novel *Maus* by Art Spiegelman provided the inspiration for this argument. *Maus* had been a reading assignment in her writing class. It tells the story of Spiegelman's parents' experiences during the Holocaust. Excerpts from *Maus* appear on pages 498–509.

1   In 1938 Hitler and the Nazi government began a reign of terror and death that would leave over ten million people dead through pogroms and in prison camps. The book *Maus* tells one survivor's story, and I have tried to speak with this work of art of the horror that these people endured, just as the author of the book does. The skeletal figures of my piece are made of clay because it creates the closest appearance to human bones, and the figures are skeletal because this is the way many of the survivors looked when they were rescued from the camps. I have also left them in various sizes and shapes just as real people are; however, my figures are left incomplete (no hands or feet) because this is how the Germans viewed them, as less than human beings.

2   Even though the figures are skeletal, they have taken on an almost lifelike quality of expression in the way some heads are bowed, while others are held up. Some of the figures lean as if in pain or fatigue, and others seem to look at those standing nearby or into space. The longer I look at them, the more human they become to me, and I hope I have been able to impart this to the viewer as well.

3   I have also included, on the box below, pictures of victims and survivors of the Holocaust so that the observer will know that this work is more than just the artist's imagination, and that these horrors really did occur. I also chose to place the title across the front of the piece so that, like the group who first used it in the Holocaust museum, I might impart to the viewer the reminder that those who died during this terrible time of death and horror will not have done so in vain, and they will be remembered. Something like this will happen NEVER AGAIN.

For Discussion:

What do you find most striking about this visual argument? What pulls you in as you look at this photograph of it? How is juxtaposition used, and what is the effect? Are the words written on the front of the visual argument sufficient to suggest the claim it is making? How does the analytical essay help you further understand this visual argument?

STUDENT VISUAL ARGUMENT 3

FARM TOWN NEWS
Debbie Bryan

Debbie Bryan, the student who made this visual argument, describes it as a graphic novel. She created it for a children's audience. The artist explains how she made it: "The artwork is completely my own and is totally drawn and colored in the creative art program Adobe Photoshop CS3. After the graphic novel was completed frame by frame, I transferred the files to Adobe InDesign CS3. There I added the storyline text to each page of the novel. This program also enabled me to line up and link the pages for viewing ease."

As Torny and Bonter left the newspaper stand, Torny said, "Have you read today's issue of *Big Town News* yet, Bonter? This article is ridiculous!"

"According to Reverend Jason Jokestone, cows and horses are mortal enemies. He says historically cows have caused every problem that horses have today. Horses have to work and herd cows, while the cows just graze all day. There are even reports that cows are getting out of their pastures just to get horses in trouble."

"Jokestone warns horses not to trust any cows in their town. 'Cows are really prejudiced against horses,' he says. 'Don't turn your back on them or they might gore you,' he warns. He says that cows and horses are being involved in race riots all over the country."

"That is so silly! Just look at Grumdo and Fark. They have been best friends since they were born."

"*Big Town News* just doesn't have a grasp on the truth in our town. *Farm Town News* is much more accurate."

"They live here and see how it really is between horses and cows. They are really great companions."

The following month peace in Farm Town would come to an end. Grumdo and Fark began to constantly argue.

"Torny," said Bonter, "just look at Grumdo and Fark! It is so upsetting to see them fighting like that! What could have happened to make them hate each other in such a short time?"

"I don't understand it," Torny replied. "Seeing them act that way just makes me want to cry. Look! They are hitting each other, and all over a silly patch of fresh grass! There is plenty for both of them here. If they keep this up, I don't know how they can ever be friends again!"

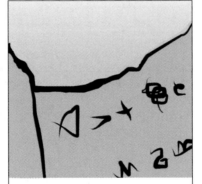

"Torny, you know that the *Farm Town News* has been reporting that pressure is building between horses and cows in Farm Town for two weeks now. An article in yesterday's paper read that cows are hogging all the fresh grass. But Grumdo and Fark never fought like this before."

"Now *both* newspapers are printing the same information. Since they both say the same thing, I guess it *has* to be true. See, the headlines read . . . Wait! Look at the small print under the title *Farm Town News*! It reads, 'now a member of the Big Town News Corporation.'"

ANALYTICAL ESSAY OF STUDENT VISUAL ARGUMENT 3

FARM TOWN NEWS
Debbie Bryan

Debbie Bryan was a student at the University of Texas at Arlington when she created her graphic novel *Farm Town News*. Ideas and discussions from her writing class inspired her to create this visual argument.

1   The news media has an obligation to tell the truth from an unbiased point of view. However, in the race to be first with sensational stories, sometimes the truth becomes less important than the breaking story. Some news media show disregard for the injuries to innocent individuals by hastily reported stories.

The general public has an unquestioning trust of newspapers and television news programs, but this trust should not be given so lightly. As portrayed in *Farm Town News*, damage is done through the unethical telling of a story. In my graphic novel, a friendship was lost because Fark and Grumdo believed information reported by two newspapers that were, in fact, owned by the same corporation and were, therefore, printing the story from the same point of view.

2   Any major story that can be reported will vary from station to station or newspaper to newspaper. Sometimes, in the case of covering politicians, these stories can be skewed by the writer's or the newspaper owner's political views. In a time when a few multimedia information companies own a vast portion of the news networks and newspapers, this is detrimental for the public. The trust that the viewing public puts in the media affects their choices for political leaders. Without the opportunity to hear, see, and gauge for themselves the issues and characters of the potential political leaders, blind and uninformed choices are made.

3   Until the news media reclaims the ethics of telling only the proven facts and not just the sensational tidbits, bad leadership choices will be made. Worse yet, people will have their lives changed in negative ways.

For Discussion:

What is your understanding of the claim made in this graphic novel? Is the graphic novel format an effective way to make such a claim? Elaborate on your answer. Can you provide an example of unethical reporting or advertising through the media that misled an audience from your own experience? Describe it. Besides the collage, the sculpture, and the graphic novel that are used as examples of student-made visual argument, how else might you and your fellow students create visual arguments? What materials would you use? What would these arguments finally look like? What do you need to present it to the class?

| Worksheet 3 | **Visual Argument Development** |

1. Write an issue question to focus your issue (example: *How can the unemployed be put back to work?*)

2. Write a claim that answers your issue question (example: *The government should create green-collar jobs to help the the unemployed and the environment.*) Refer to the "Claim Development Worksheet" on page 378 to help you get ideas to develop your claim.

3. Check the type of visual argument you will create (check more than one, if necessary):

   _____ stand-alone argument   _____ composite image

   _____ support for my essay   _____ single image

   _____ still image   _____ painting

   _____ moving image   _____ collage of images

   _____ all original   _____ graphic story (comics)

   _____ images from print sources   _____ 3-dimensional installation

   _____ images from Internet   _____ PowerPoint

   _____ photograph   _____ sculpture

   _____ drawing   _____ video

4. Check the materials you will need:

   _____ computer   _____ video camera

   _____ Paint Shop Pro   _____ poster board

   _____ Photoshop   _____ colored markers

   _____ PowerPoint   _____ scissors and paste

   _____ magazines   _____ paints

   _____ newspapers   _____ other art supplies

   _____ still camera   _____ objects for installation

5. Which of the eight special features of visual argument will be evident in my work?

6. What words should I add to make it clear to my audience?

10

Rogerian Argument and Common Ground

To this point, you have been studying traditional argument that has its origin in classical sources. It is the form of argument that predominates in American culture, and it is what you are used to when you listen to people argue on television or when you read arguments in current periodicals or books. In traditional argument, the arguer states a claim and proves it by drawing on various types of proofs, including reasoning and evidence. The object is to convince an audience that the claim is valid and that the arguer is right. In this traditional model, the arguer uses the rebuttal to demonstrate how the opposition is wrong and to state why the audience should reject that position. Thus the emphasis is on winning the argument. Debate, with participants on both sides trying to win by convincing a third-party judge, is one form of traditional argument, as is courtroom argument and all other single-perspective argument in which one person argues to convince one or more people of a particular point of view.

As you know from your own experience and from reading about argument in this book, traditional argument does not always achieve its aims with the audience. Indeed, in certain situations when strongly held opinions or entire value systems are challenged, traditional argument may not be effective at all. The audience might simply stop listening or walk away. When that happens, it is useful to have another argumentation strategy to turn to, one that might work better in cases in which there seems to be a standoff or a lack of common ground among the arguing parties.

Rogerian argument, so called because it evolved from techniques originally applied by psychotherapist Carl Rogers, is a technique that is particularly useful for reducing conflict and establishing common ground between people who hold divergent positions and who may at times express hostility toward each other. Common ground often seems impossible to achieve in such situations, but two opposing parties can almost always find something to agree on if they try hard enough. Here is an anecdote that shows two hostile individuals establishing common ground. This comes from a column titled "In Politics, It Does Help to Be Smart" by Molly Ivins. Ivins always claimed that this is a true story. (The "Lege" in the passage refers to the Texas legislature.)

> This is the perfect political story and also true, but the names have been changed to protect the players.
>
> Many years ago in the Texas Lege lurked two senators who loathed one another with livid passion. One was conservative, the other liberal; one from a rural area, the other urban; one a mean old bull and the other a witty cosmopolite. We'll call them Bubba and Cary.
>
> One afternoon, Bubba is drinking with a friend in a local dive when in walks Cary. Bubba looks at him and snarls, "You're a sorry———!"
>
> Cary continues to the bar without comment. But after he gets a drink, he passes Bubba's table again, stops and says: "You think I'm a sorry———, right?"
>
> "Right," says Bubba.
>
> "Well, I think you're a sorry———."
>
> Bubba rears back, ready to rise and fight. Cary continues. "But we both *know* Senator Doakes is a sorry———."
>
> Bubba laughs and says, "I'll drink to that."
>
> They were both smart politicians. And that's what smart politicians do: concentrate on the areas where they can agree, even if there's only one. That's how deals get done, the ball is moved forward, the system works and the people's interest is more or less served.[1]

While establishing common ground in Rogerian argument, as in this example, uncovers what two parties have in common, Rogerian argument also involves more than that. Rogerian argument employs rebuttal differently. Instead of using rebuttal to show how the opposition is wrong, as in traditional argument, Rogerian argument requires that the arguer spend at least some time at the beginning of the argument not only explaining how the opposition's position is right but also identifying situations in which it might be valid. The arguer cannot do this very successfully without finding some common ground with the opposition. It is almost impossible to show how any part of another individual's opposing position is valid if you disagree with it totally.

Look back at the example in Chapter 1 (page 12) about the two individuals who are seeking common ground on methods for stopping random shooters. One of these individuals advocates that private citizens arm themselves with handguns as a deterrent to shooters. Another believes that the availability of handguns is the problem and advocates that private gun ownership be abolished. Common ground exists between the two parties because of their common concern for personal safety. To use Rogerian argument in this situation, the anti-handgun party would restate the pro-handgun party's position and would emphasize the common concern they both have for protecting their safety, before they search together for a solution on which they can agree.[2]

---

[1]Molly Ivins, "In Politics, It Does Help to Be Smart," *Fort Worth Star-Telegram,* October 28, 1999, 9B.
[2]I am indebted to Jenny Edbauer for this example.

Additional descriptions and examples of Rogerian argument in this chapter and in the "Exercises and Activities" at the end of it will demonstrate how various people achieve common ground through restatement and validation of their opponents' positions in Rogerian argument.

You may find Rogerian argument frustrating at first, especially if you favor contention and agonistic debate in situations in which your ideas and values seem to be under threat. Because Rogerian argument emphasizes making connections with the opposition and reducing hostility in such situations, you will need to curb your instincts to launch your argument by letting the opposition know how wrong you think they are. You can learn to use Rogerian argument, even if it is not your preferred or most natural style of arguing, in situations in which traditional argument is no longer effective. It is a useful strategy when other strategies are failing. Let us look at a couple of examples.

Achieving Common Ground in Rogerian Argument

In 2005, Cal Thomas, a politically conservative newspaper columnist, and Bob Beckel, a liberal political analyst and consultant, began co-authoring their popular column "Common Ground" that appears in the newspaper *USA Today*. In 2007, they published *Common Ground: How to Stop the Partisan War That Is Destroying America*, and in it Cal Thomas describes their collaboration.

> We're a good example of how common ground can work. Before we knew each other, we only knew "about" each other. I saw you [Beckel] as a liberal Democrat with "evil" ideas and positions conservatives associate with that label. You saw me as a conservative Republican with similar "evil" ideas and suspect friends. When we got to know each other and talked about politics, as well as personal and family challenges, we stopped seeing each other in stereotype and came first to respect and then (shock, shock) even to admire each other. The politics became less important than the relationship. And, most surprising of all, we found ourselves in agreement about quite a number of things, though we occasionally still differ on the best ways to achieve our common goals.[3]

Their purpose in writing the book, they make clear, is to encourage U.S. politicians to follow their example and make it a rule to seek common ground as part of the political process for resolving difficult and divisive issues. Indeed, Thomas and Beckel claim they are presenting "a plan that makes polarization the issue and common ground the solution." They "believe the time is right to challenge polarization and for common ground to become the next dominant strategic force in national politics."[4] To support this idea, they argue that the public prefers this

---

[3]Cal Thomas and Bob Beckel, *Common Ground: How to Stop the Partisan War That Is Destroying America* (New York: Harper-Collins, 2007), 257.
[4]Thomas and Beckel, 12.

approach: "Surveys conducted over several years have found that Americans believe even the most partisan issues—from abortion to the Iraq war—can be resolved with an honest commitment by elected leaders in Washington to finding consensus."[5]

Rogerian argument, with its emphasis on finding common ground and reaching consensus, can sometimes help people who differ strongly in their views find a bedrock of values and ideas that they can all hold in common. As a result, divided individuals are often able to resolve at least some of their differences. The process of seeking political common ground that Thomas and Beckel believe is beginning to occur in political discussions, and that they hope will occur more often, includes listening, understanding, and accepting points of view different from one's own, recognizing that both positions have some merit, and finally finding a way to resolve some of the differences. This process is at the heart of Rogerian argument strategy.

Let us look at another real-life example of building common ground between disagreeing parties with each side demonstrating an understanding of the other's point of view. Environmentalists, who typically want to protect the environment at all costs, often find themselves in opposition to individuals who make their living by exploiting the environment. Loggers, ranchers, mill owners, and other industrialists, for example, can fall into this second category. Individuals from both groups, stereotyped as "nature haters" and "eco-freaks" by the press, met in Idaho to discuss efforts for protecting endangered wildlife in the area. The environmentalists went to the meeting with some trepidation, but "as they joked and sparred over steak and beer, they discovered that neither side lived up to its stereotype. 'We found that we didn't hate each other,' said Alex Irby, a manager at the Konkolville sawmill. 'Turns out, we all like to do a lot of the same things. We love the outdoors.'" Timothy Egan, who wrote about the details of the meeting, makes this comment: "Loggers in the back country sitting down with environmentalists is an astonishing change."[6] One can infer that the common ground established in this meeting was brought about by each side describing to the other the value they placed on the environment and on outdoor activity in general. In such an exchange, both parties perceived that they had been heard, and further dialogue was then possible.

As you can see from both of these examples, understanding the rhetorical situation in general and the audience in particular by analyzing the thoughts and values of the parties involved is of critical importance in Rogerian argument. In Chapter 3 you learned how to analyze an audience as part of the planning process for writing argument papers. As you read the rest of this chapter, including the examples of Rogerian arguments written by students at the end of the chapter, pay particular attention to how Rogerian arguers analyze their audiences' dissenting opinions and values and then respond to them as part of their overall strategy.

---

[5]Thomas and Beckel, 10.
[6]Timothy Egan, "Look Who's Hugging Trees Now," *New York Times Magazine*, July 7, 1996, 28.

Rogerian Argument as Strategy

Carl Rogers was a psychotherapist who was well known for the empathetic listening techniques he used in psychological counseling. Here is how he describes the importance of listening:

> I like to be heard. A number of times in my life I have felt myself bursting with insoluble problems, or going round and round in tormented circles, or during one period, overcome by feelings of worthlessness and despair. I think I have been more fortunate than most in finding at these times individuals who have been able to hear me and thus to rescue me from the chaos of my feelings. I have been able to find individuals who have been able to hear my meanings a little more deeply than I have known them. These individuals have heard me without judging me, diagnosing me, appraising me, evaluating me. They have just listened and clarified and responded to me at all levels at which I was communicating. I can testify that when you are in psychological distress and someone really hears you without passing judgment on you, without trying to take responsibility for you, without trying to mold you, it feels damn good. At these times it has released the tension in me. It has permitted me to bring out the frightening feeling, the guilts, the despair, the confusions that have been a part of my experience. When I have been listened to and when I have been heard, I am able to reperceive my world in a new way and to go on. It is astonishing how elements which seem insoluble become soluble when someone listens, how confusions which seem irremediable turn into relatively clear flowing streams when one is heard. I have deeply appreciated the times that I have experienced this sensitive, empathic, concentrated listening.[7]

Rogers later became interested in how listening techniques could be used to improve communication in other difficult, emotionally charged situations. Richard Young and his colleagues Alton Becker and Kenneth Pike built on Rogers's ideas to formulate Rogerian argument, a method for helping people in difficult situations make connections, create common ground, and understand one another. The object was to avoid undue conflict or, even worse, a mutual standoff.[8]

According to Young, Becker, and Pike, written Rogerian argument reduces the reader's sense of threat and conflict with the writer so that alternatives can be considered. Four goals are met with this strategy.

Goal 1. Writers let readers know they have been understood. To accomplish this purpose, the writer restates the opponent's position in summary form by using dispassionate, neutral language. The writer demonstrates that the reader has been heard and that the writer understands the issue exactly as the reader does. The loggers and the environmentalists listened and understood one another in the example cited earlier.

Goal 2. Writers show how readers' positions are valid in certain contexts and under certain conditions. The writer demonstrates to the reader that at least part of the reader's position is both valid and acceptable and thereby makes it easier for the reader to reciprocate and accept part of the writer's position. Both the loggers and

---

[7]Carl R. Rogers, *A Way of Being,* Boston: Houghton Mifflin, 1980, 12–13. I thank Barbara Ciarello for calling this to my attention.
[8]Richard Young, Alton Becker, and Kenneth Pike, *Rhetoric: Discovery and Change* (New York: Harcourt, Brace, and World, 1970), 7–8, 274–90.

319

the environmentalists discovered validity in each other's positions since neither group wanted to destroy wildlife.

Goal 3. Writers help readers understand that both of them share the same values, types of experience, attitudes, and perceptions and are thus similar in significant ways. The loggers and environmentalists made it clear to each other that they both shared a love of the outdoors, held some of the same values, and enjoyed the same types of experience.

Goal 4. Writers propose solutions made up of elements from both sides that can be agreed to by both parties. At this point, environmentalists discovered that loggers were quite willing to pursue ways to preserve wildlife.

The most important feature of Rogerian argument is listening empathetically and nonjudgmentally. Rogers perceived that people usually listen judgmentally and evaluatively. They are eager to jump in, point out what is right or wrong, and make corrections or refutations, whereas Rogerian listening requires that insight into the other's position precede evaluation. Thus a writer of Rogerian argument takes the reader's place, and this is achieved by requiring that the writer provide neutral summaries of the reader's position that show sympathetic understanding of it and its context. In doing this the writer encourages a continued and open exchange of ideas with the reader. In Rogers's words, the writer "listens with" as opposed to "evaluating about."

Beyond empathic understanding, writers should also show congruence, or genuine agreement, and an unconditional positive regard for the opposition. In communicating these attitudes, Rogerian argument takes the heat out of difficult argument that might otherwise result in a stalemate. Rogerian strategy cools the emotions and makes consensus more likely. The aim of the final reconciliation at the close of Rogerian argument attempts to show that the best solution to the issue may be a combination of what both parties want.

In real life, Rogerian argument is used frequently, particularly in business and perhaps increasingly in politics, where agreement is indispensable. Some people in business claim they could not get anything done if they did not use Rogerian strategies on a daily basis. William L. Ury, one of the founders of the Program on Negotiation at Harvard Law School, claims that in business now, the best way to compete is to be able to cooperate. Cooperation is necessary because of the numerous mergers and cooperative ventures between companies. Many companies now work with the same markets and the same customers, and they cannot compete, as in former times, without weakening themselves as much as their competitors.[9] Some politicians may have to resort to Rogerian strategies to resolve difficult issues like health care and Social Security. Allowing tentative solutions to problems such as these to split along partisan lines and stay that way is not always productive. Reaching across the lines to harness the best ideas from both political parties can be much more productive and usually leads to better solutions.

Box 10.1 ▪ contrasts Rogerian argument, as explained by Young, Becker, and Pike, with the traditional model of argument.

---

[9]William L. Ury, "Getting Past No . . . to Yes! The Art of Negotiation." Workshop, Dallas, October 12, 1999.

| Box 10.1 | Traditional and Rogerian Argument Compared. |

▷▷▷ What Is Rogerian Argument?

	TRADITIONAL ARGUMENT	ROGERIAN ARGUMENT
Basic strategy	Writer states the claim and gives reasons to prove it. Writer refutes the opponent by showing what is wrong or invalid.	The writer states opponent's claim to demonstrate understanding and shows how it is valid.
Ethos	Writer establishes own character by demonstrating fair-mindedness, competence, and goodwill.	Writer builds opponent's *ethos* and enhances own character through empathy.
Logos	Writer appeals to reason to establish a claim and refute the opponent's claim.	Writer proceeds in an explanatory fashion to analyze the conditions under which the position of either side is valid.
Pathos	Writer arouses emotions with evocative language to strengthen the claim.	Writer uses descriptive, dispassionate language to cool emotions on both sides.
Goal	Writer seeks to change opponent's mind and thereby win the argument.	The writer creates cooperation, the possibility that both sides might change, and a mutually advantageous outcome.
Use of argument techniques	Writer draws on the conventional structures and techniques taught in Chapters 5–8 of this book.	Writer throws out conventional structures and techniques because they may be threatening and focuses instead on connecting empathetically.

321

In Chapter 5 you learned about the Toulmin model for argument. The Toulmin model and Rogerian argument have one extremely important feature in common. Even though the Toulmin model includes rebuttal, it also provides for the creation of common ground in the shared warrants between arguer and audience. Rogerian argument provides for common ground as well, but this is accomplished through the shared values and assumptions established through the summary and restatement of the opponent's position.

Writing Rogerian Argument

To write Rogerian argument, according to Young, Becker, and Pike, the writer proceeds in phases rather than following set organizational patterns or argumentation strategies. These phases are as follows:

1. The writer introduces the issue and shows that the opponent's position is understood by restating it.

2. The writer shows in which contexts and under what conditions the opponent's position may be valid. Note that the opponent is never made to feel completely wrong.

3. The writer then states his or her own position, including the contexts in which it is valid.

4. The writer states how the opponent's position would benefit if the opponent were to adopt elements of the writer's position. An attempt is finally made to show that the two positions complement each other and that each supplies what the other lacks.

Variations of Rogerian Argument

Rogerian argument as described by Young, Becker, and Pike is rarely, if ever, written exactly according to their format. You can learn more about Rogerian argument, however, by using their format as practice. The "Exercises and Activities" section of this chapter provides four examples of Rogerian argument papers written by students who followed Young, Becker, and Pike's formulations. You also will be invited to write a Rogerian argument paper using this format.

As you read professionally written argument, however, you are much more likely to find elements or variations of Rogerian argument rather than arguments that include all of the parts of the Young, Becker, and Pike model. Here are some variations of Rogerian argument that you may encounter in your academic reading.

1. *Report on past research at the beginning of an academic argument.* Authors of academic argument, as a matter of convention, often begin with a review of what previous writers have contributed to the subject. They identify the writers by name and summarize their contributions before identifying and developing their own contribution to the subject. Thus an ongoing chain of conversation is established that acknowledges what has gone before the new material that is the actual subject of the article.

2. *Research proposal.* Research proposals that request funds and resources from granting agencies typically begin with a positive summary of the contributions of past researchers. Only after this former work has been acknowledged does the researcher explain how the new proposed research will build on what has gone before.[10]

---

[10]I am indebted to Mary Stanley for alerting me to this use of Rogerian argument.

3. *Rogerian response paper.* This paper is written in response to an essay written by another person with whom the author disagrees. The author of a response paper typically rejects the position that the author of the other essay presents but hopes to create common ground and understanding with that person to keep a dialogue on the issue going. The goal is to make a connection with the author of the other essay and thus create a context of understanding so that both authors can continue exploring the issue. Such papers usually begin with a restatement of the other author's position along with an acknowledgment of what is valuable about that position before the author goes on to present a different view of the matter. You will be invited to try writing a Rogerian response paper yourself in Exercise B (page 325).

As you read arguments written by other authors, look for elements of Rogerian argument. The three examples just cited by no means exhaust the possibilities.

Unethical and Ethical Rogerian Argument

Rogerian argument can yield significant benefit in difficult situations characterized as having unclear outcomes or in situations involving high stakes, strong emotions, unequal power relations, and no other obvious way to settle the differences. Situations like these can tempt some people to resort to unethical argument strategies. In fact, one criticism that is sometimes leveled at Rogerian argument when it is first encountered is that it can be perceived to be manipulative. Though it can be used in this way, it is not inherent to this form of argumentation.

People who use Rogerian argument in unethical ways to manipulate other people may only appear to listen and understand when, in fact, their minds are elsewhere. Indeed, they may decline to look for common ground by prior intention or because it is a too-difficult task. Unethical arguers sometimes exhibit a condescending attitude or a fake sincerity, as they seem to listen to the people who present a view different from their own. They may also use some of the same tactics that unethical arguers use in traditional argument: for example, hiding the real purpose of the argument by misrepresenting the issue; using inappropriate emotional appeals, including emotionally loaded language; manufacturing evidence; or the use of inaccurate evidence, exaggerations, or lies. Unethical argumentation harms honest communication, especially when the arguer changes the definition of words or substitutes unusual words for commonly used words to cloud the opponent's perception of the issue, or when the arguer recasts or rewords the issue to reduce its threat though it actually represents a significant threat.

Now, let's consider ethical Rogerian argument. Individuals who practice ethical Rogerian argument need to believe that they are involved in an ethical process right from the beginning. This means that both participants have to make an adequate effort to understand the issue and its consequences along with the positions they both hold. They need to be just and fair-minded and speak in a fair, accurate, and convincing manner. The participants have to sincerely believe that the position they propose is in the best interests of both parties and, possibly, the larger society as well. They need to be able to answer the questions, *Who are benefited by what I want?* and *Who are burdened or hurt?* and to scrupulously consider the consequences of their answers to those questions. Finally, ethical participants need to listen and hear nonjudgmentally; they need to seek genuine agreement with at least part of the opponent's position; and they need to develop some unconditional positive regard for the individuals with whom they are engaged and show that regard in all that they say. Rogerian argument is polite, and it takes the high road in human discourse.

The Advantages and Disadvantages of Rogerian Argument

The advantages of Rogerian argument are clear. Such an approach helps release tension and disagreement and encourages negotiation and cooperation when values and aims are in conflict. Also, Rogerian argument has the potential of leveling or at least controlling uneven power relationships that can interfere with the peaceful resolution of conflicting issues.

There are perceived disadvantages of Rogerian argument to consider. It is sometimes difficult for the writer to understand and restate the reader's position, particularly when the opponent is not present and no written material is available to explain the opposing position. Then too, connecting with the opponent by restating the opposing position may be extremely difficult if the writer is emotionally involved and strongly dislikes the opposing ideas. It takes courage, Rogers says, to listen to and restate ideas that are strongly antithetical to your own. You have to want to make connections to succeed. You also have to be willing to risk change. After totally committing yourself to understanding a different viewpoint, your own ideas will almost inevitably shift and change somewhat.[11]

Rogerian argument has also been criticized as annoying to women. Some researchers claim that women have always been expected to understand others, sometimes even at the expense of understanding themselves. As one female critic puts it, Rogerian argument "feels too much like giving in."[12] (Of course, men might equally find "giving in" aspects of Rogerian argument annoying, even it for different reasons.) Another critic finds the advice that the writer should always use unemotional, dispassionate language to restate the opponent's argument unrealistic and constraining. Avoiding rude or insulting language is necessary, a matter of common sense, but to avoid all emotionally connotative language may be impossible.[13]

Rogerian argument persists as a viable model in spite of some of its shortcomings. Its central notion, that it is important to understand and see some validity in other people's opposing positions, is often the only viable way to create common ground in difficult situations.

---

[11]I am indebted to Paul Parmeley for this insight.

[12]See Catherine Lamb, "Beyond Argument in Feminist Composition," *College Composition and Communication.* February 1991, 11–24. See also Phyllis Lassner, "Feminist Response to Rogerian Rhetoric," *Rhetoric Review* 8 (1990): 220–32.

[13]Doug Brent, "Young, Becker, and Pike's 'Rogerian' Rhetoric: A Twenty-Year Reassessment," *College English* 53 (April 1991): 446–52.

Review Questions

1. What are the four goals of Rogerian argument, and how do they differ from those of traditional argument?

2. What are some of the advantages and disadvantages of Rogerian argument?

3. In what type of argumentation situation do you think you might find Rogerian argument more productive than traditional argument? Describe an issue, along with the rhetorical situation, which might prompt you to resort to Rogerian argument.

4. In what type of argumentation situation do you think you might find traditional argument more productive than Rogerian argument? Describe an issue, along with the rhetorical situation, which might prompt you to use traditional argument instead of Rogerian argument.

5. What difficulties, if any, do you personally contemplate in using Rogerian argument? How do you feel about using this strategy?

Exercises and Activities

A. Class Discussion: Understanding Rogerian Argument as a Strategy

The excerpt below is taken from Edward O. Wilson's book *The Future of Life*. Read the passage, analyze the Rogerian strategy, and answer the questions at the end.

> **BEFORE YOU READ:** What is your present attitude about preserving the environment? Do you know of anyone who holds a different view? What is it?

ESSAY #1   **THE FUTURE OF LIFE***

Edward O. Wilson

Wilson, a well-known scientist and Harvard professor, has been called the father of the modern environmental movement. His book *The Future of Life* provides plans for conserving earth's biodiversity.

1   Everyone has some kind of environmental ethic, even if it somehow makes a virtue of cutting the last ancient forests and damming the last wild rivers. Done, it is said, to grow the economy and save jobs. Done because we are running short of space and fuel. *Hey, listen, people come first!*—and most certainly before beach mice and louseworts. I recall vividly the conversation I had with a cab driver in Key West in 1968 when we

*From Edward O. Wilson, *The Future of Life* (New York: Knopf, 2002), 151–52.

touched on the Everglades burning to the north. Too bad, he said. The Everglades are a wonderful place. But wilderness always gives way to civilization, doesn't it? That is progress and the way of the world, and we can't do much about it.

2   Everyone is also an avowed environmentalist. No one says flatly, "To hell with nature." On the other hand, no one says, "Let's give it all back to nature." Rather, when invoking the social contract by which we all live, the typical people-first ethicist thinks about the environment short-term and the typical environmental ethicist thinks about it long-term. Both are sincere and have something true and important to say. The people-first thinker says we need to take a little cut here and there: the environmentalist says nature is dying the death of a thousands cuts. So how do we combine the best of short-term and long-term goals? Perhaps,

despite decades of bitter philosophical dispute, an optimum mix of the goals might result in a consensus more satisfactory than either side thought possible from total victory alone. Down deep, I believe, no one wants a total victory. The people-firster likes parks, and the environmentalist rides petroleum-powered vehicles to get there.

For Discussion:

What is the issue in this passage? What two groups of people are identified? Why might they feel hostile? What are their differences? How does Wilson create common ground between the two groups? How does Wilson use Rogerian strategy? Summarize the two positions and describe the Rogerian elements in the passage. Why do you think Wilson uses Rogerian strategy in this part of his book? How do you think Wilson might describe his audience for this passage?

B. **Writing Assignment: Write a Rogerian Response**

Read the following essays that appear in other chapters and select the one you disagree with the most: " 'A' Is for 'Absent' " (page 76); "Sexual Harassment and the Feminist 'Front' " (pages 271–273); "Calling Blue: And on That Farm He Had a Cellphone" (page 171), or "Why I Want a Wife" (pages 64–65). As an option, find a letter to the editor in a newspaper that you disagree with and write a Rogerian response to it. Use either essay or personal letter format. Your paper should be from 300 to 500 words long.

Prewriting

Write a brief summary of the position taken by the author of the essay you have selected. Then write a brief summary of your position. Make certain you understand both positions clearly.

Writing

Do all of the following in your paper:

1. State the opposition's position as presented in the article (or letter) and describe in what instances this position might work or be acceptable. As you write, imagine that the individual who wrote the article or letter will be reading your response. Write so that that person will feel "heard."

2. Write a clear transition to your position on the issue.

3. State how your position would also work or be acceptable.

4. Try to reconcile the two positions.

C. Class Discussion: Creating Images for Visual Rogerian Argument

Creating images to support visual arguments, or creating stand-alone Rogerian visual arguments, can be challenging because not one, but two positions need to be portrayed as equal and potentially correct. Further, the idea of consensual agreement needs to be part of the picture as well. Images 1, 2, and 3 can be used as images to represent Rogerian argument. No detailed captions appear with these images. They speak for themselves. Look at each of them, and then answer the "For Discussion" questions.

Image 1:
Hands across the World.

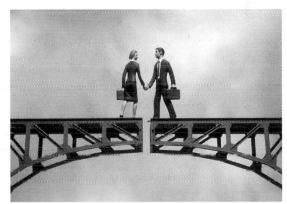

Image 2:
Bridging the Gap.

Image 3:
Bipartisanship and What It Can Achieve.

For Discussion: What do these three images have in common? In what argumentation contexts and for what types of issues would each be appropriate? To answer this question, study the icons used in each visual. What do they communicate about the broader context of each argument? The book jacket for *Common Ground: How to Stop the Partisan War That Is Destroying America*, quoted earlier in this chapter (page 317), shows the two authors in four small photos frowning, angry, and aggressively pointing their fingers at each other as they argue, and then, in a larger photo, they are standing with their arms on each other's shoulders while smiling at the camera. Do you have any ideas for visual argument that communicate the methods and goals of Rogerian argument? Use your imagination, and describe your ideas for the class.

D. Writing Assignment: Rogerian Argument

You are now going to write a Rogerian argument of around 1,000 words on an issue of your choice. There are several ways to set up this assignment. Read through the following options, select one that appeals to you, and proceed with the rest of the instructions for the assignment. The basic instructions in option 1 apply to all four options. Examples for options 1, 2, and 3 are provided at the end of this exercise.

Option 1. If you wrote an exploratory paper, write a Rogerian argument in response to the position you discovered that is most unlike the position you favor. You may have already articulated this opposing position in your exploratory paper. Move this position to the beginning of your Rogerian argument paper, and rewrite it until you believe you have fairly and dispassionately represented that other point of view. People who hold that view need to be able to agree that you have heard and understood them.

Look for common ground with that other view. Use that common ground to describe contexts and conditions in which the opponent's position might be valid. Do not show what is wrong with this other position.

Now write a transition that changes the subject to your position. Describe your position, and show the contexts in which is it valid.

Finally, reconcile the two positions. Show how they can complement each other, how one supplies what the other lacks, and how everyone would benefit if elements of both were finally accepted. (See Example 1.)

Option 2. Select any issue that you understand from at least two opposing points of view. You should feel strongly about your point of view, and you should have strong negative feelings about opposing viewpoints. Write a Rogerian argument in response to an opposing viewpoint. (See Example 2.)

Option 3. Recall the last time you were in an argument in which there was a stalemate and no one seemed to win. Write a letter to the individual with whom you were arguing. Use Rogerian strategy. (See Example 3.)

Option 4. Team up with a classmate who disagrees with you on a specific issue. Take turns articulating your partner's position until that person feels "heard" and understood. Then write a Rogerian argument in response to that position.

Prewriting

Write a one-paragraph summary of the opposing position and also a one-paragraph summary of your position. Refer to these summaries when you write your paper.

Writing

Write your paper, making sure you do all of the following:

1. Introduce the issue and restate the opposing position to show you understand it.

2. Show in which contexts and under what conditions the opposing position may be valid. State it so that it is acceptable to the opposition.

3. Write a clear transition that moves the reader from the position you have just explained to the position that you favor and will now defend.

4. State your own position and describe the context in which it is valid.

5. Show how the opposing position would be strengthened by adding elements of your position. Then try to reconcile the two positions.

Examples

Here are three examples of Rogerian argument written by students.

Example 1 *(Option 1)*. "Human Cloning: Is It a Viable Option?" was written by a student in an argument class who had also written an exploratory paper on this subject. The student conducted research for that paper, and items from her annotated bibliography appear on pages 402–404. In writing this paper, the student began with the position she had researched that was most unlike her own and rewrote it until she thought it would satisfy the individuals who hold that position. Notice that she was able to use the research for her other paper to add support for this paper as well. The marginal annotations make it easier for you to distinguish the parts of her paper.

Following the student's paper is a Rogerian argument evaluation sheet that has been filled out to show how her argument conforms to the recommended parts of a Rogerian argument. The requirements for the Rogerian argument paper are described in the left column, and the right column shows how well this paper met those requirements. When you have finished reading the papers in Examples 2 and 3, see if you can identify and describe the parts of those papers well enough to complete evaluation sheets like the sample. These analyses will help you understand how to write your own Rogerian argument.*

STUDENT PAPER #1   Angela A. Boatwright
                     Rogerian Argument
                     Professor Thorne
                     English 1302
                     30 April 2008

Human Cloning: Is It a Viable Option?

Introduction to issue and summary of rhetorical situation

1   Well, hello Dolly! Although research in animal or human cloning is not new, the technology has never had as much potential as it does today. Interest in what is and is not considered ethical in cloning

---

*For all the student papers in Chapter 10, see the Appendix to Chapter 13 for the actual MLA format guidelines.

research has surfaced since the historic announcement in Scotland of the existence of a cloned sheep named Dolly. Scientists were able to create a cloned sheep by taking the genes from a six-year-old sheep and putting them into an enucleated egg from another sheep. This egg was then implanted in the womb of yet another sheep, resulting in the birth of an identical twin that is six years younger than its sister (Bailey). This is the first known asexual reproduction of a mammal. It seems a reasonable assumption that a human clone is the next logical step down this technological pathway.

Explanation of opposing position to create common ground

2   Those who support unregulated human cloning experimentation justify their position by citing the medical gains and potential benefits the technology has to offer. They believe that the possible benefits of this technology far outweigh the risks and, furthermore, that it is an ethical practice because of its potential benefits. Some of these benefits include the generation of skin grafts for burn victims and bone marrow for patients undergoing cancer chemotherapy (Butler and Wadman 8). Cloning also shows promise for treating infertility and could become an option either for infertile couples or for people who have genetic defects and fear passing these defects on to their offspring.

3   Supporters of cloning believe that the arguments against cloning are vague and speculative and that they simply do not justify a ban. It is not the technology that frightens people so much as it is a lack of understanding. When people picture the result of an attempt at human cloning, they see images of Frankenstein or an army of Hitlers. Researchers believe that given time to digest the information, the public will one day regard cloning with the same openness and sense of normalcy that it now regards blood transfusions and organ transplants. They also reason that a ban on cloning could drive the technology underground, leading to a greater potential for unsafe, unregulated, and exploitative misuse.

Description of context in which opposing position is valid

4   Everyone would probably agree that technological advances have changed our lives in positive ways, and cloning research is not likely to be an exception. The fear held by cloning supporters, that the sensationalism created by this issue has clouded the judgment of the public and lawmakers who support a ban on cloning, is certainly a valid concern. Although it is not clear that human cloning will offer any great benefits to humanity, no one has yet made a persuasive case that it would do any real harm either (Macklin 64). It would be an injustice to completely abandon the possibilities that could enhance the lives of so many people based solely on hypothetical applications of a technology that may never be realized. Each disease we are able to eradicate is another huge step for humankind.

Transition to author's view

5   I agree that we should do everything in our power to improve the longevity and quality of life of all people, but I do not believe it should be at the expense of the dignity of human life. Many people who oppose cloning view it as an "invasion of personality." Even Dr. Ian Wilmut and his colleagues, the creators of Dolly, hold the position that

Explanation of author's view

cloning of humans would be unethical (64). He points out that it took 277 attempts to produce one live lamb. Of the 277 "reconstructed" embryos, 29 were implanted into recipient ewes, and 3 out of 5 lambs showed developmental abnormalities and died soon after birth. He believes similar tests with humans would not be acceptable.

6   Those of us who advocate anticloning measures believe that the potential abuse of such power could have disastrous consequences. The fear of the creation of human clones for the sole purpose of harvesting them for "spare parts" is too great to ignore. Another concern is that cloning will lead to efforts to breed individuals with perceived exceptional genetic qualities, eliminating the diversity that makes the human race what it is. There is a widespread belief that parents might create unrealistic expectations for cloned children, believing they no longer have the potential limitations of their genetic ancestors (Pence 135). Cloning is really a major step toward regarding our children as acceptable only if they conform to the choices of our will (Carey).

7   Many of us are also bound by the religious ideas we have been brought up with, telling us that only God has the right to create life. It is sinful to think of removing that sovereign right from an omnipotent God and placing it in the hands of mere mortals. Like the majority of Americans, I believe that human cloning experimentation should be banned before it can become an out-of-control reality.

331

Personal example to introduce idea of reconciliation of the two opposing positions

8   I am fortunate to be the mother of a wonderful and beautiful baby girl. If I had been given the opportunity to choose her characteristics, would I have elected to change my child? I absolutely would not. I would not trade any of her personal traits for something "better." I love her just as God gave her to me. Yet with absolute certainty, I can admit that if she developed a life-threatening ailment, I would not hesitate for a second to utilize any cloning technology available to cure her. This is not to say I would sacrifice another life for hers, only that I would employ any and all resources available short of that alternative.

Reconciliation of positions

9   If we can agree that human life should always be held in the highest esteem, we have the basis for reconciling our positions. Cloning should not be used to pick and choose the type of people who are allowed to exist, but we should explore the potential medical benefits of cloning technology research. Many of the medical procedures we take for granted every day were once as controversial as cloning is at this very moment. Most of these procedures became successful at the cost of testing on live beings, but with their consent. We must never allow human beings to be the subjects of experimentation without their knowledge or permission. We may not impose conditions on human beings that they might not have consented to if allowed to make the decision for themselves.

10   A moratorium might be a better solution than an outright ban. A moratorium would authorize a temporary delay of human cloning research and allow us the time to sort out the details and ensure that

an educated decision is made. It is easier to make an intelligent decision when there is not a feeling of impending doom hanging over our heads. "In a democratic society we don't usually pass laws outlawing something before there is actual or probable evidence of harm" (Macklin 64). This statement can serve as a guide for future policy on human cloning.

Works Cited

Bailey, Ronald. "The Twin Paradox: What Exactly Is Wrong with Cloning People?" *Reason* May 1997. *Reasononline*. Web. 12 Mar. 2008.

Butler, Declan, and Meredith Wadman. "Calls for Cloning Ban Sell Science Short." *Nature* 6 Mar. 1997: 8–9. Print.

Carey, John. "Human Clones: It's Decision Time." *Business Week* 10 Aug. 1998: 32. Print.

Macklin, Ruth. "Human Cloning? Don't Just Say No." *U.S. News & World Report* 10 Mar. 1997: 64+. Print.

Pence, Gregory E. *Who's Afraid of Human Cloning?* Lanham: Rowman, 1998. Print.

Wilmut, Ian. "Roslin Institute Experiments: Creation of Dolly the Sheep." *Congressional Digest* Feb. 1998: 41+. Print.

For Discussion:

Describe a rhetorical situation in which it would be better to write this paper about cloning in this form, using Rogerian strategy, than it would be to write it as a position paper, using traditional argument. Describe the readers, constraints, and, in particular, the exigence as you imagine the rhetorical situation for this paper.

Evaluation Sheet for Rogerian Argument Paper

REQUIREMENTS OF ROGERIAN ARGUMENT	WHAT THE AUTHOR DID
1. Introduce the issue and state the opposing position to show that you understand it.	1. Introduced the issue in paragraph 1 and presented the opposing view accompanied by good reasons in paragraphs 2 and 3.
2. Show how the opposition might be right.	2. Showed the contexts in which the other position might be valid in paragraph 4.
3. Write a clear transition from the opposing position to your position.	3. Wrote a transition in the first sentence of paragraph 5 to move from opposing to own position.
4. Give your position and show how you might be right.	4. Presented own position in paragraphs 5, 6, and 7.
5. Reconcile the two positions.	5. Reconciled the two views in paragraphs 8, 9, and 10.

Example 2 *(Option 2).* "Let Those Who Ride Decide!" was written by a student who depends on his motorcycle for all of his transportation. When you have finished reading this paper, see if you can identify and describe its parts and complete an evaluation sheet like the sample on page 331. This analysis will help you understand how to write your own Rogerian argument.

STUDENT PAPER #2

Eric Hartman
Rogerian Argument Paper
Professor Wood
English 1302
30 April 2008

Let Those Who Ride Decide!

1   Should the law mandate that motorcyclists wear a helmet? Texas law presently does not require that a helmet be worn by those over twenty-one who have taken a motorcycle safety course or who have at least $10,000 in health insurance coverage for injuries sustained while operating a motorcycle. In the past, Texas has had a helmet law that was universal, and many neighboring states still do. There are many in Texas who would like to see the old law reinstated so that all motorcyclists, regardless of their age, would be required to wear a helmet at all times.

2   Proponents of helmet laws are concerned with motorcyclists' safety. Their argument, that one is more likely either to survive a motorcycle wreck or to minimize physical damage if wearing a helmet, is very strong. Thus the value put on safety clearly is significant, especially for those who have lost a loved one in a motorcycle fatality. Similarly, because damage is less likely for helmet wearers, a motorcyclist in an accident is perceived as less likely to become disabled and require monetary support from the government (i.e., the taxpayers). The argument here is that a motorcyclist is potentially not only hurting him or herself but also those who might have to financially support these unfortunate motorcyclists.

3   It is not too difficult to see why one would be a proponent of mandatory helmet laws. Indeed, it would be unfortunate and unfair for anyone to have to support financially an incapacitated individual who might not be in such a condition had he or she been wearing a helmet. It is also almost inconceivable to argue that one is safer on a motorcycle without a helmet. Certainly the arguments in favor of mandatory helmet laws are so strong that it is difficult to imagine any alternative position.

4   However, there is another position, and one that is held just as passionately by some people as the one just described. As unlikely as it seems, there is a debate about the effectiveness of helmets. I agree with many people who ride motorcycles who believe helmet laws should be completely abolished. If that cannot be accomplished, the mandatory

age should at least be lowered from twenty-one to eighteen. Individuals who hold this point of view cite studies that suggest helmets have the potential to severely damage the spinal cord and/or vertebrae in an accident, causing varying degrees of paralysis and death. Full-face helmets are criticized for obstructing a rider's hearing and vision, especially peripheral vision. Helmets, furthermore, prevent the body's natural process of cooling through the head and can contribute to heat exhaustion or heat stroke, as riders in Texas are aware (Quigley).

5   Even the notion that is often termed the "social burden" theory is questionable. The famous Harborview Medical Center study showed that injured motorcyclists relied on public funds 63.4 percent of the time, which is significant. But it was later determined that 67 percent of the general population relied on public funding for hospital bills over the same period of time. Statistically, there does not seem to be any significant distinction between the reliance of motorcyclists and the general public on public funding. Thus the social burden theory seems primarily to be just that, a theory. It sounds good, but it seems to lack statistical validation ("Critics").

6   Even though I can see the validity of some of the arguments made by the proponents of helmet laws, I think there is ultimately some question regarding the strength of their arguments, and even some question of whether their arguments address the real issue that is built on a different value altogether, namely freedom. We have certain inalienable rights, rights to life, liberty, and the pursuit of happiness. It seems to me that mandatory helmet laws are in violation of such rights. Governments have a responsibility to protect their inhabitants from being harmed by each other in reasonable situations. It is not necessarily the responsibility of the government to try to prevent people from ever encountering danger. One could die on a plane or in a car or in an electrical fire in one's house, but the government would not think to outlaw airplanes, automobiles, or electricity. The fact that one incurs danger without a helmet is not a sufficient reason to mandate use of a helmet.

7   There is understandably a tension between safety and freedom, and these two values are often in conflict. In many instances people may not be in a position to make an educated decision with regard to their safety, and we understand such decisions being made for them. For example, children are not seen as capable of making certain decisions concerning the use of seat belts in automobiles or watching certain movies. Making those decisions for them seems reasonable as does requiring those under eighteen to wear a helmet. Yet, for those of sound mind who are deemed responsible, it seems unreasonable to strip away their freedom to choose by requiring them to wear a helmet.

8   I appreciate the care and concern of those proponents of helmet laws and understand their passion, and I am not unilaterally against helmets. When I ride on the highways, I tend to use mine. You might say that I am pro-choice when it comes to helmets. I believe in the rider's right to choose whether or not he or she wants to wear a helmet. I am in no way

opposed to educating and informing riders about helmets as part of the licensing process. Then riders are more likely to make the best decision with the best information at their disposal. I just want the riders to decide whether or not to wear a helmet instead of someone else making that decision for them as if they were children. In short, I echo many of my fellow motorcyclists who say, "Let those who ride decide."

Works Cited

"Critics Falsely Claim That Bikers Are a Burden on Society." *Bikers Rights Online!* N.p., 2001. Web. 27 Apr. 2008. <http://www.bikersrights.com/ama/ABCWNTBurden.html>.

Quigley, Richard. "NHTSA's Safety Standards Are Shown to Be Anything but Safe." *Helmet Law Defense League Report.* 3rd ed. N.p., Mar. 1994. Web. 27 Apr. 2008. <http://usff.com/hldl/report/3rdEditiona.html#R302>.

For Discussion:

Describe a rhetorical situation in which you think it would be better to write this paper about helmets in this form, using Rogerian strategy, than it would be to write it as a position paper, using traditional strategy. Describe the readers, constraints, and, in particular, the exigence as you imagine the rhetorical situation that might have prompted this paper.

Example 3 *(Option 3).* "Dear Boss" was written by a student who worked part-time while going to college and needed to change her working hours and some of her responsibilities. She had already spoken to her boss about making some changes but ended up with more responsibility instead of less. She was worried that her boss might think she was selfish and unconcerned about the welfare of the company. She was also worried that working too many hours would endanger her scholarship. It was very important to her that she reach a resolution to her problem. She decided to use Rogerian strategy to come to a better resolution of her dilemma with her boss. (After reading "Dear Boss," complete on evaluation using the sheet on page 332.)

STUDENT PAPER #3   Elizabeth Nabhan
Rogerian Argument Paper
Professor Wood
English 1302
30 April 2008

Dear Boss

1 Dear Boss,

I am writing to you in response to our recent conversation regarding my responsibilities as an employee of Smith and Smith. You indicated to me that you felt I had a surplus of free time at work and suggested that I was obviously capable of handling a greater workload.

Shortly thereafter, you delegated to me several new tasks that are to be performed on a regular basis. I understand that you believe I should pick up the additional workload to ensure that I am performing at a maximum level of output on a day-to-day basis. Also, you think I would complete the tasks more effectively than the individuals previously assigned to them.

2   I understand your reasoning that I should maintain a high level of output on a daily basis. As an employee of the company, it is my obligation to be productive for the duration of my workday. Not producing enough work results in idle time that, in turn, results in a loss to the company. It is intrinsic to the very nature of my role as a corporate auditor to ensure that the company does not engage in wasteful expenditures. If I worked nonstop every workday I would maximize my rate of efficiency and save the company the cost of hiring an additional employee. Furthermore, I accept your opinion that I am the employee who could most efficiently handle the new tasks you would like me to take on. My knowledge and experience with the required tasks puts me at an advantage over the employees previously delegated this work. Because of this, I would be able to complete the tasks much more quickly than other employees who would likely require more research time. Your perspective is fundamentally valid. However, I would like to introduce several factors that I believe may also bear consideration. In doing so, I believe it will be possible to reach a satisfactory conclusion regarding the issue of my workload and responsibilities.

3   According to the terms of my employment, I am required to complete a minimum of twenty hours per week. It was mutually agreed that any time I am not enrolled in school, I am free to work up to forty hours per week. The period during which I had an unusually ample amount of "down time" occurred during the summer months when I was not enrolled in school. As a result, I did briefly have an increased number of work hours. During this interim period I could have easily increased my workload, but I was not assigned any new tasks. In fact, additional duties were not assigned to me until after I commenced the fall semester. My hours are now reduced by nearly one-half, and, as a result, my idle time has diminished significantly. An increased workload now will limit the time I spend on each project and could result in a decrease in the quality of the work I complete.

4   I do not think there is any great concern as to whether the employees originally assigned to my newest tasks are able to complete them satisfactorily. These employees were hired based on their skills for completing the tasks at hand, and none of these tasks could be considered as falling outside of the scope of their regular duties. Furthermore, I believe it would be counterproductive to reassign their tasks to me, as it would essentially undermine these other employees' expertise. This type of situation can often lead to a decrease in morale, which would in turn affect each employee's total output. Finally, I would like to reconsider the belief that idle time on my part

results in decreased productivity. During my free time I am in a position to assist other staff members as necessary. I also utilize this time to observe subordinate employees, which is consistent with my role as the corporate auditor.

5   Our individual points of view share the common purpose of doing what is best for the company as a whole. Therefore, I believe it is possible to accomplish this goal via compromise. According to your perspective, I should take on additional responsibilities to fill gaps in my productivity while relieving less-qualified employees. From my point of view, I feel that my time is already effectively spent. I suggest the following steps be taken in order to ensure that each of our needs are met: First, my reduced hours must be taken into consideration when assigning me work. When I am in a position to take on additional duties, I feel I should be assigned those most compatible with my job description. More general tasks should be delegated to other employees. To alleviate your hesitation regarding their ability to perform these, I accept the responsibility of overseer and will offer them any help they may need. In doing so, I will apply my own expertise to more specific tasks without overburdening myself in such a way as to reduce my overall efficiency. Additionally, this will allow other employees the opportunity to sharpen their skills, while remaining under my observation. I propose this delegation of duties be put into effect under a probationary period, during which time we can observe the success of the program, and, if needed, redelegate tasks. Thank you for your consideration.

Sincerely,
Elizabeth Nabhan

For Discussion:

What is the issue? What is the boss's position? What is the student's position? If you were the boss, how would you respond to this letter?

E. Class Project: Combining Strategies in a Class Debate with Attempts to Reconcile the Opposing Positions

This activity provides the opportunity to combine elements of traditional and Rogerian argument theory that you have learned in Chapters 5–10.

Debate is a traditional forum for argument, and a common model for debate is to have two people on each side of the issue present their views and a judge who declares a winner. Your class can set up a debate in which everyone participates. For this class debate, however, we will use a somewhat different strategy that involves not only stating the opposing viewpoints but also working to find some common ground between the two opposing positions to achieve more productive argument and to avoid a standoff with no agreement and no resolution of the issue.

We draw on *social judgment theory* to help organize the debate. Social judgment theorists, who study the positions that individuals take on issues, plot positions on a continuum that ranges from extremely positive to extremely negative. They then describe these positions in terms of latitudes of acceptance. Individuals at the extremes of the continuum have narrow latitudes of acceptance and can usually tolerate only positions that are very close to their own. Somewhere in the middle is a latitude of noncommitment. People in this area, who are not strongly involved with the issue, have comparatively wide latitudes of acceptance and can tolerate a wide range of positions. The object of this debate is to increase everyone's latitudes of acceptance so that productive argument can take place.

Preparing for the Debates

1. *Select an Issue*

   The class can either nominate possible issues from the following list of topics and articles in this book or make recommendations of their own. They can then vote on which one of them is to be the topic for debate. The issue should be written in statement form, as in the list, so that individuals can either agree or disagree with it.

   Resolved: Traditional families are best, with the mother taking care of the children and the father working to support the family. See the articles by Pederson (pages 532–533), Cullen and Grossman (pages 533–536), and Cabot (pages 536–537).

   Resolved: Dating services in America and arranged marriages in other countries are the best ways of finding a suitable husband or wife. See the articles by Jain (pages 545–550) and Tierney (pages 553–555).

   Resolved: Facebook is a waste of time and lures people away from the real world. See the articles by Soller (pages 564–565) and Kliff (pages 566–567).

   Resolved: Relying on egg donors and sperm banks can be the best way to conceive brilliant and successful children. See the articles by Kolata (pages 134–136) and Orenstein (pages 584–587).

   Resolved: People who have broken the law and are incarcerated should have access to enriching activities while they are in prison. See the articles by Gilligan (pages 592–594), Wiltenburg (pages 595–597), and Quintanilla (pages 598–599).

   Resolved: The United States should build a fence along the United States–Mexico border to control illegal immigration. See the articles by Goldberg (pages 688–689), Hall (pages 689–690), McClatchy Newspapers Staff Writer (pages 690–691), and Bustillo (pages 692–695).

   Resolved: Wars are inevitable. See the articles by James (pages 708–711), Mead (pages 713–717), Hedges (pages 717–721), and Rhodes (pages 734–737).

Or: Brainstorm campus or current events issues and then vote on which one to debate.

2. *Create Three Groups*

The class will divide into three groups. Two groups are encouraged to take strong affirmative and negative positions and to argue from those points of view, presenting pro and con arguments, with presumably narrow latitudes of acceptance. A third group with a wider latitude of acceptance will take the middle-ground positions and present suggestions for resolving some of the conflict. This group will look for common ground in the extreme positions, try to resolve conflict, and work to achieve better understanding and perhaps even a change of views in the opposing groups.

Group 1 is the affirmative group that is in favor of the subject for debate. Group 2 is the negative group that is against it. Group 3 is the moderate group that will attempt to resolve the conflict. The groups should be equal in size. To achieve this equality, some students may have to argue for positions that they do not in fact actually hold.

3. *Do Background Reading and Writing*

All three groups should do some background reading on the subject for debate. The negative and affirmative teams will read to get ideas for their arguments and to develop ideas for refutation. The moderates should read to understand the opposing positions. Students in groups 1 and 2 will write 250-word papers outside of class that present some arguments to support their positions. After they have listened to the debate, the moderates will write 250-word papers that make an effort to resolve the conflict.

Conducting the Debate

Day One

1. *Begin with the opening papers* (10 minutes). Two students from the affirmative group and two from the negative group agree to start the debate by reading their papers. The first affirmative, first negative, second affirmative, and second negative read papers in that order.

2. *Others join in* (20 minutes). Students may now raise their hands to be recognized by the instructor to give additional arguments from their papers. Each person should stand to speak. The speakers should represent each side in turn. The class should decide whether everyone should first be allowed to speak before anyone is permitted to speak a second time. The instructor should cut off speakers who are going on too long.

3. *Caucus and closing remarks* (15 minutes). The affirmative and negative groups caucus for 5 minutes to prepare their closing arguments. Each group selects a spokesperson who then presents the group's final, strongest arguments in a 2-minute closing presentation.

4. *Moderates prepare responses.* The moderates write 250-word responses outside of class that answer the following question: Now that you have heard both sides, how would you resolve the conflict?

Day Two

1. *Moderates read* (20 minutes). All moderates read their papers. Each paper should take about 2 minutes to read.

2. *Analyze outcomes* (30 minutes). The class should now discuss the outcomes of the debate by addressing the following questions:

   a. What, in general, were some of the outcomes?

   b. Who changed their opinions? Which opinions? Why?

   c. Who did not change? Why?

   d. What are some of the outcomes of the attempts to reduce conflict and establish common ground?

   e. What strategies have you learned from participating in this debate that can help you in real-life arguments?

   f. Did you detect any fallacies that weakened the arguments?

Review and Synthesis of the Strategies for Reading, Writing, and Viewing Argument

The purpose of this appendix is to provide you with the opportunity to review and synthesize what you have learned about reading, writing, and viewing argument in the first ten chapters of this book. Your task here is to apply argument theory as you read and analyze two letters. The first, "A Call for Unity. A Letter from Eight White Clergymen" was published in a Birmingham, Alabama, newspaper in April 1963. The second, "A Letter from Birmingham Jail," was written shortly thereafter by Martin Luther King Jr. in response to the clergymen's letter.

As you read the two letters, assess the rhetorical situation from visual as well as textual material, notice the positions both parties take on the issue, and identify the claims, support, warrants, and backing for the warrants in each letter. Look for and analyze fallacies and refutation. As part of a final evaluation, decide whether each letter is primarily ethical or unethical. Consider that you must formulate reasons and evidence for your final evaluation. Plan to make some notes on these matters as you read.

Then, in the "Exercises and Activities" section that follows these example arguments, you are asked to apply your understanding to write an argument analysis paper. In this paper, you will explain the results of your reading and analysis. You will not be criticizing or showing what is wrong with the letters; you will not be arguing with the ideas or attempting to refute them. Instead, your purpose will be to explain the argumentation methods that these authors use to make their arguments. You will rely on information about argument theory that you have learned in earlier chapters in this book to help you make your evaluations and write a thorough analysis paper. A side benefit of this assignment is that you will learn to write a type of paper that is sometimes required in other classes.

Reading for the Argument Analysis Paper

Use the following information to help you read and analyze the letters:

1. The rhetorical situation for the letters is detailed on pages 341–343. Read this section first to help you situate these letters in their historical context.

2. Focus topics that identify relevant argument theory are listed along with directed questions on pages 343–344. Page numbers for each topic are provided, if you need to review. When you finish reading the two letters, you should be able to answer the questions that accompany each of the topics. A group work and discussion exercise to help you understand and work with these topics is provided on pages 359–360.

3. Questions appear in the margins of the letters that will direct your attention to various argumentation techniques and methods that the clergymen and King are employing. Answer these questions as you read. Your answers will help you understand the letters, respond to the questions that accompany the topics, and gather the information you will need to write your paper. Underline the information in the letters that answers the questions in the margins. Write your own insights and thoughts in the margins. These activities will help you generate plenty of material for your paper.

Writing the Argument Analysis Paper

The complete assignment for the argument analysis paper appears at the end of this chapter on page 360. You may want to read it now so that you will know what you will finally be asked to do. Here are some ideas to help you write this paper.

1. Create a structure for your essay, even if it is little more than a list of your main points. Or, if you prefer, make an outline. Place your ideas in an order that makes sense to you. Since you will be comparing and contrasting the two letters in this paper, you may want to write first about the clergymen's letter and then about King's letter and draw conclusions about both of them last. Or, as an alternative, set up topics, such as *emotional proof* or *writing style,* and then describe how each author, in turn, employs each technique in their letters.

2. You will be asked to explain the rhetorical situation. Be sure to place each letter in historical context and to describe the audiences each one addresses. Then explain the issue from both points of view and summarize the authors' positions. An example of a summary appears on page 126. Your summaries should be no longer than this example. You may be able to make them shorter, but plan to include enough detail to help your reader understand the ideas in each letter and how each is organized. Make a brief outline of each letter to guide your summary writing.

3. You will be asked to state the claims and describe the support in both let-ters. The following example, written about Anna Quindlen's claim and support in "Undocumented, Indispensable," pages 247–249, provides one way to do this. The following sentence not only states the claim but also lists the types of support Quindlen uses. More information about the support can be provided in the para-graphs that follow.

> In her essay "Undocumented, Indispensable," Anna Quindlen uses all three kinds of proof—*logos, ethos,* and *pathos*—to support her claim that many undocumented work-ers in America are valuable and contributing members of society and that decisions made about their future should be influenced by the same American values that have driven immigration policy in earlier centuries, including the values of free enterprise and human rights.

4. Include summarized, paraphrased, or quoted material from the letters to provide evidence to support your main points. Here is an example, again using Quindlen, that illustrates how a summary and a direct quote could pro-vide support.

> Quindlen uses an historical analogy to suggest that protest marches in the past, includ-ing those associated with the Vietnam War and feminism, are similar to the protest marches associated with the treatment of undocumented workers today. All of these protests result in change. "Immigration," she says, "is the leading edge of a deep and wide sea change in the United States today, just as those issues were in their own time (247).

Place page numbers in parentheses at the end of each summarized, para-phrased, or quoted passage to show where you found it in this textbook, as in the example above.

5. Write a conclusion in which you evaluate these letters. Are they ethical or unethical? Is one more effective and convincing than the other? Why? Write a final evaluative claim about the letters that is based on the ideas and evidence in your paper. At this point, decide whether you want to leave your claim at the end of your paper or to move it to an earlier position in your paper. Where would it be most effective?

6. Read your draft, revise it, and submit it.

Rhetorical Situation for "A Call to Unity: A Letter from Eight White Clergymen" and "Letter from Birmingham Jail"

Birmingham, Alabama, was a very strange place in 1963. Black people were allowed to sit only in certain parts of buses and restaurants, they were required to drink from separate water fountains, and they were not allowed in white churches, schools, or various other public places. The Reverend Mar-tin Luther King Jr. was a well-known minister in the black Baptist church and

Dr. Martin Luther King Jr. was jailed more than once during the civil rights movement. In this 1960 photo, police in Atlanta, Georgia, are taking him to court in handcuffs for participating in a sit-in at a segregated lunch counter in a department store. He was sentenced in this instance to four months of hard labor and was released on bail pending appeal only after Bobby Kennedy[1] phoned the judge.

For Discussion: What special features of visual argument are apparent in this photograph? (Review pages 282–289)

a leader in the civil rights movement at that time. The purpose of the movement was to end segregation and discrimination and to obtain equal rights and access for African Americans in the United States, but especially in the South.

Dr. King and others carefully prepared for demonstrations that would take place in Birmingham in the spring of 1963. The demonstrators began by "sitting in" at lunch counters that had never served blacks before and by picketing stores. Twenty people were arrested the first day on charges of trespassing. The civil rights leaders then applied for permits to picket and hold parades against the injustices of discrimination and segregation. They were refused permission, but they demonstrated and picketed anyway. Dr. King was served with an injunction granted by a circuit judge. It said civil rights leaders could not protest, demonstrate, boycott, or sit in at any facilities. King and other leaders decided that this was an unfair and unjust application of the law, and they decided to break the law by ignoring the injunction.

---

[1]Bobby Kennedy, brother of President John F. Kennedy, was the U.S. Attorney General at this time.

King himself decided to march on Good Friday, and he expected to go to jail. (As the photograph and caption document, Dr. King had long been aware that nonviolent civil disobedience required acceptance of any consequent punishments so as to create the tension of protest.) Indeed, before he had walked half a mile, he was arrested and jailed, along with fifty other people. King stayed in jail for eight days. During that time he wrote his famous letter. It was written in response to a letter signed by eight white clergymen that had been published in a local newspaper.

After King left jail, there were further protests and some violence. Thousands of people demonstrated, and thousands were jailed. Finally, black and white leaders began to negotiate, and some final terms were announced on May 10, 1963. All lunch counters, restrooms, fitting rooms, and drinking fountains in downtown stores were to be desegregated within ninety days; blacks were to be hired in clerical and sales jobs in stores within sixty days; the many people arrested during the demonstrations were to be released on low bail; and permanent lines of communication were to be established between black and white leaders. The demonstrations ended then, and the city settled down and began to implement the agreements.[2]

Focus Topics to Help You Analyze the Letters

Answer the questions that accompany the eight focus topics listed. Use the questions in the margins of the letters to help you locate the information you need to address the questions as well as suggestions posted under each topic.

1. *Rhetorical situation (pages 73–75).* Consider each of these points.
   a. What is the *exigence* for these two letters? What caused the authors to write them? What was the problem? Was it a new or recurring problem?
   b. Who is the *audience* for the clergymen's letter? For King's letter? What is the nature of these audiences? Can they be convinced? What are the expected outcomes?
   c. What are the *constraints*? Speculate about the beliefs, attitudes, habits, and traditions that were in place that limited or constrained both the white clergymen and King. How did these constraining circumstances influence the audience for both letters at that time?
   d. Think about the *authors* of both letters. Who are they? Speculate about their backgrounds, experience, affiliations, and values. What motivated them to write?
   e. What kind of *text* is each letter? What effect do its special qualities and features have on the audience?

---

[2]This account is drawn from Lee E. Bains Jr., "Birmingham, 1963: Confrontation over Civil Rights," in *Birmingham, Alabama, 1956–1963: The Black Struggle for Civil Rights,* ed. David J. Garrow (Brooklyn: Carlson, 1989), 175–83.

f. Think about *yourself as the reader.* What is your position on the issue? Do you experience constraints as you read? Do you perceive common ground with either the clergymen or King, or both? Describe it. Are you influenced by these letters? How?

2. *Organization and claims (pages 181–197).* Divide each letter into its main parts. What is the subject of each part? Why have the parts been placed in this particular order? What is the relationship between them? What is the main claim in each letter? What types of claims are they? What are some of the subclaims? What types of claims are they?

3. *Logical proofs and style (pages 222–235 and 240–241).* Analyze the use of logical proof in each of the letters. Provide examples. Describe their effect on the audience. Provide an example of the language of rational style in one of the letters.

4. *Emotional proofs and style (pages 237–239 and 242–244).* Analyze the use of emotional proof in each of the letters. Provide examples. Describe their effect on the audience. Provide an example of the language of emotional style in one of the letters.

5. *Proofs and style that establish* ethos *(pages 235–237 and 241–242).* Analyze the use of proofs that establish *ethos* or credibility in the letters. Provide examples. Describe their effect on the audience. Provide an example of language that establishes *ethos* in one of the letters.

6. *Warrants and Backing (pages 161–164 and 164).* Identify the warrants in each of the letters. What appeals to community values provide backing for the warrants? How much common ground do you think exists between the authors of the letters? How much common ground do you share with the authors? As a result, which letter do you find more convincing? Why?

7. *Fallacious thinking and rebuttals (pages 258–266 and 164–165).* Provide examples of reasoning that is considered fallacious or wrongheaded by the opposing parties in each of the letters. What rebuttals are made in response to these? How effective are they?

8. *Ethical or Unethical (pages 266–267).* Do the clergymen and King both make an adequate effort to understand the issue and its consequences? Does each also understand the position held by the other? How just and fair-minded is each party? Is their support fair, accurate, and/or convincing? Can you, as the reader, accept their warrants? Can you accept the references to community values that serve as backing for these warrants? Should the claims be qualified, if they are not already? Do the clergymen and King sincerely believe their positions are in the best interests of the people in Birmingham as well as of the larger society? Do you agree with them? Who is benefited, and who is burdened by their positions? Do you find evidence that either the clergymen or King are trying to manipulate the audience by hiding their real purpose, using inappropriate emotional appeals, manufacturing evidence, using inaccurate evidence, or telling lies? Do either of the arguers change the usual definitions of words to cloud perceptions, or do they minimize issues to trivialize them? What do you conclude about the ethical and unethical qualities of the letters?

ESSAY #1   # A CALL FOR UNITY: A LETTER FROM EIGHT WHITE CLERGYMEN

The eight white Alabama clergymen who wrote this letter to the editor of a Birmingham, Alabama, newspaper represent various religious denominations.

April 12, 1963

What is the issue?

What is the clergymen's position?

What is the claim?

What type of claim is it?

What are the rebuttals?

How do the authors build *ethos*?

How do they appeal to logic?

How do they appeal to emotion?

What are the warrants?

Describe the predominant style.

1   We the undersigned clergymen are among those who, in January, issued "An Appeal for Law and Order and Common Sense," in dealing with racial problems in Alabama. We expressed understanding that honest convictions in racial matters could properly be pursued in the courts, but urged that decisions of those courts should in the meantime be peacefully obeyed.

2   Since that time there had been some evidence of increased forebearance and a willingness to face facts. Responsible citizens have undertaken to work on various problems which cause racial friction and unrest. In Birmingham, recent public events have given indication that we all have opportunity for a new constructive and realistic approach to racial problems.

3   However, we are now confronted by a series of demonstrations by some of our Negro citizens, directed and led in part by outsiders. We recognize the natural impatience of people who feel that their hopes are slow in being realized. But we are convinced that these demonstrations are unwise and untimely.

4   We agree rather with certain local Negro leadership which has called for honest and open negotiation of racial issues in our area. And we believe this kind of facing of issues can best be accomplished by citizens of our own metropolitan area, white and Negro, meeting with their knowledge and experience of the local situation. All of us need to face that responsibility and find proper channels for its accomplishment.

5   Just as we formerly pointed out that "hatred and violence have no sanction in our religious and political traditions," we also point out that such actions as incite to hatred and violence, however technically peaceful those actions may be, have not contributed to the resolution of our local problems. We do not believe that these days of new hope are days when extreme measures are justified in Birmingham.

6   We commend the community as a whole, and the local news media and law enforcement officials in particular, on the calm manner in which these demonstrations have been handled. We urge the public to continue to show restraint should the demonstrations continue, and the law enforcement officials to remain calm and continue to protect our city from violence.

7   We further strongly urge our own Negro community to withdraw support from these demonstrations, and to unite locally in working peacefully for a better Birmingham. When rights are consistently denied, a cause should be pressed in the courts and in negotiations

347

among local leaders, and not in the streets. We appeal to both our white and Negro citizenry to observe the principles of law and order and common sense.

(Signed)
C.C.J. Carpenter, D.D., L.L.D., Bishop of Alabama; Joseph A. Durick, D.D., Auxiliary Bishop, Diocese of Mobile-Birmingham; Rabbi Milton L. Grafman, Temple Emanu-El, Birmingham, Alabama; Bishop Paul Hardin, Bishop of the Alabama–West Florida Conference of the Methodist Church; Bishop Nolan B. Harmon, Bishop of the North Alabama Conference of the Methodist Church; George M. Murray, D.D., L.L.D., Bishop Coadjutor, Episcopal Diocese of Alabama; Edward V. Ramage, Moderator, Synod of the Alabama Presbyterian Church in the United States; Earl Stallings, Pastor, First Baptist Church, Birmingham

ESSAY #2   **LETTER FROM BIRMINGHAM JAIL***

Martin Luther King Jr.

Martin Luther King Jr. was a Baptist minister who preached nonviolence and equal justice. He was a pivotal leader in the civil rights movement of the 1960s.

April 16, 1963

My Dear Fellow Clergymen:

What is the issue?
What is King's position?

Identify and describe the Rogerian elements and efforts to establish common ground throughout this letter.

1   While confined here in the Birmingham city jail, I came across your recent statement calling my present activities "unwise and untimely." Seldom do I pause to answer criticism of my work and ideas. If I sought to answer all the criticisms that cross my desk, my secretaries would have little time for anything other than such correspondence in the course of the day, and I would have no time for constructive work. But since I feel that you are men of genuine good will and that your criticisms are sincerely set forth, I want to try to answer your statement in what I hope will be patient and reasonable terms.

2   I think I should indicate why I am here in Birmingham, since you have been influenced by the view which argues against "outsiders coming in." I have the honor of serving as president of the Southern Christian Leadership Conference, an organization operating in every southern state, with headquarters in Atlanta, Georgia. We have some eighty-five affiliated organizations across the South, and one of them

---

*Author's Note: This response to a published statement by eight fellow clergymen from Alabama (Bishop C.C.J. Carpenter, Bishop Joseph A. Durick, Rabbi Milton L. Grafman, Bishop Paul Hardin, Bishop Nolan B. Harmon, the Reverend George M. Murray, the Reverend Edward V. Ramage, and the Reverend Earl Stallings) was composed under somewhat constricting circumstances. Begun on the margins of the newspaper in which the statement appeared while I was in jail, the letter was continued on scraps of writing paper supplied by a friendly Negro trusty, and concluded on a pad my attorneys were eventually permitted to leave me. Although the text remains in substance unaltered, I have indulged in the author's prerogative of polishing it for publication.

is the Alabama Christian Movement for Human Rights. Frequently we share staff, educational and financial resources with our affiliates. Several months ago the affiliate here in Birmingham asked us to be on call to engage in a nonviolent direct-action program if such were deemed necessary. We readily consented, and when the hour came we lived up to our promise. So I, along with several members of my staff, am here because I was invited here. I am here because I have organizational ties here.

3   But more basically, I am in Birmingham because injustice is here. Just as the prophets of the eighth century B.C. left their villages and carried their "thus saith the Lord" far beyond the boundaries of their home towns, and just as the Apostle Paul left his village of Tarsus and carried the gospel of Jesus Christ to the far corners of the Greco-Roman world, so am I compelled to carry the gospel of freedom beyond my own home town. Like Paul, I must constantly respond to the Macedonian call for aid.

4   Moreover, I am cognizant of the interrelatedness of all communities and states. I cannot sit idly by in Atlanta and not be concerned about what happens in Birmingham. Injustice anywhere is a threat to justice everywhere. We are caught in an inescapable network of mutuality, tied in a single garment of destiny. Whatever affects one directly, affects all indirectly. Never again can we afford to live with the narrow, provincial "outside agitator" idea. Anyone who lives inside the United States can never be considered an outsider anywhere within its bounds.

5   You deplore the demonstrations taking place in Birmingham. But your statement, I am sorry to say, fails to express a similar concern for the conditions that brought about the demonstrations. I am sure that none of you would want to rest content with the superficial kind of social analysis that deals merely with effects and does not grapple with underlying causes. It is unfortunate that demonstrations are taking place in Birmingham, but it is even more unfortunate that the city's white power structure left the Negro community with no alternative.

6   In any nonviolent campaign there are four basic steps: collection of the facts to determine whether injustices exist; negotiation; self-purification; and direct action. We have gone through all these steps in Birmingham. There can be no gain-saying the fact that racial injustice engulfs this community. Birmingham is probably the most thoroughly segregated city in the United States. Its ugly record of brutality is widely known. Negroes have experienced grossly unjust treatment in the courts. There have been more unsolved bombings of Negro homes and churches in Birmingham than in any other city in the nation. These are the hard, brutal facts of the case. On the basis of these conditions, Negro leaders sought to negotiate with the city fathers. But the latter consistently refused to engage in good-faith negotiation.

7   Then, last September, came the opportunity to talk with leaders of Birmingham's economic community. In the course of the negotiations, certain promises were made by the merchants—for example, to remove

How does King build *ethos*?

What is the effect of the comparison with Paul?

Draw a line at the end of the introduction.

Draw a line at the end of each of the other major sections of material. Label the subject of each section in the margin.

What is the subject of this first section?

What is the claim?

What type of claim is it?

Is it qualified?

Identify and analyze the effect of the emotional appeals.

349

the stores' humiliating racial signs. On the basis of these promises, the Reverend Fred Shuttlesworth and the leaders of the Alabama Christian Movement for Human Rights agreed to a moratorium on all demonstrations. As the weeks and months went by, we realized that we were the victims of a broken promise. A few signs, briefly removed, returned; the others remained.

8   As in so many past experiences, our hopes had been blasted, and the shadow of deep disappointment settled upon us. We had no alternative except to prepare for direct action, whereby we would present our very bodies as a means of laying our case before the conscience of the local and the national community. Mindful of the difficulties involved, we decided to undertake a process of self-purification. We began a series of workshops on nonviolence, and we repeatedly asked ourselves: "Are you able to accept blows without retaliating?" "Are you able to endure the ordeal of jail?" We decided to schedule our direct-action program for the Easter season, realizing that except for Christmas, this is the main shopping period of the year. Knowing that a strong economic-withdrawal program would be the by-product of direct action, we felt that this would be the best time to bring pressure to bear on the merchants for the needed change.

9   Then it occurred to us that Birmingham's mayoral election was coming up in March, and we speedily decided to postpone action until after election day. When we discovered that the Commissioner of Public Safety, Eugene "Bull" Connor, had piled up enough votes to be in the runoff, we decided again to postpone action until the day after the runoff so that the demonstrations could not be used to cloud the issues. Like many others, we waited to see Mr. Connor defeated, and to this end we endured postponement after postponement. Having aided in this community need, we felt that our direct-action program could be delayed no longer.

10   You may well ask: "Why direct action? Why sit-ins, marches and so forth? Isn't negotiation a better path?" You are quite right in calling for negotiation. Indeed, this is the very purpose of direct action. Nonviolent direct action seeks to create such a crisis and foster such a tension that a community which has constantly refused to negotiate is forced to confront the issue. It seeks so to dramatize the issue that it can no longer be ignored. My citing the creation of tension as part of the work of the nonviolent-resister may sound rather shocking. But I must confess that I am not afraid of the word "tension." I have earnestly opposed violent tension, but there is a type of constructive, nonviolent tension which is necessary for growth. Just as Socrates felt that it was necessary to create a tension in the mind so that individuals could rise from the bondage of myths and half-truths to the unfettered realm of creative analysis and objective appraisal, so must we see the need for nonviolent gadflies to create the kind of tension in society that will help men rise from the dark depths of prejudice and racism to the majestic heights of understanding and brotherhood.

What are some of the values expressed in this argument?

Identify and describe the rebuttals.

What is the effect of the comparison with Socrates?

What is King's
planned
argumentation
strategy?

Why does King refer
to history?

Why does he refer to
Niebuhr?

Identify and analyze
the emotional proof.

To what human
motives and values
does King appeal?

Identify emotional
language, examples,
and vivid description.

11   The purpose of our direct-action program is to create a situation so crisis-packed that it will inevitably open the door to negotiation. I therefore concur with you in your call for negotiation. Too long has our beloved Southland been bogged down in a tragic effort to live in monologue rather than dialogue.

12   One of the basic points in your statement is that the action that I and my associates have taken in Birmingham is untimely. Some have asked: "Why didn't you give the new city administration time to act?" The only answer that I can give to this query is that the new Birmingham administration must be prodded about as much as the outgoing one, before it will act. We are sadly mistaken if we feel that the election of Albert Boutwell as mayor will bring the millennium to Birmingham. While Mr. Boutwell is a much more gentle person than Mr. Connor, they are both segregationists, dedicated to the maintenance of the status quo. I have hope that Mr. Boutwell will be reasonable enough to see the futility of massive resistance to desegregation. But he will not see this without pressure from devotees of civil rights. My friends, I must say to you that we have not made a single gain in civil rights without determined legal and nonviolent pressure. Lamentably, it is a historical fact that privileged groups seldom give up their privileges voluntarily. Individuals may see the moral light and voluntarily give up their unjust posture; but, as Reinhold Niebuhr has reminded us, groups tend to be more immoral than individuals.

13   We know through painful experience that freedom is never voluntarily given up by the oppressor; it must be demanded by the oppressed. Frankly, I have yet to engage in a direct-action campaign that was "well-timed" in the view of those who have not suffered unduly from the disease of segregation. For years now I have heard the word "Wait!" It rings in the ear of every Negro with piercing familiarity. This "Wait" has almost always meant "Never." We must come to see, with one of our distinguished jurists, that "justice too long delayed is justice denied."

14   We have waited for more than 340 years for our constitutional and God-given rights. The nations of Asia and Africa are moving with jetlike speed toward gaining political independence, but we still creep at horse-and-buggy pace toward gaining a cup of coffee at a lunch counter. Perhaps it is easy for those who have never felt the stinging darts of segregation to say, "Wait." But when you have seen vicious mobs lynch your mothers and fathers at will and drown your sisters and brothers at whim; when you have seen hate-filled policemen curse, kick and even kill your black brothers and sisters; when you see the vast majority of your twenty million Negro brothers smothering in an airtight cage of poverty in the midst of an affluent society; when you suddenly find your tongue twisted and your speech stammering as you seek to explain to your six-year-old daughter why she can't go to the public amusement park that has just been advertised on television, and see tears welling up in her eyes when she is told that Fun-town is closed to colored children, and see ominous clouds of inferiority beginning to form in her little mental sky, and see

351

What is the effect of the emotional proof?

her beginning to distort her personality by developing an unconscious bitterness toward white people; when you have to concoct an answer for a five-year-old son who is asking, "Daddy, why do white people treat colored people so mean?"; when you take a cross-country drive and find it necessary to sleep night after night in the uncomfortable corners of your automobile because no motel will accept you; when you are humiliated day in and day out by nagging signs reading "white" and "colored"; when your first name becomes "nigger," your middle name becomes "boy" (however old you are) and your last name becomes "John," and your wife and mother are never given the respected title "Mrs."; when you are harried by day and haunted by night by the fact that you are a Negro, living constantly at tiptoe stance, never quite knowing what to expect next, and are plagued with inner fears and outer resentments; when you are forever fighting a degenerating sense of "nobodiness"—then you will understand why we find it difficult to wait. There comes a time when the cup of endurance runs over, and men are no longer willing to be plunged into the abyss of despair. I hope, sirs, you can understand our legitimate and unavoidable impatience.

What is the predominant type of proof in the first section of the letter?

15   You express a great deal of anxiety over our willingness to break laws. This is certainly a legitimate concern. Since we so diligently urge people to obey the Supreme Court's decision of 1954 outlawing segregation in the public schools, at first glance it may seem rather paradoxical for us consciously to break laws. One may well ask: "How can you advocate breaking some laws and obeying others?" The answer lies in the fact that there are two types of laws: just and unjust. I would be the first to advocate obeying just laws. Conversely, one has a moral responsibility to disobey unjust laws. I would agree with St. Augustine that "an unjust law is no law at all."

Draw a line where the subject changes. What is the subject of the second section?

How and why does King use definition?

16   Now, what is the difference between the two? How does one determine whether a law is just or unjust? A just law is a man-made code that squares with the moral law or the law of God. An unjust law is a code that is out of harmony with the moral law. To put it in the terms of St. Thomas Aquinas: An unjust law is a human law that is not rooted in eternal law and natural law. Any law that uplifts human personality is just. Any law that degrades human personality is unjust. All segregation statutes are unjust because segregation distorts the soul and damages the personality. It gives the segregator a false sense of superiority and the segregated a false sense of inferiority. Segregation, to use the terminology of the Jewish philosopher Martin Buber, substitutes an "I-it" relationship for an "I-thou" relationship and ends up relegating persons to the status of things. Hence segregation is not only politically, economically, and sociologically unsound, it is morally wrong and sinful. Paul Tillich has said that sin is separation. Is not segregation an existential expression of man's tragic separation, his awful estrangement, his terrible sinfulness? Thus it is that I can urge men to obey the 1954 decision of the Supreme Court, for it is morally right; and I can urge them to disobey segregation ordinances, for they are morally wrong.

How does he support the definition?

What is the effect of the support?

Explain the example
of just and unjust
laws.

17   Let us consider a more concrete example of just and unjust laws. An unjust law is a code that a numerical or power majority group compels a minority group to obey but does not make binding on itself. This is *difference* made legal. By the same token, a just law is a code that a majority compels a minority to follow and that it is willing to follow itself. This is *sameness* made legal.

How does King
further elaborate
on this idea?

18   Let me give another explanation. A law is unjust if it is inflicted on a minority that, as a result of being denied the right to vote, had no part in enacting or devising the law. Who can say that the legislature of Alabama which set up the state's segregation laws was democratically elected? Throughout Alabama all sorts of devious methods are used to prevent Negroes from becoming registered voters, and there are some counties in which, even though Negroes constitute a majority of the population, not a single Negro is registered. Can any law enactment under such circumstances be considered democratically structured?

19   Sometimes a law is just on its face and unjust in its application. For instance, I have been arrested on a charge of parading without a permit. Now, there is nothing wrong in having an ordinance which requires a permit for a parade. But such an ordinance becomes unjust when it is used to maintain segregation and to deny citizens the First-Amendment privilege of peaceful assembly and protest.

Analyze the
deductive reasoning
in this paragraph.

20   I hope you are able to see the distinction I am trying to point out. In no sense do I advocate evading or defying the law, as would the rabid segregationist. That would lead to anarchy. One who breaks an unjust law must do so openly, lovingly, and with a willingness to accept the penalty. I submit that an individual who breaks a law that conscience tells him is unjust, and who willingly accepts the penalty of imprisonment in order to arouse the conscience of the community over its injustice, is in reality expressing the highest respect for law.

Identify and describe
the effect of the
historical analogies.

21   Of course, there is nothing new about this kind of civil disobedience. It was evidenced sublimely in the refusal of Shadrach, Meshach and Abednego to obey the laws of Nebuchadnezzar, on the ground that a higher moral law was at stake. It was practiced superbly by the early Christians, who were willing to face hungry lions and the excruciating pain of chopping blocks rather than submit to certain unjust laws of the Roman Empire. To a degree, academic freedom is a reality today because Socrates practiced civil disobedience. In our own nation, the Boston Tea Party represented a massive act of civil disobedience.

What type of proof
predominates in the
second part of the
letter?

Draw a line where
the subject changes.
What is the subject of
the third section?

22   We should never forget that everything Adolf Hitler did in Germany was "legal" and everything the Hungarian freedom fighters did in Hungary was "illegal." It was "illegal" to aid and comfort a Jew in Hitler's Germany. Even so, I am sure that, had I lived in Germany at the time, I would have aided and comforted my Jewish brothers. If today I lived in a Communist country where certain principles dear to the Christian faith are suppressed, I would openly advocate disobeying that country's antireligious laws.

What are King's
warrants in this
passage?

How do King's
warrants differ from
the clergymen's?

How and why does
King use definition
here?

Identify and describe
the effects of the
analogies in these
paragraphs.

What is the fallacious
thinking King
complains of here?

23   I must make two honest confessions to you, my Christian and Jewish
brothers. First, I must confess that over the past few years I have been
gravely disappointed with the white moderate. I have almost reached the
regrettable conclusion that the Negro's great stumbling block in his stride
toward freedom is not the White Citizen's Councilor or the Ku Klux
Klanner, but the white moderate, who is more devoted to "order" than to
justice; who prefers a negative peace which is the absence of tension to a
positive peace which is the presence of justice; who constantly says: "I
agree with you in the goal you seek, but I cannot agree with your
methods of direct action"; who paternalistically believes he can set the
timetable for another man's freedom; who lives by a mythical concept
of time and who constantly advises the Negro to wait for a "more convenient season." Shallow understanding from people of good will is more
frustrating than absolute misunderstanding from people of ill will.
Lukewarm acceptance is much more bewildering than outright rejection.

24   I had hoped that the white moderate would understand that law and
order exist for the purpose of establishing justice and that when they fail
in this purpose they become the dangerously structured dams that block
the flow of social progress. I had hoped that the white moderate would
understand that the present tension in the South is a necessary phase of
the transition from an obnoxious negative peace, in which the Negro
passively accepted his unjust plight, to a substantive and positive peace,
in which all men will respect the dignity and worth of human personality.
Actually, we who engage in nonviolent direct action are not the creators
of tension. We merely bring to the surface the hidden tension that is
already alive. We bring it out in the open, where it can be seen and dealt
with. Like a boil that can never be cured so long as it is covered up but
must be opened with all its ugliness to the natural medicines of air and
light, injustice must be exposed, with all the tension its exposure creates,
to the light of human conscience and the air of national opinion before
it can be cured.

25   In your statements you assert that our actions, even though peaceful,
must be condemned because they precipitate violence. But is this a
logical assertion? Isn't this like condemning a robbed man because his
possession of money precipitated the evil act of robbery? Isn't this like
condemning Socrates because his unswerving commitment to truth and
his philosophical inquiries precipitated the act by the misguided populace
in which they made him drink hemlock? Isn't this like condemning
Jesus because his unique God-consciousness and never-ceasing devotion
to God's will precipitated the evil act of crucifixion? We must come to
see that, as the federal courts have consistently affirmed, it is wrong to
urge an individual to cease his efforts to gain his basic constitutional
rights because the quest may precipitate violence. Society must protect
the robbed and punish the robber.

26   I had also hoped that the white moderate would reject the myth
concerning time in relation to the struggle for freedom. I have just
received a letter from a white brother in Texas. He writes: "All Christians

know that the colored people will receive equal rights eventually, but it is possible that you are in too great a religious hurry. It has taken Christianity almost two thousand years to accomplish what it has. The teachings of Christ take time to come to earth." Such an attitude stems from a tragic misconception of time, from the strangely irrational notion that there is something in the very flow of time that will inevitably cure all ills. Actually, time itself is neutral; it can be used either destructively or constructively. More and more I feel that the people of ill will have used time much more effectively than have the people of good will. We will have to repent in this generation not merely for the hateful words and actions of the bad people but for the appalling silence of the good people. Human progress never rolls in on wheels of inevitability; it comes through the tireless efforts of men willing to be coworkers with God, and without this hard work, time itself becomes an ally of the forces of social stagnation. We must use time creatively, in the knowledge that the time is always right to do right. Now is the time to make real the promise of democracy and transform our pending national elegy into a creative psalm of brotherhood. Now is the time to lift our national policy from the quicksand of racial injustice to the solid rock of human dignity.

27   You speak of our activity in Birmingham as extreme. At first I was rather disappointed that fellow clergymen would see my nonviolent efforts as those of an extremist. I began thinking about the fact that I stand in the middle of two opposing forces in the Negro community. One is a force of complacency, made up in part of Negroes who, as a result of long years of oppression, are so drained of self-respect and a sense of "somebodiness" that they have adjusted to segregation; and in part of a few middle-class Negroes who, because of a degree of academic and economic security and because in some ways they profit by segregation, have become insensitive to the problems of the masses. The other force is one of bitterness and hatred, and it comes perilously close to advocating violence. It is expressed in the various black nationalist groups that are springing up across the nation, the largest and best-known being Elijah Muhammad's Muslim movement. Nourished by the Negro's frustration over the continued existence of racial discrimination, this movement is made up of people who have lost faith in America, who have absolutely repudiated Christianity, and who have concluded that the white man is an incorrigible "devil."

28   I have tried to stand between these two forces, saying that we need emulate neither the "do-nothingism" of the complacent nor the hatred and despair of the black nationalist. For there is the more excellent way of love and nonviolent protest. I am grateful to God that, through the influence of the Negro church, the way of nonviolence became an integral part of our struggle.

29   If this philosophy had not emerged, by now many streets of the South would, I am convinced, be flowing with blood. And I am further convinced that if our white brothers dismiss as "rabble-rousers" and "outside agitators" those of us who employ nonviolent direct action, and if they

Summarize King's reasoning about time.

Describe the two opposing forces.

How and why does King attempt to reconcile the opposing forces?

Identify and describe the causal proof.

355

refuse to support our nonviolent efforts, millions of Negroes will, out of frustration and despair, seek solace and security in black-nationalist ideologies—a development that would inevitably lead to a frightening racial nightmare.

Summarize King's reasoning about the effects of oppression.

30   Oppressed people cannot remain oppressed forever. The yearning for freedom eventually manifests itself, and that is what has happened to the American Negro. Something within has reminded him of his birthright of freedom, and something without has reminded him that it can be gained. Consciously or unconsciously, he has been caught up by the *Zeitgeist,* and with his black brothers of Africa and his brown and yellow brothers of Asia, South America and the Caribbean, the United States Negro is moving with a sense of great urgency toward the promised land of racial justice. If one recognizes this vital urge that has engulfed the Negro community, one should readily understand why public demonstrations are taking place. The Negro has many pent-up resentments and latent frustrations, and he must release them. So let him march; let him make prayer pilgrimages to the city hall; let him go on freedom rides—and try to understand why he must do so. If his repressed emotions are not released in nonviolent ways, they will seek expression through violence; this is not a threat but a fact of history. So I have not said to my people: "Get rid of your discontent." Rather, I have tried to say that this normal and healthy discontent can be channeled into the creative outlet of nonviolent direct action. And now this approach is being termed extremist.

What is the effect of these comparisons?

31   But though I was initially disappointed at being categorized as an extremist, as I continued to think about the matter I gradually gained a measure of satisfaction from the label. Was not Jesus an extremist for love: "Love your enemies, bless them that curse you, do good to them that hate you, and pray for them which despitefully use you, and prosecute you." Was not Amos an extremist for justice: "Let justice roll down like waters and righteousness like an everflowing stream." Was not Paul an extremist for the Christian gospel: "I bear in my body the marks of the Lord Jesus." Was not Martin Luther an extremist: "Here I stand; I cannot do otherwise, so help me God." And John Bunyan: "I will stay in jail to the end of my days before I make a butchery of my conscience." And Abraham Lincoln: "This nation cannot survive half slave and half free." And Thomas Jefferson: "We hold these truths to be self-evident, that all men are created equal. . . ." So the question is not whether we will be extremists, but what kind of extremists we will be. Will we be extremists for hate or for love? Will we be extremists for the preservation of injustice or for the extension of justice? In that dramatic scene on Calvary's hill three men were crucified. We must never forget that all three were crucified for the same crime—the crime of extremism. Two were extremists for immorality, and thus fell below their environment. The other, Jesus Christ, was an extremist for love, truth and goodness, and thereby rose above his environment. Perhaps the South, the nation and the world are in dire need of creative extremists.

Summarize King's description of the oppressor race.

What types of proof are used in this third section?

32   I had hoped that the white moderate would see this need. Perhaps I was too optimistic; perhaps I expected too much. I suppose I should have realized that few members of the oppressor race can understand the deep groans and passionate yearnings of the oppressed race, and still fewer have the vision to see that injustice must be rooted out by strong, persistent and determined action. I am thankful, however, that some of our white brothers in the South have grasped the meaning of this social revolution and committed themselves to it. They are still all too few in quantity, but they are big in quality. Some—such as Ralph McGill, Lillian Smith, Harry Golden, James McBride Dabbs, Ann Braden and Sarah Patton Boyle—have written about our struggle in eloquent and prophetic terms. Others have marched with us down nameless streets of the South. They have languished in filthy, roach-infested jails, suffering the abuse and brutality of policemen who view them as "dirty nigger-lovers." Unlike so many of their moderate brothers and sisters, they have recognized the urgency of the moment and sensed the need for powerful "action" antidotes to combat the disease of segregation.

Draw a line where the subject changes. What is the subject of the fourth section?

Reconsider the rhetorical situations: What went before? What will come later?

33   Let me take note of my other major disappointment. I have been so greatly disappointed with the white church and its leadership. Of course, there are some notable exceptions. I am not unmindful of the fact that each of you has taken some significant stands on this issue. I commend you, Reverend Stallings, for your Christian stand on this past Sunday, in welcoming Negroes to your worship service on a non-segregated basis. I commend the Catholic leaders of this state for integrating Spring Hill College several years ago.

34   But despite these notable exceptions, I must honestly reiterate that I have been disappointed with the church. I do not say this as one of those negative critics who can always find something wrong with the church. I say this as a minister of the gospel, who loves the church; who was nurtured in its bosom; who has been sustained by its spiritual blessings and who will remain true to it as long as the cord of life shall lengthen.

How does King build ethos in this fourth section?

35   When I was suddenly catapulted into the leadership of the bus protest in Montgomery, Alabama, a few years ago, I felt we would be supported by the white church. I felt that the white ministers, priests and rabbis of the South would be among our strongest allies. Instead, some have been outright opponents, refusing to understand the freedom movement and misrepresenting its leaders; all too many others have been more cautious than courageous and have remained silent behind the anesthetizing security of stained-glass windows.

What common ground did King hope would be clear? How was he disappointed?

36   In spite of my shattered dreams, I came to Birmingham with the hope that the white religious leadership of this community would see the justice of our cause and, with deep moral concern, would serve as the channel through which our just grievances could reach the power structure. I had hoped that each of you would understand. But again I have been disappointed.

357

How and why does King use vivid description?

37   I have heard numerous southern religious leaders admonish their worshipers to comply with a desegregation decision because it is the law, but I have longed to hear white ministers declare: "Follow this decree because integration is morally right and because the Negro is your brother." In the midst of blatant injustices inflicted upon the Negro, I have watched white churchmen stand on the sideline and mouth pious irrelevancies and sanctimonious trivialities. In the midst of a mighty struggle to rid our nation of racial and economic injustice, I have heard many ministers say: "Those are social issues, with which the gospel has no real concern." And I have watched many churches commit themselves to a completely other-worldly religion which makes a strange, unBiblical distinction between body and soul, between the sacred and the secular.

38   I have traveled the length and breadth of Alabama, Mississippi and all the other southern states. On sweltering summer days and crisp autumn mornings I have looked at the South's beautiful churches with their lofty spires pointing heavenward. I have beheld the impressive outlines of her massive religious-education buildings. Over and over I have found myself asking: "What kind of people worship here? Who is their God? Where were their voices when the lips of Governor Barnett dripped with words of interposition and nullification? Where were they when Governor Wallace gave a clarion call for defiance and hatred? Where were their voices of support when bruised and weary Negro men and women decided to rise from the dark dungeons of complacency to the bright hills of creative protest?"

39   Yes, these questions are still in my mind. In deep disappointment I have wept over the laxity of the church. But be assured that my tears have been tears of love. There can be no deep disappointment where there is not deep love. Yes, I love the church. How could I do otherwise? I am in the rather unique position of being the son, the grandson and the great-grandson of preachers. Yes, I see the church as the body of Christ. But, oh! How we have blemished and scarred that body through social neglect and through fear of being nonconformists.

What is the effect of the historical analogy?

40   There was a time when the church was very powerful—in the time when the early Christians rejoiced at being deemed worthy to suffer for what they believed. In those days the church was not merely a thermometer that recorded the ideas and principles of popular opinion; it was a thermostat that transformed the mores of society. Whenever the early Christians entered a town, the people in power became disturbed and immediately sought to convict the Christians for being "disturbers of the peace" and "outside agitators." But the Christians pressed on, in the conviction that they were "a colony of heaven," called to obey God rather than man. Small in number, they were big in commitment. They were too God-intoxicated to be "astronomically intimidated." By their effort and example they brought an end to such ancient evils as infanticide and gladiatorial contests.

41   Things are different now. So often the contemporary church is a weak, ineffectual voice with an uncertain sound. So often it is an arch-defender of the status quo. Far from being disturbed by the presence of the church, the power structure of the average community is consoled by the church's silent—and often even vocal—sanction of things as they are.

42   But the judgment of God is upon the church as never before. If today's church does not recapture the sacrificial spirit of the early church, it will lose its authenticity, forfeit the loyalty of millions, and be dismissed as an irrelevant social club with no meaning for the twentieth century. Every day I meet young people whose disappointment with the church has turned into outright disgust.

How does King contrast organized religion and the inner church? What is the effect?

43   Perhaps I have once again been too optimistic. Is organized religion too inextricably bound to the status quo to save our nation and the world? Perhaps I must turn my faith to the inner spiritual church, the church within the church, as the true *ekklesia* and the hope of the world. But again I am thankful to God that some noble souls from the ranks of organized religion have broken loose from the paralyzing chains of conformity and joined us as active partners in the struggle for freedom. They have left their secure congregations and walked the streets of Albany, Georgia, with us. They have gone down the highways of the South on tortuous rides for freedom. Yes, they have gone to jail with us. Some have been dismissed from their churches, have lost the support of their bishops and fellow ministers. But they have acted in the faith that right defeated is stronger than evil triumphant. Their witness has been the spiritual salt that has preserved the true meaning of the gospel in these troubled times. They have carved a tunnel of hope through the dark mountain of disappointment.

359

Why does King use historical analogies here?

44   I hope the church as a whole will meet the challenge of this decisive hour. But even if the church does not come to the aid of justice, I have no despair about the future. I have no fear about the outcome of our struggle in Birmingham, even if our motives are at present misunderstood. We will reach the goal of freedom in Birmingham and all over the nation, because the goal of America is freedom. Abused and scorned though we may be, our destiny is tied up with America's destiny. Before the pilgrims landed at Plymouth, we were here. Before the pen of Jefferson etched the majestic words of the Declaration of Independence across the pages of history, we were here. For more than two centuries our forebears labored in this country without wages; they made cotton king; they built the homes of their masters while suffering gross injustice and shameful humiliation—and yet out of a bottomless vitality they continued to thrive and develop. If the inexpressible cruelties of slavery could not stop us, the opposition we now face will surely fail. We will win our freedom because the sacred heritage of our nation and the eternal will of God are embodied in our echoing demands.

What types of proof are used in the fourth section?

Draw a line where the subject changes. What is the subject of the fifth section?

45   Before closing I feel impelled to mention one other point in your statement that has troubled me profoundly. You warmly commended the Birmingham police force for keeping "order" and "preventing

What is the predominant type of proof in this fifth section?

Provide some examples.

Describe the effect.

violence." I doubt that you would have so warmly commended the police force if you had seen its dogs sinking their teeth into unarmed, nonviolent Negroes. I doubt that you would so quickly commend the policemen if you were to observe their ugly and inhumane treatment of Negroes here in the city jail; if you were to watch them push and curse old Negro women and young Negro girls; if you were to see them slap and kick old Negro men and young boys; if you were to observe them, as they did on two occasions, refuse to give us food because we wanted to sing our grace together. I cannot join you in your praise of the Birmingham police department.

46   It is true that the police have exercised a degree of discipline in handling the demonstrators. In this sense they have conducted themselves rather "nonviolently" in public. But for what purpose? To preserve the evil system of segregation. Over the past few years I have consistently preached that nonviolence demands that the means we use must be as pure as the ends we seek. I have tried to make clear that it is wrong to use immoral means to attain moral ends. But now I must affirm that it is just as wrong, or perhaps even more so, to use moral means to preserve immoral ends. Perhaps Mr. Connor and his policemen have been rather nonviolent in public, as was Chief Pritchett in Albany, Georgia, but they have used the moral means of nonviolence to maintain the immoral end of racial injustice. As T. S. Eliot has said: "The last temptation is the greatest treason: To do the right deed for the wrong reason."

47   I wish you had commended the Negro sit-inners and the demonstrators of Birmingham for their sublime courage, their willingness to suffer and their amazing discipline in the midst of great provocation. One day the South will recognize its real heroes. They will be the James Merediths, with the noble sense of purpose that enables them to face jeering and hostile mobs, and with the agonizing loneliness that characterizes the life of the pioneer. They will be old, oppressed, battered Negro women, symbolized in a seventy-two-year-old woman in Montgomery, Alabama, who rose up with a sense of dignity and with her people decided not to ride segregated buses, and who responded with ungrammatical profundity to one who inquired about her weariness: "My feets is tired, but my soul is at rest." They will be the young high school and college students, the young ministers of the gospel and a host of their elders, courageously and nonviolently sitting in at lunch counters and willingly going to jail for conscience's sake. One day the South will know that when these disinherited children of God sat down at lunch counters, they were in reality standing up for what is best in the American dream and for the most sacred values in our Judaeo-Christian heritage, thereby bringing our nation back to those great wells of democracy which were dug deep by the founding fathers in their formulation of the Constitution and the Declaration of Independence.

Draw a line to set off the conclusion. What is the concluding idea?

48   Never before have I written so long a letter. I'm afraid it is much too long to take your precious time. I can assure you that it would have been much shorter if I had been writing from a comfortable desk, but

what else can one do when he is alone in a narrow jail cell, other than write long letters, think long thoughts and pray long prayers?

What is King's purpose in this conclusion?

49   If I have said anything in this letter that overstates the truth and indicates an unreasonable impatience, I beg you to forgive me. If I have said anything that understates the truth and indicates my having a patience that allows me to settle for anything less than brotherhood, I beg God to forgive me.

Do you find the two letters convincing? Why or why not?

50   I hope this letter finds you strong in the faith. I also hope that circumstances will soon make it possible for me to meet each of you, not as an integrationist or a civil-rights leader but as a fellow clergyman and a Christian brother. Let us all hope that the dark clouds of racial prejudice will soon pass away and the deep fog of misunderstanding will be lifted from our fear-drenched communities, and in some not too distant tomorrow the radiant stars of love and brotherhood will shine over our great nation with all their scintillating beauty.

Are the clergymen's and King's arguments moral or immoral according to your values and standards?

Yours for the cause of Peace and Brotherhood,
Martin Luther King, Jr.

Review Questions

1. Describe the argument analysis paper.
2. What is the purpose of this paper?
3. What do you need to avoid doing in this paper that might be a part of other types of argument papers?
4. Describe the rhetorical situation for the letters by the eight white clergymen and Dr. Martin Luther King Jr.
5. What are the focus topics? Provide three examples of them.

Exercises and Activities

A. Group Work and Discussion: Understanding the Focus Topics

Divide the class into eight groups, and assign each group one of the eight focus topics listed on pages 345–346. Here are the topics: **rhetorical situation; organization and claims; logical proofs and style; emotional proofs and style; proofs and style that establish** *ethos;* **warrants and backing; fallacious thinking and rebuttals;** and **ethical or unethical qualities**. Utilize the questions that accompany each focus item on the list. To prepare for the group work, all students will read the two letters outside of class and make notes individually on the focus topic assigned to their group. The brief questions in the margins of the letters will facilitate this reading and note taking. In class the groups will meet briefly to consolidate their views on their topic. Each of the groups will then make a brief oral report on their topic, and other class members will discuss the results and take some notes. These notes will be used as prewriting materials for the argument analysis paper.

B. **Writing Assignment: An Argument Analysis Paper**

Write a four-page double-spaced argument analysis paper of at least 1,000 words in which you analyze the two letters by the clergymen and King. Put the letters in historical context by describing the rhetorical situation, with particular emphasis on the exigence, the audiences, and the constraints. Explain the issue from both points of view. Summarize the positions taken on the issue in both letters. State the claims in both letters. Describe and evaluate the support, warrants, and backing in both. Identify any fallacies and describe how the authors use rebuttal. Finally, evaluate the ethical or unethical qualities that appear in these letters and write a conclusion in which you make a claim about the relative effectiveness of the two letters. Which letter is more effective? Why? Have your own views been modified or changed? How?

3

Writing a Research Paper That Presents an Argument

The purpose of the next three chapters is to teach you to write an argument paper that is from your own perspective and incorporates research materials from outside sources. Since other professors or even employers may ask you to produce such papers, this instruction should be useful to you not only now but also in the future. Chapter 11 teaches you to write a claim, clarify the purpose for your paper, and analyze your audience. Chapter 12 teaches you various creative strategies for gathering and evaluating both print and online research materials for your paper. Chapter 13 teaches ways to think about and organize your material, write and revise the paper, and prepare the final copy. When you finish reading Part Three:

▶ You will know how to write your claim and determine the main argumentation purpose of your research paper.

▶ You will know how to analyze your audience and predict how it might change.

▶ You will know how to think about your claim and gather material from your own background and experience to support it.

▶ You will know how to organize and conduct library and online research to support your claim further.

▶ You will know a variety of possible ways to organize the ideas for your paper.

▶ You will know how to incorporate research materials into your paper and prepare the final copy.

11

The Research Paper: Clarifying Purpose and Understanding the Audience

This chapter and the two that follow form a self-contained unit. You may think of them as one long assignment. They present the information you will need to help you plan, research, and write a researched position paper. You will be familiar with some of the information in these chapters because you have encountered it in earlier chapters. The basic process for writing a researched position paper is much like the process for writing the position paper based on "The Reader" explained in Chapters 1–8. Some of the procedures for the researched position paper, however, are more elaborate than those you have encountered before in this book because a research paper is more complicated than the other papers you have written. As you read Chapters 11, 12, and 13, you can expect to encounter some familiar information along with some new material and ideas. All of this information, including the assignments in the "Exercises and Activities" at the end of each chapter, is included for one purpose: to help you plan and write a successful and well-researched argument paper. Stay on top of these assignments, and you will be pleased with the final results.

The definition of argument presented in Chapter 1 will help you focus on your final objective in writing this paper: you will try to persuade your reading audience to agree, at least to some extent, with your claim and the ideas you use to support it.

Understanding the Assignment and Getting Started

You may want to turn to pages 425–426 now to read the assignment for preparing the final copy of the researched position paper so that you will know from the outset what this paper should finally look like. Then, to get you started on your paper, consider following some of the suggestions made in earlier chapters. They will ease you into this assignment, help you think, and make you feel knowledgeable and confident.

1. *Decide on an issue and write an issue proposal.* An issue may be assigned by the instructor, which can be inspired by "The Reader" or a set of readings provided by your instructor, or it can be left entirely up to you. There is often a stronger personal exigence for writing when you select the issue yourself. You may have made lists of issues as subjects for future papers when you finished reading Chapter 1. Look back at them now. If your concerns have shifted, think instead about the unresolved issues in your other classes or in current newspapers and television newscasts. Work to find an issue that captures your attention and interest. Submit it to the twelve tests of an arguable issue in Box 1.3 (page 30). These tests will help you ascertain whether or not your issue is potentially arguable. If it is, write an issue proposal to focus the issue and help you think about what more you need to learn. Follow the assignment and model on pages 30–32.

2. *Do some initial reading.* If you are not familiar enough with your issue, locate one or more sources about it and begin to do some background reading. Read enough material to form an idea of the various positions that people are likely to take on this issue. If you need advice about locating sources, read pages 380–385, which provide information you can use to find material in the library and on the Internet.

3. *Write an exploratory paper.* You can list and explain three or more perspectives on your issue or write an exploratory paper in which you explain multiple perspectives. The exploratory paper is described on pages 127–130. This process of exploring the different views on or approaches to the issue will help you find an original and interesting perspective of your own, as it also deepens your understanding of the perspectives others take on it. You must gain a good grasp of the various viewpoints to better refute them when you write your research paper.

Writing a Claim and Clarifying Your Purpose

Whether you write an issue proposal and an exploratory paper or not, you will want to write your claim for your position paper as early in the process as possible. Your claim is important because it provides purpose, control, and direction for everything else that you include in your paper. Mapping your issue or freewriting about it (Chapter 4) can help you narrow and focus an issue and write a claim. The five claim questions from Chapter 6 can also help you write a claim and establish the fundamental purpose of your paper. Write your issue as a question, and then freewrite in response to each of the claim questions to get a sense of the best purpose and claim for your paper. Here is an example of how the claim questions can be answered in response to an issue that came out of a specific rhetorical situation.

THE RHETORICAL SITUATION

A teenage white supremacist murdered a black middle-class family man. This crime was committed in Texas, where the same jury is impaneled to decide guilt or innocence and to impose the sentence. The jury in this case decided the white supremacist was guilty and, in ignorance, sentenced him both to probation and a jail term. The law does not permit two such contrary sentences, and so the murderer ended up with probation. As you can imagine, there was public concern, and issues regarding the sentence surfaced. Here are the claim questions used to focus purpose and a claim.

QUESTIONS TO PLAN CLAIM AND PURPOSE

The issue question is, *How should I think about this sentence for murder?*

1. *To establish a claim of fact,* ask: What happened? Does it exist? Is it a fact? Is it true?

   Example: Something seems very wrong. I could analyze what is wrong, especially since some people are satisfied and others are dissatisfied with the sentence. My claim could be a claim of fact, *The murderer escaped an appropriate sentence.* I could organize the paper chronologically, giving a history of what has happened and quoting both facts and expert opinion to prove my claim.

2. *To establish a claim of definition,* ask: What is it? What is it like? How should we interpret it? How does its usual meaning change in this context?

   Example: There may be a definition problem in the sentencing procedure. The jury was supposed to assign an appropriate sentence for a murder. The audience needs a definition of an appropriate sentence for a murder. My claim could be, *Probation is not an appropriate sentence for murder.* I would rely on expert opinion and the citation of similar cases to illustrate what an appropriate sentence for murder should be.

3. *To establish a claim of cause,* ask: What caused it? Where did it come from? Why did it happen? What are the effects? What will the short-term and long-term results be?

   Example: Personal conversations and media reports indicate considerable confusion over the cause of the sentence. Some people think the jury was racially prejudiced, others think the murderer was assigned probation because he is young, and others are baffled. I think the cause was the jury's lack of information, and my claim could be, *The jury did not know and did not receive information about how to sentence murderers, and as a result, it recommended an inappropriate sentence.* To prove this claim, I will examine the training provided to jurors in this court. I will interview people who have served on juries. I will learn what training was available for this particular jury. I will also read the charge—that is, the instructions about what must be decided—that the judge made to these jurors to learn whether it was clearly stated and correct in terms of the law.

4. *To establish a claim of value,* ask: Is it good or bad? How bad? How good? Of what worth is it? Is it moral or immoral? Who thinks so? What criteria should I use to decide goodness or badness? Are these the same criteria the audience would apply?

Example: There seems to be some disagreement about whether this sentence was good or bad, but I think it is a bad sentence. My claim could be, *It was wrong of the jury to assign the murderer both probation and a jail sentence, which permitted him to get off with probation.* To prove this, I will appeal to the standard needs and values I assume my audience holds, including a desire for physical safety, a sense of fairness and justness, and a respect for the jury system, which, I argue, has failed in this case.

5. *To establish a claim of policy,* ask: What should we do about it? What should be our future course of action? How can we solve the problem?

Example: Almost everyone thinks that the jury made a mistake. In fact, the criminal is back in jail on another charge awaiting a new trial. I could write a policy paper in which I recommend jury training so that this same problem will not recur. My claim would be, *Juries need pretrial training in order to make competent judgments.*

Try writing in response to the claim questions in this way yourself. Then read what you have written. Decide which of the potential claims seems most promising to develop in a paper. Determine your main purpose and write your claim. Now you can begin to think about ways to develop your claim.

Some Preliminary Questions to Help You Develop Your Claim

Ask the following questions to clarify and develop your claim. Some tentative answers to these questions now can help you stay on track and avoid problems with the development of your paper later.

Is the Claim Narrow and Focused?

You may have started with a broad issue area, such as technology or education, that suggests many specific related issues. If you participated in mapping sessions in class, you discovered a number of the specific related issues in your issue area.

This work likely helped you narrow your issue. However, you may now need to narrow your issue even further by focusing on one prong or aspect of it. Here is an example.

Issue area: The environment

Specific related issue:
What problems are associated with nuclear energy?

Aspects of that issue:
What should be done with nuclear waste?
How hazardous is nuclear energy, and how can we control the hazards?
What are the alternatives to nuclear energy?

In selecting a narrowed issue to write about, you may want to focus on only one of the three aspects of the nuclear energy problem. You might, for instance, decide to make this claim: *Solar power is better than nuclear energy.* Later, as you write, you may need to narrow this topic even further and revise your claim: *Solar power is better than nuclear energy for certain specified purposes.* Any topic can turn out to be too broad or complicated when you begin to write about it.

You could also change your focus or perspective to narrow your claim. You may, for example, begin to research the claim you have made in response to your issue but discover along the way that the real issue is something else. As a result, you decide to change your claim. For example, suppose you decide to write a policy paper about freedom of speech. Your claim is, *Freedom of speech should be protected in all situations.* As you read and research, however, you discover that an issue for many people is a narrower one related to freedom of speech, specifically as it relates to violence on television and children's behavior. In fact, you encounter an article that claims that television violence should be censored even if doing so violates free speech rights. You decide to refocus your paper and write a value paper that claims, *Television violence is harmful and not subject to the protection of free-speech rights.*

Which Controversial Words in Your Claim Will You Need to Define?

Identify the words in your claim that may need to be defined. In the example just used, you would need to be clear about what you mean by *television violence, censorship,* and *free-speech rights.*

Can You Learn Enough to Cover the Claim Fully?

If the information for an effective paper is unavailable or too complicated, write another claim, one that you know more about and can research more successfully. You could also decide to narrow the claim further to an aspect that you understand and can develop.

What Are the Various Perspectives on Your Issue?

Make certain that the issue you have selected invites two or more perspectives. If you have written an exploratory paper on this issue, you already know what several views are. If you have not written such a paper, explore your issue by writing several claims that represent a number of points of view, and then select the one you want to prove. For example:

Solar power is better than nuclear energy.
Solar power is worse than nuclear energy.
Solar power has some advantages and some disadvantages when compared with nuclear energy.
Solar power is better than nuclear energy for certain specified purposes.

As you identify the perspectives on the issue, you can also begin to plan some refutation that will not alienate your audience. An angry or insulted audience is not likely to change.

How Can You Make Your Claim both Interesting and Compelling to Yourself and Your Audience?

Develop a fresh perspective on your issue when writing your claim. Suppose you are writing a policy paper that claims public education should be changed. However, you get bored with it. You keep running into old reasons that everyone already knows. Then you discover new aspects of the issue that you could cover with more original ideas and material. You learn that some people think parents should be able to choose their children's school, and you learn that competition among schools might lead to improvement. You also learn that contractors can take over schools and manage them in order to improve them. You refocus your issue and your perspective. Your new fact claim is, *Competition among schools, like competition in business, leads to improvement.* The issue and your claim now have new interest for you and your audience because you are looking at them in a whole new way.

At What Point Are You and the Audience Entering the Conversation on the Issue?

Consider your audience's background and initial views on the issue to decide how to write a claim about it. If both you and your audience are new to the issue, you may decide to stick with claims of fact and definition. If your audience understands the issue to some extent but needs more analysis, you may decide on claims of cause or value. If both you and your audience have adequate background on the issue, you may want to write a policy claim and try to solve the problems associated with it. Keep in mind also that issues and audiences are dynamic. As soon as audiences engage with issues, both begin to change. So you need to be constantly aware of the current status of the issue and the audience's current stand on it.

What Secondary Purpose Do You Want to Address in Your Paper?

Even though you establish your predominant purpose as fact, for example, you may still want to answer the other claim questions, particularly if you think your audience needs that information. You may think it is important to speculate about cause and provide definitions for the key words. You might also choose to address value questions to engage your audience's motives and values. Finally, you may think it's important to suggest policy even though your paper has another predominant purpose.

Developing a Research Plan

A research plan will guide your future thinking and research and help you maintain the focus and direction you have already established. Even though you may not know very much about your issue or your claim at this point, writing out what you do know and what you want to learn can be valuable. Add some ideas to the plan for beginning research and getting started on a first draft. Box 11.1 ■ provides an example.

Box 11.1	A Research Plan Helps You Get Started.

▶▶▶ A Research Plan

Value Claim Plus Reasons.
Television violence is harmful and should not be subject to the protection of free speech rights because

> violence on television and violence in life seem to be related.
>
> children do not always differentiate between television and reality.
>
> parents do not supervise their children's television viewing.
>
> even though free speech is a constitutional right, it should not be invoked to protect what is harmful to society.

Research Needs.
I need to find out how free speech is usually defined. Does it include all freedom of expression, including forms of violence on television? Also, I will need to find the latest studies on television violence and violent behavior, particularly in children. Will I find that there is a cause–effect relationship? Even though I want to focus mainly on value and show that violent television is bad, I will also need to include definition and cause in this paper.

Plan for First Draft.
I will define television violence and free speech. I need to do some background reading on censorship and freedom of speech and summarize some of this information for my readers. My strongest material will probably be on the relationship between violence on television and violence in real life. I think now I'll begin with that and end with the idea that the Constitution should not be invoked to protect harmful elements like television violence. I'm going to write for an audience that either has children or values children. I will use examples from an article I clipped about how children imitate what they see on television.

You now have the beginning of an argument paper: a claim, some reasons, and some ideas to explore further. Your claim may change, and your reasons will probably change as you think, read, and do research. Before going further, however, you need to think more about the audience. The nature of your audience can have a major influence on how you will finally write the argument paper.

Understanding the Audience

Why is it important to understand your audience? Why not just argue for what you think is important? Some definitions and descriptions of effective argument emphasize the techniques of argument rather than the outcomes. They encourage the arguer to focus on what he or she thinks is important. For example, an argument with a clear claim, clear logic and reasoning, and good evidence will be described by some theorists as a good argument. The position in this book, however, has been different. If the argument does not reach the audience and create some common ground in order to convince or change their views in some way, the argument, no matter how skillfully crafted, is not productive. Productive argument, according to the definitions we used in Chapter 1, must create common ground and achieve some definable audience outcomes.

In order for the writer of argument to reach the audience, create common ground, and bring about change, two essential requirements need to be met. First, the audience must be willing to listen and perhaps also be willing to change. Second, the author must be willing to study, understand, and appeal to the audience. Such analysis will enable the author to relate to the audience's present opinions, values, and motives and to show as often as possible that the author shares them in ways that reveal or highlight the common ground essential for effective argument. Thus both audience and author need to cooperate to a certain degree for argument to achieve any outcomes at all.

Four strategies will help you begin the process of understanding and appealing to your audience: assess the audience's size and familiarity to you, determine how much you have in common with your audience, determine the audience's initial position and what changes in views or actions might occur as a result of your argument, and identify the audience's discourse community. You may want to go back and review the information on audience analysis in Chapter 3, pages 83–86. Here is a quick summary of what you were advised to do there.

Assess the Audience's Size and Familiarity

Audiences come in all sizes and may or may not include people you know. Audiences often include specific, known groups such as family members, classmates, work associates, or members of an organization to which you belong. You may also at times write for a large, unfamiliar audience composed of local, national, or international members. Of course, some audiences are mixed, with people you know and people you do not know. Your techniques will vary for building common ground with large and small, familiar and unfamiliar audiences, but the aim of your argumentation will not change.

Determine What You and the Audience Have in Common

You may or may not consider yourself a member of your audience, depending on how closely you identify with them and share their views. For example, if you are a member of a union, you probably identify and agree with its official positions, particularly on work-related issues. If you work with management, you likely hold other views about work-related issues. The methods you use to achieve common ground with each of these audiences will be somewhat different, depending on whether you consider yourself a member of the group or not.

Determine the Audience's Initial Position and How It Might Change

Remember that there are several possible initial audience positions and several ways in which they might change. For example, a friendly audience might read your argument, confirm their original belief, and strengthen their commitment; an audience that mildly agrees or mildly opposes your position may finally agree with you, become interested in the issue for the first time, or tentatively accept your views, at least for now; a neutral audience may become less neutral and may even decide to accept your position; and a hostile audience might be willing to consider some of your views, or agree to compromise, agree to disagree, or actually change and agree with you. It is possible that you have fellow students in your class who represent all of these potential initial positions.

Your task will be to create some changes in the starting or initial positions of your audience. You probably will be assigned to a small group of students who will read various drafts and versions of your paper. In your first meeting with this group, ask them for their initial positions on your issue. When you complete your project, you can then ask how their initial ideas have changed.

Analyze the Discourse Community in Your Class

As a member of a college class in argumentation, your discourse community will be quite well defined, and as a result, you will have already developed a significant amount of common ground with your audience because of your common background, assignments, and course goals. Your instructor is also a member of your discourse community, and by now you should have some good ideas about the quality of writing that is expected of you. Keep these individuals and what you have in common with them in mind when you write your paper.

Analyzing Your Class as Your Audience

At an early stage in the writing process, you need to answer certain key questions about your audience. To get this information, you can simply ask members of your audience some questions. Asking questions isn't always possible or advisable, however. More often, you will have to obtain your own answers by studying the audience and doing research.

The following list presents thirteen questions to ask about a familiar audience. You do not have to answer every question about every audience. You may need to add a question or two, depending on your audience. Answer questions that are suggested by the particular rhetorical situation for your argument. For example, the age range of the audience might be a factor to consider if you are writing about how to live a successful life; the diversity of the class might be important if you are writing about racial issues; or class member interests, particularly outdoor interests, might be useful to know if you are writing about the environment.

Exercise F in Chapter 3 (pages 96–97) directed you to ask some general information questions about your class as an audience. Therefore, if you completed this assignment, you already have answers to the first four questions on this list. Compare your answers with the examples below, and then ask the rest of the questions to learn what your audience thinks now about your issue.

As you read through the audience analysis questions, imagine that you are continuing to work on the argument paper on the topic of jury trials. Recall that your claim is, *Juries need pretrial training in order to make competent judgments.* The information that you uncover about your audience follows each question.

1. Describe the audience in general. Who are its members? What do you have in common with them?

   Example: My audience is my argument class. We have common educational goals, language, assignments, campus interests, and experiences.

2. What are some of the demographics of the group? Consider size, age, gender, nationality, education, and professional status.

   Example: Two-thirds of the twenty-four students are eighteen to twenty years old, and one-third are over thirty. Fifty-eight percent are female, and 42 percent are male. Slightly less than half are white; about a third are African American, Hispanic, and Asian; and the rest are international students. About three-fourths are first- and second-year students and the rest are upper-division students. More than half of the class work at part-time outside jobs. Two have full-time professions in insurance and sales.

3. What are some of their organizational affiliations? Consider political parties, religion, social and living groups, and economic status.

   Example: Roughly half say they are Democrats and half Republicans. Three say they are Libertarians. Fifty percent say they attend Christian churches, 20 percent are Jewish, and the rest either are Muslim or Hindu or say they are not religious. Four belong to fraternities or sororities, a few live in the dorms, and the rest live at home or in apartments. Most are in the middle or lower-middle class with aspirations to graduate, get better jobs, and move up.

4. What are their interests? Include outside interests, reading material, and perhaps majors.

   Example: The group lists the following interests and activities: sports, movies, television, exercise and fitness, camping and hiking, attending lectures, repairing and driving cars, listening to music, reading local newspapers, and reading newsmagazines. They are all college students. Five are in engineering, six are in business, one is in nursing, and the rest are in humanities and social sciences.

5. What is their present position on your issue? What audience outcomes can you anticipate?

   Example: My issue is jury trials, and my claim is, *Juries need pretrial training in order to make competent judgments.* Most members of the class have not thought about this issue and either are neutral or mildly agree. A show of hands reveals that five think juries need more training, fifteen don't know, and four indicate they favor the status quo. I can expect the neutral and status quo members to become interested and perhaps even agree. I can expect the others to agree more strongly than they do now.

6. Will they interpret the issue in the same way you have?

   Example: This issue comes from a local event, and some class members may see a double-jeopardy issue or some other issue emerging from it. I will have to focus their attention on my issue and make it important to them.

7. How significant is your issue to the audience? Will it touch their lives or remain theoretical for them?

   Example: This is a personally significant issue for the people planning to be lawyers. It has some personal significance for most of the others also because everyone who votes is a potential jury member. The international students will have interest in it, depending on their background and experience. I need to find out what their experiences have been.

8. Are there any obstacles that will prevent your audience from accepting your claim as soon as you state it?

   Example: Part of this audience believes that juries are always effective and need no improvement. I will have to challenge that idea.

9. How involved are audience members in the ongoing conversation about the issue? Will they require background and definitions? Are they knowledgeable enough to contemplate policy change?

   Example: Ninety percent know about the recent local case in which the jury made a poor judgment because of ignorance of procedures and a lack of information. Half of the class members have been called for jury duty, and two have served. Three intend to go to law school and have considerable background and interest in juries. This audience knows enough to think about policy changes.

10. What is the attitude of your audience toward you?

    Example: I think I have a friendly audience, and I am an insider, a part of the group. We have established an open atmosphere in this class, and there are no personal hostilities that I can foresee. We share the same discourse community.

11. What beliefs and values do you and your audience share?

    Example: In regard to my issue, we all value trial by jury, a job well done, and education.

12. What motivates your audience? What are the members' goals and aims?

    Example: The people in my audience would be motivated to do a good job were they on a jury.

13. What argument style will work best with your audience?

Example: I don't want to debate this issue. I would like to get consensus and a sense of cooperation instead. In fact, I picked this issue because it is one that people will probably not fight about. I want to use examples that will appeal to my audience's experiences. I am willing to negotiate or qualify my conclusion if the class members who critique my paper have trouble with it.

Go through these questions, and try to answer them for your potential audience at an early stage of the writing process. To help you answer questions 11 and 12 about values and motives, refer to Box 3.1 (page 81).

Constructing an Unfamiliar Audience

When the information about your audience elicited by these questions is not available, you will have to construct the audience you will be addressing by imagining what they might be like. As a student writing college papers, you can safely imagine an educated audience with a broad range of interests. Any time you construct an unknown audience, remember that it is best to assume that this group is either neutral or mildly opposed to what you will write. If you assume that your audience is either friendly or hostile, you may cause them to take unexpected and extreme positions.

The following excerpt from a speech report illustrates some of the problems that were created when the speaker assumed total agreement from the audience. Notice that the author, who describes himself as an audience member, is obviously different from the audience members imagined by the speaker. How is he different? What is the effect? What changes could this speaker make to create better common ground with all of her audience members? Consider what this speaker might have done differently if she had imagined a neutral or mildly opposed audience instead of a strongly friendly audience.

I am listening to a lecture by Helen Caldicott, the environmental activist. Dr. Caldicott is in top form, holding forth with her usual bracing mixture of caustic wit and prophetical urgency. All around me, an audience of the faithful is responding with camp-meeting fervor, cheering her on as she itemizes a familiar checklist of impending calamities: acid rain, global warming, endangered species.

She has even come up with a fresh wrinkle on one of the standard environmental horrors: nuclear energy. Did we know, she asks, that nuclear energy is producing scores of anencephalic births in the industrial shantytowns along the Mexican border? "Every time you turn on an electric light," she admonishes us, "you are making another brainless baby."

Dr. Caldicott's presentation is meant to instill unease. In my case, she is succeeding, though not in the way she intends. She is making me worry, as so many of my fellow environmentalists have begun to make me worry—not simply for the fate of the Earth, but for the fate of this movement on which so much depends. As much as I want to endorse what I hear, Dr. Caldicott's effort to shock and shame just isn't taking. I am as sympathetic a listener as she can expect to find, yet rather than collapsing into self-castigation, as I once might have, I find myself going numb.

Is it possible that green guilt, the mainstay of the movement, has lost its ethical sting?

Despite my reservations, I do my best to go along with what Dr. Caldicott has to say—even though I suspect (as I think most of her audience does) that there is no connection between light bulbs and brainless babies.[1]

Using Information about Your Audience

When you complete the analysis of your audience, examine all the information you have gathered and consciously decide which audience characteristics to appeal to in your paper. Look at the cartoon on this page. In this humorous example the speaker thinks he has assessed what concerns motivate his audience. For another kind of example, look back through the audience analysis of the argument class that was done for you. Suppose that you are the student who is planning to write the paper about jury training. You decide that the general questions about the makeup of the group suggest that you have a fairly typical college audience. Its members are varied enough in their background and experience so that you know they will not all share common opinions on all matters. They do have in common, however, their status as college students. Furthermore, all of you belong

376

The Results of a Careful Audience Analysis.

"I'll tell you what this election is about. It's about homework, and pitiful allowances, and having to clean your room. It's also about candy, and ice cream, and staying up late."

For Discussion: Describe the appeals this speaker makes to this audience. Why might they be effective?

[1]Theodore Roszak, "Green Guilt and Ecological Overload," *New York Times,* June 9, 1992, A27.

to the same group, so you can assume some common values and goals. All of them, you assume, want to be successful, to graduate, and to improve themselves and society; you can appeal to these common motives. All or most of them read local newspapers or watch local news programs, so they will have common background on the rhetorical situation for your issue. You have asked about their present views on jury training, and you know that many are neutral. Your strategy will be to break through this neutrality and provoke commitment for change.

You decide, furthermore, that you may have to focus the issue for them because they are not likely to see it your way without help. They should also, you decide, know enough to contemplate policy change. You can appeal to their potential common experience as jurors and their need for physical safety, fairness, and good judgment in dealing with criminals. You can further assume that your audience values competence, expertise, and reasonableness, all important outcomes of the training system you intend to advocate. Your argument style will work with the group members because you have already analyzed styles, and yours is familiar to them. They either share your style or are flexible enough to adapt to it.

With this audience in mind, you can now gather materials for your paper that audience members can link to their personal values, motives, beliefs, knowledge, and experience. Odd or extreme perspectives or support will usually not be acceptable to this audience. An example is the electric light causing brainless babies in "Green Guilt and Ecological Overload." This example does not have universal appeal. Your classmates are reasonable and well educated, and they should inspire a high level of argumentation. Careful research, intelligent reasoning, and clear writing style are requirements for your audience of fellow students.

Review Questions

1. What are the claim questions, and how can they be used to establish major and minor purposes in your position paper?

2. What are some additional preliminary questions that you can ask to help you develop your claim?

3. What is the purpose of the research plan? What three main types of information are included on it?

4. What would you need to consider about an audience to discover how much common ground you share?

5. What are a few items described in this chapter that you consider particularly important in conducting an audience analysis?

Exercises and Activities

A. The Researched Position Paper: Creating Peer Writing Groups

List and briefly discuss the issues that class members have selected for research. Place related issues in categories. Use these categories to form groups of four or five students each for future group work.

B. **The Researched Position Paper: Writing a Claim and Clarifying Your Purpose**

Complete Worksheet 4 by writing answers to the questions. The questions will help you focus on your claim and on ways to develop it. Discuss your answers with the members in your peer writing group, or discuss some of your answers with the whole class.

Worksheet 4   Claim Development

1. Write an issue question to focus your issue.
2. Freewrite in response to the claim questions. They are as follows:

   Fact: Did it happen? Does it exist?

   Definition: What is it? How can I define it?

   Cause: What caused it? What are the effects?

   Value: Is it good or bad? What criteria will help us decide?

   Policy: What should we do about it? What should be our future course of action?

3. Read what you have written and decide on a purpose. Write your claim as a complete sentence.
4. Which will be your predominant argumentation purpose in developing the claim: fact, definition, cause, value, or policy?
5. What is your original slant on the issue, and is it evident in the claim?
6. Is the claim too broad, too narrow, or manageable for now? Elaborate.
7. How will you define the controversial words in your claim?
8. Do you predict at this point that you may have to qualify your claim to make it acceptable to the audience? How?

C. **The Researched Position Paper: Starting to Think and Write about Your Issue**

   a. *Freewrite what you know about your issue.* Write rapidly, do not bother about exact phrasing or punctuation, and include details, descriptions, and examples. Explain the position you think you will take.
   b. *Apply the critical thinking prompts (page 104) to your issue and write out the results.* Keep these to use later in your argument papers.
   c. Develop a research plan using Worksheet 5 on page 379.

D. **The Researched Position Paper: Analyzing Your Peer Writing Group as an Audience**

   Do an analysis of the small group of four or five individuals in your class who will serve as readers and critics of your paper from now until you hand it in. Your aim is to get an idea of how your audience regards your issue before you write, and also to help your audience become interested in your paper. Do this as a group project, with each group member in turn interviewing the others and jotting down answers to the questions in Worksheet 6 on page 379.

Worksheet 5 | Research Plan

▶▶▶ Claim Plus Reasons

Write your claim, write the word *because* after the claim, and then list three to five possible reasons or subclaims that you might develop in your paper.

▶▶▶ Research Needs

Anticipate your research needs: What parts of your paper can you develop with your present knowledge and information? What parts will you need to think about and research further? Can you learn enough to develop the claim, or should you simplify it? What types of research materials will you seek, and where will you seek them?

Make a list of key words related to your issue to help you search.

How much preliminary background reading do you need to do, and where should you do it?

▶▶▶ Plan for Your First Draft

How much background information will you need to provide your readers?

What terms will you need to define?

What are your strongest opinions? Your best reasons?

What is a reasoned way to begin your paper? What is a reasoned way to end it?

What original examples, descriptions, or comparisons occur to you now?

Worksheet 6 | Audience Analysis

1. Describe your issue. What is your audience's present position on this issue? Describe some other perspectives on your issue, and ask for reactions to those ideas. State your claim and ask if there is anyone who cannot accept it as stated. If there is, ask why.

2. How significant is your issue to the audience? If it is not considered significant, describe why it is significant to you. Talk about ways you can make it more significant to the audience.

3. How involved are audience members in the ongoing conversation about the issue? What do they already know about it?

4. How will you build common ground? What beliefs and values do you and your audience share about your issue? What motivates audience members in regard to your issue?

5. What argument style will work best with them? A direct adversarial style? Or a consensual style? Why?

6. Write what you have learned from this analysis to help you plan your appeal to this audience. Include values and motives in your discussion. (See Box 3.1 on page 81.)

12

The Research Paper: Research and Invention

T he reading and writing process requires both creative thinking and critical thinking. For example, research and invention call for creative thinking but also for critical thinking about your sources; and rewriting and revision call for critical thinking but also for creative thinking in language use and in reshaping or qualifying your claim. This chapter is mainly about creativity. The first part of the chapter is about research. It describes how to find both print and online materials to help you develop the ideas in your research paper. It also teaches how to assemble a bibliography and take reading notes. As you research your topic, remember to think about what you already know and what you have come to believe as you seek the opinions of others. It is your voice, as a result, that will be the major voice in your paper, and your ideas will predominate over those of others. Information and ideas from other sources are brought into your writing chiefly as back up for your main ideas and arguments.

The last part of the chapter is about invention. In classical times, *invention,* or gathering material and creating ideas, was one of the five canons of rhetoric. These canons identified the important aspects of building an argument that every orator of the time needed to know. Besides invention, the canons included: *arrangement,* or organizing the material in an argument; *style,* or using appropriate language to explain it; *memory,* or committing the ideas in a speech to memory; and *delivery,* or making good use of voice and gestures. Three of these canons, invention, arrangement, and style, are important to writers as well as to speakers of argument. You have already learned to use a number of invention strategies for argument in previous chapters (e.g., the critical thinking prompts, the rhetorical situation questions, the Toulmin questions, and the claim and proof questions). You have learned about style in Chapter 7, and you will learn about arrangement in the next chapter.

In this chapter you will expand your resources for creative thinking by adding two additional invention strategies: Burke's pentad and chaining reasons to develop lines of argument. Both of these strategies help you think through your research materials so that you can integrate them with your own ideas. They may also, at times, show that you need to do additional research in some areas. These strategies, along with the other methods for invention taught in this book, are summarized in Worksheet 9, on pages 406–407. When you finish the research and invention activities described in this chapter, you will have gathered ample material to organize and write your research paper, which is the subject of the next chapter.

Get Organized for Research

You can prepare for your research by implementing some of the initial ideas about reading, thinking, and writing described in Chapter 4 to help you get off to a strong start (pages 102–105). As recomended there, begin by writing what you already know and think about your issue and by reading broadly to both expand your background information and refine your research. You may also want to use the critical thinking prompts to help you generate ideas (Box 4.1, page 104). Most of your effort, however, will be guided by the research plan you completed in Exercise C in Chapter 11 (page 379) using Worksheet 5. The plan helps you do directed reading to fill in your initial brief outline (the claim plus reasons section of the worksheet) and to answer the questions about your research needs and your first draft. The following suggestions will aid you in reading efficiently to meet these prerequisites for your paper.

▶ **Link your research to your research plan.** As you read, expand on the brief outline you wrote using the research plan worksheet. You do not need to make the plan elaborate, but you will need some kind of list or outline to help you decide on tentative content and a possible order for your ideas. Chapter 13 provides some standard patterns of organization to consider in developing this outline.

Each piece of research material that you gather and each creative idea should be related to an item on your list or outline. Change the outline when necessary. Once you begin research, you may find you need to narrow your topic and write on only one aspect of it, add additional reasons as support, or even change the pattern of organization. Stay flexible and adjust your outline or list as you go along so that it continues to focus and guide your research.

▶ **Think about your audience.** Write out what your audience needs as background. Also, consider what reasons and evidence they might find particularly convincing.

▶ **Think of some search keywords.** Make a list of keywords associated with your issue that will help you locate sources on library and online search engines. For example, if you are writing about college entrance tests, you could enter terms such as *testing, standardized testing, college entrance tests, standardized college entrance tests,* or *tests and college admission.* To focus your search more specifically, enter a less broad term such as *new SAT.* Keyword searches will help you find both relevant and irrelevant information. Refine and narrow sources by trying different combinations of keywords and, as you proceed, by using terms that are less broad.

❱ **List the types of research materials you will seek.** Jot down where you can find them as well. Books and articles will be high on your list, but you may also want to use other sources, such as personal interviews, speeches, television programs, radio programs, advertisements, song lyrics, graphs, photographs, drawings or paintings, maps, letters, or any other types of material that would help you write an argument that is convincing to your audience.

❱ **Gather research supplies.** You will need pens, sheets of paper, and, possibly, 3 by 5 inch note cards, if you decide to use them, plus a large envelope or folder to keep everything together. Also, bring money for the copy machine. If you print online materials or photocopy print materials, you will be able to mark what you want to use in your paper right on your personal copies themselves and thus save the time it takes to transfer the same information onto handwritten cards or into your computer notebook. Acquire a highlighter or color pencil to mark this information.

Locating Sources for Research

Begin your research by becoming acquainted with the general layout of your library. Locate the library's online catalog, which indexes all its holdings; find out where the books, magazines, and journals are located; and then find the microforms, the government documents, the reference books, and the media section that houses video and audio materials. In addition, learn where the copy center or copy machines are located. Then find the reference desk and the reference librarians who will help you whenever you are stuck or need advice.

Learn to Use the Library's Online Catalog

Most libraries now store information about all of their holdings, including all books and periodicals (magazines, journals, and newspapers), in an online index. Note that the periodicals are indexed in the online catalog and not the articles themselves. You will learn how to use library online databases to find articles in a following section.

Any computer with access to the Internet will allow you to search your library's online catalog. Search for a book by entering the author's name, the title, or the subject, and look for a particular magazine or journal by entering the title or the subject. Online catalogs also permit you to search by keyword. The keyword search is a powerful and effective research tool that can help you find mainly books but also other materials relevant to your topic, such as reference books, government documents, and various magazines and newspapers that have been reduced in size and preserved on microfilm.

Start with a keyword that represents your topic, such as *clear-cutting*, and the computer will display all titles of the books and other holdings in the library that contain that word. Read the titles as they appear on the screen and identify those that might be useful. When you have found a title that looks promising, move to the screen that gives complete information about that book. There you will find all of the other subject headings under which that book is listed in the index. Use those subject headings, or keywords extracted from them, to expand your search. For instance, you might move from your first keyword, *clear-cutting,* to a new keyword, *erosion,* in order to access more varied material. Online catalogs are user-friendly and will tell you on the screen how to use them. Follow the directions exactly, and ask for help if you get frustrated.

Learn to Find a Library Book

To locate the actual books or other research materials you think you want to use, copy the *call number* listed with the title in the online catalog. Copy it exactly; find out where the source is located by consulting a directory, which is usually in plain sight in the lobby of the library, and go to the shelf where the source belongs. If you cannot find it, look at the other books and resources in the area. They will often be on the same or a similar subject, and one of them may serve you just as well as the one you cannot find. Some libraries allow you to click on the call number of a book in the online catalog to find a list of the volumes that are shelved in close proximity. Books often contain bibliographies, or lists of related books and articles, which can lead you to additional sources.

Use Library Subscription Services to Find Articles

Most libraries now subscribe to huge licensed online databases that allow you, with a single command, to search through articles from a large number of different print periodicals for information on your topic. All of these databases provide full publishing information about the articles they index, including the author, title, and date and place of publication. Some databases also provide either abstracts or full-text versions of the articles themselves. Since the library pays for these databases, you will need to obtain a password to use them. A librarian can help you with that. When you have your password, you will be able to search for articles related to your research project with any computer linked to the Internet. Many students now conduct at least some of their research on their home computers, printing copies of the material at home. Also, most of these databases allow the user to forward either article information or an entire article to one's e-mail account to be read later.

Verify which database services your library subscribes to before you begin. Here are a few of the most common ones: *Academic Search Complete* describes itself as the "world's largest scholarly, multi-discipline, full text database," with peer-reviewed articles from more than four thousand periodical titles; *CQResearcher* provides full-text articles on topics of current interest that include a wide range of issues; *LexisNexis Academic* indexes six thousand international titles, including national and international newspapers, provides full text, and is updated hourly; and EBSCO*host* allows you to search multiple databases at the same time. Some databases specialize in particular areas of research and list journals, magazines, newspapers, books, and other media related to that area. Check each database you use to see how far back in time it goes. Some cover only the last twenty to twenty-five years, while others go back one hundred years or more.

Use databases by typing in subjects or keywords and executing a search. A list of associated articles in periodicals and scholarly journals will be displayed on the screen, with the most current appearing first. Read the title and, if there is one, the brief annotation of what the article is about to help you decide which articles to locate and read.

Learn to Use *Research Navigator*

If your library lacks databases such as those described, or if they are difficult for you to access, help is available. Pearson Education, which publishes this textbook, maintains a Web site, called *Research Navigator*, that, with the purchase of this or any other Pearson book, gives you access to four huge databases that will enable you to locate credible and reliable sources on your issue. These are free and available twenty-four hours a day. The first of these, EBSCO's *ContentSelect*, is an academic journal and abstract database. It is organized by subject and indexes thousands of articles that are organized by discipline and drawn from many periodicals, including leading academic journals for each discipline it covers. The second, *The New York Times on the Web*, is a search-by-subject archive that provides one year of full-text articles by the world's leading journalists who write for this respected newspaper. The third, *Link Library*'s "*Best of the Web*," is organized by subject and provides access to Web sites that have been selected by editors as the "best of the Web." These are updated on a regular basis to provide relevant links to help you find material for your research paper. Finally, *FT.com* is a one-year archive from the *Financial Times*, a daily business newspaper that provides news stories about companies, industries, and economies as well as financial information for the five hundred largest U.S. companies. Also available on the *Research Navigator* Web site are tips to help you conduct online research successfully and write a research paper. Go to www.researchnavigator.com to visit the site, or, if you have trouble, ask your instructor to help you access this resource.

See Figure 12.1, a reproduction of the *Research Navigator* Web page, which provides more information about the databases and other research services to be found there.

Learn to Find a Printed Journal or Magazine Article

If the database does not provide you with the full text of an article, you will have to find it in the printed periodical in which it first appeared. Look up the name of the periodical, including the volume number, issue number or month, and year, in the online catalog and copy the call number. Then look for it in the same way you would a book. You can learn additional information about the magazine or journal itself, including who publishes it and why, the types of material it publishes, and its overall quality by visiting its Web site and reading about it. Scholarly journals, for example, are often described as "refereed," which means the

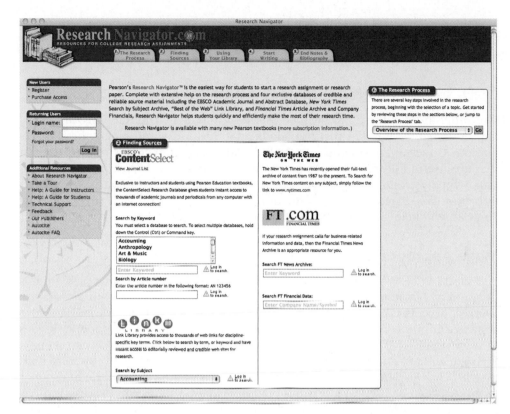

Figure 12.1
The Web Page for Research Navigator. It provides help with all phases of the research process.

articles in them are read by several expert reviewers before they are accepted for publication and appear in print. As a general rule, such articles are very reliable sources.

Be forewarned—some issues of a periodical may be in bound volumes in the book stacks, some may be on microfilm, and the newest issues may be stacked on shelves in the current periodicals section of the library. You may have to search to find what you want. Ask a librarian to help you. If you discover that your library does not own the journal in which your article appears, it is usually possible for you to order it through an Interlibrary Loan system and have a copy from another library mailed directly to you.

Learn to Find Newspaper Articles

The databases we have just described will lead you to newspaper articles as well as journal and magazine articles, and many of them are full text. When they are not, you may be able to find the newspaper in which the article appeared in the microfilm section of the library. Newspapers such as the *New York Times,* the *Wall Street Journal,* the *Christian Science Monitor,* and the *London Times,* along with newsmagazines like *Time* and *Newsweek,* are kept in this special section of the library. Some books and many other journals are kept in this form also. When you encounter the abbreviations *mic, mf, cm,* or *mfc* as part of the catalog information for a book or magazine, you will need to find these sources in the microfilm section of the library.

Machines are available there that enlarge the tiny images so that you can read them. Other machines enable you to print copies of microfilm material. Indexes to newspapers and some magazines are available in the microfilm section as well.

Learn to Find Reference Materials and Government Documents

Two other areas of the library can be useful for research. The reference area contains a variety of volumes that provide factual, historical, and biographical information. Government documents contain data and other forms of information that are useful for argument. Indexes, such as the *Public Affairs Information Bulletin,* which your library may have online, show you the types of factual information you can expect to find in documents printed by the government. Your librarian will help you locate the actual documents themselves.

Make Appropriate Use of the World Wide Web

The World Wide Web, unlike library databases that you access with a password, is free and available to everyone. Not all of the materials on the Web are quality sources, however. Unlike the sources indexed in library databases that have also appeared in print, not all of the material you find on the World Wide Web goes through a publisher or editor. In fact, anyone familiar with computers can set up a Web site and put articles or other documents on it. To maintain your own credibility with your audience, a good rule of thumb is that no source from the Internet or in print should be used unless it has gone through a submission process and has been selected for publication by an editor of a reputable publication. While finding sources from well-known magazines and journals or professional organizations is generally safe, selecting sources from second-rate publications or from individuals lacking credentials reflects negatively on your credibility. Consequently, it is wise to use online articles and information sparingly, unless directed otherwise by your instructor. Your paper will benefit from your use of a variety of sources.

Use Web Browsers and Search Engines

Use a browser such as Safari, Firefox, Netscape Navigator, or Microsoft Internet Explorer to gain access to the World Wide Web. You can then surf the Internet to find information for your paper by using search engines like *Google* at www.google.com, *Yahoo!* at www.yahoo.com, or *Firefox* at www.firefox.com. These search engines take the search terms (keywords) that you enter, comb the Net, and give you a search report, which is a list of titles and descriptions along with hypertext links that take you directly to the documents. The results that the engine measures most relevant (often based on frequency of visits) will be at the top of the list.

Vary Keyword Searches

Some engines allow you to use operators like *and, or,* and *not* to combine your search terms in a more focused way so that the results can be more relevant. By using specific keywords and their grammatical variations and synonyms along with these operators, you can find more particular information. Some of the search engines take you directly to your subject, and others first present a directory of categories that are generated by the authors of the Web sites. They include subject guides (lists of categories like *science* and *education*) that can lead you to good general information about your issue as well as sites that serve as good starting points by offering lots of links.

Use *Wikipedia*, Blogs, E-mail, and Chat Rooms Carefully

Wikipedia, the free, online encyclopedia that is open to anyone who has information to contribute, can be a good source of background information when you begin to think about your topic. Some of the entries, for example, are accompanied by useful bibliographies that can lead you to additional sources. Be cautious, however, about quoting *Wikipedia* in your paper. Some schools have policies that discourage the use of *Wikipedia* as a source for a scholarly paper because the entries have not been refereed by panels of experts and because anyone can write or edit material on this site at any time. Ask about the policy at your school. If you do use *Wikipedia* as a source, use it in a limited way just as you would any encyclopedia, to provide a few basic facts or definitions. Do cite it as a source for any information you use from it that is not general knowledge. It should not be the only source you cite for that information, however.

Blogs (the shortened name for Web logs) are virtual journals that may be written by anyone who wants to do this type of writing on the Internet. Blogs are personal, opinionated, and idiosyncratic. Explain exactly why you are quoting a blog. For example, you might quote a sampling of opinions on an issue from a few blogs. If you do, make your sources of information clear, explain how they contribute to your paper, and say why you have used them. Follow this same general advice for material you quote from e-mail, chat rooms, or personal networking sites like MySpace.

The Internet also offers a forum for you to discuss your issue with other interested people: you can send e-mail to addresses made available on Web sites, and you can take part in "live" chats in discussion rooms. Remember that e-mail and chatting are potential sources for your paper, so always generate a print copy of any exchanges you think are particularly interesting or pertinent. Your instructor may in fact want you to submit print copies of all electronic material you quote or paraphrase in your final paper, so it is best to keep print copies of everything you use from the Internet.

387

Evaluate both Print and Online Sources

As you locate the sources you think you will use for your paper, take a few minutes to evaluate each of them, and discard those that don't meet your standards. Good, reliable sources add to your credibility as an author, making your argument more convincing. In the same way, bad sources reflect poorly on your judgment and detract from your credibility. It is essential that you evaluate every source you use in your paper, whether it is a print or an online source. Print sources that are also to be found online, such as those you access through the library's databases, should be evaluated as published print sources.

Analyze the Author's Purpose

Look back at the continuum of the different purposes for writing argument, ranging from obvious argument at one extreme to objective reporting at the other and including extremist, hidden, unconscious, and exploratory argument (see Chapter 4, pages 105–106). Getting an idea of how the author's argumentation purpose is presented in each of your sources will help you both understand the argument better and analyze the rhetorical situation.

Analyze Web Address Extensions to Determine the Purpose of Web Sites

Web sites have a variety of purposes. A site may be created to sell a product, persuade the reader to vote for a political candidate, provide entertainment, or offer educational information. Understanding how to read a Web site address can provide valuable clues to help you determine the purpose of a site. The following examples demonstrate common Web site extensions that provide information about the general category of a Web site and an indication of its basic purpose:

▶ The *.gov* extension means the Web site was created by a government agency. An example is *irs.gov*.

▶ The *.edu* extension means an educational institution produced the Web site. An example is *stanford.edu*.

▶ The *.mil* extension means the site is produced by the military. An example is *army.mil*.

▶ The *.com* extension means the Web site has a commercial purpose. An example is *honda.com*. The most common Web extension on the Internet is *.com*.

▶ The *.org* extension means the Web site was produced by a nonprofit organization. An example is *npr.org*.

▶ The *.net* extension stands for network. An example is *asp.net*.

▶ The *.int* extension stands for international. An example is *who.int*, the address of the World Health Organization.

▶ The *.us* extension stands for the United States, and *.uk* for the United Kingdom. Every country (and in the United States every state) has its own extension. An example is *lib.ks.us*, the Kansas State Library.

It is difficult to generalize about the reliability of the different types of sites. Consider, however, that *.gov*, *.edu*, *.lib*, and *.mil* sites are created by established institutions with stated public purposes, and *.com*, *.net*, and *.org* can be set up by any person or group with a particular self-interest. Knowing you are on a commercial or special interest site can be useful when you are trying to access reliable information for a research paper.

Analyze the Rhetorical Situation of Your Sources

This will help you gain even more insight into them. Remember TRACE. Consider the *text:* analyze its point of view on the issue, compare it with other sources on the same subject, analyze the values implicit in it, look at the types of support it contains, and examine its conclusions. Ask, Who is the intended *reader?* Notice where (in what city or nation or which institution) the publication is from and when (the date of publication). Is the source intended for a particular category of readers or a universal audience? Would you classify yourself as one of the intended readers?

Learn more about the *author.* Read the preface of a book or the beginning or end of an article for author information (if there is any). Use the Internet for additional information by accessing *Google* and entering the author's name. Many authors have individual Web sites where you can learn more about their interests and other publications. You can also type in an author's name at www.amazon.com and see what other books he or she has written or edited. By clicking on various links on the Amazon page, parts of the author's book, such as the Contents page, or a list of other authors who cite this author or this text are sometimes available as well.

Imagine each source in a context, and think about the *constraints* that may have influenced the author to write about an issue in a certain way. Also think about the constraints that might influence you as you read it. Try to understand the author's motivation or *exigence* for writing on the issue.

Evaluate the Credibility of Your Sources

To help you determine the credibility of all sources, but particularly online sources, ask the following questions.

1. ***Is the source associated with an organization that is recognized in the field?*** For example, an American Civil Liberties Union Web site on capital punishment is credible because the ACLU is a nationally known organization that deals with issues of civil rights.

2. ***Is the source listed under a reputable domain?*** Look at what comes after "www" in the URL. For example, information found at www.stanford.edu has some credibility because it is associated with a university. Universities are considered reliable sources of information. Of course, any Stanford student, faculty member, or staff member with authorized access to the domain can publish material online. The material would not automatically be credible, so you still must review it carefully.

3. ***Is the source published in a print or online journal that is peer-reviewed?*** Check the journal's Web site or look at a print copy. The journal will usually advertise this on its front page. For example, *Modern Language Notes,* published by Johns Hopkins University Press, is credible because everything

389

written in it has been reviewed by a panel of experts to ensure that the work meets a high standard of scholarship. Articles in such sources also meet the standards for academic writing, which makes them valuable potential sources for your research.

4. ***Is the online source duplicated in print?*** For example, material appearing on www.nytimes.com is credible because the *New York Times,* a nationally respected edited newspaper, sponsors it.

5. ***Is the source accessed by a large number of people?*** For example, a daily up-dated news site, www.cnn.com, is read and talked about across the country.

6. ***Is the source directed mainly to extremists?*** You will recognize such sources by their emotional language, extreme examples, and implicit value systems associated with extremist rather than mainstream groups. Learn what you can about such groups and try to determine whether or not they have a wide appeal. Your goal should be to find information with sufficiently wide appeal so that it might be acceptable to a universal audience.

7. ***Is the evidence in the source stacked to represent one point of view?*** Again, an unusual amount of emotional language, carefully selected or stacked evidence, and quotations from biased sources and authorities characterize this material. You can attack the obvious bias in this material, if you want to refute it.

8. ***Is the source current?*** Check to see when a Web site was published and last updated. Many topics are time sensitive. A Web site that discusses foreign policy in the Middle East, but is dated before 2001 (especially before 9/11), might have limited value unless you are examining the history of American foreign policy in this area. If you are looking for the latest ideas about global warming or immigration, check the date of the Web site, which is sometimes at the bottom of the document or on the home page.

9. ***Is the source sloppily edited, undocumented, or unreasonable?*** Material that is poorly edited, infrequently updated, or old may be untrustworthy. Other red flags are inflammatory language and no identified author. Sweeping generalizations made without evidence, undocumented statistics, or unreasonable arguments indicate questionable sources for research.

10. ***Is the source moral or immoral or ethical or unethical, according to your values?*** This is the bottom-line question that will help you differentiate credible from noncredible sources for research.

Create a Bibliography

The bibliography is the alphabetically arranged (by author's last name) list of evaluated sources you have decided are credible, related to your issue, and potentially valuable to your research. You will begin by reading them. You may not use all of them, and some of them may lead you to other sources that you will add later. You will either enter these items directly into a computer or write them on note cards to be typed later.

USING A COMPUTER

Copy and paste bibliographical information for each of your sources into a computer file. Use the journalist's questions to help you get the basic information you will need: *who* is the author, *what* is the title, *where* was the source published, *when* was it published, *which* medium of publication is it,[1] and *why* would I use it? For each source, add a note to suggest why you might use it in your paper. You will need this information later when you assemble the bibliography or list of works cited in your paper, so write or type all of it out accurately. You will not want to have to find a source again later. Here are some examples in MLA style.

In examples 1 and 3, a search by author and title on a search engine such as *Google* or a database such as *JSTOR* locates the source, and no URL is necessary.[2]

▶ ***Bibliographical information for a book*** must include the author, the title italicized (underlined in handwritten notes),[3] the place of publication, publisher, date of publication, and medium of publication. To help you, add the call number so that you can find it later in the library.

Example:
Stock, Gregory. *Redesigning Humans: Our Inevitable Genetic Future*. Boston: Houghton, 2002. Print.
[Call number in stacks, QH438.7 S764]

▶ ***Bibliographical information for a printed article*** must include the author's name (if there is one), title of the article (in quotation marks), name of the publication (italicized), volume. Issue numbers (for scholarly journals), date of publication, page numbers, and medium of publication. Add the call number or a location.

Example:
Sandel, Michael J. "The Case Against Perfection: What's Wrong with Designer Children, Bionic Athletes, and Genetic Engineering." *Atlantic Monthly*, Apr. 2004: 51–62. Print.
[photocopied article; in research file folder]

▶ ***Bibliographical information for online material accessed on the Web or a database*** must include as many of the following elements as are available or needed for the type of source: author's (editor's, etc.) name; title of article (in quotation marks); title of the journal or book (italicized); volume. Issue numbers (for a scholarly journal) and date of publication (or last update); page or paragraph numbers (if numbered, N. pag. when unpaged) for articles; name of the Web site or database (italicized); sponsor, owner, or publisher of the site (or N.p. if not available), date of sponsorship, publication, or update (use n.d. when

---

[1]The medium of publication is required for all bibliography entries in MLA style. The medium is listed after the other publication information. Examples include Print, Web, E-mail, DVD, Radio, Performance, and so on. For a list of mediums, see the Appendix to Chapter 13 (page 437).
[2]This is a new MLA documentation standard, published in 2008. See the third example in this list as well. For more complete information, see the Appendix to Chapter 13, pages 437–456.
[3]Italicize the titles of books and journals in your bibliography when following both MLA style and APA style. Underlining in written notes is understood to mean "place in italics." See additional MLA and APA information and examples in the Appendix to Chapter 13, pages 429–479.

unavailable); medium; access or use date; and the address (URL, within angle brackets for MLA) of the service or site when an author-title search does not locate the source. A URL follows the access date.

Example:

Hayden, Thomas. "The Irrelevant Man." *US News & World Report* 3 May 2004. *Academic Search Complete.* Web. 15 May 2008.

USING NOTE CARDS

Another way to record bibliographical information should you not be recording directly into a computer file is on 3 by 5 inch index cards. Write out a bibliography card for each separate source you are likely to utilize and include the same items of information you have just been advised to include in a computer file. Figures 12.2, 12.3, and 12.4 provide examples of bibliography cards for an online article, for a book, and for an article from a magazine in MLA style. Notice that each card provides publication information, a summary of the contents, and a brief evaluation. Use underlining to represent italics. Additional information on how to format bibliographical sources appears in the Appendix to Chapter 13 (pages 429–479).

Figure 12.2
Bibliography Card for an Online Article.

> McVay, Douglas A.,ed. "Drug War Facts." 6th ed.
> Common Sense for Drug Policy. Jan. 2008. Web. 21 Apr. 2008.
> <http://www.drugwarfacts.org/index2.htm>.
>
> Use for statistics to support more treatment and less imprisonment. Click on entries under "Prisons" and "Treatment" in list of Chapters.
>
> 1. "Treatment is 10 times more cost effective than interdiction in reducing the use of cocaine in the United States."
>
> 2. "Over 80% of the increase in the federal prison population from 1985–1995 was due to drug convictions."

Figure 12.3
Bibliography Card for a Book.

> Gray, Mike. Drug Crazy: How We Got into This Mess and How We Can Get Out. New York: Random, 1998. Print.
>
> Cite text to show historical failures and drawbacks of the current laws and systems in place to fight the drug war. Author has produced award-winning documentaries and written three books, all of which deal with investigative reporting.
>
> Fairly objective. The author consulted various agencies, including the DEA, U.S. Border Patrol, and U.S. Customs.
>
> Wide audience appeal.
>
> Call number:
> HV
> 5825
> .G6955

Massing, Michael. "It's Time for Realism." <u>Nation</u>
   20 Sept. 1999: 11+. Print.

Use for arguments against harsh drug laws and for better
rehabilitation programs. Also use for statistics on drug crimes.
Author has researched historical and current drug war information
for his article. He's written a text on which this article is based.

Very objective source—written by a journalist and journalism professor.
Wide appeal.

Figure 12.4
Bibliography Card for an Article in a Magazine.

ADD ANNOTATIONS TO YOUR BIBLIOGRAPHY

Your instructor may ask you to create an annotated bibliography to help you organize the research for your paper. Even when not required, it is important to the quality of your research that you hone your critical and evaluative skills with this practice. The annotation is a critical or explanatory note. An annotated bibliography is an alphabetical listing of all of the sources you might use in your paper, with notes or annotations that explain, describe, or critically evaluate the material. That is, your written assessment accompanies each listing. These can include a summary of the argument and authority of the source; a description of the contents and a brief, critical evaluation; and an interpretation of how you could use the material in your paper. An example of an annotated bibliography appears on pages 402–404.

Survey, Skim, and Read Selectively

When you have located your research material, do not try to read all of it. You will never finish. It is important, however, to understand the context of the material you quote and to learn something about the author. Survey and skim rather than read books and articles (see Chapter 4, pages 109–111).

Surveying and skimming may not always yield the understanding that you require, particularly if the material is difficult or dense or if you do not know exactly what information you are looking for. In these situations, switch from surveying or skimming to critical and creative reading to help you think about and get additional ideas for your paper.

Critical and creative reading are different from some of the other types of reading that you do. For example, *leisure reading* is done for relaxation and pleasure. *Study reading* requires you to understand, learn, and remember material so that you can pass a test. *Critical reading,* which you learned to do in Parts One and Two of this book, requires that you identify and analyze the parts of an argument within an overall context. *Creative reading* enables you to form original ideas and think critically. Here are some questions that you can keep in mind to guide creative reading.

▶ What strikes me in this text? What interests me? Why?

▶ What new ideas and answers are occurring to me as I read?

▶ How does this new material fit with what I already know?

▶ Do these new ideas challenge any of my existing ideas? How? Can I reconcile the differences?

▶ What are the implications of these new ideas?

▶ How can I use these new ideas in my paper?

Using the Toulmin model to read will also help you find information quickly. The focus is on the important parts of a written argument: the claim, the support, the warrants, and the backing. The model also calls your attention to the different ways that other authors handle rebuttal. You may want to follow someone's example when you write your own.

Develop a System for Taking and Organizing Your Notes

You may want to open a file in your computer where you will enter your own ideas and as well as the various types of reading notes you want to record, including material you *quote* word for word, the material you *paraphrase* or rephrase in your own words, and the material you *summarize*. On the other hand, you may prefer to keep such materials in a research notebook, in a paper folder, or on note cards. A combination of these possibilities may work best for you. **The cardinal principle in whatever note taking system you use is to clearly indicate on every note which ideas and language belong to other authors and which of them are your own.** Add the author's name and the page number to all quoted, paraphrased, or summarized material; place direct quotations in quotation marks; and set off your own ideas and comments in square brackets [ ], place them in a different font or color in your computer files, or label them "mine."

USING A COMPUTER

Use your research plan both to guide your research and to help you organize your notes and ideas. Arrange your notes as you go along and enter them under appropriate headings in a computer file like those on your research plan worksheet (see page 379), or on the list or outline that you have prepared to guide your research. Add additional headings to this plan when you need them. One way to accomplish this on a computer is to open two windows or document pages side by side. One window displays the headings from your research plan that may become major sections in your paper, and the other window displays an online article you are reading and noting. Copy and paste quoted material from the article and drop it into your outline. Get in the habit of *always* enclosing such material in quotation marks, and then add the name of the author at the end. Add the page number as well, if you can. Many online sources do not have page (or paragraph) numbers. You do not need at this point to add the title, place, or date of publication of each source since that information is available in your bibliography by author name. If you are using more than one book by the same author, write both the author's name and a short version of the title at the end of the citation.

When you are taking notes, you can omit words in a direct quotation to make it shorter and more to the point; indicate where words have been omitted with three spaced periods, known as an *ellipsis*. If the omitted material occurs at the end of a sentence, add a period immediately after the last quoted word, followed by the three spaced periods. Add the page number after the closing quotation mark.

If your research leads you to a new source and you want to use it, add full information about it to your bibliography. Every source you quote should be represented in your bibliography. Conversely, you should not have any items in your eventual Works Cited list that you do not quote, paraphrase, or summarize in your paper.

Clearly distinguish paraphrased and summarized material from your own ideas, just as you would quoted material. Introduce each paraphrase or summary that you enter into your document with a phrase that attributes it to its original author. "According to Scott . . ." or "Jones points out . . ." will make it clear who is responsible for the material that follows, even if it has been reworded and does not appear in quotation marks. Add a page number at the end, if it is from a paged source.

USING NOTE CARDS

You may prefer to take notes on 3 by 5 inch cards. When using note cards, you must also be careful to differentiate the material you quote, the material you write in your own words (paraphrase), the material you summarize, and your own ideas. Code the different types of information by using different colors of cards, by writing with different colors of pens, or by labeling each type of information. When you intersperse your own insights with material quoted from others, place your ideas in brackets [ ] to set them off or label them "mine." Always indicate directly quoted material by placing it in quotation marks. See Figure 12.5 for an example of a note card with a direct quotation using ellipses and a page number.

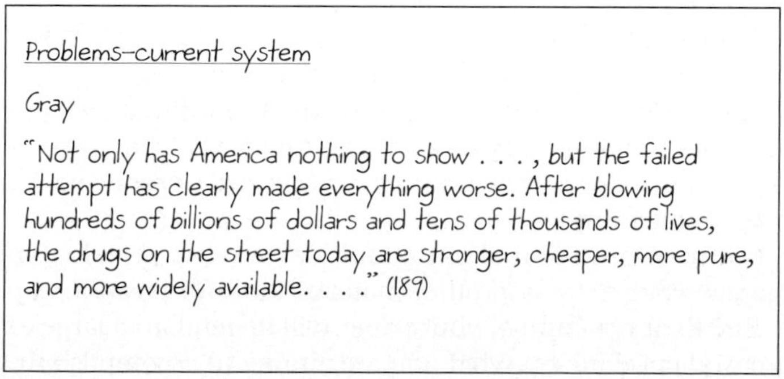

Problems–current system

Gray

"Not only has America nothing to show . . . , but the failed attempt has clearly made everything worse. After blowing hundreds of billions of dollars and tens of thousands of lives, the drugs on the street today are stronger, cheaper, more pure, and more widely available. . . ." (189)

Figure 12.5 *Note Card with Quoted Material.*

Indicate at the top of the card where you intend to use the source in your paper. Use a brief heading from your list of ideas, outline, or research plan for this cross-referencing. Look again at the example in Figure 12.5, which shows one way to do this.

Paraphrased or summarized material should also be recorded carefully and accurately with the page number at the end. Since you are condensing or changing the wording of this material, do not place it in quotation marks. You will still have to let your reader know who and from what source you are paraphrasing or summarizing when you write your paper, so include on the card the author's name and the page number. Also indicate where you will use it in your paper. Figure 12.6 provides an example of paraphrased material. Figure 12.7 provides an example of a note card with the student essayist's original idea on it. Whether you use cards or some other method for recording notes, you will need to include the same information illustrated in Figures 12.5–12.7.

Figure 12.6
Note Card with Paraphrases.

> Introduction–statistics
>
> Massing
>
> He quotes figures indicating there are more than 1.5 million drug arrests per year. Laws are discriminatory in that a large percentage of drug arrests are of black and Latino men. (11)
>
> U.S. spends 18 billion annually to fight the war on drugs. (14)

Figure 12.7
Note Card with an Original Idea or Reaction.

> Need for change
>
> Mine
>
> If harsh laws for minor drug possession were reformed, and if more money were spent on treatment of hard-core drug users, jails would have more room for dangerous criminals.

Arrange these cards as you go along according to the categories that are written at the top. Then place the categories in the sequence you think you will follow in your paper. The cards are now ready to work into your paper when you write the first draft.

More information about additional ways to develop your research plan and organize your notes and other material for your position paper appears in Chapter 13. The final structure of your paper will depend, to a large extent, on the nature of your audience and on what you are aiming to accomplish in your argument paper.

Two Invention Strategies to Help You Think Creatively about Your Research and Expand Your Own Ideas

When you have completed or nearly completed your research, try using one or both of the following invention strategies to help you gain a more comprehensive idea of what you want to do in your paper and also to help you develop specific lines of argument in your paper.

USE BURKE'S PENTAD TO GET THE BIG PICTURE AND ESTABLISH CAUSE

Asking *why* will help you establish cause for controversial incidents and human motives. So too will a systematic application of Kenneth Burke's pentad, as he describes it in his book *A Grammar of Motives*.[2] In his first sentence, Burke poses the question, "What is involved, when we say what people are doing and why they are doing it?" Burke identified five terms and associated questions that can be used to examine possible causes for human action and events. Since establishing cause is an important part of many arguments, and especially of fact, cause, and policy arguments, the pentad is potentially very useful to the writer of argument.

Here are Burke's terms and questions along with an example to demonstrate an application of the pentad. The example describes a controversial art exhibition that political leaders tried to shut down by withholding public funds from the art museum. Controversies about public funding of art occur from time to time. This specific example took place in Brooklyn, New York. After you have read the example, apply Burke's questions to your own issue to help you think about possible ways to describe its cause. The questions force a close analysis of an issue, and they will help you gain additional insight into the controversy associated with your issue. Burke's pentad, by the way, is similar to the journalist's questions *who, what, where, when, why,* and *how,* except that it yields even more information than they do.

1. *Act: What was done?* What took place in thought or deed?

   Example: An exhibit of works by modern British artists opened at the Brooklyn Museum of Art. It was controversial because it included some objects that are not usually considered art, including animal parts and an unusual presentation of the Virgin Mary. Some people objected.

2. *Scene: When or where was it done?* What is the background or scene in which it occurred?

   Example: The primary scene was the art museum and the exhibition. The scene also extended beyond the museum to include the art scene, made up of art lovers, museum directors, and art connoisseurs who saw the exhibition,

---

[2]Kenneth Burke, *A Grammar of Motives* (New York: Prentice Hall, 1945), xv. James Wood pointed out to me the value of Burke's pentad in attributing cause in argument.

titled *Sensation*, as a bold and interesting experiment in modern art; the political and religious scene, made up of political and religious leaders who saw the exhibition as outrageous and blasphemous and tried to shut it down as a result; and the judicial scene, made up of the judge and the court that ruled against withholding funds and declared that act a form of censorship, contrary to the First Amendment guarantee of freedom of speech. Thus the long tradition of constitutional law is also part of the scene.

3. *Agent: Who did it?* What person or kind of person performed the act?

   Example: The British artists who created the works in the exhibition, and their sponsors who hoped to make money on it, are agents, as are the museum directors and art lovers, the mayor and the religious leaders, and the judge. Other agents include the individuals who visited the art show and either liked it or did not and the other individuals who only read or heard about the exhibition but formed opinions about it anyway.

4. *Agency: How was it done?* What means or instruments were used?

   Example: The unusual materials used in the art exhibition are part of the agency: elephant dung adorned with sequins, flies and rotting meat, obscene body parts glued to the Virgin Mary's gown, mattresses, buckets, and so on. The mass media were also part of the agency: numerous articles in newspapers and magazines either praised or condemned the exhibition. The availability of the museum, the funding for the show provided by outside individuals as well as by the city, and the desire to profit from the exhibition are part of the agency, as are the power of the mayor's office to withhold money and the power of the law to declare the mayor's actions unconstitutional.

5. *Purpose: Why did it happen?* What was the main motivation?

   Example: The artists had several purposes: for example, to extend the definition of art by creating new forms, to create more tolerance for contemporary art by creating extreme examples, and to stimulate critical thinking and debate about art and its materials. The artists and their sponsors also wanted to exhibit the art, improve their own artistic reputations, and make money. The mayor and the religious leaders wanted to shut down the exhibition because they regarded it as offensive and irreligious and believed that the public would not want to support it. The judge's purpose was to uphold constitutional law.

Notice that you can focus on a part of an answer to any one of the five questions and argue that it is the main cause of the controversy. Notice also that each of the five questions provides a different perspective on the cause. Furthermore, the answers to these questions stir controversy. You may in fact have found yourself disagreeing with the answers in the examples. As Burke puts it, "Men may violently disagree about the purposes behind a given act, or about the character of the person who did it, or how he did it, or in what kind of situation he acted; or they may even insist upon totally different words to name the act itself."[3] Still, he goes on to say, one can begin with some kinds of answers to these questions,

---

[3]Ibid., xv.

which then provide a starting point for inquiry and argument. Apply Burke's pentad to every issue you write about to provide you with a deeper perspective on it, including the causes or motives behind it.

USE CHAINS OF REASONS TO DEVELOP LINES OF ARGUMENT

Another method of developing a claim or subclaim in your paper is to use chains of reasons to help you get a line of thinking going. You use this method quite naturally in verbal argument when you make a claim: someone asks you questions like *why* or *what for,* and you give additional reasons and evidence as support. For example:

You claim: The university should be more student-friendly.

Someone asks: Why do you think so? I think it's okay.

You answer: Because students are its customers, and without us, it would not exist.

Someone asks: Why wouldn't it?

You answer: Because we pay the money to keep it going.

Someone asks: Why do students keep it going? There are other sources of income.

You answer: Because our tuition is much more income than all of the other sources of funding combined.

You get the idea. Imagining that you are in a dialogue with another person who keeps asking *why* enables you to create quantities of additional support and detailed development for your claim. Also, by laying out your argument in this way, you can see where you need more support. In the preceding example, you need to provide support to show what portion of the operating budget is funded by student tuition. You might also give examples of insensitive treatment of students and explain what students have in common with customers.

To chain an argument, repeat the *why . . . because* sequence three or four times, both for your main claim and for each of your subclaims. Add evidence in all the places where your argument is sketchy. You will end up with a detailed analysis and support for your claim that will make it much less vulnerable to attack. You are now ready to think about how to organize all of this material and write your paper, which is the subject of the next chapter.

Review Questions

1. What is the difference between library subscription databases, such as *JSTOR* and *LexisNexis Academic,* and the World Wide Web? What types of material might you find by using each of them?

2. What is a bibliography? What is an annotated bibliography? How might writing an annotated bibliography help you research and write your paper?

3. Name some of the characteristics of a credible source.

4. Why would you create a research plan to guide your research?

5. Why would you use Burke's pentad and chains of reasons as part of the process of gathering material for a research paper?

Exercises and Activities

A. Pairs of Students: Becoming Familiar with the Library

Visit the library with a classmate or with your entire class and learn how to access the online catalog, the subscription databases of periodical articles, and the World Wide Web. Find out how to print full-text articles in the library or send them to your e-mail address at home. Arrange for passwords, if those are required. Then learn to locate the following: books and bound periodicals in the stacks; current periodicals; microfilm or microfiche, including how to use the viewers; and the government documents. Finally, locate the reference desk and the reference librarians, who are always willing to help you with a research project.

B. The Researched Position Paper: Conducting Research

Follow the steps delineated in the research worksheet below.

Worksheet 7	Research

1. Get organized for research: gather cards, pencils, money for the copy machine, paper, and a big envelope or folder. Review your research plan (Worksheet 5, page 379).

2. Locate a variety of sources on your issue and make evaluative judgments about each of them.

3. Gather ten to twelve of your most reliable sources. Include books, print and online articles, and other potential sources. Create a bibliography. Add annotations.

4. Survey and skim for specific information. Take notes.

5. Read critically to understand, and read creatively for original ideas. Take notes.

C. The Researched Position Paper: Writing an Annotated Bibliography

a. *Collect ten quality sources about your issue.* Make certain that your sources express several different perspectives or ways of thinking about your issue. Copy all the publisher's information needed to cite your sources in MLA or APA format, and assemble your bibliography in alphabetical order. See the Appendix to Chapter 13 (pages 429–479) and the examples on pages 391–392 and 392–393 to help you. Notice that the example of an annotated bibliography (pages 402–404) includes both print and online sources and that more than two perspectives on the issue are represented in these bibliographical items. Your bibliography should include the same, unless your instructor indicates otherwise.

b. *Survey, skim, and read selected parts of each source.*

c. *Write a summary, a response, and an indication of how you might use each source in your paper after each item.* The example on pages 402–404 provides selected items from a student's annotated bibliography and demonstrates how to record information from different types of sources, how to summarize, how to respond to the sources, and how to indicate where you might use them in your paper.

D. The Researched Position Paper: Adding Visual Materials to the Annotated Bibliography

If the assignment calls for it, add related images, graphs, or charts to your bibliography to use later in your paper. Add publisher's information needed to cite your sources in MLA and APA format just as you would an essay or book. Here is an example of an image that might be used in a paper about cloning humans. Publisher's information in MLA format follows the description of the image. It would now be ready to move into your paper.

Image 1: Welcome Clones of 2012!

Staged photograph by Berton Chang, a depiction of a 40th reunion of women cloned in 2012. From Sean Hamilton Alexander, "Artifacts from the Future," *Wired* (May, 2007): 188. Print.

(Use at beginning of paper to help readers visualize what human cloning might look like should it ever become a reality.)

STUDENT PAPER #1

Angela A. Boatwright
Annotated Bibliography
Professor Thorne
English 1302
15 March 2008

Human Cloning: An Annotated Bibliography

Online journal (appeared earlier in print)

Bailey, Ronald. "The Twin Paradox: What Exactly Is Wrong with Cloning People?" *Reason* May 1997. *Reasononline*. Web. 12 Mar. 2008.

This article explains simply, in nonscientific terms, exactly what was done to clone Dolly the sheep. The author briefly explains the legislation that has resulted from the first asexual reproduction of a mammal. Bailey explains what a clone would be and discusses the reasons why human clones could in no way be exact copies of their predecessors. Clones would have different personalities and would be as different as identical twins. He doesn't feel it is unethical to clone humans because they would be treated with the same moral status as any identical twins or triplets. He states that as long as we treat cloned individuals as we would treat any other human being, all other ethical problems we have concerning cloning would essentially disappear.

This article answers the questions I had regarding exactly what a clone would be like in relation to the "original model." It reinforces the belief I had that clones would be different people because of different social influences and environmental factors that have so much to do with the personality of an individual.

I will use information about Dolly and the uniqueness of clones in my discussion about the feasibility of cloning people.

Web site (online publication)

U.S. Dept. of Energy Office of Science. "Cloning Fact Sheet." *Genomics. energy.gov*. Human Genome Project Information, 23 July 2008. Web. 14 Feb. 2008.

According to this government Web site, which is maintained by the Human Genome Project, both scientists and physicians at present advise against cloning humans. When the first cloned animal, Dolly, died in 2003, she had developed both arthritis and cancer. Since that time, animal cloning has been very difficult. Only one or two tries out of one hundred are successful with animals. Also, many cloned animals are born with "large offspring syndrome" and other birth defects. They often die prematurely. There is fear that cloning humans could lead to similar problems. For these reasons, human cloning at this time is considered unethical and dangerous.

This Web site also provides links to anti-cloning legislation information and answers many other questions about all types of cloning issues. It is a credible Web site.

I will draw some information from this Web site to use in the introduction to my paper; and I will also use the information about the dangers of human cloning in my conclusion.

Magazine article (print)

Mann, Charles C. "The First Cloning Superpower." *Wired* (Jan. 2003): 116+. Print.

The author has interviewed a number of scientists in China who are working on therapeutic cloning techniques that employ stem cell research with the ultimate end of growing human replacement organs and tissues. China does not have as many regulations against experimenting with human stem cells as do the United States and other Western countries. China allows almost complete freedom to scientists in this field, disallowing only human reproductive cloning experiments. This means that scientists can experiment with embryonic stem cells to clone spare human parts, to regenerate damaged nerve and other tissue, and to find cures for diseases that have had no cures in the past. The author gives several examples of Chinese scientists who received their education in the United States but could not conduct stem cell research there because of bans on such research, and who have now returned to China where they have the freedom and access to funding and materials to conduct such research. The Chinese government hopes to win a Nobel Prize for China's work with therapeutic cloning.

While the United States debates the morality of this technology, China, with a different set of values, pursues it. Stem cell research and therapeutic cloning will be carried on in other parts of the world as well, even while being banned in the United States. This science is not likely to go away, and it is potentially extremely valuable to humans.

I will use this article to develop my section on the feasibility of therapeutic cloning.

Book (print)

Pence, Gregory E. *Who's Afraid of Human Cloning?* Lanham: Rowman, 1998. Print.

This is a comprehensive source of information on cloning. The book provides a complete overview, including discussions on the misconceptions, ethics, regulations, and arguments regarding human cloning. This author is most definitely an advocate of human cloning technology. He feels the discussion of this issue to date has been horribly one-sided. He states that never in the history of modern science has the world seen such an instant, overwhelming condemnation of an application to humanity of a scientific breakthrough. His aim is to correct this problem of a one-sided debate over the issue.

I will probably cite this book because of the wealth of information it contains. Although the author advocates human cloning, his book is a fairly good source of material for arguing against human cloning.

I will use ideas from this book in my introduction to show how some people are in favor of cloning and how some are not. I will also make

403

the distinction between cloning humans and therapeutic cloning, both of which are controversial.

Article in print and online (accessed on database)

Wilson, Jim. "Cloning Humans." *Popular Mechanics* June 2002: 42-44. *Academic Search Complete*. Web. 11 Mar. 2008.

This article discusses the technological progress of cloning and the "inevitability" that humans will soon be cloned. Wilson begins by showing that cloning humans is not different from the procedure used for in vitro fertilization (IVF). For IVF, a human conception (the union of a male sperm and female egg) takes place in a glass lab dish, grows into an embryo, and is then implanted in a human uterus. Human clones will go through the same process, Wilson tells us. The difference between IVF and cloned embryos is that the genetic blueprint for IVF cases comes from two parents, whereas clones require only one. Wilson traces the potential for human cloning back to 1997 and shows that while the world marveled at the cloning of Dolly the sheep, the scientific community marveled that researchers from Duke University Medical Center had learned that cloning humans would be simpler than cloning sheep.

Once this discovery was made, Italian researcher Severino Antinori argued that the genetic pattern of sterile males could be passed on via clones. Antinori, who successfully performed IVF for a woman 62 years of age, presented his findings at the International Cloning Consortium in Rome in 2001. His case was taken quite seriously by the scientific community, and since then a number of cloning projects have emerged. The formation of the first human-cloning company, Clonaid, was announced by founder Claude Vorilhon. Clonaid's chief scientist, Brigitte Boisselier, is a chemist who perfected the process of forcing DNA-inoculated cells to divide successfully. Thanks to Boisselier, this cloning process is no less successful than that of standard fertility techniques. The market for this process is fertility clinics.

This article shows how the technology for cloning may be used in a way that is more insidious than many may have previously thought. Combining cloning with fertility treatment to allow couples and individuals to pass along their genetic traits may be a way for cloning to become silently mainstreamed.

I will use this material at the end of my paper to suggest what could happen if this technology is not carefully monitored.

E. The Researched Position Paper: Evaluating Your Research

Look back over your bibliography and the other research and ideas you have gathered and complete the worksheet on the next page. Make certain all of the information you want to use is complete and that you have the information you need to cite all sources. Add, correct, or eliminate any material that might weaken your argument.

Worksheet 8   Research Evaluation

Examine the research you have done so far.

a. Do I have enough information to be convincing? What can I add?

b. Is my information reliable and convincing? How can I make it more so?

c. Is anything exaggerated or oversimplified? How can I be more accurate?

d. Do I rely too much on my own authority ("This is true because I say it is") instead of giving support? Can I add opinions of other authorities to be more convincing?

e. Am I weakening this argument with too much emotional material? Should any of it be eliminated?

F. The Researched Position Paper: Using Burke's Pentad to Develop an Expanded Perspective on Your Issue

Use Burke's pentad to analyze the whole context and, in particular, the cause for your issue. Write out your issue so that you will focus on it, and then answer the following questions.

  1. *Act:* What was done?

  2. *Scene:* When or where was it done?

  3. *Agent:* Who did it?

  4. *Agency:* How was it done?

  5. *Purpose:* Why did it happen?

Indicate how you can use the information generated by these questions in your paper.

G. Pairs of Students: Using Chains of Reasons to Develop Lines of Argument for the Researched Position Paper

  1. Write a 100-word synthesis of your thinking and research on your issue to this point.

  2. Exchange your synthesis with a classmate. Read each other's syntheses, and write a thought-provoking question that asks for additional information or clarification about the topic or about the author's point of view. Return the paper to its author. Each author should read the question and write a reasoned response of two or three sentences. Exchange papers again, read the responses, and ask another question. Continue this questioning and answering until time is called.

  3. When the time is up, read over the questions and answers you have developed for your issue. What surprises you? What do you need to research more? Where do you think your answers were the strongest? Once you have examined this material closely, add to your outline or draft plan to indicate how this additional information might apply when you write your paper.

H. The Researched Position Paper: Inventing Ideas

Read through the list of invention strategies on Worksheet 9, which follows on this page and the next. The list is a composite of the approaches described in this and earlier chapters. Some of them will be "hot spots" for you. That is, they will immediately suggest profitable activity for developing your paper. Check those that you want to use at this point and complete them. There may be only two or three. You should include the Toulmin model, nevertheless. It is one of the best invention activities for argument.

Worksheet 9	**Invention**

Your claim: _____

Begin to develop your claim by using some of the following invention strategies. If you cannot generate information and ideas, do some background reading and then return to these strategies.

1. Freewrite for five minutes.
2. Brainstorm additional ideas and details in brief phrases for another five minutes.
3. Make a list or map that shows the parts of your paper.
4. Explain to someone in your class or group what you expect to accomplish in your paper, or talk into a tape recorder about it.
5. Write your insights in a computer file, a journal, or on sheets of paper filed in a folder.
6. Mentally visualize and write a description of a scene related to your claim.
7. Make a research plan. Write your claim plus three to five reasons. Add ideas for research and a draft plan.
8. Think about possible organizational patterns to shape your paper. What might work best—a claim with reasons, problem–solution, cause and effect, compare and contrast, chronology or narrative, or a combination of two or more patterns? (Refer to pages 410–413 for help.)
9. Think through the rhetorical situation. Remember TRACE: text, reader, author, constraints, exigence.
10. Use the Toulmin model to come up with the key parts of your paper. Consider the claim, support, warrants, backing for the warrants, possible rebuttals, and qualifiers.
11. Ask the claim questions: Did it happen? What is it? What caused it? Is it good or bad? What should we do about it?
12. Decide on proofs that are suited for your type of claim. Recall SICDADS—sign, induction, cause, deduction, analogies (literal, figurative, historical), definition, and sign—and VAM—value, authoritative, and motivational proofs.
13. Utilize critical thinking prompts. Start with your claim, but then make these recursive; that is, apply them at any point and more than once during the process.

Associate it.	Think about it as it is now.	Evaluate it.
Describe it.	Think about it over time.	Elaborate on it.
Compare it.	Decide what it is a part of.	Project and predict.
Apply it.	Analyze its parts.	Ask why.
Divide it.	Synthesize it.	

continued

Worksheet 9 *continued*

14. Use Burke's pentad to establish cause: act, scene, agent, agency, purpose.
15. Use chains of reasons to develop your ideas through five repetitions of *claim* (or *subclaim*)-*why-because*. Describe where you need to add evidence.
16. Make a more complete outline, set of notes, or list to guide your writing.
17. Write chunks or bits of your paper as they begin to form in your mind.

I. The Researched Position Paper: Adding Proofs

If either your evaluation of your research or your answer to item 12 on the invention worksheet about adding proofs indicate that you need more proof in your paper, use Worksheet 10 to help you plan additional proofs. Proofs are powerful. They help make your paper convincing to your audience.

Worksheet 10 Proofs and Language Development

Write your claim: _____

a. *Signs:* What symptoms or signs will demonstrate that this might be true?
b. *Induction:* What examples can I use? What conclusions can I draw from the examples? Can my readers make the "inductive leap" from the examples to an acceptance of the conclusion?
c. *Cause:* What is the main cause of the controversy? What are the effects?
d. *Deduction:* What conclusions will I draw? On what general principles, warrants, and examples are they based?
e. *Analogies:* What comparisons can I make? Can I show that what happened in the past might happen again or that what happened in one case might happen in another? Can I use a figurative analogy to compare items from different categories?
f. *Definition:* What words or concepts will I need to define?
g. *Statistics:* What statistics can I use? How should I present them? Would they be more convincing in graph form? (If yes, see examples of graphs in Chapter 9, pages 294–296.)
h. *Values:* What values can I appeal to? Should I spell them out, or is it best to leave them unstated? What emotional narratives, examples, descriptions, and emotional language would make my appeals to values stronger?
i. *Authority:* Whom should I quote? What background information should I supply both for myself and for those I quote to establish our expertise? How can I use language to create common ground and establish *ethos*?
j. *Motives:* What do my readers need and want in regard to my issue? How can I appeal to those needs? What emotional material might help?
k. *Language:* What type of language do I want to predominate in my paper: the language of reason? emotional language? language that establishes *ethos*? a mix of styles? Make a few notes to help you plan language.

The Research Paper: Organizing, Writing, and Revising

I n this chapter you will learn to write a research paper in which you take a position on your issue, organize the research materials and idea notes that you have collected, and write a paper that is convincing to your audience of readers. You may want to take a look at the assignment for this paper now, on pages 425–426, to get a sense of what you will be doing. Instruction in this chapter includes organizing and outlining the paper, incorporating research into your first draft, and revising and preparing the final copy.

Organization, or deciding on a framework of ideas for your paper, will be dealt with first. As you go back and reread the material you have gathered for your paper, you will need to think about (1) how this material can be divided into *parts;* (2) how these parts can be placed in an *order;* and (3) what the logical *relationships* are among the parts.

To help you accomplish this, let's look first at the advice classical rhetoricians give on these matters. Recall that you learned about the five canons of classical rhetoric in Chapter 12 (page 380). Now read more about the part of the canon that the classical authors called arrangement and that we usually refer to as organization.

Classical Organization of Arguments

Occasional disagreement exists among some of the classical authors regarding the parts and the order of the parts in an argument. In the *Rhetoric,* Aristotle complains about earlier writers who present elaborate organizational schemes that he considers unnecessarily complicated. For Aristotle, an argument only has to have two essential parts, the proposition (or claim), which is stated first, and the proof that follows. He allows that an arguer might want to expand on this core structure by adding other parts, including an introduction and a conclusion. He emphasizes, however, that anyone planning an argument needs to remain flexible and consider the purpose, the audience, and the occasion, since any one of these variables could influence the way in which an argument is finally put together. Furthermore, according to Aristotle, if you have no reason to include one of the parts, then leave it out.

After Aristotle, Cicero and other Roman orators made minor modifications to Aristotle's structure. As a result, classical organization is usually explained as having six parts, with the following specified functions.

THE SIX PARTS OF CLASSICAL ORGANIZATION

Introduction. Makes the subject and purpose clear right from the start. Also includes information that will interest the audience so that they will want to keep reading.

Statement of proposition and division. States claim at or near the end of the introduction. Sometimes names the major sections of the paper so that it is easier for readers to follow along.

Narration. Provides background about the subject and the events that led up to the controversy. Indicates why the subject is important. Gives the author an opportunity to establish *ethos* by citing reasons for an interest in the subject and qualifications for writing about it. May describe other positions on the issue or summarize the scholarship to date.

Proof. Provides reasons and evidence that are acceptable to the audience to prove the proposition or claim.

Refutation. Refutes opposing positions. May be placed after the proof, before the proof, or at various points among the items of proof. (According to Aristotle, if the opposition has a lot of objections to your position, it is better to remove these objections early, before you give your reasons. Otherwise, state your position, prove it, and then refute others.)

Conclusion. Emphasizes the most important point and reminds the audience of the other important points.

You will find classical organization useful when you plan your position paper, particularly if you remain flexible and adapt it to your needs.

Classical and Modern Organization

When you look back at the classical structure just described, much of it may seem familiar to you. Did you think of the Toulmin model? Toulmin is a modern writer. Your study of the Toulmin model in Chapter 5 introduced you to the usual *parts* of an argument. These include a claim, support, warrants, backing for the warrants, and possibly also a rebuttal and a qualifier for the claim. The Toulmin model only identifies parts and does not specify the order in which they should appear, so it is not a model for structuring an argument. When you begin to think about the claim, the subclaims that represent the major sections of a paper, and the facts, examples, and opinions that support them, however, you begin to imagine various possibilities for ordering these parts of your paper. You could, for example, easily move the Toulmin model's parts into the classical framework.

You are also probably familiar with the introduction-body-conclusion format that frequently is used to organize modern essays and speeches. These parts have their origin in classical rhetoric. The usual functions mentioned for a modern introduction are to focus and introduce the topic, to provide some background, to get the attention of the audience, and sometimes, to present the claim. The conclusion either states the claim or refocuses it through restatement and final, compelling reasons.

Regarding *order,* students are often advised to think of the beginning of the paper as a strong position but the end as even stronger. Thus you would place your strongest material at or near the end, other strong material at the beginning, and the less impressive material in the middle.

Both classical and modern theorists advise you to think about your audience when determining the order of ideas in a paper. For instance, for a hostile audience, consider beginning your paper with material that your readers can agree with so that they will want to continue reading. For a neutral audience, you might want to present strong and interesting examples at the beginning to get their attention and create interest. For a friendly audience, you can show in your introduction how you agree with them and confirm their already favorable opinion of you.

Now let's look at some additional ideas that will help you organize your paper and establish *relationships* among the ideas and sections in it.

Use Organizational Patterns to Help You Think and Organize

Organizational patterns represent distinct ways to think about the parts of your paper, the order in which you will place them, and the relationships among the parts. They can be incorporated into the overall structure of the classical model, particularly in the proof section (body) of the paper. You were introduced to some of the organizational patterns that are particularly useful for argument in Chapters 6 where we identified patterns appropriate for different types of claims. This chapter provides additional information about these same patterns, which by the way, can shape your paper as the dominant pattern or can be combined as minor patterns within the dominant pattern to organize some of the sections. Imagine them alone or in combinations accompanied by an introduction and a conclusion. Use them to help you think about your ideas as well as to organize them.

CLAIM WITH REASONS (OR REASONS FOLLOWED BY CLAIM)

This pattern takes the following form.

Statement of claim
Reason 1
Reason 2
Reason 3, and so forth

Set this pattern up by writing the claim, following it with the word *because*, and listing some reasons. Or, list some reasons, follow them with the word *therefore,* and write the claim. For example, you may present the claim that we need a national health care program, which is followed by reasons: the unemployed have no insurance, many employed people have no insurance, the elderly cannot afford medicine, many children do not receive adequate health care. The reasons may be distinct and different from one another and set up like separate topics in your paper. Alternatively, you may create a chain of related reasons by asking *why* and answering *because* five or six times. Also, some of your reasons may be used to refute, others to prove, and still others to show how your claim will meet the needs and values of the audience. Support all reasons with facts, examples, and opinions. You can use transitional phrases such as *one reason, another reason, a related reason,* and *a final reason* to emphasize each reason and also make the arrangement of the reasons in your paper stand out.

CAUSE AND EFFECT (OR EFFECT AND CAUSE)

The cause-and-effect pattern may be used to identify one or more causes, followed by one or more effects or results. You can reverse this sequence and describe effects first and then the cause or causes if it works better. For example, the causes of water pollution might be followed by its effects on both humans and animals. Use obvious transitions to clarify cause and effect, such as "What are the results? Here are some of them," or simply the words *cause, effect, finding, follows, consequence,* and *result.*

APPLIED CRITERIA

This pattern establishes criteria or standards for evaluation and judgment and then shows how the claim meets them. For example, in an argument about children in day care, you might set out physical safety, psychological security, sociability, and creativity as criteria for measuring the success of day care. Then you might claim that day care centers meet those criteria as well as or even better than home care and provide support. The applied criteria pattern is obviously useful for value arguments. It is also useful in policy arguments to establish a way of evaluating a proposed solution. Use such words and phrases as *criteria, standards, needs, best practice,* and *meets those criteria* or *needs* to clarify the parts of this kind of paper.

PROBLEM–SOLUTION

The problem–solution pattern is commonly used in policy papers. There are at least three ways to organize these papers. The problem is described, followed by the solution. In this case, the claim is the solution, and it may be stated at the beginning of the solution section or at the end of the paper. An alternative is to propose the solution first and then describe the problems that motivated it. A third arrangement is to state a problem followed by several solutions, one of

411

which is then selected as the best. When the solution or claim is stated at the end of the paper, the pattern is sometimes called the *delayed proposal.* For a hostile audience, it may be effective to describe the problem, show why other solutions do not work, and finally suggest the favored solution. For example, you may want to claim that labor unions are the best solution for reducing unemployment. First, you describe the unemployment problem in vivid detail so that the audience really wants a solution. Next, you show that government mandates and individual company initiatives have not worked. Finally, you show how labor unions protect employment for workers. Use such words as *problem* and *solution* to signal the main sections of the paper for your reader. Language that shows the logic of your connections, such as *since, because, if so,* or *similar to,* is also helpful.

CHRONOLOGY OR NARRATIVE

Material arranged chronologically is explained as it occurs in time. This pattern can be used to establish what happened for an argument of fact. For example, you may want to give a history of childhood traumas to account for an individual's current criminal behavior. Or you may want to tell a story to develop one or more points in your argument. Use transitional words like *once, before, then, next,* and *finally* to make the parts of the chronology clear.

DEDUCTION

Recall that deductive reasoning involves reasoning from a generalization, applying it to cases or examples, and drawing a conclusion. For instance, you may generalize that the open land in the West is becoming overgrazed; follow this assertion with specific cases of erosion, threatened wildlife, and other environmental harms; and conclude that the government must restrict grazing to designated areas. The conclusion is the claim. You can use such transitional phrases as *for instance, for example,* and *to clarify* to set your cases and examples off from the rest of the argument and *therefore, thus, consequently,* or *in conclusion* to lead into your claim.

INDUCTION

The inductive pattern involves citing one or more examples and then making the "inductive leap" to the conclusion. For instance, five or six examples of illegal immigrants crossing over into the United States who require expensive social services lead some people to conclude that they should be sent home. Other people may conclude that the immigrants ought to be allowed to stay. No matter which claim or conclusion is chosen, it can be stated at the beginning or at the end of the paper. The only requirement is that it be based on the examples. The same transitional words used for the deductive pattern are also useful for the inductive: *for instance, for example,* or *some examples* to emphasize the examples; *therefore; thus,* or *consequently* to lead into the claim.

COMPARE AND CONTRAST

This pattern is particularly useful in definition arguments and in other arguments that show how a subject is like or unlike similar subjects. It is also often used to demonstrate a variety of similarities or differences. For example, the claim is made that drug abuse is a medical problem instead of a criminal justice problem. The proof consists of literal analogies that compare drug abuse to AIDS, cancer, or heart disease to redefine it as a medical problem. The transitional words such as *similarly, by contrast, in comparison, while, separate from, opposite,* and *others* are used to clarify the ideas in this pattern.

Incorporate Ideas from Your Exploratory Paper

The pattern you used to write your exploratory paper can be expanded for a researched position paper. Recall that you may have explained the positions of those in favor of the issue, those against it, and those with various views in between. Your objective there was to explain the range of different perspectives on the issue. Having stated these positions, you can now expand your exploratory paper by refuting some of these positions and by stating and supporting your own. You may decide to use another pattern, such as the claim with reasons, to organize your own position on the issue.

    As an alternative, you can explain the various positions from your exploratory paper at the beginning of your position paper and show the advantages of each of them; then identify one position as probably best; and finally develop that idea in the rest of your paper. This strategy impresses readers as fair-minded and convincing because each major perspective is acknowledged. To write such a position paper, go to your exploratory paper file in your computer and build parts of it into your position paper.

How to Match Patterns and Support to Claims

Some of the organizational patterns are particularly appropriate for specific types of claims. Table 13.1 (page 414) suggests patterns you might want to consider as promising for particular argumentation purposes. You could, of course, combine more than one pattern to develop a paper. For example, you may begin with a narrative of what happened, then describe its causes and effects, and finally propose a solution for dealing with the problems created by the effects.

    When you use organizational patterns to help you think, these same patterns can function to organize your ideas into a complete argument. However, the patterns may be too constraining if you start with one and try to fill it in

413

Table 13.1	Appropriate Patterns for Developing Types of Claims—in Descending Order of Suitability.			
CLAIMS OF FACT	**CLAIMS OF DEFINITION**	**CLAIMS OF CAUSE**	**CLAIMS OF VALUE**	**CLAIMS OF POLICY**
Claim with reasons	Deduction	Cause and effect	Applied criteria	Problem–solution
Induction	Claim with reasons	Claim with reasons	Cause and effect	Applied criteria
Chronology or narrative	Compare and contrast	Rogerian argument	Claim with reasons	Cause and effect
Cause and effect	Rogerian argument	Deduction	Chronology or narrative	Claim with reasons
Rogerian argument	Exploration	Exploration	Rogerian argument	Rogerian argument
Exploration	Induction		Induction	Exploration
			Deduction	
			Compare and contrast	
			Exploration	

with your material. If you prefer to work with ideas first, without the conscious constraints of a pattern to guide you, though, at some point, patterns of argumentation must be considered. When you are finished or nearly finished organizing your research and ideas, move out of the creative mode and into the critical mode to analyze what you have done. You may find that you have arranged your ideas according to one or more of the patterns without being consciously aware of it. This is a common discovery. Now use what you know about the patterns to improve and sharpen the divisions among your ideas and to clarify these ideas with transitions. You will ultimately improve the readability of your paper by making it conform more closely to one or more specific patterns of organization.

Some proofs and support work better than others to establish different types of claims.[1] Table 13.2 (page 415) offers suggestions, not rules, for you to consider. Remember that a variety of types of proof and a generous amount of specific support create the best, most convincing argument papers.

---

[1] I am indebted to Wayne E. Brockriede and Douglas Ehninger for some of the suggestions in Table 13.2. They identify some types of proof as appropriate for different sorts of claims in their article "Toulmin on Argument: An Interpretation and Application," *Quarterly Journal of Speech* 46 (1960): 44–53.

Table 13.2	**Proofs and Support That Are Particularly Appropriate for Developing Specific Types of Claims.**			
CLAIMS OF FACT	**CLAIMS OF DEFINITION**	**CLAIMS OF CAUSE**	**CLAIMS OF VALUE**	**CLAIMS OF POLICY**
Facts	Reliable authorities	Facts	Value proofs	Facts
Statistics	Accepted sources	Statistics	Motivational proofs	Motivational proofs
Real examples	Analogies with the familiar	Historical analogies	Literal analogies	Value proofs
Quotations from reliable authorities	Examples (real or made up)	Literal analogies	Figurative analogies	Literal analogies
Induction	Signs	Signs	Quotations from reliable authorities	Reliable authorities
Literal and historical analogies		Induction	Induction	Deduction
Signs		Deduction	Signs	Definition
Informed opinion		Quotations from reliable authorities	Definition	Statistics
			Cause	Cause

Outline Your Paper and Cross-Reference Your Notes

You have already been provided with a rationale and some ideas for outlining in Chapters 4 and 11. Some people find they can draft simple papers that require little or no research without an outline or list. They can later rearrange material on the computer until it is in a logical order. Most people, however, need some sort of outline or list to guide their writing when they are working with their own ideas or with material from outside sources.

If you have not already, try making an outline or list for your research paper, and make one that works best for you. Think of your outline as a guide that will help you write later. At the very least, indicate on your outline the major ideas, in the order you intend to write about them, and add the ideas and research you will use for support and development. Read your original ideas and research notes, and check to make certain that all are cross-referenced in some way to the outline. Identify the places where you need more information and research. If you have stored research material in computer files, reread each item, check to make certain you have placed quotation marks around quoted material, and make certain you have recorded the original source for every quoted, paraphrased, or summarized item. Arrange the items under headings on your outline in the order you think you are likely to use them. If you have photocopied or printed material from online, use numbers to cross-reference to your outline the highlighted passages you intend to quote. If you have gathered research material on cards, paper-clip the cards to the places on the outline where you will use them later. Work with your outline until it flows logically and makes sense. Pay attention to the parts, the order of the parts, and the relationships among the parts.

If you have the opportunity, discuss your outline or plan with your instructor, a peer editing group, or a friend. Someone else can often tell you whether the organization is clear and logical, whether you have sufficient support or will need more support and evidence, and whether the warrants will be generally acceptable.

The following sample outline is more complete than the research plan described on page 379. It is an outline of the student-written researched position paper that appears in the Appendix to Chapter 13, on pages 446–455. This outline would be complete enough to guide writing for some people. Other people might want to add more detail to it before attempting the first draft. It is the sort of outline one might take to a peer editing group to discuss and receive suggestions for the actual writing of the paper.

Sample Outline   Working Title: "The Big Barbie Controversy"

▶▶▶ Strategy for Paper:

Summarize positions in exploratory paper in introductory paragraphs and describe personal interest in Barbie to create my own *ethos;* establish and apply criteria for judging Barbie doll as both good as a role model for building girls' self-esteem and bad for that purpose; conclude by stating that Barbie is neither good nor bad and should not be the focus of this issue; instead, parents and community are responsible for helping children build self-esteem. Value claim at the end.

▶▶▶ Introduction (Summary of Positions in Exploratory Paper and Background History):

▶ My childhood interest in Barbie—loved her. My sister's disinterest
▶ Feminism—how changed my view: new respect for sister

continued

Sample Outline   *continued*

▶ New commonsense view: Barbie just a doll with marketable appeal

▶ History of Barbie doll: new concept in 1959; offers choices to girls; evidence of success

▶▶▶ Is Barbie Good for Building Girls' Confidence and Self-Esteem?

▶ A powerful icon; evidence of doll's popularity

▶ Criteria for showing Barbie is good: Barbie is everywhere; people all over the world play with these dolls; it is fun to play with Barbie; Barbie stimulates imagination and is a good role model because she can take on many roles.

▶▶▶ Is Barbie Bad for Harming Girls' Confidence and Self-Esteem?

▶ Criteria for showing Barbie is bad for girls: she creates a poor body image; encourages eating disorders; encourages stereotypes; is a negative role model.

▶▶▶ Refutation: Does Barbie Have to Be Either Good or Bad?

▶ Refute those who say all bad: anorexia older than Barbie; cannot protect children from everything that might be a negative influence

▶ Refute those who say all good: people who played with Barbie still self-critical and have limited insight into themselves

▶▶▶ Conclusion:

It is not Barbie's responsibility to create a self-image in children.

▶▶▶ Claim:

Adults and society are responsible for children's self-images. Barbie is being used as a scapegoat.

Note that this outline is worked out in detail in some areas but not in others. The ideas in it so far, however, belong to the author. The peer group that critiques it at this stage would be able to help the author decide whether she has gathered enough source material to write a credible paper or whether she needs to read and take more notes. When your own research seems to be complete, and the notes you intend to include in the paper are either copied in a computer file, on cards, or highlighted on photocopies, they can now be cross-referenced to your outline and stacked in the order in which you will use them in the paper. You are ready to write the draft next. Most of the material in the paper will be your own insights, observations, ideas, and examples. The researched material will be incorporated into the paper to add information, interest, clarity, and credibility.

Incorporating Research into Your First Draft

Use common sense in working your research materials into your draft. Your objective is to create a smooth document that can be read easily while, at the same time, demonstrating to your readers exactly which materials are yours and which are drawn from outside sources. Here are some suggestions to help you accomplish this. We draw our examples from an article by Johanne Mednick, "The Highs of Low Technology," from the Toronto *Globe and Mail,* July 23, 1993, page 16.* Mednick is a teacher who lives in Canada, and her article is about her old bicycle.

1. *Use quoted material sparingly.* You want to have the controlling voice in your paper. No more than 20 percent of your paper should be made up of direct quotations of other people's words. When you do quote, select material that is interesting, vivid, and best stated in the quoted words.

   Here is an example of a direct quote that you could have marked on a photocopy of the article or copied onto a note card with the author's name and the page number recorded in MLA style to use later in your paper. In this first example, the author's name is cited with the page number at the end of the quote since she is not named in the text. This signals the reader that the full citation is available in the alphabetized list of sources at the end of the paper. The two ellipses in this quotation show that the writer omitted words before or at the end of the source's sentence and omitted at least another full sentence. This shortened quotation efficiently expresses what you want to say:

   Example: "Perhaps my bike is representative of a world gone by. . . . My bike is certainly not built for speed. . . . It's built for taking time. It makes people feel relaxed" (Mednick 16).

2. *Paraphrase or summarize when you do not know enough to use your own explanations.* Use your own words to rephrase or summarize other people's explanations and ideas so that yours is the dominant voice in your paper.

   Here is an example of paraphrased material from the same article, followed by the page number only since the author is mentioned in the text:

   Example: Mednick says that her microwave and her computer make her feel that life is getting too complicated and out of control (16).

   Here is a summary of Mednick's article, again with the author mentioned in the text so that only the page number is necessary at the end.

---

*The examples on pages 418–420 show how and when to use research and credit its source in your writing; for teaching purposes, we are treating the Mednick article as a source longer than one page. To find more complete MLA instructions, see the *MLA Style Manual and Guide to Scholarly Publishing,* third edition, 2008, or the seventh edition of the *MLA Handbook for Writers of Research Papers,* due to be available in 2009.

Example: Mednick claims that people still long for the older, simpler machines like her old bicycle and the simpler way of life they represented (16).

3. *Begin and end your paper with your own words instead of a quotation, paraphrase, or summary of other people's ideas.* The beginning and end are emphatic places in a paper. Put *your* best ideas there, not someone else's.

4. *Whenever you can, introduce each quotation, paraphrase, or summary in your paper so that your readers will know who wrote the original material.* Make it clear where your words and ideas leave off and where someone else's begin. Introduce each quotation, paraphrase, or summary with the name of the person you are quoting or otherwise citing. Consider adding a description of that person's credentials to establish his or her *ethos* and authority.

Example: According to Johanne Mednick, a teacher in Canada, an old bicycle is better than newer models (16).

5. *Integrate every quotation into your paper so that it flows with the rest of the text and makes sense to the reader.* Work in the quotations so that they make sense in context.

Example: People have various reasons for preferring the old to the new. Mednick's reasons for preferring her old bicycle are clear in her concluding statement. In describing her bicycle, she says, "It allows me the opportunity to relax and, at best when I'm heading down the road, escape what I don't understand" (16).

6. *If your author quotes someone else and you want to use that quote in your own paper, introduce the quotation by indicating who originated it.* Make clear you are quoting someone your source quoted.

Example: Mednick declares that other people show a great deal of interest in her old bicycle. Strangers come up to her regularly and make such comments as "Where did you get that thing?" and "I haven't seen one of those in ages" (16).

7. *Cite the source of the quotation, paraphrase, or summary in parentheses at the end of it.* Further instructions for writing in-text parenthetical citations are given in the Appendix to Chapter 13.

Write all quotations, paraphrases, and summaries into your first draft so that your entire paper will be in place for smooth reading. The following three paragraphs show the quoted, paraphrased, and summarized material from the Mednick article worked into the first draft so that it is absolutely clear what is the author's and what is Mednick's.

Many people become nostalgic for the ways things were. Some people keep old cash registers at their businesses to remind customers of days gone by. Other people fire up wood stoves to help them remember earlier times. Johanne Mednick, a teacher in Canada, claims that many people still long for older, simpler machines and also for the way of life they represent (16).

Mednick uses her old bicycle as an example. "Perhaps my bike is representative of a world gone by . . . ," she says. "My bike is certainly not built for speed. . . . It's built for taking time. It makes people feel relaxed" (16).

New computers and microwave ovens, by contrast, make people feel that life is getting too complicated and out of control (Mednick 16).

Notice that in the first paragraph, Johanne Mednick's entire name is used to introduce her material, and in subsequent references she is referred to as Mednick. Notice also that in the first two paragraphs, Mednick's name is used to introduce the material that is attributed to her. Since it is clear from the context where her material begins and where it leaves off, it is only necessary to insert the page number of her article at the end of the borrowed material. In the third paragraph, Mednick's name is not included in the text, and it is less clear whose idea this is. To make it absolutely clear to the reader that this is another idea of Mednick's, her last name along with the page number is placed at the end of the borrowed idea. The full information about this source and where it was first located will be placed on bibliography pages at the end of the paper. The reader who wants to know when and where Mednick published her article can refer to those pages.

CLEARLY IDENTIFY WORDS AND IDEAS FROM ALL SOURCES TO AVOID PLAGIARISM

Whenever you use quoted, paraphrased, and summarized material from other sources in your paper, you must indicate where your words leave off and someone else's begin, and you must identify the original source for all borrowed material.

Sometimes students mix their words in with the words of the author they are quoting and, as a result, the reader cannot easily sort out the students' words from those of the person being quoted. This is a form of plagiarism. You have seen a real example of this error in Chapter 4, page 117. Let's look at another example. The underlined words and phrases in the paragraph below have been copied exactly as the author wrote them. Notice, however, that the student does not place any of this material in quotes to show these words belong to the author and not to the student.

Low technology can be a high for many people. A wonderful bicycle that most people would refer to as an <u>old clunker</u> might bring its owner considerable pleasure. Its <u>two large wheels, seat, handle bars, basket, bell</u>, and pedals help its owner <u>glide past all of the riders on racers and mountain bikes who are intent on engaging the right gear for the occasion</u>. People admire her bike because it gives them a sense of <u>something manageable, not too complicated</u> (Mednick 16).

Even though the citation at the end of the paragraph indicates that some of the ideas and language are Mednick's, the reader does not know which words came directly from Mednick's essay and which have been supplied by the author.

Now let's examine two better ways to incorporate research. One is to *paraphrase the ideas in your own words.*

Not everyone likes new bicycles. Johanne Mednick describes her old bicycle and the pleasure it brings her. She never envies people who pass her by on new bikes. She prefers the familiar comfort of her old bicycle (16).

An alternative is to *combine your words with the author's, but place the author's words in quotation marks.*

Johanne Mednick claims in her essay "The Highs of Low Technology" that she prefers her old bicycle to new racing bikes or mountain bikes. She describes her old bicycle in admiring terms. It has, she says, "two large wheels, seat, handle bars, basket, bell and the simple mechanism that allows me to pedal my way to wherever I'm going" (16). She is often able to pass people on newer bikes because they have to slow down to shift gears (16).

DOCUMENT YOUR SOURCES

Some of the main features of source acknowledgment are explained in the Appendix to Chapter 13, pages 429–479. Use this appendix as a reference guide when you are working borrowed material into your paper and also when you are preparing the final list of the works you have used. These methods will inform your reader about exactly what material in your paper is yours, what belongs to other people, and where you found the material in your research. In the Appendix to Chapter 13 you will first be shown examples of ways to incorporate borrowed material into the text of your paper and how to cite them in the text to indicate succinctly where they originally appeared. You will then be shown how to prepare entries for the list of sources that you have used. This list will appear at the end of your paper. Take a look at the types of sources listed in the Appendix to Chapter 13. Some of them may suggest resources you have not yet thought of for your paper.

As you incorporate borrowed material from other sources, you will need to follow a system and a set of conventions that has been prescribed for this purpose. Two such systems are described in the Appendix to Chapter 13. MLA style, which is recommended by the Modern Language Association for papers written in the humanities, is explained first. MLA documentation style provides advice on how to acknowledge the work of other individuals in your paper itself and also how to give full information about these sources in a list of "Works Cited" at the end of your paper. Following the discussion of MLA style is a researched position paper in MLA style format (pages 446–455). It was written by a student, and you can use it as an example when you write your own paper. Study the annotations in the margins of this paper. They demonstrate how quoted and summarized material can be incorporated into papers and acknowledged according to MLA style. Answer the questions that accompany this paper (page 456) to further develop your expertise in using MLA style.

The second documentation style taught in the Appendix to Chapter 13 is APA style, recommended by the American Psychological Association for papers written in education and the social sciences. APA documentation calls for a somewhat different system from MLA. Information is provided for citing sources in the text of an APA style paper and listing these sources on a "References" page at the end. A student paper written in APA style provides an illustration of this documentation format (pages 469–478).

Other documentation styles, not described in the Appendix to Chapter 13, include CSE style, which is recommended by the Council of Science Editors for scientific papers, including natural sciences, chemistry, geography, and geology; and Chicago style, the style recommended by the University of Chicago Press. Chicago style is followed throughout this book. If an instructor asks you to use CSE or Chicago style in a paper, consult the Internet or a published manual for guidelines. No matter which system you use while writing a paper, be consistent, and never mix styles.

Make Revisions and Prepare the Final Copy

Review Chapter 4 for additional information to help you write and revise your paper. It may take several tries, but you will eventually get a version of your paper that you are content to show to other readers. Seek the help of your peer editing group, a tutor, your instructor, or other readers once again, when you have improved your paper as much as possible on your own. When you arrive at this point, you will think your paper is pretty good. However, a new reader will always find ways to improve your paper. This is the time, then, to put aside pride and let others take a final look at what you have written. A fresh set of eyes (and ears) usually adds to the careful refining you are trying to accomplish. During this final revision process, you and your readers can also use the Toulmin model to help you identify and revise the major elements in your paper.

1. Find your claim. Is it clear? Is it well-positioned?

2. Check the quantity and quality of your support. Is there enough? Is it relevant? Is it authoritative and accurate?

3. Check your warrants. Are they likely to be acceptable to your audience?

4. Think about backing for your warrants. Should you explain backing for your warrants to make them stronger and more acceptable to your audience?

5. Focus on your rebuttal, if you have one. Does it effectively address the opposing arguments?

6. Consider a qualifier. Ask yourself, Would a qualified claim make your argument stronger?

As you go through your paper these final times, make all the remaining changes, large and small. If you have not done so, write a meaningful title that reflects the content of your paper; rewrite parts by using more evocative words; cut out anything that does not contribute to the meaning and add text where necessary; rearrange sentences or parts if you have a good reason to do so; read your paper aloud to catch additional problems; and make all final corrections. You will reach a point where you are finally satisfied. Now it is time to prepare the final copy.

Type your paper on standard 8½ by 11 inch paper, and double-space all of it, including the "Works Cited" (MLA) or "References" (APA) pages. See pages 437–445 and 461–468 for further instructions. If you are following MLA style, leave 1-inch margins all around. Type your last name and the page number 1/2 inch from the top of the right-hand corner. Repeat this on all subsequent pages, including the Works Cited list. One inch from the top of the first page, by the left-hand margin, type and double-space your name, your instructor's name, the course name and number, and the date. (Your instructor may ask you to add the type of assignment.) Double-space again, and type the title, centered. Double-space once more, and begin typing your paper. Attach the list of "Works Cited" at the end, beginning on a new page.

If you are following APA style, prepare a title page (if your professor requires it) on which you type a short version of your title and the page number in the top right-hand corner and on all subsequent pages. For example, the author of the paper "Alaskan Wolf Management" uses the short title "Alaskan Wolf" on each page of his paper (page 469). Next, drop down to midpage and type the title, centered. Then double-space and type your name; double-space again and type the name of your school. Begin your paper on the next page with the short title and page number in the top right-hand corner. Then double-space and type the title. Double-space again and begin your paper. Attach the list of "References" at the end, starting on a new page, numbered sequentially.

Spell-check your paper if you are using a computer, and proofread it one last time. Correct all of the errors that you can find. Errors in a research paper damage your *ethos* with your readers. Careless errors communicate that you do not really value your own work or your audience. When your paper is as error-free as you can make it, it is ready for submission.

Present Your Paper Orally to the Class

Your instructor may ask you and your classmates to present the results of your research to the class in the form of oral argument. Like written and visual argument, oral argument possesses special features that make it uniquely effective for presenting arguments. Oral argument has been around much longer than written argument. In earlier chapters you read about Aristotle's *Rhetoric*, which was written twenty-five hundred years ago to train public speakers to be convincing to audiences. Then, as now, people recognized that speakers have certain advantages over writers in presenting effective argument. Here are a few of these advantages.

1. *Oral argument is immediate.* When the speaker and the audience are together in the same physical location, face to face, the potential for effective argument is greatly enhanced. This is true of all forms of oral argument, whether spoken, chanted, or sung. The physical presence of an effective speaker intensifies what is said, and the audience is thus more likely to pay attention and be influenced. Furthermore, a good speaker is always aware of the audience and can adapt both words and delivery to keep listeners' attention and influence them in desired ways. Oral argument delivered through the media, such as television, the Internet, print, radio, or film, usually lacks some of the sense of immediacy and consequent power that the actual presence of the speaker provides, but it can still be very effective.

2. *Oral argument employs physical as well as verbal strategies.* Speakers are able to influence perception in ways that writers cannot. For example, speakers can use physical gestures, vocal inflections, facial expressions, eye contact, physical setting, dress, and physical appearance in effective and dramatic ways to strengthen delivery and make their words more powerfully convincing. Combine these physical attributes with a strong message and a sincere motivation to persuade the audience through direct speech, and the potential for successful and productive argument is usually stronger than in a written essay.

3. *Oral argument is a continuous stream of fleeting content that is sometimes difficult to monitor and evaluate.* A reader of written argument can always stop to reread or turn back to find a previous passage that could illuminate a confusing passage. Listeners do not have this advantage. They have only one chance to understand the speaker. Sometimes, of course, listeners have the opportunity to interrupt and ask the speaker to repeat or clarify what has just been said. This is often not the case, however. As a result, the listener does not have the same opportunity the reader has to accomplish a close evaluation of the speaker's content. Instead, a listener is usually left with a powerful impression of the main argument that the speaker wants to communicate, along with some of the ideas and examples that support that argument. This fact can be an advantage to a speaker who wants to overwhelm and convince the audience. The listener, always hearing the next words, has a diminished opportunity to consciously monitor and critique everything that is said during the speech. Think of evangelists and politicians you have heard who rely on physical setting, their voice, gestures, and appearance, and a stream of content that often includes emotionally loaded language and examples that are crafted to convince you. In many cases such speakers can be more powerfully convincing than writers.

4. *Oral argument usually employs a less formal style than written argument and can be easier to respond to and understand.* When compared with written argument, oral argument usually has fewer main points, more support of all kinds, and more obvious transitions to help the listener move from one idea to another. Oral argument is usually also more repetitious, contains more personal pronouns (*I, you, we, us*), includes direct questions that engage the audience, and contains less perfect sentence structure than written argument. Such informality results in an enhanced rapport and the establishment of more common ground between the speaker and the audience. The informality of spoken argument, when compared with written argument, is often more inviting to an audience and makes it easier for listeners to pay attention, believe the speaker, and become convinced.

Analyze oral argument just as you would written or visual argument. That is, when listening to oral argument, you can recognize and understand the rhetorical situation; analyze the use of *logos, ethos,* and *pathos*; identify and expose fallacies; apply the Toulmin model; and make ethical judgments, just as you would when reading an essay or viewing a visual argument. Apply these methods of analysis when you create oral argument. Exercise B on pages 426–427 explains how to prepare your researched position paper for oral presentation in a class symposium.

Review Questions

1. Name five examples of organizational patterns that you might use in a position paper, describe their main features or rationale, and name the type of claim typically associated with each of them.

2. Name at least one type of proof that would be appropriate for developing each of the five types of claims.

3. What steps can you take to avoid plagiarism when you are incorporating research materials into your draft and when you are preparing the final copy?

4. What is the purpose of the "Works Cited" page (MLA) and the "References" page (APA)?

5. What are some of the special features of oral argument?

Exercises and Activities

A. Writing Assignment: The Researched Position Paper

1. *Write a list, outline, or partial manuscript that will serve as a plan for your paper, and bring it to class.* Refer to the example on pages 416–417 in this chapter. In peer editing groups of three or four students, explain to the group what your paper is about and how you plan to organize and develop it. Suggestions from the others can help with ideas and organization and also with adding research. Decide whether or not to add visual images as support.

2. *Create a class peer critique sheet.* The peer critique sheet provides a guide for critiques and revision. Make a list of all of the special requirements for a researched position paper: a title, a clear claim, adequate support, clear organization, accurate documentation, and so on. Select five to ten items from this list that you believe are essential elements to consider during revision. Organize them on a peer critique sheet. Use these sheets in your peer editing group to critique individual student papers and make good recommendations for revision.

3. *Write a draft of your paper, revise it, and bring it to class.* At this point it is useful to have one or more people read your paper and give you ideas for improving it. Your readers may use the peer critique sheets created in Exercise A2 above, either writing their comments on them or on the papers. This can be accomplished in one of the following ways:

   a. Groups in class: The members of your peer group should first read all of the papers written by your group and make a few notes about each of them on the peer critique sheets or on the papers. As an alternative, the authors can read their papers aloud, with each paper discussed in turn. Members of the group should offer observations and recommendations for improvement to each author, and as the discussion progresses, they may continue to add suggestions to the peer critique sheets, which should be given to the authors at the end of the session.

   b. Individuals outside of class: Exchange papers with a classmate and critique each other's work outside of class. Before the next class period, read the paper you have been assigned carefully and make as many useful suggestions as you can on the paper itself and on the peer critique sheet. When you return to class, talk through your suggestions with the author. Then listen to that individual's ideas for improving your paper.

4. *Make final revisions, and then prepare the final copy.* Your researched position paper should be a length specified by your instructor. It should be

double-spaced and should use a specified number of outside sources. Use MLA or APA format throughout. The student paper on pages 446–455 demonstrates general format, in-text citations, and "Works Cited" requirements for MLA style. The student paper on pages 469–478 does the same for APA style. Notice that in these papers the ideas that control them are the authors' original ideas and opinions and that the quoted and paraphrased material is used to provide support.

5. *Write a one-page Toulmin analysis of your paper.* Submit it with your final paper.

6. *Write a submission letter to your instructor.* Submit a letter to your instructor with your final paper, and in it describe what you like about your paper and what still dissatisfies you. Identify problems or passages on which you would like some feedback.

B. Class Project: Conducting a Class Symposium and Presenting Your Research

Adapt your researched position paper to create a five-minute oral presentation of the research you have completed. Follow these instructions:

1. Work with your written manuscript to change it into an oral report. Underline and number the most important ideas. Since oral argument usually has fewer main ideas than written argument, limit yourself to three to five main ideas so that you can explain them in the time you have.

2. Think about your audience. How much background information about your topic will you have to present or possibly add at the beginning of your speech to help your audience understand it?

3. Remember, also, that your listeners have only one chance to understand the main ideas. Add some obvious transitions to clarify your main ideas and make them stand out. These might include, for example, explaining your main points in your introduction, numbering them as you explain them, and restating and summarizing them at the end of your speech.

4. You will not read your speech, but you will probably want some speaking notes to refer to as you speak. Accomplish this by writing a 250-word abstract of your researched position paper. State the claim, the main points made about it, some of the evidence, and your conclusion. Now go back and underline the points in the abstract that you want to talk about and number these in the margin. While you are speaking, you might need to glance at your abstract from time to time to remind yourself of the next point, and, if you find that you are stuck, you can read a sentence or two. Writing the abstract in sentences will also help you get the phrasing right so that you will speak more fluently.

5. Organize members of your class in groups around the same or related topics. The best group size is five to seven students with a moderator. The moderator will call on the students in your group to present your abstracts of your research papers.

6. Practice your speech and time it. If anything in the speech seems to be unclear or awkward, make revisions. Work with the speech until it fits the time frame of five minutes.

7. Add a visual to your presentation to make it more forceful and memorable. Copy or create single or composite pictures, graphs, or other visuals than can be used to make your claim more convincing. Or, you may want to include visuals in a PowerPoint presentation. Here are the rules for using visuals during an oral presentation: (a) make it large enough for your audience to read easily, and (b) do not put it in front of your audience until you are ready to discuss it.

8. Practice the speech several times until you can give it fluently.

9. When you give your speech, use eye contact and experiment with some gestures. Above all, concentrate on communicating with your audience.

10. Answer questions from the class. Participate in a brief class discussion of the ideas presented by your group.

C. **Analyzing a Student's Researched Position Paper**

An example of a researched position paper, written in MLA style by the same student who wrote the issue proposal on page 31 and the exploratory paper on pages 144–145, appears in the Appendix to Chapter 13 on pages 446–455. Take a few minutes to read this paper along with the labels in the margins. Then work in pairs to answer the questions that follow the paper on page 456. If you have difficulty answering the questions about quotations and in-text page references or the list of "Works Cited," refer to pages 431–445 for help. Report your answers to the questions to the class.

How to Document Sources

Using
MLA Style
and
APA Style

How to Document Sources Using MLA Style

The following material will demonstrate, first, how to use in-text citations to show your readers exactly what material you have included in your paper from outside sources; and, second, how to prepare a final list of sources with publication details at the end of your paper. This list is called either Works Cited, if you are following MLA style, or References, if you are following APA style. In-text citations are structured to make clear to the reader who is to be credited with the words or ideas and where in the Works Cited or References list to find the full documentation of that source. You will have noted that this book utilizes the footnote style preferred by the University of Chicago Press and described in the *Chicago Manual of Style* (15th ed., 2003) to make the same information clear to the reader.

The first section of this appendix discusses MLA documentation. If you need information on APA style, turn to page 457. For additional detail on how to use MLA style, consult the *MLA Style Manual and Guide to Scholarly Publishing* (3rd ed., 2008) or the *MLA Handbook for Writers of Research Papers* (due to publish in a 7th ed., 2009),* both published by the Modern Language Association; for APA style, consult the *Publication Manual of the American Psychological Association* (5th ed., 2001), and the *APA Style Guide to Electronic References* (2007), both published by the American Psychological Association.

The MLA portion of this appendix is itself divided into two sections, as described above: (1) how to cite sources in the body of the text, and (2) how to cite sources in the Works Cited list. If you need information only on how to format sources for the Works Cited page, turn to page 437.

---

*The Modern Language Association has determined to alter some of the standard formats published in 2003. The 2008 changes have been included in this text.

MLA: How to Cite Sources in the Body of the Text

The MLA system of documentation is very simple to learn and understand. The system asks that you show where you originally found a direct quotation or the information for a paraphrase or a summary by inserting a brief parenthetical citation at the end of the borrowed material in your written text. The typical in-text parenthetical citation contains the author's last name and the page number: (Jones 5). However, if you include the author's name in the text, then you do not need to include it in the citation. If you include a book or journal title because no author is available, place the title in italics (for a book) or quotation marks (for an article).

To help you quickly find what you need, use the following list.

1. A direct quotation with the author mentioned in the text—page 432
2. A direct quotation with the author not mentioned in the text—page 432
3. A paraphrase or summary with the author mentioned in the text—page 432
4. A paraphrase or summary with the author not mentioned in the text—page 433
5. Two or more authors—page 433
6. Two books by the same author—page 433
7. A corporate or group author—page 433
8. An unknown author—page 433
9. A work reprinted in a book or journal—pages 433–434
10. Short quotations versus block quotations—page 434
11. Ellipsis points and quoted material—pages 434–435
12. Tables—page 435
13. Graphs, artwork, photographs, and other illustrations—page 435
14. Poetry and song lyrics—page 436
15. Electronic sources—page 436

1. *A direct quotation with the author mentioned in the text* If you introduce the author's name in the body of the text before you quote directly, then there is no need to include the name in the parenthetical citation.

> Although various critics have accused Arnold Schoenberg's musical compositions of being "atonal," Alex Ross points out that the composer was "simply offering a tonality of a less familiar kind" (176).

2. *A direct quotation with the author not mentioned in the text*

> Although various critics have accused Arnold Schoenberg's musical compositions of being "atonal," others argue that the composer was "simply offering a tonality of a less familiar kind" (Ross 176).

3. *A paraphrase or summary with the author mentioned in the text*

> According to Calvin Tomkins, the rebuilding and expansion of the New York Museum of Modern Art proves that modern art has not reached its end (72).

4. *A paraphrase or summary with the author not mentioned in the text*

If the rebuilding and expansion of the New York Museum of Modern Art is any indication, claims that modern art has reached its end may soon be proven wrong (Tomkins 72).

5. *Two or more authors* If two or three authors have written the material you have borrowed, include all of their last names in either the introductory wording or the citation.

Pimentel and Teixeira remind us, "Virtual reality is all about illusion" (7).

"Virtual reality is all about illusion" (Pimentel and Teixeira 7).

For more than three authors, use only the first author's last name and add *et al.* to the citation. (*Et al.* is an abbreviation of the Latin *et alii,* meaning "and others." It is not italicized in your paper.)

"Television is not primarily a medium of entertainment in all societies" (Comstock et al. 25).

6. *Two books by the same author* To indicate which book you are citing, either include the name of the book in the introductory material or add a shortened title to the parenthetical information to differentiate between the books. For example, if you are using *The Second Self: Computers and the Human Spirit* (1984) and *Life on the Screen: Identity in the Age of the Internet* (1995), both by Sherry Turkle, document as follows:

Sherry Turkle says the computer is like a mirror that has a strong psychological hold over her (*Second Self* 306). She explains further that "the computer tantalizes me with its holding power" (*Life* 30).

If the author is not mentioned in the text, include the author's name followed by a comma before the shortened title of the work: (Turkle, *Life* 30).

7. *A corporate or group author* Sometimes written materials are attributed to a corporate or group author (e.g., a corporation, company, association, or organization) rather than to an individual author. In this case, use the name of the corporation or group, preferably in the wording that precedes the quotation.

The RAND Corporation observes that "when the No Child Left Behind Act was passed into law in January 2002, it heralded the beginning of one of the most expansive efforts to reform public education" (7).

If the corporate author is not mentioned in the text, include the corporate author's name as part of the citation before the page number.

(RAND Corporation 7)

8. *An unknown author* When no author is listed for either a book or an article, use the title or the first words of an abbreviated title in your citation.

Article: ("Creativity and Television" 14)

Book: (*World Almanac* 397)

9. *A work reprinted in a book or journal* If you quote an article, poem, story, or any other work that is reprinted not in its original but in another compilation, cite the author you are quoting in the text and the page number. The author or editor of the compilation is not cited in the parenthetical citation, but is fully cited in the Works Cited. Thus a quotation that includes words from both pages of the essay by

Edward O. Wilson on pages 325–326 of this book by Nancy V. Wood would be cited in the text as **(Wilson 325-26)**.* (See page 441, Works Cited example 18.)

10. *Short quotations versus block quotations*   Short quotations do not exceed four lines of text. For short quotations, place quotation marks around the quoted material, insert the citation information in parentheses, and place the period outside it.

> According to Nate Stulman, many college students in his dormitory "routinely stay awake all night chatting with dormmates online. Why walk 10 feet down the hall to have a conversation when you can chat on the computer—even if it takes three times as long?" (268).

Quotations that exceed four lines of text should be blocked. To block a quotation, you should eliminate the quotation marks and indent each line 1 inch (or ten spaces) from the left margin, including the first line if you quote all or part of a single paragraph (that is, do not set a paragraph indent). If you quote two or more full paragraphs, indent the first line of each paragraph an additional ¼ inch (or three spaces), as in the example below. Place the period at the end of the text, followed by the parenthetical citation. Use double-spacing, as you do throughout your paper. It is good writing style to provide a brief introduction to a long quote and to finish the quote with a concluding thought.

> Nate Stulman describes some of the uses of computers by the students at his school that he has observed:
>
> > Several people who live in my hall routinely stay awake all night chatting with dormmates online. Why walk 10 feet down the hall to have a conversation when you can chat on the computer—even if it takes three times as long?
> > You might expect that personal computers in dorm rooms would be used for nonacademic purposes, but the problem is not confined to residence halls. The other day I walked into the library's reference department, and five or six students were grouped around a computer—not conducting research, but playing Tetris. Every time I walk past the library's so-called research computers, it seems that at least half are being used to play games, chat, or surf the Internet aimlessly. (268)
>
> These experiences may be typical of students' computer use at other colleges as well.

11. *Ellipsis points and quoted material*   Occasionally, you will want to delete material from the original source either to make your document shorter or to make the writing that includes the quote more readable. If you do so, indicate by inserting ellipsis points to signal that you have removed words. The following example shows how to use ellipsis points to indicate you have omitted words in the middle of a sentence. (Other information on ellipsis points can be found in Chapter 12, page 395).

> "If there were a wider appreciation for motherhood in society, women might . . . hold their heads high when going to the boss and asking for a reduced hour work schedule" (Hewlett 308).

When deleting the ending of a sentence in a short quotation, indicate that deletion by using three spaced points and a fourth after the parenthetical citation. The fourth point serves as the period to the sentence.

> "A weakness of mass entertainment is its impersonality . . ." (Jones 226).

---

*Note that inclusive page ranges in MLA style ellide the hundred- or thousand-place numeral for the closing page in the range, as long as it is clear which pages are being cited. For example, 199–203 would not be ellided.

When there is no parenthetical citation (for example, within a large block quotation), then the sentence is completed by placing the period before the ellipsis.

12. *Tables* Place tables as close as possible to the text they explain or illustrate. At the top, place with the word *Table* and assign an arabic numeral. On a new line, give it a caption capitalized headline style. Provide source information immediately below the table. Notes, if any, follow, numbered with lowercase letters (*a, b, c,* etc.). Double-space throughout (for a small table) and align as shown. Indent the second or more lines in the caption and source line two spaces; indent the first line of notes five spaces.

Table 1

Travel and Entertainment Cost Savings Using Electrovision

Source of Savings	Amount Saved per Year[a]
Switching from first-class to coach airfare	$2,300,000
Negotiating preferred hotel rates	940,000
Negotiating preferred rental car rates	460,000
Systematically searching for lower airfares	375,000
Reducing interdivisional travel	675,000
Reducing seminar and conference attendance	1,250,000
Total Potential Savings	$6,000,000

Source: Courtland L. Bovee and John V. Thill, *Business Communication Today,* 6th ed. (Upper Saddle River: Prentice, 2000) 539. Print.
[a]In U.S. dollars.

13. *Graphs, artwork, photographs, and other illustrations* Graphs, artwork, photographs, and other illustrations are labeled Fig., the abbreviation for *Figure,* followed by an arabic numeral; the caption (see format below) is followed on the same line by any source material. This is an example created in a word processing program.

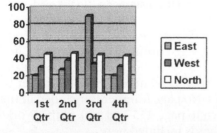

Fig. 1. Quarterly earnings according to region.

14. *Poetry and song lyrics* Quote three lines or less of poetry in your text by using quotation marks and a slash with spaces on each side [/] to separate the lines. The parenthetical citation should contain the line numbers.

> As "Gacela of the Dead Child" shows, Lorca's goal was to express the character of *duende:* "The dead wear mossy wings. / The cloudy wind and the clear wind / are two pheasants in flight through the towers," (5-7).

For more than three lines, indent the quotation 1 inch (or ten spaces) from the left margin.

> In fact, *duende* invades much of Lorca's work:
>
> > Death goes in
> > and death goes out
> > of the tavern
> > Black horses
> > and sinister people
> > roam the hidden trails
> > of the guitar. (1-7)

15. *Electronic sources* Cite electronic sources in the text just as you would print sources. Introduce the quotation with the author's name, or cite the author's last name (or a short title, if there is no author) with a page or paragraph number in parentheses at the end. If the source has no page or paragraph numbers or if you are citing or quoting from the whole source as a single document, place only the author's name in the parentheses. Here is an example of a quotation from an online journal that numbers paragraphs.

> "Rose represents the unnamed multitude of women who were placed in the same circumstances but whose stories were never told" (Mason, par. 8).

If you use the author's name in the body of the text introducing the quotation, then place only the paragraph number in the citation.

> According to Mason, "Rose represents the unnamed multitude of women who were placed in the same circumstances but whose stories were never told" (par. 8).

Some online sources do not provide page or paragraph numbers. There are two ways to cite such sources. If you place the author's name in the text, there is no parenthetical citation at the end.

> Carlos Oliveira phrases the question about media and reality this way: "Take, for instance, the alteration of our reality through the mass media. Do the media create reality? Or do they alter or destroy it?"

If you do not mention the author in the text, place only the author's name in the citation.

> "Take, for instance, the alteration of our reality through the mass media. Do the media create reality? Or do they alter or destroy it?" (Oliveira).

Also, some online sources are a single page, which may or may not be numbered. When your source is a single page, include any page number in the Works Cited entry but use the no-page-number model in your text. For example, look at the quotation from Rachel Sa in paragraph 15 of the MLA student research paper titled "The Big Barbie Controversy" on page 453. No page number is included in the text since this is a single-page source. Now turn to page 455 and look at the Works Cited entry for Sa. Notice that the page number is included here.

MLA: How to Cite Sources in the Works Cited Page

Attach to the draft a list of all the works you have quoted, paraphrased, or summarized in your paper along with full publication information for each source. This list is titled Works Cited, and it begins on a new page, which is numbered consecutively. It is alphabetized according to the last names of the authors or, if no author is listed, by the title of the works, ignoring any initial *A, An,* or *The*. Note: *All the information on the list should be double-spaced, just like the rest of your final paper.*

Look at the Works Cited page at the end of the MLA-style student paper appearing on pages 454–455. Include on any works cited list only those works actually cited or borrowed from in your paper. The easiest way to prepare this list for your paper is to alphabetize your bibliography cards or notes, in the manner just explained. If you have prepared an annotated bibliography, simply eliminate the annotations to create the Works Cited list. Start each citation at the left margin and indent each successive line ½ inch (or five spaces; this is called a hanging indent). Note: Use day, month (abbreviated), year order for dates.

The Internet has increased not only personal access to printed source material but also proliferated the number and type of published forms or mediums available as credible source material. A writer's ethical responsibility in documenting sources requires that the audience be able to locate and examine the cited sources readily. Accordingly, the Modern Language Association now requires that the medium of publication be clearly documented in all citations in MLA style. That is, all mediums or vehicles or forms of publication will be identified as a standard element of citation. Here is a list of mediums, which will usually appear at the end of an entry, followed by a period.

Print.	Web.	CD.
CD-ROM.	DVD.	DVD-ROM.
Radio.	Television.	Performance.
Audiocassette.	LP.	Film.
Videocassette.	Laser disc.	Address.
MS.	E-mail.	Microform.
Microsoft Word file.	MP3 file.	Digital file.

Examine the basic formats provided next, and then locate and use the many specific examples for documenting sources in specific mediums that follow in this section on MLA style.

Basic Format for Books, Articles, and Electronic Sources

Books

Author. *Title of Book*. City: Publisher Name in Shortened Form, year of publication. Medium of publication.

Articles in newspapers

Author. "Title of Article." *Name of Newspaper* date of publication, edition, if relevant: page numbers. Medium.

Articles in magazines

Author. "Title of Article." *Name of Magazine* date of publication: page numbers. Medium.

Articles in scholarly journals

Author. "Title of Article." *Name of Journal* volume number.issue number, if available (year of publication): page numbers. Medium.

Documents from the Internet that can be located by author and title search

Author. "Title."/*Title*. Print publication information. *Site*. Web. Access date.

or

Author. "Title."/*Title Database/Site.* Sponsor/Owner/Publisher, Publication date or latest update. Web. Access date.

Documents from the Internet that require a URL to be located

Author. "Title"/*Title Database*. Print publication date. *Site.* Sponsor, publication date or latest update. Web. Access date. <URL>.*

*Note: If you can find an Internet site easily by entering the author and title into a search engine, like *Google* or *Firefox*, omit the Web address or URL (for uniform resource locator). Add the URL when a site or document would be difficult to locate without it.

Documents from online scholarly articles located through library subscription services

Author. "Title of Article." [Follow the basic model for either a Newspaper, Magazine, or Journal article]. *Database Name*. Medium. Access date.

Note that in book titles, article titles, names of periodicals, names of Web sites, and other titles of works or publications, MLA capitalizes all important words, headline style. Also note that article, short story, and poem titles are placed within quotation marks, whereas titles of books, newspapers, journals, magazines, Web sites, databases, software, and so forth are italicized. For electronic sources, print publication information (when it exists) is listed first, followed by the electronic publication information, medium of publication, date of access, and uniform resource locator (URL) in angle brackets (included only when it is needed to access that specific source). A period ends the entry. Eliminate the volume number, issue number, and parentheses around the date when citing newspaper or magazine articles.

Examples of many of the types of sources most commonly cited for argument papers are provided on the next several pages. Consult the following list to quickly find the formats you need.

How to List Print Books

How to List Print Articles

How to List Electronic Sources

How to List Other Nonprint Sources

How to List Print Books

1. *A book by one author*

Melvern, Linda. *Conspiracy to Murder: The Rwandan Genocide.* London: Verso, 2004. Print.

2. *A book by two or three authors*

Chayes, Antonia H., and Martha Minow. *Imagine Coexistence: Restoring Humanity after Violent Ethnic Conflict.* San Francisco: Jossey, 2003. Print.

3. *A book by more than three authors*

Stewart, Charles J., et al. *Persuasion and Social Movements.* 3rd ed. Prospect Heights: Waveland, 1994. Print.

4. *Two or more books by the same author* As demonstrated in the first entry of this example, an initial *The* (or *A* or *An*) is disregarded in the alphabetized titles. Replace the author's name after the first entry with three hyphens followed by a period. Shorten the words *University* and *Press* as U and P in the publisher information; note other standard abbreviations in various entries.

Shaviro, Steven. *The Cinematic Body.* Minneapolis: U of Minnesota P, 1993. Print.

---. *Connected, Or, What It Means to Live in the Networked Society.* Minneapolis: U of Minnesota P, 2003. Print.

5. *A book by a corporate or group author*

Harvard Business School Press. *The Results-Driven Manager: Winning Negotiations That Preserve Relationships: A Time-Saving Guide.* Boston: Harvard Business School P, 2004. Print.

6. *A book with no author named*

The World Almanac and Book of Facts. New York: World Almanac, 2007. Print.

7. *A republished book*

Locke, John. *An Essay Concerning Human Understanding.* 1690. New York: Dover, 1959. Print.

8. *A translation*

Virilio, Paul. *Ground Zero.* Trans. Chris Turner. London: Verso, 2002. Print.

9. *A second or subsequent edition*

Wood, Nancy V. *Perspectives on Argument.* 6th ed. Upper Saddle River: Prentice, 2009. Print.

10. *Proceedings from a conference or symposium*

Medhurst, Martin J., and H. W. Brands, eds. *Presidential Rhetoric: Critical Reflections on the Cold War Linking Rhetoric and History.* Texas A&M Conf. on Presidential Rhetoric, 5-8 Mar. 1998. College Station: Texas A&M UP, 2000. Print.

11. *An introduction, preface, foreword, or afterword*

Rajchman, John. Introduction. *Pure Immanence.* By Gilles Deleuze. Trans. Anne Boyman. New York: Zone, 2001. 7-23. Print.

12. *A government document*

United States. FBI. Dept. of Justice. *National Instant Criminal Background Check System.* Washington: GPO, 2004. Print.

How to List Print Articles

Include all the page numbers of the article. Use a plus sign when the pages are not consecutive; otherwise, cite the range of inclusive pages. Elide the first digit of the ending page above 99 (e.g., *122–25*), but only when elliding a digit will not cause confusion (see examples 20 and 40).

13. *An article from a magazine*

Tomkins, Calvin. "The Modernist." *New Yorker* 5 Nov. 2001: 72-83. Print.

14. *An article from a newspaper*

Rutenberg, Jim, and Micheline Maynard. "TV News That Looks Local, Even If It's Not." *New York Times* 2 June 2003: C1+. Print.

15. *An article in a periodical with no author listed*

"Metamorphosis." *New Yorker* 5 Nov. 2001: 10. Print.

16. *An article in a journal*

Mountford, Roxanne. "The Rhetoric of Disaster and the Imperative of Writing." *Rhetoric Society Quarterly* 31.1 (2001): 41-48. Print.

17. *An edited collection of articles or an anthology*

Handa, Carolyn, ed. *Visual Rhetoric in a Digital World.* Boston: Bedford, 2004. Print.

18. *An article in an edited collection or an anthology*

Stroupe, Craig. "Visualizing English: Recognizing the Hybrid Literacy of Visual and Verbal Authorship on the Web." *Visual Rhetoric in a Digital World.* Ed. Carolyn Handa. Boston: Bedford, 2004. 13-37. Print.

19. *A cross-reference to an edited collection or an anthology* To avoid duplicating information when citing more than one source from a collection or anthology, set up a cross-reference in the Works Cited list. Cite the whole anthology or collection as you would any source. For the entire collection, the editor is the author.

Handa, Carolyn, ed. *Visual Rhetoric in a Digital World.* Boston: Bedford, 2004. Print.

Cite each article from the anthology that you have used but instead of duplicating the anthology's full publication information, include the last name of the editor of the collection and pertinent page numbers only. Alphabetize each entry in this case by the cited article author's last name.

> Stroupe, Craig. "Visualizing English: Recognizing the Hybrid Literacy of Visual and Verbal Authorship on the Web." Handa 13-37.

20. *A reprinted article in an edited volume or collection* The following shows a chapter from Gunther Kress's book *Literacy in the New Media Age* reprinted in the collection by Handa.

> Kress, Gunther. "Multimodality, Multimedia, and Genre." *Literacy in the New Media Age.* London: Routledge, 2003.106–21. Rpt. in *Visual Rhetoric in a Digital World.* Ed. Carolyn Handa. Boston: Bedford, 2004. 38-54. Print.

21. *A signed article in a reference work* Omit page numbers for reference works that arrange entries alphabetically.

> Davidson, W. S., II. "Crime." *Encyclopedia of Psychology.* Ed. Raymond J. Corsini. 4 vols. New York: Wiley, 1984. Print.

22. *An unsigned article in a reference work*

> "Quindlen, Anna." *Current Biography Yearbook.* Ed. Judith Graham. New York: Wilson, 1993. Print.

23. *A review*

> Ottenhoff, John. "It's Complicated." Rev. of *The Moment of Complexity: Emerging Network Culture,* by Mark C. Taylor. *Christian Century* 119.21(2002): 56-59. Print.

24. *A letter to the editor*

> Cooper, Martin. Letter. *Business Week* 17 May 2004: 18. Print.

25. *An editorial*

> "Consider Cloning Source of Organs." Editorial. *USA Today* 22 Oct. 2003: 19A. Print.

26. *A published interview*

> Rice, Condoleeza. Interview by Nathan Gardels. *New Perspectives Quarterly* 18.1 (2001): 35-38. Print.

27. *A personal interview*

> Wick, Audrey. Personal interview. 27 Dec. 2008.

28. *A lecture, speech, or address*

> King, Martin Luther, Jr. "I Have a Dream." March on Washington. Lincoln Memorial, Washington, DC. 28 Aug. 1963. Address.

How to List Electronic Sources

A helpful rule for electronic sources is to use Web sites that are as unchanging as possible so the reader will be able to access the information at a later date. Sites that are refereed, authoritative, or based on historical texts or that have print counterparts should prove to be stable, at least in the immediate future. Entries for Internet sources consist of six basic divisions: the author's name, title of the document, print publication information (where applicable), electronic publication information, medium, date of access, and URL (required only when it is necessary to lead a reader to the source directly).

29. *A document from an Internet site* List print publication information, if any, first. If none is available, list only the electronic publication information: author's name, document title or short selection (in quotes), Internet site name or title (italicized), sponsor or host (if applicable), date of electronic publication or last update (if available), medium (Web.), and date of access, ended by a period. Add a URL (in angle brackets) if a Google search does not lead to the article, as in this example. This is an online source with no print version. The journal is archived, and this specific article can be located by using the Search box on the journal's home page, as shown here, or the URL for the document page, as in example 43. (In MLA style, break a URL *only* after a slash.)

McPhaul, Kathleen M., and Jane A. Lipscomb. "Workplace Violence in Health Care: Recognized but Not Regulated." *Online Journal of Issues in Nursing* 9.3 (2004). American Nurses Association, 2008. Web. 20 June 2008. <http://www.nursingworld.org/MainMenuCategories/ANAMarketplace/ANAPeriodicals/OJIN.aspx>. Search path: McPhaul and Lipscomb.

30. *A digital file* A digital file is a document created electronically, either on a computer using a software program or on some other digital producer—a camera, sound equipment, and so on. Digital files can be uploaded to the Internet, where they can be researched on a search engine, or they can exist and be exchanged and utilized independently from it. To cite such a document, identify its form or type (a book, recorded music, a manuscript, etc.) and follow the citation model for that kind of document. The file format, for example, *PDF, XML, MP3,* or *JPEG,* is the medium of publication. When the format is not known, use *Digital file.* (The file format or medium is not italicized unless a software name is part of its name, as in *Microsoft Word.*) If the file has versions, name the version or identify the one cited as shown in the example.

Norman. Don. "Attractive Things Work Better." *Emotional Design*, Ch. 1. File last modified 24 Feb. 2003. PDF file. 22 Aug. 2008.

31. *An entire Internet site* Include the site name (its title) italicized, name of the editor (if available), name of any sponsoring organization, date of electronic publication, date of access.

CNN.com. Cable News Network, 2008. Web. 24 May 2008.

32. *A home page for a course* Include the instructor's name, the course title, the label *Course home page,* dates or semester of the course, names of the department and the institution, date of access, and the URL.

Stern, David. Heidegger. Course home page. Fall 2000. Dept. of Philosophy, U of Iowa. Web. 15 June 2008. <http://www.uiowa.edu/~c026036/>.

33. *A personal home page* Include the owner's name, title of the site (if available), the label *Home page,* date of the last update (if available), and an access date. Add the URL only if a name search does not lead directly to the page.

Blakesley, David. Home page. 18 Sept. 2003. Web. 22 Nov. 2008.

34. *An online book* Include the author, title of the book (italicized), print publication information (if available), title of the Web site (italicized), date of electronic publication, medium of publication, and date of access. The following is an example of an online book that is out of print.

443

Mussey, R. D. *An Essay on the Influence of Tobacco Upon Life and Health.* Boston: Perkins and Marvin, 1836. *Project Gutenberg.* Project Gutenberg Online Book Catalog, 2006. Web. 31 Mar. 2008.

35. *A part of an online book*

Mussey, R. D. "Cases Illustrative of the Effects of Tobacco." *An Essay on the Influence of Tobacco Upon Life and Health.* Boston: Perkins and Marvin, 1836. *Project Gutenberg.* Project Gutenberg Online Book Catalog, 2006. Web. 31 Mar. 2008.

36. *An article in an online newspaper* Include the author, title of the article, name of the newspaper, date of publication, page or paragraph numbers (if available), medium of publication, and date of access.

Webb, Cynthia L. "The Penguin That Ate Microsoft." *Washington Post.* Washington Post, 27 May 2004. Web. 28 May 2008.

37. *An article in an online magazine*

Reiss, Spencer. "The Wired 40." *Wired* July 2006. CondéNet, 2008. Web. 6 Aug. 2008.

38. *An article in an online scholarly journal* If the article is included within a database, state the name of the database (italicized) after the print publication information.

Wishart, Jocelyn. "Academic Orientation and Parental Involvement in Education during High School." *Sociology of Education* 74.3 (2001): 210–30. *JSTOR.* Web. 27 Oct. 2008.

39. *A review*

Gray, Donna. Rev. of *Psychic Navigator,* by John Holland. *BookReview.com.* 18 Oct. 2004. Web. 20 Oct. 2008.

40. *A publication on a CD-ROM or DVD-ROM* Cite as you would a book or a work in a book, and add the label *CD-ROM* or *DVD-ROM* after the publication information. The CD-ROM is the medium of publication.

Leston, Robert. "Drops of Cruelty: Controlling the Mechanisms of Rhetorical History." *Proceedings of the Southwest/Texas Popular and American Culture Associations: Years 2000–2003.* Ed. Leslie Fife. Emporia: SW/TX PCA/ACA P, 2003. 681–91. CD-ROM.

41. *A work from a library subscription service* In addition to the print information, you should include the name of the database (italicized), the name of the service, medium, and the date of access. Omit the URL assigned by the service to the article itself.

Goldwasser, Joan. "Watch Your Balance." *Kiplinger's Personal Finance* 58.3 (2004): 96. *LexisNexis Academic.* LexisNexis. Web. 22 June 2008.

42. *A television or radio program* If you are citing the transcript of a program instead of the program itself, at the end of the entry write *Print. Transcript.* (not italicized).

Rehm, Diane. *The Diane Rehm Show.* With E. L. Doctorow. American University Radio, 24 May 2004. Web. 12 June 2008.

43. *An advertisement* Cite the product's name or company name, followed by the label *Advertisement.*

Lanvin. Advertisement. *Haut Fashion.* Web. 17 June 2008. <http://www.hautfashion.com/fashion-ads/lanvin-spring-summer-2008-ad-campaign>.

For advertisements found in a print source, include the print publication information and eliminate the electronic publication information.

44. *A cartoon or comic strip* Include the creator's name and the title, followed by the label *Comic strip* and the publication and/or electronic access information.

> Adams, Scott. "Dilbert." Comic strip. *Dilbert.com.* United Feature Syn., 27 Sept. 2004. Web. 20 Oct. 2008 <http://www.dilbert.com/> Search path: 27 Sept. 2004.

For cartoons or comic strips found in a print source, include the print publication information and eliminate the electronic publication information. (Typically, a print archive is a more secure resource.)

How to List Other Nonprint Sources

If the sources in this section are accessed online, add the medium of publication, date of access, and the URL to the entry, if needed. See model 30 for a digital file.

45. *An audio recording* Include the name of the performer (or conductor or composer), the title of the recording, the manufacturer, and the date. Song titles appear in quotation marks; album titles are italicized.

> James, Bob. *Dancing on the Water.* Warner Bros., 2001. Audiocassette.

46. *A film or video recording* Begin with the title, list the director, distributor, and year of release. However, if you are citing a particular individual contributor, first, begin with the person's name, followed by their title or functions: Capra, Frank, dir. or Chaplin, Charles, perf.

> *Rabbit-Proof Fence.* Dir. Phillip Noyce. Miramax, 2002. Film.

47. *A videotape or DVD* Insert the type of publication medium at the end of the entry.

> *Composition.* Prod. ABC/Prentice Hall Video Library. Prentice, 1993. Videocassette.

48. *A painting, sculpture, or photograph* Cite the artist's name, the title of the work, the date of creation (optional), and the name and city of either the institution that houses the work or the individual who owns it.

> Klee, Paul. *Red Balloon.* 1922. Guggenheim Museum, New York. Visual artwork.

49. *A map or chart* Include the title of the map or chart, the label *Map* or *Chart,* and the publication information.

> *Oregon.* Map. Chicago: Rand, 2000. Print.

For an online map or chart, include the title (in quotation marks), the label *Map* or *Chart,* name of the reference source (italicized), sponsoring organization, date of publication or update, medium, date of access, and the URL, if needed.

> "New York City Transit." Map. *Mta.info.* Metropolitan Transportation Authority. Web. 3 July 2007.

50. *A e-mail message* Here the medium of publication is *E-mail.* The title is the subject line enclosed in quotation marks.

> Harris, Omar. "Re: Artist Statement." Message to [Your Name]. 25 Apr. 2008. E-mail.

AUTHOR'S LAST NAME ⟶ Virasin 1

1/2 INCH

1 INCH

DOUBLE-SPACE

PAGE NUMBER

Prisna Virasin

Researched Position Paper

Professor Wood

English 1302

19 April 2008

The Big Barbie Controversy

DOUBLE-SPACE

1   As a twenty-something female who grew up in America, I am very

interested in the Barbie debate. I played with Barbie dolls almost

Author establishes ethos in first three paragraphs

obsessively from first to third grade. I designed clothes for them out of

handkerchiefs and tissues and dreamed about becoming a fashion

designer. I remember envying the girls who had Barbie Ferraris and dream

1 INCH

houses. I looked on in horror as my little sister cut her Barbie's hair short

1 INCH

and colored it hot pink with a marker.

2   I would later learn, as a first-year student in a small, liberal arts

college, that by turning Barbie into a punk rocker, my sister was actually

Summaries of positions in exploratory paper in paragraphs 2 and 3

"queering Barbie" or using the doll in a way unintended by Mattel (the

makers of Barbie). I was proud of my sister for this creative venture

because this was around the time I was introduced to feminism. Through

the lens of feminism, the horror I felt by watching my sister destroy

Barbie transformed into a reverence for my little sister. At the age of five,

she acted on her instinct to deconstruct Barbie, and I could not see her

Personal narrative

political defiance for what it was until I was nearly twenty. In my women's

studies classes, I tried to deny any past connection to Barbie. I was

ashamed to have ever associated with this figure. I felt duped by Barbie. I

thought that she had tricked me into wanting to be seven feet tall with

1 INCH

(continued)

long blond hair and a body that wouldn't quit. I felt sorry for the girls who looked like walking Barbie dolls, always worried about looking perfect. It was obvious that they were still under "the Barbie spell."

3   Now, as a returning student, with a few years of working "in the real world" behind me, I'm not sure whether my feminist instinct to hate Barbie is lying dormant or whether it has been replaced by common sense. I have seen little girls playing with Barbies, and I do not have the urge to snatch the dolls out of their hands. However, I still feel a twinge of guilt because a part of my mind continues to wonder if Barbie or the image of Barbie is doing irreparable damage to the self-image of children everywhere.

4   There are many people who say that Barbie is "just a doll." These people believe that the Barbie debate is a "FemiNazi" creation to breed fear in the hearts of parents. These skeptics in the Barbie debate view Barbie as a toy, stating that she does not have power or influence over little girls or grown women. If Barbie is just a doll, then the Barbie debate is indeed without foundation. In reviewing Barbie's history, I found that she was created to make a difference in girls' lives and has succeeded in becoming a very marketable product.

5   The Barbie doll was created in 1959 by Ruth Handler, the cofounder of Mattel. Handler created the doll after seeing her daughter, whose nickname was Barbie, and her daughter's friends play with their paper dolls. According to Gaby Wood and Frances Stonor Saunders, Handler realized that little girls wanted a doll "they could aspire to be like, not aspire to look after" (38). This was a revolutionary idea because before

Focus on issue

Transition to Barbie's history

Quotation: authors identified in text

1 INCH · 1/2 INCH · 1 INCH · 1 INCH · 1 INCH

(continued)

1 INCH

1/2 INCH

Virasin 3

the creation of Barbie, the toy store doll selection mainly consisted of baby dolls, which encouraged little girls to pretend to be mothers. Ruth Handler states that Barbie "has always represented the fact that a woman has choices" (39). In 1959, Mattel sold 350,000 Barbie dolls. In 2004, according to the "Barbie Dolls" discussion on the History Channel Web site, "ninety percent of all American girls in the last forty years have owned at least one Barbie." This Web site provides additional evidence of Barbie's continued popularity: "If every Barbie doll ever manufactured were laid end-to-end, they would circle the earth three-and-one-half times." The Barbie doll and other Barbie products average sales of 1.9 billion dollars a year.

Online source mentioned in text; no page number available

1 INCH

6   Barbie is also marketed internationally, in more than 140 countries. Stephanie Deutsch, who has written a book about collecting Barbie dolls and who is a collector herself, says, "It is fascinating to see how Barbie dolls from other countries reflect the ideals of foreign societies," and she goes on to describe the "wild and sexy" dolls of Brazil, and the Barbie dolls strapped to candles for little girls in Greece to carry in religious processions (5). In 1968, Barbie dolls were first provided with the mechanism to talk. Besides English, some Barbie dolls spoke Spanish, and others spoke French, German, or Japanese. One of Barbie's friends spoke with a British accent (34).

1 INCH

7   I believe that Barbie's influence lies in her pervasiveness. She is everywhere, and therefore she is on the minds of many people. I don't think that Barbie is "just a doll." With the overarching product placement, marketing force, and popularity of the Barbie doll, she is undeniably a powerful icon of American society.

Transition to why Barbie's good

1 INCH

(continued)

1 INCH   1/2 INCH

Virasin 4

8   Avid Barbie fans span many different age groups. There are three-to six-year-olds who play with Barbie dolls, wear Barbie brand clothes, and sleep on Barbie brand beds with matching sheet sets. Barbie doll collectors have met for over twenty years to celebrate all things Barbie. Special collection Barbies are auctioned for thousands of dollars. Supporters of Barbie state that, apart from being a national icon, Barbie is just a fun part of growing up. They refer to the simple fun of playing with Barbie dolls. They believe that Barbie is a tool in building

Fig. 1 *A President 2000 Barbie.*
Source: Carlos Osorio/ AP Wide World Photos. Web.

girls' imaginations. They also maintain that Barbie is a positive role model because she is able to do almost anything. Barbie was an astronaut before the first woman went into space. Barbie is a veterinarian, a doctor, a businesswoman, and to top it all off, a presidential candidate. Figure 1 shows the Barbie that was dressed to run for President of the United States in 2000. Included in the package are a blue campaign suit, a red

ball gown, campaign material, and an Internet Web site. In her article about growing up with Barbie, Patricia O'Connell reminisces:

> What always facinated me about Barbie was that she could be—and was—anything I wanted her to be. By extension, I felt the same was true for me. That's the real magic of Barbie. Deciding which career she ought to pursue on any given day fired my imagination far more than pushing a baby-size doll around in a carriage ever did.

Criteria for goodness

Appeals to motives and values

1 INCH

1 INCH

449

Quote longer than four lines

1 INCH

(continued)

1/2 INCH

1 INCH

Virasin 5

9   Handler's creation of Barbie as a challenge to the idea that the proper role

for a woman was that of a mother has become ironic in light of feminist

protests against the Barbie doll. Barbie protesters have stated

that Barbie is responsible for the development of poor body image in girls.

They believe that Barbie's proportions create impossible images of beauty

toward which girls will strive. If Barbie were human, she would be seven feet

tall with a thirty-nine-inch chest measurement, twenty-two inch waist

measurement, and thirty-three inch hip measurement ("History of Toys"). The

Barbie protesters also believe that the poor body image resulting from playing

with Barbie could lead to eating disorders such as anorexia and bulimia.

10   In addition to protests of Barbie's physical appearance, there is also the

issue of Barbie's intellectual image. Barbie detractors have criticized the Barbie

lifestyle, which seems to center around clothes, cars, dream homes, and other

material possessions. According to Jacqueline Reid-Walsh and Claudia Mitchell,

the feminist leader Betty Friedan believed that "Barbie was a product of

consumerism who spent all her time shopping, a model for women who are

defined by their relationships with men rather than their accomplishments as

people" (184). Protests followed the release of the talking Barbie, which was

enabled with such expressions as "Math is hard" and "Let's go shopping."

Parents feared that the first sentence would reinforce the stereotype that girls

were less skilled at math than boys. The second sentence seemed to reinforce

the importance of clothes, physical appearance, and material goods. Writing

for the Barbieology Web site, Ophira Edut criticizes educational materials

based on Barbie for the image they reinforce. Edut states that the Barbie

computer is bundled with typing tutor software, while the boy's Hot Wheels

Transition to why
Barbie's bad

Criteria for
badness

Two authors
quoting another
author

Appeals to values

1 INCH

1 INCH

1 INCH

450

(continued)

½ INCH

1 INCH

Virasin 6

(a kind of tricycle) computer is bundled with adventure games. Also, the Barbie Rapunzel CD-ROM is touted by Mattel to expose girls to fine art and creativity, when the only creative function of the program is the option of changing Barbie's clothes and hairstyle interactively on the computer screen.

11   Some people have questioned whether or not Barbie is a suitable American icon. They challenge Barbie's ability to represent the all-American woman positively. In 2004, Mattel announced the release of a new California Barbie doll that would more accurately reflect the times ("It's Splittsville"). This Barbie has broken up with Ken, who is now "just a friend," and has taken up with Blaine, an Australian surfer. California Barbie uses modern "instant messaging to stay connected to her game. Her ears can be pierced. Her car has a working CD player" (Verdon 18A). Still, a television advertisement following the release of the Cali Girl

1 INCH

Barbie shows she has not changed that much from the old Barbie. In this ad, Barbie says she is "born to shop," and she can "never have too much stuff" or "too many friends."

12   According to Seth M. Siegel, the government of Iran has banned Barbie, and police officers are confiscating Barbie dolls from toy stores all over that country. The Iranian government believes that Barbie is "un-Islamic" because of the way she represents Western immorality. She dresses provocatively and has a close relationship with a man who is not her husband. For many Iranians, Barbie has become a

Fig. 2 *Jenna Debryn shows off her Razanne doll, a modest Muslim alternative to Barbie.*
Source: Reed Saxon/ AP Wide World Photos. Web.

Summary of an article

1 INCH

(continued)

451

symbol of American women in a very negative sense (22–24). As an alternative, little Muslim girls are encouraged to play with the Razanne doll that better reflects Muslim culture and values. Figure 2 provides a picture of a Muslim girl, who lives in the United States, and her Razanne doll.

13   Does the Barbie debate boil down to whether Barbie is good or bad? I believe that if she has the power to convey all of the positivity that Barbie fans believe she embodies, then the same power can be used to contaminate the world with all of the negativity that the Barbie protesters warn us against. She is a pervasive image in American society, but that does not necessarily mean that we have to label her as either good or bad. As a feminist, I am willing to concede that women are neither all good nor all bad. As a female image, Barbie plays the dual role quite well. We can make Barbie into whatever we want. She can be an astronaut or a punk rocker or a punk-rock astronaut. I believe that Barbie supporters have made her into a goddess, while Barbie protesters have turned her into a demon. In both cases, I believe she has become a scapegoat.

14   In addressing the issue that Barbie causes poor body image that could lead to eating disorders, the obvious statement that I can make is that eating disorders were around long before Barbie was created. Also, because of Barbie's immense popularity, if the doll truly caused eating disorders, eating disorders would have reached epidemic proportions. In actuality, only about five percent of women suffer from eating disorders. Barbie supporters also ask why male action dolls are not protested against when they have similar unattainable proportions.

Transition to refutation

Refutation of those who say Barbie's all bad

(continued)

452

1/2 INCH

1 INCH

Virasin 8

15   By banning Barbie, we will not be solving the problem of poor body

image. Also, Barbie's image is so pervasive that it would be almost

No need to cite a page number for a one-page source

impossible to shelter children from her. In a satirical editorial by Rachel Sa,

she muses on the absurdity of sheltering children from all things Barbie:

"Maybe the safest thing is to just keep your little girls in their bedrooms.

Yes! Just keep them shut away until all of that icky stuff disappears or

until they grow up—surely by then they will have figured out how to deal

with it all on their own."

16   If one were to believe the argument made by Barbie supporters that

1 INCH

Barbie creates positive self-image in girls, and combine this belief with

Refutation of those who say Barbie's all good

the fact that Barbie is very pervasive in the United States, it should follow

that American females who have played with Barbie would have nearly

1 INCH

eradicated any thoughts of negative self-image. Theoretically then, at

least ninety percent of American women would have conquered self-

critical thoughts about their physical or intellectual state as a result of

their contact with Barbie. However, women know that these self-critical

thoughts are a part of many women's daily lives, and even the most

ardent Barbie fanatic has "bad hair days" or "fat days."

17   It is not the responsibility of the Barbie doll to create positive or

The real issue

negative self-images in children. The ability to influence children falls

mainly on the shoulders of all adults in the communities in which these

children live. This includes the global community in which we now find

ourselves living. The issue of self-image should be addressed by all

cultures early on and continuously in children's lives. Only by positively

reinforcing unconditional acceptance of children's physical appearance

1 INCH

(continued)

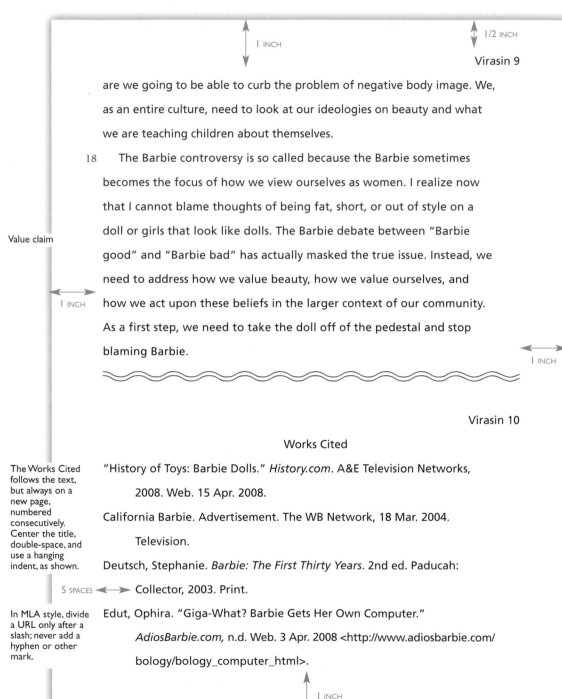

Virasin 9

are we going to be able to curb the problem of negative body image. We, as an entire culture, need to look at our ideologies on beauty and what we are teaching children about themselves.

18   The Barbie controversy is so called because the Barbie sometimes becomes the focus of how we view ourselves as women. I realize now that I cannot blame thoughts of being fat, short, or out of style on a doll or girls that look like dolls. The Barbie debate between "Barbie good" and "Barbie bad" has actually masked the true issue. Instead, we need to address how we value beauty, how we value ourselves, and how we act upon these beliefs in the larger context of our community. As a first step, we need to take the doll off of the pedestal and stop blaming Barbie.

Value claim

1 INCH

1 INCH

Virasin 10

Works Cited

The Works Cited follows the text, but always on a new page, numbered consecutively. Center the title, double-space, and use a hanging indent, as shown.

"History of Toys: Barbie Dolls." *History.com*. A&E Television Networks, 2008. Web. 15 Apr. 2008.

California Barbie. Advertisement. The WB Network, 18 Mar. 2004. Television.

Deutsch, Stephanie. *Barbie: The First Thirty Years*. 2nd ed. Paducah:

5 SPACES Collector, 2003. Print.

In MLA style, divide a URL only after a slash; never add a hyphen or other mark.

Edut, Ophira. "Giga-What? Barbie Gets Her Own Computer." *AdiosBarbie.com*, n.d. Web. 3 Apr. 2008 <http://www.adiosbarbie.com/ bology/bology_computer_html>.

1 INCH

(continued)

Virasin 11

"It's Splitsville for Barbie and Ken." *CNN.com.* 12 Feb. 2004. Web.

15 Apr. 2008.

O'Connell, Patricia. "To Ruth Handler: A 21 Barbie Salute." *BusinessWeek Online*

1 May 2002. *Academic Search Complete.* EBSCO. Web. 11 Apr. 2008.

Reid-Walsh, Jacqueline, and Claudia Mitchell. "Just a Doll? Liberating

Accounts of Barbie-Play." *Review of Education/Pedagogy/Cultural*

Studies 22.2 Aug. 2000: 175-90. *Academic Search Complete.* EBSCO.

Web. 3 Apr. 2008.

Sa, Rachel. "Blame It on Barbie: How Was I Supposed to Know She Was

Warping Our Minds?" *Toronto Sun* 4 May 2002: 15. *LexisNexis.* Reed

Elsevier. Web. 3 Apr. 2008.

Seigel, Seth M. "Sell the West as a Brand." *Brandweek* 10 June 2002: 22-

24. *Academic Search Complete.* EBSCO. Web. 3 Apr. 2008.

Verdon, Joan. "Barbie Says, Bye-Bye Doll." *Fort Worth Star-Telegram* 13

Feb. 2004: 1A+. Print.

Wood, Gaby, and Frances Stonor Saunders. "Dream Doll." *New Statesman* 15

Apr. 2002: 38-40. *Academic Search Complete.* EBSCO.Web. 3 Apr. 2008.

(continued)

Questions on the Researched Position Paper, MLA Style (Pages 446–455)

1. This author could have put her claim at the beginning, end, or somewhere in the middle of her paper. Where did she put it? What is her claim? What type of claim is it? Why do you think she placed it where she did?

2. How does this author use the ideas from her exploratory paper at the beginning of her paper? What is accomplished by this strategy?

3. What are some of the types of proofs and support that this student uses in her paper? Identify some of them. Comment on the images. What do these images accomplish?

4. What warrants does the author expect you to accept?

5. What major ideas does the author refute in this paper?

6. What organizational pattern does the author use to organize some of the major parts of her paper?

7. Identify and underline the transitional sentences. Read some of them aloud in class.

8. Find an example of a quotation that is introduced with the author's or organization's name in the text, followed by a page reference in parentheses.

9. Find an example of two authors who quote another author.

10. Find an example of a quotation that is identified at the end of a sentence by the author and page number because the author is not mentioned in the text.

11. Locate an example of an online quotation that is identified by the title in the text but that has no available page number to place at the end of the quotation.

12. Find an example of a summarized article that is introduced with the author's name and concludes with page references.

13. Find a long quotation and explain how and why it is punctuated as it is.

14. Roughly what percent of this paper is made up of quotations from other people's writings and what percent is the author's own writing?

15. Read the "Works Cited" page and identify the different types of sources this author used.

How to Document Sources Using APA Style

This section is provided as a concise resource for documenting sources in APA style. If you need similar information on MLA style, go to page 431. For additional detail on how to use APA style, consult the *Publication Manual of the American Psychological Association* (5th ed., 2001) and the *APA Style Guide to Electronic References* (2007), both published by the American Psychological Association.

The APA portion of this appendix is itself divided into two sections: (1) how to cite sources in the body of the text, and (2) how to cite sources in the References list. If you need information on how to format sources for the References page, go to pages 461–468.

APA: How to Cite Sources in the Body of the Text

As in MLA style, the APA system of documentation asks that you show where you originally found a direct quotation or the information for a paraphrase or a summary by inserting a brief parenthetical citation at the end of the borrowed material in your written text. The APA system requires that you provide the author's last name, the date of publication, and the page numbers, which are introduced by *p.* or *pp.*: **(Jones, 2003, p. 5)**. If, however, you mention the name of the author in the text, you do not need to repeat the author's name in the parenthetical material.

To help you quickly find what you need, use the following list.

1. A direct quotation with the author mentioned in the text—page 458
2. A direct quotation with the author not mentioned in the text—page 458
3. A paraphrase or summary with the author mentioned in the text—page 458

1. *A direct quotation with the author mentioned in the text* If you introduce the author's name in the body of the text before you quote directly, then there is no need to include the name in the parentheses. Note that the year of publication follows the author's name, while the page number follows the quotation.

> Although various critics have accused Arnold Schoenberg's musical compositions of being "atonal," Alex Ross (2001) points out that the composer was "simply offering a tonality of a less familiar kind" (p. 176).

2. *A direct quotation with the author not mentioned in the text* Note that in this case, the author's last name, year of publication, and page number appear together in parentheses after the quotation.

> Although various critics have accused Arnold Schoenberg's musical compositions of being "atonal," others argue that the composer was "simply offering a tonality of a less familiar kind" (Ross, 2001, p. 176).

3. *A paraphrase or summary with the author mentioned in the text*

> According to Calvin Tomkins (2001), the rebuilding and expansion of the New York Museum of Modern Art proves that modern art has not reached its end (p. 72).

4. *A paraphrase or summary with the author not mentioned in the text*

> If the rebuilding and expansion of the New York Museum of Modern Art is any indication, claims that modern art has reached its end may soon be proven wrong (Tomkins, 2001, p. 72).

5. *Two or more authors* If two authors have written the material you have borrowed, list both of their last names in either the introductory wording or the citation for all references. In APA style, use *and* in your text, but use the & sign inside parentheses and in tables or other context features.

> Pimentel and Teixeira (1993) remind us, "Virtual reality is all about illusion" (p. 7).

> "Virtual reality is all about illusion" (Pimentel & Teixeira, 1993, p. 7).

If a work has three, four, five, or six authors, list all of the authors' last names for the first reference, then use only the first author's last name and the abbreviated term *et al.* (but not italicized) for subsequent references.

458

"Television is not primarily a medium of entertainment in all societies" (Comstock et al., 1978, p. 25).

For more than six authors, use only the first author's last name followed by et al. (an abbreviation for *et alii,* "and others") in all citations.

6. *Two books by the same author* To indicate which book you are citing, use the publication dates to distinguish between the books. For example, if you are using *The Second Self: Computers and the Human Spirit* (1984) and *Life on the Screen: Identity in the Age of the Internet* (1995), both by Sherry Turkle, document as follows:

The computer can have a strong psychological hold over some individuals (Turkle, 1984, p. 306). In fact, the computer can tantalize "with its holding power—in my case, the promise that if I do it right, *it* will do it right, and right away" (Turkle, 1995, p. 30).

7. *A corporate or group author* Sometimes written materials are attributed to a corporate or group author (e.g., a corporation, company, association, or organization) rather than to an individual author. In this case, use the name of the corporation or group, preferably in the wording that precedes the quotation.

The RAND Corporation (2004) observes that "when the No Child Left Behind Act was passed into law in January 2002, it heralded the beginning of one of the most expansive efforts to reform public education" (p. 7).

Otherwise, mention the corporate author in the citation after the quotation.

(RAND Corporation, 2004, p. 7)

8. *An unknown author* When no author is listed for either a book or an article, use the title or the first words of an abbreviated title in your citation.

Article: ("Creativity and Television," 1973, p. 14)

Book: (*World Almanac,* 2003, p. 397)

9. *A work reprinted in a book or journal* If you quote an article, poem, story, or any other work that is reprinted from its original publication, cite the author of the work you are quoting, not the author or editor who reprinted it, but use the date of the reprint. Thus a quotation from the Edward O. Wilson essay on pages 324–325 of this book would be cited as (Wilson, 2008, pp. 325–326). Note that in APA style, no numbers are ellided in page ranges.

10. *Short quotations versus block quotations* Quotations should not be formatted as block quotations unless they exceed forty words. For short quotations, place quotation marks around the quoted material, insert the citation information, and place the period outside of the parentheses.

Author Benjamin Cheever (1999) says he uses his computer to "write and read letters, and if it did not involve the elimination of envelopes and a certain parallel loosening of style, the process would be similar to the one that once involved lambskins and sharpened feathers" (p. 7).

Quotations that exceed forty words are blocked. To block a quotation, you eliminate the quotation marks and indent each line 1/2 inch (or five spaces) from the left margin. Blocked quotations are double-spaced like all of your text.

If you quote two or more paragraphs, indent the first line of the second and each subsequent paragraph an additional 1/2 inch (or five spaces). Place the period at the end of the text, followed by the parenthetical citation. It is good

459

writing style to provide a brief introduction to a long quote and to finish the quote with a concluding thought.

> Author Benjamin Cheever (1999) contrasts his use of the computer with that of individuals who spend a lot of time on the Internet.

> The news bulges with stories about dispensing therapy on the Net, doing business on the Net, trolling for unsuspecting sexual prey on the Net. Not on this computer. Most of what I do on the electronic superhighway is write and read letters, and if it did not involve the elimination of envelopes and a certain parallel loosening of style, the process would be similar to the one that once involved lambskins and sharpened feathers. (p. 7)

> Cheever has essentially substituted his computer and its word processing program for his old typewriter.

11. *Ellipsis points and quoted material* Occasionally, you will want to delete material from the original source either to make your document shorter or more readable. Always indicate that you have removed words by inserting ellipsis points. The following example shows how to use ellipsis points to indicate you have omitted words in the middle of a sentence.

> "If there were a wider appreciation for motherhood in society, women might . . . hold their heads high when going to the boss and asking for a reduced hour work schedule" (Hewlett, 2002, p. 308).

Do not insert ellipsis points at the beginning or ending of a quotation except in the unusual instance that you want to emphasize that it begins or ends in mid-sentence, as in the following example.

> "A weakness of mass entertainment is its impersonality . . ." (Jones, 2002, p. 226).

To indicate an omission between two sentences of a quotation, however, you must use a period followed by three spaced ellipsis points.

12. *Tables* Tables should be placed as closely as possible to the text they explain or illustrate. Label with the word *Table* (not italicized), assign it an arabic numeral, and give it a brief explanatory title, which appears above the table on a

Table 1

Travel and Entertainment Cost Savings Using Electrovision

Source of savings	Amount saved
Switching from first-class to coach airfare	$2,300,000
Negotiating preferred hotel rates	940,000
Negotiating preferred rental car rates	460,000
Systematically searching for lower airfares	375,000
Reducing interdivisional travel	675,000
Reducing seminar and conference attendance	1,250,000
Total potential savings	$6,000,000

Note. From *Business Communication Today* (p. 539), by C. L. Bovee and J. V. Thill, 2000, Upper Saddle River: Prentice Hall.

new line and is italicized. Provide the citation information immediately below the table, labeled with the word *Note* in italics followed by a period. Double-space throughout and align to the left margin. (Note that APA style requires that you use italics, not underlining, when you have access to a computer.)

13. *Graphs, artworks, photographs, and other illustrations* Graphs, artworks, photographs, and other illustrations should be placed close to the text they illustrate. Below each visual, place the label *Figure*, assign a number in sequence, followed by a period, all italicized. A caption (if there is one), formatted sentence style as shown, and then the source information follows on the same line. See page 469 for an example of a visual image used as an illustration in a student paper. The example below was created in a word processing program.

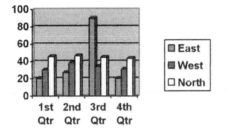

Figure 1. Quarterly earnings according to region.

14. *Electronic sources* If a page number is available in an electronic source, cite as you would a print source. Some electronic journals number paragraphs rather than providing page numbers. If this is the case, then include the author's name, the year, and the page or paragraph number (if available) in parentheses, just as you would for a print source. If paragraph numbers are available, use the symbol ¶ or use the abbreviation *para.* (not italicized) to show you are citing a paragraph number. For more information, see the next section or consult more complete APA publications.

> "Rose represents the unnamed multitude of women who were placed in the same circumstances but whose stories were never told" (Mason, 2003, ¶ 8).

If no page or paragraph number is provided, cite a heading in the work and direct the reader to the paragraph in that section by number:

> (Regelin, 2002, Management plan section, para. 4)

If no author is listed, cite a short title, headline style, and place it in quotes.

> ("Wolf in Alaska," 2003)

APA: How to Cite Sources in the References Page

Attach to your draft a list of all the works you have quoted, paraphrased, or summarized in your paper along with full publication information for each of them. This list begins on a new page, is titled References, and is alphabetized according to the last names of the authors or, if no author is listed, by the title of the work, ignoring any initial *A, An,* or *The* when alphabetizing. For exceptions to this rule, consult the latest edition of the APA style manual. All the information on the list should be double-spaced, just like the rest of your final paper.

Look at the References list at the end of the APA-style student paper appearing on pages 469–478. Include on your list only the works you have actually cited in your paper. The easiest way to prepare this list is to alphabetize your bibliography cards or notes, as explained in the previous paragraph. If you have prepared an annotated bibliography, simply eliminate the annotations to create the References list. Start each citation at the left margin and indent each successive line 1/2 inch (or five spaces).

Basic Format for Books, Articles, and Electronic Sources

Books

Author, A. A. (year of publication). *Title of book.* Location: Publisher name in full.

Articles in periodicals

Author, A., & Author, B. (Date of publication). Title of article. *Name of the Periodical, volume number* (issue number), page numbers in full.

Online documents

Author, A. (Date of publication). *Title of document.* Retrieved month, day, year, from source URL or DOI (Digital Object Indentifier)

Online periodicals with or without print version

Author, A. (Date of publication). Title of article [Electronic version]. *Title of Periodical, volume number* (issue number), page numbers. Retrieved month, day, year, from source URL or DOI

A document from an online periodical located through a library subscription service

Author, A. (Date of publication). Title of article. *Title of Periodical, volume number,* (issue number, if applicable), page numbers. Retrieved month, day, year, from name of subscription service.

Note that in book and article titles, APA capitalizes only the first word of the title, the first word of a subtitle, and all proper nouns, sentence style. Also note that APA does not require quotation marks for article titles. Titles of periodicals are written headline style with important words capitalized. Titles of books, newspapers, and journals or magazines are italicized. The volume numbers of periodicals are also italicized, but the issue numbers are not. For electronic sources, print publication information is listed first, followed by the date of retrieval and, if it is a source likely to change, the name of the source or service. *Note:* If the electronic version is exactly the same as the print version, including the same paging, the date and URL can be omitted. (According to the APA, this is especially the case with scholarly online articles in the behavioral sciences.)

Here are examples of the types of sources most commonly cited for argument papers. To help you quickly find what you need, consult the following list.

How to List Other Nonprint Sources

How to List Print Books

1. *A book by one author*

Melvern, L. (2004). *Conspiracy to murder : The Rwandan genocide.* London: Verso.

2. *A book by two to six authors*

Chayes, A. H., & Minow, M. (2003). *Imagine coexistence: Restoring humanity after violent ethnic conflict.* San Francisco: Jossey-Bass.

Comstock, G., Chaffee, S., Katzman, N., McCombs, M., & Roberts, D. (1978). *Television and human behavior.* New York: Columbia University Press.

3. *A book by more than six authors* When a book has more than six authors, list the first six names, just as in the example above that lists five, followed by et al.

4. *Two or more books by the same author* Alphabetize the titles by publication date, with the earliest date first.

Shaviro, S. (1993). *The cinematic body.* Minneapolis: University of Minnesota Press.

Shaviro, S. (2003). *Connected, or, what it means to live in the networked society.* Minneapolis: University of Minnesota Press.

5. *A book by a corporate or group author* When the author and the publisher are the same, as they are in the following example, use the word *Author* (not italicized) as the name of the publisher.

Harvard Business School Press. (2004). *The results-driven manager: Winning negotiations that preserve relationships.* Boston: Author.

6. *A book with no author named*

The world almanac and book of facts. (2007). New York: World Almanac Books.

7. *A republished book*

Locke, J. (1959). *An essay concerning human understanding.* New York: Dover. (Original work published 1690)

8. *A translation*

Virilio, P. (2002). *Ground zero* (C. Turner, Trans.). London: Verso.

9. *A second or subsequent edition*

Bovee, C. L., & Thill, J. V. (2000). *Business communication today* (6th ed.). Upper Saddle
River, NJ: Prentice Hall.

10. *Proceedings from a conference or symposium* Treat the title of the conference or symposium as a proper noun.

Gray, W. D. (Ed.). (2004). *Proceedings of the Twenty-Fifth Annual Conference of the
Cognitive Science Society.* Mahwah, NJ: Erlbaum.

11. *An introduction, preface, foreword, or afterword*

Rajchman, J. (2001). Introduction. In G. Deleuze, *Pure immanence* (A. Boyman, Trans.)
(pp. 7–23). New York: Zone.

12. *A government document*

Federal Bureau of Investigation. U.S. Department of Justice. (2004). *National instant
criminal background check system.* Washington, DC: U.S. Government Printing Office.

How to List Print Articles

List all the pages on which the article is printed, whether they are successive or
interrupted by other pages. Insert *p.* or *pp.* only for newspaper articles and articles
or chapters in books. Omit *p.* or *pp.* for journal and magazine articles.

13. *An article from a magazine*

Tomkins, C. (2001, November 5). The modernist. *The New Yorker,* 72–83.

If a volume number is available, insert it in italics after the comma following the
magazine title: *Natural History, 96,* 12–15.

14. *An article from a newspaper*

Rutenberg, J., & Maynard, M. (2003, June 2). TV news that looks local, even if it's not.
The New York Times, p. C1.

15. *An article in a periodical with no author listed*

Metamorphosis. (2001, November 5). *The New Yorker,* 10.

16. *An article in a journal with continuous pagination in each volume*

Hanlon, J. (2004). It is possible to give money to the poor. *Development and Change, 35,*
375–384.

17. *An article in a journal*

Kruse, C. R. (2001). The movement and the media: Framing the debate over animal
experimentation. *Political Communication, 18*(1), 67–88.

18. *An edited collection of articles or an anthology*

Johnson, V. D., & Lyne, B. (Eds.). (2002). *Walkin' the talk: An anthology of African American
literature.* Upper Saddle River, NJ: Prentice-Hall.

19. *An article in an edited collection or an anthology*

Willis, C. (2002). Heaven defend me from political or highly educated women! Packaging
the new woman for mass consumption. In A. Richardson & C. Willis (Eds.), *The*

new woman in fact and in fiction: Fin-de-siècle feminisms (pp. 53–65). New York: Palgrave Macmillan.

20. *A reprinted article in an edited volume or collection*

Kress, G. (2004). Multimodality, multimedia, and genre. In C. Handa (Ed.), *Visual rhetoric in a digital world* (pp. 106–121). Boston: Bedford/St. Martin's. (Original work published 2003)

21. *A signed article in a reference work*

Davidson, W. S., II. (1984). Crime. In R. J. Corsini (Ed.), *Encyclopedia of psychology* (Vol. 1, pp. 310–312). New York: Wiley.

22. *An unsigned article in a reference work*

Quindlen, Anna. (1993). In J. Graham (Ed.), *Current biography yearbook* (pp. 477–481). New York: Wilson.

23. *A review*

Ottenhoff, J. (2002). It's complicated. [Review of the book *The moment of complexity*]. *Christian Century, 119* (21), 56–59.

24. *A letter to the editor*

Cooper, M. (2004, May 17). [Letter to the editor]. *Business Week,* 18.

25. *An editorial*

Consider cloning source of organs. (2003, October 22). [Editorial]. *USA Today,* p. A19.

26. *A published interview*

Gardels, N. (2001, January). [Interview with C. Rice]. *New Perspectives Quarterly, 18* (1), 35–38.

27. *A personal interview* You would not cite this in the References list. Cite it instead in the text.

Audrey Wick (personal communication, December 27, 2008) holds a different perspective.

28. *A lecture, speech, or address*

King, M. L., Jr. (1963, August 28). I have a dream. Speech delivered at the Lincoln Memorial, Washington, DC.

How to List Electronic Sources

A helpful rule to keep in mind in your research and when citing electronic sources is to use Web sites that are as reliable and unchanging as possible so a reader can access the information at a later date. Web sites that are refereed, authoritative, based on historical texts, have print counterparts, or provide archival versions of articles and other material should prove to be stable.

The basic elements of an electronic APA References list entry are author, publication date in parentheses, title of the article, title of the periodical or electronic text, volume and issue number, and pages (if any), date retrieved from the World Wide Web for undated or changeable content, and the URL with no brackets and no period at the end. Provide URLs that link as directly as possible to the work or to the document page. If doing so is not possible, provide the URL for the home page.

Like some content, URLs are changeable. Increasingly, publishers of scholarly and stable or archival content are assigning a Digital Object Identifier (DOI) to journal articles and other documents. The DOI is linked to the content no matter its portability from location to location on the Internet. When you have a DOI for your source, it replaces the URL. To cite a source with a DOI, first list the publication information as in example 17. The retrieval or access date is next, entered as follows: **Retrieved month day, year.** Then, if there is a DOI, enter *doi:* (not italicized) followed by the number. No final period is used.

29. *An entire Internet site* For a multipage document Internet site, provide the URL for the home page that contains the document. It can also be cited within the text, with the URL, in parentheses, rather than in the References page.

CNN.com. (2004). Retrieved from http://www.cnn.com

30. *A document from a professional Web site* Use n.d. (no date) when a publication date is not available, and provide a URL that links directly to the chapter or section. URLs can be divided at the end of a line *after* a slash or *before* a period or symbol.

Herman, P. (n.d.). Events. *Milton-L Home Page.* Retrieved January 15, 2003, from http://www.richmond.edu/~creamer/milton/events.html

31. *A home page for a course* Include the name of the instructor, date of publication or latest update, course title, and retrieval information.

Stern, D. (2000). Heidegger. Retrieved June 15, 2008, from http://www.uiowa.edu/~c026036/

32. *A personal home page* Include the name of the owner, date of publication or latest update, title of the site (if available), and retrieval information.

Blakesley, D. (2003, September 18). Home page. Retrieved May 18, 2008, from http://web.ics.purdue.edu/~blakesle/

33. *An online book*

Mussey, R. D. (1836). *An essay on the influence of tobacco upon life and health.* Retrieved from http://www.gutenberg.org/dirs/1/9/6/6/19667/19667.txt

34. *A part of an online book* Provide the URL that links directly to the book chapter or section. If the URL leads to a page that directs the reader to locate the text within it, use the language *Available from* (not italicized) instead.

Mussey, R. D. (1836). Cases illustrative of the effects of tobacco. *An essay on the influence of tobacco upon life and health.* Retrieved from http://www.gutenberg.org/dirs/1/9/6/6/19667/19667.txt

35. *An article in an online newspaper* Include the author, date of publication, title of the article, and name of the periodical, and URL.

Webb, C. L. (2004, May 27). The penguin that ate Microsoft. *The Washington Post.* Retrieved from http://www.washingtonpost.com/wp-dyn/articles/A59941-004May27.html

36. *An article in an online magazine*

Reiss, S. (2006, July). The wired 40. *Wired, 14* (07). Retrieved from http://www.wired.com/wired/archive/14.07/wired40.html

37. *An article in an online scholarly journal* If the article is included within a library subscription database, state the name of the database rather than providing the URL.

> Wishart, J. (2001). Academic orientation and parental involvement in education during high school. *Sociology of Education, 74,* 210–230. Available from *JSTOR* database.

38. *A review*

> Gray, D. (2004). [Review of the book *Psychic Navigator*]. *BookReview.com.* Available from http://www.bookreview.com

39. *A publication on a CD-ROM or DVD-ROM*

> Leston, R. (2002). Drops of cruelty: Controlling the mechanisms of rhetorical history. *Proceedings of the Southwest/Texas Popular and American Culture Associations: Years 2000–2003.* Ed. Leslie Fife. [CD-ROM]. (681–691). Emporia, KS: SW/TX PCA/ACA Press, 2003.

40. *Electronic mail (e-mail)* You would not cite this in the References list. Cite it instead in the text, as in this example.

> Byron Hawks (personal communication, October 4, 2008) suggests a different approach.

41. *A work from a library subscription service* See also *An article in an online scholarly journal,* item 37, above.

> Goldwasser, J. (2004, March). Watch your balance. *Kiplinger's Personal Finance, 58* (3), 96. Available from *LexisNexis Academic* database.

42. *A television or radio program* Include the URL if an archive version or transcript exists online so a reader may access the program in the future.

> Rehm, D. (Executive producer & host). (2004, May 24). *The Diane Rehm Show* with E. L. Doctorow. [Radio broadcast]. Washington, DC: American University Radio.

How to List Other Nonprint Sources

43. *An audio recording*

> James, B. (Artist). (2001). *Dancing on the water.* [CD]. New York: Warner Brothers.

44. *A motion picture* Include the name of the director or producer or both, the title, the label *Motion picture* (not italicized) in square brackets, the country of origin of the motion picture, and the name of the studio.

> Noyce, P. (Director). (2002). *Rabbit-proof fence* [Motion picture]. United States: Miramax Films.

45. *A videotape or DVD* Place the type of medium in square brackets.

> ABC/Prentice Hall Video Library (Producer). (1993). *Composition* [Videotape]. Englewood Cliffs, NJ: Prentice Hall.

46. *Graphs, artworks, photographs, advertisements, and other illustrations* Illustrations such as artworks, photographs, maps, comic strips, and advertisements are not included in the References list. They are documented within the text. See *Graphs, artworks, photographs, and other illustrations* on page 461.

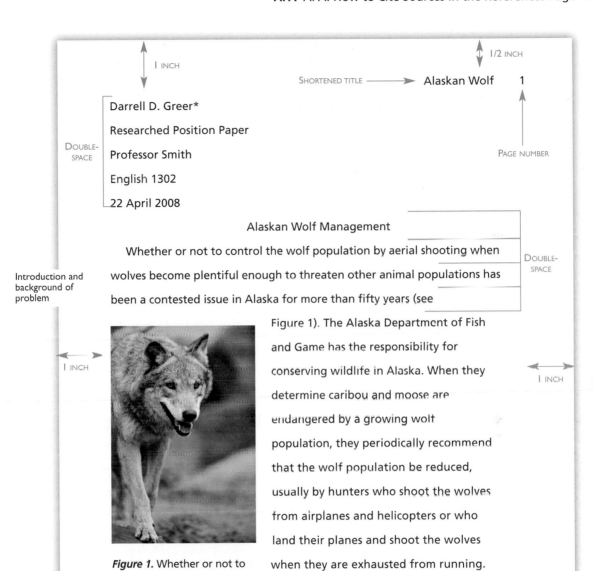

Within the illustrated manuscript page:

SHORTENED TITLE → Alaskan Wolf 1

1 INCH

1/2 INCH

PAGE NUMBER

DOUBLE-SPACE

Darrell D. Greer*

Researched Position Paper

Professor Smith

English 1302

22 April 2008

Alaskan Wolf Management

DOUBLE-SPACE

Introduction and background of problem

Whether or not to control the wolf population by aerial shooting when wolves become plentiful enough to threaten other animal populations has been a contested issue in Alaska for more than fifty years (see Figure 1). The Alaska Department of Fish and Game has the responsibility for conserving wildlife in Alaska. When they determine caribou and moose are endangered by a growing wolf population, they periodically recommend that the wolf population be reduced, usually by hunters who shoot the wolves from airplanes and helicopters or who land their planes and shoot the wolves when they are exhausted from running. The position of the Department of Fish and Game is that the wolf population must be reduced at times in Alaska when the

1 INCH

Figure 1. Whether or not to thin out the wolf population by aerial shooting when these animals are believed to threaten other wildlife is a persistent issue in Alaska. From www.shutterstock.com

1 INCH

(continued)

---

*APA guidelines call for a separate title page, which includes a running head for publication, the full title, and the author's name and institutional affiliation (see the *Publication Manual of the American Psychological Association,* 5th ed., 2001). Your professor, however, may ask you to present your identifying information as shown here.

caribou and moose populations become endangered because predators, like wolves, "kill 80 percent of the moose and caribou that die during an average year, while humans kill less than 10 percent." Even when many wolves are killed, the wolf population is only temporarily reduced, and it soon recovers ("Wolf Control," 2008). The animal rights advocates, many of whom are members of the Defenders of Wildlife organization in Alaska, passionately oppose this practice, arguing that shooting wolves from airplanes is unsporting and unethical and that it upsets the natural ecology of the region ("History," 2008).

According to Wayne L. Regelin (2002), past director of Wildlife Conservation for the Alaska Department of Fish and Game, public attitudes "are based on deeply held values," and that makes it extremely difficult to set wildlife policy in Alaska.

Regelin (Brief History section, 2002) details some of the history of aerial shooting of wolves in Alaska. It began officially in 1948 and was conducted by federal agents until the late 1950s. When Alaska became a state in 1959, legislation was passed to protect the wolf population. The issue did not go away, however. Aerial shooting resumed in the 1960s, and periodic efforts to control the wolf population in Alaska in this manner continued through the early 1980s.

Since 1986, the policy on wolf control in Alaska seems to change with the election of each new governor. Governor Steve Cooper (1986–1990) opposed wolf control and suspended the aerial shooting of wolves while he was governor. Cooper was followed by Governor Walter Hickel (1990–1994), who reinstated the practice. Public reaction

Two main positions

Quotation from authority to show difficulty of problem

History of problem

1 INCH

1/2 INCH

1 INCH

1 INCH

1 INCH

(continued)

against killing wolves was so strong during Governor Hickel's term that the governor commissioned "The Wolf Conservation and Management Policy for Alaska," in 1993, to set an official state policy on wolf control. This document is still the guiding policy for the state (Regelin, 2002).

Governor Tony Knowles (1994–2002) followed Hickel. Under Knowles, voters showed their support of animal rights groups by voting in 1996 and 2000 to ban the aerial shooting of wolves ("History," 2008). Governor Knowles not only suspended the wolf control program, he also assigned it to the U.S. National Academy of Sciences to study for a year. That group concluded that wolf control could be effective in Alaska and that current practices were based on sound science, but cautioned that control could be costly and controversial (Regelin, 2002) Governor Frank Murkowski (2002–2006), reinstated the aerial shooting of wolves, and the controversy surrounding this practice continued to rage throughout his term. In March 2004 *The New York Times* published an editorial in support of the animal rights activists and warned that the wolf population in Alaska could be wiped out if present policy is not changed. This editorial states: "Thanks to the compliance of Gov. Frank Murkowski and the state's official game board, the legal protections for Alaska's 7,000 to 9,000 wolves have been seriously eroded ("Wolf 'Control,'" 2004, p. 12). The current governor, Sarah Palin, who took office in 2006, is continuing Murkowski's policy and has proposed legislation to make it difficult for conservation groups, like the Defenders of Wildlife, to sue the government for killing wolves from planes (Cockerham, 2008).

(continued)

1/2 INCH

I INCH

Comparison

The situations in 1993 and 2008 have a lot in common. In the early 1990s Alaska witnessed a decline in the populations of caribou and moose in the Fortymile, Delta, and Nelchina Basin areas. This decline in the caribou and moose populations was due mainly to the increase of the wolf populations in these three areas. Robert Stephenson of the Alaska Department of Fish and Game claimed at that time, "Wolf packs will kill one caribou every two days or so, and one moose every three to ten days" (Keszler, 1993, p. 65). The Delta caribou herd alone declined from about eleven thousand in 1989 to fewer than four thousand just four

I INCH

years later ("Alaska Wolf," 1993). With statistics such as these, the size of the caribou and moose populations in Alaska was clearly a problem that needed ongoing attention.

I INCH

Now, as then, a rapid decline in caribou and moose populations can be devastating to the state. Not only are they a valuable resource for Alaska in terms of nonresident hunting and tourist sightseeing, but for many remote residents, caribou and moose are the main source of food.

The way of life for many Alaskans is one that the average American cannot begin to understand. Max Peterson, the executive director of the International Association of Wildlife Agencies, says that in Alaska,

Quotations worked into text suggest the unique character of the problem in Alaska.

"people interact as another predator in the ecosystem," and as a result, "the interest in Alaska by people outside Alaska certainly is greater than their knowledge of Alaska" (Keszler, 1993, p. 67). Ted Williams (1993) clarifies the lifestyle that many rural Alaskans lead:

Genuine subsistence is the most environmentally benign of all possible lifestyles. Subsisters do not—indeed cannot—deplete fish

I INCH

(continued)

472

and wildlife because if they do, they will subsist no more. But even

in the remotest native villages, Alaska as trackless wilderness

where people blend with nature is just an old dream. Many

villagers are now on social welfare programs and are therefore

cash dependent. (p. 49)

Failing to protect existing caribou and moose populations can lower

the subsistence level for some Alaskans, even more than it is at

present.

    The biologists of the state of Alaska commonly believe that wolf

populations are nowhere close to being endangered, and that the current

wolf control programs will sustain future wolf populations ("Wolf

Control," 2008). The total wolf population in Alaska at present is

estimated to be between 7,700–11,200. According to the Division of

Wildlife Conservation in Alaska, the wolf population has never been

endangered, and the future of the wolf in Alaska is secure ("Wolf in

Alaska," 2008). In 2008 five wolf control programs are in place in about

9.4% of the total area of Alaska. Aerial shooting that is designed to

protect other animal populations is permitted in these areas. "In these

areas, wolf numbers will be temporarily reduced, but wolves will not be

permanently eliminated from any area" ("Wolf Control," 2008). In the

past five years, gunners in airplanes who carry state permits have killed

more than 700 wolves (Cockerham, 2008).

    In 1993, when Governor Walter Hickel and the Alaska Department of

Fish and Game announced the new "Wolf Conservation and Management

Policy for Alaska" that allowed for the aerial shooting of wolves, the

A long quotation of more than forty words is indented and written in block form. No quotation marks are necessary for indented quotations. The page number is indicated at the end, and the author is mentioned in the text.

Statistics and quotations from authorities to strengthen the solution preferred by this author

(continued)

473

I INCH

animal rights groups started an all-out war on the state. They organized

widespread mailings to the governor and threatened massive boycotts of

tourism in Alaska if the plan was not repealed (Keszler, 1993, p. 65). The

animal rights groups believed that other methods of management could

increase caribou and moose populations. Such methods included reducing

bag limits, shortening hunting seasons, or totally eliminating hunting in

Refutation of the animal rights groups and their solution to the problem

the three main areas. This type of management was not effective,

however, since hunters were not the real cause of the problem. Pete

Buist, a Fairbanks, Alaska, resident, pointed out at the time, "In control

areas, hunters are taking less than five percent of the annual production

of meat animals. Predators are taking more than seventy-five percent"

(1993). Animal rights groups commonly point to hunters as the culprits in

I INCH

animal conservation efforts. According to Arms (1994), however,

I INCH

"Nowadays in developed countries, groups representing hunting and

fishing interests are the most active conservationists. They understand

that their sport and, sometimes, their livelihood depend on sustained or

increasing populations of the organisms they hunt or fish" (p. 347). As

mentioned earlier, rural Alaskans who depend on caribou and moose for

subsistence are some of these hunters who continue to take these animals

but not in dangerously large numbers.

Another alternative management method that has been brought up by

the animal rights groups is tranquilizing and capturing the wolves and

chemically sterilizing them or using some other sort of contraception. This

method was tried from 1997–2001. Alpha males and females in wolf packs

I INCH

(continued)

474

Alaskan Wolf   7

in control areas were sterilized. During these years the caribou population
experienced an increase from 22,000 to 38,000. Whether or not the wolf
sterilization program caused this increase in the caribou population is still
being studied. Even if it is finally judged to be the main cause of the
increase in caribou, the sterilization program has been accounted
unfeasible for implementation throughout Alaska because of its scope and
cost (Regelin, 2002). In the long run, sterilization is less effective than
killing wolves for another reason. It would take too long to be effective in
reducing an existing wolf population. Sterilization only deals with the wolf
numbers in the future, not with existing numbers, which would remain the
same for the present. Existing wolves in the immediate future could
devastate the caribou and moose populations in the meantime.

In the U.S. Constitution, the management of fish and wildlife is left up
to the individual states. When Alaska made the professional decision that
the best way to control its wolf population was by aerial shootings, the
animal rights groups picked only that part of a larger plan to attack. In
media reports, activists "portrayed the plan simply as a mass
extermination of wolves designed to increase game numbers for
out-of-state hunters and wildlife watchers" (Keszler, 1993, p. 39). The
Defenders of Wildlife claim now that Governor Palin's proposed bill,
which makes it difficult for conservation groups to sue the government
for killing wolves, will take "science and public input out of the process";
the current wildlife director counters that people will still be able to
state their views

Refutation of other
solutions and
evaluation of
evidence

(continued)

(Cockerham, 2008). After all these years, the issue of wolf population control in Alaska is still far from settled. In August 2008 the citizens of Alaska will vote for the third time on whether or not to ban aerial hunting of wolves. The 1996 and 2000 propositions of Governor Knowles's term passed by 58.5% and 53% of the votes, respectively. Each propositions either banned or limited the killing of wolves ("History," 2008).

Animal rights commercials in 1993 showed "visions of helicopter gunships slaughtering wolves by the hundreds" (Keszler, 1993, p.39). Since then other images of wolves in distress have been distributed to influence public opinion on this issue (Regelin, 2002). What is not always clear to the public, however, is that the aerial shooting of wolves is just one small part of the plan that also includes protecting the wolves themselves when their numbers become too low. The animal rights groups have not focused on those parts of the wolf plan that deal with restrictions to help the wolves in areas where their populations are sparse. The Alaska Department of Fish and Game, Division of Wildlife Conservation in Alaska, makes it clear that the long-term conservation of wolves is a major goal. Furthermore, when wolves are killing other important animal populations, they must be reduced ("Wolf Control," 2008).

The professional wildlife biologists at the Alaska Department of Fish and Game have taken a lot of heat from the animal rights media reports on their decision to go ahead with the original plan to manage wolf populations through aerial shootings and other methods not mentioned by the media. Governor Hickle in 1991 and Governor Palin in 2008 have both been besieged with requests from animal rights activists

Establishment of the *ethos* of conservationists in Alaska to make their plan acceptable

476

(continued)

Author has identified a problem, evaluated several solutions, and arrived at this solution as the best possible one. This is a value argument because it claims that one of several considered solutions is the best.

to discontinue aerial hunting of wolves. The biologists of the state of Alaska have devoted their lives to the preservation of wildlife. They know Alaska and Alaska's wildlife better than anyone else. After researching and trying other methods, they believe the best solution to their problem is aerial shootings. Their main concern is to protect the wildlife population as a whole, not just to wage a "war on wolves." While the animal rightists are sitting in their offices wondering which animals to save, the biologists at the Alaska Department of Fish and Game are in the field researching the range conditions and overall population conditions to manage the wildlife community as a whole.

Problem–solution and policy are also strong features in this argument.

Value claim in last sentence

The resolution of the Alaskan wolf management issue needs to be left to the experts. As inhumane and immoral as it might seem to many citizens, the aerial shooting of wolves is periodically the best solution for game management in Alaska.

(continued)

1/2 INCH

1 INCH

References

Alaska wolf update. (1993, August). *American Hunter,* 6.

Arms, K. (1994). *Environmental science* (2nd ed.). Fort Worth, TX: Harcourt Brace.

Buist, P. (1993, September). [Letter to the editor]. *American Hunter,* 12.

Cockerham, S. (2008, January 30). Palin wants to shoot down wolf
    lawsuits [Electronic version]. *Anchorage Daily News*. Retrieved from
    http://www.adn.com/news/alaska/wildlife/wolves/story/298522.html

History of wolf control in Alaska (2008). Retrieved April 10, 2008, from
    Defenders of Wildlife Web site: http://www.defenders.org

Keszler, E. (1993, May). Wolves and big game: Searching for balance in
    Alaska. *American Hunter,* 38–39, 65–67.

1 INCH

Regelin, W. L. (2002, March). *Wolf management in Alaska with an historic
    perspective.* Retrieved April 12, 2008, from http://www.wc.adfg
    .state.ak.us/index.cfm?adfg=wolf.wolf_mgt

1 INCH

Williams, T. (1993, May–June). Alaska's war on the wolves. *Audubon,*
    44–47, 49–50.

Wolf control in Alaska (2003, December 29). Retrieved April 12, 2008,
    from Alaska Department of Fish and Game—Division of Wildlife
    Conservation Web site: http://www.wildlife.alaska.gov/index
    .cfm?adfg=wolf.control

Wolf "control" in Alaska. (2004, March 14). [Editorial]. *The New York
    Times,* A12.

The wolf in Alaska (2008). Retrieved April 16, 2008, from Alaska
    Department of Fish and Game—Division of Wildlife Conservation
    Web site: http://www.wildlife.alaska.gov

1 INCH

In APA format,
break long URLs
before a period or
after a slash. Never
add a hyphen.

478

(continued)

Questions on the Researched Position Paper, APA Style (Pages 469–478)

1. Where did the author place his claim? What type of claim is it? Why do you think he placed it where he did?

2. What are the two conflicting positions on wolf management described in this paper? How much common ground would you say there is between the two positions?

3. What are some of the types of proofs and support that this student uses in his paper? Comment on the use of *logos, ethos,* and *pathos* in general, as well as on specific types of proofs, including the image of the wolf.

4. What warrants are held by the conservationists? What warrants are held by the animal rights advocates? What warrants does this author expect you to accept?

5. What major ideas does this author refute in this paper?

6. What organizational pattern do you detect in this paper?

7. Find an example of a summary of information from a document on an Internet site with no available author.

8. Find an example of a quotation that is longer than forty words.

9. Roughly what percent of this paper is made up of quotations from other people's writings and what percent is the author's own writing?

10. Read the "References" list and identify the different types of sources this author used.

Further Applications: Argument and Literature

Chapter 14 suggests some ways to apply argument theory to reading and writing about literature. When you finish reading Part Four:

▶ You will know how to apply argument theory to literary works.

▶ You will know how to analyze arguments made by literary works.

▶ You will know how to analyze arguments made by characters in literary works.

▶ You will know how to write your own arguments about literary works.

CHAPTER 14

Argument and Literature

T
he purpose of this chapter is to extend the applications of argument theory and to suggest that you apply this theory, as one of many possible theories, when you read imaginative literature and when you write papers about literature, including poetry, short stories, plays, and novels. Any theory that is applied to literature can help you look at it in whole new ways, and so it is with argument theory. In particular, argument theory is useful for speculating about the ideas and themes in literature, especially when there is no general agreement about what these ideas are exactly. It can also provide insight into literary characters, especially into how they argue and interact with one another. Finally, argument theory can help you write papers about literature and argue in favor of your own understandings and insights.

A basic idea in this book has been that argument can be found everywhere—particularly where people are. Creative writers, along with the imaginative characters they create, are as given to argument as any other people. It should not surprise you that argument is as pervasive in literature as it is in real life. In fact, literature often raises issues, takes positions on them, and even changes people's views about them. Literature can be convincing because it invites readers to identify with the characters, which creates empathy and common ground, and because it almost always employs effective emotional tone, vivid language, and emotional examples. Literature has high interest appeal as well. Argument achieved through literary narrative can be one of the most convincing forms of argument.

This chapter will provide you with examples and focus questions to help you apply argument theory to literature. The exercises and activities provide sufficient practice to get you started. Note also that in the introductory material to each of the seven issues in "The Reader," the suggestion is made to expand your perspective on the issues through literature and film. Specific examples of relevant literature and film are

provided. Literature, like film, raises issues, makes claims, and changes people's views about complex and controversial subjects. You can analyze arguments in literature and write arguments about literature just as you would with film.

Finding and Analyzing Arguments in Literature

When you apply argument theory to the reading of literature, you will be "inside the text," so to speak, analyzing what is there and working to understand it. Your focus may be on the main argument made by the text, or it may be on one or more of the characters and the arguments they make. Let's consider first how to analyze the main argument.

WHAT IS AT ISSUE? WHAT IS THE CLAIM?

To use argument theory to read a literary text and analyze the main argument, focus on the issues raised in the work, the perspectives that are expressed, and the claims that are made. The claims may be explicit, overt and openly expressed, or they may be implicit, covert and merely suggested, so that you will need to infer them yourself. There may also be conflicting claims in a single work that seem at times to contradict each other. The Toulmin model is useful for analyzing and understanding the main line of argument in a literary work.

For example, here is a poem by Robert Herrick (1591–1674) that makes an explicit argument.

To the Virgins, to Make Much of Time
Gather ye rosebuds while ye may,
    Old Time is still a-flying;
And this same flower that smiles today,
    Tomorrow will be dying.

The glorious lamp of heaven, the sun,
    The higher he's a-getting,
The sooner will his race be run,
    And nearer he's to setting.

That age is best which is the first,
    When youth and blood are warmer;
But being spent, the worse, and worst
    Times still succeed the former.

Then be not coy, but use your time,
    And while ye may, go marry:
For having lost but once your prime,
    You may forever tarry.

In applying the Toulmin model to this poem, most readers would agree that a policy claim is stated in the first line and restated in different language in the last stanza. There would not be much disagreement, furthermore, about that claim: "Young people should marry in their prime and not later" would be one way of putting it. Or the poet's first line, "Gather ye rosebuds while ye may," taken metaphorically to mean that one should take advantage of good things when they are before you and available, serves as well to express the claim of this poem. The support is supplied in the form of reasons: time is flying, and it is better to marry when one is young than when one is old. The warrant that connects the support to the claim is that people will want to marry in the first place. Individuals who accept this warrant may be persuaded that they should, indeed, seize the day and wait no longer.

The claims in imaginative literature are not always this easy to identify. In many cases, it is necessary to ask questions to uncover what is at issue and to formulate the claim. Here are some questions to help you make these determinations.

1. *What is most of this work about?* The answer will help you identify the subject of the work.

2. *Can the subject be regarded as controversial?* That is, would it invite more than one perspective? This question will help you discover the issues.

3. *What positions are taken on the issue, and who takes them?* This question will help you discover both explicit and implicit claims along with who is making them: the author, a narrator, or various characters in the text.

4. *If the claim is not stated, what evidence can I use from the text to help me state it myself?* Draw on such evidence to help you make the claim explicit.

5. *Will everyone agree that this is a viable claim, or will I need to make a case for it?* Paper topics often come from disagreements over how to state the main argument in a literary work.

In her poem "The Mother," Gwendolyn Brooks begins, "Abortions will not let you forget." She continues by saying that she has never forgotten her "killed children," and she ends the poem:

> oh, what shall I say, how is the truth to be said?
> You were born, you had body, you died.
> It is just that you never giggled or planned or cried.
>
> Believe me, I loved you all.
> Believe me, I knew you, though faintly, and I loved,
>   I loved you all.

One could argue that the claim of the poem is in the first sentence, "Abortions will not let you forget," a claim of fact in the poet's experience. However, by the time one has read the entire poem, one can also infer and make a case for a value claim, that abortions cause the mothers who seek them considerable psychological pain and that, as with any experience of death, an absence is born or created that is difficult for them to endure as time goes on. There is sufficient evidence in the poem to make an argument for that second claim as well.

Still other literary texts express conflicting claims about an issue. In poet Robert Frost's "Mending Wall," two claims are made about the issue concerning the value of fences. The two claims are "Something there is that doesn't love a wall" and "Good fences make good neighbors." These claims contradict each other. Furthermore, careful readers have pointed out that convincing arguments are made for both of these positions in the poem. In the case of "Mending Wall," the poem tends to start an argument rather than deliver one.[1] Once again, paper topics come out of such disagreements and can provide you with material for lively writing. You can always take a position yourself on any argument started by a literary work.

In other literary texts, arguments are made entirely through metaphor, as in Frost's poem "Birches," in which swinging on birch trees becomes a way of escaping from the cares of life, or in another Frost poem, "The Road Not Taken," in which the two roads in the poem become metaphors for two possible life choices. Metaphors are comparisons of items from two different categories. They work like figurative analogies since they invite readers to make unique mental connections and to expand their perspective on a subject in new and original ways. The meanings of metaphors in a literary work are often difficult to pin down exactly. Thus they become the subject of controversy and are often open to a variety of interpretations. The disputed meaning of a key metaphor in a literary work can become a fruitful paper topic.

CHARACTERS MAKING ARGUMENTS

The second way to employ argument theory to analyze literature is to apply it to specific arguments that are made by characters in the context of a literary text. Also enlightening is to consider how these individual characters' arguments contribute to the main argument of the text. Focusing on the rhetorical situation and the modes of appeal, identifying fallacies, and applying the Toulmin model all help with this type of analysis.

Further, it is useful to identify the type of argument (see Chapter 1, pages 5–7). For example, a character may argue internally with himself, as Hamlet does when he asks, "To be or not to be, that is the question" in Shakespeare's *Hamlet*. A character may also argue with an imaginary audience, like the woman who constructs an imaginary argument with her child's counselor in the short story "I Stand Here Ironing" by Tillie Olsen. Two individuals may argue one on one, both trying to convince the other, as in the poem "Myth" by Muriel Rukeyser; or the character may make a single-perspective argument to convince a mass audience, as Marc Antony does in his speech that begins "Friends, Romans, countrymen, lend me your ears" in Shakespeare's *Julius Caesar*. The characters may argue in front of a third-party judge, as they do in the play *Inherit the Wind*. Identifying the type of argument will help you understand the rhetorical situation in which it takes place. It will focus your attention on who is arguing, with whom these characters are arguing, and to what end.

A famous literary argument is Satan's persuasion of Eve in John Milton's seventeenth-century epic *Paradise Lost*. The story is familiar. Adam and Eve have been placed in the garden of Eden by God and have been told they may eat

---

[1]Tim Morris provided me with some of the examples and insights in this chapter, such as this one, as well as with some of the literary examples in "The Reader."

anything in the garden except the fruit from the tree of knowledge. The rhetorical situation can be narrated like this: Satan is the arguer. He sneaks into the garden, inhabits the serpent, and in that guise tempts Eve, his audience, to eat the forbidden fruit. This is a one-on-one argument with Satan trying to convince Eve. The exigence of Satan's argument is that he needs to get a foothold on earth so that he can spend more time there and less time in Hell, a very unpleasant place in this poem. Satan's constraints are that he must get Eve alone because he's afraid he cannot persuade Adam; Eve is a bit vain, as he has discovered, and there are good angels around who could also frustrate his plan. Thus he decides to hide in the serpent. Satan's persuasive argument, full of fallacies as it is, is successful with Eve. She eats the fruit, she persuades Adam to eat it also, and as a result, they are expelled from the garden (paradise) forever.

In the poem, we witness the entire persuasive process that involves Satan and Eve, from the audience analysis carried on by Satan as he hides in the garden, watching Eve and analyzing her weaknesses, to the final changes in Eve's thought and action brought about by Satan's argumentative speeches. As part of this process, we overhear Satan's initial planning of his argument, and as he schemes and plans, we observe that there is a vast difference between his private feelings and beliefs and the roles he adopts to establish *ethos* with Eve. Satan is not an ethical arguer; he is an immoral manipulator. We also watch Satan deliberately plant a highly emotional version of the temptation in Eve's mind in the form of a dream. The remembered pleasure and emotional appeal of this dream will help make the later logical argument even more readily acceptable to Eve.

When Satan-in-the-serpent delivers the speeches in Book 9 of the poem that finally convince Eve that she should eat the apple, he employs *ethos, pathos,* and *logos* to strengthen his argument. He flatters Eve; he appeals to her desire to be more powerful; he refutes what God has told her with fallacious reasoning; he uses induction to show that he ate the fruit and did not die and, therefore, Eve will not die either; he points to himself as a sign of the intelligence and power that can come from eating the fruit; and he uses a deductive argument that can be summarized as follows:

> Eve should know evil in order to recognize good.
> Eating the fruit will help Eve know evil.
> Therefore, Eve should eat the fruit in order to recognize good.

There are other examples of logical and emotional appeal in this argument that are not detailed here. Furthermore, if the Toulmin model is also employed to analyze Satan's argument, his purpose and strategy become even clearer, particularly as we examine some of his warrants. One of these, for example, is that humans want to become gods. Satan himself envies God and assumes that humans will also.

Another unique feature of the argument in *Paradise Lost* is that we are allowed to witness the argument outcomes. Not only do we observe Eve's outward actions, but we are also a party to her inner thoughts following Satan's speech. We see her eat the fruit. We also learn from her private musings how her reasoning, her emotional state, and the credibility she places in the serpent have been changed by Satan's speeches. We have a full explanation of what has convinced Eve to disobey God and why the argument has been successful.

If you become interested in analyzing the argument in *Paradise Lost*, you might also like to know that Satan makes no fewer than twenty public addresses in the poem and that his audiences range in size from the single listener Eve to the multitudes of the fallen angels. Furthermore, Adam, Eve, God, the Son, and some of the angels in the poem make arguments of their own that can be profitably analyzed with argument theory.

Consider this list of questions for you to use to analyze the arguments of fictional characters in literature. Any one of these questions could help you discover a claim for a paper on a literary work. You would develop your claim by drawing examples from the literary work itself to illustrate your argument.

1. What is at issue in the literary work?
2. Who is the character taking a position on this issue, and what is the character's position on the issue?
3. What is the rhetorical situation for the argument?
4. What is the claim made by the character? Is it stated overtly? Is it implied? Write it yourself as a statement, and identify its type.
5. How does the character establish credibility? What logical and emotional proofs does the character use?
6. What type of language predominates: language that appeals to reason, language that appeals to emotion, or language that establishes credibility? Describe the language.
7. What are the warrants?
8. How does the character establish common ground? Through warrants? Through Rogerian argument? What else?
9. Are rebuttals used? How effective are they?
10. Are there fallacies? How do they distort the argument?
11. What are the outcomes of the argument? Is it convincing? To whom? What happens as a result?
12. Is the argument moral or immoral by the standards established in the text itself? How would you evaluate the argument according to your own standards and values?
13. How does the argument made by the character contribute to the main argument of the text?

Writing Arguments about Literature

Argument theory can also be used to help you formulate your own argument about your insights and understanding of a literary text. At this point you will move "outside the text," and you will begin by identifying an issue about the text on which there is no general agreement. You will then take a position on that issue, state your position in a claim, and present evidence from the text to prove it. Argument theory can be extremely beneficial in writing scholarly argument of this type. The Toulmin model will help you the most. It can help you identify an issue to write about in the first place, and it can also help you set up the elements of your argument.

Your first challenge will be to move from reading the piece of literature to writing about it. First, you will need to find an issue to write about. To help you find an issue, ask, *What is unclear about this text that I think I can explain?* or *What is left out by the author that I think I can explain?* Focus on the main argument of the text, on the characters themselves, on what the narrator says about the characters, or on the meaning of metaphors to help you discover possible issues to write about. Controversy often resides in those locations. Also, issues may emerge in class discussion, or issues may come from the questions in your literature anthology. If all else fails, write a summary of a literary text along with your reaction to it. Then read your reaction and circle the most promising idea in it. It should be an idea that you think you can make a claim about and defend with evidence from the text.

Consider some examples of issues that appear in literary texts. In Henry James's novel *The Turn of the Screw*, there is an unresolved question about whether the ghosts are real or not. One student actually went through the novel and highlighted in one color all of the evidence that suggests they are real and then highlighted in another color all of the evidence that suggests they are imaginary. According to this student, the quantity of evidence for both explanations was roughly comparable in the novel. If you decided to write about that issue, you could argue for either position and find many people who would agree with you. Your instructor would evaluate your paper on the quality of its argument rather than on whether you had resolved the controversy or not. Some literary controversies cannot be finally resolved any more than many issues in life can be finally resolved.

Look at another example of a literary issue. At the end of Ernest Hemingway's short story "The Short Happy Life of Francis Macomber," a wounded and enraged buffalo charges the main character, who is on an African safari. His wife shoots, but the bullet kills her husband instead of the buffalo. The "great white hunter" who is leading this expedition assumes the wife meant to kill her husband instead of the buffalo, and there is plenty of evidence in the story to suggest that this might have been her intent. However, it is equally possible to argue that she was really shooting at the buffalo and hit her husband by mistake. You could write a paper in which you argue for either position, as long as you provide evidence from the story to support your position. In other words, you could make either position convincing.

One student wrote a paper about a poem by William Butler Yeats in which she argued in favor of one interpretation, and she received an A. The next year, in another class, she argued in favor of a completely different interpretation of the same poem, and she merited another A. In both cases, she provided evidence from the poem to support the claims she made. Both of her arguments were convincing. Here are some questions to help you make a claim about a literary work and write a convincing argument to support it.

1. What is an issue raised by this text that needs clarification?

2. What are the different perspectives that can be taken on this issue?

3. Which perspective will I take?

4. What support from the text will I use to defend my position?

5. What warrants are implicit in my argument, and will they be acceptable to the person who will evaluate this paper? Should I make the backing explicit to strengthen the warrants?

6. Would my paper be more convincing if I include a rebuttal of the opposing positions?

7. Will my claim be more acceptable to my audience if I qualify it?

Once you have read and thought about a literary text, and you have answered these questions, you will write your paper just like you would write any other position paper in which your aim is to state what you think and provide evidence to support it. You can use suggestions from the other chapters in this book to help you meet this aim.

Review Questions

1. How can argument theory be used in the study of literature? Name and describe the three approaches described in this chapter.

2. What are some of the questions the reader can ask to arrive at a claim in a work of literature? What are some of the ways in which claims are expressed in literature?

3. Describe the argument theory you would employ to help you analyze an argument that a character makes in a literary work.

4. What are some of the suggestions made in this chapter to help you find a topic for a position paper you might write about an issue in literature?

5. What is your main responsibility as a writer when you argue on one side or the other of a literary issue?

Exercises and Activities

A. **Writing Assignment: Analyzing Arguments in Poems**

The three poems on the following pages all present arguments.

1. Read the poems; then freewrite for five minutes on each of them to capture your original thoughts and reactions.

2. Discuss the answers to the "For Discussion" questions that appear at the end of each poem.

3. Describe the rhetorical situation for each poem: Describe the text. Who is the author? What audience does the author seem to have in mind, and how closely do you match that imagined audience? What are the author's constraints regarding the issue? What are your constraints? What is the exigence for the poem?

4. Write a 350- to 400-word paper on one of the poems that explains the issue, the claim (or claims) made in the poem, the support, the expected warrants, and your final reaction to the claim(s), including the degree of common ground you share either with the author or with another character in the poem.

POEM #1   THEME FOR ENGLISH B*

Langston Hughes

Hughes, an African American author who wrote about the black experience in twentieth-century America, is best known for his poetry. He wrote this poem in 1926 while he was a student at Columbia University in New York City.

The instructor said,

    Go home and write
      a page tonight,
    And let that page come out of you—
5   Then, it will be true.

I wonder if it's that simple?

I am twenty-two, colored, born in Winston-Salem.
    I went to school there, then Durham, then here
to this college on the hill above Harlem.
10   I am the only colored student in my class.

The steps from the hill lead down to Harlem,
    through a park, then I cross St. Nicholas,
Eighth Avenue, Seventh, and I come to the Y,
    the Harlem Branch Y, where I take the elevator
15 up to my room, sit down, and write this page:
    It's not easy to know what is true for you or me
at twenty-two, my age. But I guess I'm what

I feel and see and hear. Harlem, I hear you:
    hear you, hear me—we two—you, me talk on this page.
(I hear New York, too.) Me—who?
20

Well, I like to eat, sleep, drink, and be in love.
    I like to work, read, learn, and understand life.
I like a pipe for a Christmas present,
    or records—Bessie, bop, or Bach.

25 I guess being colored doesn't make me not like
    the same things other folks like who are other races.
So will my page be colored that I write?
    Being me, it will not be white.
But it will be
30   a part of you, instructor.
You are white—
    yet a part of me, as I am a part of you.
That's American.

---

*Used with permission of Alfred A. Knopf, Inc.

35	Sometimes perhaps you don't want to be a part of me.
	Nor do I often want to be a part of you.
	But we are, that's true!
	As I learn from you,
	I guess you learn from me—
	although you're older—and white—
40	and somewhat more free.
	This is my page for English B.

For Discussion:

What is the relationship established between the teacher and the student in this poem? Think about similarities, differences, and common ground or lack of common ground between them. How does the student in the poem interpret the writing assignment and respond to it? How would you describe the issue in this poem? Is there a possibility of disagreement on this issue? What is the author's claim? How do you think the teacher will respond to this student's interpretation of this assignment?

POEM #2   **TOTALLY LIKE WHATEVER, YOU KNOW?***

Taylor Mali

Mali is a contemporary poet who is well known for his oral performances of his poetry.

	In case you hadn't noticed,
	it has somehow become uncool
	to sound like you know what you're talking about?
	Or believe strongly in what you're saying?
5	Invisible question marks and parenthetical (you know?)'s
	have been attaching themselves to the ends of our sentences?
	Even when those sentences aren't, like, questions? You know?
	Declarative sentences— so-called
	because they used to, like, DECLARE things to be true
10	as opposed to other things which were, like, not—
	have been infected by a totally hip
	and tragically cool interrogative tone? You know?
	Like, don't think I'm uncool just because I've noticed this;
	this is just like the word on the street, you know?
15	It's like what I've heard?
	I have nothing personally invested in my own opinions, okay?
	I'm just inviting you to join me in my uncertainty?
	What has happened to our conviction?
	Where are the limbs out on which we once walked?

*Taylor Mali, *What Learning Leaves*. Newtown, CT: Hanover Press, 2002, 37–38.

20   Have they been, like, chopped down
       with the rest of the rain forest?
       Or do we have, like, nothing to say?
       Has society become so, like, totally . . .
       I mean absolutely . . . You know?
25   That we've just gotten to the point where it's just, like . . .
       whatever!

       And so actually our disarticulation . . . ness
       is just a clever sort of . . . thing
       to disguise the fact that we've become
30   the most aggressively inarticulate generation
       to come along since . . .
       you know, a long, long time ago!

       I entreat you, I implore you, I exhort you,
       I challenge you: To speak with conviction.

35   To say what you believe in a manner that bespeaks
       the determination with which you believe it.
       Because contrary to the wisdom of the bumper sticker,
       it is not enough these days to simply QUESTION AUTHORITY.
       You have to speak with it, too.

For Discussion:

What is the issue that is addressed in this poem? What is the author's position on the issue? What is the claim, and what type of claim is it? What is the organizational pattern in the poem? What support is presented for the claim? What warrants does the author hope you will share with him? How much common ground do you have with this author? What is your own experience with this issue? What is your personal response to the author's claim?

POEM #3 ## MENDING WALL*

Robert Frost

Frost is a well-known American poet who often wrote about people and settings in New England. He wrote this poem in 1914.

       Something there is that doesn't love a wall,
       That sends the frozen-ground-swell under it,
       And spills the upper boulders in the sun;
       And makes gaps even two can pass abreast.
5   The work of hunters is another thing:
       I have come after them and made repair
       Where they have left not one stone on a stone,

*From *The Norton Anthology of American Literature*, ed. Nina Baym et al. (New York: W. W. Norton, 1989), 1719–1720.

But they would have the rabbit out of hiding,
To please the yelping dogs. The gaps I mean,
10　No one has seen them made or heard them made,
But at spring mending-time we find them there.
I let my neighbor know beyond the hill;
And on a day we meet to walk the line
And set the wall between us once again.
15　We keep the wall between us as we go.
To each the boulders that have fallen to each.
And some are loaves and some so nearly balls
We have to use a spell to make them balance:
'Stay where you are until our backs are turned!'
20　We wear our fingers rough with handling them.
Oh, just another kind of outdoor game.
One on a side. It comes to little more:
There where it is we do not need the wall:
He is all pine and I am apple orchard.
25　My apple trees will never get across
And eat the cones under his pines, I tell him.
He only says, 'Good fences make good neighbors.'
Spring is the mischief in me, and I wonder
If I could put a notion in his head:
30　'*Why* do they make good neighbors? Isn't it
Where there are cows? But here there are no cows.
Before I built a wall I'd ask to know
What I was walling in or walling out,
And to whom I was like to give offense.
35　Something there is that doesn't love a wall,
That wants it down.' I could say 'Elves' to him,
But it's not elves exactly, and I'd rather
He said it for himself. I see him there
Bringing a stone grasped firmly by the top
40　In each hand, like an old-stone savage armed.
He moves in darkness as it seems to me,

Not of woods only and the shade of trees.
He will not go behind his father's saying,
And he likes having thought of it so well
45　He says again, 'Good fences make good neighbors.'

For Discussion:

What is the issue in this poem? Describe the perspectives that are presented on this issue. State the conflicting claims. Who makes these claims? How are the individuals who make them characterized in the poem? Is the conflict of views resolved? Can you imagine Rogerian argument being employed in this situation to resolve the conflict? Why or why not? With whom do you identify in this poem and share the most common ground? Why?

B. **Writing Assignment: An Argument about a Literary Work**

The purpose of this assignment is to discover an issue, make a claim, and write about your interpretation of a story. The author of the reading for this assignment, Ursula Le Guin, has said that she was prompted to write the story by a remark she came across in William James's story "The Moral Philosopher and the Moral Life." In it, James suggests that if multitudes of people could be "kept permanently happy on the one simple condition that a certain lost soul on the far-off edge of things should lead a life of lonely torment," our moral sense would make us immediately reject that bargain. Le Guin's story is written as a parable—that is, it is written to illustrate a principle. Think about these things as you read it.

1. When you have finished reading the story, freewrite for five minutes to capture your original thoughts and reactions.

2. As a class, discuss answers to the following questions:

   a. What is this story about? What issues are raised by this story?
   b. What are some of the perspectives in the story? Who takes them? With which do you identify?
   c. Write a claim made by this story; then help list a few of these claims on the board. Which of these claims could be supported with evidence from the text? Which would you like to write about? Write your claim. Read with the class some of these claims.

3. Answer the next three questions to plan your paper.

   a. What evidence from the text can you use to support your claim (examples, quotations, etc.)? Underline it.
   b. What warrants are implicit in your argument? Will they be acceptable to the person who reads your paper, or should you provide backing?
   c. Would your paper be more convincing if you included a rebuttal? What would it be?
   d. Will your claim be more acceptable if you qualify it? How would you do that?

4. Write a 500-word position paper defending the claim you have made about this story.

STORY #1   **THE ONES WHO WALK AWAY FROM OMELAS***

Ursula K. Le Guin

Le Guin is a contemporary author of science fiction and fantasy.

1 With a clamor of bells that set the swallows soaring, the Festival of Summer came to the city Omelas, bright-towered by the sea. The rigging of the boats in harbor sparkled with flags. In the streets between houses with red roofs and painted walls, between old moss-gardens and under avenues of trees, past great parks and public buildings, processions moved. Some were decorous: old people in long stiff robes of mauve and gray, grave master workmen, quiet, merry women carrying their babies and chatting as they walked. In other streets

———————————————
*Used with permission of the author.

the music beat faster, a shimmering of gong and tambourine, and the people went dancing, the procession was a dance. Children dodged in and out, their high calls rising like the swallows' crossing flights over the music and the singing. All the processions wound towards the north side of the city, where on the great water-meadow called the Green Fields boys and girls, naked in the bright air, with mud-stained feet and ankles and long, lithe arms, exercised their restive horses before the race. The horses wore no gear at all but a halter without bit. Their manes were braided with streamers of silver, gold, and green. They flared their nostrils and pranced and boasted to one another; they were vastly excited, the horse being the only animal who has adopted our ceremonies as his own. Far off to the north and west the mountains stood up half encircling Omelas on her bay. The air of morning was so clear that the snow still crowning the Eighteen Peaks burned with white-gold fire across the miles of sunlit air, under the dark blue of the sky. There was just enough wind to make the banners that marked the racecourse snap and flutter now and then. In the silence of the broad green meadows one could hear the music winding through the city streets, farther and nearer and ever approaching, a cheerful faint sweetness of the air that from time to time trembled and gathered together and broke out into the great joyous clanging of the bells.

2 Joyous! How is one to tell about joy? How describe the citizens of Omelas?

3 They were not simple folk, you see, though they were happy. But we do not say the words of cheer much any more. All smiles have become archaic. Given a description such as this one tends to make certain assumptions. Given a description such as this one tends to look next for the King, mounted on a splendid stallion and surrounded by his noble knights, or perhaps in a golden litter borne by great-muscled slaves. But there was no king. They did not use swords, or keep slaves. They were not barbarians. I do not know the rules and laws of their society, but I suspect that they

were singularly few. As they did without monarchy and slavery, so they also got on without the stock exchange, the advertisement, the secret police, and the bomb. Yet I repeat that these were not simple folk, not dulcet shepherds, noble savages, bland utopians. They were not less complex than us. The trouble is that we have a bad habit, encouraged by pedants and sophisticates, of considering happiness as something rather stupid. Only pain is intellectual, only evil interesting. This is the treason of the artist: a refusal to admit the banality of evil and the terrible boredom of pain. If you can't lick 'em, join 'em. If it hurts, repeat it. But to praise despair is to condemn delight, to embrace violence is to lose hold of everything else. We have almost lost hold, we can no longer describe a happy man, nor make any celebration of joy. How can I tell you about the people of Omelas? They were not naïve and happy children—though their children were, in fact, happy. They were mature, intelligent, passionate adults whose lives were not wretched. O miracle! but I wish I could describe it better. I wish I could convince you. Omelas sounds in my words like a city in a fairy tale, long ago and far away, once upon a time. Perhaps it would be best if you imagined it as your own fancy bids, assuming it will rise to the occasion, for certainly I cannot suit you all. For instance, how about technology? I think that there would be no cars or helicopters in and above the streets; this follows from the fact that the people of Omelas are happy people. Happiness is based on a just discrimination of what is necessary, what is neither necessary nor destructive, and what is destructive. In the middle category, however—that of the unnecessary but undestructive, that of comfort, luxury, exuberance, etc.—they could perfectly well have central heating, subway trains, washing machines, and all kinds of marvelous devices not yet invented here, floating light-sources, fuelless power, a cure for the common cold. Or they could have none of that: it doesn't matter. As you like it. I incline to think that people from towns up and down the coast have been coming in to Omelas during the last days before the Festival on very fast little trains and double-decked trams, and that the train station of Omelas is actually the handsomest building in town, though plainer than the magnificent Farmer's Market. But even granted trains, I fear that Omelas so far strikes some of you as goody-goody. Smiles, bells, parades, horses, bleh. If So, please add an orgy. If an orgy would help, don't hesitate. Let us not, however, have temples from which issue beautiful nude priests and priestesses already half in ecstasy and ready to copulate with any man or woman, lover or stranger, who desires union with the deep god-head of the blood, although that was my first idea. But really it would be better not to have any temples in Omelas—at least, not manned temples. Religion yes, clergy no. Surely the beautiful nudes can just wander about, offering themselves like divine soufflés to the hunger of the needy and the rapture of the flesh. Let them join the processions. Let tambourines be struck above the copulations, and the glory of desire be proclaimed upon the gongs, and (a not unimportant point) let the offspring of these delightful rituals be beloved and looked after by all. One thing I know there is none of in Omelas is guilt. But what else should there be? I thought that first there were no drugs, but that is puritanical. For those who like it, the faint insistent sweetness of *drooz* may perfume the ways of the city, *drooz* which first brings a great lightness and brilliance to the mind and limbs, and then after some hours a dreamy languor, and wonderful visions at last of the very arcana and inmost secrets of the Universe, as well as exciting the pleasure of sex beyond all belief; and it is not habit-forming. For more modest tastes I think there ought to be beer. What else, what else belongs in the joyous city? The sense of victory, surely, the celebration of courage. But as we did without clergy, let us do without soldiers. The joy built upon successful slaughter is not the right kind of joy; it will not do; it is fearful and it is trivial. A boundless and generous contentment, a magnanimous triumph felt not against some outer enemy but in

communion with the finest and fairest in the souls of all men everywhere and the splendor of the world's summer: this is what swells the hearts of the people of Omelas, and the victory they celebrate is that of life. I really don't think many of them need to take *drooz*.

4 Most of the processions have reached the Green Fields by now. A marvelous smell of cooking goes forth from the red and blue tents of the provisioners. The faces of small children are amiably sticky; in the benign grey beard of a man a couple of crumbs of rich pastry are entangled. The youths and girls have mounted their horses and are beginning to group around the starting line of the course. An old woman, small, fat, and laughing, is passing out flowers from a basket, and tall young men wear her flowers in their shining hair. A child of nine or ten sits at the edge of the crowd, alone, playing on a wooden flute. People pause to listen, and they smile, but they do not speak to him, for he never ceases playing and never sees them, his dark eyes wholly rapt in the sweet, thin magic of the tune.

5 He finishes, and slowly lowers his hands holding the wooden flute.

6 As if that little private silence were the signal, all at once a trumpet sounds from the pavilion near the starting line: imperious, melancholy, piercing. The horses rear on their slender legs, and some of them neigh in answer. Sober-faced, the young riders stroke the horses' necks and soothe them, whispering, "Quiet, quiet, there my beauty, my hope. . . ." They begin to form in rank along the straight line. The crowds along the racecourse are like a field of grass and flowers in the wind. The Festival of Summer has begun.

7 Do you believe? Do you accept the festival, the city, the joy? No? Then let me describe one more thing.

8 In a basement under one of the beautiful public buildings of Omelas, or perhaps in the cellar of one of its spacious private homes, there is a room. It has one locked door, and no window. A little light seeps in dustily between cracks in the boards, secondhand from a

cobwebbed window somewhere across the cellar. In one corner of the little room a couple of mops, with stiff, clotted, foul-smelling heads, stand near a rusty bucket. The floor is dirt, a little damp to the touch, as cellar dirt usually is. The room is about three paces long and two wide: a mere broom closet or disused tool room. In the room a child is sitting. It could be a boy or a girl. It looks about six, but actually is nearly ten. It is feeble-minded. Perhaps it was born defective, or perhaps it has become imbecile through fear, malnutrition, and neglect. It picks its nose and occasionally fumbles vaguely with its toes or genitals, as it sits hunched in the corner farthest from the bucket and the two mops. It is afraid of the mops. It finds them horrible. It shuts its eyes, but it knows the mops are still standing there; and the door is locked; and nobody will come. The door is always locked; and nobody ever comes, except that sometimes—the child has no understanding of time or interval—sometimes the door rattles terribly and opens, and a person, or several people are there. One of them may come in and kick the child to make it stand up. The others never come close, but peer in at it with frightened, disgusted eyes. The food bowl and the water jug are hastily filled, the door is locked, the eyes disappear. The people at the door never say anything, but the child, who has not always lived in the tool room, and can remember sunlight and its mother's voice, sometimes speaks. "I will be good," it says. "Please let me out. I will be good!" They never answer. The child used to scream for help at night, and cry a good deal, but now it only makes a kind of whining, "eh-haa, eh-haa," and it speaks less and less often. It is so thin there are no calves to its legs; its belly protrudes; it lives on a half-bowl of corn meal and grease a day. It is naked. Its buttocks and thighs are a mass of festered sores, as it sits in its own excrement continually.

9   They all know it is there, all the people of Omelas. Some of them have come to see it, others are content merely to know it is there. They all know that it has to be there. Some of

them understand why, and some do not, but they all understand that their happiness, the beauty of their city, the tenderness of their friendships, the health of their children, the wisdom of their scholars, the skill of their makers, even the abundance of their harvest and the kindly weathers of their skies, depend wholly on this child's abominable misery.

10   This is usually explained to children when they are between eight and twelve, whenever they seem capable of understanding; and most of those who come to see the child are young people, though often enough an adult comes, or comes back, to see the child. No matter how well the matter has been explained to them, these young spectators are always shocked and sickened at the sight. They feel disgust, which they had thought themselves superior to. They feel anger, outrage, impotence, despite all the explanations. They would like to do something for the child. But there is nothing they can do. If the child were brought up into the sunlight out of that vile place, if it were cleaned and fed and comforted, that would be a good thing, indeed; but if it were done, in that day and hour all the prosperity and beauty and delight of Omelas would wither and be destroyed. Those are the terms. To exchange all the goodness and grace of every life in Omelas for that single, small improvement: to throw away the happiness of thousands for the chance of the happiness of one: that would be to let guilt within the walls indeed.

11   The terms are strict and absolute; there may not even be a kind word spoken to the child.

12   Often the young people go home in tears, or in a tearless rage, when they have seen the child and faced this terrible paradox. They may brood over it for weeks or years. But as time goes on they begin to realize that even if the child could be released, it would not get much good of its freedom: a little vague pleasure of warmth and food, no doubt, but little more. It is too degraded and imbecile to know any real joy. It has been afraid too long ever to be free of fear. Its habits are too uncouth for it to respond to humane treatment. Indeed, after so long it

would probably be wretched without walls about it to protect it, and darkness for its eyes, and its own excrement to sit in. Their tears at the bitter injustice dry when they begin to perceive the terrible justice of reality, and to accept it. Yet it is their tears and anger, the trying of their generosity and the acceptance of their helplessness, which are perhaps the true source of the splendor of their lives. Theirs is no vapid, irresponsible happiness. They know that they, like the child, are not free. They know compassion. It is the existence of the child, and their knowledge of its existence, that makes possible the nobility of their architecture, the poignancy of their music, the profundity of their science. It is because of the child that they are so gentle with children. They know that if the wretched one were not there sniveling in the dark, the other one, the flute-player, could make no joyful music as the young riders line up in their beauty for the race in the sunlight of the first morning of summer.

13   Now do you believe in them? Are they not more credible? But there is one more thing to tell, and this is quite incredible.

14   At times one of the adolescent girls or boys who go to see the child does not go home to weep or rage, does not, in fact, go home at all.

Sometimes also a man or woman much older falls silent for a day or two, and then leaves home. These people go out into the street, and walk down the street alone. They keep walking, and walk straight out of the city of Omelas, through the beautiful gates. They keep walking across the farmlands of Omelas. Each one goes alone, youth or girl, man or woman. Night falls; the traveler must pass down village streets, between the houses with yellow-lit windows, and on out into the darkness of the fields. Each alone, they go west or north, towards the mountains. They go on. They leave Omelas, they walk ahead into the darkness, and they do not come back. The place they go towards is a place even less imaginable to most of us than the city of happiness. I cannot describe it at all. It is possible that it does not exist. But they seem to know where they are going, the ones who walk away from Omelas.

For Discussion:

How is happiness defined in this story? Who gets to define it? Why? Why do some walk away? Make some connections: What actual societies or organized groups of people existing either now or in history might be suggested by this parable? Why do you think so?

C. **Writing Assignment: Analyzing the Argument in a Graphic Novel**

The following excerpts are from the graphic novel *Maus: A Survivor's Tale* by Art Spiegelman. It is a visual memoir, in comic book format, that depicts the author's parents' experiences in German death camps during World War II. The novel moves back and forth between conversations Spiegelman has with his elderly Jewish father and Spiegelman's depiction of his father's Auschwitz experiences. Volume 1 of *Maus, My Father Bleeds History*, was published in 1986, and Volume 2, *And Here My Troubles Began*, was published in 1991. Spiegelman won a Pulitzer Prize special category award for *Maus* in 1992.

Vladek and Anja Spiegelman, the author's parents, like so many other Jews from Poland and other parts of Europe, were sent to Auschwitz in 1944 where either death or a terrible struggle to remain alive, to survive, awaited them. Volume 1 of *Maus* relates their war experiences in Poland before they were imprisoned in Auschwitz, and Volume 2 is about their actual lives in the death camps, where they were when Germany surrendered in 1945. In 1951, the Spiegelman family immigrated to America.

Throughout *Maus*, the Jews are depicted as mice and the Germans are depicted as cats; modern-day Jews wear masks that look like mice. Spiegelman draws himself wearing a black vest. His father wears glasses. Two short excerpts from *Maus* are included here. The first excerpt comes from Volumn II, Chapter 2, "Auschwitz (Time Flies)." The author is experiencing severe writer's block as he contemplates writing about Auschwitz. The second excerpt from the same chapter is set in Auschwitz. Speigelman shows some of his conversations with his father and then draws what his father describes. His father speaks with an East European accent. In the excerpts, Françoise is Art Spiegelman's wife.

1. When you have finished reading, write brief answers to the following questions. Discuss your answers as a class after writing is completed.

    a. What is Spiegelman's implied claim about the experience of drawing and writing about extremely unpleasant personal experiences? How does he show the difficulty in images? How does he describe it in words?

    b. What claim does he make about Auschwitz? Who states this claim?

    c. How does the author employ emotional appeal and logical appeal? How does he portray his and his father's personal *ethos*?

    d. What values are implicit in this work?

    e. Describe the eight special features of visual argument in this work: What pulls you in? Do you experience common ground with any of the characters? Do the images arouse your emotions, and what is your reaction? What is placed in juxtaposition, and what is the effect? What icons are employed? What symbols? To what do they refer? What has been selected, what has been left out, and what is the effect? What is your personal interpretation of these excerpts from *Maus*? What is the artist's purpose? What is the effect?

    f. What can a graphic novelist accomplish with visual images and words that might not be possible with words alone?

2. Write a 500- to 750-word paper about one of these topics.

    a. What are the claims, and how are they developed through *ethos, pathos,* and *logos*? What values are implicit?

    b. How does the author employ the eight special features of visual argument?

    c. Describe some of the unique features of the graphic novel. What can a graphic novelist achieve visually that would not be as effective with words alone?

MAUS: A SURVIVOR'S TALE*

Art Spiegelman

The author is one of the world's best known and most influential graphic novelists. He started drawing professionally when he was 16. He has spent most of his life in New York City where he has drawn for magazines such as *The New Yorker*, for which he was staff artist and writer for ten years; has served as creative consultant for a children's candy business; has taught at the School for Visual Arts; and has founded his own avant-garde comics magazine, *RAW*.

*Art Spiegelman, *Maus: A Survivor's Tale*, vol. 2, *And Here My Troubles Began*. New York: Pantheon Books, 1991. 41–46, 49–51.

Excerpt 1:
Getting Ready
to Write

501

Excerpt 1:
(Continued)

Excerpt 1:
(Continued)

Excerpt 2:
Auschwitz

Excerpt 2:
(Continued)

507

Excerpt 2:
(Continued)

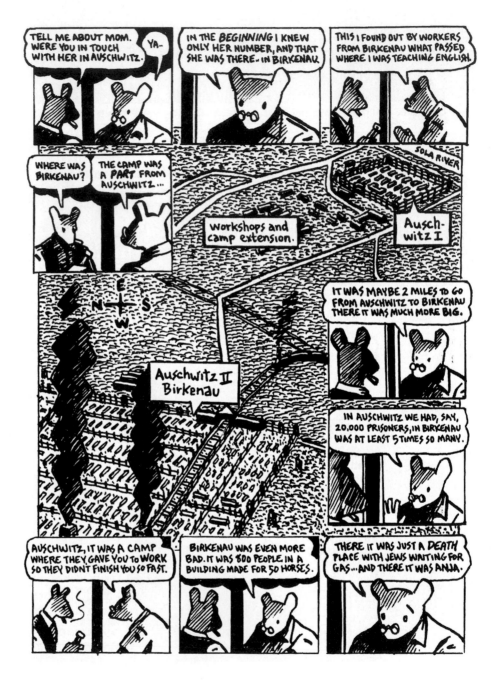

For Discussion:

What dilemmas does the author face in the first excerpt? How does he depict the media and others who want to capitalize on his success? What is the effect on him, and how does he show that visually? Where does he seek help? Look carefully at the way he has drawn himself throughout this section of *Maus*. How does he show that he has conquered his writer's block? In the second excerpt, how does he visually separate his conversations with his father, aside from the images of Auschwitz? How does he distinguish his father's story about his experiences in Auschwitz from the day-to-day activities and conversations in the death camp?

Summary Charts

TRACE

THE RHETORICAL SITUATION

FOR THE TARGETED READER AT THE TIME THE TEXT WAS WRITTEN

Text. What kind of text is it? Is it unique to its time?

Reader. Who were the targeted readers? What qualities did they have as the original audience? Were they convinced? How are they different from other or modern readers?

Author. Who is the author? What influenced the author? Why was the author motivated to write?

Constraints.* What beliefs, attitudes, habits, affiliations, or traditions influenced the author's and the readers' views in this argument?

Exigence. What happened to cause the argument? Why was it a problem? Has it recurred?

FOR YOU AS THE READER

Text. What kind of text is it? What are its special qualities and features? What is it about?

Reader. Are you one of the readers the writer anticipated? Do you share common ground with the author and other audience members? Are you open to change?

Author. Who is the author? How is the author influenced by background, experience, education, affiliations, or values? What is the author's motivation to write?

Constraints.* What beliefs, attitudes, habits, affiliations, or traditions will influence the way you and the author view the argument?

Exigence. What caused the argument, and do you perceive it as a defect or problem?

FOR YOU AS THE WRITER

Text. What is the assignment? What should your completed paper look like?

Reader. Who are your readers? Where do they stand on the issue? How can you establish common ground? Can they change?

Author. What is your argumentation strategy? What is your purpose and your perspective? How will you make your paper convincing?

Constraints.* How are your training, background, affiliations, and values either in harmony or in conflict with your audience? Will they drive you apart or help build common ground?

Exigence. What happened? What is motivating you to write on this issue? Why is it compelling to you?

*Do not confuse constraints with warrants. Constraints are a broader concept. See page 161.

The Process

...and flexible in using the strategies, and remember that there is no best order. You will backtrack and repeat.

WHEN YOU ARE THE READER

Prereading Strategies

▶ **Read the title and first paragraph; consult your background.** Identify the issue. Free-associate and write words and phrases that the issue brings to mind.

▶ **Evaluate and improve your background.** Do you know enough? If not, read or discuss to get background. Look up a key word or two.

▶ **Survey the material.** Locate the claim (the main assertion) and some of the subclaims (the ideas that support it); notice how they are organized. Do not slow down and read.

▶ **Write out your present position on the issue.**

▶ **Make some predictions, and write one big question.** Jot down two or three ideas that you think the author may discuss, and write one question you would like to have answered.

Reading Strategies

▶ **Pick up a pencil, underline, and annotate** the ideas that seem important. Write a brief summary.

▶ **Identify** and **read** the information in the **introduction, body,** and **conclusion.**

▶ **Look for the claim, subclaims, and support.** Box the **transitions** to highlight relationships between ideas and changes of subject.

▶ **Find the key words** that represent major concepts, and jot down meanings as needed.

▶ **Analyze the rhetorical situation.** Remember TRACE: Text, Reader, Author, Constraints, Exigence.

▶ **Analyze argument strategies.**

▶ **Read with an open mind, and analyze the common ground** between you and the author.

Strategies for Reading Difficult Material

▶ **Read all the way through once** without stopping.

▶ **Write a list** of what you understand and what you do not understand.

▶ **Identify words and concepts** you do not understand, look them up, and analyze how they are used in context.

WHEN YOU ARE THE WRITER

Prewriting Strategies

▶ **Get organized to write.** Set up a place with materials. Be motivated.

▶ **Understand the writing assignment,** and **schedule time.** Break a complicated writing task into manageable parts, and set aside time to write.

▶ **Identify an issue, and do some initial reading.** Use the twelve tests to make certain you have an arguable issue (Box 1.3).

▶ **Analyze the rhetorical situation,** particularly the exigence, the audience, and the constraints.

▶ **Focus** on your issue and **freewrite.**

▶ **Brainstorm, make lists, and map ideas.**

▶ **Talk it through** with a friend, your instructor, or members of a peer editing group.

▶ **Keep a journal, notebook, or folder of ideas.**

▶ **Mentally visualize** the major concepts.

▶ Do some directed **reading and thinking.**

▶ Use **argument strategies.**

▶ Use **reading strategies.**

▶ Use **critical thinking prompts.**

▶ Plan and conduct **library research.**

▶ Make an **expanded list or outline** to guide your writing.

▶ **Talk it through again.**

Drafting Strategies

▶ **Write the first draft.** Put your ideas on paper so that you can work with them. Use your outline and notes to help you. Either write and rewrite as you go or write the draft quickly with the knowledge that you can reread and rewrite later.

Strategies to Use When You Get Stuck

▶ **Read more** and **take more notes.**

▶ **Read your outline, rearrange parts, and add information to it.**

▶ **Freewrite** on the issue, **read some more,** and then **freewrite** some more.

513

(continued)

The Process *(continued)*

WHEN YOU ARE THE READER

▶ **Reread the material,** and add to your list of what you can and cannot understand.

▶ **Reread again** if you need to do so.

▶ **Discuss the material** with someone who has also read the material for further clarification and understanding.

Postreading Strategies

▶ **Monitor your comprehension.** Insist on understanding. Check the accuracy of your **predictions,** and answer your **question.**

▶ **Analyze the organization,** and write a **simplified outline,** a **map,** or a **summary** to help you understand and remember.

▶ **Write a response** to help you think.

▶ **Compare your present position** with your position before you began to read.

▶ **Evaluate the argument.** Decide whether it is ethical or unethical and convincing or not convincing.

WHEN YOU ARE THE WRITER

▶ **Talk about your ideas** with someone else.

▶ **Lower your expectations for your first draft.** At this point, the writing does not have to be perfect.

Postwriting Strategies

▶ **Read your draft critically** and also **have someone else read it.** Put it aside for 24 hours, if you can, to develop a better perspective for reading and improving.

▶ **Rewrite and revise.** Make changes and additions until you think the paper is ready for others to read. Move sections, cross out material, add other material, and rephrase for clarity, as necessary.

▶ **Check your paper** for final mechanical and spelling errors, **write the final title,** and **type or print the paper.**

The Toulmin Model

WHEN YOU ARE THE READER

1. *What is the claim?* What is this author trying to prove? Look for the claim at the beginning or at the end, or infer it.

2. *What is the support?* What information does the author use to convince you of the claim? Look for reasons, explanations, facts, opinions, personal narratives, and examples.

3. *What are the warrants?* What assumptions, general principles, values, beliefs, and appeals to human motives are implicit in the argument? How do they link the claim and the support? Do you share the author's values? Does the support develop the claim? Are the warrants stated, or must they be inferred?

4. *Is backing supplied for the warrants?* See whether additional support or appeals to widely accepted values and belief systems are provided to make the warrants more acceptable to the reader.

5. *Is there a rebuttal?* Are other perspectives on the issue stated in the argument? Are they refuted? Are counterarguments given?

6. *Has the claim been qualified?* Look for qualifying words such as *sometimes*, *probably*, *most*, and *possibly*. Decide what is probably the best position to take on the issue, for now.

WHEN YOU ARE THE WRITER

1. *What is my claim?* Decide on the type of claim and the subclaims. Decide where to put the claim in your paper.

2. *What support will I use?* Invent reasons, opinions, and examples. Research and quote authorities and facts. Consider using personal narratives.

3. *What are my warrants?* Write out the warrants. Do they strengthen the argument by linking the support to the claim? Do you believe them yourself? Will the audience share them or reject them?

4. *What backing for the warrants should I provide?* Add polls, studies, reports, expert opinion, or facts to make your warrants convincing. Refer to generally accepted values and widely held belief systems to strengthen the warrants.

5. *How should I handle rebuttal?* Include other perspectives and point out what is wrong with them. Make counterarguments.

6. *Will I need to qualify my claim?* Decide whether you can strengthen your claim by adding qualifying words such as *usually*, *often*, or *probably*.

Types of Claims

CLAIMS OF FACT

What happened? Is it true? Does it exist? Is it a fact?

Examples:

Increasing population threatens the environment.
Television content promotes violence.
Women are not as effective as men in combat.

READERS

❱ Look for claims that state facts.

❱ Look for facts, statistics, real examples, and quotations from reliable authorities.

❱ Anticipate induction, analogies, and signs.

❱ Look for chronological or topical organization or a claim plus reasons.

WRITERS

❱ State the claim as a fact, even though it is controversial.

❱ Use factual evidence and expert opinion.

❱ Use induction, historical and literal analogies, and signs.

❱ Consider arranging your material as a claim with reasons.

CLAIMS OF DEFINITION

What is it? What is it like? How should it be classified? How should it be interpreted? How does its usual meaning change in a particular context?

Examples:

We need to define what constitutes a family before we discuss family values.
A definition will demonstrate that the riots were an instance of civil disobedience.
Waterboarding can be defined as a form of torture.

READERS

❱ Look for a claim that contains or is followed by a definition.

❱ Look for reliable authorities and sources for definitions.

❱ Look for comparisons and examples.

❱ Look for compare-and-contrast, topical, or deductive organization.

WRITERS

❱ State your claim, and define the key terms.

❱ Quote authorities, or go to dictionaries, encyclopedias, or other reliable sources for definitions.

❱ If you are comparing to help define, use compare-and-contrast organization.

❱ Use vivid description and narrative.

❱ Use deductive organization.

CLAIMS OF CAUSE

What caused it? Where did it come from? Why did it happen? What are the effects? What probably will be the results on both a short-term and a long-term basis?

Examples:

Clear-cutting is the main cause of the destruction of ancient forests.
Censorship can result in limits on freedom of speech.
The American people's current mood has been caused by the state of the economy.

READERS

❱ Look for a claim that states or implies cause or effect.

WRITERS

❱ Make a claim that states or implies cause or effect.

❱ Use facts and statistics.

(continued)

Types of Claims *(continued)*

READERS

▶ Look for facts and statistics, comparisons such as historical analogies, signs, induction, deduction, and causal arguments.

▶ Look for cause-and-effect or effect-and-cause organization.

WRITERS

▶ Apply Burke's pentad to focus the main cause.

▶ Use historical analogies, signs, induction, and deduction.

▶ Consider using cause-and-effect or effect-and-cause organization.

CLAIMS OF VALUE

Is it good or bad? How good? How bad? Of what worth is it? Is it moral or immoral? Who thinks so? What do those people value? What values or criteria should I use to determine its goodness or badness? Are my values different from other people's or the author's?

Examples:

Computers are a valuable addition to modern education.
School prayer has a moral function in the public schools.
Animal rights are as important as human rights.

READERS

▶ Look for claims that make a value statement.

▶ Look for value proofs, motivational proofs, literal and figurative analogies, quotations from authorities, signs, and definitions.

▶ Expect emotional language.

▶ Look for applied criteria, topical, and narrative patterns of organization.

WRITERS

▶ State your claim as a judgment or value statement.

▶ Analyze your audience's needs and values, and appeal to them.

▶ Use literal and figurative analogies, quotations from authorities, signs, and definitions.

▶ Use emotional language appropriately.

▶ Consider the applied criteria, claim with reasons, or narrative organizational patterns.

CLAIMS OF POLICY

What should we do? How should we act? What should future policy be? How can we solve this problem? What course of action should we pursue?

Examples:

The criminal should be sent to prison rather than to a mental hospital.
Sex education should be part of the public school curriculum.
Battered women who take revenge should not be placed in jail.

READERS

▶ **Look for claims** that state that something **should be done.**

▶ Look for statistical data, motivational appeals, literal analogies, and argument from authority.

▶ Anticipate the problem–solution pattern of organization.

WRITERS

▶ **State the claim as something that should be done.**

▶ Use statistical data, motivational appeals, analogies, and authorities as proof.

▶ Use emotional language appropriately.

▶ Consider the problem–solution pattern of organization.

Types of Proof and Tests of Validity

LOGICAL PROOFS

Don't confuse proofs with support. A proof represents a complete line of argument that includes a claim, support, and warrant. A proof demonstrates a particular way of thinking about and developing the main claim of the argument. The logical proofs have been arranged according to the mnemonic SICDADS: Sign, Induction, Cause, Deduction, Analogies, Definition, Statistics.

WHEN YOU ARE THE READER

WHEN YOU ARE THE WRITER

Sign

Look for clues, symptoms, and occurrences that are explained as signs or symptoms that something is so.

Pointing out the symptoms or signs that something is so.

Example:
Claim: The child has chickenpox.
Support: The child has spots.
Warrant: Those spots are a sign of chickenpox.

Test of Validity: Ask whether this is really a sign of what the author claims, or is there another explanation.

Think of symptoms or signs that you can use to demonstrate that something is so.

Induction

Look for a conclusion or claim based on examples or cases.

Drawing a conclusion (claim) from a number of representative cases or examples.

Example:
Claim: Everyone liked that movie.
Support: I know three people who liked it.
Warrant: Three examples are enough.

Tests of Validity: Ask whether there are enough examples, or is this a "hasty" conclusion or claim. Try to think of an exception that would change the conclusion or claim. See if you can make the "inductive leap" from the examples to the conclusion or claim and accept it as probably true.

Give some examples and draw a conclusion/claim based on them; *or* make the claim and back it up with a series of examples.

(continued)

Types of Proof and Tests of Validity *(continued)*

LOGICAL PROOFS

WHEN YOU ARE THE READER	WHEN YOU ARE THE WRITER
### Cause	
Look for examples, trends, people, or events that are cited as causes for the claim. Look for effects of the claim.	Placing the claim in a cause-and-effect relationship to show that it is either the cause of an effect or an effect of a cause.	Make a claim, and ask what caused it. Apply Burke's pentad to focus the main cause.
	Example:	What was done?
	Warrant: Depression in a group of people has also increased.	Where was it done?
	Support: This group of people has also increased its use of the Internet.	Who did it?
	Claim/conclusion: The Internet may be causing depression	How was it done?
		Why did it happen?
	Tests of Validity: Ask whether these causes alone are sufficient to create these effects, or is it that these effects result from other causes. Try to think of exceptions to the cause-and-effect outcome.	
### Deduction	
Locate or infer the general principle (warrant). Apply it to the example or case. Draw a conclusion or claim.	Applying a general principle (warrant) to an example or a case and drawing a conclusion.	Make a general statement. Apply it to an example or a case. Draw a conclusion.
	Example:	Decide whether to make the general statement (warrant) explicit or implicit.
	Warrant: Most uneven footprints are left by people who limp.	
	Support: These footprints are uneven.	
	Claim: The person who left these footprints walks with a limp.	
	Test of Validity: Ask whether the general principle (warrant) and the support are probably true, because then the claim is also probably true.	

(continued)

Types of Proof and Tests of Validity *(continued)*

LOGICAL PROOFS

Analogies: Literal, Historical, and Figurative

Literal and historical analogy:
Look for items, events, people, or periods of time that are being compared.

Interpreting what we do not understand by comparing it with something we do. Literal and historical analogies compare similar items, and figurative analogies compare items from radically different categories.

Example of historical analogy:
Claim: Many people will die of AIDS.
Support: Many people died of the Black Death.
Warrant: AIDS and the Black Death are similar.

Example of literal analogy:
Claim: The state should spend more money on education.
Support: Another state spent more money with good results.
Warrant: The two states are similar, and the results of one will be the results of the other.

Example of figurative analogy:
Claim: Reading a difficult book should take time.
Support: Digesting a large meal takes time.
Warrant: Reading and eating are sufficiently alike that they can be compared.

Figurative analogy:
Look for extended metaphors or items being compared that are from totally different categories.

Tests for Validity: For literal analogies, ask whether the cases are so similar that the results of one will be the results of the other. For historical analogies, ask whether history will repeat itself. For figurative analogies, ask whether the qualities of the items being compared are real enough to provide logical support or are they so dissimilar that they do not prove anything.

WHEN YOU ARE THE WRITER

Literal and historical analogy:
Think of items in the same category that can be compared. Show that what happened in one case will also happen in the other. Or, demonstrate that history repeats itself.

Figurative analogy:
Think of comparisons with items from other categories. Try to compare items that have similar qualities, characteristics, or outcomes.

(continued)

Types of Proof and Tests of Validity *(continued)*

LOGICAL PROOFS

WHEN YOU ARE THE READER	WHEN YOU ARE THE WRITER 

Definition

WHEN YOU ARE THE READER

Look for definitions of key words or concepts.

Definitions can be short (a word or sentence) or long (several paragraphs or an entire essay).

Notice whether the reader is supposed to accept the claim "by definition" because it has been placed in an established category.

Describing the fundamental properties and qualities of a term or placing an item in a category and proving it "by definition."

Example:
Warrant: Family values characterize the good citizen.
Support: Radical feminists lack family values.
Claim: Radical feminists are not good citizens.

Tests of Validity: Ask whether the definition is accurate and reliable, or are there exceptions or other definitions that would make it less reliable. Ask whether the item belongs in the category in which it has been placed.

WHEN YOU ARE THE WRITER

Define the key terms and concepts in your claim.

Define all other terms that you and your reader must agree on for the argument to work.

Place some ideas or items in established categories and argue that they are so "by definition."

Statistics

WHEN YOU ARE THE READER

Look for numbers, data, and tables of figures along with interpretations of them.

Using figures or data to prove a claim.

Example:
Claim: We should end draft registration.
Support: It costs $27.5 million per year.
Warrant: This is too much; it proves we should end it.

Tests of Validity: Ask where the statistics came from, to what dates they apply, and whether they are fair and accurate. Ask whether they have been exaggerated or skewed. Ask whether they prove what they are supposed to prove.

WHEN YOU ARE THE WRITER

Find data, statistics, and tables of figures to use as evidence to back up your claim.

Make clear where you find the statistics, and add your interpretations and those of experts.

(continued)

521

Types of Proof and Tests of Validity *(continued)*

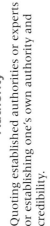

PROOF TO ESTABLISH *ETHOS*

WHEN YOU ARE THE READER

Look for references to the author's credentials, background, and training.
Look for credential statements about quoted authorities.

Authority

Quoting established authorities or experts or establishing one's own authority and credibility.

Example:
Claim: California will have an earthquake.
Support: Professors and scientists say so.
Warrant: These experts are reliable.

Tests of Validity: Ask whether the experts, including both outside authorities and the author, are really experts. Remember that argument from authority is only as good as the authorities themselves.

WHEN YOU ARE THE WRITER

Refer to your own experience and background to establish expertise.
Quote the best and most reliable authorities.
Establish common ground and respect by using appropriate language and tone.

EMOTIONAL PROOFS

Motives

Look for references to items or qualities you might need or want and advice on how to get them.
Look for emotional language, description, and tone.

Appealing to what all audiences are supposed to need, such as food, drink, warmth, shelter, sex, security, belonging, self-esteem, creativity, and self-expression. Urging audiences to take steps to meet their needs.

Example:
Claim: You should support this candidate.
Support: The candidate can help you get job security and safe neighborhoods.
Warrant: You want job security and safe neighborhoods.

Tests of Validity: Ask whether you really need what the author assumes you need. Ask whether doing what is recommended will satisfy the need as described.

Think about what the members of your audience need, and show how your ideas will help them meet these needs.
Use emotional language and tone where appropriate.

(continued)

Types of Proof and Tests of Validity *(continued)*

EMOTIONAL PROOFS

WHEN YOU ARE THE READER

Look for examples or narratives that display values.

Infer values (warrants) that are not explicitly stated.

Look for emotional language and tone.

Values

Appealing to what all audiences are supposed to value, such as reliability. honesty, loyalty, industry, patriotism. courage, conviction, faithfulness, dependability, creativity, integrity, freedom, equality, devotion to duty, and acceptance by others.

Example:

Claim: The curriculum should be multicultural.

Support: A multicultural curriculum will contribute to equality and acceptance.

Warrant: You value equality and acceptance.

Tests of Validity: Ask whether you share the author's values. Ask about the effect that differences in values will have on the argument.

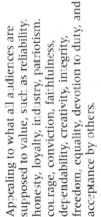

WHEN YOU ARE THE WRITER

Appeal to your audience's values through warrants, explicit value statements, and narratives that illustrate values.

Use emotional language and tone where appropriate.

The Reader

Introduction to "The Reader"
Reading and Writing about Issue Areas

"The Reader" contains seven sections that introduce you to broad issue areas that engage modern society: families and personal relationships; technology; crime and the treatment of criminals; race, culture, and identity; the environment; immigration; and war and peace. Essays are then organized under specific related issues in each broad category. "The Reader" contains essays that explore some of the individual perspectives and positions people have taken in regard to these issues both now and in the past. You may expand your information and understanding of these issues by doing additional research and reading in other reliable sources on the Internet, in the library, or elsewhere.

Internet sources for further online research appear in the introduction to each issue area of "The Reader." You can also expand your perspective on each of these issues through film and literature; a list of related films and literary works that treat these issues in interesting ways is provided in the introduction to each issue area. The films are available on DVD and videotape, and the literature is available in anthologies and in the library.

Purpose of "The Reader"

"The Reader" serves three main purposes.

1. It introduces you to big issue areas and a few of their specific related issues. It also helps you build background and provides you with information to quote in your papers.

2. It provides you with models of different types of arguments and thus gives you a better idea of how argument works in general. It provides you with examples and strategies for improving your own written arguments.

3. It helps you think and invent arguments and ideas of your own by providing you with essays that function as springboards for your own thoughts and reactions.

How to Use "The Reader"

Refer to the chapters indicated for details or review.

1. Select an issue area that is compelling for you. Understand why it is compelling. Assess your background on it. Anticipate ways to build common ground with those who oppose you. (Chapters 1 and 10)

2. Survey it: read the titles and summaries of the articles in the table of contents, read the introductory material and "The Rhetorical Situation" at the beginning of the issue area, and read the introductions to the articles. (Chapters 3 and 4)

3. Select the specific related issue that interests you the most. (Chapters 1 and 4)

4. Read the articles about the related issue, and jot down the claim and some of the major support and warrants for each article. (Chapters 4 and 5)

5. Make a map or write a list of all of the smaller related issues that you can think of that are related to the issue you have read about. Discover the aspect of the issue that interests you the most. This will be your issue. (Chapter 4)

6. Understand the perspectives presented by the articles in "The Reader" on your issue. You may also want to do outside research. Write an exploratory paper in which you explain at least three perspectives on your issue. (Chapter 4)

7. Take a position on your issue, and phrase it as a question. Apply the twelve tests in Box 1.3 to make certain you have an arguable issue. (Chapter 1)

8. State your claim, clarify your purpose, and plan and write an argument paper that presents your position on the issue. (Chapters 8 and 11–13)

QUESTIONS TO HELP YOU READ CRITICALLY AND ANALYTICALLY

1. What is at issue?
2. What is the claim? What type of claim is it?
3. What is the support?
4. What are the warrants?
5. What are the weaknesses in the argument, and how can I refute them?
6. What are some other perspectives on the issue?
7. Where do I stand now in regard to this issue?

QUESTIONS TO HELP YOU READ CREATIVELY AND MOVE FROM READING TO WRITING

1. What is my exigence for writing about this topic?
2. What is my general position compared to the author's?
3. With which specific ideas do I agree or disagree?
4. Do the essays confirm what I think, or do they cause me to change my mind?

5. What original or related ideas are occurring to me as I read?

6. What original perspective can I take?

7. What type of claim do I want to make?

8. What can I quote, paraphrase, or summarize in my paper?

SECTION 1

Issues concerning Families and Personal Relationships

The Issues

A. What Is the Status of the Traditional American Family? How Is the Family Being Redefined?

What we think of as the "traditional family" is a unit composed of a man and a woman—the man acting as the breadwinner and the woman as the homemaker—plus children. The articles in this section work with and against this definition. In the epilogue to Megan Kelso's graphic novel *Watergate Sue*, we see how families persist and reshape themselves after the traditional nuclear family unit has been dissolved. The next essay, by Sarah Yoest Pederson, offers a different perspective on same-sex parenting and therefore on the concept of "family" itself. The essays "Fatherhood 2.0" and "Loving Late Motherhood" consider why some mothers and fathers have chosen to redefine their relationship to traditional notions of family. Finally, the lyrics to the song "Love and Marriage," made popular by Frank Sinatra in the 1950s, ask whether "love and marriage" really do go together like a "horse and carriage." What do you think? See also "Bringing Up Adultolescents" (pages 211–213) and "Kids and Chores: All Work and No Pay" (pages 139–141).

B. What Causes Personal Relationships to Succeed or Fail?

The articles in this section take a close look at how relationships are constructed in today's world and consider what makes them either successful or difficult to establish and sustain. "Crazy Love" and "Why We Flirt" were both published in an issue of *Time* on the relationship of the mind to the body. Psychologist Steven Pinker examines the all-consuming nature of passion and Belinda Luscombe the social dynamics of flirting. The next two articles expand our idea of personal relationships by considering the role of arranged marriages for contemporary young people in America (Anita Jain) and of same-sex friendship as an important relationship (Jennifer 8 Lee). Finally, in "Hitting It Off, Thanks to Algorithms of Love," John Tierney examines contemporary efforts to use science to "fine-tune" love relationships. See also "Why I Want a Wife" (pages 64–65), and the TAG Body Spray ad (page 270).

Web Sites for Further Exploration and Research

CYFERnet (Children, Youth, and Families Educational and Research Network)	http://www.cyfernet.org
All Family Resources™	http://www.familymanagement.com/
Children and Family Research Center	http://cfrcwww.social.uiuc.edu/
Harvard Family Research Project	http://www.hfrp.org
National Marriage Project	http://marriage.rutgers.edu/
National Fatherhood Initiative	http://www.fatherhood.org/
Relationship Web	http://www.relationshipweb.com/
National Association of Mothers' Centers	http://www.motherscenter.org/
"Famous Couples" (*Time* photo essay)	http://www.time.com/time/photogallery/ 0,29307,1704127,00.html

529

Films and Literature Related to Families and Personal Relationships

Films *Annie Hall,* 1977; *The Birdcage,* 1996; *The Brady Bunch Movie,* 1995; *Brokeback Mountain,* 2005; *Daddy Day Care,* 2003; *Kramer vs. Kramer,* 1974; *Mr. Mom,* 1983; *Mrs. Doubtfire,* 1993; *Pat and Mike,* 1952; *Pride and Prejudice* (television mini-series), 1995; *Smoke Signals,* 1998; *Ten Things I Hate about You,* 1999; *That's a Family,* 2000; *Tru Loved,* 2008; *When Harry Met Sally,* 1989.

Literature novels: *Pride and Prejudice* by Jane Austen; *A Thousand Acres* by Jane Smiley; plays: *Death of a Salesman* by Arthur Miller; *A Doll's House* by Henrik Ibsen; *King Lear* by William Shakespeare; *Pygmalion* by George Bernard Shaw; short stories: "The Chrysanthemums" by John Steinbeck; "Sweat" by Zora Neale Hurston; poem: "One Art" by Elizabeth Bishop.

The Rhetorical Situation

The organization of families and the nature and quality of human relationships have always been a source of controversy. The world's religions, along with different social customs and traditions, provide both the constraints and some of the warrants for the positions that many individuals take on issues associated with families and personal relationships. This is particularly true in the case of marriage as a social and religious institution. Much of the controversy centers around the ideal—or, from some perspectives, the myth—of the happy, healthy American nuclear family consisting of one man, one woman, and an unspecified number of children.

In Shakespeare's day, marriages were arranged, largely by the bride and groom's families, on the grounds that elders were more knowledgeable about relationships and that families were the best resource for ensuring a comfortable, stable, and financially healthy marriage. Numerous cultures across the globe rely on arranged marriages, and many members of those cultures, both here and abroad, continue to negotiate their way between traditional customs and emerging concepts of romance, dating, and marriage. Finally, many kinds of nontraditional families—single-parent families, blended families created by remarriage, multigenerational families, grandparent-led families, adoptive families, and even commuter families—are not necessarily new in America, but are receiving more attention, both positive and negative, from politicians, psychologists, and community activists.

While multiple models for family structure have, to some extent, always existed, romantic and familial relations probably have undergone a more radical change in the twentieth and twenty-first centuries. Some people think that the women's movement in the second half of the twentieth century changed what women and men expect from one another, although that process probably began much earlier. Nevertheless, such events as women's acquisition of the right to vote (1920), the entrance of women into the work force during World War II, and the eventually unsuccessful fight in the 1970s for the Equal Rights Amendment pushed both men and women to reevaluate their social roles. Social customs and the law have begun to reflect some of these changes. The legal status of single-sex marriage in the United States remains unresolved. On the other hand, the Family and Medical Leave Act of 1993 allows an employee of either gender to take up to twelve weeks of unpaid leave from work to care for a new baby, a newly adopted child, or a sick spouse, child, or parent; thus the definition of family acknowledged in this legislation is broad.

The science of romance has also been a subject of much attention. While Romeo and Juliet may have fallen in love at first sight, for ordinary humans, factors ranging from hormone production to smell help to bring human beings together. Not merely the sexual drive but romance itself is influenced by the body's chemistry, for Mother Nature wants humans not only to reproduce but to stick together and raise their offspring to maturity, a process that takes at least eighteen years. Thus the testosterone decrease men experience after a partner gives birth may be an effect designed to make males better caretakers of a newborn. Even that most idealized symbol of romantic love, the kiss, not only unleashes a chemical cocktail that releases stress and promotes social bonding but also likely communicates information about the genetic compatibility of two people as potential mates. Some modern young people embrace science as a way to find a life partner, while others turn to the Internet, and still others return to traditional methods such as arranged marriage or engaging a matchmaker.

A. What Is the Status of the Traditional American Family? How Is the Family Being Redefined?

> **BEFORE YOU READ:** Think about your own family: How does it fit or not fit the model of the American nuclear family, consisting of mother, father, and one or more children?

WATERGATE SUE: EPILOGUE*

Megan Kelso

Cartoonist Megan Kelso was born in Seattle, then moved to Brooklyn, New York, with her husband. She plans to keep drawing cartoons until she is an old lady.

Context: The graphic novel *Watergate Sue* (see full novel at URL below) follows two generations of one family. During Sue's pregnancy with baby Mathilda, she and her sister, Josie, reminisce with their mother, Eve, about Sue's own conception and birth during the Watergate hearings of 1973–1974. The epilogue reveals what has happened to the family later in their lives.

For Discussion: The novel ends with an image of Eve (the grandmother in this episode) silently smoking a cigarette. Based on the conversation, what might she be thinking?

For Writing: What definition of the contemporary family is expressed in this epilogue? What holds people together as a family?

531

---

*Megan Kelso, *Watergate Sue: Epilogue*, *New York Times Magazine*, "The Funny Pages," September 9, 2007, http://www.nytimes.com/ref/magazine/funnypagesWatergate.html?_r=1&oref=slogin (accessed June 18, 2008).

> **BEFORE YOU READ:** Think of a childhood book or story that you remember fondly or know well. How does that narrative describe children's relations to parents or other adults in the family?

A FAMILY OF A DIFFERENT FEATHER*

Sarah Yoest Pederson

Sarah Yoest Pederson is Op-Ed editor for the *Fort Worth Star-Telegram*.

1   There are books on the most-challenged list that probably won't surprise you—works with sexually explicit language, stories that contain violence. But that last year's most-challenged book was the children's story *And Tango Makes Three* makes me a bit sad. We could have used it at our house last fall.

2   I'm a mom of two, one of whom is a voracious reader. She's also 5, and a lot of books that she might be ready for intellectually aren't really appropriate for her emotionally. *Tango* is. And it would have been a godsend a year ago, when the debate about same-sex couples hit home.

3   The Princess had a classmate—let's call him Sam—who happens to have two moms. My husband and I had talked about that and decided that the best way to respond, if Her Highness ever raised the topic, was something simple: "Well, honey, there are lots of ways to be a family. We happen to think our way works best for us. [Sam's] moms feel like theirs works best for them."

4   Dodging the Larger Issue? Maybe. But c'mon—kids that age are egocentric little things. Other peoples' sexuality isn't something they're going to spend a lot of time on. . . . "Hey, Mom," came the voice from the back seat. "How can [Sam] have two moms and no dad? Doesn't every baby have to have a dad?"

5   I took a deep breath and started in.

6   "Well, you're right—God takes a seed from the mom and a seed from the dad to make a baby. But with [Sam's] family, the dad isn't there now. There are all kinds of ways to be a family. Daddy and I think our way is best for our family. [Sam's] moms probably think their way is best for their family."

7   She didn't spend much time chewing on that, picking out the unanswered questions in the deliberately vague answer. "Oh," she said. "I get it." She paused. "Can I open my presents as soon as we get home?" And that was that.

8   Little Tango "was the very first penguin in the zoo to have two daddies," the book says. In classrooms all across this country, there are kids in Tango's boat. And straight parents would be well-served to read the book and figure out how they'll respond when the issue is raised in their home. Of course, to do that, they'd have to be able to find it. I tried six large bookstores; finally, at the seventh, I got the only copy they had.

9   There are lots of ways to be a family. And there are lots of ways to lead a family. You can choose to acknowledge differences and to show respect for love and kindness, as *Tango* does, or you can choose to act like a bird of a different feather.

10   It's called an ostrich.

*Sarah Yoest Pederson, "A Family of a Different Feather," *Fort Worth Star-Telegram*, September 30, 2007, 3E.

532

> **BEFORE YOU READ:** Think of a family film, television sitcom, or drama, ranging from *The Brady Bunch* to *The Cosby Show* to *The Sopranos*. What actions and behaviors define the father of this fictional family? What really makes him the "dad"?

FATHERHOOD 2.0*

Lisa Takeuchi Cullen and Lev Grossman

Lisa Takeuchi Cullen is a New York–based staff writer for *Time* magazine. Born and raised in Kobe, Japan, she now lives in New Jersey with her husband, daughter, and basset hound. Lev Grossman grew up in a suburb of Boston and graduated from Harvard with a degree in literature. After leaving graduate school, he wrote freelance articles for magazines such as *Lingua Franca*, the *Village Voice*, and *Time Out New York*. In 2002, he was hired by *Time* and became the magazine's book critic and a technology writer. In 2006, he won the Deadline Club Award for Arts Reporting.

For Discussion: Look at the posture of the two figures in this photograph. From the way in which their bodies are posed, what can you tell about the relation between father and daughter?

For Writing: In this photograph, ordinary objects, clothing, and even furniture can be used to define what it means to be a man as well as a father. Based on the father's dress, actions, and his surroundings, how would you articulate the photograph's definition of "real masculinity" or of "fatherhood 2.0"?

533

Context: The caption to this photograph reads: "A Girl's Best Friend. True, Doug Ranno, 41, is a hard-driving medical equipment salesman in Denver. But he's also a tea-sipping, ballet-recital-attending dad to Reese, 4, and her younger sister. Becoming a dad, he says, 'made me more of a man.'"

1   Does being more of a father make you less of a man? To a group of committed dads assembled one night in a New Jersey diner, the answer is obvious. Sort of. Paul Haley, 38, a father of two, says women look at him when he walks down the street with his kids. "I think it's admiration," he says. Adam Wolff, also 38—with two kids and one on the way—ponders what it means to be a man. "Is my man-ness about being the breadwinner or being a good father to my kids or something else?" Michael Gerber, 36, father of a

---

*Lisa Takeuchi Cullen and Lev Grossman, "Fatherhood 2.0," *Time*, October 4, 2007, http://www.time.com/time/magazine/article/0,9171,1668449,00.html (accessed June 18, 2008).

7-month-old, asks, "Do you mean, Do we feel whipped?"

2   "I'm probably a little whipped," shrugs Lee Roberts, 45. He's a part-time copy editor, married to a full-time journalist, who has stayed home for nine years to raise their two children. "There are definitely some guys who look at me and think, 'What's up with him?' Do I care? Well, I guess I do a little because I just mentioned it," he says. Haley speaks up to reassure him: "Kids remember, man. All that matters is that you're there. Being there is being a man."

3   But what does it mean, exactly, to be a man these days? Once upon a Darwinian time, a man was the one spearing the woolly mammoth. And it wasn't so long ago that a man was that strong and silent fellow over there at the bar with the dry martini or a cold can of beer—a hardworking guy in a gray flannel suit or blue-collar work shirt. He sired children, yes, but he drew the line at diapering them. He didn't know what to expect when his wife was expecting, he didn't review bottle warmers on his daddy blog, and he most certainly didn't participate in little-girl tea parties. Today's dads plead guilty to all of the above—so what does that make them? [. . .]

4   "Men today are far more involved with their families than they have been at virtually any other time in the last century," says Michael Kimmel, author of *Manhood in America: A Cultural History*. In the late 1970s, sociologists at the University of Michigan found that the average dad spent about a third as much time with his kids as the average mom did. By 2000, that was up to three-fourths. The number of stay-at-home fathers has tripled in the past 10 years. The Census counts less than 200,000, but those studying the phenomenon say it's probably 10 times that number. Fathers' style of parenting has changed, too. Men hug their kids more, help with homework more, tell kids they love them more. Or, as sociologist Scott Coltrane of the University of California,

534

Riverside, says, "Fathers are beginning to look more like mothers."

5   Many dads are challenging old definitions of manliness. "Masculinity has traditionally been associated with work and work-related success, with competition, power, prestige, dominance over women, restrictive emotionality—that's a big one," says Aaron Rochlen, an associate professor of psychology at the University of Texas who studies fatherhood and masculinity. "But a good parent needs to be expressive, patient, emotional, not money oriented." Though many fathers still cleave to the old archetype, Rochlen's study finds that those who don't are happier. Other research shows that fathers who stop being men of the old mold have better-adjusted children, better marriages and better work lives—better physical and mental health, even. "Basically," says Rochlen, "masculinity is bad for you." [. . .]

6   But how to forge a new idea of manhood for this brave new two-income world? Hollywood hasn't been much help. From Michael Keaton in the 1983 movie *Mr. Mom* to Adam Sandler in *Big Daddy* (1999) to Eddie Murphy in *Daddy Day Care* (2003), the sight of a man caught in the act of parenting has been a reliable laugh getter—always a good indicator of what the culture considers uncomfortable material. For every *Pursuit of Happyness*, there's a movie like . . . *Knocked Up*, which plays not so much as a tribute to fatherhood as an effort by men to convince themselves that fatherhood is all right—and the movie's happy ending is the least plausible thing about it. One show at least managed to capture the tension: What were those seven seasons of *The Sopranos* about if not a man fighting to reconcile the tender pangs of a caring, new-style father with the old-school masculine ideals of violence and stoicism—not to mention the psychological damage wreaked on him by his own old-school father?

7   Society hasn't made it easy for newly evolved dads to feel manly, either. In Rochlen's study of stay-at-home dads, those who scored low on measures of traditional

masculinity professed higher degrees of happiness in their roles—as well as in their marriages, with their children and with their health. But even they worried about how the rest of the world viewed their choice—with some reason. "There's definitely a stigma out there," says Rochlen. "The dads tell stories about mothers on the playground looking at them like they're child molesters or losers."

8   Ironically, dads who take on parenting roles once considered emasculating may simply be responding to nature. Studies have shown that men experience hormonal shifts during their female partner's pregnancy. A man's testosterone level drops after settling down to marriage and family, perhaps in preparation for parenthood, as the male hormone is thought to be incompatible with nurturing behavior. In one study, for example, men with lower amounts of testosterone were willing to hold baby dolls for a longer period of time than those with a higher count. In another, the very act of holding dolls lowered testosterone.

9   More evidence of nature's intent to design men as active parents might be seen in the effects of involved fathering on children. Given the politically charged debates over same-sex unions and single parenting, it is perhaps not surprising that the richest area in the nascent field of fatherhood research is in the results of fathers' absence. David Popenoe of Rutgers University has pointed to increased rates of juvenile delinquency, drug abuse and other problems among children raised without a male parent present. Research on the unique skills men bring to parenting is sparse, but intriguing. Eleanor Maccoby of Stanford University has found that fathers are less likely than mothers to modify their language when speaking to their children, thus challenging their kids to expand vocabulary and cognitive skills. Fathers also tend to enforce rules more strictly and systematically in reaction to children's wrongdoing, according to educational psychologist Carol Gilligan. "Having a father isn't magic," says Armin Brott,

author of seven books about fatherhood, "but it really does make a difference for the kids."

10   When men take on nontraditional roles in the home and family, it also makes a difference to the marriage. Coltrane of UC Riverside and John Gottman at the University of Washington found in separate studies that when men contribute to domestic labor (which is part and parcel of parenting), women interpret it as a sign of caring, experience less stress, and are more likely to find themselves in the mood for sex. This is not to say that more involved fathering has erased marital tensions or that it hasn't introduced new ones. Dads admit they get fussed over for things moms do every day. "Sometimes you're treated like a dog walking on its hind legs—'Oh, look, he can do laundry!'" says Jim O'Kane, 47, a father of two in Blackstone, Mass. And some women resent ceding their role as top parent. When her daughter fell down at a birthday party, Amy Vachon, 44, of Watertown, Mass., recalls that the girl ran crying all the way across the room—to her husband Marc. "I admit it hurt at the time," she says, "mostly because I wondered what everyone thought. There's such a high standard in society for the good mother."

11   It's a slippery slope: a recent Pew survey found that increasingly, parents rank their relationships with their kids as more important than their relationship with their spouse. Just as interesting, they rank their job dead last. That most masculine of traits—the ability to go out into the world and bring home a buck—is receding in importance for the men of Generation X. Men's rates of labor-force participation have dropped from just above 90% in 1970 to just above 80% in 2005. Almost a third of young fathers (32%) say they dedicate more time to their children, while 28% say they devote more time to their jobs. [. . .]

12   Today's fathers aren't the men their own fathers were but only if you insist that the nature of masculinity doesn't change—that it's a biological fact and not a mutable cultural

construct. The new fathers are creating a new ideal of masculinity. It's not as *Mad Men* cool, but it is healthier. "The emerging and evolving norms of fatherhood and masculinity challenge men to be a different kind of guy," says Rochlen. "But on the positive side, it gives them new opportunity to embrace and enact these dimensions that are good for them and good for their families." It's even good for their emotional health. Coltrane says fatherhood is proving a "safe pathway" for men to develop and explore their nurturing side. "It's not considered wimpy . . . to hug your daughter," he adds. That's something we can all embrace.

> **BEFORE YOU READ:** What goals do you (or did you) want to accomplish before becoming a parent? What is the ideal time for starting a family and why? Are you certain that you want to become a parent?

LOVING LATE MOTHERHOOD[*]
Heather Cabot

Heather Cabot is the founder and editor of the e-zine *The Well Mom* (www.thewellmom.com) and is also Web-life editor for *Yahoo!* Previously she spent fifteen years working in television, co-anchoring *World News Now* and *World News This Morning* for ABC.

1   From Halle to J. Lo to Julia, the public is going ga-ga over celebrity offspring. And with the spotlight shining bright on baby bumps galore, it seems that Hollywood starlets are starting families later and later (Jamie Lynn Spears aside). But deciding to become a first-time mom after 35 or 40 isn't pioneering anymore. It's the new norm.

2   The number of women who've delayed first-time motherhood until their mid-thirties or beyond has grown tenfold over the past 30 years according to researcher Elizabeth Gregory, associate professor and director of the Women's Studies Program at the University of Houston and the author of the new book titled, *Ready: Why Women Are Embracing the New Later Motherhood* (Basic Books 2008).

3   Gregory, a first-time mother herself at age 39, spent two and a half years interviewing 113 women who had children in their mid-thirties or older about their choices and the consequences. "Women are choosing when they want to have children for the first time in history," she told me in an interview this week. She says their decisions, due in part to birth control, longer life expectancy, and new fertility technologies are spurring societal changes including more participatory dads and more employers accommodating family-friendly schedules.

4   "Most consistently, I heard (from the women) that waiting offered them the chance to establish themselves, as individuals and in their work, to find the right partners . . . and to achieve a measure of financial stability. When they did have their kids, they felt ready to focus on their children's development rather than their own," Gregory says. So maybe us Gen-X slackers had it right all along. We've been delaying marriage and parenthood to find ourselves and at the same time maturing so we could actually handle the responsibility of raising a child.

5   Motherhood unfolded so differently for our own moms. When my mom gave birth to

*Heather Cabot, "Loving Late Motherhood," *The Huffington Post*, January 16, 2008, http://www.huffingtonpost.com/heather-cabot/loving-late-motherhood_b_81648.html (accessed June 18, 2008).

me in 1970, the average age of a new mother in the U.S. was 21. And while my aspirations as a little girl included being a mom someday, it was never in the context of choosing to pursue a profession or not. Thanks to Title IX and the feminist voices who really changed the landscape for me and my contemporaries, I grew up thinking I could be anything I wanted to be and have it all.[1]

6   But somewhere along the way, I became aware of biological realities. Despite advances in fertility treatments, it's tough to ignore the ticking clock at some point. Gregory found that her research subjects were keenly aware of the timeline. I was, when I finally hit thirty. But the chance to live the life of a single working person, to pay my own bills, to bask in my own professional accomplishments, and most importantly, to know I can support myself and live independently were tremendously important lessons for me. And now at age 37, with two-year-old twins, I think I am a better mother for it.

7   When I turned 23, a year older than the age my mom had me, motherhood was the last thing on my mind. Fresh from grad school, I was in hot pursuit of my first TV reporting job

and had somehow patched together a bunch of freelance gigs to make my rent. I was living in New York City in a crowded apartment with four, sometimes five female roommates who all had lots of drama in their lives (or so it seemed at the time). I remember sipping wine on Sunday nights while we gabbed for hours about our work, our love lives, politics, not to mention our worried parents, anxious about us single gals living in the big city. It was heaven. Looking back, I wouldn't trade that indulgent time in my life for anything. And I hope my daughter won't either.

8   "If you are perfectly set up to have a family at 32, then fine. But if you are not, why add the burden of all this anxiety?" asks Gregory. She hopes her research will empower other women to feel confident in their decisions to choose motherhood when it feels right.

Editor's note:

1. Title IX is a 1972 law that states: "No person in the United States shall, on the basis of sex, be excluded from participation in, be denied the benefits of, or be subjected to discrimination under any education program or activity receiving Federal financial assistance."

BEFORE YOU READ: The principal metaphor for marriage offered by this song, which was popularized by singer Frank Sinatra, is "love + marriage" = "horse + carriage." Before you consider the entire lyric, what does this equation suggest about the nature of marriage?

"LOVE AND MARRIAGE"

1955, Lyrics by Sammy Cahn, Music by Jimmy Van Heusen

Love and marriage, love and marriage
Go together like a horse and carriage
This I tell you brother
You can't have one without the other.

Love and marriage, love and marriage   5
It's an institute you can't disparage
Ask the local gentry
And they will say it's elementary.

Try, try, try to separate them
It's an illusion   10
Try, try, try, and you will only come
To this conclusion.

Love and marriage, love and marriage
Go together like a horse and carriage
Dad was told by mother   15
You can't have one without the other.

B. **What Causes Personal Relationships to Succeed or Fail?**

> **BEFORE YOU READ:** The title of Steven Pinker's essay, "Crazy Love," was also the title of a 2007 movie about jealousy, violence, and love. Think, by contrast, of your own definition of "true love"? What are its causes?

CRAZY LOVE[*]

Steven Pinker

Steven Pinker, the Johnstone Professor of Psychology at Harvard University, is the author of *The Language Instinct* and *The Stuff of Thought: Language as a Window into Human Nature.*

Context: The caption reads: Crazy Love. This image appears after the lead-in to Pinker's article, which states: "Our partners may be obsessive, possessive, even dangerous. There's a reason we stick around—even at our own peril."

For Discussion: This is a particularly symbolic, even an allegorical cartoon. What does the image of a woman who wears a large bow and black stockings emerging from a box or suitcase suggest about the nature of "crazy love"?

For Writing: The cartoonist makes a particular claim about "crazy love," using points from Pinker's essay for its evidence and supports. What argument do the essay and cartoon together make about love and its dark counterpart, "crazy love"?

*Steven Pinker, "Crazy Love," *Time*, January 28, 2008, 82–83.

1 Why do fools fall in love? And when we do fall, why do our faculties of reason—and decency and self-respect and even right and wrong—sometimes not come along? For that matter, why would anyone reciprocate the love of a partner who has come so romantically unhinged?

2 The thought of a loved one can turn our wits upside down, ratchet up our heart rate, impel us to slay dragons and write corny songs. We may become morose, obsessive, even violent. Lovesickness has been blamed on the moon, on the devil, but whatever is behind it, it doesn't look like the behavior of a rational animal trying to survive and reproduce. But might there be a method to this amorous madness?

3 During the decades that the concept of human nature was taboo in academia, many scholars claimed that romantic love was a recent social construction. It was an invention of the Hallmark-card poets or Hollywood scriptwriters or, in one theory, medieval troubadours extolling the adulterous love of a knight for a lady.

4 For anyone who has been under love's spell, these theories seem preposterous, and so they are. Nothing so primal could have been created out of thin air as a mere custom or product. To the contrary, romantic love is a human universal. In 1896 a Kwakiutl Indian in southern Alaska wrote the lament "Fire runs through my body—the pain of loving you," which could be the title of a bad power ballad today. Similar outpourings of passion can be found all over the world from those with broken hearts.

5 Romantic infatuation is different from both raw lust and the enduring commitment that keeps lovers together long after their besot-tedness has faded. We all know the symptoms: idealized thoughts of the loved one; swings of mood from ecstasy to despair; insomnia and anorexia; and the intense need for signs of reciprocation. Even the brain chemistry is dif-ferent: lust is fueled (in both sexes) by testos-terone, and companionate love by vasopressin and oxytocin.[1] Romantic passion taps the same dopamine system that is engaged by other obsessive drives like drug addiction.[2]

6 For all this, there may be a paradoxical logic to romantic love. Imagine a world without it, a world of rational shoppers looking for the best available mate. Unsentimental social scientists and veterans of the singles scene know that this world is not entirely unlike our own. People shop for the most desirable person who will accept them, and that is why most marriages pair a bride and a groom of roughly equal desirability. The 10s marry the 10s, the 9s marry the 9s and so on. That is exactly what should happen in a marketplace where you want the best price you can get (the other person) for the goods you're offering (you).

7 But we also know this isn't the whole picture. Most daters find themselves at some point with a match who ought to be perfect but with whom for some reason the chemistry isn't there. Why do the principles of smart shopping give us only the rough statistics of mate choice, not the final pick?

8 The reason is that smart shopping isn't enough; both parties have to close the deal. Somewhere in this world lives the best-looking, richest, smartest person who would settle for you. But this ideal match is hard to find, and you may die single if you insist on waiting for such a mate to show up. So you choose to set up house with the best person you have found so far.

9 Your mate has gone through the same reasoning, which leaves you both vulnera-ble. The law of averages says that someday one of you will meet an even more desirable person; maybe a newly single Brad Pitt or Angelina Jolie will move in next door. If you are always going for the best you can get, at that point you will dump your partner pronto. But your partner would have invested time, child rearing and forgone opportunities in the relationship by that point. Anticipating this, your mate would have been foolish to enter the relationship in the first place, and the same is true for you. In this world of rational actors, neither of you could thus take the chance on the other. What could make you trust the other person enough to make that leap?

539

Reading Images: Movie Madness

Image 1:
Loony (*Fatal Attraction*)

Image 2:
Furry (*King Kong*)

Image 3:
Loony—Again (*Play Misty for Me*)

Image 4:
Scheming (*Vertigo*)

Image 5:
Ill Clad (*Basic Instinct*)

Context: The caption reads: "Don't Go There: Bad lovers come in many forms in film."

For Discussion: Consider the kinds of bad lovers listed in the caption to this photograph: "loony," "furry," "scheming," and "ill clad." Based on your own knowledge of contemporary films, which kind of bad lover is the most frightening?

For Writing: The figure who might not fit in this group of "bad lovers" is King Kong, who is a beast. Defend Kong against the charge that he is a crazy, evil, or just plain "bad" lover.

10   One answer is, don't accept a partner who wanted you for rational reasons to begin with. Look for someone who is emotionally committed to you because you are you. If the emotion moving that person is not triggered by your objective mate value, that emotion will not be alienated by someone who comes along with greater mate value than yours. And there should be signals that the emotion is not faked, showing that the person's behavior is under the control of the involuntary parts of the brain—the ones in charge of heart rate, breathing, skin flushing and so on. Does this emotion sound familiar?

11   This explanation of infatuation was devised by the economist Robert Frank on the basis of the work of Nobel laureate Thomas Schelling. Social life is a series of promises, threats, and bargains; in those games it sometimes pays to sacrifice your self-interest and control. An eco-protester who handcuffs himself to a tree guarantees that his threat to impede the logger is credible. The prospective home buyer who makes an unrecoverable deposit guarantees that her promise to buy the house is credible. And suitors who are uncontrollably smitten are in effect guaranteeing that their pledge of love is credible.

12   And this gets us to the dark side of romance. Threats, no less than promises, must be backed up by signs of commitment. A desperate lover in danger of being abandoned may resort to threatening his wife or girlfriend (yes, his; it's usually a man). The best way to prevent her from calling his bluff is in fact not to bluff—to be the kind of hothead who is crazy enough to do it. Of course, if he does make good on the threat, everyone loses (which is why the judicial system must make good on its threat to punish violent thugs).

13   This perverse logic of promises and threats lies behind the observation on romance offered by George Bernard Shaw: "When we want to read of the deeds that are done for love, whither do we turn? To the murder column."

Editor's notes:

1. Testosterone is the principal male sex hormone in humans. Vasopressin is a hormone that retains water in the human body but has also been known to encourage pair-bonding between male and female voles, a kind of small mammal. Oxytocin is a hormone released in women during labor, birth, and breastfeeding.

2. Dopamine is a hormone that increases heart rate and blood pressure.

BEFORE YOU READ: Consult your own experience and common sense. Why do you think that people flirt?

WHY WE FLIRT*

Belinda Luscombe

Belinda Luscombe is arts editor of *Time* magazine. Among her special interests are fashion, architecture, and design, but she has also written about divorce, kidnapping, and motherhood.

For Discussion: The environment depicted in this image sets the stage for the couple's flirtation. How does the social situation allow for them to flirt? What conditions make flirting easy or difficult?

For Writing: The caption to this photo suggests that the man is attractive to this woman. We could also argue that the two figures make an argument from personal *ethos* recommending themselves to the other. Focusing either on the man or the woman, how does the figure's stance make an argument from *ethos*? How do posture, clothing, and accessories help to create that gendered *ethos*?

Context: The caption to this photograph reads: "Affectionate Young Couple on Balcony Smiling." This couple's proximity to each other suggests that neither the woman nor the man is about to flee or fight.

---

*Brenda Luscombe, "Why We Flirt," *Time*, January 28, 2008, 62–65.

1   Contrary to widespread belief, only two very specific types of people flirt: those who are single and those who are married. Single people flirt because, well, they're single and therefore nobody is really contractually obliged to talk to them, sleep with them, or scratch that difficult-to-reach part of the back. But married people, they're a tougher puzzle. They've found themselves a suitable—maybe even superior—mate, had a bit of productive fun with the old gametes, and ensured that at least some of their genes are carried into the next generation. They've done their duty, evolutionarily speaking. Their genome will survive. Yay them. So for Pete's sake, why do they persist with the game?

2   And before you claim, whether single or married, that you never flirt, bear in mind that it's not just talk we're dealing with here. It's gestures, stance, eye movement. Notice how you lean forward to the person you're talking to and tip up your heels? Notice the quick little eyebrow raise you make, the sidelong glance coupled with the weak smile you give, the slightly sustained gaze you offer? If you're a woman, do you feel your head tilting to the side a bit, exposing either your soft, sensuous neck or, looking at it another way, your jugular? If you're a guy, are you keeping your body in an open, come-on-attack-me position, arms positioned to draw the eye to your impressive lower abdomen?

3   Scientists call all these little acts "contact-readiness" cues, because they indicate, nonverbally, that you're prepared for physical engagement. (More general body language is known as "nonverbal leakage." Deep in their souls, all scientists are poets.) These cues are a crucial part of what's known in human-ethology circles as the "heterosexual relationship initiation process" and elsewhere, often on the selfsame college campuses, as "coming on to someone." In primal terms, they're physical signals that you don't intend to dominate, nor do you intend to flee—both useful messages potential mates need to send before they can proceed to that awkward talking phase. They're the opening line, so to speak, for the opening line.

4   One of the reasons we flirt in this way is that we can't help it. We're programmed to do it, whether by biology or culture. The biology part has been investigated by any number of researchers. Ethnologist Irenaus Eibl Eibesfeldt, then of the Max Planck Institute in Germany, filmed African tribes in the 1960s and found that the women there did the exact same prolonged stare followed by a head tilt away with a little smile that he saw in America. (The technical name for the head movement is a "cant." Except in this case it's more like "can.")

5   Evolutionary biologists would suggest that those individuals who executed flirting maneuvers most adeptly were more successful in swiftly finding a mate and reproducing and that the behavior therefore became widespread in all humans. "A lot of people feel flirting is part of the universal language of how we communicate, especially nonverbally," says Jeffry Simpson, director of the social psychology program at the University of Minnesota.

6   Simpson is currently studying the roles that attraction and flirting play during different times of a woman's ovulation cycle. His research suggests that women who are ovulating are more attracted to flirty men. "The guys they find appealing tend to have characteristics that are attractive in the short term, which include some flirtatious behaviors," he says. He's not sure why women behave this way, but it follows that men who bed ovulating women have a greater chance of procreating and passing on those flirty genes, which means those babies will have more babies, and so on. Of course, none of this is a conscious choice, just as flirting is not always intentional. "With a lot of it, especially the nonverbal stuff, people

may not be fully aware that they"re doing it," says Simpson. "You don't see what you look like. People may emit flirtatious cues and not be fully aware of how powerful they are."

FLIRTING WITH INTENT

7   Well, some people anyway. But then there are the rest of you. You know who you are. You're the gentleman who delivered my groceries the other day and said we had a problem because I had to be 21 to receive alcohol. You're me when I told that same man that I liked a guy who knew his way around a dolly. (Lame, I know. I was caught off guard.) You're the fifty-something guy behind me on the plane before Christmas telling his forty-something seatmate how sensual her eyes were —actually, I hope you're not, because if so, you're really skeevy. My point is, once you move into the verbal phase of flirtation, it's pretty much all intentional.

8   And there are some schools of thought that teach there's nothing wrong with that. Flirtation is a game we play, a dance for which everyone knows the moves. "People can flirt outrageously without intending anything," says independent sex researcher Timothy Perper, who has been researching flirting for 30 years. "Flirting captures the interest of the other person and says 'Would you like to play?'" And one of the most exhilarating things about the game is that the normal rules of social interaction are rubberized. Clarity is not the point. "Flirting opens a window of potential. Not yes, not no," says Perper. "So we engage ourselves in this complex game of maybe." The game is not new. The first published guide for how to flirt was written about 2,000 years ago, Perper points out, by a bloke named Ovid. As dating books go, *The Art of Love* leaves more recent publications like *The Layguide: How to Seduce Women More Beautiful Than You Ever Dreamed Possible No Matter What You Look Like or How Much*

You Make in its dust. And yes, that's a real book.

9   Once we've learned the game of maybe, it becomes second nature to us. Long after we need to play it, we're still in there swinging (so to speak) because we're better at it than at other games. Flirting sometimes becomes a social fallback position. "We all learn rules for how to behave in certain situations, and this makes it easier for people to know how to act, even when nervous," says Antonia Abbey, a psychology professor at Wayne State University. Just as we learn a kind of script for how to behave in a restaurant or at a business meeting, she suggests, we learn a script for talking to the opposite sex. "We often enact these scripts without even thinking," she says. "For some women and men, the script may be so well learned that flirting is a comfortable strategy for interacting with others." In other words, when in doubt, we flirt.

10   The thing that propels many already committed people to ply the art of woo, however, is often not doubt. It's curiosity. Flirting "is a way of testing one's mate-value and the possibility of alternatives—actually trying to see if someone might be available as an alternative," says Arthur Aron, professor of psychology at the State University of New York at Stony Brook. To evolutionary biologists, the advantages of this are clear: mates die, offspring die. Flirting is a little like taking out mating insurance.

11   If worst comes to worst and you don't still have it (and yes, I'm sure you do), the very act of flirting with someone else may bring about renewed attention from your mate, which has advantages all its own. So it's a win-win.

12   Flirting is also emotional capital to be expended in return for something else. Not usually for money, but for the intangibles— a better table, a juicier cut of meat, the ability to return an unwanted purchase without too many questions. It's a handy social lubricant, reducing the friction of everyday

transactions, and closer to a strategically timed tip than a romantic overture. Have you ever met a male hairdresser who wasn't a flirt? Women go to him to look better. So the better they feel when they walk out of his salon, the happier they'll be to go back for a frequent blowout. Flirting's almost mandatory. And if the hairdresser is gay, so much the better, since the attention is much less likely to be taken as an untoward advance.

IT'S DANGEROUS OUT THERE

13 But outside the hairdresser's chair, things are not so simple. Flirt the wrong way with the wrong person, and you run the risk of everything from a slap to a sexual-harassment lawsuit. And of course, the American virtue of plainspokenness is not an asset in an activity that is ambiguous by design. Wayne State's Abbey, whose research has focused on the dark side of flirting—when it transmogrifies into harassment, stalking or acquaintance rape—warns that flirting can be treacherous. "Most of the time flirtation desists when one partner doesn't respond positively," she says. "But some people just don't get the message that is being sent, and some ignore it because it isn't what they want to hear."

14 One of the most fascinating flirting laboratories is the digital world. Here's a venue that is all words and no body language; whether online or in text messages, nuance is almost impossible. And since text and e-mail flirting can be done without having to look people in the eye, and is often done with speed, it is bolder, racier and unimpeded by moments of reflection on whether the message could be misconstrued or is wise to send at all. "Flirt texting is a topic everyone finds fascinating, although not much research is out there yet," says Abbey. But one thing is clear: "People are often more willing to disclose intimate details via the Internet, so the process may escalate more quickly."

15 That's certainly the case on sites like *Yahoo!*'s Married and Flirting e-mail group, as well as on Marriedbutplaying.com and Married-but-flirting.com. "Flirting" in this sense appears to be a euphemism for talking dirty. A University of Florida study of 86 participants in a chat room published in *Psychology Today* in 2003 found that while nearly all those surveyed felt they were initially simply flirting with a computer, not a real person, almost a third of them eventually had a face-to-face meeting with someone they chatted with. And all but two of the couples who met went on to have an affair. Whether the people who eventually cheated went to the site with the intention of doing so or got drawn in by the fantasy of it all is unclear. Whichever, the sites sure seem like a profitable place for people like the guy behind me on the pre-Christmas flight to hang out.

16 Most people who flirt—off-line at least—are not looking for an affair. But one of the things that sets married flirting apart from single flirting is that it has a much greater degree of danger and fantasy to it. The stakes are higher and the risk is greater, even if the likelihood of anything happening is slim. But the cocktail is in some cases much headier. It is most commonly the case with affairs, therapists say, that people who cheat are not so much dissatisfied with their spouse as with themselves and the way their lives have turned out. There is little that feels more affirming and revitalizing than having someone fall in love with you. (It follows, then, that there's little that feels less affirming than being cheated on.) Flirting is a decaf affair, a way of feeling more alive, more vital, more desirable without actually endangering the happiness of anyone you love—or the balance of your bank account. So go ahead and flirt, if you can do it responsibly. You might even try it with your spouse.

544

BEFORE YOU READ: From your own family history—perhaps in the case of your parents, grandparents, or cousins—what social and cultural traditions are followed for courtship and marriage?

IS ARRANGED MARRIAGE REALLY ANY WORSE THAN CRAIGSLIST?*
Anita Jain

Anita Jain is currently a technology and telecommunications reporter for *Crain's New York Business*.

For Discussion: This photograph functions in many ways as a form of autobiography. What can you tell about Anita Jain as a person from the iconographic details in the photograph (e.g., clothing, flowers, pictures, furniture, etc.)?

For Writing: Think of this image as evidence for the claim made by the article that follows it. What is the article's principal claim? How does the image function as evidence for the main essay's argument from the writer's personal *ethos*?

545

Context. The caption to this photograph reads: The author in her Fort Greene apartment. This casually posed photograph shows the author of the article at home in her urban apartment. The image shows a combination of Indian and American, and traditional and modern influences on the writer's *ethos*.

1 Recently, I was cc'd on an e-mail addressed to my father. It read, "We liked the girl's profile. The boy is in good state job in Mississippi and cannot come to New York. The girl must relocate to Mississippi." The message was signed by Mr. Ramesh Gupta, "the boy's father."

2 That wasn't as bad as the time I logged on to my computer at home in Fort Greene and got a message that asked, forgoing any preamble, what the date, time, and location of my birth were. Presumably sent to determine how astrologically harmonious a match with a Hindu suitor I'd be, the e-mail was

*Anita Jain, "Is Arranged Marriage Really Any Worse Than Craigslist?" *New York Magazine,* March 28, 2005, http://nymag.com/nymetro/news/culture/features/11621/index.html (accessed June 18, 2008).

dismayingly abrupt. But I did take heart in the fact that it was addressed only to me.

3   I've been fielding such messages—or, rather, my father has—more and more these days, having crossed the unmarriageable threshold for an Indian woman, 30, two years ago. My parents, in a very earnest bid to secure my eternal happiness, have been trying to marry me off to, well, just about anyone lately. In my childhood home near Sacramento, my father is up at night on arranged-marriage Websites. And the result— strange e-mails from boys' fathers and stranger dates with those boys themselves— has become so much a part of my dating life that I've lost sight of how bizarre it once seemed.

4   Many women, Indian or not, whose parents have had a long, healthy marriage hope we will, too, while fearing that perhaps we've made everything irreparably worse by expecting too much. Our prospective husbands have to be rich and socially conscious, hip but down-to-earth.

5   For some Indians, the conundrum is exacerbated by the fact that our parents had no choice for a partner; the only choice was how hard they'd work to be happy. My father saw my mother once before they got married. He loves to shock Americans by recounting how he lost sight of her at a bazaar the day after their wedding and lamented to himself that he would never find her again, as he'd forgotten what she looked like. So while we, as modern Indian women, eschew the idea of marrying without love, the idea that we're being too picky tends to nag even more than it otherwise would.

6   Still, for years, I didn't want to get married the way my brother did. He'd met his wife through a newspaper ad my parents had taken out. He's very happily married, with a baby daughter, but he also never had a girlfriend before his wedding day. I was more precocious when it came to affairs of the heart, having enjoyed my first kiss with cute Matt from the football squad at 14.

7   Perhaps it was that same spirit of romantic adventurism that led me, shortly after college, to go on the first of these "introductions," though I agreed to my parents' setup mainly with an eye toward turning it into a story for friends.

8   At the time, I was working as a journalist in Singapore. Vikram, "in entertainment," took me to the best restaurant in town, an Indonesian place with a view of the skyscrapers. Before long, though, I gathered that he was of a type: someone who prided himself on being modern and open-minded but who in fact had horribly crusty notions passed down from his Indian parents. I was taken aback when he told me about an Indian girl he'd liked. "I thought maybe she was the one, but then I found out she had a Muslim boyfriend in college," he said. I lodged my protest against him and arranged marriage by getting ragingly intoxicated and blowing smoke rings in his face. Childish? Maybe, but I didn't want to be marriageable back then. Indeed, I rarely thought of marriage at the time.

9   But for Indians, there's no way to escape thinking about marriage, eventually. It wouldn't be a stretch to say that *shaadi*, the word for marriage in many Indian languages, is the first word a child understands after *mummy* and *papa*. To an Indian, marriage is a matter of karmic destiny. There are many happy unions in the pantheon of Hindu gods—Shiva and Parvati, Krishna and Radha.[1] [. . .]

10   The pressure on me to find a husband started very early. A few days after my 1st birthday, within months of my family's arrival in the U.S., I fell out the window of a

three-story building in Baltimore. My father recalls my mother's greatest concern, after learning that I hadn't been gravely injured: "What boy will marry her when he finds out?" she cried, begging my father to never mention my broken arm—from which I've enjoyed a full recovery—to prospective suitors out of fear my dowry would be prohibitively higher. (A middle-class family can easily spend $100,000 these days on a dowry in India.) Much savvier in the ways of his new country, my father laughed it off. "But there is no dowry in America!"

11 Fulfilling his parental duty, my father placed matrimonial ads for me every couple of years during my twenties in such immigrant newspapers as *India Abroad*. They read something like, "Match for Jain girl, Harvard-educated journalist, 25, fair, slim."[. . .]

12 Depending on whether my father was in a magnanimous mood, he would add "caste no bar," which meant suitors didn't have to belong to Jainism, an offshoot of Hinduism with the world's most severe dietary restrictions. [. . .]

13 This desultory casting around to see what was out there has become much more urgent now that I'm in my thirties, and in their quest, my parents have discovered a dizzying array of Websites: *shaadi.com*, *indiamatrimony.com*, etc. Within these sites are sub-sites for Indian regions, like *punjabimatrimony.com*. You might be surprised at who you'd find on them: the guy in the next cubicle, your freshman-year roommate at NYU, maybe even the cute girl you tried to pick up at a Lower East Side bar last night.

14 Far from being a novel approach to matrimony, these sites are a natural extension of how things have been done in India for decades. Even since well before the explosion of the country's famously vibrant press in the fifties, Indians were coupling up via matrimonial ads in national papers ("Match sought for Bengali Brahmin, wheatish complexion," etc.).

15 My father took to the Websites like a freshly divorced 42-year-old who's just discovered Craigslist. He uploaded my profile on several, indicating that only men living in New York City need apply (*nota bene*, Mr. Ramesh Gupta). Unfortunately, in the world of *shaadi.com*, this means most of the men live in New Jersey, while working in IT departments all around New York.

16 My father also *wrote* my profile. This may be why dates are surprised to discover I enjoy a glass of wine or two with dinner, and another couple afterward, even though the profile says "I never drink." And he writes back to those who appear aboveboard. This is no small task, as anyone who's done any online dating can attest. As my father puts it, wagging his head, "You get a lot of useless types."

17 Like most Indians of their generation, my parents believe there are only two legitimate professions: doctor and engineer (not medicine and engineering, but doctor and engineer). . . . The problem is that while he wants doctor or engineer, my heart beats for the diametric opposite. Take the aging but rakish foreign correspondent I was smitten with last year. Nearing 50, he'd just seen his marriage fall apart, and he mourned its passing by plastering his body with fresh tattoos and picking bar fights. I found it terribly sexy that he rode a Harley, perhaps less so that his apartment was decorated with Wonder Woman paraphernalia. He was on a downward spiral, but perhaps my parents might appreciate that he'd won a Pulitzer earlier in his career?

18 The relationship didn't go anywhere, as my father might have warned me if I'd told him about such things. I will admit to needing a little romantic assistance. Since moving here a few years ago, I'd hardly describe my dating life as successful. There was Sadakat, the half-Finnish, half-Pakistani barrister from London who slept most of the

day and worked most of the night writing a book on criminal justice. Circumscribed within this schedule, our dates would begin at midnight. Once I fell asleep on the bar during the middle of one.

19   Then there were the ones who simply never called again. The boy from Minnesota who imported women's leather clothing from Brazil, the Cockney songwriter, the French dot-com millionaire. Perhaps I didn't want to marry these men, but I certainly wanted to see them again. I began to feel baffled by Western norms of dating, what one Indian friend calls "dating for dating's sake." [. . .]

20   Given such escapades, it may come as no surprise that I've started to look at my father's efforts with a touch less disdain. At least the messages aren't as mixed, right? Sometimes they're quite clear. One of the first setups I agreed to took place a year ago. The man—I'll call him Vivek—worked in IT in New Jersey and had lived there all his life. He took the train into the city to meet me at a Starbucks. He was wearing pants that ended two inches before his ankles. We spoke briefly about his work before he asked, "What are you looking for in a husband?" Since this question always leaves me flummoxed—especially when it's asked by somebody in high-waters within the first few minutes of conversation—I mumbled something along the lines of, "I don't know, a connection, I guess. What are you looking for?" Vivek responded, "Just two things. Someone who's vegetarian and doesn't smoke. That shouldn't be so hard to find, don't you think?"

21   It's a common online-dating complaint that people are nothing like their profiles. I've found they can be nothing but them. And in their tone-deafness, some of these men resemble the parents spurring them on. One Sunday, I was woken by a call at 9 A.M. A woman with a heavy Indian accent asked for Anita. I have a raspy voice at the best of times, but after a night of "social" smoking, my register is on par with Clint Eastwood's. So when I croaked, "This is she," the perplexed lady responded, "She or he?" before asking, "What are your qualifications?" I said I had a B.A. "B.A. only?" she responded. "What are the boy's qualifications?" I flung back in an androgynous voice. She smirked: "He is M.D. in Kentucky *only*." Still bleary-eyed, but with enough presence of mind to use the deferential term for an elder, I grumbled, "Auntie, I will speak to the boy only." Neither she, nor he, called back. [. . .]

22   My father's screening method is hardly foolproof. Once, he was particularly taken with a suitor who claimed to be a brain surgeon at Johns Hopkins and friends with a famous Bollywood actress, Madhuri Dixit.[2] I was suspicious, but I agreed to speak to the fellow. Within seconds, his shaky command of English and yokel line of questioning— "You are liking dancing? I am too much liking dancing"—told me this man was as much a brain surgeon as I was Madhuri Dixit. I refused to talk to him again, even though my father persisted in thinking I was bullheaded. "Don't you think we would make sure his story checked out before marrying you off?" he said.

23   Sometimes, though, you get close, really close. A year ago, I was put in touch with a McKinsey consultant in Bombay whom I'll call Sameer. I liked the fact that he was Indian-American but had returned to India to work. We had great conversations on the phone— among other things, he had interesting views on how people our age were becoming more sexually liberated in Indian cities—and I began envisioning myself kept in the finest silk saris. My father kept telling me he wanted it all "wrapped up" by February—it was only Christmas! Sameer had sent a picture, and while he wasn't Shah Rukh Khan, he wasn't bad.[3]

24   Back for a break in New York, Sameer kindly came to see me in Brooklyn. We went to a French bistro, where he leaned over the table and said, "You know, your father really shouldn't send out those photos of you. They don't do justice to your

beauty." Sameer was generous, good-natured, engaging, seemingly besotted with me, on an expat[riate] salary—and also on the Atkins diet to lose 50 pounds. *My* Bombay dreams went up in smoke.

25   In this, I guess I am like every other woman in New York, complaining a man is too ambitious or not ambitious enough, too eager or not eager enough. But they are picky, too. These men, in their bid to fit in on Wall Street or on the golf course, would like a wife who is eminently presentable—to their boss, friends, and family. They would like a woman to be sophisticated enough to have a martini, and not a Diet Coke, at an office party, but, God forbid, not "sophisticated" enough to have three. Sometimes I worry that I'm a bit too sophisticated for most Indian men.

26   That's not to say I haven't come to appreciate what Indian men have to offer, which is a type of seriousness, a clarity of intent. I've never heard from an Indian man the New York beg-off phrase "I don't think I'm ready for a relationship right now. I have a lot of things going on in my life."

27   Indian men also seem to share my belief that Westerners have made the progression toward marriage unnecessarily agonizing. Neal, a 35-year-old Indian lawyer I know, thinks it's absurd how a couple in America can date for years and still not know if they want to get married. "I think I would only need a couple of months to get to know a girl before I married her," he says.

28   In more traditional arranged marriages—which are still very much alive and well in India—couples may get only one or two meetings before their wedding day. In America, and in big Indian cities, a couple may get a few months before they are expected to walk down the aisle, or around the fire, as they do seven times, in keeping with Hindu custom. By now, I certainly think that would be enough time for me.

29   Other Indian women I know seem to be coming to the same conclusion. My friend Divya works the overnight shift at the BBC in London and stays out clubbing on her nights off. Imagine my surprise when I discovered she was on *keralamatrimony.com*, courtesy of her mother, who took the liberty of listing Divya's hobbies as shopping and movies. (I was under the impression her hobbies were more along the lines of trance music and international politics.) Though she's long favored pubgoing blokes, Divya, like me, doesn't discount the possibility that the urologist from Trivandrum or the IT guy could just be the one—an idea patently unthinkable to us in our twenties.

30   It's become second nature for women like us to straddle the two dating worlds. When I go out on a first date with an Indian man, I find myself saying things I would never utter to an American. Like, "I would expect my husband to fully share domestic chores." Undeniably, there's a lack of mystery to Indian-style dating, because both parties are fully aware of what the endgame should be. But with that also comes a certain relief.

31   With other forms of dating the options seem limitless. The long kiss in the bar with someone I've never met before could have been just that, an exchange that has a value and meaning of its own that can't be quantified. Ditto for the one-night stand. (Try explaining that one to my parents.) The not-knowing-where-something-is-headed can be wildly exciting. It can also be a tad soul-crushing. Just ask any single woman in New York.

32   Indians of my mother's generation—in fact, my mother herself—like to say of arranged marriage, "It's not that there isn't love. It's just that it comes after the marriage." I'm still not sure I buy it. But after a decade of Juan Carloses and short-lived affairs with married men and Craigslist flirtations and emotionally bankrupt boyfriends and, oddly, the most painful of all, the guys who just never call, it no longer seems like the most outlandish possibility.

33   Some of my single friends in New York say they're still not convinced marriage is what they really want. I'm not sure I buy that, either. And no modern woman wants to close

549

the door on any of her options—no matter how traditional—too hastily.

34 My friend Radhika, an unmarried 37-year-old photographer, used to hate going to her cousins' weddings, where the aunties never asked her about the famines in Africa or the political conflict in Cambodia she'd covered. Instead it was, "Why aren't you married? What are your intentions?" As much as she dreaded this, they've stopped asking, and for Radhika, that's even worse. "It's like they've written me off," she says.

35 On a recent trip to India, I was made to eat dinner at the children's table—they sent out for Domino's pizza and Pepsis—because as an unmarried woman, I didn't quite fit in with the adults. As much as I resented my exile, I realized that maybe I didn't want to be eating vegetable curry and drinking rum with the grown-ups. Maybe that would have meant they'd given up on me, that they'd stopped viewing me as a not-yet-married girl but as an unmarriageable woman who'd ruined

her youth by being too choosy and strong-headed.

36 This way, the aunties can still swing by the kids' table as I'm sucking on a Pepsi and chucking a young cousin on the chin, and ask me, "When are you getting married? What are your intentions?" And I can say, "Auntie, do you have a boy in mind?"

Editor's notes:

1. The god Krishna and Radha are legendary Hindu lovers. So are Shiva and Parvati, although they did not have an easy life together. Shiva was originally married to Sati, but her father did not approve of the marriage and ignored him. Humiliated, Sati threw herself into the sacrificial fire. Shiva was so inconsolable that the gods decided to revive Sati. Reborn as Parvati, she danced in front of Shiva and drew him back from his ascetic life into marriage.

2. "Bollywood" is the term applied to the Hindu-language film industry in India; the parallels with Hollywood are obvious. Madhuri Dixit is an award-winning actress and an icon of the Bollywood film industry.

3. Shahrukh Khan is a famous Bollywood actor.

BEFORE YOU READ: What kinds of relationships (family, same-sex friendships, romantic partner, etc.) do you rely on the most for emotional support? How does the way you interact with friends of the same gender compare to the way you interact with a romantic interest?

THE MAN DATE*

Jennifer 8. Lee

The author is a reporter for the *New York Times.* Her middle name, 8, was given to her by her Taiwanese parents since 8 is a symbol for prosperity and good luck in China. In the following article, Lee writes about the difficulty men sometimes have in forming close relationships.

1 The delicate posturing began with the phone call.

2 The proposal was that two buddies back in New York City for a holiday break in December

meet to visit the Museum of Modern Art after its major renovation.

3 "He explicitly said, 'I know this is kind of weird, but we should probably

---

New York Times, April 10, 2005, sec. 9, 1–2.

go,'" said Matthew Speiser, 25, recalling his conversation with John Putman, 28, a former classmate from Williams College.

4   The weirdness was apparent once they reached the museum, where they semi-avoided each other as they made their way through the galleries and eschewed any public displays of connoisseurship. "We definitely went out of our way to look at things separately," recalled Mr. Speiser, who has had art-history classes in his time.

5   "We shuffled. We probably both pretended to know less about the art than we did."

6   Eager to cut the tension following what they perceived to be a slightly unmanly excursion—two guys looking at art together—they headed directly to a bar. "We couldn't stop talking about the fact that it was ridiculous we had spent the whole day together one on one," said Mr. Speiser, who is straight, as is Mr. Putman. "We were purging ourselves of insecurity."

7   Anyone who finds a date with a potential romantic partner to be a minefield of unspoken rules should consider the man date, a rendezvous between two straight men that is even more socially perilous.

8   Simply defined a man date is two heterosexual men socializing without the crutch of business or sports. It is two guys meeting for the kind of outing a straight man might reasonably arrange with a woman. Dining together across a table without the aid of a television is a man date; eating at a bar is not. Taking a walk in the park together is a man date; going for a jog is not. Attending the movie *Friday Night Lights* is a man date, but going to see the Jets play is definitely not.

9   *Sideways*, the Oscar-winning film about two buddies touring the central California wine country on the eve of the wedding of one of them, is one long and boozy man date.

10   Although "man date" is a coinage invented for this article, appearing nowhere in the literature of male bonding (or of homosexual panic), the 30 to 40 straight men interviewed, from their 20's to their 50's, living in cities across the country, instantly recognized the peculiar ritual even if they had not consciously examined its dos and don'ts. Depending on the activity and on the two men involved, an undercurrent of homoeroticism that may be present determines what feels comfortable or not on a man date, as Mr. Speiser and Mr. Putman discovered in their squeamishness at the Modern.

11   Jim O'Donnell, a professor of business and economics at Huntington University in Indiana, who said his life had been changed by a male friend, urges men to get over their discomfort in socializing one on one because they have much to gain from the emotional support of male friendships. (Women understand this instinctively, which is why there is no female equivalent to the awkward man date; straight women have long met for dinner or a movie without a second thought.)

12   "A lot of quality time is lost as we fritter around with minor stuff like the Final Four scores," said Mr. O'Donnell, who was on the verge of divorce in the mid-1980's before a series of conversations over meals and walks with a friend 20 years his senior changed his thinking. "He was instrumental in turning me around in the vulnerability that he showed," said Mr. O'Donnell, who wrote about the friendship in a book, *Walking With Arthur.* "I can remember times when he wanted to know why I was going to leave my wife. No guy had ever done that before."

13   While some men explicitly seek man dates, and others flatly reject them as pointless, most seem to view them as an unavoidable form of socializing in an age when friends can often catch up only by planning in advance. The ritual comes particularly into play for many men after college, as they adjust to a more structured, less spontaneous social life. "You see kids in college talking to each other, bull sessions," said Peter Nardi, a sociology professor at Pitzer College in Claremont, Calif., who edited a book called *Men's Friendships.* "But the opportunities to get close to

another man, to share and talk about their feelings, are not available after a certain age."

14   The concern about being perceived as gay is one of the major complications of socializing one on one, many straight men acknowledge. That is what Mr. Speiser, now a graduate student at the University of Virginia, recalled about another man date he set up at a highly praised Italian restaurant in a strip mall in Charlottesville. It seemed a comfortable choice to meet his roommate, Thomas Kim, a lawyer, but no sooner had they walked in than they were confronted by cello music, amber lights, white tablecloths and a wine list.

15   The two exchanged a look. "It was funny," Mr. Speiser said. "We just knew we couldn't do it." Within minutes they were eating fried chicken at a "down and dirty" place down the road.

16   Mr. Kim, 28, who is now married, was flustered in part because he saw someone he knew at the Italian restaurant. "I was kind of worried that word might get out," he said. "This is weird, and now there is a witness maybe."

17   Dinner with a friend has not always been so fraught. Before women were considered men's equals, some gender historians say, men routinely confided in and sought advice from one another in ways they did not do with women, even their wives. Then, these scholars say, two things changed during the last century: an increased public awareness of homosexuality created a stigma around male intimacy, and at the same time women began encroaching on traditionally male spheres, causing men to become more defensive about notions of masculinity.

18   "If men become too close to other men, then they are always vulnerable to this accusation of, 'Oh, you must be gay,'" said Gregory Lehne, a medical psychologist at the Johns Hopkins School of Medicine who has studied gender issues. At the same time, he added, "When you have women in the same world and seeking equality with men, then all of a sudden issues emerge in the need to maintain the male sex role."

19   And thus a simple meal turns into social Stratego. Some men avoid dinner altogether unless the friend is coming from out of town or has a specific problem that he wants advice about. Otherwise, grabbing beers at a bar will do just fine, thank you.

20   Other men say dinners may be all right, but never brunch, although a post-hangover meal taking place during brunch hours is O.K. "The company at that point is purely secondary," explained Steven Carlson, 29, a public relations executive in Chicago.

21   Almost all men agree that beer and hard alcohol are acceptable man date beverages, but wine is risky. And sharing a bottle is out of the question. "If a guy wants to get a glass of wine, that's O.K.," said Rob Discher, 24, who moved to Washington from Dallas and has dinner regularly with his male roommate. "But there is something kind of odd about splitting a bottle of wine with a guy."

22   Other restaurant red flags include coat checks, busboys who ask, "Still or sparkling?" and candles, unless there is a power failure. All of those are fine, however, at a steakhouse. "Your one go-to is if you go and get some kind of meat product," explained James Halow, 28, who works for a leveraged buyout firm in San Francisco.

23   Cooking for a friend at home violates the man date comfort zone for almost everyone, with a possible exemption for grilling or deep-frying. "The grilling thing would take away the majority of the stigma because there is a masculine overtone to the grill," Mr. Discher said.

24   And man dates should always be Dutch treat, men agree. Armen Myers, 28, a lawyer in New York who is an unabashed man dater, remembers when he tried to pay for dinner for a friend. "I just plopped out the money and didn't even think about it," Mr. Myers said. "He said, 'What are you doing?' And I'm like: 'I was going to pay. What's the big deal?' And he said something like, 'Guys don't pay for me,' or 'No one pays for me.' There was a certain slight power issue."

25   When attending a movie together—preferably with explosions or heavy special effects, never a romantic comedy—guys prefer to put a nice big seat between each other. (This only sounds like an episode of *Seinfeld*.) "Going to the movie with one other guy is sort of weird, but you can balance it out by having a seat space between you," explained Ames McArdle, a financial analyst in Washington.

26   Men who avoid man dates altogether are often puzzled by the suggestion that they might like to spend time with male friends. "If you're buddies with another guy, there shouldn't be any work involved," Mr. Halow of San Francisco said. Which is why many men say that a successful man dates requires a guy to demonstrate concern for his friend without ever letting on. "The amount of preparation that the other guy is making is directly proportional to how awkward it is," Mr. McArdle of Washington said.

27   When man daters socialize with non–man daters, the activities always fall to the lowest common denominator. Mr. Myers of New York remembers how he would ask his roommate Jonathan Freimann out for dinner by himself. But Mr. Freimann would instinctively pre-empt, by asking other guys along.

28   "If I had known he wanted to spend one-on-one time, I would have," Mr. Freimann explained, adding that group dinners had simply seemed "more fun." (The two had dinner in San Diego last week.)

29   Jeffrey Toohig, 27, is a more reliable bet for Mr. Myers. They regularly have dinner together to discuss women, jobs and whatever else is on their minds, because, as Mr. Toohig put it, "the conversation is more in depth than you can have at a bar." Mr. Toohig, who is looking for a job helping underdeveloped countries, divides his male friends into two groups: "good friends who I go out one on one with, and guys I go out with and we have beers and wings." And, he pointed out, dinner with Mr. Myers has the advantage of not making his girlfriend jealous, the way dinners with his female friends do.

30   All men, however, agree that one rule of guy meets-guy time is inviolable: If a woman enters the picture, a man can drop his buddies, last minute, no questions asked.

31   A romantic date always trumps a man date.

BEFORE YOU READ: Based on your experience, what do you think are the most important factors (similarity of religion, region, family values, ethnicity, etc.) in having a good romantic relationship?

HITTING IT OFF, THANKS TO ALGORITHMS OF LOVE*
John Tierney

John Tierney writes for the *New York Times*. He has written extensively about science and technology, economics, and environmental controversies.

1   Pasadena, Calif.—The two students in Southern California had just been introduced during an experiment to test their "interpersonal chemistry." The man, a graduate student, dutifully asked the undergraduate woman what her major was.

---

*John Tierney, "Hitting It Off, Thanks to Algorithms of Love," *New York Times*, January 29, 2008, D1.

2   "Spanish and sociology," she said.

3   "Interesting," he said. "I was a sociology major. What are you going to do with that?"

4   "You are just full of questions."

5   "It's true."

6   "My passion has always been Spanish, the language, the culture. I love traveling and knowing new cultures and places."

7   Bogart and Bacall it was not. But Gian Gonzaga, a social psychologist, could see possibilities for this couple as he watched their recorded chat on a television screen.

8   They were nodding and smiling in unison, and the woman stroked her hair and briefly licked her lips—positive signs of chemistry that would be duly recorded in this experiment at the new eHarmony Labs here. By comparing these results with the couple's answers to hundreds of other questions, the researchers hoped to draw closer to a new and extremely lucrative grail—making the right match.

9   Once upon a time, finding a mate was considered too important to be entrusted to people under the influence of raging hormones. Their parents, sometimes assisted by astrologers and matchmakers, supervised courtship until customs changed in the West because of what was called the Romeo and Juliet revolution. Grown-ups, leave the kids alone.

10   But now some social scientists have rediscovered the appeal of adult supervision—provided the adults have doctorates and vast caches of psychometric data. Online matchmaking has become a boom industry as rival scientists test their algorithms for finding love.

11   The leading yenta is eHarmony, which pioneered the don't-try-this-yourself approach eight years ago by refusing to let its online customers browse for their own dates.[1] It requires them to answer a 258-question personality test and then picks potential partners. The company

554

estimates, based on a national Harris survey it commissioned, that its matchmaking was responsible for about 2 percent of the marriages in America last year, nearly 120 weddings a day.

12   Another company, Perfectmatch.com, is using an algorithm designed by Pepper Schwartz, a sociologist at the University of Washington at Seattle. Match.com, which became the largest online dating service by letting people find their own partners, set up a new matchmaking service, Chemistry.com, using an algorithm created by Helen E. Fisher, an anthropologist at Rutgers who has studied the neural chemistry of people in love.

13   As the matchmakers compete for customers—and denigrate each other's methodology—the battle has intrigued academic researchers who study the mating game. On the one hand, they are skeptical, because the algorithms and the results have not been published for peer review. But they also realize that these online companies give scientists a remarkable opportunity to gather enormous amounts of data and test their theories in the field. EHarmony says more than 19 million people have filled out its questionnaire.

14   Its algorithm was developed a decade ago by Galen Buckwalter, a psychologist who had previously been a research professor at the University of Southern California. Drawing on previous evidence that personality similarities predict happiness in a relationship, he administered hundreds of personality questions to 5,000 married couples and correlated the answers with the couples' marital happiness, as measured by an existing instrument called the dyadic adjustment scale.

15   The result was an algorithm that is supposed to match people on 29 "core traits," like social style or emotional temperament, and "vital attributes" like

relationship skills. (For details: *nytimes.com/tierneylab*.)

16 "We're not looking for clones, but our models emphasize similarities in personality and in values," Buckwalter said. "It's fairly common that differences can initially be appealing, but they're not so cute after two years. If you have someone who's Type A and real hard charging, put them with someone else like that. It's just much easier for people to relate if they don't have to negotiate all these differences."

17 Does this method actually work? In theory, thanks to its millions of customers and their fees (up to $60 a month), eHarmony has the data and resources to conduct cutting-edge research. It has an advisory board of prominent social scientists and a new laboratory with researchers lured from academia like Gonzaga, who previously worked at a marriage-research lab at UCLA.

18 So far, except for a presentation at a psychologists' conference, the company has not produced much scientific evidence that its system works. It has started a longitudinal study comparing eHarmony couples with a control group, and Buckwalter says it is committed to publishing peer-reviewed research, but not the details of its algorithm. That secrecy may be a smart business move, but it makes eHarmony a target for scientific critics, not to mention its rivals.

19 In the battle of the matchmakers, Chemistry .com has been running commercials faulting eHarmony for refusing to match gay couples (eHarmony says it can't because its algorithm is based on data from heterosexuals), and eHarmony asked the Better Business Bureau to stop Chemistry.com from claiming its algorithm had been scientifically validated. The bureau concurred that there was not enough evidence, and Chemistry.com

agreed to stop advertising that Fisher's method was based on "the latest science of attraction."

20 Fisher now says the ruling against her last year made sense because her algorithm at that time was still a work in progress as she correlated sociological and psychological measures, as well as indicators linked to chemical systems in the brain. But now, she said, she has the evidence from Chemistry.com users to validate the method, and she plans to publish it along with the details of the algorithm.

21 "I believe in transparency," she said, taking a dig at eHarmony. "I want to share my data so that I will get peer review."

22 Until outside scientists have a good look at the numbers, no one can know how effective any of these algorithms are, but one thing is already clear. People aren't so good at picking their own mates online. Researchers who studied online dating found that the customers typically ended up going out with fewer than 1 percent of the people whose profiles they studied, and that those dates often ended up being huge letdowns. The people make up impossible shopping lists for what they want in a partner, says Eli Finkel, a psychologist who studies dating at Northwestern University's Relationships Lab.

23 "They think they know what they want," Finkel said. "But meeting somebody who possesses the characteristics they claim are so important is much less inspiring than they would have predicted."

24 The new matchmakers may or may not have the right formula. But their computers at least know better than to give you what you want.

Editor's note:

1. *Yenta* is a Yiddish word for a gossip, but also a matchmaker; see the musical *Fiddler on the Roof*.

Questions to Help You Think and Write about Family and Personal Relationships

1. How have the opinions of Pederson and Cullen and Grossman influenced your views on the traditional family? What were your views before reading these essays? What are your views now?

2. Cullen and Grossman quote sociologist Scott Coltrane, who says that today, "Fathers are beginning to look more like mothers." Define the cultural images or ideals of "motherhood" and "fatherhood" and analyze ways in which today's fathers either are or are not becoming more like mothers. Conversely, are today's mothers more like fathers? You can choose to focus on a real-life situation or on a fictional representation of family in literature or film.

3. Using Heather Cabot's essay "Loving Late Motherhood" as a starting point, consider what you think would be the right time to start a family. What do you need to achieve and what goals do you need to meet before making your own family and why?

4. Song lyrics are also poems; analyze the lyrics to "Love and Marriage" as a poetic comment on the relationship between love as an emotional state and marriage as a social institution. What in the logic of the poem suggests that "you can't have one without the other"? Do you think that conclusion is true or false and why?

5. In "Crazy Love," Steven Pinker argues that although romance is not governed by logical considerations, such as finances or social compatibility, there is nevertheless "method in the madness." The article also references films of "bad" or "dangerous" love. Choosing one film or fictional work, analyze the "method" behind the madness of one example of "crazy love." What motivates both lovers in this situation?

6. Using either the reprinted panel *Watergate Sue: Epilogue,* which concludes Megan Kelso's graphic novel, or the image that accompanies Belinda Luscombe's article on flirting, construct an imaginary monologue or dialogue for the characters. What would the people in each of these situations be thinking about family and/or personal relationships?

7. Luscombe suggests that flirting offers a generally safe way to let potential partners in romance get to know one another, although if not handled properly, flirting can be dangerous. Describe a popular social situation or event familiar from your school or town and analyze how it allows individuals to get to know one another, either through flirting or some other means.

8. Anita Jain, as a modern young woman with traditional parents, has experienced both the pros and cons of having family manage or even arrange a young person's dating and possible marriage. What are the advantages and disadvantages of involving family in such decisions? What, in the end, do you think is the best way to find a romantic partner or spouse?

9. Jennifer Lee and John Tierney discuss the problems people have establishing both friendships and romantic relations. Many of the essays in this section also suggest ways in which contemporary technology can both foster and interfere with strong personal relationships. What has been the effect of the Internet on making and sustaining such human ties?

SECTION 2

Issues concerning Modern Technology

The Issues

A. **How Are Web 2.0 Technologies Changing the Way We Live and Our Knowledge of the World?**

People are always divided about technology, and computer technologies are no exception. The first essay in this section reports on the theories of Stanford legal scholar Lawrence Lessig, who argues that the new Web 2.0 technologies are creating an "amateur culture" that is creative and empowering for ordinary individuals. Silicon Valley entrepreneur Andrew Keen, perhaps the most outspoken critic of the Web 2.0 phenomenon, thinks that amateur culture promotes both narcissism and ignorance. The next three essays examine two popular Web 2.0 phenomena. Facebook, as social network software, is intended to bring people together into an ever-growing digital community that transcends geographical limitations. Kurt Soller and Sarah Kliff, respectively, tell why they "love" or "hate" Facebook. YouTube's motto is "Broadcast Yourself," but Ashley Jones shows how broadcasting yourself can subject you unwittingly to surveillance and the long arm of the law. Finally, critics of multimedia communication lament the loss of traditional reading and writing skills. Edward Tenner considers whether or not "Googling" a subject produces solid information. By contrast, Michael Kirschenbaum argues that computers can foster intense, sustained acts of reading and writing. See also "The Laptop Ate My Attention Span" (pages 26–27).

B. **What Are the Benefits and Dangers of Genetic Engineering for Individuals and for Society?**

As the first decade of the twenty-first century moves forward, technologies for human engineering are becoming not only possible but commonplace. Ray Kurzweil, an important inventor and an enthusiastic promoter of biological and computer science, gives us his vision of the decades to come. Jeremy Rifkin provides an overview of the promise and perils of eugenics and of the commercialization of genetic technologies. Peggy Orenstein reports on in vitro fertilization as an increasingly common choice for Americans seeking to have children; she describes the human faces, fears, and aspirations behind the science and explores ethical issues involved in the choice to use an egg donor. See also "Psst! Ask for Donor 1913" (pages 134–136), "Welcome Clones of

2012!" (page 401), "Human Cloning: An Annotated Bibliography" (pages 402–404), "Human Cloning: Is It a Viable Option?" (pages 329–332).

Web Sites for Further Exploration and Research

Institute for the Future of the Book	http://www.futureofthebook.org/
Web 2.0: The Machine Is Us/ing Us (YouTube)	http://www.youtube.com/watch?v=6gmP4nk0EOE
Lawrence Lessig's Blog	http://lessig.org/blog/
Stanford Center for Internet and Society (CIS)	http://cyberlaw.stanford.edu/
Electronic Frontier Foundation	http://www.eff.org/
Creative Commons	http://creativecommons.org/
Facebook	http://www.facebook.com/
YouTube	http://www.youtube.com/
Wikipedia	http://www.wikipedia.org/
Open Content Alliance	http://www.opencontentalliance.org/
To Read or Not to Read (PDF)	http://www.nea.gov/research/ToRead.pdf

Films and Literature Related to Modern Technology

Films *2001: A Space Odyssey*, 1968; *Avalon*, 2001; *Bladerunner*, 1982; *The Fly*, 1986; *Gattaca*, 1997; *I Robot*, 1984; *Johnny Mnemonic*, 1995; *The Matrix*, 1999; *Murderers on the Dancefloor* (television documentary on YouTube video), 2008; *Terminator*, 1984; *X-Men*, 2000.

Literature novels: *1984* by George Orwell; *Brave New World* by Aldous Huxley; *Cast of Shadows* by Kevin Guilfoyle; *Chromosome 6* by Robin Crock; *The Experiment* by John Darnton; *Frankenstein* by Mary Shelley; *The Handmaid's Tale* by Margaret Atwood; *The Man without Qualities* by Robert Musil; *Overdrive* and *Neuromancer*, both by William Gibson; *Prey* by Michael Crichton; *Society of the Mind* by Eric L. Harry; essay: "The Total Library" by Jorge Luis Borges.

The Rhetorical Situation

The technologies examined in this section of "The Reader" have been progressing at a rapid rate. The first computer, with its seventeen thousand vacuum tubes, was invented at the University of Pennsylvania in 1946. Personal computers have been widely available since 1981, and open Internet use dates only from 1983. Yet, by July 2007, 210,575, 287 Americans were Internet users; there were 162,000,000 users in China.

The World Wide Web, now known as Web 1.0, was created by Tim Berners Lee in 1991. His dream was twofold: first, to create a common space in which anyone, worldwide, could share information with anyone else; second, to use this huge collection of information to understand ourselves and our relations to one another. Web 2.0 refers to a collection of new Web technologies developed since the late 1990s. Web 2.0 invites a broader participation than the original Web, in part because posting videos to YouTube or constructing a Facebook page requires no technical skills—that is taken care of by the service providers—and in part because these new technologies, at least according to enthusiasts, encourage individual creativity and sustain a whole new "amateur culture." Web 2.0 afficionados write and publish their own work rather than passively absorb online documents, "broadcast" themselves rather than just shop online for commodities.

The potential problems with Web 2.0, on the other hand, are threefold. First, the creativity fostered by new technologies can involve appropriation of existing materials, an infringement of copyright or theft of intellectual property. Second, according to opponents, the quality of knowledge available through the Web is being degraded. Sites such as *Wikipedia*, which welcome authors in a very democratic manner, have been accused of failing to review adequately the work provided by their contributors. Some universities have gone so far as to ban *Wikipedia* as a source for student essays. In a similar manner, search engines such as *Google* do the hard work of research for us, but studies may show that we are becoming dumber in the process. Finally, the social consequences of computer use and computer technologies continue to be debated. For some parents, for instance, Facebook has replaced television as the biggest threat to a healthy family life; many limit their children's time on Facebook, encouraging them instead to read, talk, and go outside to play.

Other essays in this section of "The Reader" focus on the potential benefits and ethical drawbacks of using bioengineering to improve human life. Ray Kurzweil looks forward to a time, not too far in the future, when tiny robots can enter the body to trigger reactions ranging from an attack on cancer cells to turning off an enzyme that destroys "good" cholesterol. He thinks that with science, we can soon extend and improve the lives of many people. The ethical dilemmas posed by genetic engineering become most pronounced in the creation of human life. Efforts to "perfect" the human species by ruling out genetic defects from the beginning may be hubris in the face of nature and, for many religions, a usurpation of divine authority. On the other hand, new technologies such as in vitro fertilization (I.V.F.) are giving parents expanded options for creating a loving family. Genetic engineering has already become a factor of everyday life. In 2007, cloned meat was approved by the FDA for sale in the United States; the next year Europeans were told that although cloned meat was safe to eat, the cloning process may cause animals to suffer. Where once we had to worry about the ethics of cloning a sheep like Dolly, we now have the additional burden of wondering whether it is not just safe, but morally right, to eat Dolly.

A. How Are Web 2.0 Technologies Changing the Way We Live and Our Knowledge of the World?

> **BEFORE YOU READ:** Lawrence Lessig is a champion of "free culture" and thinks that restrictions on use of digital materials is unnecessary. When in your life do you appropriate freely the work of other people or put your own creations out there for others to read, reproduce, and even remix? (Some of these creations may not necessarily be digital. Use your imagination.)

"AMATEUR CULTURE" SET TO EXPLODE*

BBC News Staff

Lawrence Lessig, the subject of this essay, is a professor of law at Stanford Law School and founder of the school's Center for Internet and Society. He has won numerous awards, including the Free Software Foundation's Freedom Award, and was named one of *Scientific American's* Top 50 Visionaries for arguing "against interpretations of copyright that could stifle innovation and discourse online."

1 The 21st century is seeing an explosion in the field of amateur culture and creativity, according to leading digital commentators. Professor Lawrence Lessig, a champion of so-called "free culture," told the BBC digital technology was inspiring new forms of creativity. Blogs, podcasts and digital photos are examples of amateur culture, he said. "Digital tools are inspiring creativity in a way that I do not think we have seen in a very long time," he said.

2 Professor Lessig, who teaches law at Stanford University in the U.S., is a founder of Creative Commons, a set of copyright licenses which help creators share and protect their works. He said: "If you think of the 20th Century as this period of professionalizing creativity—you've got the film and recording industries which become the professional creators, separating and stifling in many ways the popular culture.

3 "I do not think you are going to see the elimination of the professional creators but you are going to see it complemented by a much wider range of amateur culture in the original sense of the word amateur— in that people do it purely for the love of creating."

4 Millions of people now have blogs— websites which are created using simple and free tools—and thousands of people are now podcasting, creating radio-style programs which are distributed over the internet and can be transferred to MP3 players.

PARTICIPATORY CULTURE

5 There are a reported 60 million bloggers— writing everything from personal diaries to

---

*"'Amateur Culture' Set to Explode," *BBC NEWS*, July 18, 2005, http://news.bbc.co.uk/go/2/hi/entertainment/4685471.stm (accessed June 18, 2008).

influential political rhetoric—and research firm The Diffusion Group recently predicted there will be 60 million podcasters in the U.S. by 2010. Thousands of other people are remixing songs, making their own films and TV programs and generally participating in culture rather than being passive consumers. Professor Lessig said this rise in amateur culture was not without its problems as the desire to be creative often clashes with that of traditional creators and content distributors.

"EXTRAORDINARY POTENTIAL"

6 "Many of the professional creators don't get it—they can't imagine a world where creativity is not controlled," he said. "But they should recognize this amateur creativity has extraordinary potential for them too." Cory Doctorow, a campaigner for digital rights with lobby group Electronic Frontier Foundation, agreed. "We are in a pretty pitched battle on many, many fronts," he said.

7 Big media companies are imposing copy protection restrictions on what consumers can do with their purchases—whether they are CDs, DVDs, or digital songs—in an effort to prevent piracy. But Mr. Doctorow said: "All the copy protection in the world won't stop Ukrainian pirate gangs from stamping out millions of high-quality counterfeits a month." Professor Lessig and Mr. Doctorow believe the attitude of big business is stifling amateur creativity.

REMIX

8 [Lessig and Doctorow] want to see consumers take professional creative works they have bought and then alter them and share them with other people. Professor Lessig gave an example of how it could work with the television industry. "Imagine you are Channel 4 and you have a new series to be released.

What you do is each week put the latest episode online and invite people to remix it. So you create this huge community of people remixing your content and you create this huge community of people watching your program each week."

9 The BBC is undertaking a long-term project to release hundreds of hours of its TV and radio archive online so that people can use it in creative ways. Paul Gerhardt, head of the BBC's Creative Archive scheme, said: "We see moving image and audio as having the same potential for contributing to people's lives as books and the written word did."

"INSPIRED"

10 "In other words, we all get inspired by what we read and we share it with others and we think nothing of quoting from it or building our creativity on it. Yet it is almost impossible to access moving images or audio with the same ease and to use it in the same way."

11 Mr. Doctorow said the digital age—plus the growth in use of the Creative Commons license—was also fuelling collaborations between artists and authors, some of whom may never have met in real life. Creative Commons is a license which sets out in simple terms what others can or cannot do with any creative work. "We wanted a set of tools that would make it easy for artists to mark their creativity with the freedoms that they intended to carry," said Professor Lessig. "Just as Apple and Microsoft provide tools for people to make music or documents we provide tools for people to solve legal problems. Some creators will be happy for people to make non-commercial use of their work and we have a simple way of showing that."

12 "Others are happy for people to make commercial use and we have a simple way for them to enforce that."

BEFORE YOU READ: Andrew Keen considers amateur culture to be not truly culture; he uses the term *amateur* in a negative sense. What does the word *amateur* mean to you?

INTRODUCTION, *THE CULT OF THE AMATEUR**
Andrew Keen

Andrew Keen is a Silicon Valley media entrepreneur who founded Audiocafe.com in 1995 and built it into a well-known Internet music company. Since then, however, he has become one of the leading critics of Web 2.0 technologies and their social impact.

For Discussion: This iconic image comes from the *Wikipedia* site on the "infinite monkey theorem" (http://en.wikipedia.org/wiki/Infinite_monkey_theorem). What does the image of an infinite number of monkeys typing *Hamlet* convey about the relationship between technology and art?

Context: The caption to this image reads: Monkey Typing. The idea that an infinite number of monkeys typing could eventually produce *Hamlet* is a byword of the technological era. The notion is derived from a mathematical theorem.

1   If I didn't know better, I'd think it was 1999 all over again. The boom has returned to Silicon Valley, and the mad utopians are once again running wild. I bumped into one such evangelist at a recent San Francisco mixer.

2   Over glasses of fruity local Chardonnay, we swapped notes about our newest things. He told me his current gig involved a new software for publishing music, text, and video on the Internet. "It's MySpace meets YouTube meets *Wikipedia* meets *Google*," he said, "On steroids."

3   In reply, I explained that I was working on a polemic about the destructive impact of the digital revolution on our culture, economy, and values. "It's ignorance meets egoism meets bad taste meets mob rule," I said, unable to resist a smile, "On steroids."

4   He smiled uneasily in return. "So it's Huxley meets the digital age," he said. "You're

*Andrew Keen, *The Cult of the Amateur: How Today's Internet Is Killing Our Culture* (New York: Doubleday, 2007), 1–9.

For Discussion: This image is an updated version of the single monkey at the typewriter. How does this image elaborate on the infinite monkey theorem? How might it be related to the modern Internet?

For Writing: Do you think that the images of the single monkey at a typewriter and of 100 monkeys at computers are fair depictions of today's amateur authors, filmmakers, and artists who broadcast their work over the World Wide Web? State the claims of the two images. Which image makes the better argument about the modern Internet? Why?

Context: The caption to this image reads: One Hundred Monkeys Typing.

rewriting Huxley for the twenty-first century." He raised his wine glass to my honor. "To *Brave New World 2.0!*" We clinked wine glasses. But I knew we were toasting the wrong Huxley. Rather than Aldous, the inspiration behind this book comes from his grandfather, T. H. Huxley, the nineteenth-century evolutionary biologist and author of the "infinite monkey theorem." Huxley's theory says that if you provide infinite monkeys with infinite typewriters, some monkey somewhere will eventually create a masterpiece—a play by Shakespeare, a Platonic dialogue, or an economic treatise by Adam Smith.[1]

5   In the pre-Internet age, T. H. Huxley's scenario of infinite monkeys empowered with infinite technology seemed more like a mathematical jest than a dystopian vision. But what had once appeared as a joke now seems to foretell the consequences of a flattening of culture that is blurring the lines between traditional audience and author, creator and consumer, expert and amateur. That is no laughing matter.

6   Today's technology hooks all those monkeys up with all those typewriters. Except in our Web 2.0 world, the typewriters aren't quite typewriters, but rather networked personal computers, and the monkeys aren't quite monkeys, but rather Internet users. And instead of creating masterpieces, these millions and millions of exuberant monkeys—many with no more talent in the creative arts than our primate cousins—are creating an endless digital forest of mediocrity. For today's amateur monkeys can use their networked computers to publish everything from uninformed political commentary to unseemly home videos, to embarrassingly amateurish music, to unreadable poems, reviews, essays, and novels. . . . What happens, you might ask, when ignorance meets egoism meets bad taste meets mob rule?

7   The monkeys take over. Say good-bye to today's experts and cultural gatekeepers—our reporters, news anchors, editors, music companies, and Hollywood movie studios. In today's cult of the amateur, the monkeys are running the show. With their infinite typewriters, they are authoring the future. And we may not like how it reads.

Editor's note:

1. For more about Huxley's theory, see Jorge Luis Borges's 1939 essay, "The Total Library."

Reading Images: Today's Technology

For Discussion: This cartoon implies that our machines rule our lives. Can you think of some concrete evidence in support of the claim?

For Writing: This cartoon also makes a particular claim about the influence of technology on families and personal relationships. What is that claim and what evidence for it is provided by the image itself?

CONTEXT: Dick Locher has been an editorial cartoonist at the *Chicago Tribune* since 1973, and in 1983 he won the Pulitzer Prize. His work focuses on life's absurdities and on politics.

BEFORE YOU READ: If you had to explain to a skeptic why you do or do not belong to Facebook, what would be your number 1 reason?

FACEBOOK: WHY I LOVE IT . . .*

Kurt Soller

Kurt Soller is a staff writer for *Newsweek*.

1 I have three fond memories from my senior year of high school: the day I got my college acceptance letter, the day I graduated, and the day I joined Facebook. The latter

---

*Kurt Soller, "Facebook: Why I Love It . . . ," *Newsweek*, August 14, 2007, 44.

happened on a May afternoon before graduation, when a college friend e-mailed me an invitation to join. I was 17, and anything the older kids were doing was automatically cool. All I needed was an attractive profile photo (easier said than done) and a well-curated list of interests to meet the friends I always dreamed I'd have in college: people who preferred Faulkner over Hemingway, liked thrift shopping, and wanted to sneak into Chicago jazz clubs. Facebook became my dry-erase tabula rasa. Under favorite quote, I wrote "True friends stab you in the front," as Oscar Wilde said. For the section titled "About Me," I said, "I like to write, but writing 'about me' is difficult."

2   As summer days passed and friend requests poured in, it didn't matter that I'd never met these people, because soon we'd be on campus together at Northwestern. When I landed at O'Hare that September, I met a girl who had seen my profile and wanted to introduce herself. Later, when I walked in on her in bed with a dormmate, she told me, "Don't be awkward." After all, we'd already met on Facebook.

3   As Facebook grew up alongside us, it improved our collective social lives—all 1,042 friends of mine and counting. I can't go to a sorority formal or football game without photos from the event winding up on Facebook, uploaded by me or a friend. Sure, it may be overly indulgent, and some of the pictures are unflattering, but this constant chronicling of life eliminates the secret diary or crafty scrapbook. Before Facebook, I may have written some words in my journal about a wild night in Chicago; now my friends and I are building each other's collective stories—one photo, caption, and poke at a time.

4   Facebook is my personal assistant, allowing me to catch up on my social life without telephone tag, awkward lunches, and 5-, 10-, 15-year reunions. We write on each other's Wall, a message board, when we want to say happy birthday without singing into an answering machine. When I'm having a hectic week at my internship, I can change my status so that people know why I haven't returned their telephone calls— much better than wasting time calling people to tell them you're too busy to talk.

5   It may seem artificial that I don't have to go out of my way to get in touch. But in the end, I've beaten the system. I have more time for my closest friends, those whose relationships transcend computers. And Facebook enriches those close friendships: when a best friend changed her dating status from "In a Relationship" to "Single," I brought over a movie, one that she had listed as a fave.

6   You've heard criticism that Facebook makes us robotic, but history shows we've always feared new communication tools. In 360 B.C., Plato criticized writing, saying that it would induce forgetfulness; 2,200 years later, the telephone was seen as invasive and unnecessary. Mark Zuckerberg is no more, or no less, than the next Samuel Morse or Alexander Graham Bell.[1] We all want to interact as best we can, and Facebook allows us to do that. That said, if you're thinking of friending me after reading this, you should know: I'm not in the market for any more friends.

Editor's note:

1. Mark Zuckerberg invented Facebook when he was just nineteen years old. Samuel Morse invented the telegraph, and Alexander Graham Bell invented the telephone.

> **BEFORE YOU READ:** Contemporary technologies such as Facebook help to keep us "connected" with friends and loved ones. What is your favorite way of staying in touch with others?

FACEBOOK: WHY I HATE IT . . .*

Sarah Kliff

Sarah Kliff is a staff writer for *Newsweek*.

1   I have no idea how many hours of my life I've wasted on Facebook. When I wake up each morning, with my laptop sitting on the edge of my futon, I check it. Before I've thought about brushing my teeth, I have already seen the photographs of my brother's new apartment in San Francisco and discovered the evidence of my friend's tumultuous breakup: she changed her relationship status from "In a Relationship" to "Single" to "It's Complicated," all while I was sleeping. As best I can figure, since joining the site in 2004 when I was a freshman at Washington University in St. Louis, I've been logging on a dozen times a day. When I should have been studying or working, I found myself instead doing tasks like flipping through 400 photos of myself online, debating whether I wanted the picture where I have food in my hair to be on display to the world. (I decided to leave it: while it's not the most attractive pose, I think it indicates that I am a laid-back, good-humored person.)

2   I spend an inordinate amount of time like this, worrying about what's in my online profile. When I graduated from college this May, I decided it was time for a Facebook makeover. Looking to present a more "professional" image, I stripped my profile of many of my collegiate interests—you'll no longer know from Facebook that I'm obsessed with penguins—and I purged my membership in questionable Facebook groups such as "Scotland? Sounds more

like Hotland" (tamer than it sounds). I know I'm not the only one constantly revamping my cyber-image: according to my Facebook account, 109 of my friends have changed something over the past two days. One friend added "goofy dads" to her interests, and another let it be known that he "falls asleep easily" and "loses things all the time."

3   What is with all this time we've spent, thinking about ourselves and creating well-planned lists of our interests? Facebook is much worse than e-mail, cell phones, instant messaging and the other devices that keep me constantly connected. It nurses every self-indulgent urge I could possibly have. I hate that Facebook encourages me to home in on each of my idiosyncrasies—that I like running in Central Park, for example, or that my favorite forms of punctuation are the dash and semicolon—and broadcast them to a largely uninterested world. I have a sneaking suspicion that very few people want to know that I am particularly fond of bagels. And no one really cares when I change my Facebook status, a fill-in-the-blank feature where users can let people know what they're up to at any moment. Mine is currently set to "Sarah is trying to write an article about Facebook . . . but is ironically too distracted by Facebook." The network is as much about obsessing over the dull details of my life as it as about connecting with others.

*Sarah Kliff, "Facebook: Why I Hate It . . . ," *Newsweek,* August 14, 2007, 45.

4   As a recent college graduate, with my friends scattered across the globe, I understand the communicative value of Facebook. Right now, I have 469 "friends"—though I admit many of these virtual relationships are tenuous at best. Still, I would be hard-pressed to give up my four-year-long membership or leave Facebook out of my early morning routine. But who knows what I'm missing out on in the real world while sitting at my laptop, debating whether penguins or bagels are more respectable?

> **BEFORE YOU READ:** If you enjoy watching YouTube, what kinds of videos do you, your friends, and family enjoy the most?

YOUTUBE'S LEGAL ISSUES GROW*

Ashley Jones

Ashley Jones publishes articles regularly in *EContent*.

1   Copyright lawsuits have become commonplace for YouTube. People post videos without the right to do so, leaving YouTube to clean up the mess before the video-sharing site finds itself embroiled in yet another, much larger, legal mess. Some, like Brian Banner, a Washington, D.C., attorney who specializes in copyright law, believe that YouTube may be a bit lax up front. He says: "Service providers like YouTube don't want to exercise any control. They just want to provide a service without verifying what the content is." Lately, though, YouTube has found itself facing a whole new slew of legal issues beyond copyright, which may force the site to take control over its content.

2   This past August in Thailand, Thai censors finally lifted a 5-month, countrywide YouTube ban. The censors were originally put in place because some material posted on the site was deemed insulting to the Thai king. The ban was lifted on a conditional basis. If Thai censors find a video on YouTube that they believe to be inappropriate per Thai standards, the censors will notify YouTube, and if YouTube agrees that the material is against Thai law, YouTube will block said material from Thai viewers.

3   YouTube recently received hundreds of complaints from a German government agency about posted videos that included Nazi imagery and promoted racism. YouTube responded by removing all of the objectionable videos from its site, rather than only blocking German viewers' access.

4   Here in the United States, where "questionable" content surrounds us on a near-constant basis, one might think that copyright laws are the extent of YouTube's woes. Americans, after all, have the First Amendment, which protects us from censorship and allows us to freely express our beliefs, no matter how unpopular they may be. What the First Amendment fails to do, however, is protect us from ourselves.

5   Take the Columbus, Ohio, cop, for example, whose YouTube video post resulted in her reassignment. In August, Susan Purtee, a 15-year veteran of the Columbus police force, was seen on YouTube blaming the Jewish population for problems in the United States. Following the incident, Purtee was reassigned to a non-enforcement position, and Columbus Mayor Michael

---

*Ashley Jones, "YouTube's Legal Issues Grow," *EContent* 30.9 (November 2007), 10–11.

Coleman commented, "While we respect the right of free speech, we also demand that every officer meet the highest standard of conduct on and off the job."

6   Also in August, an unnamed 19-year-old boy was arrested after allegedly posting a YouTube video of himself driving at speeds topping 140 mph. Another YouTube video left a group of teenagers answering authorities' questions after a clip showing the teens trespassing in an old, rundown mill was posted on YouTube.

7   According to Banner, "The First Amendment is obviously more important than YouTube or anything else on the Internet. People claim their right to free speech under the First Amendment, but those rights are limited." Once you post racist rants or illegal actions on YouTube for all to see, it then becomes an issue of self-incrimination. If you post a video of yourself doing some-

thing wrong, it makes denial pretty difficult. In fact, the video could quickly become the most damning piece of evidence in the case against you.

8   Some of these problems arise from the myth of online anonymity. People create user names on YouTube or bump up their privacy settings on MySpace and then assume that they are hidden behind some mysterious, anonymous cloak of protection. However, the truth is that wherever you go and whatever you do during your online journeys, you leave a trail.

9   YouTube encourages its users to broadcast themselves, but in light of this new wave of litigation, it might not hurt to exercise some inhibition before doing so. The question, however, is if YouTube needs to build inhibitors—content regulation mechanisms— into its network to protect itself . . . and maybe even protect us from ourselves.

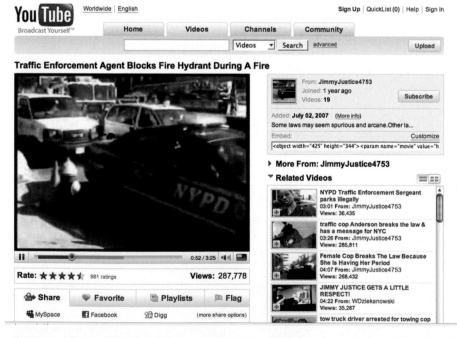

For Discussion: What kind of an argument does this image make, and how effective is it?

For Writing: The name of this amateur journalist, "Jimmy Justice," makes an implicit argument about the nature of his documentary investigation. YouTube lists other videos by the same contributor and also lists the number of hits it has received. How do these features of YouTube technology provide support for Jimmy Justice's personal *ethos*?

Context: The caption reads: "Jimmy Justice," "Traffic Enforcement Agent Blocks Fire Hydrant During a Fire," YouTube, viewed February 14, 2007. This image chronicles a vigilant citizen's efforts to uncover abuses by law enforcement. He himself was later investigated by law enforcement, and his work was discussed on MSNBC and elsewhere.

> **BEFORE YOU READ:** Whenever someone wants an answer to a question, the most common response is probably "Google it!" For what kinds of information, entertainment, and other purposes do you use *Google*?

SEARCHING FOR DUMMIES*

Edward Tenner

Edward Tenner, the author most recently of *Our Own Devices: How Technology Remakes Humanity*, is working on a book about positive unintended consequences.

1   Talk of decline was old news in academia even in 1898, when traditionalists blasted Harvard for ending its Greek entrance requirement. But today there's a new twist in the story: Are search engines making today's students dumber?

2   In December, the National Center for Education Statistics published a report on adult literacy revealing that the number of college graduates able to interpret complex texts proficiently had dropped since 1992 from 40 percent to 31 percent. As Mark S. Schneider, the center's commissioner of education statistics, put it, "What's disturbing is that the assessment is not designed to test your understanding of Proust, but to test your ability to read labels."

3   The Higher Education Supplement of *The Times of London* reports that a British survey also finds that the ability of undergraduates to read critically and write cogently has fallen significantly since 1992. Students are not just more poorly prepared, a majority of queried faculty members believe, but less teachable.

4   While some blame reality television, MP3 players, cellphones, or the multitasking that juggles them all, the big change has been the Web. Beginning in the early 1990's, schools, libraries, and governments embraced the Internet as the long promised portal to information access for all. And at the heart of their hopes for a cultural and educational breakthrough were superbly efficient search engines like *Google* and those of its rivals *Yahoo!* and *MSN*. The new search engines not only find more, they are more likely to present usable information on the first screen.

5   *Google* modestly declares its mission "to organize the world's information and make it universally accessible and useful." But convenience may be part of the problem. In the Web's early days, the most serious search engine was *AltaVista*. To use it well, a searcher had to learn how to construct a search statement, like, say, "Engelbert Humperdinck and not Las Vegas" for the opera composer rather than the contemporary singer. It took practice to produce usable results. Now, thanks to brilliant programming, a simple query usually produces a first page that's at least adequate—"satisficing," as the economist Herbert Simon called it.[1] The efficiency of today's search engines arises from their ability to analyze links among Web sites. *Google* led in ranking sites by how often

569

*Edward Tenner, "Searching for Dummies," *New York Times*, March 26, 2006: 12.

they are linked to other highly ranked sites. It did so using an elaborate variation of a concept familiar in natural science, citation analysis. Instead of looking at which papers are cited most often in the most influential journals, it measures how often Web pages are linked to highly ranked sites—ranked by links to themselves.

6   Citation analysis has been attacked in library circles for inflating the ratings (and indirectly the subscription prices) of certain journals. Search engines have the opposite problem: dispersion rather than concentration of interest. Despite constant tweaking, their formulas display irrelevant or mediocre sites on a par with truly expert ones.

7   Curious about the academic field of world history? A neophyte would find little help entering "world history" in *Google*. When I tried, the only article on the world history movement, from the open-source *Wikipedia* project, didn't appear until the fifth screen and was brief and eccentric, erroneously dating the field from the 1980's. (In fairness to *Wikipedia*, that entry has since been corrected and improved; moreover, the paid-access *Encyclopaedia Britannica* site has no specific article at all.) Only on the seventh screen did I find the World History Network site, financed by the National Endowment for the Humanities, and it is not yet a good portal for beginners.

8   Many students seem to lack the skills to structure their searches so they can find useful information quickly. In 2002, graduate students at Tel Aviv University were asked to find on the Web, with no time limit, a picture of the Mona Lisa; the complete text of either *Robinson Crusoe* or *David Copperfield*; and a recipe for apple pie accompanied by a photograph. Only 15 percent succeeded at all three assignments.

9   Today, *Google* may have expedited such tasks, but the malaise remains. In the February newsletter of the American Historical Association, the reference librarian Lynn D. Lampert notes the prevalence of "ill-conceived (or often nonexistent) student research practices." As another university librarian, Pamela Martin, observed, "*Google*'s simplicity and impressive search prowess trick students into thinking they are good all-around searchers, and when they fail in library searches, they are ashamed as well as confused."

10   Higher education is fighting back. Librarians are teaching "information literacy" and establishing alternative Web indexes. Graduate students, in the front lines as teaching assistants, are starting to discuss joining *Wikipedia* rather than fighting it, as many instructors still, quixotically, do.

11   Can better information in the classroom produce the literate, numerate society the Web once promised? There are two ways to proceed. More owners of free high-quality content should learn the tradecraft of tweaking their sites to improve search engine rankings. And *Google* can do more to educate users about the power—and frequent advisability—of its advanced search options. It would be a shame if brilliant technology were to end up threatening the kind of intellect that produced it.

Editor's note:

1. According to *Wikipedia*, the term *satisficing* signifies a "decision-making strategy which attempts to meet criteria for adequacy, rather than to identify an optimal solution." Among the cognitive tasks that Herbert Simon considers as relying on this strategy are games, problem-solving situations, and financial decisions.

Reading Images: Ways of Reading

Image 1:
Girl Reading

Image 2:
Diverse et Artificiose Machine (1588)

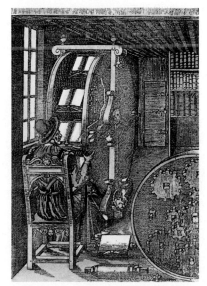

Image 3:
The Multitasking Generation

571

Context: These images offer different ideas about the nature of reading raised by Matthew Kirschenbaum. The first image, from the NEA report *To Read or Not to Read*, reveals the ideal of reading held by the authors of that report. The second, an image from a Renaissance book, shows a reader working his way through parallel passages in many works, comparing the passages rather than reading a single book from cover to cover. Image 3 is a portrait of a girl multitasking that gives several views of digital reading.

For Discussion: These three images of readers reflect different approaches to text, which require different acts of attention and imply different purposes. What do you think is the purpose of reading, as represented by each of these examples?

For Writing: Using these three images as a starting point, construct your own definition of what constitutes an act of "reading" in the computer age. Which image fits best your own way of reading, whether a book or some other piece of writing?

> **BEFORE YOU READ:** Think about the ways in which you use your computer on a daily basis. Which activities would you generally characterize as "reading," and which activities as "writing"?

HOW READING IS BEING REIMAGINED*

Matthew Kirschenbaum

Matthew Kirschenbaum is an associate professor of English and the associate director of the Maryland Institute for Technology in the Humanities at the University of Maryland at College Park.

1   There is no doubt that it is time for a serious conversation about reading, not least because books themselves are changing.

2   *Google,* in cooperation with several dozen research libraries worldwide, is digitizing books at the rate of 3,000 a day. The noncommercial Open Content Alliance is scanning at a more modest pace but gaining ground, especially among institutions who chafe at some of the restrictions imposed by *Google* and its competitors. LibraryThing, an online book catalog that allows readers to list their books and find other readers with (sometimes uncannily) similar tastes, has almost 300,000 users who have collectively tagged some 20 million books. *Newsweek* ran a cover story on "The Future of Reading" in their November 26, [2007] issue. And on Monday, the same day that the National Endowment for the Arts released *To Read or Not to Read: A Question of National Consequence,* the follow-up to its controversial 2004 *Reading at Risk: A Survey of Literary Reading in America* report, Amazon.com launched Kindle, an e-book reader device that the *Newsweek* story describes as the "iPod of reading."

3   My purpose is not to debunk the NEA's most recent report, which synthesizes a number of studies to conclude that Americans—especially younger ones—are reading less, that they are reading "less well," and that these trends have disturbing implications for culture, civics, and even the national economy. The data are significant to anyone who cares about reading and its place in a 21st-century society, and deserve to be treated seriously. But clearly the report comes to us at a moment when reading and conversations about reading are in a state of flux. It's worth taking a moment to account for this broader context. High-profile projects like *Google*'s and new devices like Kindle suggest what I call the remaking of reading, meaning that reading is being both reimagined and re-engineered, made over creatively as well as technologically.

4   Historically, we've placed very different values on different kinds of reading. The reading of novels and other "literary" works—precisely the core concern of the earlier NEA report—has not always enjoyed the pride of place it has in the current cultural canon. When Cervantes sent poor, mad Don Quixote on his delirious adventures at the beginning of the 17th century,

---

*Matthew Kirschenbaum, "How Reading Is Being Reimagined," *Chronicle of Higher Education* 54.15 (December 7, 2007), B20.

there existed a popular prejudice surrounding the reading of chivalric romances. Until well into the 19th century, novel-reading was regarded in Europe as a pastime fit mostly for women and the indolent—and a potentially dangerous one, since women, especially, could not be trusted to distinguish fiction from reality. But both the 2004 and the current report are curiously devoid of historical awareness, as though there is but a single, idealized model of reading from which we have strayed.

5   *To Read or Not to Read* deploys its own self-consistent iconography to tell us what reading is. In the pages of the report we find images of an adolescent male bent over a book, a female student sitting alone reading against a row of school lockers, and a white-collar worker studying a form. These still lives of the literate represent reading as self-evident—we know it when we see it. Yet they fail to acknowledge that such images have coexisted for centuries with other kinds of reading that have their own iconography and accouterments: Medieval and early modern portraits of scholars and scribes at work at their desks show them adorned with many books (not just one), some of them bound and splayed on exotic devices for keeping them open and in view; Thomas Jefferson famously designed a lazy susan to rotate books in and out of his visual field. That kind of reading values comparison and cross-checking as much as focus and immersion—lateral reading as much as reading for depth.

6   That is the model of reading that seems compatible with the Web and other new electronic media. Yet it also raises fundamental questions about what it means to read, and what it means to have read something. When can we claim a book to have been read? What is the dividing line between reading and skimming? Must we consume a book in its entirety—start to finish, cover to cover—to say we have read it? Pierre Bayard, a literature professor in France, recently made a stir with a naughty little volume called *How to Talk about Books You Haven't Read.* When I read it (well, most of it), the book provoked the most intense author envy I have ever felt—not because I too secretly enjoy perpetuating literary frauds, but because Bayard speaks to a dilemma that will be familiar to every literate person: namely, that there are far more books in the world (50 million or 60 million by the estimates I've seen) than any of us will ever have time to read. Reading, Bayard says, is as much about mastering a system of relationships among texts and ideas as it is about reading any one text in great depth. He quotes the extreme case of the fictional librarian in Robert Musil's *The Man without Qualities* (a book Bayard admits to having only skimmed): The librarian resolutely reads no books whatsoever for fear that undue attention to any one of them will compromise the integrity of his relation to them all.

7   The structure of *To Read or Not to Read* presents itself as tacit acknowledgment that not all of its own text will likely be read by any one reader, since it is clearly designed to be "not read" in at least some of the ways that accord with Bayard's observations. The report is accompanied by an Executive Summary, a condensed version of the major findings. Its internal organization is carefully laid out, with summary points at the head of each chapter, topic sentences, extensive notes, sidebars, and sections labeled as conclusions.

8   The authors of the report would doubtlessly insist that the kind of person who reads (or doesn't read) books by French intellectuals writing about books they haven't read (or have only skimmed) is not the kind of reader who has them much worried. It's the people, especially the

573

young ones, who are simply not reading at all that are cause for alarm. But the new report also places extreme emphasis on what it repeatedly terms "voluntary" reading. Reading that one does for work or for school doesn't "count" in this regard. While one can appreciate the motivations here—the NEA is interested in people who read because they choose to, not because they have to—it seems oddly retrograde. How many of us who count ourselves as avid readers are able to maintain clear boundaries between work and leisure anymore?

9   Likewise, while the authors of the report repeatedly emphasize that they include online reading in their data, the report sounds most clumsy and out of touch when referring to new media. The authors of the report tend to homogenize "the computer" without acknowledging the diversity of activity—and the diversity of reading—that takes place on its screen. Our screens are spaces where new forms like blogs and e-mail and chats commingle with remediations of older forms, like newspapers and magazines—or even poems, stories, and novels. Reading your friend's blog is not likely a replacement for reading Proust, but some blogs have been a venue for extraordinary writing, and we are not going to talk responsibly or well about what it means to read online until we stop conflating genre with value.

10   The report also fails to acknowledge the extent to which reading and writing have become commingled in electronic venues. The staccato rhythms of a real-time chat session are emblematic in this regard: Reading and writing all but collapse into a single unified activity. But there is a spectrum of writing online, just as there is a spectrum of reading, and more and more applications blur the line between the two. Many electronic book interfaces allow users to annotate their texts, for example; some

allow users to share those notes and annotations with others (CommentPress, from the Institute for the Future of the Book, is exemplary in this regard, as is Zotero, from the Center for History and New Media at George Mason University). Alph, a project directed by Nancy Kaplan at the University of Baltimore, is developing new online reading interfaces for children; the ability to leave notes and marks behind for these young readers' peers is a signature design feature. Book Glutton, a Web service still in beta mode, provides adult users with a shared electronic library; readers write notes for other readers in the margins of the books, and this virtual marginalia persists over time, accreting in Talmudic fashion.[1] Moreover, readers can choose to chat in real time with other readers perusing the same chapter that is on their screens.

11   What kind of activity is taking place here? What are the new metrics of screen literacy? I don't have that data, it's not my field, but anecdotally my instinct is that computer users are capable of projecting the same aura of deep concentration and immersion as the stereotypical bookworm. Walk into your favorite coffee shop and watch the people in front of their screens. Rather than bug-eyed, frenzied jittering, you are more likely to see calm, meditative engagement—and hear the occasional click of fingers on keyboards as the readers write.

Editor's note:

1. The Talmud is a record of rabbinic discussions pertaining to Jewish law, ethics, customs, and history. The Talmud is perhaps second in authority only to the Jewish Bible (Old Testament). Here Kirschbaum refers to the cumulative and encyclopedic nature of the Talmud.

B. What Are the Benefits and Dangers of Genetic Engineering for Individuals and for Society?

> **BEFORE YOU READ:** Kurzweil talks about a number of technologies that, in the near future, will let us control our bodies and biological predispositions. At this point in time, what do you think is the most amazing or interesting way in which science is letting us control our bodies?

OUR BODIES, OUR TECHNOLOGIES*

Ray Kurzweil

Ray Kurzweil has been described as "the restless genius" by the *Wall Street Journal*. He invented the first flat-bed scanner, pioneered omni-font optical character recognition, the first print-to-speech reading machine for the blind, the first text-to-speech synthesizer, and the first music synthesizer capable of recreating orchestral instruments. This essay is an abridged version of Kurzweil's Cambridge Forum Lecture.

1 In the 2020s, we'll see nanobots, blood-cell-sized devices that can go inside the body and brain to perform therapeutic functions. But what happens when we have billions of nanobots inside the capillaries of our brains, non-invasively, widely distributed, expanding human intelligence, or providing full-immersion virtual reality? It turns out that information technology is increasingly encompassing everything of value. It's not just computers, it's not just electronic gadgets. It now includes the field of biology. We're beginning to understand how life processes, disease, aging, are manifested as information processes and gaining the tools to actually manipulate those processes. It's true of all of our creations of intellectual and cultural endeavors, our music, movies are all facilitated by information technology, and are distributed, and represented as information.

2 Evolutionary processes work through indirection. Evolution creates a capability, and then it uses that capability to evolve the next stage. That's why the next stage goes more quickly, and that's why the fruits of an evolutionary process grow exponentially. The first paradigm shift in biological evolution, the evolution of cells, and in particular DNA (actually, RNA came first)—the evolution of essentially a computer system or an information processing backbone that would allow evolution to record the results of its experiments—took billions of years. Once DNA and RNA were in place, the next stage, the Cambrian explosion, when all the body plans of the animals were evolved, went a hundred times faster. Then those body plans were used by evolution to concentrate on higher cognitive functions. Biological evolution kept accelerating in this manner. *Homo sapiens*, our species, evolved in only a few hundred thousand years, the blink of an eye in evolutionary terms.

3 Then again working through indirection, biological evolution used one of its creations,

---

*Ray Kurzweil, "Our Bodies, Our Technologies," Cambridge Forum Lecture (abridged), originally transcribed from the Cambridge Forum Lecture on May 4, 2005, and reprinted in *Science & Theology News*. Reprinted on *KurzweilAI.net,* March 16, 2006, http://www.kurzweilai.net/meme/frame.html?main=/articles/art0649.html (accessed June 18, 2008).

the first technology-creating species to usher in the next stage of evolution, which was technology. The enabling factors for technology were a higher cognitive function with an opposable appendage, so we could manipulate and change the environment to reflect our models of what could be. The first stages of technology evolution—fire, the wheel, stone tools—only took a few tens of thousands of years.

4   Technological evolution also accelerated. Half a millennium ago the printing press took a century to be adopted, half a century ago the first computers were designed pen on paper. Now computers are designed in only a few weeks' time by computer designers sitting at computers, using advanced computer-assisted design software. When I was at MIT [Massachusetts Institute of Technology, in the mid-1960s] a computer that took about the size of this room cost millions of dollars yet was less powerful than the computer in your cell phone today.

5   One of the profound implications is that we are understanding our biology as information processes. We have 23,000 little software programs inside us called genes. These evolved in a different era. One of those programs, called the fat insulin receptor gene, says, basically, hold onto every calorie because the next hunting season might not work out so well. We'd like to change that program now. We have a new technology that has just emerged in the last couple years called RNA interference, in which we put fragments of RNA inside the cell, as a drug, to inhibit selected genes. It can actually turn genes off by blocking the messenger RNA expressing that gene. When the fat insulin receptor was turned off in mice, the mice ate ravenously and remained slim. They didn't get diabetes, didn't get heart disease, lived 20% longer: they got the benefit of caloric restriction without the restriction.

6   Every major disease and every major aging process has different genes that are used in the expression of these disease and aging processes. Being able to actually select when we turn them off is one powerful methodology. We also have the ability to turn enzymes off. Torcetrapib, a drug that's now in FDA Phase 3 trials, turns off a key enzyme that destroys the good cholesterol, HDL, in the blood. If you inhibit that enzyme, HDL levels soar and atherosclerosis slows down or stops.

7   There are thousands of these developments in the pipeline. The new paradigm of rational drug design involves actually understanding the information processes underlying biology, the exact sequence of steps that leads up to a process like atherosclerosis, which causes heart attacks, or cancer, or insulin resistance, and providing very precise tools to intervene. Our ability to do this is also growing at an escalating rate.

8   Another exponential process is miniaturization. We're showing the feasibility of actually constructing things at the molecular level that can perform useful functions. One of the biggest applications of this, again, will be in biology, where we will be able to go inside the human body and go beyond the limitations of biology. Rob Freitas has designed a nanorobotic red blood cell, which is a relatively simple device, it just stores oxygen and lets it out. A conservative analysis of these robotic respirocytes shows that if you were to replace ten percent of your red blood cells with these robotic versions you could do an Olympic sprint for 15 minutes without taking a breath, or sit at the bottom of your pool for four hours. It will be interesting to see what we do with these in our Olympic contests. Presumably we'll ban them, but then we'll have the specter of high school students routinely outperforming the Olympic athletes.

9   A robotic white blood cell is also being designed. A little more complicated, it downloads software from the Internet to combat specific pathogens. If it sounds very futuristic to download information to a device inside

your body to perform a health function, I'll point out that we're already doing that. There are about a dozen neural implants either FDA-approved or approved for human testing. One implant that is FDA-approved for actual clinical use replaces the biological neurons destroyed by Parkinson's disease. The neurons in the vicinity of this implant then receive signals from the computer that's inside the patient's brain. This hybrid of biological and non-biological intelligence works perfectly well. The latest version of this device allows the patient to download new software to the neural implant in his brain from outside his body.

10   These are devices that today require surgery to be implanted, but when we get to the 2020s, we will ultimately have the "killer app" of nanotechnology, nanobots, which are blood cell-sized devices that can go inside the body and brain to perform therapeutic functions, as well as advance the capabilities of our bodies and brains. If *that* sounds futuristic, I'll point out that we already have blood cell-size devices that are nano-engineered, working to perform therapeutic functions in animals. For example, one scientist cured type I diabetes in rats with this type of nanoengineered device. And some of these are now approaching human trials. The 2020s really will be the "golden era" of nanotechnology.

11   It is a mainstream view now among informed observers that by the 2020s we will have sufficient computer processing to emulate the human brain. The current controversy, or I would say, the more interesting question is, will we have the software or methods of human intelligence? To achieve the methods, the algorithms of human intelligence, there is underway a grand project to reverse-engineer the brain. And there, not surprisingly, we are also making exponential progress. If you follow the trends in reverse brain engineering it's a reasonable conclusion that we will have reverse-engineered the

several hundred regions of the brain by the 2020s.

12   By early in the next decade, computers won't look like today's notebooks and PDAs, they will disappear, integrated into our clothing and environment. Images will be written to our retinas for our eyeglasses and contact lenses, we'll have full-immersion virtual reality. We'll be interacting with virtual personalities; we can see early harbingers of this already. We'll have effective language translation. If we go out to 2029, there will be many turns of the screw in terms of this exponential progression of information technology. There will be about thirty doublings in the next 25 years. That's a factor of a billion in capacity and price performance over today's technology, which is already quite formidable.

13   By 2029, we will have completed reverse engineering of the brain, we will understand how human intelligence works, and that will give us new insight into ourselves. Non-biological intelligence will combine the suppleness and subtlety of our pattern-recognition capabilities with ways computers have already demonstrated their superiority. Every time you use *Google* you can see the power of non-biological intelligence. Machines can remember things very accurately. They can share their knowledge instantly. We can share our knowledge, too, but at the slow bandwidth of language.

14   This will not be an alien invasion of intelligent machines coming from over the horizon to compete with us, it's emerging from within our civilization, it's extending the power of our civilization. Even today we routinely do intellectual feats that would be impossible without our technology. In fact our whole economic infrastructure couldn't manage without the intelligent software that's underlying it.

15   The most interesting application of computerized nanobots will be to interact with our biological neurons. We've

577

already shown the feasibility of using electronics and biological neurons to interact non-invasively. We could have billions of nanobots inside the capillaries of our brains, non-invasively, widely distributed, expanding human intelligence, or providing full immersion virtual reality encompassing all of the senses from within the nervous system. Right now we have a hundred trillion connections. Although there's a certain amount of plasticity, biological intelligence is essentially fixed. Non-biological intelligence is growing exponentially; the crossover point will be in the 2020s. When we get to the 2030s and 2040s, it will be the non-biological portion of our civilization that will be predominant. But it will still be an expression of human civilization.

16 Every time we have technological gains we make gains in life expectancy. Sanitation was a big one, antibiotics was another. We're now in the beginning phases of this biotechnology revolution. We're exploring, understanding and gaining the tools to reprogram the information processes underlying biology; and that will result in another big gain in life expectancy. So, if you watch your health today, the old-fashioned way, you can actually live to see the remarkable 21st century.

BEFORE YOU READ: Rifkin's article discusses some ways in which human genetics can be engineered to "improve" society. Can you think of more ordinary ways in which people are always trying to improve their bodies, minds, and social identities?

ULTIMATE THERAPY:
COMMERCIAL EUGENICS IN THE 21ST CENTURY*

Jeremy Rifkin

Rifkin is author of *The Biotech Century,* president of the Foundation on Economic Trends in Washington, D.C., and a fellow in the Wharton's Executive Program at the University of Pennsylvania.

1 While the 20th century was shaped largely by spectacular breakthroughs in the fields of physics and chemistry, the 21st century will belong to the biological sciences. Scientists around the world are quickly deciphering the genetic code of life, unlocking the mystery of millions of years of biological evolution on Earth. Global life science companies, in turn, are beginning to exploit the new advances in biology in a myriad of ways, laying the economic framework for the coming Biotech Century.

2 Genes are the raw resource of the new economic epoch and are already being used in a variety of international business fields—including agriculture, animal husbandry, energy, bioremediation, building and packing materials, and pharmaceuticals—to fashion a bio–industrial world. Nowhere is the new genetic commerce likely to have a bigger impact,

*Harvard International Review, *Spring* 2005, 44–48.

however, than in human medicine. For the first time in history, the scientific tools are becoming available to manipulate the genetic instructions in human cells. Human gene therapy raises the very real possibility that we might be able to engineer the genetic blueprints of our own species and begin to redirect the future course of our biological evolution on Earth. Breakthroughs in genetic technology are bringing us to the edge of a new eugenics era with untold consequences for present and future generations and for civilization itself.

3   In less than ten years, the global life science companies will hold patents on many of the 30,000 or so genes that make up the human race as well as patents on the cell lines, tissues, and organs of our species, giving them unprecedented power to dictate the terms by which we and future generations live our lives. The concentration of power in the global pharmaceutical industry has already reached staggering proportions. The implications of a new market-driven eugenics are enormous and far reaching. Indeed, commercial eugenics could become the defining social dynamic of the new century.

FRIENDLY EUGENICS

4   The term "eugenics" was conceived by Sir Francis Galton, Charles Darwin's cousin, in the 19th century and is generally divided along two lines. Negative eugenics involves the systematic elimination of so-called biologically undesirable traits. Positive eugenics is concerned with the use of genetic manipulation to "improve" the characteristics of an organism or species.

5   The prospect of creating a new eugenic man and woman is becoming ever more likely as a result of the steady advances in somatic and germ line genetic engineering technology. In somatic therapy, intervention takes place only within somatic cells and the genetic changes do not transfer into the offspring. In germ line therapy, genetic changes are made in the sperm, egg, or embryonic cells, and are passed along to future generations. Somatic gene surgery has been carried out in limited human clinical trials for more than a decade. Germ line experiments have been successfully carried out on mammals for more than 15 years and researchers expect the first human trials to be conducted in the near future.

6   Despite years of favorable media reports on various somatic gene therapy experiments and the high expectations voiced by the medical establishment and the biotech industry, the results have, thus far, been disappointing. So disappointing, in fact, that the National Institutes of Health (NIH) itself was forced to acknowledge the results and issue a sober warning to scientists conducting the experiments to stop making promises that could not be kept. After surveying all 106 clinical gene therapy trials conducted over a five-year period, involving more than 597 patients, a panel of experts convened by the NIH reported that "clinical efficacy has not been definitively demonstrated at this time in any gene therapy protocol, despite anecdotal claims of successful therapy." Still, many of the staunchest supporters of the new gene therapies remain convinced that the techniques will bear fruit as methodologies and procedures are refined and new knowledge of the workings of genes become more available to researchers and clinicians.

7   Far more controversial is the prospect of conducting human germ line therapy. Programming genetic changes into the human germ line to direct the evolutionary development of future generations may be the most radical human experiment ever contemplated and raises unprecedented moral, social, and environmental risks for the whole of humanity. Consequently, debate over genetic manipulation of human eggs, sperm, and embryonic cells has raged for more than 20 years.

579

8   Even so, a growing number of molecular biologists, medical practitioners, and pharmaceutical companies are anxious to take the gamble, convinced that controlling our evolutionary destiny is humankind's next great social frontier. Their arguments are couched in terms of personal health, individual choice, and collective responsibility for future generations.

9   Writing in *The Journal of Medicine and Philosophy,* Dr. Burke Zimmerman makes several points in defense of germ line cell therapy over somatic cell therapy. To begin with, he argues that the increasing use of somatic therapy is only likely to increase the number of survivors with defective genes in their germ lines, who will pass an increasing number of genetic problems onto succeeding generations. Second, although this therapy may be able to treat many global disorders by replacing populations of cells, it may never prove effective in addressing diseases involving solid tissues, organs, and functions dependent on structure, like, for example, the brain, making germ line therapy the only likely solution to such disorders.

10   Proponents of germ line therapy argue for broadening the ethical mandate of the global health profession to include responsibility for the health of those not yet conceived. The interests of the patient, says Zimmerman, should be extended to include the interests of "the entire genetic legacy that may result from intervention in the germ line." Moreover, parents ought not to be denied their right as parents to make choices on how best to protect the health of their unborn children during pregnancy. Therefore, it is argued that to deny parents the opportunity to take corrective action in the germ line would be a serious breach of medical responsibility.

11   Finally, the health costs to global society need to be factored into the equation, say the advocates of germ line therapy. Although the costs of genetic intervention into the germ line to cure diseases will likely remain high in the early years, the cost should drop dramatically as the methods and techniques become more refined. The lifetime cost of caring for generations of patients suffering from Parkinson's disease or severe Down's syndrome is likely to be far greater than simple prevention in the form of genetic intervention at the germ line level.

12   In the coming decades, scientists will learn more about how genes function. They will become increasingly adept at turning genes "on" and "off." They will become more sophisticated in the techniques of recombining genes and altering genetic codes. At every step of the way, conscious decisions will have to be made as to which kinds of permanent changes in the biological codes of life are worth pursuing and which are not. A global society steeped in "engineering" the gene pool of the planet cannot possibly hope to escape the kind of on-going eugenics decisions that go hand-in-hand with each new advance in biotechnology. There will be enormous social pressure to conform with the underlying logic of genetic engineering, especially when it comes to its human applications.

13   Parents in the biotech century will be increasingly forced to decide whether to take their chances with the traditional genetic lottery and use their own unaltered egg and sperm, knowing their children may inherit some "undesirable" traits, or undergo corrective gene changes on their sperm, egg, embryo, or fetus, or substitute egg or sperm from a donor through in vitro fertilization and surrogacy arrangements. If they choose to go with the traditional approach and let genetic fate determine their child's biological destiny, they could find themselves culpable if something goes dreadfully wrong in the developing fetus, something they could have avoided had they made use of corrective genetic intervention at the sex cell or embryo stage.

14   In the biotech century, a parent's failure to correct genetic defects in utero might well be regarded as a heinous crime. Society may

conclude that every parent has a responsibility to provide as safe and secure an environment as humanly possible for their unborn child. Not to do so might be considered a breach of parental duty for which the parents could be held morally, if not legally, liable. Mothers have already been held liable for having given birth to cocaine-addicted babies and babies with fetal alcohol syndrome. Prosecutors have argued that mothers passing on these painful addictions to their unborn children are culpable under existing child abuse statutes and ought to be held liable for the effect of their life style on their babies.

15   Proponents of human genetic engineering argue that it would be cruel and irresponsible not to use this powerful new technology to eliminate serious "genetic disorders." The problem with this argument, says the *New York Times* in an editorial entitled, "Whether to Make Perfect Humans," is that "there is no discernible line to be drawn between making inheritable repair of genetic defects and improving the species." The *Times* rightly points out that once scientists are able to repair genetic defects, "it will become much harder to argue against additional genes that confer desired qualities, like better health, looks, or brains."

16   If diabetes, sickle cell anemia, and cancer are to be prevented by altering the genetic makeup of individuals, why not proceed to other less serious "defects": myopia, color blindness, dyslexia, obesity, left-handedness? Indeed, what is to preclude the world from deciding that a certain skin color is a disorder? In the end, why would we ever say no to any alteration of the genetic code that might enhance the well-being of our offspring? It would be difficult to imagine parents rejecting genetic modifications that promised to improve, in some way, the opportunities for their progeny.

17   Despite the growing enthusiasm among some molecular biologists for engineering fundamental changes in the genetic code of human sex cells, it should be emphasized that treating genetic disorders by eliminating them at the germ line level is far different from treating genetic disorders by way of somatic gene surgery after birth. In the former instance, the genetic deletions can result, in the long run, in a dangerous narrowing of the human gene pool, which future generations rely on for making evolutionary adaptations to changing environments. On the other hand, if somatic gene surgery proves to be a safe, therapeutic way to treat serious diseases that cannot be effectively treated by more conventional approaches, it would appear to have potential value.

18   While the notion of consumer choice would appear benign, the very idea of eliminating so-called genetic defects raises the troubling question of what is meant by the term "defective." Ethicist Daniel Callahan of the Hastings Center penetrates to the core of the problem when he observes that "behind the human horror at genetic defectiveness lurks . . . an image of the perfect human being. The very language of 'defect,' 'abnormality,' 'disease,' and 'risk' presupposes such an image, a kind of proto-type of perfection."

19   The very idea of engineering the human species—by making changes at the germ line level—is not too dissimilar from the idea of engineering a piece of machinery. An engineer is constantly in search of new ways to improve the performance of a machine. As soon as one set of defects is eliminated, the engineer immediately turns his attention to the next set of defects, always with the idea in mind of creating a more efficient machine. The very idea of setting arbitrary limits as to how much "improvement" is acceptable is alien to the entire conception of engineering.

20   The new language of the information sciences has transformed many molecular biologists from scientists to engineers, although they are, no doubt, scarcely aware of the metamorphosis. When molecular biologists speak of

mutations and genetic diseases as errors in the code, the implicit, if not explicit, assumption is that they should never have existed in the first place, that they are "bugs," or mistakes that need to be deprogrammed or corrected. The molecular biologist, in turn, becomes the computing engineer, the writer of codes, continually eliminating errors and reprogramming instructions to upgrade both the program and the performance. This is a dubious and dangerous role when we stop to consider that every human being brings with him or her a number of lethal recessive genes. Do we then come to see ourselves as miswired from the get-go, riddled with errors in our code? If that is the case, against what ideal norm of perfection are we to be measured? If every human being is made up of varying degrees of error, then we search in vain for the norm, the ideal. What makes the new language of molecular biology so subtly chilling is that it risks creating a new archetype, a flawless, errorless, perfect being to which to aspire—a new man and woman, like us, but without the warts, wrinkles, vulnerabilities, and frailties that have defined humanity's essence from the very beginning of our existence.

21   No wonder so many in the disability rights community are becoming increasing frightened of the new biology. They wonder, if in this new world, people like themselves will be seen as errors in the code, mistakes to be eliminated, lives to be prevented from coming into being. We are not likely to be tolerant when we come to see everyone around us as defective.

22   The question, then, is whether or not humanity should begin the process of engineering future generations of human beings by technological design in the laboratory. What are the potential consequences of embarking on a course whose final goal is the "perfection" of the human species?

23   Many in the life sciences field would have us believe that the new gene splicing technologies are irrepressible and irreversible and that any attempt to oppose their introduction is both futile and retrogressive. They never stop to even consider the possibility that the new genetic science might be used in a wholly different manner than is currently being proposed.

24   While the global life science companies favor the introduction and widespread use of gene therapy to cure diseases and enhance the physical, emotional, and mental well-being of individuals, a growing number of holistically-minded geneticists and health practitioners are beginning to use the new data generated by the Human Genome Project in a very different way. They are exploring the relationship between genetic mutations and environmental triggers with the hope of fashioning a more sophisticated, scientifically-based understanding and approach to international health. More than 70 percent of all deaths in the United States and other industrialized countries are attributable to what physicians refer to as "diseases of affluence." Heart attacks, strokes, diabetes, and breast, colon, and prostate cancer are among the most common diseases of affluence. While each individual has varying genetic susceptibilities to these diseases, environmental factors, including diet and lifestyle, are major contributing elements that can trigger genetic mutations. Heavy cigarette smoking, high levels of alcohol consumption, diets rich in animal fats, the use of pesticides and other poisonous chemicals, contaminated water and food, polluted air, and sedentary living habits with little or no exercise, have been shown in study after study to cause genetic mutations and lead to the onset of many of these high-profile diseases.

25   The mapping and sequencing of the human genome is providing researchers with vital new information on recessive gene traits and genetic predispositions for a range of illnesses. Still, little research has been done, to date, on how genetic predispositions interact with toxic materials in the environment, the metabolism of different

BIOLOGICAL SELECTION

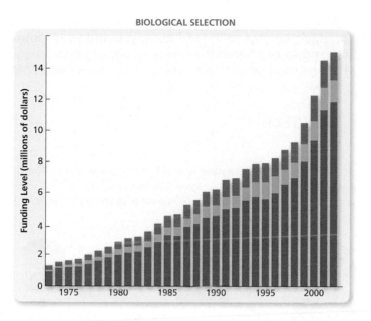

The figure shows the rapid increases in government funding for life sciences (orange) when compared to engineering sciences (green) and physical sciences (purple) since 1973. Increases for biological sciences funding are likely to be even more pronounced in the 21st century as scientists develop more advanced therapies. The data for the years 2001 and 2002 are projected.

foods, and lifestyle to affect genetic mutations and phenotypic expression. The new holistic approach to human medicine views the individual genome as part of an embedded organismic structure, continually interacting with and being affected by the environment in which it unfolds. The effort is geared toward using increasingly sophisticated genetic and environmental information to prevent genetic mutations from occurring.

26   The new "soft path" approach to the age of biology represents a change in the way researchers harness the new scientific and technological breakthroughs in the genetic sciences. While the "hard path" approach favors using the new genetic science to engineer changes in the very blueprint of a human being to advance medical progress, the soft path uses the same genetic information to create a more sustainable relationship between individual human beings and their environments. Although there is certainly a growing market for preventive health practices, programs, and products, far more money is invested in "illness-based" medicine. That could change, but it would require a paradigm shift in the way we think about science and its applications.

27   In closing, the biotech revolution will affect many aspects of our lives. The way we eat, the way we date and marry, the way we have our babies, the way our children are raised and educated, the way we perceive the world around us and our place in it— many of our individual and shared realities will be deeply touched by the new technologies of the Biotech Century. Surely, these very "personal" technologies deserve to be widely discussed and debated by the public at large before they become a ubiquitous part of our daily lives.

BEFORE YOU READ: If, either now or in the future, you and your spouse or partner were unable to have a child and were offered the choice of either using an egg donor or adopting a child, which method do you think you would choose and why?

YOUR GAMETE, MYSELF*

Peggy Orenstein

Peggy Orenstein is a contributing writer for the *New York Times Magazine* and author of the memoir *Waiting for Daisy: A Tale of Two Continents, Three Religions, Five Infertility Doctors, an Oscar, an Atomic Bomb, a Romantic Night and One Woman's Quest to Become a Mother.*

For Discussion: What comment on the process of selecting an egg donor does this collage of women's faces with labels make?

For Writing: Using the categories offered by this collage, describe what combination of qualities would make a "perfect" child. Would you feel comfortable "engineering" a child by genetic means?

584

Context: The caption reads: *Your Gamete, Yourself* by Balint Zesko. This image is an illustration to the essay with which it appears, and so comments directly on its themes.

1   Two years ago, when Catherine was in sixth grade, she was given a school assignment that would have been unremarkable for most kids: make a timeline for history class in which half the events occurred before she was born and half after. For a while, she worked quietly at the dining-room table of her family's rambling Northern California home. Then she looked up.

2   "Mom?" she asked. "What was the year that you and Dad met our donor?"

3   Sitting with me in May, Catherine's mother, Marie, a 59-year-old therapist, smiled wryly, remembering the incident. The crinkling of Marie's eyes gave her a passing resemblance to the actress Anne Bancroft—but not to her own daughter. Marie, who asked me to use only her middle name and a family name for

*Peggy Orenstein, "Your Gamete, Myself," *New York Times Magazine*, July 15, 2007: 36–63.

her daughter to protect their privacy, is dark where Catherine is blond, olive-skinned where Catherine is fair, brown-eyed where the girl's are hazel. There is no similarity to their jaw lines, their cheekbones, the shapes of their faces. Of course, lots of kids don't look like their mothers; few people would consider that odd, though they might—often incessantly—comment on it in conversation.

4   "So, what's going to happen with this project?" Marie recalled responding to Catherine at the time, being careful to keep her voice neutral. "Is it going to be put up in the hallway? In the classroom?"

5   Catherine shrugged. "I don't know," she said. And later, "Mom, this is my timeline."

6   "I got the message," Marie told me. "But in essence, I was outed on the wall of the middle school. It was there in black and white for everyone to see. They'd all know we used an egg donor. We'd been committed to openness from the beginning, but my first reaction was, 'No!'"

7   If Marie and Catherine are unusual, it is only because of Catherine's age. In 1992, the year she was conceived, there were just 1,802 attempts by women to become pregnant using someone else's eggs, according to the Centers for Disease Control. Three years later, there were more than 4,738 such cycles; by 2004, the most recent year for which data has been published, there were 15,175 cycles, resulting in 5,449 babies. By comparison, some 22,911 children were adopted from abroad that year, and although there are no official figures, one survey estimated that at least the same number are conceived annually via donor insemination. Donor eggs are now used in 12 percent of all in vitro fertilization (I.V.F.) attempts, making it among the fastest-growing infertility treatments. Despite the portentous hype around women like Frieda Birnbaum, a 60-year-old New Jersey resident who in May used donor eggs to become the oldest American to give birth to twins, the bulk of intended mothers are in their 40s. The

birthrate among women ages 40–44 has risen 62 percent since 1990, while the rate among those in their late 40s has more than doubled. Among those who used I.V.F. in 2004, about a third of the 43-year-olds used someone else's eggs; by 47 years old, 91 percent did. [. . .]

8   One day this spring, Becky, who is 38, met me at the airy loft in a sketchy neighborhood of Oakland, Calif., where she works in the music industry. She is a tiny woman—just over five feet tall—with dark blond ringlets pulled back in a ponytail and three earrings ascending one ear. A wedding photo on her desk, taken last summer, showed her tucked beneath the arm of her husband, Russell, a public-school teacher who is a more than a foot taller than she and who asked that I use only his middle name. [. . .]

9   Becky, who asked me to use a nickname, sat down and began scrolling through pictures on the Web site of Ova the Rainbow, one of the (regrettably named) agency sites she browsed last fall during her search for an egg donor. "When I first started doing this it was really emotional for me," she said. "I kept thinking about that kids' book, 'Are You My Mother?' I'm looking through these pictures of young women and feeling like: 'Oh, my God! Is this the mother of my future child? Is this the mother of my future child?'"

10   I stood behind her, watching the young women go by. Each was accompanied by an assortment of photos: girls in caps and gowns graduating from high school, sunburned and smiling on family vacations, as preschoolers in princess frocks, sporting supermodel pouts in shopping-mall glamour portraits. Sperm banks rarely provide such visuals, which is just one disparity in the packaging and treatment of male and female donors, according to a study published last month in *The American Sociological Review*. Egg donors are often thanked with presents and notes by recipients for their generous "gift." [. . .]

11   It was weird to look at these pictures with Becky. I inevitably objectified the young women in them, evaluating their component

585

parts; it made me feel strangely like a guy. Becky clicked on a photo of a 22-year-old brunette with a toothy grin. Each profile listed the donor's age (many agencies consider donors to be over the hill by 30), hair color (there seemed to be a preponderance of blondes), eye color, weight, ethnicity, marital status, education level, high school or college G.P.A.'s, college major, evidence of "proved" fertility (having children of their own or previous successful cycles). Some agencies include blood type for recipients who don't plan to tell their child about his conception. Others include bust size and favorite movies, foods and TV shows. [. . .]

12 "Why don't you just adopt?" That is the first question most people ask if you say you're considering egg donation. It's the question I asked myself, as had every potential donor recipient I spoke with. Why create a child where none existed? Why spend the money on something that's not a sure bet? Why ask another woman, even (or maybe especially) a friend, to inject herself with drugs—drugs whose side effects, although unlikely, could require hospitalization and even, in extremely rare instances, be fatal. (Recipients of donor eggs are required to buy supplementary health insurance for the donors in case something untoward occurs.)

13 The answers among the women I met were both deeply personal and surprisingly consistent. Like Becky, these women longed for the experience of pregnancy, childbirth and breastfeeding. Often they (or, more often, their husbands) resisted adoption, reasoning that egg donation would be psychologically easier on the child, who would be born—rather than relinquished—into its family. They wanted the opportunity to handpick a donor's genes rather than gamble on a birth mother's and father's. And they wanted to be able to see at least their husbands, if not themselves, reflected in their children's faces. [. . .]

14 Yet there is often no way to know whether the information the donor gives, including her medical history and educational background, is accurate. A 2006 study conducted by researchers at New York University found that donors routinely lowballed their weight, and the heavier they were, the more they fudged. Agencies, too, which are unregulated and unlicensed, can easily manipulate the truth. Many advertise I.Q. and psychological testing as part of their services, though there is no independent verification of either the results or the protocols used. Even if there were, jacking up fees for smarts is a dubious prospect. "Fees for donors are based on time and trouble, so I don't see how someone who goes to Brown has more time or trouble doing this than someone who didn't go to college at all," Feingold, the psychologist, told me. "Parents are vulnerable. People would be willing to do a lot to take charge so that they didn't need to feel so sad, bad, fearful, and out of control. They'll pay more money, do testing. But it's impossible to do intelligence testing on an egg."

15 To discourage both fraud and undue inducement, the ethics committee of the American Society for Reproductive Medicine (A.S.R.M.) issued a position paper in 2006 on donor compensation: $5,000, they determined, was a reasonable, but not coercive fee. Anything beyond that needed "justification," and sums over $10,000 went "beyond what is appropriate." What's more, the committee denounced paying more for "personal attributes," saying that the practice commodifies human gametes. [. . .]

16 The agency Becky eventually used charged her a flat $6,500 donor fee (there would've been a comparatively reasonable $500 premium if she had requested a Jewish or Asian donor) along with a $3,800 agency fee. Additionally, there were the costs of the donor's medical screening and health insurance; legal fees; reimbursement for the donor's and possibly a companion's travel expenses if the donor was from out of the area (Becky's wasn't); and reimbursement for lost wages and child care. There were also the costs associated with any I.V.F. cycle: not only the

fertility drugs, but also physician, clinic, and lab fees. And fees for freezing any unused embryos, in case the transfer failed or the couple wanted to have another child. Becky estimated that she and Russell would eventually be out about $35,000. [. . .]

17   According to several studies, most donor recipients haven't told their children about their origins, though some researchers argue that this trend is reversing. . . . In truth, it isn't clear that secrecy is necessarily damaging. In the most extensive longitudinal study to date, Susan Golombok, the director of the Center for Family Research at Cambridge University in England, has compared families who have sperm-donor children with those who have egg-donor children, as well as with those who used conventional I.V.F. and those who conceived naturally. In 2006, when her team last checked in with the donor-conceived children, they were 12, and most had not been told the nature of their conception. The kids in all of the groups were equally well adjusted. What's more, parents of donor-conceived kids (and those who used conventional I.V.F.) were more involved with their kids' lives than those who had conceived naturally. [. . .]

18 Once a child knows she was donor-conceived, what then? How far do her rights extend? Should she be able to meet her donor, and who gets to decide? It was clear to Marie, the donor recipient who is also an adoptee, that knowing one's genetic lineage should not just be an option, it should be an entitlement. . . . [Marie and Catherine] have been in phone and e-mail contact with the donor, who at the time of the donation was a college student interning for an acquaintance of Marie's, ever since. Catherine has known about the woman since preschool. "The comments she'd make about it at 5 were different than at 10," Marie said. "At 5, we'd be driving to Safeway, and this little voice in the back of the car would say, 'Now, what's an egg donor again?' At 10 there were a lot of questions about who she looked like and 'Why don't I look like you?'"

19   Then, when Catherine was 12, came the moment that all of the donor recipients I spoke to told me they dreaded. "She turned to me in this relaxed, 'Hey, Mom, isn't this interesting' kind of voice and said, 'You know, technically speaking, you're not actually my mother.'"

20   This, Marie said, is where it helped to be a trained therapist—and perhaps an adoptee as well, someone who has understood from experience both the salience and limits of genetic relationships, that DNA doesn't make the mom, but children need to figure out what, if anything, it signifies. "It was her way of acknowledging that this means something to her that's completely independent of her relationship to me. And that's inevitable: no amount of being wanted, planned for or loved eliminates that piece of the experience."

21   Last winter, the donor, who is now 36, single and childless, began pressing for a closer relationship with Catherine. She invited the girl and her parents to her house for dinner, the first time they had gotten together in several years. Halfway through the meal, and against Marie's explicit instructions, she pulled out a collection of family photos: her mother, brothers, sisters, nieces, and nephews. Catherine recoiled. "The donor has this great need to make Catherine into family because she doesn't have children of her own," Marie said. "My husband and I had to tell her: 'That's Catherine's decision. It's not yours or even ours.' So now the two continue to e-mail but rarely get together." [. . .]

22   A few days after my conversation with Marie, I talked to Becky. She had just found out she was pregnant with twins. . . . She paused a moment, thinking about her future. "I'm just happy," she said. Finally, Becky would be a mother, her husband a father, the two of them building a family with all the conflict, joy and unpredictability that entails—regardless of whose genes are involved.

Questions to Help You Think and Write about Modern Technology

1. Lessig tells us that Web 2.0 is creating an exciting new amateur culture, while Keen thinks that the ability to broadcast widely our thoughts, actions, and feelings breeds narcissism and sheer silliness. Take one example of a Web 2.0 technology—a blog written by someone famous or just someone you know, a YouTube video, or a Facebook profile—and, for the sake of argument, defend that piece of amateur culture from Keen's criticisms. How is the online community alive and creative?

2. Dick Locher's cartoon and the essays by Kurt Soller and Sarah Kliff explore the ways in which our lives are being governed by the machines that make social communication simple and easy. For one full day, make an hourly chart and keep a record of how much time you spend doing different kinds of activities: reading, writing, eating, exercising, thinking, catching up on the news, communicating, doing homework, praying, and so on. For which of these activities do you need technology? Is technology making your life easier and more efficient or is it just eating up your time?

3. While the Jones essay surveys the legal problems that YouTube posting can cause, both here and worldwide, consider instead the ways in which YouTube can give you a glimpse of people, places, ideas, and activities that otherwise you would not have access. Find one YouTube video on a topic of your choice, then look at four or five videos on related topics that the YouTube search function offers you. Argue the claim that the positives of YouTube outweigh the negatives, using the videos you have watched as your supports. What new information, skills, or social/cultural knowledge have you gained from this activity?

4. Test how well you know how to use *Google* by replicating the test Tenner talks about that was given to graduate students at Tel Aviv University: find "a picture of the Mona Lisa; the complete text of either *Robinson Crusoe* or *David Copperfield*; and a recipe for apple pie accompanied by a photograph." How well did you do? Then pick another search term of your choice and see how well the first page of sites listed fits the requirement of being adequate or "satisficing." Try some variations on your search term to see whether you can get better results. From your practical experiences, what do students need to know in order to do Web research intelligently and efficiently?

5. Using Matt Kirschenbaum's observation that the line between reading and writing is becoming blurred by computers, consider an online or computer-facilitated method of communication with which you are familiar. List the ways in which the activity could be described as one that involves "reading," then list the ways in which the activity could be described as "writing." What do you think is the relationship between reading and writing in a computer environment?

6. Kurzweil and Rifkin present the pros and cons of genetic engineering for the improvement of both individuals and human society. Take one aspect of life that, according to these authors, could be improved by genetic science and consider whether intervening in the "genetic lottery" is a good or bad thing. In what ways can science help to overcome this problem? Are there other ways to accomplish the goal of making people lead longer and better lives? Which way is preferable?

7. Some of the essays in Section 1 of "The Reader" consider how concepts of family, motherhood, and fatherhood have been changing. How would creating a child by using an egg donor influence what defines a family? Who is the true mother of such a child? How is this situation like and unlike adopting a child?

SECTION ③

589

Issues concerning Crime and the Treatment of Criminals

The Issues

A. How Should We Treat Convicted Criminals?

This section considers how society and the legal system should treat convicted criminals and incarcerated prisoners. James Gilligan argues that education is the best antidote to the cycle of violence that entraps many prisoners. The next two essays analyze the beneficial effects of educational prison programs: Mary Wiltenburg examines a project in which maximum-security prisoners perform Shakespeare, while Ray Quintanilla investigates a program in which women prisoners train dogs for the disabled, giving both humans and canines a "second chance." Following two historically based visual arguments about execution are a final pair of essays (one by Robert Tanner and an article from *The Economist* magazine) evaluating the claim that capital punishment deters violent crime. See also "Giving People a Second Chance" (pages 60–61).

B. What Should Be Done with Young Offenders?

The focus here is on the escalating problem of children and teenagers who commit crimes and acts of violence. Aristotle, in an excerpt from the *Rhetoric*, describes the characteristics of young people as he perceived them in 350 B.C., and you may find these surprisingly modern. Claudia Wallis explains the 2005 Supreme Court ruling that makes it unlawful to administer the death penalty to 16- and 17-year-old convicted criminals, and Daniel Weinberger presents one reason the Supreme Court was prompted to make this ruling: the adolescent brain does not have mature judgment. A new development in youth crime is the rise of children's participation in international terrorism; William Glaberson reports on the youngest detainee at Guantánamo. Finally, Alan Feuer follows a young man from the Bronx who is released from prison on a drug charge, showing readers the vicious cycle of poverty, drugs, and crime that some young offenders contend with daily. See also "Minor Problems?" (pages 277–279).

Web Sites for Further Exploration and Research

Alcatraz History	http://www.alcatrazhistory.com/
Death Penalty Information Center	http://www.deathpenaltyinfo.org/
Shakespeare Behind Bars Web Site	http://www.shakespearebehindbars.com/
National Center for Victims of Crime	http://www.ncvc.org/
"An Abolitionist's View of the Death Penalty," ReligiousTolerance.org	http://www.religioustolerance.org/ whitson01.htm
ACLU Capital Punishment Project	http://www.aclu.org/capital/index.html
Youth Violence: A Report of the Surgeon General (2001)	http://www.surgeongeneral.gov/library/ youthviolence/
Coalition for Juvenile Justice	http://www.juvjustice.org/

Films and Literature Related to Crime

Films *A Clockwork Orange*, 1971; *Boyz N the Hood*, 1991; *Capote*, 2005; *Dead Man Walking*, 1996; *Escape from Alcatraz*, 1979; *The Green Mile*, 1996; *No Country for Old Men*, 2007; *Shakespeare Behind Bars*, 2005; *The Shawshank Redemption*, 1994.

Literature novels: *The Green Mile* by Stephen King; *In Cold Blood* by Truman Capote; *Native Son* by Richard Wright; *No Country for Old Men* by Cormac McCarthy; short stories: "Billy Budd" by Herman Melville; "A Good Man Is Hard to Find" by Flannery O'Connor; poems: "The Ballad of Reading Gaol" by Oscar Wilde; "Danny Deever" by Rudyard Kipling.

The Rhetorical Situation

There is a continued exigence for the issues associated with crime and the treatment of criminals both in the United States and worldwide. Motivational warrants linked to the needs for safety and for justice, often in the form of retribution, are implicit in many of the arguments about crime and criminals.

Before the eighteenth century, as social historians argue, criminals were punished in physical ways, such as by a clipping of the ear or loss of a hand for smaller felonies or by hanging, drawing, and quartering for capital offenses such as treason or attempted regicide. The prison grew in social importance during the eighteenth and nineteenth centuries, when discipline replaced punishment as the social goal for the justice system. Many of the features we associate with prisons today—isolation of prisoners, surveillance by officials, and regimented life—emerged during this period. The idea that penitentiaries should not only discipline criminals but rehabilitate them as well was also established in the late eighteenth century. The first U.S. penitentiary of this kind was the Walnut Street Jail of Philadelphia (1790). On the other hand, prisons could be constructed as warnings to future criminals. The famous island prison at Alcatraz (also called "The Rock"), which was known for its horrible living conditions, gave the prisoners who endured under these circumstances a clear view of San Francisco and the surrounding water, reminding them continually of what they had lost. This, prison officials believed, was a deterrent to the most hardened, violent prisoners in other penitentiaries; no one wanted to be sent to Alcatraz.

Two areas in which contemporary attitudes toward crime and punishment have become complicated are in the legal institution of capital punishment and in the treatment of young offenders. The institution of capital punishment, although designed as retribution for the most heinous crimes, also goes against the imperative to rehabilitate criminals and help them reenter society as useful citizens. Debates over how to treat young offenders, on the other hand, must deal with the possibility that children's violence is neither so ingrained as that of adults and with the equally serious possibility that children and teenagers have less developed brains and moral understanding than do adults. At the same time, they may be vulnerable to the same social prejudices as their adult peers and may have been trained by adults from an early age to commit violence.

591

A. How Should We Treat Convicted Criminals?

BEFORE YOU READ: The essays in this section implicitly consider the question of what prisons are intended to accomplish (e.g., to remove offenders from society, to punish them, to reeducate them, etc.) What are your opinions about the social purpose of prisons?

REFLECTIONS FROM A LIFE BEHIND BARS: BUILD COLLEGES, NOT PRISONS*

James Gilligan

James Gilligan is the former director of mental health for the Massachusetts prison system. He is also a clinical instructor in psychiatry at Harvard Medical School who has twenty-five years of experience as a prison psychiatrist. He believes that education is the key to preventing recidivism.

1   Neither words nor pictures, no matter how vivid, can do more than give a faint suggestion of the horror, brutalization, and degradation of the prisons of this country. I speak from extensive personal knowledge of this subject, for I have spent 25 years of my professional life behind bars—not as an inmate, but as a prison psychiatrist.

2   I am a physician, and I see violence (whether it is legal or illegal, homicidal or suicidal, intentional or careless) as a public-health problem—indeed, the most important and dangerous threat to public health in our time. Because it affects mostly the young, violence kills more people under the age of 65 in this country than do cancer and heart disease, the two illnesses that are often (and mistakenly) thought to be the most significant causes of death.

3   So I cannot emphasize too strongly how seriously I take the problem of violence. Far from being tolerant or permissive toward it, I am far more strongly opposed to violence in all its forms and in all its legal statuses, and far less tolerant and permissive toward it than are those who believe that our salvation lies in building more and more punitive (i.e., violent) prisons.

4   There is a widespread misimpression that punishment deters violence—in other words, that punishment is one means of preventing violence. However, the overwhelming weight of empirical evidence suggests that exactly the opposite is true—namely, that punishment, far from inhibiting or preventing violence, is the most potent stimulus or cause of violence that we have yet discovered. Several different lines of evidence, from several different populations and stages of the life cycle, converge in supporting that conclusion.

5   For example, child-rearing is such an inherently and inescapably complicated subject that there are relatively few findings from the past several decades of research on it that are so clear, so unmistakable, and so consistently replicated that they are virtually universally agreed on. But among those few is this: The more severely punished children are, the more violent they become, both as children and as adults. This is especially true of violent punishments. For example, children who are subjected to corporal discipline

*Chronicle of Higher Education, October 16, 1998, B7–B9.

592

are significantly more likely to subject other people to physical punishments (i.e., inflict violence on them), both while they are still children and after they have reached adulthood. That is hardly surprising, of course, for corporal discipline is simply another name for physical violence; it would be called assault and battery if committed against an adult.

6   In fact, even with respect to nonviolent behavior, such as bed-wetting or excessive dependency or passivity ("laziness"), punishment has a counterproductive effect; that is, the more severely children are punished for a given behavior, the more strongly they persist in repeating it. To put it the other way around: If we want to produce as violent a generation of children and adults as possible, the most effective thing we can do is to punish our children and adults as severely as possible.

7   While the research just referred to can be found in the literature on child development and child abuse, there is no reason to think that the psychology of adults differs in this respect from that of children, and every reason to think that it is the same. In fact, 1 have been able to confirm those findings on children from my own clinical experience of over 25 years with violent adult criminals and the violent mentally ill. The degree of violent child abuse to which this population had been subjected was so extreme that the only way to summarize it is to say that the most violent people in our society—those who murder others—are disproportionately the survivors of attempted murder themselves, or of the completed murders of their closest relatives, siblings, or parents.

8   Thus, if punishment could prevent violence, these men would never have become violent in the first place, for they were already punished, even before they became violent, as severely as it is possible to punish a person without actually killing him. Many were beaten nearly to death as children, so when they became adults, they did beat someone else to death.

9   Fortunately, we not only know what stimulates violence (punishment, humiliation), we also know what prevents violence, both in society in general and in the criminal-justice and prison systems in particular. Unfortunately, we Americans have been dismantling the conditions that do prevent violence as rapidly as we could over the past 25 years, with the entirely predictable result that the levels of violent crimes, such as murder, have repeatedly reached the highest recorded levels in our history. For example, for the last quarter of a century our murder rates have been twice as high as they were 40 years ago, and five to ten times as high as they currently are in any other democracy and developed economy on earth.

10   What are the conditions that prevent violence? Among general social conditions, there are several, but space permits mentioning only the most powerful one: a relatively classless society, with an equitable social and economic system in which there are minimal discrepancies in wealth, income, and standard of living between the poorest and the wealthiest factions of the population (people are vulnerable to feelings of shame and inferiority if they are poor, or economically inferior, while other people are rich, or economically superior).

11   Around the world, the nations with the most equitable economic systems, such as Sweden and Japan, are significantly more likely to have the lowest murder rates. And those with the greatest economic discrepancies between the rich and the poor (of which the United States is the world leader among developed democracies) have the highest murder rates (a statistic in which the United States is also the world leader). Even within the United States, the most equitable or "classless" states have the lowest murder rates, and those with the most inequitable degrees of class stratification have the highest. Yet the last Congress dismantled one of the few programs we had that tended to equalize income in this country—the earned-income tax credit.

12   Among the conditions in the prison system that prevent violent behavior (both during imprisonment and after release to the community), the most powerful is education. In Massachusetts, for example, when I headed the prison mental-health service, we did a study to see what programs within the prison had been most effective in preventing recidivism among prison inmates after they had been released from prison and returned to the community. While several programs had worked, the most successful of all, and the only one that had been 100 percent effective in preventing recidivism, was the program that allowed inmates to receive a college degree while in prison. Several hundred prisoners in Massachusetts had completed at least a bachelor's degree while in prison over a 25-year period, and not one of them had been returned to prison for a new crime.

13   Immediately after I announced this finding in a public lecture at Harvard, and it made its way into the newspaper, our new governor, William Weld, who had not previously been aware that prison inmates could take college courses, gave a press conference on television in which he declared that Massachusetts should rescind that "privilege," or else the poor would start committing crimes in order to be sent to prison so they could get a free college education! And lest one think that that was merely the rather bizarre response of one particularly cynical demagogue, it is worth noting that the U.S. Congress responded the same way. The last Congress declared that inmates throughout the federal prison system would no longer be eligible to receive Pell grants.

14   It is too late now to even begin to attempt to "reform" prisons. The only thing that can be done with them is to tear them all down, for their architecture alone renders them unfit for human beings. Or even animals: No humane society permits animals in zoos to be housed in conditions as intolerable as those in which we cage humans. The reason for the difference, of course, is clear: Zoos are not intended for punishment; prisons are. That is why it would benefit every man, woman, and child in this country, and it would hurt no one, to demolish the prisons and replace them with much smaller, locked, secure residential schools and colleges in which the residents could acquire as much education as their intelligence and curiosity would permit.

15   Such institutions would of course be most effective in their only rational purpose, which would be to prevent crime and violence, if they were designed to be as humane and homelike as possible, and as near the prisoners' own homes as possible, so that their families could visit as freely as possible (including frequent conjugal visits), and so they could visit their families as freely as possible. (For conjugal and home visits have repeatedly been shown, in this country and around the world, to be associated with lowered rates of violence, both during incarceration and after release into the community—which is probably why both have been effectively abolished in this country.)

16   Since there is no reason to isolate anyone from the community against his will unless he poses a danger of physically harming others, these residential schools would need to be limited to those who have been, or have threatened or attempted to be, violent. (Very few, if any, nonviolent "criminals" need to be removed from the community at all. Nor should those who have committed only nonviolent crimes ever have to be housed with those who have been seriously violent; and there are many reasons why they should not be.)

17   Thus one of the most constructive responses I can think of . . . would be the designing of an "anti-prison"—not prison reform, but prison replacement; not prison construction, but prison deconstruction. If we replaced prisons with a boarding-school "home away from home" for many people who are literally homeless in the so-called community, and provided them with the tools they need in order to acquire knowledge and skill, self-esteem and self-respect, and the

esteem and respect of others, these new facilities could actually reduce the rates of crime and violence in our society, instead of feeding them, as our current prisons do.

18   Of course, before we could do that, we would need to overcome our own irrational need to inflict revenge (i.e., punishment) on those who are weaker than we. Nothing corrodes the soul of the vengeful person as thoroughly as his own vengeful impulses. Thus the main reason we need to abolish [prisons] is not only, or even primarily, for the sake of those who get imprisoned in them, but in order to heal our own souls—and indeed, our whole society, which is sick with an epidemic of violence, both legal and illegal.

BEFORE YOU READ: You might be surprised to hear that Shakespeare is being performed in prison. What is your general understanding of Shakespeare's cultural status and the meaning of his plays? Why might *Hamlet* be a good choice for a prison performance?

SHAKESPEARE BEHIND BARS: *HAMLET**

Mary Wiltenburg

In 2001, photographer Andy Nelson and writer Mary Wiltenburg traveled to a Kentucky prison, where inmates were putting the final touches on their production of a long-anticipated play, Shakespeare's *Titus Andronicus*. They returned to Luther Luckett Correctional Complex for this production of *Hamlet* in 2002. Wiltenburg is on the staff of the *Christian Science Monitor*.

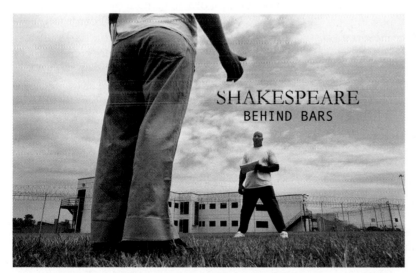

FOR DISCUSSION: In this image, the physical relation of the figures to the prison structure in the background is important to its claim. What can you tell from the pictorial arrangement and posture of the actors and from their spatial relation to the prison building?

For Writing: This poster makes a claim about the effect that participating in this program has on the prisoners mentally, emotionally, and spiritually. How does the image itself provide evidence in support of that claim? What are the underlying warrants?

Context: The caption reads: Poster for *Shakespeare Behind Bars*. A film about the Shakespeare Behind Bars project was released in 2005. This poster conveys the project's values rather than providing a record of an actual performance.

---

*Mary Wiltenburg, "Shakespeare Behind Bars: *Hamlet*," *Christian Science Monitor*, 2002, http://www.csmonitor.com/specials/shakespeare/act6.html (accessed June 18, 2008).

1   He killed a cop; I know that. He almost got the death penalty. I know that, too. So tonight, listening to Kentucky inmate Jerry Guenthner deliver Hamlet's famous soliloquy, it seems to me that "To be, or not to be" is very much the question.

2   Partly that's because of the life that, 17 years ago, he cut short—and the one, as many years ago, he himself almost lost. But even more, it's because of a choice he made during his time behind bars—the one that helped land him on this stage, playing one of Shakespeare's most difficult roles.

3   He and the other inmates in this cast of *Hamlet: Prince of Denmark* have all faced that choice: whether "to be"—to begin a new life in prison, by coming to terms with what they've done and making what amends they can, or "not to be"—never to outgrow the men they were when they committed their crimes; not to do the hard work that reformation takes. Even if they didn't realize it when they signed on as the cast of this year's Shakespeare Behind Bars production, Mr. Guenthner and the company playing opposite his tortured prince have chosen to do that work. [. . .]

4   [A]s the actors struggle to identify with the characters they're playing in *Hamlet*, it becomes clear that the year's real changes have occurred within them: Each has come a little further toward taking responsibility for his crime.

5   Take Lavassa Anderson. In for life without possibility of parole for 25 years for robbing, sodomizing, and shooting two liquor store clerks (one of whom died), Mr. Anderson found God in prison and committed himself to a fierce prison ministry. Last year, his first in the theater group, he talked angrily about how he'd "had to" kick a gay inmate out of his Christian Fellowship because "he had gone against God and how God wanted him to live."

6   Over the past year, Anderson says, he's learned from other members of the Shakespeare program—particularly from Mr. Cobb, who is very open about being gay—not to be so quick to pass judgment. "I still don't agree with that lifestyle," he says, "but it was wrong of me to close [that inmate] out, wrong not to find room for him in my heart."

7   This year, Anderson plays Laertes, a friend of Prince Hamlet who turns on him when the prince accidentally kills Laertes's father. Anderson says he doesn't like the character because he's a coward: Laertes abandons his commitments, betrays his friends, and doesn't know how to fight—qualities Anderson doesn't see in himself, or doesn't want to. But thinking back to his crime, he says: "As far as being stupid and treacherous, I guess I can relate to him in that way."

8   Fellow actor Leonard Ford has also had a difficult time with his role. Playing Hamlet's uncle, Claudius, who murders the prince's father and marries his mother, Mr. Ford delivers one of the play's famous speeches. "O, my offense is rank," it begins, "it smells to heaven." Ford, serving a 50-year sentence for sexual abuse of minors, still can't talk directly about his crimes. But he has a lot to say about mercy, repentance, forgiveness. . . . Claudius's signature speech is particularly difficult for him to deliver, Ford says, because in it, his character's inability to pray reveals that he has not yet fully repented of his crime. [. . .]

9   Sammie Byron has been acting with the Shakespeare Behind Bars program since its founding almost seven years ago. "The dad of the group"—according to its prison sponsor, classification and treatment officer Karen Heath—he is serving a life sentence for murdering his girlfriend. Until this year, Mr. Byron says, he always felt he had to play villains, because acting those roles allowed him to exorcise his own capacity for villainy. But tonight Byron is playing Polonius, an overearnest comic character. "I wanted to do something a little lighter, [and] this role is similar to where I'm at," he explains. "Polonius never really has any ill intent, and I've never

played a character who didn't possess that quality, because I always kind of viewed myself—or what I had done in the past—as something really bad." Now "I've pretty much come to terms with that," he says. "Maybe I will play the villain again—but I'm just not as attracted to the villain." Byron speculates that his fellow actors are still facing down their own demons in the roles they play—particularly in those roles they're struggling to play.

10   Curt Tofteland, director of the program and of the Kentucky Shakespeare Festival, agrees. In the prison company, he says, "We challenge each other to say: 'Well, dig deeper. You've resonated that in your intellect, now can you resonate that in your heart? Oh, there it is in your heart, now can you find it in your soul? Oh, OK, now can you find it in the metaphysical?'" [. . .]

11   The company does four performances of each of its annual productions. This year, the first two shows were for inmates; tonight's and tomorrow's are for family members and other visitors. Most of those in attendance this evening are actors from the Kentucky Shakespeare Festival or members of the press.

12   But one of tonight's visitors is unique. Mike Smith is returning to Luther Luckett for the first time since he served out his sentence almost a year ago. Though he's the 14th Shakespeare Behind Bars alumnus to leave prison and stay out, Mr. Smith is the first to come back to see a performance. (Two alumni have returned to prison the other way—because of parole violations.) While serving eight years for assault and theft, Smith played a major role in the 1999 production of *Othello* and a smaller role last spring in *Titus Andronicus*.

13   Since his release last June, Smith has found a job doing deliveries and soliciting business for a dry cleaning service, and recently bought his own house. He met his girlfriend nine months ago; they're happy together, he says, and she's patient with him

when he has trouble keeping up with the demands of free life. "I'm used to life going 30 miles an hour" in prison, he explains, "but out here it's a hundred and ten." [. . .]

14   When the guests are seated and hushed, Tofteland gives a simple introduction and the play begins. Bush, wide-eyed in a cape and tam, convincingly sees a ghost coming through the gloom. Guenthner has no lines when he first comes onstage. Even so he's impossible to ignore: Hamlet's anger seems to boil through his skin.

15   The show is a success—not flawless, but hard-won. Anderson makes good use of his dislike for Laertes in his portrayal of the character's vengeful side. Ford begins Claudius's repentance speech uncertainly, but by the time he looks skyward and begs, "Help, angels! Make assay," it doesn't even sound as if he's acting.

16   When Guenthner tackles his "To be, or not to be" speech, I'm paying special attention. Earlier this afternoon, I asked him how he related to those lines, thinking he might talk about his crime, or the sentence he almost received for it. "I don't," he said. Of the 1,600 lines he's memorized to play the Danish prince, that famous one has given him the most trouble. He can't see himself in it, the 38-year-old murderer says, because "bad as I've messed up—and I would give anything to undo what I done—I never thought about taking my life." Guenthner was considered a suicide risk when he was first locked up: Guards checked on him regularly, expecting him to make an attempt. That baffled him. "Maybe they thought I should want to die," he says, "but I never did." It must sound strange, he says, but in a way, taking a life shows you how important life is. [. . .]

17   In the past year, there've been no flash-bang conversions, no sudden contrition among these players. But maybe this slow growth, these lonely revelations—maybe this incremental change is what begins to happen when a man chooses to be.

DOG TRAINING IN WOMEN'S PRISON*

Ray Quintanilla

Ray Quintanilla is a reporter for the *Chicago Tribune.*

For Discussion: The setting for this photograph, as with the image in the previous article, is a real place, the Dwight Correctional Center. How does the relation of the women and dogs to that building contribute to your sense of the significance of this training program?

For Writing: This image can be considered an argument from *ethos*. From the arrangement of human and canine figures in space, what claim does the photographer make about the dogs and their inmate handlers?

Context: The caption reads: Women inmates prepare to walk their dogs at the Dwight Correctional Center in Dwight, Ill. This is an example of photojournalism, an image that is meant to visually tell a news story. The women who train the disability dogs are pictured with their canines outside the prison facility. The photographer, Alex Garcia, also produced a video titled *Prison Dogs* that won an award for multimedia photojournalism in Illinois. See it at http://ippaonline.com/multimedia/2008contest/55=IVP.mov (accessed September 6, 2008).

1 Dwight, Ill.—As several hundred women dressed in dark canvas uniforms marched across the prison grounds under the watchful eyes of heavyset guards, inmate Jennifer Lawson stood outside her unlocked cell and smiled as she quietly trained a black poodle to turn on a light and open a heavy steel door.

2 She once was quick to anger and even assaulted a guard, but thanks to an innovative type of rehabilitation that pairs inmates with dogs, Lawson is now considered a model prisoner. "Working with a dog has helped me grow up, and it's given me something to look forward to, which I have never had before," said Lawson, 30, who

*Ray Quintanilla, "Dog Training in Women's Prison Helps Inmates and the Clients Who Get Companions," *Chicago Tribune,* February 11, 2008, n.p. http:www//chicagotribune.com/ (accessed February 11, 2008).

once lived in Chicago's west suburbs and is serving an 18-year sentence at Dwight Correctional Center for robbery and home invasion.

3   Lawson is among nine inmates at the state's largest women's prison who train dogs for the disabled, many of them children. So far, more than 150 dogs have been placed since the first service animals arrived at the prison seven years ago.

4   The dogs fill an emotional void for inmates, and the program has helped put many on a path to lasting rehabilitation, officials said. Only two of the 39 women who have trained dogs and completed their sentences returned to prison. That compares with recent data showing nearly half of all women released from Illinois prisons in 2001 were back behind bars within three years.

5   "Many of us have household pets that bring a lot of love into the home, and it's no different here," said Warden Mary Sigler, who directs the Illinois Department of Correction's only dog-training project. "The inmates bond with these dogs and that bond serves the inmate and the dogs really well."

6   Lawson has certainly benefited, she said. When the former Bensenville resident arrived at Dwight in 1999, she often fought with other inmates and over the next five years drifted in and out of solitary confinement. "I got here thinking my being in prison was an injustice," said Lawson, who was arrested in Chicago in 1997 for a string of robberies and home invasions. "I was angry back then, and that made it difficult for me to get along with anyone."

7   Her breakthrough came about two years ago when she enrolled in a prison pet-grooming class. She enjoyed the work so much, she said it helped her channel her anger into positive energy. Before long, Lawson was earning good-behavior credit. She also liked the idea of having a partner by her side 24 hours a day, so she asked to join the dog training program.

8   Since Lawson received the poodle, Gracie, last summer, the two have become inseparable. If she remains on good behavior, Lawson could be discharged later this year, prison officials said. "I'm trying not to look back," she said. "My success with Gracie is helping me look forward."

9   Marcia Ramirez, who oversees job training at Dwight, said a trainer supervises every inmate's interaction with a dog. The animals are trained to carry backpacks, walk obediently alongside wheelchairs and, in some instances, summon help. On a typical day, inmates groom the dogs, walk them around the prison yard and prepare them for drills such as opening doors and carrying cargo. At night, the dogs sleep in cages in the prisoners' cells.

10   Ann Galassi, Dwight's dog trainer, said it can take a year or longer of daily effort to prepare a dog to become a service animal. "It's very heartwarming to see all the care and love these women show the dogs," she said. "This is giving the dogs a second chance, and it may do the same thing for the women."

11   Renee Allen, a former drug addict from Rockford, said training a yellow Labrador named Zen makes it easier for her to serve her 15-year sentence. Caring for the dog helped Allen rebuild her confidence after hitting bottom two years ago when she was convicted of drug-induced homicide, a crime stemming from injecting a man with an overdose of heroin during a night of drug use. "I know this experience is making me into a better person," said Allen, 30. "I am learning to be so much more tolerant, and it reminds me there are good things in all of us."

12   But Allen said she's warned her friend Lawson about getting too close to Gracie. The day will come when the dog will have to be given to someone who needs it most, she

said. "Jennifer is going to be heartbroken when that dog is placed," said Allen, who found that out for herself a year ago. "It really hurts."

13   Elena Winters, 15, of Lockport received her dog, Jewel, in 2006 through an agency that works with the disabled. Winters is barely 3 feet tall, and the prison-trained dog helps her stand, walk and grab things she can't reach. It even presses elevator buttons for her. "When I drop my cane, Jewel will pick it up for me," Winters said. "Before I got her, people would see me and just turn away. Now, Jewel helps break the ice so people come up to talk with me more often."

Reading Images: Methods of Execution

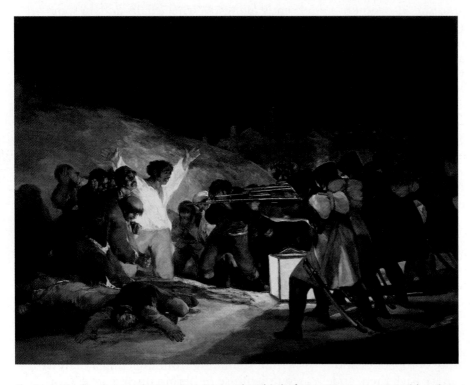

Image 1:
Firing Squad.

Context: The caption reads: Francisco Goya, *The Third of May.* Goya was a Spanish painter who experienced the occupation of Madrid in 1808 by the French armies of Napoleon. On the second of May, there was a riot in the Puerto del Sol, and on the third, a firing squad was deployed to execute rebels, although random citizens were also rounded up and killed. Goya, who painted this image six years after the event, had not been an eyewitness. He depicts the scene not as an execution, but as a massacre, raising issues about the relationship between power, punishment, and justice.

For Discussion: Formal composition is important to Goya's artistry. What does the composition tell you about the artist's attitude toward the soldiers and those they execute?

For Writing: The focus of this highly artistic composition is the central figure, whom lighting and color make the center of the viewer's interest. Think of this as a visual argument. What is the claim, the support, and the warrants?

Reading Images: Methods of Execution, cont.

Image 2:
Old Sparky: The Electric Chair.

Context: The caption reads: *Old Sparky*. This image was published by ABC News. The caption reads: "Aaron Dickson, President of the Board of Directors of the Texas Prison Museum stands with Old Sparky, November 19, 2002, the Texas electric chair in which 361 killers were executed." You can see the image in its original context at http://www.abc.net.au/news/photos/2007/08/14/2004269.htm.

For Discussion: Analyze Old Sparky in its rhetorical context. What does the juxtaposition of electric chair and guard tell you about the symbolic function of capital punishment in contemporary America?

For Writing: Some of the debate over capital punishment focuses on the methods used to execute condemned criminals: their relative humanity, their cost, and even their cultural symbolism. Images 1 and 2 present two iconic images of methods of execution. Compare and contrast "Old Sparky" with the Goya painting. What do these images communicate about execution? What makes each of these images effective as visual argument?

601

BEFORE YOU READ: The essay below considers studies that support or contradict the idea that the death penalty acts as a deterrent to violent crime. Can you think of other ways to prevent or discourage crime, especially violent crime? What might be alternatives to capital punishment?

STUDIES SAY DEATH PENALTY DETERS CRIME*

Robert Tanner

Robert Tanner writes for the *Fort-Worth Star Telegram*.

1   Anti-death penalty forces have gained momentum in the past few years, with a moratorium in Illinois, court disputes over lethal injection in more than a half-dozen states, and progress toward outright abolishment in New Jersey. What gets little notice, however, is a series of academic studies over the last half-dozen years that claim to settle a once hotly debated argument: whether the death penalty acts as a deterrent to murder. The analyses say yes. They say between 3 and 18 lives would be saved by the execution of each convicted killer. The reports have horrified death penalty opponents and some scientists, who vigorously question the data and their implications.

*Robert Tanner, "Studies Say Execution Deters Crime," *Fort Worth Star-Telegram*, June 11, 2007, 4A.

2   So far, the studies have had little effect on public policy. New Jersey's commission on the death penalty this year dismissed the body of knowledge on deterrence as "inconclusive." But the ferocious argument in academic circles could eventually spread to a wider audience. "Science does really draw a conclusion. It did. There is no question about it," said Naci Mocan, an economics professor at the University of Colorado at Denver, who has done some of the research. "The conclusion is there is a deterrent effect."

DETERRENT EFFECTS

3 A 2003 study Mocan co-wrote, and a 2006 study that re-examined the data, said that each execution results in five fewer homicides and that commuting a death sentence means five more. "The results are robust, they don't really go away," he said. "I oppose the death penalty. But my results show that the death penalty [deters]. What am I going to do, hide them?"

4   Statistical studies like his are among a dozen papers since 2001 that show capital punishment has deterrent effects. They all explore the same basic theory: If the cost of something (be it the purchase of an apple or the act of killing someone) becomes too high, people will change their behavior (forgo apples or shy from murder).

5   In 2005, there were 16,692 cases of murder and non-negligent manslaughter nationally. There were 60 executions. Texas, which is responsible for two-thirds of all executions, had its 15th execution Wednesday.

DEATH PENALTY

6 To explore the question of whether the death penalty deters homicide, researchers look at executions and homicides, by year, state or county, trying to tease out the effect of the death penalty on homicides by accounting for other factors, such as unemployment data and per capita income, the probabilities of arrest and conviction, and more.

7   Among the conclusions:

> ◗ A 2003 nationwide study by professors at Emory University says each execution deters an average of 18 murders. Other studies have estimated deterred murders per execution at 3, 5, and 14.

> ◗ A 2006 study by professors at the University of Houston said the Illinois moratorium on executions in 2000 led to 150 additional homicides over the next four years.

> ◗ A 2004 study by an Emory University professor said that speeding up executions would strengthen the deterrent effect: For every 2.75 years cut from time spent on Death Row, one murder would be prevented.

RESPONSE

8 The studies' conclusions drew a philosophical response from a well-known liberal law professor and death penalty critic, Cass Sunstein of the University of Chicago. In 2005, he co-wrote a paper titled *Is Capital Punishment Morally Required?*

9   "If it's the case that executing murderers prevents the execution of innocents by murderers, then the moral evaluation is not simple," he told The Associated Press. "Abolitionists or others, like me, who are skeptical about the death penalty haven't given adequate consideration to the possibility that innocent life is saved by the death penalty." Sunstein said that moral questions aside, the data need more study.

10   Some critics say that the deterrent-supporting studies made profound mistakes in their methodology, so their results are untrustworthy. One critic argues that the studies wrongly count all homicides, rather than just those homicides where a conviction could bring the death penalty. And several argue that there are simply too few executions each year in the United States to make a judgment.

11   "We just don't have enough data to say anything," said Justin Wolfers, an economist at the Wharton School of Business who last year co-wrote a sweeping critique of several studies and said they were "flimsy" and appeared in "second-tier journals."

BEFORE YOU READ: Before you began to study the subject of capital punishment, were you for or against the death penalty in the United States? What are your reasons for this position?

REVENGE BEGINS TO SEEM LESS SWEET*
The Economist *Staff*

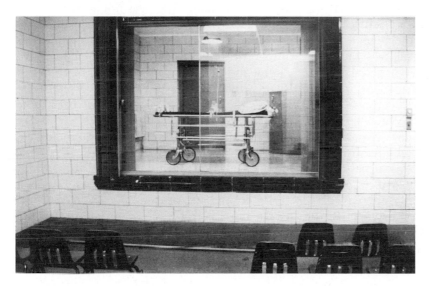

For Discussion: Few people are allowed to witness a prison execution in the United States. What does this image tell you (and also not tell you) about the process of the prisoner's death? What does the absence of human beings in the photograph suggest about the photographer's or article writer's attitude toward the subject?

For Writing: There are no people in this picture, but there are many clues about the relation of the convicted criminal about to be executed and the society that requires his or her death. Consider this photograph as an argument based on a claim of value. How does the photo provide evidence and support for that claim?

Context: The caption reads: Setting for Execution by Legal Injection. This photograph shows the trolley used for execution by lethal injection behind the window that separates the prisoner from observers.

603

1   Joseph Nichols did not fight the guards at his execution, but he did not co-operate, either. He had to be lifted onto the trolley on which he was to die, and then strapped down. A needle was thrust into his arm. Asked if he had any last words, he said, "Yes, yes I do," and then swore at a guard. There followed a gurgling sound as his lungs collapsed and, for about a minute, an animal-like noise issued from the back of his throat. After that came silence, broken only by a few people in the room clearing their throats. Then a doctor pulled out his stethoscope and pronounced the condemned man dead. The execution had taken six minutes.

2   Mr. Nichols was one of 22 people put to death in Texas this year (as this was written, two more were scheduled to die). His story was fairly typical. He had been convicted for the murder of a delicatessen clerk during a robbery in 1980. It had not been much of a

*"Revenge Begins to Seem Less Sweet," *The Economist,* August 30, 2007, http://www.economist.com/displaystory.cfm?story_id=9719806 (accessed June 18, 2008).

heist; he said his accomplice "got some change" but he got nothing. The victim was killed by a single bullet. It was unclear which of the two men had fired it, but under Texan law it made no difference, since both admitted to shooting at him. Mr. Nichols was 20 when he arrived on death row and 45 when he died. His accomplice was executed in 1995.

3   Capital punishment is hardly controversial in Texas. Nearly three-quarters of Texans approve of it. In June the governor signed a law that would make some people who rape children eligible for it. But Texas is special. It now accounts for nearly half of all executions in America, of which there have been over 1,000 since 1976. During the six years in which George Bush was governor, the state put 152 people to death. No other governor in America's recent history except his successor, Rick Perry, has overseen so many executions.

4   Elsewhere, the death penalty is increasingly controversial. . . . Unlike most Texans, the people of New Jersey have strong doubts about the death penalty. Most would prefer to see murderers locked up forever. Their representatives are listening: no one has been executed in New Jersey since the 1960s. A state Senate committee has approved a bill to end capital punishment formally; the full legislature [passed] it later [in 2007]. [. . .]

5   For a few years in the 1970s, America joined most other rich countries in revoking the death penalty. This was not done by passing a law. Rather, the Supreme Court decided, in 1972, that capital punishment was unconstitutional, since it broke the ban on "cruel and unusual" punishment. In 1976 a slightly different set of justices reversed the court's ruling and handed the issue back to the states.

6   Since then, the states have gone their own ways (see map). Twelve have no death penalty on their statute books. Of the 38 that do, some apply it often, some never. Texas has executed 401 people since 1976, the entire north-eastern region only four. By and large, the way the penalty is applied mirrors local preferences.

604

HAPHAZARD RETRIBUTION

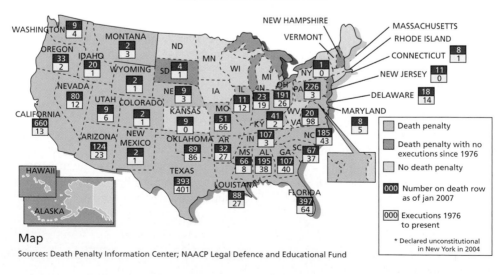

Map

Sources: Death Penalty Information Center; NAACP Legal Defence and Educational Fund

7   Asked by pollsters whether they think murderers should be put to death, two-thirds of Americans say yes, down from four-fifths in 1994. If asked to choose between the death penalty and a life sentence with no chance of parole, however, they are evenly divided. Life that means life is relatively new. Before the 1990s, juries used to worry that if they did not send the man in the dock to his death, he would be freed to kill again after a decade or two. Now nearly every state allows the option of life without parole (Texas introduced it only in 2005). For the first time last year, a Gallup poll reported that a slim plurality of Americans found this option preferable to a capital sentence (48–47%).

8   Campaigners against the death penalty have been making their case state by state, with little fanfare but some success. The number of executions has fallen by 46% from its modern peak in 1999, to 53 last year (see chart 1). Two-thirds of states executed no one last year, and only six carried out multiple executions. The number of death sentences has fallen even more sharply, by 60% from a peak of about 300 a year in the mid-1990s.

9   The arguments for and against capital punishment have evolved. Thirty years ago, says Mr. Radelet, Americans supported the death penalty for three main reasons: deterrence, religious conviction (an eye for an eye) and taxes (the idea of spending public money to feed and clothe murderers for the rest of their lives seemed outrageous). This last argument no longer applies. It is now far more expensive to execute someone than to jail him for life; in North Carolina, for instance, each capital case costs $2 million more. Ordinary inmates need only to be fed and guarded. Those on death row must have lawyers arguing expensively about their fate, sometimes for a decade or more (see chart 2). The system of appeals has grown more protracted because of fears that innocent people may be executed. Few would argue that such safeguards are not needed, but their steep cost gives abolitionists a new line of attack.

10   Martin O'Malley, the governor of Maryland, says that, but for the death penalty, his state would have been $22.4 million richer since 1978. That money would have paid for 500 extra policemen for a year, or provided drug treatment for

605

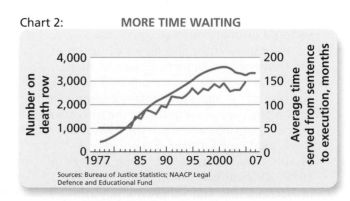

Chart 1:   **FEWER EXECUTIONS**
US JUDICIAL KILLINGS

Sources: Bureau of Justice Statistics;
Death Penalty Information Center. *to August 28th 2007

Chart 2:   **MORE TIME WAITING**

Number on death row

Average time served from sentence to execution, months

Sources: Bureau of Justice Statistics; NAACP Legal
Defence and Educational Fund

10,000 addicts. "Unlike the death penalty, these are investments that save lives and prevent violent crime," he told the state legislature in February, in a speech urging it to repeal capital punishment in Maryland. He failed by the narrowest of margins: a state Senate committee was deadlocked by five votes to five, preventing the bill from advancing. [. . .]

11 Abolitionists have had more luck, at least temporarily, by arguing that lethal injection, the form of execution most widely adopted, is excruciatingly painful. The cocktail used generally contains sodium thiopental (to anaesthetize the condemned man), pancuronium bromide (to paralyze his muscles) and potassium chloride (to stop his heart). Some studies suggest that prisoners are sometimes inadequately sedated, and perhaps die in silent agony from asphyxiation. Since last year, ten states have halted executions because of fears that lethal injection may be cruel, and therefore unconstitutional. In Florida, for example, Governor Jeb Bush [. . .] suspended executions after a fiasco last December in which the executioner missed a vein and pumped the drugs into muscle. The condemned man took 34 minutes to die, during which he grimaced and writhed, suggesting acute agony. [. . .]

12 For many, the death penalty holds a deep emotional appeal. It is "an expression of society's ultimate outrage," says Bob Grant, a former prosecutor and now a professor at the University of Denver, Colorado. Some acts, he argues, are so heinous that no other punishment is appropriate. One example he cites is the case of Gary Davis, the only man executed in Colorado since the 1960s. Mr. Davis kidnapped, tortured, sexually assaulted and murdered a young mother in 1986. His guilt was not in doubt. Mr. Grant prosecuted him and watched him put to death. Mr. Grant says his views on the

death penalty have nothing to do with religion, but many who agree with him do so for religious reasons. A prosecutor in Texas cites Genesis 9:6: "Whoso sheddeth man's blood, by man shall his blood be shed." This, he says, is "pretty compelling."

13 Opponents of capital punishment tend to respond by saying that juries, being human, err. If you find you have jailed the wrong man, you can free and compensate him. If you have executed him, however, it is too late. Jurors increasingly balk at imposing the death penalty, even when they are convinced of a defendant's guilt. Governors, who must review every capital conviction, are also becoming hesitant. In 2000, for example, after journalism students dug up evidence that a man about to be executed was innocent, Illinois's governor, George Ryan, commuted all death sentences in the state and imposed a moratorium that still stands, despite challenges.

14 Since 1973, 124 Americans have been released from death row because of doubts about their guilt; and of the 7,662 sentenced to death between 1973 and 2005, 2,190 had their sentence or conviction overturned. But in no case has it been legally proven—for example, with DNA evidence—that an innocent person has been executed. Mr. Grant says it simply does not happen. "The fact that some people are released from death row is proof that the safeguards work," he says. Abolitionists suspect he is wrong. The Death Penalty Information Centre, a lobby group, lists eight executed men for whom there is "strong evidence of innocence." [. . .]

DETERRENCE WORKS—OR DOES IT?

15 Although DNA testing has yet to show that an innocent American has been executed, it has proved beyond question that miscarriages of justice occur. Widely

606

reported exonerations have alerted the public to the uncomfortable fact that juries are sometimes biased, that the police sometimes lie and that snitches often do. But what if executions save lives by deterring potential murderers? That would "greatly unsettle moral objections to the death penalty," argue Cass Sunstein and Adrian Vermeule, two law professors. Abolitionists say there is no proof that capital punishment deters. Death-penalty enthusiasts say several studies suggest it does.

16　A crude way of trying to settle which camp is correct is to compare murder rates in jurisdictions with and without capital punishment. This offers no support for the notion of deterrence. In 2005 there were 46% more murders per head in states with the death penalty than in those without it, and that gap has widened since 1990. The murder rate in the United States as a whole, moreover, is far higher than in western Europe, where capital punishment is a thing of the past. Yet many other factors influence murder rates—unemployment, the probability of getting caught, the availability of guns, the proportion of young men in the population and so on. More sophisticated studies attempt to control for such factors.

17　Joanna Shepherd, of Emory School of Law in Atlanta, for example, looked at monthly data for executions and murders between 1977 and 1999 and controlled for age, sex, race and labour-market conditions. She found that each execution deterred on average three murders, and that swift executions deterred even more. Other researchers at Emory found that each execution deterred a startling 18 murders. In another study Naci Mocan of the University of Colorado and Kaj Gittings of Cornell University found that each execution deterred five murders, and that

each time a death sentence was commuted, five more murders were committed.

18　The trouble with all these studies is that they draw firm conclusions from sparse data. America has executed on average fewer than 40 people a year since 1976. Even if each execution had a strong deterrent effect, it would be hard to detect against the background of a murder toll that has fluctuated from 24,703 in 1991 to 15,522 in 1999, before rising again to 16,692 in 2005. Researchers' calculations are further distorted by the fact that one state dominates the data. "Any regression study will be primarily a comparison of Texas with everywhere else," writes Ted Goertzel in *Skeptical Enquirer* magazine.

19　The chance of being executed in America is so remote that it cannot plausibly be a significant deterrent, argues Steven Levitt, of the University of Chicago. Even if you are on death row—a fate over 99% of murderers escape—the chance of being put to death in any given year is only about 2%. Members of a crack gang studied by one of Mr. Levitt's colleagues had a 7%-a-year chance of being murdered. For them, death row would be safer than the street.

20　There are other arguments against the death penalty. Some opponents complain of a racial bias in its application. This is disputed. Mr Radelet thinks the race of the perpetrator makes little difference, but juries respond more vengefully when the victim is white. In a study of murders in California, he found that those who killed non-Hispanic whites were twice as likely to be sentenced to death as those with darker victims.

21　Capital punishment is not about to end in America. But, as voters lose their appetite for it, states will use it less or even give it up completely. How closely America follows the global trend towards abolition will depend less on academic arguments than on emotional ones.

B. **What Should Be Done with Young Offenders?**

> **BEFORE YOU READ:** Aristotle's descriptions of different ages from Book 2 of the *Rhetoric* detail the characteristics of young men in classical Greece. Before you read, what are the characteristics of today's American young men (and young women, a category of audience not considered by Aristotle)?

THE CHARACTERISTICS OF YOUTH[*]

Aristotle

In the second book of the *Rhetoric,* written between 360 and 334 B.C., Aristotle characterizes different types of audiences to help the orator with audience analysis. By understanding a particular audience, the orator could more easily persuade them. No young women are mentioned in the *Rhetoric,* but you may want to apply relevant parts of this description of youth to them as well. Compare this description of the young with modern perceptions of the young reflected in the other essays in this section. How would you describe the characteristics of youth?

1 We shall begin with the characteristics of youth. Young men have strong desires, and whatever they desire they are prone to do. Of the bodily desires the one they let govern them most is the sexual; here they lack self-control. They are shifting and unsteady in their desires, which are vehement for a time, but soon relinquished; for the longings of youth are keen rather than deep—are like sick people's fits of hunger and thirst. The young are passionate, quick to anger, and apt to give way to it. And their angry passions get the better of them; for, since they wish to be honored, young men cannot put up with a slight; they are resentful if they only imagine that they are unfairly treated. Fond of honor, they are even fonder of victory, for youth likes to be superior, and winning evinces superiority. They love both honor and victory more than they love money. Indeed, they care next to nothing about money, for they have not yet learned what the want of it means. . . . The young think no evil [are not cynical], but believe in human goodness, for as yet they have not seen many examples of vice. They are trustful, for as yet they have not been often deceived. And they are sanguine; for young men

glow with a natural heat as drinkers are heated with wine, while as yet their failures have not been many. They live their lives for the most part in hope [anticipation], as hope is of the future and memory of the past; and for young men the future is long, the past but short; on the first day of life there is nothing to remember, everything to expect. They are easily deceived, and for the same reason, since they are quick to hope. Being passionate as well as hopeful, they are relatively brave; the passion excludes fear, and the hope inspires confidence—no one is afraid when he is angry, and an anticipation of good makes one confident. And they are shy; for as yet they have no independent standard of good conduct, but only the conventional standards in which they were reared. They are high-minded [have lofty aspirations]; first, because they have not yet been humbled by life, nor come to know the force of circumstances; and secondly, because high-mindedness means thinking oneself fitted for great things, and this again is characteristic of the hopeful. In their actions they prefer honor to expediency; for their lives are rather lives of good impulse [moral instinct or feeling] than of calculation

---

[*]"Types of Character," *The Rhetoric of Aristotle*. 2.12. Lane Cooper, ed. and trans. (New York: Appleton-Century-Crofts, 1932), 32–34.

[reason]; and calculation aims at the expedient, virtue at the honorable. They are fond of their friends, intimates, and associates—more so than are men in the other two periods of life; this comes from their love of company, and from the fact that as yet they judge nothing, and hence do not judge their friends, by the standard of expediency. All their mistakes are on the side of intensity and excess, running counter to the maxim of Chilon ['Moderation in all things']. They carry everything too far: they love to excess, they hate to excess—and so in all else.

They think they know everything, and are positive about everything; indeed, this is why they always carry their doings too far. When they wrong other people, the injuries are wanton [insolent], not malicious. The young are prone to pity, because they think every one good, or at all events better than people really are. That is, they judge their fellow man by their own guilelessness, and hence assume that his sufferings are undeserved. . . . They are fond of laughter, and therefore facetious, facetiousness being a subdued insolence.

BEFORE YOU READ: Since the death penalty can no longer be imposed on young criminal offenders, what do you think the justice system should do with them?

TOO YOUNG TO DIE*
Claudia Wallis

Wallis, an editor at large at *Time* magazine, describes the overturn of the juvenile death penalty and provides reasons for the decision.

1 In his Norman, Okla, law office, attorney Steven Presson stores two unusual keepsakes. One is a leather pouch that holds the ashes of Sean Sellers, the only person executed for a crime committed as a 16-year-old since the death penalty was reinstated in the U.S. in 1976. Sellers—who murdered his mother, his stepfather and a store clerk—was dispatched by lethal injection in 1999, when he was 29. Presson's other memento is a plastic box containing the ashes of Scott Hain, who, it now seems fair to say, was the last juvenile offender to be executed in the U.S. Hain, sent to his death in 2003 at the age of 32, was 17 when he and a friend committed a grisly double murder.

2 Presson, who represented both boys, found it "very bittersweet" when the U.S. Supreme Court ruled last week that it was cruel and unusual to sentence anyone to death for crimes committed before the age of 18. "I'm happy for those on death row, but it came six years too late

for Sean and two years too late for Scott," says Presson. "We've been arguing for decades that kids don't have the same moral culpability that adults have, and finally, finally, they listened."

3 It took 16 years for the high court to come around to Presson's point of view, by a narrow 5-to-4 vote. In 1989 the court ruled 5 to 4 the other way. Justice Antonin Scalia, who wrote the 1989 decision, argued that there was neither a "historical nor a modern societal consensus" forbidding capital punishment for 16- or 17-year-olds (though the court had found such a consensus for those under 16 a year earlier). Last week, however, Scalia was on the short side of the decision.

4 What changed? The views of Justice Anthony Kennedy, for one thing. While Kennedy voted with Scalia in 1989, he wrote a very different majority opinion this time around. Why did Kennedy change his mind? Legal tradition invites him to do so. Since

---

Time, March 14, 2005, 40.

1958 the court has applied a flexible standard to interpreting the Eighth Amendment's ban on "cruel and unusual punishments." What we mean by the phrase, wrote then Chief Justice Earl Warren in *Trop* v. *Dulles,* depends on "the evolving standards of decency that mark the progress of a maturing society."

5   How do you know that society no longer believes in sentencing a 17-year-old killer to death? Kennedy's argument mirrors his reasoning in a 2002 decision that outlawed death sentences for the mentally retarded. He notes that since 1989 five states have banned capital punishment for juveniles, making the practice illegal in 30 states, including the 12 with an outright ban on executions. Second, Kennedy cites scientific literature showing that, like the retarded, adolescents lack mature judgment and a full appreciation of the consequences of their actions. They are also more vulnerable than adults to peer pressure. Third, Kennedy points out that only seven other countries have executed juvenile offenders since 1990, and all seven have repudiated the practice: "The United States now stands alone in a world that has turned its face against the juvenile death penalty."

6   "This reference to international practices is a very big deal," says Cass Sunstein, a constitutional scholar at the University of Chicago Law School, and is part of a surprising new trend in Supreme Court thinking. Overseas legal practices were also cited by the court in the 2002 ruling on the mentally retarded and in a 2003 decision overturning a Texas law banning gay sex. For his part, Scalia blasted his brethren for suggesting that "American law should conform to the laws of the rest of the world" and pointed out that the U.S. has unique legal traditions.

7   In the 12 states where juvenile offenders have been languishing, death sentences will be lifted for 72 offenders. That brought dismay to many victims' families. Martin Soto-Fong was 17 in 1992 when he and two accomplices robbed the EI Grande Market in Tucson, Ariz. for $300 and shot three workers. Richard Gee, who lost a brother and an uncle that day, is not happy to see the murderer exit death row. "We had him at the gates of hell," he says, "and he got kicked back."

BEFORE YOU READ: Based on your personal knowledge and what you read in the news, what do you think are the principal reasons why young people commit violent crimes?

A BRAIN TOO YOUNG FOR GOOD JUDGMENT*

Daniel R. Weinberger

This article first appeared in the Op-Ed section of the *New York Times* following a high school shooting. The author is director of the Clinical Brain Disorders Laboratory at the National Institutes of Health. Do adolescents possess brains that are biologically mature enough for them to exhibit rational behavior? What do you think?

1   This week's shootings at Santana High School in California led quickly to now-familiar attempts to explain the seemingly unexplainable in terms of culture and circumstance: violent entertainment, a lack of accountability for deviant behavior, broken homes. While each of these issues may play some role in the tragedies of school shootings, to understand what goes wrong in the teenagers who fire the guns, you have to understand something about the biology of the teenage brain.

New York Times, March 10, 2001, A27.

2   Andy Williams, the boy held in the Santana shootings, is 15. Many other school shooters have been about the same age or even younger. And the brain of a 15-year-old is not mature—particularly in an area called the prefrontal cortex, which is critical to good judgment and the suppression of impulse.

3   The human brain has required many millennia and many evolutionary stages to reach its current complex status. It enables us to do all kinds of amazing and uniquely human things: to unravel the human genome, to imagine the future, to fall in love. As part of its capacity for achievement, it must also be able to exercise control that stops maladaptive behavior. Everyone gets angry; everybody has felt a desire for vengeance. The capacity to control impulses that arise from these feelings is a function of the prefrontal cortex.

4   This is the part that distinguishes our brain most decisively from those of all other animals, even our closest relatives. It allows us to act on the basis of reason. It can preclude an overwhelming tendency for action (e.g., to run from a fire in a crowded theater), because an abstract memory (e.g., "don't panic,") makes more sense. It knows that all that glitters is not gold. Without a prefrontal cortex, it would be impossible to have societies based on moral and legal codes.

5   Sometimes violent behavior may be adaptive (for example, in self-defense), in which case the prefrontal cortex will help plan an effective strategy. However, controlling violent impulses when they are maladaptive can be a very taxing duty for the prefrontal cortex, especially if the desire for action is great or if the brain is weakened in its capacity to exercise such control.

6   Many factors can impair the capacity of the prefrontal cortex to serve its full impulse-control function: for example, neurological diseases that kill cells in the prefrontal cortex, head injuries that damage these cells, alcohol and drugs that impair their function, and biological immaturity.

7   The inhibitory functions are not present at birth; it takes many years for the necessary biological processes to hone a prefrontal cortex into an effective, efficient executive. These processes are now being identified by scientific research. They involve how nerve cells communicate with each other, how they form interactive networks to handle complex computational tasks and how they respond to experience. It takes at least two decades to form a fully functional prefrontal cortex.

8   Scientists have shown that the pace of the biological refinements quickens considerably in late adolescence, as the brain makes a final maturational push to tackle the exigencies of independent adult life. But the evidence is unequivocal that the prefrontal cortex of a 15-year-old is biologically immature. The connections are not final, the networks are still being strengthened and the full capacity for inhibitory control is still years away.

9   The 15-year-old brain does not have the biological machinery to inhibit impulses in the service of long-range planning. This is why it is important for adults to help children make plans and set rules, and why institutions are created to impose limits on behavior that children are incapable of limiting. Parents provide their children with a lend-lease prefrontal cortex during all those years that it takes to grow one, particularly when the inner urges for impulsive action intensify. [. . .]

10   Adolescents have always had to deal with feeling hurt, ashamed and powerless. In the face of ridicule they may want revenge. Thirty years ago, a teenager in this position might have started a fight, maybe even pulled a knife. If he was afraid that he could not defend himself, he might have recruited a tough guy to help him out. One way or another, he would have tried to teach his tormentors a lesson. Very likely, however, no one would have died.

11   But times have changed, and now this angry teenager lives in a culture that romanticizes gunplay, and he may well have access to guns. I doubt that most school shooters intend to kill, in the adult sense of permanently ending a life and paying the price for the rest of their own lives. Such intention would require a fully developed prefrontal cortex, which

611

could anticipate the future and rationally appreciate cause and effect. The young school shooter probably does not think about the specifics of shooting at all. The often reported lack of apparent remorse illustrates how unreal the reality is to these teenagers.

12 This brief lesson in brain development is not meant to absolve criminal behavior or make the horrors any less unconscionable.

But the shooter at Santana High, like other adolescents, needed people or institutions to prevent him from being in a potentially deadly situation where his immature brain was left to its own devices. No matter what the town or the school, if a gun is put in the control of the prefrontal cortex of a hurt and vengeful 15-year-old, and it is pointed at a human target, it will very likely go off.

BEFORE YOU READ: How do you distinguish between what it means to be an adult and to be a child? How do you define a violent crime committed by a child or teenagar? Is it the same as a crime committed by an adult, or are there significant differences?

A LEGAL DEBATE IN GUANTÁNAMO ON BOY FIGHTERS[*]

William Glaberson

William Glaberson writes regularly for the *New York Times*.

1 The facts of Omar Ahmed Khadr's case are grim. The shrapnel from the grenade he is accused of throwing ripped through the skull of Sgt. First Class Christopher J. Speer, who was 28 when he died.

2 To American military prosecutors, Mr. Khadr is a committed Al Qaeda operative, spy and killer who must be held accountable for killing Sergeant Speer in 2002 and for other bloody acts he committed in Afghanistan. But there is one fact that may not fit easily into the government's portrait of Mr. Khadr: He was 15 at the time.

3 His age is at the center of a legal battle that is to begin tomorrow with an arraignment by a military judge at Guantánamo Bay, Cuba, of Mr. Khadr, whom a range of legal experts describe as the first child fighter in decades to face war-crimes charges. It is a battle with implications as large as the growing ranks of child fighters around the world. Defense lawyers argue that military prosecutors are violating international law by filing charges that date from events that occurred when

Mr. Khadr was 15 or younger. Legal concepts that are still evolving, the lawyers say, require that countries treat child fighters as victims of warfare, rather than war criminals.

4 The military prosecutors say such notions may be "well-meaning and worthy," but are irrelevant to the American military commissions at Guantánamo. Mr. Khadr is one of only three Guantánamo detainees to face charges under the law establishing the commissions, passed by Congress last year. "International law," the Justice Department asserted in a court filing in the case last week, "does not prohibit an individual under 18 from being prosecuted for war crimes." Even so, prosecutors said that if they won a conviction, they would seek something less than a life term, given Mr. Khadr's age. He is 20 now.

5 Whatever the outcome, his case seems destined to become a landmark, though some scholars say not enough attention has been given to its importance. "What is the precedent that we are setting with this unique step?"

---

*William Glaberson, "A Legal Debate in Guantánamo on Boy Fighters," *International Herald-Tribune*, June 2, 2007, http://www.iht.com/articles/2007/06/03/asia/03gitmo-web.php (accessed June 18, 2008).

asked Peter W. Singer, a senior fellow at the Brookings Institution who has written about child fighters.

6   Mr. Khadr's case offers a snapshot of relatively new questions surrounding the legal treatment of child fighters globally, though advocates for children have tended to focus less on young terrorists and more on children who fight in civil wars, like Ishmael Beah, whose best-selling memoir, "A Long Way Gone: Memoirs of a Boy Soldier," recounts his bloody days as a child soldier in Sierra Leone's civil war.

7   Mr. Khadr may not be the most sympathetic figure for those pressing for the more forgiving interpretation of international law. He was born in Canada to a family with such deep Al Qaeda ties that some newspapers there have called them Canada's first family of terrorism.

8   He is the youngest detainee at Guantánamo Bay, nearly blind in one eye from injuries sustained during the July 2002 firefight in which Sergeant Speer was mortally wounded and another American soldier was severely injured.

9   It is an appeal to emotion that the prosecutors are likely to meet with their own. Sergeant Speer left a wife and two small children. His widow, Tabitha, said in an e-mail exchange with a reporter last week that Mr. Khadr's youth entitled him to no special consideration. "Given the opportunity, he would do it all over again," she wrote. "He was trained to do exactly what he did, regardless of his age."

10   To the prosecutors, Mr. Khadr is the essence of a young man who should be held to adult standards. American officials say his father, Ahmed Said Khadr, who was killed in a shootout with Pakistani forces in 2003, was a senior deputy to Osama bin Laden.

11   One of Mr. Khadr's brothers is in a wheelchair as a result of that 2003 shootout; another told the Canadian Broadcasting Corporation "we are an Al Qaeda family." Ahmed Khadr traveled internationally from Canada nder the auspices of handling charity money for Muslims. In the mid-1990s, he was held for a time in Pakistan on suspicion of helping finance the bombing of the Egyptian embassy in Islamabad.

Editor's note:

1. In May 2008 the military judge who was presiding over Khadr's case decided he would be tried as an adult.

BEFORE YOU READ: How do you think that released prisoners can escape the "cycle of crime" that often sends them back repeatedly to prison?

OUT OF JAIL, INTO TEMPTATION: A DAY IN A LIFE[*]

Alan Feuer

The following article appeared in the *New York Times.* In it, journalist Alan Feuer reports on the day in the life of a New York City convict, Nando, on the day of his release from prison. Given the world that Nando was released back into, what are his chances for success?

1   Nando came home from jail to a small apartment in the Bronx that stank like a backed-up toilet.

2   He had been gone eight months, behind bars for selling crack, and as he came through the door from Rikers Island, he wrinkled his nose at the smell. His spider plant was dead. Its blackened leaves crumpled under his touch. His telephone was dead. He blew in the receiver, but the line was out.

3   The bathroom faucet spewed brown water. A bag of chips in the kitchen was covered in dust.

New York Times, February 28, 2002, A1+.

4   "It's like a garbage dump," he said. "I've got a lot of work to do."

5   The work would not be easy. What lay ahead for Nando, a 20-year-old man who agreed to spend his first day out of jail with a reporter and photographer as long as his last name did not appear in print, would prove to be a veil of dark temptation, a toxic mix of the traps and troubles that sent him off to prison to begin with.

6   Each year, more than 20,000 inmates are released from the C-76 jail on Rikers Island, which houses those serving terms of a year or less. Unlike state prisoners, these city convicts have no probation or parole officers to report to once they are released. They are free to find jobs, or buy drugs, without the authorities watching.

7   Nando was released at 5 A.M. on Feb. 4. By 7 A.M. he had learned that his best friend had just been arrested on a crack charge. By 9 A.M., he was languishing in a welfare office. By 10, he had been offered a joint. By 10:15, he had been offered his old job back, selling crack and marijuana.

8   By the end of the day, he had watched an old friend try to hide her drug habit from her curious toddler son. He had stood at the hospital bed of his catatonic mother. He had sorted through the mail that had piled up for months. The electric company was threatening to shut his power off.

9   He chose to return to his fifth-floor walk-up in the Morrisania section of the Bronx. His girlfriend and his old pals were still in the neighborhood; so was his past as an addict and a dealer. Though home seemed the natural place to go, it was also where his problems had started. Nando knew that in advance. He knew it the moment he stepped off the Rikers Island bus in northern Queens at 5:16 A.M.

10   It was still dark and the other men ran for the subway. Nando sniffed the air and smiled. "It's good to be out," he said.

11   Nando, short for Fernando, is a skinny man with scruff on his chin and Chinese characters tattooed along his neck. He started peddling drugs at 14, started using them at 15. He was jailed last June for selling 200 grams of crack to an undercover officer.

12   The city releases Rikers Island inmates on a squalid street corner in Queens Plaza every day between 3 and 5:30 A.M. Each one carries a $3 MetroCard provided by the prison and his jailhouse chattel in a paper bag. Nando got off the bus with a Hermann Hesse novel in his bag and an ambitious to-do list in his head: Reconnect with family. Stay off drugs. Enroll in college. Find a job.

13   His first stop was his father's apartment in Co-op City. He arrived about 6. His younger brother, David, hugged him in the kitchen, still wearing his pajamas. His father, Fernando Sr., handed him a winter coat, a videotape of the Super Bowl and a couple of $20 bills.

14   "I never expected any kid of mine to wind up where he wound up," the father said. "I ain't never going back, not even on a visit. Don't know about him, but I ain't never going back."

15   It was a brief reunion. Nando's father was due at the factory where he works and his brother was due at school. His father gave Nando keys to the apartment. Nando mused that he might just buy a dog.

16   It was a terrible idea, his father said. "No dogs," he ordered. "Right now, you can't afford to feed yourself."

17   East Tremont Avenue cuts through the Bronx like a swollen femoral artery. It is a wide urban boulevard of barber shops and Spanish greasy spoons. But to Nando, it might as well have been the only road in a tiny town.

18   He knew everyone. The woman walking by was the manager of a grocery store, he said. The crumpled man on the corner was a crackhead. An unmarked Chevrolet rolled by and, out of instinct, Nando ducked; it was a prowling team of undercover cops.

19   "I don't want to be here, but there's nowhere else to go," he muttered as the car drove by. "Lots of us end up right back in the same damn place. It makes me want to blow up the 'hood."

BAD NEWS ABOUT A FRIEND

20   He turned down Boston Road until he came to a dim apartment house on Crotona Park East. Nando put his hands to his mouth and

hooted like an owl. "Hey yo, Chuckie!" he yelled. "Hey yo, where's Chuck?"

21   A woman appeared in a fourth-floor window and shouted for him to come inside. The lobby smelled like feces. Its ceiling light was smashed. The walls looked like a notebook, covered in graffiti. The scrawl praised murder and masturbation.

22   The woman in the window was Nando's former girlfriend, Jackie, who quickly gave him the news: Chuckie—her brother and Nando's friend—had been arrested the day before.

23   Nando was crushed. He had just left Rikers Island, and now Chuckie might be headed there himself.

24   Five minutes later, Nando left. "The ghetto of all ghettos," he said as he walked toward home.

25   At his old apartment, the stench got up to meet him. It smelled like a stadium men's room on a hot summer's day. Dirty dishes were piled in the sink; a box of Cheerios stood open on the table. He turned on the television, and the screen looked like a finger-painting. The picture tube was blown.

26   It was starting to dawn on him, he said: he was out of jail, responsible for himself, alone. He popped a compact disc in the player and sat down on his rocking chair. "I used to sit here for hours getting high," he said, rocking slowly, staring at his hands. "I can feel the whole thing pulling at me. What am I going to do?"

27   On the walk home from Jackie's, he had called his girlfriend, Mery, and set a date for 9 A.M. He needed to clean himself, but first he had to clean the shower. A thick layer of scum had settled in the tub.

28   He went to the bathroom with a toilet brush. There, on the sink, were his mother's false teeth.

A REMINDER OF HIS MOTHER

29   Six months ago, a guard woke him to say, "Your mother's had a heart attack. She's in the hospital in Brooklyn." The jail allowed him a visit. He went and stared at his mother. All she could do was twitch her head.

30   Nando ignored the teeth. He cleaned the tub and showered. Then he looked for clothes

in the bedroom his mother had used before she had fallen ill. The bed was stripped of sheets and gave the impression of a vacant lot. Nando ignored that, too.

31   Three hours earlier, after getting off the prison bus, Nando had laughed at a movie billboard with the slogan, "Behind every good man, there is a woman kicking his butt." At 9 A.M., Mery was waiting for him on the corner of Suburban Place and Boston Road. Her smile lit up the sidewalk two full blocks away.

32   They hugged. They kissed. She touched his hair, grown long on Rikers Island. They kissed again and didn't care who watched.

33   Mery is going to college while living in a homeless shelter. She is Nando's one good thing, and Nando freely admits it. Still, he sometimes finds her loving attention hard to take.

34   They walked down Boston Road to the subway station so Mery could head to school. She scooted up the stairs, then turned around. "Yo, behave!" was all she said.

35   At the welfare office across the street, Nando filled out forms for Medicaid. It was 9:15, and the room was already packed. Telephones rang. Babies cried. Nando put his name on the list. He was 21st in line.

36   The form asked, "Do you have any of these problems?" Nando checked the boxes next to "Urgent Personal or Family Problems" and "No Food."

37   Thirty minutes later a clerk informed him that he had come to the wrong place. The office he needed was on 138th Street, 40 blocks away.

38   He was mad at the clerk. He was mad at himself. He stormed outside to a pay phone and punched in a number. "Yeah," he said. "What up? I'm on the block. I'm home."

39   Minutes later, a bony man in a baggy sweatshirt came walking down the block. His name was Rob, and he was a member of Nando's former drug crew. On Boston Road, the two old friends bumped chests. Rob made fun of Nando's hair.

40   "What you up to, son?" Nando asked.

615

41   Rob did not waste time. "I'm smoking a blunt with you."

EVERYWHERE, TEMPTATION

42 Suddenly, a choice: Go to the welfare office or get high with Rob. The choice got harder when Rob's cellphone began to ring. The call was for Nando. It was his old crack boss, asking if he wanted to go back to work.

43   According to city officials, 80 percent of Rikers Island's inmates test positive for drug use, and drugs are why most end up on the island to begin with. In the past, Nando had taken drugs and sold drugs. Now, within 60 seconds, he'd had offers to do both again.

44   "No, I'm straight," he told the boss, "but I'll let you know." Then he turned down Rob's joint. But as he stood there talking, his old crack customers walked by. They waved and nodded. It was as if he'd never left.

45   With Rob in tow, Nando went back to Jackie's place. He wanted someplace quiet to use the phone. He wanted the address of his mother's hospital in Brooklyn. It had been six months; he wanted to see her face.

46   When Jackie opened the door, the marijuana smoke enveloped him like a blanket. He called information for the hospital's address, trying to ignore the smell. Jackie ran through the rooms, opening windows, spraying a can of air freshener. Her little boy, Aaron, came down the hallway. Aaron is 3. Jackie is 18.

47   Nando headed for the door and as he went out, Rob came in. He had bought a cheap cigar and stuffed it full of dope.

48   Nando unloaded on him on the street.

49   "Keep doing that and you'll wind up on Rikers Island," he said. Rob brushed him off. Nando let out a cold laugh at his buddy. "You best make sure you don't wind up in jail," he said.

50   The trip to the hospital took an hour. As Nando approached his mother's room, an orderly stopped him in the hall.

51   "Who are you?" she asked. She was baffled by the answer. "Her son?" the woman said.

"Why don't you ever visit? Where have you been the last six months?"

52   His mother's limbs were frozen, her eyes so empty of emotion they looked like dirty glass. Her face twitched uncontrollably, and Nando stood there, wordless. The orderly told him if he pinched her fingers she would feel it. But other than that, she would not respond.

53   Nando stared at his mother for 30 minutes, trying to fight back tears. On the nightstand was the fake red rose he had bought on the way to see her.

54   "A day in my life," he said on the street again, his voice gone soft. "Anyone want it?" It was 2:15 P.M.

A REMINDER IN THE MAIL

55 Back at home, he planned his week. Hit the job center. Hit the right welfare office.

56   Then he went downstairs to get his mail.

57   On Rikers, he had taken a writing class, and his last assignment was to write a letter to himself as a happy 70-year-old man. He was to describe that happy life, writing from the future, to himself as he was now, at 20. He had to describe the choices he had made.

58   The letter was in his mailbox.

Dear Nando,

I remember those days we spent on Rikers Island. Pretty rough, huhh! Well, as for me, I made the best of it. I chose to change a couple of things about myself in order to get where I'm at now. Let's just say I'm at a place where it's always sunny and hot and when it rains, it really rains. I got a few kids now and a beautiful wife with a handful of grandchildren. What I chose to do was leave all the drugs and negative things alone. It was really rough at first, but I never gave up. I always knew I could do more.

Sincerely,
Nando

59   He sat on the rocking chair and read the letter, twice. Then he lay down on his mother's bed.

60   It was 4 P.M. and he wasn't sleepy. Tomorrow was only eight hours away.

Questions to Help You Think and Write about Crime and the Treatment of Criminals

1. Gilligan calls for a complete renovation of the current prison system. He claims that prisons should focus on educating criminals rather than punishing them or exacting retribution for harm done to others. What are the benefits of adopting Gilligan's plan? What are the drawbacks? In your final opinion, what should be the purpose of prisons?

2. The essays on two innovative programs, Shakespeare Behind Bars and the program in which women inmates train disability dogs, draw on some basic human values that prison tends to suppress. What makes these programs succeed where other prison regimens fail to rehabilitate prisoners? What would be your ideal program for prisoner rehabilitation?

3. In the debate over capital punishment, the symbolism of execution methods and rituals is very important. Using one or more of the images in this section, either analyze an image as an argument for or against the death penalty; or analyze the relationship between society and convicted criminals that is constructed by the setting and rituals surrounding executions.

4. Analyze the arguments presented by Tanner and the essay reprinted from *The Economist* both for and against capital punishment as a deterrent to violent crime. Based on your reading, which position is supported by the statistical evidence? Does either position rely on logical fallacies? Are the underlying warrants for each position justified? Conclude by taking your own position on the question of whether capital punishment is a viable deterrent to crime.

5. The excerpt from Aristotle's *Rhetoric* suggests that human nature has not changed very much in the past twenty-four hundred years. Compare Aristotle's description of youth with Weinberger's. How are they similar, and how are they different? What can you conclude about the nature of young people who are sixteen and seventeen years old?

6. Why, according to Wallis, has the death penalty for 16- and 17-year-olds been overturned by the Supreme Court? Do you agree with this decision? Why or why not? Drawing on what you have learned from this essay and those by Aristotle and Weinberger, develop a plan for dealing with young offenders that would benefit both them and society.

7. Juvenile terrorism is a new variety of youth crime. Do you think it is right to subject young people accused of terrorist crimes to the same kind of interrogation and treatment used for adults at a facility such as Guantánamo? Why or why not?

8. Feuer's article about Nando paints a bleak picture. How long do you think that a person like Nando can last after being released from prison with nothing but a transportation pass that is good for one day? Do you think that Nando will turn back to drugs? What policies could be changed to stop the hopeless cycle described by Feuer's article?

SECTION ④

Issues concerning Race, Culture, and Identity

The Issues

A. **How Important Is Race to American Identity?**

The first set of essays considers race as cultural construct and genetic makeup. Richard Dyer claims that whites are represented in the media as existing outside of racial and ethnic categories and suggests that the concept of "whiteness" should be racialized. In the visual exercise that follows, two famous Shakespearean lovers are reversed. Emma Daly writes about college students' reactions when DNA tests show that the racial makeup of some of them differs from what they had always thought. One of these students reflects on why that knowledge seems so important. The next two essays provide a historical perspective on the role of race in American culture from the 1960s to the present. In his classic speech "I Have a Dream," Martin Luther King Jr. offers his dream of equality for "all God's children." K. A. Dilday recommends abandoning the term *African American* for the more inclusive term *black*, which acknowledges affinities Americans have with the global community of black persons. See also "We Knew What Glory Was" (pages 54–56), "A View from Berkeley (pages 58–60), "One of Our Own: Training Native Teachers for the 21st Century" (pages 62–63), "The Man behind Rosa Parks"(pages 91–92), "Fewer Call Themselves Multiracial" (pages 183–184), "A Call for Unity: A Letter from Eight White Clergymen" (pages 347–348), "Letter from Birmingham Jail" (pages 348–360), "Theme for English B" (pages 490–491), and advertisements on pages 66–69.

B. **To What Extent Does Individual Identity Depend on Ethnic Affiliation?**

The essays in this section consider the ways in which cultural identity can shape individuals, how individuals can reject ethnic identity, and the potential benefits and costs of both processes. Yahlin Chang offers examples of Asians in America who have kept their ethnic identities and others who have not. Dorinne Kondo writes about the confusion in identity that can result when trying to retain one's own cultural identity in a foreign context where there is pressure to conform to social norms. The final two essays suggest the complexity of ethnic identity for contemporary Americans. Katie Halper argues that she feels most Jewish when connected to the social ideals of her family rather than

618

to the religious rituals of Judaism. Richard Rodriguez's meditation on his own name suggests as well that while post–9/11 America fears the growth of Hispanic immigration, in fact the many "Richard Rodriguezs" already in the United States represent a myriad of ethnicities, religions, professions, and values. Hispanic culture is not monolithic, but a loose association of individuals who share the language of Spain. See also "We're Fighting Terror, But Killing Freedom" (pages 56–57), "A Simple 'Hai' Won't Do" (pages 70–71), and "What Sets Us Apart" (pages 191–193).

Web Sites for Further Exploration and Research

Interracial Voice	http://www.interracialvoice.com/
Genetic Genealogy, DNA Ancestry Project	http://www.dnaancestryproject.com/ gdna_intro_ancestry.php
Martin Luther King Jr. Research and Education Institute (Stanford University)	http://www.stanford.edu/group/King/
JewishEncyclopedia.com	http://www.jewishencyclopedia.com/
Foundation for Jewish Culture	http://www.jewishculture.org/
Anne Frank House, official Web Site	http://www.annefrank.org/content.asp? pid=1&lid=2
The Muslim News	http://www.muslimnews.co.uk/
Muslim-Answers.org	http://www.muslim-answers.org/
Information Resource Centers, U.S. Diplomatic Mission to Germany, "Multiculturalism and Race Relations at the End of the Century"	http://usa.usembassy.de/classroom/ethnic.htm
National Japanese American Historical Society	http://www.njahs.org/
Crossroads, AmericanStudiesWeb	http://lamp.georgetown.edu/asw/

619

Films and Literature Related to Race, Culture, and Identity

Films *American Ramadan*, 2006; *Brother from Another Planet*, 1984; *Citizen King* (American Experience), 2005; *Do the Right Thing*, 1989; *Guess Who*, 2005; *Guess Who's Coming to Dinner*, 1967; *Joy Luck Club*, 1993; *Malcolm X*, 1992;

Mississippi Burning, 1988; *Monster's Ball,* 2002; *O,* 2001; *A Raisin in the Sun,* 1961 and 2008; *West Side Story,* 1961.

Literature novels: *Beloved* by Toni Morrison; *Borderlands* by Gloria Azaldua; *The Joy Luck Club* by Amy Tan; *To Kill a Mockingbird* by Harper Lee; autobiography and memoir: *The House on Mango Street* by Sandra Cisneros; "How It Feels to Be Colored Me" by Zora Neale Hurston; *Hunger of Memory* by Richard Rodriguez; *I Know Why the Caged Bird Sings* by Maya Angelou; play: *A Raisin in the Sun* by Lorraine Hansbury; poem: "Incident" by Countee Cullen.

The Rhetorical Situation

Dorinne K. Kondo, one of the authors in this section, makes the assertion that "race, language, and culture are intertwined." To understand this statement, you might want to think about how your race, culture, and language intertwine to contribute to your own sense of personal identity and also how they cause other people to regard you in particular ways. How would you characterize yourself in terms of these categories? What group of people do you identify with primarily? How would you characterize the knowledge, beliefs, and behavior of this group, and how does the group itself influence your values and behavior? What aspects of your identity *cannot* be accounted for by such categories as race and ethnicity?

Throughout the history of the United States, race has been an important factor in defining American national identity. As Dr. Martin Luther King Jr. implies when articulating his "dream," the most fundamental expressions of American idealism, such as the Declaration of Independence, promote the concept of "equality." Nevertheless, as Dr. King makes clear, the institution of slavery, although in the past, existed and still makes the realization of this ideal difficult. At the same time, science is changing our understanding of race by making it possible for individuals to learn their racial DNA makeup, a process that has produced interesting and even surprising results. The African American literary scholar Henry Louis Gates Jr., for instance, recently discovered through DNA testing that his maternal ancestors were European. The essays in this section also question the importance of customs and religion in determining personal identity. The line between religion, values, and customs can be difficult to define. To what degree, for instance, are identities such as "Jewish" or "Muslim" a matter of religion or family, and to what extent are they a matter of shared values and commitments?

Another issue is the degree to which the ideal of multiculturalism remains possible or desirable in a global society. Some critics argue that in a post–9/11 world, the ability to value and celebrate all cultures within one geographic space has simply become impossible; such people think that there are unbridgeable moral gaps between the teachings of religions such as Islam, Christianity, and Judaism and that even differing cultural values can undermine national unity.

France has been the site of debates over whether Muslim women can wear head coverings in public schools. In the United States, we have seen controversy about whether women can be covered in driver's license photos and movements to make English the country's "official" language. In Britain as well, the decision of some ethnic groups to keep to themselves and maintain their own traditions rather than assimilate into their host culture has been cited as a cause of rising terrorism. Others insist on the individual's right to preserve cultural distinctions such as religion, language, and dress. The writers in this section urge us to look beyond national boundaries and consider the global connections between Americans of different racial and ethnic identities and their counterparts throughout the world.

A. How Important Is Race to American Identity?

> **BEFORE YOU READ:** Consider your own cultural, racial, and family heritage. With what media images did you or do you identify? How does your self-image fit or not fit with the images of your own type of family that have been offered in the media?

THE MATTER OF WHITENESS*
Richard Dyer

Richard Dyer is professor of film studies at the University of Warwick in England. The following piece is an excerpt from Dyer's book *White: Essays on Race and Culture*, which was published in 1997. Here Dyer explores the representation of white people in Western culture.

1 Racial[1] imagery is central to the organisation of the modern world. At what cost regions and countries export their goods, whose voices are listened to at international gatherings, who bombs and who is bombed, who gets what jobs, housing, access to health care and education, what cultural activities are subsidised and sold, in what terms they are validated—these are all largely inextricable from racial imagery. The myriad minute decisions that constitute the practices of the world are at every point informed by judgements about people's capacities and worth, judgements based on what they look like, where they come from, how they speak, even what they eat, that is, racial judgements. Race is not the only factor governing these things and people of goodwill everywhere struggle to overcome the prejudices and barriers of race, but it is never not a factor, never not in play. And since race in itself—insofar as it is anything in itself—refers to some intrinsically insignificant geographical/physical

*Richard Dyer, *White: Essays on Race and Culture* (London: Routledge, 1997), 1–4.

differences between people, it is the imagery of race that is in play.

2   There has been an enormous amount of analysis of racial imagery in the past decades, ranging from studies of images of, say, blacks or American Indians in the media to the deconstruction of the fetish of the racial Other in the texts of colonialism and post-colonialism. Yet until recently a notable absence from such work has been the study of images of white people. Indeed, to say that one is interested in race has come to mean that one is interested in any racial imagery other than that of white people. Yet race is not only attributable to people who are not white, nor is imagery of non-white people the only racial imagery.

3   [I write] about the racial imagery of white people—not the images of other races in white cultural production, but the latter's imagery of white people themselves. This is not done merely to fill a gap in the analytic literature, but because there is something at stake in looking at, or continuing to ignore, white racial imagery. As long as race is something only applied to non-white peoples, as long as white people are not racially seen and named, they/we function as a human norm. Other people are raced, we are just people.

4   There is no more powerful position than that of being "just" human. The claim to power is the claim to speak for the common-ality of humanity. Raced people can't do that—they can only speak for their race.[2] But non-raced people can, for they do not represent the interests of a race. The point of seeing the racing of whites is to dislodge them/us from the position of power, with all the inequities, oppression, privileges and sufferings in its train, dislodging them/us by undercutting the authority with which they/we speak and act in and on the world.

5   The sense of whites as non-raced is most evident in the absence of reference to whiteness in the habitual speech and writing of white people in the West. We (whites) will speak of, say, the blackness or Chineseness of friends, neighbours, col-leagues, customers or clients, and it may be in the most genuinely friendly and accept-ing manner, but we don't mention the whiteness of the white people we know. An old-style white comedian will often start a joke: "There's this bloke walking down the street and he meets this black geezer," never thinking to race the bloke as well as the geezer. Synopses in listings of films on TV, where wordage is tight, none the less squander words with things like: "Comedy in which a cop and his black sidekick investigate a robbery," "Skinhead Johnny and his Asian lover Omar set up a laun-drette," "Feature film from a promising Native American director" and so on. Since all white people in the West do this all the time, it would be invidious to quote actual examples, and so I shall confine myself to one from my own writing. In an article on lesbian and gay stereotypes,[3] I discuss the fact that there can be variations on a type such as the queen or dyke. In the illustrations which accompany this point, I compare a "fashion queen" from the film *Irene* with a "black queen" from *Car Wash*— the former, white image is not raced, whereas all the variation of the latter is reduced to his race. Moreover, this is the only non-white image referred to in the article, which does not however point out that all the other images discussed are white. In this, as in the other white examples in this paragraph, the fashion queen is, racially speaking, taken as being just human.

6   This assumption that white people are just people, which is not far off saying that

622

whites are people whereas other colours are something else, is endemic to white culture. Some of the sharpest criticism of it has been aimed at those who would think themselves the least racist or white supremacist. bell hooks, for instance, has noted how amazed and angry white liberals become when attention is drawn to their whiteness, when they are seen by non-white people as white.

> Often their rage erupts because they believe that all ways of looking that highlight difference subvert the liberal belief in a universal subjectivity (we are all just people) that they think will make racism disappear. They have a deep emotional investment in the myth of "sameness," even as their actions reflect the primacy of whiteness as a sign informing who they are and how they think.[4]

7   Similarly, Hazel Carby discusses the use of black texts in white classrooms, under the sign of multiculturalism, in a way that winds up focusing "on the complexity of response in the (white) reader/student's construction of self in relation to a (black) perceived 'other.'" We should, she argues, recognise that "everyone in this social order has been constructed in our political imagination as a racialized subject" and thus that we should consider whiteness as well as blackness, in order "to make visible what is rendered invisible when viewed as the normative state of existence: the (white) point in space from which we tend to identify difference."[5]

8   The invisibility of whiteness as a racial position in white (which is to say dominant) discourse is of a piece with its ubiquity. When I said above that [I am not] merely seeking to fill a gap in the analysis of racial imagery, I reproduced the idea that there is no discussion of white people. In fact for most of the time white people speak about nothing but white people, it's just that we couch it in terms of "people" in general. Research—into books, museums, the press, advertising, films, television, software—repeatedly shows that in Western representation whites are overwhelmingly and disproportionately predominant, have the central and elaborated roles, and above all are placed as the norm, the ordinary, the standard.[6] Whites are everywhere in representation. Yet precisely because of this and their placing as norm they seem not to be represented to themselves *as* whites but as people who are variously gendered, classed, sexualised and labeled. At the level of racial representation, in other words, whites are not of a certain race, they're just the human race.

9   We are often told that we are living now in a world of multiple identities, of hybridity, of decentredness and fragmentation. The old illusory unified identities of class, gender, race, sexuality are breaking up; someone may be black *and* gay *and* middle class *and* female; we may be bi-, poly- or non-sexual, of mixed race, indeterminate gender and heaven knows what class. Yet we have not yet reached a situation in which white people and white cultural agendas are no longer in the ascendant. The media, politics, education are still in the hands of white people, still speak for whites while claiming—and sometimes sincerely aiming—to speak for humanity. Against the flowering of a myriad postmodern voices, we must also see the countervailing tendency towards a homogenisation of world culture, in the continued dominance of US news dissemination, popular TV programmes and Hollywood movies. Postmodern multiculturalism may have genuinely opened up a space for the voices of the other, challenging the authority of the white West,[7] but it may also

623

simultaneously function as a side-show for white people who look on with delight at all the differences that surround them.[8] We may be on our way to genuine hybridity, multiplicity without (white) hegemony, and it may be where we want to get to—but we aren't there yet, and we won't get there until we see whiteness, see its power, its particularity and limitedness, put it in its place and end its rule. This is why studying whiteness matters.

10   It is studying whiteness *qua* whiteness. Attention is sometimes paid to "white ethnicity,"[9] but this always means an identity based on cultural origins such as British, Italian or Polish, or Catholic or Jewish, or Polish-American, Irish-American, Catholic-American and so on. These however are variations on white-ethnicity (though . . . some are more securely white than others), and the examination of them tends to lead away from a consideration of whiteness itself. John Ibson, in a discussion of research on white US ethnicity, concludes that being, say, Polish, Catholic or Irish may not be as important to white Americans as some might wish.[10] But being white is.

Editor's Notes:

1. I use the terms race and racial . . . in the most common though problematic sense, referring to supposedly visibly differentiable, supportedly discrete social groupings.

2. In their discussion of the extraordinarily successful TV sitcom about a middle-class, African-American family, *The Cosby Show*, Sut Jhally and Justin Lewis note the way that viewers repeatedly recognise the characters' blackness but also that "you just think of them as people"; in other words that they don't only speak for their race. Jhally and Lewis argue that this is achieved by the way the family conforms to "the everyday, generic world of white television," an essentially middle-class world. The family is "ordinary" *despite* being black; because it is upwardly mobile, it can be accepted as "ordinary," in a way that marginalises most actual African-Americans. If

the realities of African-American experience were included, then the characters would not be perceived as people. Sut Jhally and Justin Lewis, *Enlightened Racism: 'The Cosby Show,' Audiences and the Myth of the American Dream* (Boulder: Westview Press, 1992).

3. Richard Dyer, "Seen to Be Believed: Problems in the Representation of Gay People as Typical," in *The Matter of Images: Essays on Representation* (London: Routledge, 1993), pp. 19–51.

4. bell hooks, "Representations of Whiteness in the Black Imagination," in *Black Looks: Race and Representation* (Boston: South End Press, 1992), p. 167.

5. Hazel V. Carby, "The Multicultural Wars," in *Black Popular Culture*, ed. Gina Dent (Seattle: Bay Press, 1992), p. 193.

6. . . . The research findings are generally cast the other way round, in terms of non-white under-representation, textual marginalisation and positioning as deviant or a problem. Recent research in the US does suggest that African-Americans (but not other racially marginalised groups) have become more represented in the media, even in excess of their proportion of the population. However, this number still falls off if one focuses on central characters.

7. See, for example, Craig Owens, "The Discourse of Others: Feminists and Post-modernism," in *The Anti-Aesthetic: Essays on Postmodern Culture*, ed. Hal Foster (Port Townsend, Wash.: Bay Press, 1983), pp. 57–82.

8. *The Crying Game* (GB, 1992) seems to me to be an example of this. It explores with fascination and generosity, the hybrid and fluid nature of identity: gender, race, national belonging, sexuality. Yet all of this revolves around a bemused but ultimately unchallenged straight white man—it reinscribes the position of those at the intersection of heterosexuality, maleness and whiteness as that of the one group which does not need to be hybrid and fluid.

9. See, for example, Richard D. Alba, *Ethnic Identity: The Transformation of White America* (New Haven, Conn.: Yale University Press, 1990).

10. John Ibson, "Virgin Land or Virgin Mary? Studying the Ethnicity of White Americans," *American Quarterly* 33 (1981): 284–308.

Reading Images: Racial Role Reversal in William Shakespeare's *Othello*

Image 1:
A Black Othello

Paul Robeson as Othello and Peggy Ashcroft as Desdemona in the 1930 London production of Shakespeare's *Othello*

For Discussion: In the preceding article, Dyer argues that "whiteness" should be made visible as a color, not just accepted as a normative condition against which other colors and races are defined. Whether or not you have read or seen *Othello* (the plot is also familiar from the film *O*), what is the impact on your awareness of color when the races of two fictional characters (e.g., friends or lovers) are reversed? How does the photo of the Patrick Stewart production of *Othello,* when juxtaposed with the Robeson-Ashcroft photograph, make you conscious of what qualities are stereotypically associated with whiteness and blackness?

625

Image 2:
A White Othello

Patrick Stewart as Othello and Patrice Johnson as Desdemona in Jude Kelly's production of William Shakespeare's *Othello*, The Shakespeare Theatre, Washington, D.C., 1997

For Writing: Think of a short story, film, or television show you know that involves both black and white characters or characters of different ethnicities or color. Describe how the story would be changed if the race, ethnicity, or color of the characters were reversed.

Context: The famous actor, singer, and political activist Paul Robeson was one of the first African American actors to play Othello in Shakespeare's play of that name. The character is a black African Moor who is married to Desdemona, a white Venetian, and race plays a large role in their love tragedy: Othello is persuaded that Desdemona is unfaithful and ends up strangling her. In the "photo-negative" production, Royal Shakespeare actor Patrick Stewart (better known in the U.S. as Captain Picard of *Star Trek: The Next Generation*) plays Othello, while African American actress Patrice Johnson plays Desdemona; in fact, all of the characters besides Othello are played by actors of color in Jude Kelly's production.

BEFORE YOU READ: What do you know about your own family background? To when and where can you trace your ancestors? Have you ever found out some new, surprising information about your heritage?

DNA TEST GIVES STUDENTS ETHNIC SHOCKS[*]

Emma Daly

Daly is a former Balkan correspondent for the British newspaper *The Independent* and a foreign correspondent for *the New York Times.*

1   When Don R. Harrison Jr. was growing up in Philadelphia, neighborhood children would tease him and call him "white boy," because his skin was lighter than theirs. But Mr. Harrison, a "proud black man," was still unprepared for the results of a DNA test, taken as part of a class at Pennsylvania State University, to determine his genetic ancestry.

2   "I figured it would be interesting. I'm light-skinned and I wanted to know my whole makeup," said Mr. Harrison, a 20-year-old sociology major. But he was shocked by results showing him to be 52 percent African and 48 percent European: "which I had no clue about, considering both my parents are black," said Mr. Harrison. "So I'm half white."

3   Samuel M. Richards, who teaches Sociology 119, Race and Ethnic Relations, to 500 students each semester, said the DNA tests, which were conducted last year for the first time, were very popular with the class.

4   "Everyone wants to take the test, even students who think they are 100 percent one race or another, and almost every one of them wants to discover something, that they're 1 percent Asian or something.

It's a badge in this multicultural world," he said.

5   About half of the 100 students tested this semester were white, he said, "And every one of them said, 'Oh man, I hope I'm part black,' because it would upset their parents."

6   "That's this generation," he said. "People want to identify with this pop multiracial culture. They don't want to live next to it, but they want to be part of it. It's cool."

7   The tests also help to deepen conversations about race, he said.

8   "When I teach I try to demonstrate to students how complex race and ethnicity are," Dr. Richards said. "My secondary goal is to improve race relations, and when people discover that what they thought about themselves is not true—'I thought I was black, but I'm also Asian and white'—it leads them to have a different kind of conversation about race. It leads them to be less bigoted, to ask the deeper questions, to be more open to differences."

9   Mark D. Shriver, associate professor of anthropology and genetics at Penn State, took cheek swabs from about 100 student volunteers in Dr. Richards's class for the DNA tests.

---

[*]*New York Times*, April 13, 2005, A18.

10   Many students were surprised by the results of the test, which was created by Professor Shriver and his commercial partners at DNAPrint Genomics Inc. to measure genetic mixing in populations, because of the potential importance of racial or ethnic background to drug trials, and also because of the researchers' curiosity about their own ancestry. The company analyzed the test results free; the results will go into a database for Dr. Shriver's research.

11   The test compares DNA with that of four parent populations, western European, west African, east Asian and indigenous American, and the company claims it is more than 90 percent accurate.

12   Many unexpected results can be explained by family history. Mr. Harrison, for instance, recalled a great-grandfather who "would cross for white, he was so fair."

13   "The white women apparently found him attractive, and black women would flock to him because light was in back then." Mr. Harrison added, "He worked on the railroad, and he looked white in a black-and-white photo."

14   Natasha Best, a 21-year-old public relations major, has always thought of herself as half black and half white, because her mother is Irish-Lithuanian and her father West Indian. But the test proved her to be 58 percent European and 42 percent African.

15   "I was surprised at how much European I was, because though my father's family knows there is a great-great-grandfather who was Scottish, no one remembered him," said Ms. Best, who grew up in Yonkers. "I knew it was true, because I have dark relatives with blue eyes, but to bring it up a whole 8 percent, that was shocking to me."

16   But Professor Shriver explained that although a great-great-grandparent would contribute on average 6.25 percent of a person's genes, any one ancestor might be represented at a higher or lower level in today's generation.

17   Modern migration patterns are also leaving a mark. Ms. Best and Mr. Harrison are members of the fastest-growing ethnic grouping in the United States, one that was acknowledged in the 2000 census for the first time: mixed race.

18   Yet the two students identify themselves in very different ways.

19   "I am 48 percent white—genetically I am, at least, but not culturally. And the fact that I'm black is more important, because it's something I know. It's who I'm comfortable with," Mr. Harrison said.

20   "Some people think it's funny that I consider myself Irish and celebrate St. Patrick's Day," said Ms. Best, "because no matter how you cut it, when you look at me you don't think, there goes a white girl."

21   She has noted discrimination on both sides. "Black people have told me I shouldn't date white people," said Ms. Best, whose boyfriend is white. Some of her white friends say their parents, too, disapprove of interracial dating. "Other people have told me I'm not really black, or I think I'm better than other black people because I'm lighter."

22   Mr. Harrison, who says that as a child he molded himself to be more black, does not want this new information to change his identity.

23   "Just because I found out I'm white, I'm not going to act white." he said. "I'm very proud of my black side."

24   But whatever his genes say, or those of Ms. Best, they will most likely be seen as black—at least by white Americans—for the rest of their lives.

25   "I think the test is really interesting; I had to know," said Ms. Best. "But it makes me question, why are we doing this? Why do people, especially in this country, want to know? Why are we, as a people, so caught up in race? Maybe we haven't progressed as much as we thought we had."

627

BEFORE YOU READ: Martin Luther King Jr. is an American icon. What is your sense of his importance to American history?

I HAVE A DREAM*
Martin Luther King Jr.

Dr. Martin Luther King was an influential leader in the civil rights movement of the 1960s. He was assassinated on April 4, 1968, in Memphis, Tennessee.

For Discussion: Based on the themes of King's speech, why do you think that he chose to situate the event symbolically between the Lincoln Memorial and Washington Monument? Why does he call it a "hallowed spot"?

For Writing: We might say that by referring to George Washington and Abraham Lincoln, King is making an argument from authority. What other evidence does the speech provide to support his use of these authorities? How does all the evidence work together to prove the speech's central claim?

Context: The captions is: King delivering the "I Have a Dream" speech. This speech was delivered August 28, 1963, on the steps of the Lincoln Memorial on the National Mall in Washington, D.C. The Lincoln Memorial stands at one end of the Reflecting Pool and the Washington Monument, seen in the background, stands at the other. King delivered this speech to more than a quarter of a million people, the largest audience to gather for a political speech in American history. Most members of the audience were African Americans, but fifty thousand white Americans were also present. The purpose of the gathering was to demonstrate for better jobs and more freedom for African Americans. People sang freedom songs and listened to speeches all day. At the end of the day King gave this speech. It is a classic of American oratory. Visit the Web site of top 100 American speeches at http://www.americanrhetoric.com/newtop100speeches.htm and listen to the speech. It is listed there as the number one speech of the twentieth century.

1   I am happy to join with you today in what will go down in history as the greatest demonstration for freedom in the history of our nation.

2   Five score years ago, a great American, in whose symbolic shadow we stand today, signed the Emancipation Proclamation. This momentous decree came as a great beacon light of hope to millions of Negro slaves, who had been seared in the flames of withering injustice. It came as a joyous daybreak to end the long night of their captivity.

*The text of this speech comes from the Web sites listed in "Context" above and on page 619.

3   But one hundred years later, the Negro still is not free. One hundred years later, the life of the Negro is still sadly crippled by the manacles of segregation and the chains of discrimination. One hundred years later, the Negro lives on a lonely island of poverty in the midst of a vast ocean of material prosperity. One hundred years later, the Negro is still languished in the corners of American society and finds himself an exile in his own land. And so we've come here today to dramatize a shameful condition.

4   In a sense we have come to our nation's capital to cash a check. When the architects of our republic wrote the magnificent words of the Constitution and the Declaration of Independence, they were signing a promissory note to which every American was to fall heir. This note was a promise that all men, yes, black men as well as white men, would be guaranteed the inalienable rights of life, liberty, and the pursuit of happiness. It is obvious today that America has defaulted on this promissory note, insofar as her citizens of color are concerned. Instead of honoring this sacred obligation, America has given the Negro people a bad check, a check which has come back marked "insufficient funds."

5   But we refuse to believe that the bank of justice is bankrupt. We refuse to believe that there are insufficient funds in the great vaults of opportunity of this nation. And so we have come to cash this check, a check that will give us upon demand the riches of freedom and the security of justice.

6   We have also come to this hallowed spot to remind America of the fierce urgency of Now. This is no time to engage in the luxury of cooling off or to take the tranquilizing drug of gradualism. Now is the time to make real the promises of democracy. Now is the time to rise from the dark and desolate valley of segregation to the sunlit path of racial justice. Now is the time to lift our nation from the quicksands of racial injustice to the solid rock of brotherhood. Now is the time to make justice a reality for all of God's children.

7   It would be fatal for the nation to overlook the urgency of the moment. This sweltering summer of the Negro's legitimate discontent will not pass until there is an invigorating autumn of freedom and equality. Nineteen sixty-three is not an end but a beginning. Those who hope that the Negro needed to blow off steam and will now be content will have a rude awakening if the nation returns to business as usual. There will be neither rest nor tranquility in America until the Negro is granted his citizenship rights. The whirlwinds of revolt will continue to shake the foundations of our nation until the bright day of justice emerges.

8   But there is something that I must say to my people who stand on the warm threshold which leads into the palace of justice. In the process of gaining our rightful place we must not be guilty of wrongful deeds. Let us not seek to satisfy our thirst for freedom by drinking from the cup of bitterness and hatred. We must ever conduct our struggle on the high plane of dignity and discipline. We must not allow our creative protest to degenerate into physical violence. Again and again we must rise to the majestic heights of meeting physical force with soul force.

9   The marvelous new militancy which has engulfed the Negro community must not lead us to a distrust of all white people, for many of our white brothers, as evidenced by their presence here today, have come to realize that their destiny is tied up with our destiny. And they have come to realize that their freedom is inextricably bound to our freedom. We cannot walk alone.

10   And as we walk, we must make the pledge that we shall always march ahead. We cannot turn back. There are those who are asking the devotees of civil rights, "When will you be satisfied?" We can never be satisfied as long as the Negro is the victim of the unspeakable horrors of police brutality. We can never be satisfied as long as our bodies, heavy with the fatigue of travel, cannot gain lodging in the motels of the highways and the hotels of the cities. We cannot be satisfied as long as a Negro in Mississippi cannot vote and a Negro in New York believes he has nothing for which to vote. No, no, we are not satisfied and we will not be satisfied

629

until justice rolls down like waters and righteousness like a mighty stream.

11   I am not unmindful that some of you have come here out of great trials and tribulations. Some of you have come fresh from narrow jail cells. Some of you have come from areas where your quest for freedom left you battered by the storms of persecutions and staggered by the winds of police brutality. You have been the veterans of creative suffering. Continue to work with the faith that unearned suffering is redemptive. Go back to Mississippi, go back to Alabama, go back to South Carolina, go back to Georgia, go back to Louisiana, go back to the slums and ghettos of our northern cities, knowing that somehow this situation can and will be changed. Let us not wallow in the valley of despair, I say to you today, my friends. And so even though we face the difficulties of today and tomorrow, I still have a dream. It is a dream deeply rooted in the American dream.

630

12   I have a dream that one day this nation will rise up and live out the true meaning of its creed: We hold these truths to be self-evident that all men are created equal.

13   I have a dream that one day on the red hills of Georgia the sons of former slaves and the sons of former slave owners will be able to sit down together at the table of brotherhood.

14   I have a dream that one day even the state of Mississippi, a state sweltering with the heat of injustice, sweltering with the heat of oppression, will be transformed into an oasis of freedom and justice.

15   I have a dream that my four little children will one day live in a nation where they will not be judged by the color of their skin but by the content of their character.

16   I have a *dream* today!

17   I have a dream that one day, down in Alabama, with its vicious racists, with its governor having his lips dripping with the words of interposition and nullification; one day right down in Alabama little black boys and black girls will be able to join hands with little white boys and white girls as sisters and brothers.

18   I have a *dream* today!

19   I have a dream that one day every valley shall be exalted, and every hill and mountain shall be made low, the rough places will be made plain, and the crooked places will be made straight, and the glory of the Lord shall be revealed and all flesh shall see it together.

20   This is our hope. This is the faith that I will go back to the South with. With this faith we will be able to hew out of the mountain of despair a stone of hope. With this faith we will be able to transform the jangling discords of our nation into a beautiful symphony of brotherhood. With this faith we will be able to work together, to pray together, to struggle together, to go to jail together, to stand up for freedom together, knowing that we will be free one day. And this will be the day—this will be the day when all of God's children will be able to sing with new meaning,

> "My country 'tis of thee,
>   sweet land of liberty, of thee I sing.
> Land where my fathers died,
>   land of the Pilgrim's pride,
> From every mountainside, let freedom ring!"

And if America is to be a great nation, this must become true.

21   And so let freedom ring—from the prodigious hilltops of New Hampshire.

22   Let freedom ring—from the mighty mountains of New York.

23   Let freedom ring—from the heightening Alleghenies of Pennsylvania.

24   Let freedom ring—from the snow-capped Rockies of Colorado.

25   Let freedom ring—from the curvaceous slopes of California.

26   But not only that:

27   Let freedom ring—from Stone Mountain of Georgia.

28   Let freedom ring—from Lookout Mountain of Tennessee.

29   Let freedom ring—from every hill and molehill of Mississippi, from every mountainside, let freedom ring!

30   And when this happens, when we allow freedom to ring, when we let it ring from every village and every hamlet, from every

state and every city, we will be able to speed up that day when all of God's children, black men and white men, Jews and Gentiles, Protestants and Catholics, will be able to join hands and sing in the words of the old Negro spiritual,

> Free at last, free at last.
> Thank God Almighty, we are free at last.

BEFORE YOU READ: Americans are very familiar with the term *African American*, but try making up a term using a different national or geographic adjective that is less familiar (e.g., French American, Antarctican American). How would such a title alter or not alter your perception of the relation of Americans to other parts of the world?

GO BACK TO BLACK*

K. A. Dilday

K. A. Dilday is a columnist for the online magazine *Open Democracy*, according to the *New York Times* where this column was published.

1 I'm black again. I was black in Mississippi in the 1970s but sometime in the 1980s I became African-American, with a brief pause at Afro-American. Someone, I think it was Jesse Jackson, in the days when he had that kind of clout, managed to convince America that I preferred being African-American. I don't.

2 Now I live in Britain, where I'm black again. Blacks in Britain come from all over, although many are from the former colonies. According to the last census, about half of the British people who identify as black say they are black Caribbean, about 40 percent consider themselves black African, and the rest just feel plain old black. Black Brits are further divided by ancestral country of origin, yet they are united under the term black British—often—expanded to include British Asians from the Indian subcontinent.

3 The term *African-American* was contrived to give black Americans a sense of having a historical link to Africa, since one of slavery's many unhappy legacies is that most black Americans don't know particulars about their origins. Black Americans whose ancestors arrived after slavery and who can pinpoint

their country of origin are excluded from the definition—which is why, early in his [presidential] campaign, people said Barack Obama wasn't really African-American.[1] Yet, since he has one parent from the African continent and one from the American continent, he is explicitly African-American.

4 Distinguishing between American black people based on their ancestors' arrival date ignores the continuum of experience that transcends borders and individual genealogies and unites black people all over the world. Yes, scientists have shown that black means nothing as a biological description, but it remains an important signal in social interaction. Everywhere I travel, from North Africa to Europe to Asia, dark-skinned people approach me and, usually gently but sometimes aggressively, establish a bond.

5 When, early on in the race for the Democratic nomination [in 2008], people wondered if black Americans would vote for Mr. Obama, I never doubted. During the last two years I've learned to decipher his name in almost any pronunciation, because on finding out that I'm an American, all other black

631

---

*K. A. Dilday, "Go Back to Black," *New York Times*, February 27, 2008, http://www.nytimes.com/2008/02/27/opinion/27dilday.html (accessed June 25, 2008).

people I meet, whether they are Arabic-speaking Moroccans in Casablanca, French-speaking African mobile-phone-store clerks in the outer boroughs of Paris, or thickly accented Jamaican black Brits, ask me eagerly about him. Black people all over the world feel a sense of pride in his accomplishment.

6   It's hard to understand why black Americans ever tried to use the term *African-American* to exclude people. The black American community's social and political power derives from its inclusiveness. Everyone who identifies as black has traditionally been welcomed, no matter their skin color or date of arrival. In Britain, in contrast, dark-skinned people who trace their relatives to particular former colonies can be cliquish. Beyond the fact that blacks make up a smaller share of the population here, this regional identity may be a reason that the British black community isn't as powerful a social and political force.

7   I've never minded not knowing who my ancestors are beyond a few generations. My partner is an Englishman whose family

tree is the sort that professional genealogists post on the Internet because it can be traced back to the first king of England in the 11th century. To me, it's more comforting to know that, through me, our children will be black, with all of the privileges and pains.

8   On Mr. Obama's behalf, American blacks have set aside their exclusive label. Polls show that about 80 percent of blacks who have voted in the [2008] Democratic primaries have chosen him. And all of the black people in the mountains of Morocco, the poor suburbs of Paris, the little villages in Kenya and the streets of London are cheering Mr. Obama's victories because they see him as one of their own.

9   Black Americans should honor that. It's time to retire the term *African-American* and go back to black.

Editor's note:

1. Barack Obama was a Democratic candidate for President of the United States in 2008, when this essay was written and published as an Op-Ed contribution.

B. **To What Extent Does Individual Identity Depend on Ethnic Affiliation?**

BEFORE YOU READ: Where did your ancestors come from and when did they come to the United States? Were they eager to assimilate, or did they remain true to their original culture?

ASIAN IDENTITY CRISIS*

Yahlin Chang

Yahlin Chang writes for *Newsweek* and, like the other authors in this section, raises the question about assimilating one's ethnic identity with the dominant group. Do you agree that it is good for Eric Liu to give up his Chinese heritage for an American identity? What is the author's position on this question? Chang wrote this essay when Eric Liu's book *The Accidental Asian: Notes of a Native Speaker* was published in 1998. Liu is now on the faculty of the University of Washington.

1   Eric Liu has spent most of his life climbing up the social ladder without looking back.

The son of Chinese immigrants from Taiwan, he grew up learning to play down his ethnic

---

*Newsweek, June 22, 1998, 68.

identity in the mostly white community of Wappingers Falls, N.Y. Then he went on to amass a heap of power credentials: he graduated from Yale, at 25 he wrote speeches for President Clinton, and now he's at Harvard Law School. In his provocative, wonderfully honest new book, *The Accidental Asian*, Liu, 29, finally pauses long enough to reflect on his assimilationist's guilt, on the feeling that he's left something behind without knowing exactly what it is. Half cultural commentary, half memoir, *Accidental* is a remarkable accomplishment—both a defense of assimilation and an intense recounting of personal loss.

2   Though he's one of Asian America's biggest stars, Liu doesn't act or feel particularly Asian-American. He married a white woman—half of all Asian-Americans intermarry, he points out. He says he cannot escape the feeling that the Asian-American identity is "contrived" and "unnecessary." "Asian Americans are only as isolated as they want to be," he writes. "They—we—do not face the levels of discrimination and hatred that demand an enclave mentality. . . . The choice to invent and sustain a pan-Asian identity is just that: a choice, not an imperative." His book, which just hit stores, is already infuriating Asian-Americans who have a fierce sense of ethnic pride. "Liu has been totally co-opted by the white mainstream," says Bert Wang, who works on labor issues and anti-Asian violence, and christened his rock band Superchink. "But would he be where he is today if he weren't Asian? They love him because he's this novelty who's pro-assimilation." Jeff Yang, the founder of *A. Magazine*—a sort of Asian *Vanity Fair*—finds Liu's view misguided and a bit naive. "Race is an obsession in our society," he says. "To be out of the racial equation takes us away from the table of dialogue completely. But we're creating a culture out of our common experiences: immigration, being perceived as strangers in our own land, serving as a bridge between East and West."

3   But even the most militant Asian-Americans admit to an identity crisis. Chinese, Koreans, Filipinos and other "Asians" have not only different cultures and languages but deep historical antagonisms toward one another. More than anything, what binds them together in America is what they look like—the exact basis for their stigmatization. The Asian-American "race" is just three decades old, born with the immigration boom in 1965. "Race is fundamentally an invention," says Liu. "And just as something can be invented, so it can be dismantled. If you believe in the identity, I can respect that. I'm just not sure it'll last another generation."

4   The economic success many Asian-Americans have achieved may only further weaken that identity. They account for 4 percent of the population, and have the highest median income of all races, including whites. A higher percentage of them earn advanced degrees than of any other group. But those statistics hide the growing number of poor immigrants who feel increasingly alienated from upper-class Asians. "The poor are an embarrassment to professionals who don't want to be seen as peasants," says Peter Kwong, head of Asian-American Studies at New York's Hunter College. "You're taught to be ashamed of your parents," says Chinatown labor activist Trinh Duong, whose mother works in a garment factory. Some activists, who say they have a hard time drawing attention to the plight of those immigrants, try to play down the achievements of upper-class Asians and chafe at the "model minority" stereotype. "That label is clearly part of a hostile discourse between whites and blacks," says Kwong. "Whites are basically saying to blacks, 'We're not racist, and the reason you're not as successful is because you're not working as hard as Asians.'"

5   Yet the abstract debate over assimilation can't do justice to the complex emotional acrobatics of dealing with your own ethnicity. While Liu grew up trying to fit in to

white America, that was the last thing I wanted. I was taught that Asians were smarter and harder-working than everyone else and that explained their success—when the truth is that immigration laws favored professionals, a highly selective group to begin with. There seemed to be no way to have ethnic pride without ethnocentrism. The only solution, it seemed, was to try and transcend race—to erase racial concerns by ignoring them. I started to think a lot like Liu.

6   But something always comes along to jolt me out of this colorblind slumber. The rising number of incidents of anti-Asian violence. College-admission quotas against us. Coverage of the campaign-finance scandals, filled with "shadowy" Orientals creeping into

power, practicing the ancient Chinese art *guanxi*, a scarily exotic word for "connections." And why do so many articles on race neglect to mention us? Why do so many reports from the Census Bureau include only blacks, whites and Hispanics?

7   Is racial identity formed only through racial persecution? I was once berated by a white classmate for claiming I had never been persecuted—which made me wish that I had. But I can't help feeling that it would be contrived to suddenly become passionate about my ethnicity, or to dredge up racial scars that don't exist. Liu says, "Race for people of color should be as much of an option as ethnicity is for whites." But in America, trying to forget about being a minority can still get you in as much trouble as being one.

BEFORE YOU READ: Have you ever visited a place where you felt you were an outsider or been among people with whom you felt a cultural outsider? How did you respond to this feeling ? Did you feel awkward? Did you work hard to fit in with people or the customs of the place? How successful were you?

ON BEING A CONCEPTUAL ANOMALY*

Dorinne K. Kondo

Dorinne K. Kondo, a Japanese American professor of anthropology, is the author of *Crafting Selves: Power, Gender, and Discourses of Identity in a Japanese Workplace*. In this excerpt from her book, she relates her experiences in visiting Japan, where she looked Japanese but acted like an American.

1   As a Japanese American,[1] I created a conceptual dilemma for the Japanese I encountered. For them, I was a living oxymoron, someone who was both Japanese and not Japanese. Their puzzlement was all the greater since most Japanese people I knew

seemed to adhere to an eminently biological definition of Japaneseness. Race, language, and culture are intertwined, so much so that any challenge to this firmly entrenched conceptual schema—a white person who speaks flawlessly idiomatic and unaccented Japanese,

*Dorinne K. Kondo, *Crafting Selves: Power, Gender and Discourses of Identity in a Japanese Workplace* (Chicago: University of Chicago Press, 1990), 11–17.

or a person of Japanese ancestry who cannot—meets with what generously could be described as unpleasant reactions. White people are treated as repulsive and unnatural—*hen na gaijin,* strange foreigners—the better their Japanese becomes, while Japanese Americans and others of Japanese ancestry born overseas are faced with exasperation and disbelief. How can someone who is racially Japanese lack "cultural competence"?[2] During my first few months in Tokyo, many tried to resolve this paradox by asking which of my parents was "really" American.

2   Indeed, it is a minor miracle that those first months did not lead to an acute case of agoraphobia, for I knew that once I set foot outside the door, someone somewhere (a taxi driver? a salesperson? a bank clerk?) would greet one of my linguistic mistakes with an astonished "Eh?" I became all too familiar with the series of expressions that would flicker over those faces: bewilderment, incredulity, embarrassment, even anger, at having to deal with this odd person who looked Japanese and therefore human, but who must be retarded, deranged, or—equally undesirable in Japanese eyes—Chinese or Korean. Defensively, I would mull over the mistake of the day. I mean, how was I to know that in order to "fillet a fish" you had to cut it "in three pieces"? Or that opening a bank account required so much specialized terminology? Courses in literary Japanese at Harvard hadn't done much to prepare me for the realities of everyday life in Tokyo. Gritting my teeth in determination as I groaned inwardly, I would force myself out of the house each morning.

3   For me, and apparently for the people around me, this was a stressful time, when expectations were flouted, when we had to strain to make sense of one another. There seemed to be few advantages in my retaining an American persona, for the distress caused by these reactions was difficult to bear. In the face of dissonance and distress, I found that the desire for comprehensible order in the form of "fitting in," even if it meant suppression of and violence against a self I had known in another context, was preferable to meaninglessness. Anthropological imperatives to immerse oneself in another culture intensified this desire, so that acquiring the accoutrements of Japanese selfhood meant simultaneously constructing a more thoroughly professional anthropological persona. This required language learning in the broadest sense, mastery of culturally appropriate modes of moving, acting, and speaking. For my informants, it was clear that coping with this anomalous creature was difficult, for here was someone who looked like a real human being, but who simply failed to perform according to expectation. They, too, had every reason to make me over in their image, to guide me, gently but insistently, into properly Japanese behavior, so that the discrepancy between my appearance and my cultural competence would not be so painfully evident. I posed a challenge to their senses of identity. How could someone who *looked* Japanese not *be* Japanese? In my cultural ineptitude, I represented for the people who met me the chaos of meaninglessness. Their response in the face of this dissonance was to *make* me as Japanese as possible. Thus, my first nine months of fieldwork were characterized by an attempt to reduce the distance between expectation and inadequate reality, as my informants and I conspired to rewrite my identity as Japanese.

4   My guarantor, an older woman who, among her many activities, was a teacher of flower arranging, introduced me to many families who owned businesses in the ward of Tokyo where I had chosen to do my research. One of her former students and fellow flower-arranging teachers, Mrs. Sakamoto, agreed to take me in as a guest over the summer, since the apartment

635

where I was scheduled to move—owned by one of my classmates in tea ceremony—was still under construction. My proclivities for "acting Japanese" were by this time firmly established. During my stay with the Sakamotos, I did my best to conform to what I thought their expectations of a guest/daughter might be. This in turn seemed to please them and reinforced my tendency to behave in terms of what I perceived to be my Japanese persona.

5   My initial encounter with the head of the household epitomizes this mirroring and reinforcement of behavior. Mr. Sakamoto had been on a business trip on the day I moved in, and he returned the following evening, just as his wife, daughter, and I sat down to the evening meal. As soon as he stepped in the door, I immediately switched from an informal posture, seated on the *zabuton* (seat cushion), to a formal greeting posture, *seiza*-style (kneeling on the floor) and bowed low, hands on the floor. Mr. Sakamoto responded in kind (being older, male, and head of the household, he did not have to bow as deeply as I did), and we exchanged the requisite polite formulae, I requesting his benevolence, and he welcoming me to their family. Later, he told me how happy and impressed he had been with this act of proper etiquette on my part. "Today's young people in Japan," he said, "no longer show such respect. Your grandfather must have been a fine man to raise such a fine granddaughter." Of course, his statements can hardly be accepted at face value. They may well indicate his relief that I seemed to know something of proper Japanese behavior, and hence would not be a complete nuisance to them; it was also his way of making me feel at home. What is important to note is the way this statement was used to elicit proper Japanese behavior in future encounters. And his strategy worked. I was left with a warm, positive feeling toward the Sakamoto family, armed with an incentive to behave in a Japanese

way, for clearly these were the expectations and the desires of the people who had taken me in and who were so generously sharing their lives with me.

6   Other members of the household voiced similar sentiments. Takemi-san, the Sakamotos' married daughter who lived in a distant prefecture, had been visiting her parents when I first moved in. A few minutes after our initial encounter, she observed, "You seem like a typical Japanese woman" (*Nihon no Josei to iu kanji*). Later in the summer, Mrs. Sakamoto confided to me that she could never allow a "pure American" (*junsui na Amerikajin*) to live with them, for only someone of Japanese descent was genetically capable of adjusting to life on *tatami* mats, using unsewered toilets, sleeping on the floor—in short, of living Japanese style. Again, the message was unambiguous. My "family" could feel comfortable with me insofar as I was—and acted—Japanese. [. . .]

7   My physical characteristics led my friends and coworkers to emphasize my identity as Japanese, sometimes even against my own intentions and desires. Over time, my increasingly "Japanese" behavior served temporarily to resolve their crises of meaning and to confirm their assumptions about their own identities. That I, too, came to participate enthusiastically in this recasting of the self is a testimonial to their success in acting upon me. [. . .]

8   The more I adjusted to my Japanese daughter's role, the keener the conflicts became. Most of those conflicts had to do with expectations surrounding gender, and, more specifically, my position as a young woman. Certainly, in exchange for the care the Sakamotos showed me, I was happy to help out in whatever way I could. I tried to do some housecleaning and laundry, and I took over the shopping and cooking for Mr. Sakamoto when Mrs. Sakamoto was at one of the children's association meetings, her flower-arranging classes, or meetings of

ward committees on juvenile delinquency. The cooking did not offend me in and of itself; in fact, I was glad for the opportunity to learn how to make simple Japanese cuisine, and Mr. Sakamoto put up with my sometimes appalling culinary mistakes and limited menus with great aplomb. I remember one particularly awful night when I couldn't find the makings for soup broth, and Mr. Sakamoto was fed *"miso* soup" that was little more than *miso* dissolved in hot water. He managed to down the tasteless broth with good grace—and the trace of a smile on his lips. (Of course, it is also true that although he was himself capable of simple cooking, he would not set foot in the kitchen if there were a woman in the house.) Months after I moved out, whenever he saw me he would say with a sparkle in his eye and a hint of nostalgic wistfulness in his voice, "I miss Dorin-san's salad and sautéed beef," one of the "Western" menus I used to serve up with numbing regularity. No, the cooking was not the problem.

9   The problem was, in fact, the etiquette surrounding the serving of food that produced the most profound conflicts for me as an American woman. The head of the household is usually served first and receives the finest delicacies; men—even the sweetest, nicest ones—ask for a second helping of rice by merely holding out their rice bowls to the woman nearest the rice cooker, and maybe, just maybe, uttering a grunt of thanks in return for her pains. I could never get used to this practice, try as I might. Still, I tried to carry out my duties uncomplainingly, in what I hope was reasonably good humor. But I was none too happy about these things "inside." Other restrictions began to chafe, especially restrictions on my movement. I had to be in at a certain hour, despite my "adult" age. Yet I understood the family's responsibility for me as their guest and quasi-daughter, so I tried to abide by their regulations, hiding my irritation as best I could.

10   This fundamental ambivalence was heightened by isolation and dependency. Though my status was in some respects high in an education-conscious Japan, I was still young, female, and a student. I was in a socially recognized relationship of dependency vis-à-vis the people I knew. I was not to be feared and obeyed, but protected and helped. In terms of my research, this was an extremely advantageous position to be in, for people did not feel the need to reflect my views back to me, as they might with a more powerful person. I did not try to define situations; rather, I could allow other people to define those situations in their culturally appropriate ways, remaining open to their concerns and their ways of acting in the world. But, in another sense, this dependency and isolation increased my susceptibility to identifying with my Japanese role. By this time I saw little of American friends in Tokyo, for it was difficult to be with people who had so little inkling of how ordinary Japanese people lived. My informants and I consequently had every reason to conspire to re-create my identity as Japanese. Precisely because of my dependency and my made-to-order role, I was allowed—or rather, *forced*—to abandon the position of observer. Errors, linguistic or cultural, were dealt with impatiently or with a startled look that seemed to say, "Oh yes, you are American after all." On the other hand, appropriately Japanese behaviors were rewarded with warm, positive reactions or with comments such as "You're more Japanese than the Japanese." Even more frequently, correct behavior was simply accepted as a matter of course. *Naturally* I would understand, *naturally* I would behave correctly, for they presumed me to be, *au fond*, Japanese. [. . .]

11   Identity can imply unity or fusion, but for me what occurred was a fragmentation of the self. This fragmentation was encouraged by my own participation in Japanese life and by the actions of my friends and acquaintances.

At its most extreme point, I became "the Other" in my own mind, where the identity I had known in another context simply collapsed. The success of our conspiracy to recreate me as Japanese reached its climax one August afternoon.

12   It was typical summer weather for Tokyo, "like a steam bath" as the saying goes, so hot the leaves were drooping limply from the trees surrounding the Sakamotos' house. Mrs. Sakamoto and her married daughter, Takemi, were at the doctor's with Takemi's son, so Mr. Sakamoto and I were busy tending young Kaori-chan, Takemi-san's young daughter. Mr. Sakamoto quickly tired of his grandfatherly role, leaving me to entertain Kaori-chan. Promptly at four P.M., the hour when most Japanese housewives do their shopping for the evening meal, I lifted the baby into her stroller and pushed her along ahead of me as I inspected the fish, selected the freshest-looking vegetables, and mentally planned the meal for the evening. As I glanced into the shiny metal surface of the butcher's display case, I noticed someone who looked terribly familiar: a typical young housewife, clad in slip-on sandals and the loose, cotton shift called "home wear" (*hōmu wea*), a woman walking with a characteristically Japanese bend to the knees and a sliding of the feet. Suddenly I clutched the handle of the stroller to steady myself as a wave of dizziness washed over me, for I realized I had caught a glimpse of nothing less than my own reflection. Fear that perhaps I would never emerge from this world into which I was immersed inserted itself into my mind and stubbornly refused to leave, until I resolved to move into a new apartment, to distance myself from my Japanese home and my Japanese existence.

13   For ultimately this collapse of identity was a distancing moment. It led me to emphasize the *differences* between cultures and among various aspects of identity:

researcher, student, daughter, wife, Japanese, American, Japanese American. In order to reconstitute myself as an American researcher, I felt I had to extricate myself from the conspiracy to rewrite my identity as Japanese. Accordingly, despite the Sakamotos' invitations to stay with them for the coming year, I politely stated my intentions to fulfill the original terms of the agreement: to stay just until construction on my new apartment was complete. In order to resist the Sakamotos' attempts to re-create me as Japanese, I removed myself physically from their exclusively Japanese environment.

Editor's notes:

1. See Edward Said, *Orientalism* (New York: Pantheon, 1978). The issue of what to call ourselves is an issue of considerable import to various ethnic and racial groups in the United States, as the recent emphasis on the term *African American* shows. For Asian Americans, the term *Oriental* was called into question in the sixties, for the reasons Said enumerates: the association of the term with stereotypes such as Oriental despotism, inscrutability, splendor, exoticism, mystery, and so on. It also defines "the East" in terms of "the West," in a relationship of unequal power—how rarely one hears of "the Occident," for example. Asian Americans, Japanese Americans included, sometimes hyphenate the term, but some of us would argue that leaving out the hyphen makes the term "Asian" or "Japanese" an adjective, rather than implying a half-and-half status: i.e., that one's loyalties/identities might be half Japanese and half American. Rather, in the terms *Asian American* and *Japanese American,* the accent is on the "American," an important political claim in light of the mainstream tendency to see Asian Americans as somehow more foreign than other kinds of Americans.

2. Merry White, *The Japanese Overseas: Can They Go Home Again?* (New York: Free Press, 1988) offers an account of the families of Japanese corporate executives who are transferred abroad and who often suffer painful difficulties upon reentering Japan.

BEFORE YOU READ: Do you define yourself primarily as a religious or a secular person? Is this even a useful distinction?

DIGGING FOR ROOTS AT SECULAR CAMP[*]

Katie Halper

Katie Halper is a comic, writer, and filmmaker based in New York.

1 My name is Katie Halper, and I am a secular Jew. I've been secular for a little over 26 years now.

2 I recently went on a young adult retreat, whose aim was to explore the definition of Judaism. When several people assumed I was Reform I explained I was secular. When they responded, "Oh cool. What synagogue do you go to?" or "Nice. Where do you celebrate Shabbat?"[1] I started to think that not everyone was as familiar with secular Judaism as I had thought.[2]

3 One of the speakers, a female rabbi who wore a yarmulke, spoke about the Jewish tradition of social justice and the importance of the Exodus story. She asked us, rhetorically, "How can we, whose ancestors came out of slavery in Egypt, not care about current-day oppression and injustice, whether that be genocide in Darfur, or pharmaceutical companies denying access to life-saving AIDS medication and killing millions?"

4 After, one young man was visibly uncomfortable with the rabbi's message. Social justice was not an inherent part of Jewish identity, he said. He was a recovering secular Jew, he confessed, whose parents had desecrated their home with a Christmas tree every winter, and whose grandparents had been . . . Communists. Ultimately, this born-again Jew concluded, it was impossible to be Jewish without believing in God. A woman agreed:

"It's Shabbat," not justice, that defined Judaism. Hearing them, I realized that not only was secular Judaism an unknown for many, it was a rejected unknown. And I, a secular Jew who values activism but does not celebrate Shabbat, was not a real Jew.

5 This wasn't the first time I felt like the odd Jew out. I have never felt comfortable with exclusively Jewish communities. Until I was seven, I went to a Jewish day school. (I still don't know why my secular parents sent me there. They claim that it was for its warmth and minimal snobbishness, but I suspect it was because it was a walkable distance from our apartment.) The roll call gives you a good sense of the type of school it was: Malka, Brahm, Yehuda, Yael H., Yael R., Yael S. (Yes, there were three Yaels in my class of 12), Hannah, Rachel, Sarah, Samuel, Jacob, and . . . Katie. I couldn't quite put my finger on it, but even then, as early as kindergarten, I was aware that in some way or another, I wasn't part of this community.

6 I really put my un-kosher foot in my mouth when we had to go around the room and state our Hebrew names. This was a no-brainer for my classmates, (especially easy for the Yael trio), who translated effortlessly: "My name is Hannah and my Hebrew name is Chana, my name is Rebecca and my Hebrew name is Rivka." I, on the other hand, had no idea if I had a Hebrew name, much less what

---

[*]Katie Halper, "Digging for Roots at Secular Camp," *JBooks.com*, 2007, http://jbooks.com/secularculture/Halper.htm (accessed June 26, 2008). (Reprint of "My Life as a Secular Jew," *PresenTense*, April 10, 2006)

it was. I racked my brain and found nothing. Finally it was my turn. All Yahweh-fearing eyes were on me as I thought to myself, "Come on, Katie: Think, think! Rebecca is to Rivka as Katie is to . . . " And then, like lightning, it struck me. I suddenly remembered a name my uncle sometimes called me, which sounded foreign and, I deduced, had to be Hebrew: "My name is Katie," I bellowed triumphantly, "and my Hebrew name is Katchkalah!" I exhaled a breath of relief and smiled in victory. But the room grew silent, the students looked confused, and the teachers exchanged worried glances. Little did I know that katchkalah was not Hebrew at all but actually the Polish-derived Yiddish word for duckling. [. . .]

7   The retreat on the meaning of Judaism was the first time I was asked to examine my Jewish identity and my place in the Jewish community. Was I indeed less Jewish than the religious Jews on the retreat, than religious Jews in general? Was I even Jewish? [. . .] While I've found certain Jewish communities and practices alienating, I do feel Jewish. Yet the Jews I identify with are Jews who identify with Jews as well as non-Jews. And this, itself, draws from both a rich tradition of Jewish social justice and, at the same time, a universal sense of solidarity that defies religious, ethnic, and national boundaries. Just as religious Jews connect with the rituals they inherit from their families, I feel a connection to the secular traditions in which I was raised.

8   My grandmother was raised in The Coops, a workers' housing cooperative in the Bronx, inspired—in spirit and architecture—by a communal housing complex in Vienna, aptly named the Karl Marx apartments. My father's uncle died in Spain during the Spanish Civil War fighting against Franco with the Abraham Lincoln Brigade.[3] My maternal grandfather lied about his age in an attempt to join the Brigade, but a *brigadista* examining papers saw he was only 16 and sent him home. Stuck in the United States, my grandfather went to jail for climbing the flagpole outside the Austrian embassy and tearing down a swastika. And then, a few years later, as fascism marched along, my grandfather got his chance to fight fascists in Italy and North Africa during World War II.

9   My parents are almost a parody of Upper West Side [New York] secular Jews. Their apartment is filled with saints, shivas, Buddhas, and the occasional dream catcher. The only Jewish holiday we celebrate—Passover—is based in a historical story of oppression, resistance, and liberation. Until recently, I didn't even know Passover was a Jewish holiday. I thought it was a Black holiday, like Kwanzaa, but much, much older because while my family honors the Jews' Exodus out of Egypt, most of our Seder is spent discussing slavery in the United States, the Civil Rights Movement, and now, the occupation of Iraq. The story of the suffering of Jews in Egypt is a mere starting point for exploring more recent realms of oppression, wherever—and to whomever—they occur.

10   Ultimately, where I felt most connected to my Jewish identity was at summer camp. I went to a camp founded by progressive Jewish immigrants in the 1920s, welcoming Jews and non-Jews alike. Following in the footsteps of my mother and her mother before her, I made that great summertime migration north from NYC to Camp Kinderland. While other camps name their bunks after letters, numbers, or (often fictitious) Native American tribes, Kinderland names its bunks after social-justice activists, Jews like Shalom Aleichem, Emma Goldman, and Anne Frank, and non-Jews such as Joe Hill, Harriet Tubman, and Roberto Clemente. For the World Peace Olympics, Kinderland's version of the "color wars," teams are named after social movements (AIDS Education, Suffragism, Civil Rights) or activists (A. Philip Randolph, Sojourner Truth, César Chávez).[4] My first summer I was on the Martin Luther King team, and I'll never forget that MLK vs. Ghandi soccer match of '92, when Martin Luther King cleaned the floor with Ghandi. [. . .]

11   After years as a camper, I became a counselor. To this day, I try to visit every summer, and my friends from camp remain my best friends. And it was and is here, surrounded by Jews and non-Jews committed to social justice (for everyone), drawing from traditions as rich, as authentic, and as Jewish as the religious traditions that offer so much meaning to others, that I felt and feel most Jewish.

Editor's notes:

1. *Shabbat* means "Sabbath," which is celebrated by Jews from sundown on Friday through sundown Saturday.

2. The concept "secular Jew" is open to various interpretations. It refers generally to a person who is ethnically Jewish and identifies with that ethnic identity, but is not religious and perhaps may not believe in God. In this essay, the term suggests an identification with ethical and social ideals learned from the Jewish community, but also implies inclusiveness, a sense of identification as well with non-Jews who share those same ideals (e.g., "social justice").

3. The Abraham Lincoln Brigade was made of American volunteers in the Spanish Civil War against Francisco Franco and fascism.

4. Sholem Aleichem was a famous Yiddish author; *Fiddler on the Roof* is based loosely on one of his stories. Emma Goldman was an anarchist and political activist. *The Diary of Anne Frank* relates the story of a German Jewish girl whose family took refuge in the Netherlands, was betrayed to the Nazis during the German occupation, and deported to the concentration camps; she died in Bergen-Belsen concentration camp. Joe Hill was a radical American labor activist whose execution for murder was controversial and made him a folk hero. Abolitionist Harriet Tubman, herself a former slave, rescued African American slaves through the Underground Railroad during the Civil War. Roberto Clemente was born in Puerto Rico and died tragically in a plane carrying relief supplies to earthquake victims in Nicaragua, the last day of 1972. He is a member of the Baseball Hall of Fame. A. Philip Randolph was a twentieth-century African American Civil Rights leader. Sojourner Truth, an emancipated slave, was an abolitionist and women's rights activist. César Chávez was a Mexican American migrant farmer and labor activist. This diverse list of persons all embody and worked toward the ideal of social justice.

641

BEFORE YOU READ: Rodriguez's essay talks about the significance of names and their ethnic associations for personal identity. What does your name tell others (or not tell others) about you?

SURNAMES REFLECT CHANGING FACE OF AMERICA*
Richard Rodriguez

Richard Rodriguez is a contributing editor at New America Media in San Francisco. He has written an autobiographical trilogy on class, ethnicity, and race: *Hunger of Memory* (1982), *Days of Obligation: An Argument with My Mexican Father* (1992), and *Brown: The Last Discovery of America* (2002). He received a 1997 George Foster Peabody Award for his *NewsHour* essays on American life.

*Richard Rodriguez, "Surnames Reflect the Changing Face of America," *NewsHour*, PBS, January 25, 2008, http://www.pbs.org/newshour/bb/social_issues/jan-june08/name_01-25.html (accessed June 26, 2008). You can also hear the broadcast of the essay at this Web address.

For Discussion: The photo illustrates this statement from the essay: "Our ascending numbers frighten many Americans who see Hispanics as overwhelming this country." How does the photograph potentially provide support for this statement?

For Writing: The claim of Rodriguez's essay, by contrast, makes a very different claim. State the claim. Analyze the essay as refuting rather than reinforcing the message of this photo.

Context: The caption reads: An American Street Scene. Rodriguez delivered the essay below on the PBS *NewsHour*. This photograph illustrates what he refers to as "the hatinization of the United States," which some people find troubling.

1   Many Americans are troubled regarding the Latinization of the United States, the ubiquitous brown faces in the crowd, Spanish everywhere. On nativist talk radio, in the speeches of politicians, a legend of illegality as old as cowboy America attaches to anyone related to Latin America, whether or not one is legally here.

2   It made the news recently that "Garcia" and "Rodriguez" are now among the top 10 most common American surnames. We Hispanics have become a people whose presence gets told by such numbers, our ascending numbers. Our ascending numbers frighten many Americans who see Hispanics as overwhelming this country. But Hispanics are more than numbers. We are Catholics. We are Evangelical Protestants. We come in all colors, and races, and talents, and sensibilities. We are judges. We are gang-bangers. We are U.S. Marines. We are retired. We are crowding desert high schools.

3   In the 1990 census, Garcia ranked 18th, Rodriguez 22nd. A decade later, the Garcias have ascended 10 rungs, the Rodriguezs 13.

This numerical rise means simply that descendants of the Spanish empire are now living alongside descendants of the English empire in places like Kentucky and Iowa, where they have rarely lived side-by-side before.

4   Throughout the Spanish-speaking world, the habit is for her surname to be linked by a hyphen with his. In the next American census, the ranking of Spanish surnames is certain to be confused, as number 11 marries number 10. America is a generous society. But with the great thrust of immigration in the 19th century, many Americans grew uneasy with eastern and southern European names. Often the children of immigrants, a generation removed from Ellis Island, attempted discretion by shortening their name or adopting an Anglo-Saxon name. America, the great leveler.

5   On the playing field, last names were apt to get shorn. Carl Yastrzemski became "Yaz" in America. Nowadays, the nation's sports writers name America's best baseball player "A-Rod." "Rod" was also the name classmates gave me as early as grammar school. My

"Rodriguez" got shortened the same year Elvis Presley entered the Army. Rod seemed to me as American as a crew-cut.

6   Because Hispanics are an ethnic category joined loosely by culture, Hispanic advertising agencies and Spanish-language television stations daily impress on us how our cultural identity is tied to the language of Spain. Often, as Hispanics grow assimilated in the U.S., paradoxically they give their surnames baroque pronunciations. Tiffany Rodriguez goes to college and becomes "Tiffany Rodrihuez."

7   Permit me to indulge vanity by talking about my name, first and last. On *Google*, our national yellow pages, I found thousands of Rodriguez Richards. Richard Rodriguez is a building commissioner in Chicago. Richard Rodriguez is a photographer. Richard Rodriguez is under arrest. Richard Rodriguez is a high school wrestler. Richard Rodriguez is

a Protestant minister. The least-daunted among us, Richard Rodriguez holds the Guinness world's record for time spent riding on roller coasters.

8   On September 11th, America suffered a trauma from which we have not recovered. We are anxious now about people we have not seen before. In the days after, when the country was still in mourning, I found Richard Rodriguez among the lists of the dead at the World Trade Center. It is unsettling to see one's name attached to another life in the morning paper. It is disturbing to see one's own name in a list of the dead. Richard Rodriguez, from a generation younger than mine, was still early in his adult life, aged 31.

9   Richard Rodriguez was a police officer for the New York–New Jersey Port Authority, an American killed in a dangerous time.

10   Rest in peace, Richard Rodriguez.

11   I'm Richard Rodriguez.

643

Questions to Help You Think and Write about Race, Culture, and Identity

1. Demographers predict that whites will become a minority race sometime in the first half of the twenty-first century. Consider Dyer's idea that the concept of "whiteness" be racialized. What effect might that have now, at the beginning of the twenty-first century? What effect might it have later in the century, if whites become a "racial minority"?

2. Daly writes about students in a sociology class at Penn State University who participate in DNA tests to determine their genetic ancestry. How would you feel about participating in such a study? How would you adjust to learning that your racial makeup is different from what you had thought it was? Should this information matter to individuals? Why or why not?

3. Imagine that Dr. Martin Luther King Jr., and K. A. Dilday have been invited on Oprah's show to consider how Americans can better promote racial equality for all citizens. What position might each of these speakers take? What might be their claims? Would they agree or disagree in their opinions?

4. "Reading Images" in this section of "The Reader" shows how "photo-negative" images—the reversal of black and white—can alter your perception of familiar

figures, groups, and settings. Select a photograph, famous painting, advertisement, or some other image and "recolor" it to change the race/color/identity of the figures. Then write an analysis of your visual argument that examines how the color reversal either makes "whiteness visible" or calls into question some cultural assumptions embodied in the image or in the figures depicted.

5. Chang, Halper, and Rodriguez all discuss the problems of identifying with a particular religious, ethnic, or cultural group. Identify one group with which you identify. Create a chart: in the left column, list the typical, or even stereotypical, characteristics associated with this group; in the right column, consider whether you see these characteristics in yourself. What are the limits of group identification?

6. Halper's essay is based on an oxymoron, or the simultaneous existence of two incompatible things: secularism and Judaism. Write an essay about an important paradox in your own identity. Begin the essay with this statement completed: "My name is _____, and I am a ____ _____. I've been _____ for a little over ____ years now." For instance, "My name is Joe, and I am a compulsive procrastinator. I've been a compulsive procrastinator for a little over eighteen years now." Or, "My name is Joe, and I am a cheerful pessimist."

7. "I Have a Dream" is a classic piece of American oratory that, by drawing on sources ranging from the Declaration of Independence to the Bible, places its author within a certain tradition of wisdom and knowledge. Analyze the speech as an argument from authority in which King establishes a persuasive *ethos* by placing himself in this tradition of wisdom. What is the speech's claim and how does King support that claim? Look for clues to his *ethos* in the photograph of Dr. King delivering the speech and even listen to a recording of the speech. (Audio clips are readily available on the Web.) How do voice, gesture, dress, and general appearance support King's depiction of himself?

8. As background work for his essay, Richard Rodriguez Googled his own name. Try this same exercise with your name. How many different kinds of people can you find with either your first and last name (or just your last name, if the first attempt does not yield enough examples)? What can you infer or imagine about the group of people who share name as a cultural "type"? Create your own "label" for this new group or community. Is it possible to find common threads? Describe these threads or, if you find no threads at all, discuss the significance of that lack of commonality.

9. Imagine that you are going to live in another country where the race, language, religion, and culture are different from your own. What aspects of your culture would you want to keep? What would you be willing to give up? Do you think you would experience the identity crisis Kondo describes? How might your sense of personal identity be affected by such a relocation? What would you do to try to adjust to your new environment?

SECTION  5

Issues concerning the Environment

The Issues

A. Is Global Warming a Problem, and If It Is, What Can Be Done about It?

Four authors analyze the political, social, and human ramifications of the debate about global warming. Al Gore argues that global warming is a real threat and that addressing the problem is a moral imperative. Tom Harris challenges Gore's fundamental claim by citing scientists who disagree with him. Gregg Easterbrook, expressing optimism, recommends local solutions rather than international controls. Brian Clark makes practical suggestions for individual action. See also images of the polar bear (page 9), the abandoned home (page 28), the Rhône glacier (page 215) and the *Planet Gore* blog (page 271); and the essays "The Future of Life" (pages 325–326), and "Let's Stop Scaring Ourselves" (pages 201–203).

B. How Can We Resolve the Economy versus Environment Debate?

The essays in this section consider environmental issues within a global context. George Will raises the question, How much will nations be willing to pay to change the climate? "Reading Images: Coal Mining and the Environment" depicts the impact of coal production in two distant locales. Erik Reece's investigation of mountaintop removal in Appalachia argues that this method of mining coal serves the economic interests of big business at the expense of poor people's health, happiness, and traditional way of life. Claire Andre and Manuel Velasquez make the argument that not only humans but also animals should be considered when debating the priorities of the economy and the environment. Finally, Brian Wingfield reports on the ways in which the needs of environment and economy are coming together in the green-job sector. See also images of corn power (page 217), animal rights (page 288), and the advertisement "Liberate Your Cool" (page 216); and the essays "The Race for Survival" (pages 112–113) and "Alaskan Wolf Management" (pages 469–478).

Web Sites for Further Exploration and Research

U.S. Environmental Protection Agency, Climate Change	http://www.epa.gov/climatechange/
United Nations Environment Programme (UNEP), Themes, Climate Change	http://www.unep.org/themes/climatechange/
Pew Center on Global Climate Change	http://www.pewclimate.org/
Ohio Valley Environmental Coalition	http://www.ohvec.org/
Center for Virtual Appalachia	http://cva.morehead-st.edu/
Chinamining.org	http://www.chinamining.org/
Mongabay.com Preface page to Rain Forests	http://rainforests.mongabay.com/preface.htm
World Bank	http://www.worldbank.org/
World Wildlife Fund	http://www.worldwildlife.org/
Amazon Conservation Team	http://www.amazonteam.org/

Films and Literature Related to the Environment

Films *The 11th Hour*, 2007; *Big Business*, 1988; *Erin Brockovich*, 2000; *The Great Global Warming Swindle*, 2007; *An Inconvenient Truth*, 2006; *Silent Spring*, 1993; *The White Planet*, 2006; *Who Killed the Electric Car?* 2006; *The Unforeseen*, 2008.

Literature novels and nonfiction: *Arctic Dreams* by Barry Lopez; *Ecology of a Cracker Childhood* by Janisse Ray; *The Falls* by Joyce Carol Oates; *An Inconvenient Truth* by Al Gore; *Silent Spring* by Rachel Carson; *Walden* by Henry Thoreau; essays: "After the Clearcut" by Gary Snyder; "Living Like Weasels" by Annie Dillard; "Thinking Like a Mountain" by Aldo Leopold; short story: "The Sound of Thunder" by Ray Bradbury; poem: "Polar Bear Dreams Himself Swimming" by Ari Berk.

The Rhetorical Situation

Modern debates over the environment stretch back at least to the 1960s. In 1962, nature writer and marine biologist Rachel Carson published *Silent Spring*, which attacked the chemicals industry by imagining a time when pesticides would, through a chain of ecological events, kill off all the songbirds. The activism of pioneers such as Carson led to the establishment of the Environmental Protection

Agency in 1970, but many changes in the political climate and the economy have sustained ongoing conflict and negotiation among environmental groups, the levels and agencies of government, and the business sector.

In the southeastern United States, mountaintop removal, although an efficient and profitable method of mining coal, literally flattens mountains, destroys forests, and fills streams with soil. Among the problems that have been blamed on mountaintop removal are water and noise pollution, flash floods, cancer, unemployment, and the loss of community and traditional ways of life. The struggle over mountaintop removal has been complicated most recently by uncertainty about how liberally the Clean Water Act, which bans mining near streams, should and will be interpreted by the government and the courts. The northern spotted owl of the Pacific Northwest became an environmental icon in the 1990s, when this reclusive bird was placed on the Endangered Species List and logging was banned in its habitat. Today, despite these protections, the spotted owl is being threatened again, this time by barred owls who have moved into its territory. Loggers and many people in communities that formerly relied on the timber industry are calling again for the government to relax its restrictions on the logging of old growth forest. To complicate matters further, the policies and practices of one nation can affect not only its own citizens but also the global community. China, like Appalachia, relies heavily on energy from coal; sulfur dioxide pollution produced by the burning of coal in that country may have begun to affect other locales, ranging from South Korea to Hawaii.

In all of the geographical areas pictured and discussed in this section, destruction of the environment is linked in complicated ways to poverty. In the Appalachian areas where mountaintop removal occurs, unemployment can be quite high, rising as high as ten to fifteen percent of the population. Troublingly, although mining jobs pay better than average, it is not clear whether this production practice creates new jobs or further unemployment. Placing the spotted owl on the endangered species list cost 30,000 jobs in Washington State alone; loggers from the area have been forced to seek work in other regions and industries, often with a significant loss of income. Migrants have flocked to the cities in industrialized China, but many harm their health at the same time.

The rain forests in South America and Africa are some of the most delicate and damaged ecosystems in the world. They have been severely damaged from forces ranging from elephants to slash-and-burn subsistence farming, but most of all from indiscriminate logging of valuable forests, an industry that rarely benefits the inhabitants of those forest areas.

There is hope, however. For Americans there is a rising interest in so-called green collar jobs. This shift can particularly benefit low-income Americans by creating jobs that must be performed here: a job putting up solar panels in homes or constructing wind farms cannot be outsourced to developing countries. "Green careers" for scientists and engineers will also need to be developed to create the environment-saving materials used in these jobs.

International organizations are beginning to acknowledge how small the globe seems to have become. The United Nations Climate Change Conference in Bali (December 2007) recognized both the responsibility of affluent nations, such as the United States, for global environmental depletion and the rising impact of

647

developing nations, such as China, on the environment. In a world that is increasingly interdependent, what happens in one place can have unexpected consequences for other places and peoples. What has sometimes been called the "butterfly effect" suggests that humans, while responsible for the harm inflicted on others by the desecration of the environment worldwide, also have the opportunity and the power to create change by even the smallest, most ordinary attempts at resource conservation.

A. Is Global Warming a Problem, and If It Is, What Can Be Done about It?

> **BEFORE YOU READ:** Based on your own experience, are there signs of global warming in your own community? What overall effect might such an ecological change have on your local environment? What smaller effects might result?

AN INCONVENIENT TRUTH, INTRODUCTION*
Al Gore

Al Gore, former vice president of the United States, lectures on and in other ways promotes solving global warming. In 2007, Gore and the U.N.'s Intergovernmental Panel on Climate Change were awarded a Nobel Peace Prize.

1   After more than thirty years as a student of the climate crisis, I have a lot to share. I have tried to tell this story in a way that will interest all kinds of readers. My hope is that those who read the book and see the film will begin to feel, as I have for a long time, that global warming is not just about science and that it is not just a political issue. It is really a moral issue.

2   Although it is true that politics at times must play a crucial role in solving this problem, this is the kind of challenge that ought to completely transcend partisanship. So, whether you are a Democrat or a Republican, whether you voted for me or not, I very much hope that you will sense that my goal is to share with you both my passion for the Earth and my deep sense of concern for its fate. It is impossible to feel one without the other when you know all the facts.

3   I also want to convey my strong feeling that what we are facing is not just a cause for alarm, it is paradoxically also a cause for hope. As many know, the Chinese expression for "crisis" consists of two characters side by side. The first is the symbol for "danger," the second the symbol for "opportunity."

4   The climate crisis is, indeed, extremely dangerous. In fact, it is a true planetary emergency. Two thousand scientists, in a hundred countries, working for more than twenty years in the most elaborate and well-organized scientific collaboration in the history of humankind, have forged an exceptionally strong consensus that all the nations on Earth must work together to solve the crisis of global warming.

*Al Gore, from Introduction, *An Inconvenient Truth: The Planetary Emergency of Global Warming and What We Can Do about It* (New York: Rodale Books, 2006), 1–2.

5   The voluminous evidence now strongly suggests that unless we act boldly and quickly to deal with the underlying causes of global warming, our world will undergo a string of terrible catastrophes, including more and stronger storms like Hurricane Katrina, in both the Atlantic and the Pacific. We are melting the North Polar ice cap and virtually all of the mountain glaciers in the world. We are destabilizing the massive mound of ice on Greenland and the equally enormous mass of ice propped up on top of islands in West Antarctica, threatening a worldwide increase in sea levels of as much as twenty feet. The list of what is now endangered due to global warming also includes the continued stable configuration of ocean and wind currents that has been in place since before the first cities were built almost 10,000 years ago.

6   We are dumping so much carbon dioxide into the Earth's environment that we have literally changed the relationship between the Earth and the Sun. So much of that CO_2 is being absorbed into the oceans that if we continue at the current rate, we will increase the saturation of calcium carbonate to levels that will prevent formation of corals and interfere with the making of shells by any sea creature.

7   Global warming, along with the cutting and burning of forests and other critical habitats, is causing the loss of living species at a level comparable to the extinction event that wiped out the dinosaurs 65 million years ago. That event was believed to have been caused by a giant asteroid. This time it is not an asteroid colliding with the Earth and wreaking havoc; it is us.

8   Last year, the national academies of science in the eleven most influential nations came together to jointly call on every nation to "acknowledge that the threat of climate change is clear and increasing" and declare that the "scientific understanding of climate changes is now sufficiently clear to justify nations taking prompt action."

9   So the message is unmistakably clear. This crisis means "danger"! Why do our leaders seem not to hear such a clear warning? Is it simply that it is inconvenient for them to hear the truth? If the truth is unwelcome, it may seem easier just to ignore it. But we know from bitter experience that the consequences of doing so can be dire.

10   For example, when we were first warned that the levees were about to break in New Orleans because of Hurricane Katrina, those warnings were ignored. Later, a bipartisan group of members of Congress chaired by Representative Tom Davis (R-VA.), chairman of the House Government Reform Committee, said in an official report, "The White House failed to act on the massive amounts of information at its disposal," and that a "blinding lack of situational awareness and disjointed decision-making needlessly compounded and prolonged Katrina's horror."

11   Today, we are hearing and seeing dire warnings of the worst potential catastrophe in the history of human civilization: a global climate crisis that is deepening and rapidly becoming more dangerous than anything we have ever faced. And yet these clear warnings are also being met with a "blinding lack of situational awareness"—in this case, by the Congress, as well as the president. As Martin Luther King Jr. said in a speech not long before his assassination: "We are now faced with the fact, my friends, that tomorrow is today. We are confronted with the fierce urgency of now. In this unfolding conundrum of life and history, there is such a thing as being too late."[1]

12   Procrastination is still the thief of time. Life often leaves us standing bare, naked, and dejected with a lost opportunity. The tide in the affairs of men does not remain at flood—it ebbs. We may cry out desperately for time to pause in her passage, but time is adamant to every plea and rushes on. Over the bleached bones and jumbled residues of numerous civilizations are written the pathetic words, "Too late." There is an invisible book of life that faithfully records our vigilance in our neglect. Omar Khayyam is

right: "The moving finger writes, and having writ moves on."[2]

13   But along with the danger we face from global warming, this crisis also brings unprecedented opportunities. What are the opportunities such a crisis also offers? They include not just new jobs and new profits, though there will be plenty of both: we can build clean engines; we can harness the sun and the wind; we can stop wasting energy; we can use our planet's plentiful coal resources without heating the planet.

14   The procrastinators and deniers would have us believe this will be expensive. But in recent years, dozens of companies have cut emissions of heat-trapping gases while saving money. Some of the world's largest companies are moving aggressively to capture the enormous economic opportunities offered by a clean energy future.

15   But there's something even more precious to be gained if we do the right thing. The climate crisis also offers us the chance to experience what very few generations in history have had the privilege of knowing: a

generational mission; the exhilaration of a compelling moral purpose; a shared and unifying cause; the thrill of being forced by circumstances to put aside the pettiness and conflict that so often stifle the restless human need for transcendence; the opportunity to rise.

16   When we do rise, it will fill our spirits and bind us together. Those who are now suffocating in cynicism and despair will be able to breathe freely. Those who are now suffering from a loss of meaning in their lives will find hope. When we rise, we will experience an epiphany as we discover that this crisis is not really about politics at all. It is a moral and spiritual challenge.

Editor's notes:

1. From "Beyond Vietnam: A Time to Break Silence," a speech delivered by Martin Luther King Jr. on April 4, 1967, to a meeting of the Clergy and Laity Concerned, at Riverside Church in New York City.

2. Omar Khayyam was an eleventh-century Persian poet. He is best known for the *Rubaiyat of Omar Khayyam*.

BEFORE YOU READ: One problem facing ordinary citizens when evaluating scientific controversies is that we must rely on evidence and interpretations provided by experts. When you cannot judge an issue based on your own knowledge and experience, what kinds of authorities do you tend to trust?

AL GORE, GLOBAL WARMING, INCONVENIENT TRUTH: SCIENTISTS RESPOND TO GORE'S WARNINGS OF CLIMATE CATASTROPHE[*]

Tom Harris

Tom Harris is an Ottawa-based mechanical engineer and the executive director of the Natural Resources Stewardship Project. This essay was one of a group of essays critical of *An Inconvenient Truth* published in the *Canada Free Press*.

1   "Scientists have an independent obligation to respect and present the truth as they see it," Al Gore sensibly asserts in his film *An Inconvenient Truth*, showing at Cumberland 4 Cinemas in Toronto since June 2 [2006]. With that outlook in mind, what do

---

*Tom Harris, "Al Gore, Global Warming, Inconvenient Truth: Scientists Respond to Gore's Warnings of Climate Catastrophe," *Canada Free Press*, June 12, 2006, http://www.canadafreepress.com/2006/harris061206.htm (accessed June 25, 2008).

world climate experts actually think about the science of his movie?

2   Professor Bob Carter of the Marine Geophysical Laboratory at James Cook University, in Australia gives what, for many Canadians, is a surprising assessment: "Gore's circumstantial arguments are so weak that they are pathetic. It is simply incredible that they, and his film, are commanding public attention." But surely Carter is merely part of what most people regard as a tiny cadre of "climate change skeptics" who disagree with the "vast majority of scientists" Gore cites?

3   No; Carter is one of hundreds of highly qualified non-governmental, non-industry, non-lobby group climate experts who contest the hypothesis that human emissions of carbon dioxide (CO_2) are causing significant global climate change. "Climate experts" is the operative term here. Why? Because what Gore's "majority of scientists" think is immaterial when only a very small fraction of them actually work in the climate field.

4   Even among that fraction, many focus their studies on the impacts of climate change; biologists, for example, who study everything from insects to polar bears to poison ivy. "While many are highly skilled researchers, they generally do not have special knowledge about the causes of global climate change," explains former University of Winnipeg climatology professor Dr. Tim Ball. "They usually can tell us only about the effects of changes in the local environment where they conduct their studies."

5   This is highly valuable knowledge, but doesn't make them climate change cause experts, only climate impact experts. So we have a smaller fraction. But it becomes smaller still. Among experts who actually examine the causes of change on a global scale, many concentrate their research on designing and enhancing

computer models of hypothetical futures. "These models have been consistently wrong in all their scenarios," asserts Ball. "Since modelers concede computer outputs are not 'predictions' but are in fact merely scenarios, they are negligent in letting policy-makers and the public think they are actually making forecasts."

6   We should listen most to scientists who use real data to try to understand what nature is actually telling us about the causes and extent of global climate change. In this relatively small community, there is no consensus, despite what Gore and others would suggest. Here is a small sample of the side of the debate we almost never hear.

7   Appearing before the Commons Committee on Environment and Sustainable Development last year, Carleton University paleoclimatologist Professor Tim Patterson testified, "There is no meaningful correlation between CO_2 levels and Earth's temperature over this [geologic] time frame. In fact, when CO_2 levels were over ten times higher than they are now, about 450 million years ago, the planet was in the depths of the absolute coldest period in the last half billion years." Patterson asked the committee, "On the basis of this evidence, how could anyone still believe that the recent relatively small increase in CO_2 levels would be the major cause of the past century's modest warming?" Patterson concluded his testimony by explaining what his research and "hundreds of other studies" reveal: on all time scales, there is very good correlation between Earth's temperature and natural celestial phenomena such as changes in the brightness of the Sun.

8   Dr. Boris Winterhalter, former marine researcher at the Geological Survey of Finland and professor in marine geology, University of Helsinki, takes apart Gore's

dramatic display of Antarctic glaciers collapsing into the sea. "The breaking glacier wall is a normally occurring phenomenon which is due to the normal advance of a glacier," says Winterhalter. "In Antarctica the temperature is low enough to prohibit melting of the ice front, so if the ice is grounded, it has to break off in beautiful ice cascades. If the water is deep enough icebergs will form."

9   Dr. Wibjorn Karlen, emeritus professor, Dept. of Physical Geography and Quaternary Geology, Stockholm University, Sweden, admits, "Some small areas in the Antarctic Peninsula have broken up recently, just like it has done back in time. The temperature in this part of Antarctica has increased recently, probably because of a small change in the position of the low pressure systems." But Karlen clarifies that the "mass balance" of Antarctica is positive—more snow is accumulating than melting off. As a result, Ball explains, there is an increase in the "calving" of icebergs as the ice dome of Antarctica is growing and flowing to the oceans. When Greenland and Antarctica are assessed together, "their mass balance is considered to possibly increase the sea level by 0.03 mm/year—not much of an effect," Karlen concludes.

10   The Antarctica has survived warm and cold events over millions of years. A meltdown is simply not a realistic scenario in the foreseeable future. Gore tells us in the film, "Starting in 1970, there was a precipitous drop-off in the amount and extent and thickness of the Arctic ice cap." This is misleading, according to Ball: "The survey that Gore cites was a single transect across one part of the Arctic basin in the month of October during the 1960s when we were in the middle of the cooling period. The 1990 runs were done in the warmer month of September, using a wholly different technology." Karlen explains that a paper published in 2003 by University of Alaska

professor Igor Polyakov shows that the region of the Arctic where rising temperature is supposedly endangering polar bears showed fluctuations since 1940 but no overall temperature rise. "For several published records it is a decrease for the last 50 years," says Karlen.

11   Dr. Dick Morgan, former advisor to the World Meteorological Organization and climatology researcher at University of Exeter, U.K. gives the details: "There has been some decrease in ice thickness in the Canadian Arctic over the past 30 years but no melt down. The Canadian Ice Service records show that from 1971–1981 there was average, to above average, ice thickness. From 1981–1982 there was a sharp decrease of 15% but there was a quick recovery to average, to slightly above average, values from 1983–1995. A sharp drop of 30% occurred again 1996–1998 and since then there has been a steady increase to reach near normal conditions since 2001."

12   Concerning Gore's beliefs about worldwide warming, Morgan points out that, in addition to the cooling in the NW Atlantic, massive areas of cooling are found in the North and South Pacific Ocean; the whole of the Amazon Valley; the north coast of South America and the Caribbean; the eastern Mediterranean, Black Sea, Caucasus and Red Sea; New Zealand and even the Ganges Valley in India. Morgan explains, "Had the IPCC used the standard parameter for climate change (the 30 year average) and used an equal area projection, instead of the Mercator (which doubled the area of warming in Alaska, Siberia and the Antarctic Ocean), warming and cooling would have been almost in balance."

13   Gore's point that 200 cities and towns in the American West set all time high temperature records is also misleading according to Dr. Roy Spencer, Principal

Research Scientist at The University of Alabama in Huntsville. "It is not unusual for some locations, out of the thousands of cities and towns in the U.S., to set all-time records," he says. "The actual data shows that overall, recent temperatures in the U.S. were not unusual."

14   Carter does not pull his punches about Gore's activism, "The man is an embarrassment to U.S. science and its many fine practitioners, a lot of whom know (but feel unable to state publicly) that his

propaganda crusade is mostly based on junk science."

15   In April sixty of the world's leading experts in the field asked Prime Minister Harper to order a thorough public review of the science of climate change, something that has never happened in Canada. Considering what's at stake—either the end of civilization, if you believe Gore, or a waste of billions of dollars, if you believe his opponents—it seems like a reasonable request.

BEFORE YOU READ: As Easterbrook's essay points out, environmental problems are not new in the United States. What kinds of regulations, policies, and local practices are already in effect to help protect the environment in your community?

SOME CONVENIENT TRUTHS*

Gregg Easterbrook

Gregg Easterbrook is a contributing editor for *The Atlantic* magazine and a visiting fellow at the Brookings Institution, a nonprofit public policy organization. He is also the author of *The Progress Paradox.*

1   If there is now a scientific consensus that global warming must be taken seriously, there is also a related political consensus: that the issue is Gloom City. In *An Inconvenient Truth*, Al Gore warns of sea levels rising to engulf New York and San Francisco and implies that only wrenching lifestyle sacrifice can save us. The opposing view is just as glum. Even mild restrictions on greenhouse gases could "cripple our economy," Republican Senator Kit Bond of Missouri said in 2003. Other conservatives suggest that greenhouse-gas rules for Americans would be pointless anyway, owing to increased fossil-fuel use in China and India. When commentators hash

this issue out, it's often a contest to see which side can sound more pessimistic.

2   Here's a different way of thinking about the greenhouse effect: that action to prevent runaway global warming may prove cheap, practical, effective, and totally consistent with economic growth. Which makes a body wonder: Why is such environmental optimism absent from American political debate?

3   Greenhouse gases are an air-pollution problem—and all previous air-pollution problems have been reduced faster and more cheaply than predicted, without economic harm. Some of these problems once seemed scary and intractable, just as greenhouse gases

---

*Gregg Easterbrook, "Some Convenient Truths," *Atlantic Monthly*, September 2006, 29–30.

seem today. About forty years ago urban smog was increasing so fast that President Lyndon Johnson warned, "Either we stop poisoning our air or we become a nation [in] gas masks groping our way through dying cities." During Ronald Reagan's presidency, emissions of chlorofluorocarbons, or CFCs, threatened to deplete the stratospheric ozone layer.[1] As recently as George H. W. Bush's administration, acid rain was said to threaten a "new silent spring" of dead Appalachian forests.

4   But in each case, strong regulations were enacted, and what happened? Since 1970, smog-forming air pollution has declined by a third to a half. Emissions of CFCs have been nearly eliminated, and studies suggest that ozone-layer replenishment is beginning. Acid rain, meanwhile, has declined by a third since 1990, while Appalachian forest health has improved sharply.

5   Most progress against air pollution has been cheaper than expected. Smog controls on automobiles, for example, were predicted to cost thousands of dollars for each vehicle. Today's new cars emit less than 2 percent as much smog-forming pollution as the cars of 1970, and the cars are still as affordable today as they were then. Acid-rain control has cost about 10 percent of what was predicted in 1990, when Congress enacted new rules. At that time, opponents said the regulations would cause a "clean-air recession"; instead, the economy boomed.

6   Greenhouse gases, being global, are the biggest air-pollution problem ever faced. And because widespread fossil-fuel use is inevitable for some time to come, the best-case scenario for the next few decades may be a slowing of the rate of greenhouse-gas buildup, to prevent runaway climate change. Still, the basic pattern observed in all other forms of air-pollution control—rapid progress at low cost—should repeat for greenhouse-gas controls.

7   Yet a paralyzing negativism dominates global-warming politics. Environmentalists depict climate change as nearly unstoppable; skeptics speak of the problem as either imaginary (the "greatest hoax ever perpetrated," in the words of Senator James Inhofe, chairman [until January 2007] of the Senate's environment committee) or ruinously expensive to address.

8   Even conscientious politicians may struggle for views that aren't dismal. Mandy Grunwald, a Democratic political consultant, says, "When political candidates talk about new energy sources, they use a positive, can-do vocabulary. Voters have personal experience with energy use, so they can relate to discussion of solutions. If you say a car can use a new kind of fuel, this makes intuitive sense to people. But global warming is of such scale and magnitude, people don't have any commonsense way to grasp what the solutions would be. So political candidates tend to talk about the greenhouse effect in a depressing way."

9   One reason the global-warming problem seems so daunting is that the success of previous antipollution efforts remains something of a secret. Polls show that Americans think the air is getting dirtier, not cleaner, perhaps because media coverage of the environment rarely if ever mentions improvements. For instance, did you know that smog and acid rain . . . continued to diminish throughout George W. Bush's presidency?

10   One might expect Democrats to trumpet the decline of air pollution, which stands as one of government's leading postwar achievements. But just as Republicans have found they can bash Democrats by falsely accusing them of being soft on defense, Democrats have found they can bash Republicans by falsely accusing them of destroying the environment. If that's your argument, you might skip over the evidence that many environmental trends are positive. One might also

expect Republicans to trumpet the reduction of air pollution, since it signifies responsible behavior by industry. But to acknowledge that air pollution has declined would require Republicans to say the words, "The regulations worked."

11   Does it matter that so many in politics seem so pessimistic about the prospect of addressing global warming? Absolutely. Making the problem appear unsolvable encourages a sort of listless fatalism, blunting the drive to take first steps toward a solution. Historically, first steps against air pollution have often led to pleasant surprises. When Congress, in 1970, mandated major reductions in smog caused by automobiles, even many supporters of the rule feared it would be hugely expensive. But the catalytic converter was not practical then; soon it was perfected, and suddenly, major reductions in smog became affordable. Even a small step by the United States against greenhouse gases could lead to a similar breakthrough.

12   And to those who worry that any greenhouse-gas reductions in the United States will be swamped by new emissions from China and India, here's a final reason to be optimistic: technology can move across borders with considerable speed. Today it's not clear that American inventors or entrepreneurs can make money by reducing greenhouse gases, so relatively few are trying. But suppose the United States regulated greenhouse gases, using its own domestic program, not the cumbersome Kyoto Protocol; then America's formidable entrepreneurial and engineering communities would fully engage the problem.[2] Innovations pioneered here could spread throughout the world, and suddenly rapid global warming would not seem inevitable.

13   The two big technical advances against smog—the catalytic converter and the chemical engineering that removes pollutants from gasoline at the refinery stage—were invented in the United States. The big economic advance against acid rain—a credit-trading

system that gives power-plant managers a profit incentive to reduce pollution—was pioneered here as well. These advances are now spreading globally. Smog and acid rain are still increasing in some parts of the world, but the trend lines suggest that both will decline fairly soon, even in developing nations. For instance, two decades ago urban smog was rising at a dangerous rate in Mexico; today it is diminishing there, though the country's population continues to grow. A short time ago declining smog and acid rain in developing nations seemed an impossibility; today declining greenhouse gases seem an impossibility. The history of air-pollution control says otherwise.

14   Americans love challenges, and preventing artificial climate change is just the sort of technological and economic challenge at which this nation excels. It only remains for the right politician to recast the challenge in practical, optimistic tones. Gore seldom has, and [George W.] Bush seems to have no interest in trying. But cheap and fast improvement is not a pipe dream; it is the pattern of previous efforts against air pollution. The only reason runaway global warming seems unstoppable is that we have not yet tried to stop it.

Editor's notes:

1. Chlorofluorocarbons (CFCs) are organic compounds that contain carbon, chlorine, and fluorine atoms. They are highly effective refrigerants developed to replace toxic substances that were used in refrigerators, air conditioners, and aerosol sprays. The most commonly known CFC is Freon. In the 1970s, scientists at the University of California, Irvine identified CFCs as contributing to the depletion of the ozone layer, a significant factor in global warming.

2. The Kyoto Protocol, the result of the International Framework Convention on Climate Change, was put in place in 2005; the United States (under the George W. Bush administration) did not ratify the protocol. (A protocol is a rule governing procedures of diplomacy.)

> **BEFORE YOU READ:** Originally identified by Edward N. Lorenz, a mathematician and meteorologist, the concept "butterfly effect" describes complex events such as climate change in terms of small, apparently unconnected events. From your own experience (not necessarily on the subject of the environment), can you think of an example of the butterfly effect at work?

THE BUTTERFLY EFFECT AND THE ENVIRONMENT: HOW TINY ACTIONS CAN SAVE THE WORLD*

Brian Clark

Brian Clark's blog *copyblogger* was a 2007 finalist for the Best Web Development Web log in the 2007 Bloggie Awards, at http://2007.bloggies.com/. He writes that "This post is my contribution to Blog Action Day [http://blogactionday.org/], joining thousands of other bloggers to write about one topic for a single day. This year's topic is the environment."

1   The acre of land my family and I live on rests on a heavily-wooded elevation, which provides a panoramic view of a sparkling lake to the south. It's quite a departure from the suburban tract home I grew up in, and I'm hoping my kids end up with fond childhood memories of frolicking in a beautiful natural setting.

2   One remarkable thing about the property is the amount of butterflies it attracts, no doubt due to the variety of plant species that are permitted to grow undisturbed. My 5-year-old daughter and her little brother spend large chunks of time hopelessly chasing after scores of Monarchs and other brightly-colored, flitting butterflies.

3   And all I can think about is the havoc these little critters are having on the weather in China. Not the kids . . . the butterflies.

THE BUTTERFLY EFFECT

4   The Butterfly Effect is a term that has leaked into popular culture thanks to time-travel stories, but its actual meaning is steeped in no-nonsense science. From a technical standpoint, it refers to the sensitive dependence on initial conditions in chaos theory.

5   In plain language, tiny changes within a complex system lead to results that are impossible to predict. For example, the flapping of a butterfly's wings could create tiny changes in the atmosphere that lead to violent weather conditions elsewhere on the planet.

6   Although the concept has been around since 1890, the Butterfly Effect gained popular acceptance in 1961 due to weather prediction modeling performed by meteorologist Edward Lorenz. He found that changes that should have been statistically insignificant led to completely different weather scenarios. The butterfly analogy began in 1972, when Lorenz delivered a speech entitled *Predictability: Does the Flap of a Butterfly's Wings in Brazil Set Off a Tornado in Texas?*

7   What's that got to do with the environment?

8   Well, given the changes we humans have introduced into the complex ecosystem known as Planet Earth, it's fair to say that

---

*Brian Clark, "The Butterfly Effect and the Environment: How Tiny Actions Can Save the World," *copyblogger,* October 15, 2007, http://www.copyblogger.com/butterfly-effect-environment/ (accessed June 27, 2008).

we've done the work of billions of butterflies. What we're trying to figure out now is what's going to happen, but it's most likely going to be pretty significant.

WHAT IF BUTTERFLIES DISAPPEARED?

9 While there's little agreement as to what's going to happen ecologically due to human activity, there's no doubt that we've made drastic changes to just about every natural habitat on the planet. Our oceans and natural water sources are polluted, the composition of our soil has been chemically altered, the atmosphere has been heavily influenced by emissions, our forests have been dramatically reduced, and on and on.

10 One area of particular importance is biodiversity. Beyond the fact that biodiversity itself protects humans from the effects of agricultural catastrophes like the Irish Potato Famine, the loss of a species results in significant changes in natural habitats that can hurt us badly down the road.

11 Maybe you don't personally care about the Mexican long-nosed bat, but if they disappear completely, there will most assuredly be consequences that ripple well beyond Texas and New Mexico over time. We just can't predict what they'll be.

12 If butterflies disappeared, the world would most certainly be worse off for children of all ages. But it's much worse than that. Many flowering plants are so closely linked to butterflies (and vice versa) that one cannot survive without the other. When you think about the natural interdependence network that could collapse due to the extinction of one important species, it starts to get a little scary.

13 In the last 439 million years, there have been five cataclysmic extinction events, each one wiping out between 50 to 95 percent of existing life, including the dominant lifeforms of the time. Many scientists believe that:

▶ we're in the midst of the sixth extinction event

▶ we're the cause, and

▶ we're in danger of being wiped out ourselves

14 Harvard biologist Edward O. Wilson predicts that if things don't change, half of all plant and animal species will be extinct by the year 2100. Worse, a poll by the American Museum of Natural History finds that 7 in 10 biologists believe that mass extinction poses a much more dire threat to human existence than global warming does.

15 That's not good news, but let's step away from the negative. Instead, let's look at how we can put the Butterfly Effect to work for us in a good way.

THE POSITIVE SIDE OF THE BUTTERFLY EFFECT

16 Let's face it—things will likely change for the worse regarding the environment no matter what. Some of those changes will be pretty bad, and there's nothing we can do to stop it.

17 That doesn't mean we should give up. The more positive change we introduce into the system starting right now, the more bad things we avoid. Plus, we buy time for technology to help protect us from adverse conditions, and even reverse some of the damage.

18 The corollary of the Butterfly Effect is that tiny changes you make do in fact make a difference. And when those tiny changes are aggregated among millions of people, we can truly make a real difference in how much nature we save for our children, grandchildren, and beyond. We might even be saving *them*.

19 It doesn't need to be a sacrifice. Why not make changes that simply save you money? Check out these planet-saving actions that keep more coin in your pocket:

▶ **Cut out bottled water.** Producing plastic water bottles consumes massive amounts of fossil fuels only to crowd landfills. American demand alone requires 1.5 million barrels of oil annually, enough to fuel approximately 100,000 U.S. cars for a year. And if you

657

think gas prices are bad, you're paying $10 a gallon *for water* when you buy individual bottles. Get a simple home filtration solution, and a reusable stainless steel bottle.

❯ **Switch to compact fluorescent light bulbs.** CFL bulbs are more expensive, but they last 5 times longer than conventional bulbs. Save $30 in energy costs per bulb and help save the planet.

❯ **Buy a new monitor.** You know you want a new LCD monitor, so go ahead and do it. They use 1/3 the energy, and they look cool. Just hold on to your computer as long as you can stand it, or learn to recycle it when you trade up.

❯ **Quit your job.** Telecommuting twice a week can save 40 percent of your gas costs according to the Telework Coalition, or $624 per year. To further maximize your

happiness and the future health of the Earth, start that home-based business you keep talking about.

WHAT HAVE YOU GOT TO LOSE?

20 It's mid-October now, and the butterflies are just about gone for the year. My daughter provided the inspiration for this article when she asked me in a concerned voice:

21 "Daddy, where have all the butterflies gone?"

22 "It's okay sweetie . . . they'll be back in the spring."

23 I hope no parent has to answer that question differently.[1]

Editor's note:

1. To follow the author's links to external sources, read the posting online in its original form at *copyblogger.*

B. How Can We Resolve the Economy versus Environment Debate?

BEFORE YOU READ: George Will's title, which puns on that of Al Gore's book, suggests his own position on the "Economy versus Environment" debate. Can you think of an instance in which you experienced a conflict between economic reality and protecting the environment? Which priority did you choose?

AN INCONVENIENT PRICE[*]

George F. Will

Pulitzer Prize–winning author George Will has been a contributing editor for *Newsweek* since 1976.

1 Economics is "the dismal science," in part because it puts a price tag on the pleasure of moralizing. This is pertinent to the crusade, often masquerading as journalism, aimed at hectoring developed nations into taking "strong" actions against global warming. For such nations (developing nations have more pressing priorities), the question, plainly put, is: How much are they willing to pay—in direct expenditures, forgone economic growth, inefficiencies and constricted freedom—in order to have a negligible effect on climate change?

---

[*]George Will, "An Inconvenient Price," *Newsweek*, October 22, 2007, 68.

2   Zealots say fighting global warming is a moral imperative, so cost-benefit analyses are immoral. Like our Manichaean president, they have a simple fixation: Are you with us or not? But in his book *Cool It: The Skeptical Environmentalist's Guide to Global Warming*, the Danish economist Bjorn Lomborg suggests that global warming, although real, is not apt to be severe; that many of its consequences will be beneficial, and that the exorbitant costs of attempting to substantially curtail it would squander resources that, put to other uses, could have effects thousands of times more ameliorative. He offers cautionary calculations:

> The warming that is reasonably projected might be problematic, although not devastating, for the much-fretted-about polar bears, but it will be beneficial for other species. The Arctic Climate Impact Assessment anticipates *increasing* species richness.

3   Global warming was blamed for 35,000 deaths in Europe's August 2003 heat wave. Cold, however, has caused 25,000 deaths a year recently in England and Wales—47,000 in each winter from 1998 to 2000. In Europe, cold kills more than seven times as many as heat does. Worldwide, moderate warming will, on balance, save more lives than it will cost—by a 9-to-1 ratio in China and India. So, if ubstantially cutting carbon dioxide reverses warming, that will mean a large net loss of life globally.

4   How cool do we want the world to be? As cool as it was when the Arctic ice pack extended so far south that Eskimos in kayaks landed in Scotland? Just cool enough to prevent the oceans from inundating us?

5   The U.N.'s 2007 report estimates that by 2100, sea levels will rise about a foot—as much as they have risen since 1860. That will mean a number of local problems, not a planetary crisis. More people now live near coasts (which is why hurricanes have become more costly; they have not become more frequent or violent), but protecting people and property from the sea would be far less costly than attempting to turn down the planet's thermostat.

6   In an example of what has been called titillating "climate porn," we have been warned that warming might make malaria endemic in Vermont. Well. Malaria kills more than a million people a year worldwide and was endemic in parts of America's South within living memory (which is why the Centers for Disease Control are in Atlanta).[1] But Lomborg says malaria is "related strongly to economic development and weakly to changing climate." Increasing prosperity and low-tech methods like mosquito nets, not controlling climate change, is the key to preventing 85 million malaria deaths by 2100.

7   Warming will help agriculture in some regions and hurt it in others, but even a net negative effect will be less injurious than current agriculture policies are. The farm bill currently taking odious shape in Congress will be a killer—literally. Rich countries subsidizing their agriculture limit the ability of poor countries to prosper—and become healthier—by selling their products in rich countries' markets.

8   Recent loopiness about warming has ranged from the idiotic (an academic study that "associated" warming with increased Italian suicide rates) to the comic (London demonstrators chanting, "What do we want? Carbon taxes! When do we want them? Now!"). Well, you want dramatic effects *now*? We can *eliminate* what the World Health Organization says will be, by 2020, second only to heart disease as the world's leading cause of death.

9   The cause is traffic accidents. The surefire cure is speed limits of 5mph. In 2008 alone, that would save 1.2 million lives and $500 billion in damages, disproportionately in the Third World, which will be hardest hit by increasing traffic carnage. But a world moving at 5mph would be, over the years, uncountable trillions of dollars poorer, which would cost some huge multiple of 1.2 million lives through forgone nutrition, education, infrastructure—e.g., clean water—medicine, research, etc.

659

10　The costs of such global slowing would be the medievalization of the world, so the world accepts the costs of velocity. There also are high costs of what Lomborg calls "impossibly ambitious and yet environmentally inconsequential" plans for inventing a "big knob of climate change" that we can give a twist or two, thereby making the climate "better" and making nothing worse.

11　Sums that are small relative to the cost of trying to fine-tune the planet's climate could prevent scores of millions of deaths from AIDS, unsafe drinking water, and other clear and present dangers. If nations concert to impose antiwarming measures commensurate with the hyperbole about the danger, the damage to global economic growth could cause in this century more preventable death and suffering than was caused in the last century by Hitler, Stalin, Mao and Pol Pot combined.[2] Nobel Peace Prize, indeed.[3]

Editor's notes:

1. The Centers for Disease Control and Prevention (CDC) in Atlanta, Georgia, is described on the organization's Web site as the "nation's premier public health agency—working to ensure healthy people in a healthy world."

2. Pol Pot (1925–1998) was the leader of the Khmer Rouge, a communist movement in Cambodia.

3. Will refers sarcastically to the fact that in 2007, Al Gore and the U.N.'s Intergovernmental Panel on Climate Change were awarded the Nobel Peace Prize.

Reading Images: Coal Mining and the Environment

**Image 1:
Coal Mining in China.**

For Discussion: Photojournalist Chang W. Lee does not comment directly on the scenes he captures on camera. How does the artistic composition of this photo make a claim about daily life in industrialized China?

For Writing: Analyze the ways in which this photo employs *logos*, *ethos*, and/or *pathos* to create its argument.

Context: The caption reads: China's industrial growth depends on coal, plentiful but polluting, from mines like this one in Shenmu, Shaanxi Province, behind a village store. Chang W. Lee's photographs of China depict a world that has been compared to the London of Charles Dickens during the Industrial Revolution in England in the nineteenth century. The relation of people to their environment is a common theme. For more photos by Lee, see the multimedia presentation "China: The World's Smokestack," at http://www.nytimes.com/packages/html/world/20070826_ CHINA_OVERVIEW_FEATURE/index.html.

Reading Images: Coal Mining and the Environment, cont.

Image 2:
Mountaintop Removal in the United States.

For Discussion: This photo, shot from an airplane makes a claim of fact. Like Image 1 of China this image makes an appeal to *ethos* and *pathos*, giving the landscape a dignity and identity of its own, separate from human industry. How do appeals to *ethos* and *pathos* elaborate on the claim of fact in this image?

For Writing: Analyze this image as an "argument from sign," visible evidence that supports the claim that coal mining in Appalachia is changing the landscape.

Context: The caption reads: Mountaintop Removal in Appalachia. Vivian Stockman, a project coordinator with the Ohio Valley Environmental Coalition, photographs the effects of mountaintop removal in Appalachia as part of her organization's ongoing fight against what they call "King Coal." More of her photographs on this subject can be seen at http://www.ohvec.org/galleries/mountaintop_removal/index.html. Like Chang W. Lee, Stockman documents with images of precise clarity and aesthetic merit.

661

> **BEFORE YOU READ:** Erik Reece's essay argues that modern industry is destroying community and traditional ways of life in Appalachia. What natural resources are crucial to your own community and way of life?

MOVING MOUNTAINS: THE BATTLE FOR JUSTICE COMES TO THE COAL FIELDS OF APPALACHIA*

Erik Reece

Erik Reece teaches at the University of Kentucky, where he codirects the Summer Environmental Writing Program. His book, titled *Lost Mountain: Radical Strip Mining and the Devastation of Appalachia,* was published in 2006 by Riverhead Books.

1   Not since the glaciers pushed toward these ridgelines a million years ago have the Appalachian Mountains been as threatened as they are today. But the coal-extraction

---

*Erik Reece, originally published as "Moving Mountains: The Battle for Justice Comes to the Coal Fields of Appalachia" in *Orion Magazine* (January/February), 2006; available online at *Grist: Environmental News and Commentary,* "Moving Mountains: Mountaintop-removal Mining Is Devastating Appalachia, but Residents Are Fighting Back," February 16, 2006, http://www.grist.org/news/maindish/2006/02/16/reece/index.html.

process decimating this landscape, known as mountaintop removal, has generated little press beyond the region. The problem, in many ways, is one of perspective. From interstates and lowlands, where most communities are clustered, one simply doesn't see what is happening up there. Only from the air can you fully grasp the magnitude of the devastation. If you were to board, say, a small prop plane at Zeb Mountain, Tennessee, and follow the spine of the Appalachian Mountains up through Kentucky, Virginia, and West Virginia, you would be struck not by the beauty of a densely forested range older than the Himalayas, but rather by inescapable images of ecological violence. Near Pine Mountain, Kentucky, you'd see an unfolding series of staggered green hills quickly give way to a wide expanse of gray plateaus pocked with dark craters and huge black ponds filled with a toxic byproduct called coal slurry. The desolation stretches like a long scar up the Kentucky-Virginia line, before eating its way across southern West Virginia.

2   Central Appalachia provides much of the country's coal, second only to Wyoming's Powder River Basin. In the United States, one hundred tons of coal are extracted every two seconds. Around 70 percent of that coal comes from strip mines, and over the last twenty years, an increasing amount comes from mountaintop removal sites. In the name of corporate expedience, coal companies have turned from excavation to simply blasting away the tops of the mountains. To achieve this, they use the same mixture of ammonium nitrate and diesel fuel that Timothy McVeigh employed to level the Murrow Building in Oklahoma City—except each detonation is ten times as powerful, and thousands of blasts go off each day across central Appalachia.[1] Hundreds of feet of forest, topsoil, and sandstone—the coal industry calls all of this "overburden"—are unearthed so bulldozers and front-end loaders can more easily extract the thin seams of rich, bituminous coal that stretch in horizontal layers throughout these mountains. Almost everything that isn't coal is pushed down into the valleys below. As a result, 6,700 "valley fills" were approved in central Appalachia between 1985 and 2001. The Environmental Protection Agency estimates that over 700 miles of healthy streams have been completely buried by mountaintop removal and thousands more have been damaged. Where there once flowed a highly braided system of headwater streams, now a vast circuitry of haul roads winds through the rubble. From the air, it looks like someone had tried to plot a highway system on the moon. [. . .]

3   Serious coal mining has been going on in Appalachia since the turn of the twentieth century. But from the time World War II veterans climbed down from tanks and up onto bulldozers, the extractive industries in America have grown more mechanized and more destructive. Ironically, here in Kentucky where I live, coal-related employment has dropped 60 percent in the last fifteen years; it takes very few men to run a strip mine operation, with giant machines doing most of the clearcutting, excavating, loading, and bulldozing of rubble. And all strip mining—from the most basic truck mine to mountaintop removal—results in deforestation, flooding, mudslides, and the fouling of headwater streams.

4   Alongside this ecological devastation lies an even more ominous human dimension: an Eastern Kentucky University study found that children in Letcher County, Kentucky, suffer from an

alarmingly high rate of nausea, diarrhea, vomiting, and shortness of breath—symptoms of something called blue baby syndrome—that can all be traced back to sedimentation and dissolved minerals that have drained from mine sites into nearby streams. Long-term effects may include liver, kidney, and spleen failure, bone damage, and cancers of the digestive track.

5   Erica Urias, who lives on Island Creek in Grapevine, Kentucky, told me she has to bathe her two-year-old daughter in contaminated water because of the mining around her home. In McRoberts, Kentucky, the problem is flooding. In 1998, Tampa Energy Company (TECO) started blasting along the ridgetops above McRoberts. Homes shook and foundations cracked. Then TECO sheared off all of the vegetation at the head of Chopping Block Hollow and replaced it with the compacted rubble of a valley fill. In a region prone to flash floods, nothing was left to hold back the rain; this once forested watershed had been turned into an enormous funnel. In 2002, three so-called hundred-year floods happened in ten days. Between the blasting and the flooding, the people of McRoberts have been nearly flushed out of their homes.

6   Consider the story of Debra and Granville Burke. First the blasting above their house wrecked its foundation. Then the floods came. Four times, they wiped out the Burkes' garden, which the family depended on to get through the winter. Finally, on Christmas morning 2002, Debra Burke took her life. In a letter published in a local paper, her husband wrote: "She left eight letters describing how she loved us all but that our burdens were just getting too much to bear. She had begged for TECO to at least replace our garden, but they just turned their back on her. I look back now and think of all the things I wish I had done differently so that she might still be with us, but mostly I wish that TECO had never started mining above our home."

7   In the language of economics, Debra Burke's death was an externality—a cost that simply isn't factored into the price Americans pay for coal. And that is precisely the problem. Last year, American power plants burned over a billion tons of coal, accounting for over 50 percent of this country's electricity use. In Kentucky, 80 percent of the harvested coal is sold and shipped to twenty-two other states. Yet it is the people of Appalachia who pay the highest price for the rest of the country's cheap energy—through contaminated water, flooding, cracked foundations and wells, bronchial problems related to breathing coal dust, and roads that have been torn up and turned deadly by speeding coal trucks. Why should large cities like Phoenix and Detroit get the coal but be held accountable for none of the environmental consequences of its extraction? And why is a Tampa-based energy company—or Peabody Coal in St. Louis, or Massey Energy in Richmond, Virginia—allowed to destroy communities throughout Appalachia? As my friend and teacher the late Guy Davenport once wrote, "Distance negates responsibility."

8   The specific injustice that had drawn together a group of activists calling themselves the Mountain Justice Summer movement, was the violent death of three-year-old Jeremy Davidson.[2] At two-thirty in the morning on August 30, 2004, a bulldozer, operating without a permit above the Davidsons' home, dislodged a thousand-pound boulder from a mountaintop removal site in the town of Appalachia, Virginia. The boulder rolled two hundred feet down the mountain

before it crushed to death the sleeping child. [. . .]

9   But Davidson's death is hardly an isolated incident. In West Virginia, fourteen people drowned in the last three years because of floods and mudslides caused by mountaintop removal, and in Kentucky, fifty people have been killed and over five hundred injured in the last five years by coal trucks, almost all of which were illegally overloaded. [. . .]

10   The history of resource exploitation in Appalachia, like the history of racial oppression in the South, follows a sinister logic—keep people poor and scared so that they remain powerless. In the nineteenth century, mountain families were actually doing fairly well farming rich bottomlands. But populations grew, farms were subdivided, and then northern coal and steel companies started buying up much of the land, hungry for the resources that lay below. By the time the railroads reached headwater hollows like McRoberts, Kentucky, men had little choice but to sell their labor cheaply, live in company towns, and shop in overpriced company stores. . . . In nearly every county across central Appalachia, King Coal had gained control of the economy, the local government, and the land. [. . .]

11   In their own way, Mountain Justice activists worked hard to expose the injustice spreading across the coal fields of Appalachia. Through nonviolent actions and demonstrations, they attempted to show the nation how coal companies break the law with a pathological consistency and operate with little regard for the human consequences of their actions. But on the national stage, Mountain Justice Summer couldn't compete with high gas prices and a

foreign war, even though it is precisely that war over oil that is driving coal demands higher and laying mountains lower faster. That plus the fact that U.S. energy consumption increased 42 percent over the last thirty years. Urban affluence and this country's short-sighted energy policy are making Appalachia a poorer place—poorer in beauty, poorer in health, poorer in resources, and poorer in spirit. [. . .]

12   That the civil rights movement happened so recently in our country's history can seem dumbfounding, but not to the people who still live in the shadow of oppression. Those who live in the path of the coal industry—beneath sheared-off mountains, amid unnatural, treeless landscapes, drinking poisoned water and breathing dirty air—are fighting their own civil rights battle. And, as in the past, justice may be slow coming to the mountains of Appalachia. But justice delayed could mean the ruin of a place that has sacrificed much for this nation, and has received next to nothing in return.

Editor's notes:

1. Timothy McVeigh (1968–2001) is known as the Oklahoma City bomber. A former Army soldier, he was convicted and executed for the 1995 bombing of the Alfred P. Murrah Federal Building in Oklahoma City, which killed 168 and injured 850 people; among the dead were nineteen children in day care. This was considered the most devastating incident of domestic terrorism in the United States when it occurred.

2. Mountain Justice is an organization that defines itself as a broad coalition of student and community groups working against mountaintop removal. Its home page is at http://mountainjustice.org (accessed June 28, 2008).

Reading Images: The Rain Forest

Image 1:
Dipterocarpus Tree in Lowland Rain Forest in Borneo.

For Discussion: The saying "A picture is worth a thousand words" may be a cliché, but these photographs offer a particular argument within the Web sites that frame them. Look at the two photos as discrete images and describe the claims being made by them. From the evidence of the visual images, what can you infer about the goals of the Web sites themselves? What *ethos* of the photographer is being communicated, and what claims are being made about the places being represented?

Image 2:
Clear-cutting in the Amazon Rain Forest.

For Writing: Visit the sites from which these two pictures are taken. How do the photographs work within their larger contexts? How are they used to reinforce the site's *ethos* or as evidence to support claims made on the site?

Context: The top photo, of the rain forest in Gunung Palung National Park in Borneo, Indonesia, is reprinted from the Web site of photographer Cagan Sekercioglu, a Turkish photographer who is interested in the conservation of biodiversity. The bottom photo, of a deforested area in Peru, viewed from above by airplane was taken by Rhett Butler of Mongabay.com, an organization that, according to its Web site, "seeks to raise interest in wildlife and wildlands while promoting awareness of environmental issues." Image 1 is available online at http://www.naturalphotos.com/sekercioglu/asia_pacific/index.htm (accessed July 3, 2008). Image 2 can be seen at http://travel.mongabay.com/pix/peru/aerial-rainforest-Flight_1022_1553.html. More information about Mongabay.com can be found at http://www.mongabay.com/.

Reading Images: The Rain Forest, cont.

Image 3:
Logging Road and Deforestation in Loango National Park, Gabon (West Coast of Central Africa).

For Discussion: Many writers and artists in the environmental movement appeal to the experience of viewers who live far away from the areas depicted. How does this photograph visually tap into your feelings about nature?

For Writing: This photograph is intended to record damage to the environment, but the image also makes an argument of fact. What is the claim and what evidence supports it?

Image 4:
Rain Forest Logs Being Moved by Barge in Loango National Park, Gabon (West Coast of Central Africa).

For Discussion: This is a photograph of logs being transported through a national park. How does the relationship of cut logs to the natural surroundings affect your reaction to the photograph?

For Writing: Imagine seeing these photos as either advertisements or "anti-advertisements" for the eco-tourist industry; write text to accompany one of them on the Web site of an imaginary travel company. "Come to Gabon and . . . "

Context: Most Americans have never visited Gabon in Africa and therefore depend on photos and videos for their visual information. Both of these photographs of rain forest logging in Gabon were taken by Rhett Butler of Mongabay.com, an organization that promotes awareness of "environmental science and conservation news," according to its Web site. More photographs by Butler of deforestation in different parts of the rain forest can be found at http://travel.mongabay.com/deforestation_photos.html (accessed June 28, 2008). Compare these informational photographs to the illustration for the essay "Carving Up the Congo" (pages 667–669).

BEFORE YOU READ: This essay not only describes how economic interests are trumping environmental concerns in Africa, but suggests that the wealth made from logging never reaches the community. What is the most important natural resource in your own community and who benefits from it?

CARVING UP THE CONGO*

Stuart Price

Stuart Price is deputy editor of *New African* magazine.

Context: Harvested Rain Forest Timber (African mahogany) in the Republic of the Congo. In this photograph, the interplay between image and title and text is significant.

For Discussion: How does this image contribute to the essay's examination of the conflict between environment and economics in the Congo? What claim does the image make? What evidence does the essay provide in support of the image's claim? Compare this image with Images 3 and 4 on page 666, which depict logging in Gabon, a different area of the Central African rain forest. What claim do the images make as a group? How effective are they?

For Writing: Consider this image as a comment on the essay's title, "Carving Up the Congo." How does it contribute to the essay's argument, by supporting its claims or by supplying value warrants?

1   In the murky days of colonial occupation, it was ivory pillaged by Europeans from deep within the jungles of DRCongo [Democratic Republic of the Congo] that formed the core of the exploitation. Over 100 years later, the plunder continues, but this time in the form of timber and other strategic natural resources.

2   According to an investigation by the environmental pressure group, Greenpeace, international logging companies are conning forest communities with as little as a crate of beer, sugar, and salt in order to gain access to rare and lucrative tropical hardwoods worth hundreds of thousands of dollars.

3   The Greenpeace report, *Carving Up the Congo*, claims that companies operating in the country are causing social chaos and wreaking environmental havoc while the rainforest is being sold off under the illusion that logging alleviates poverty. According to the report, some companies donate "gifts" to local communities worth as little as $100. In one instance, Greenpeace found that: "Sodefor's—an NST Group[1] company—gift package often comprises

two sacks of salt, 18 bars of soap, four packets of coffee, 24 bottles of beer, and two bags of sugar, in exchange for rainforest access."

4   As a result, the communities effectively sign away their right to protection against the Company's activities within their area. "It is crunch time for the DRCongo's rainforests," says Stephan van Praet, Greenpeace International Africa Forest Campaign coordinator. "The international logging industry operating in the country is out of control. Unless the World Bank helps DRCongo to stop the sale of these rainforests, they will soon be under the chainsaws." Greenpeace claims that the World Bank's support for development through extractive industries, including logging, is set to compromise the future of DRCongo's rainforests, its people, and the global climate.[2]

5   Two thirds of Congo's population—40 million people—relies on the forest for food, traditional medicines, and energy. Ironically, the years of political turmoil and war in the Congo protected the forest from major logging companies. During the conflict of 1996–2003, timber production virtually ground to a halt, while corrupt and criminal elites, backed by foreign multinationals, joined a free-for-all to gain control of Congo's natural resources.

6   During this period, an estimated 43.5 million hectares of forest, an area twice the size of the United Kingdom, fell under the control of the logging industry.[3] At the same time, the World Bank suspended all funding and lending to the Congo, resuming its assistance in 2001. And by mid-2006, having by then approved more than $4 billion in grants, credits, and loans, the Bank was in a "unique position to influence the country's development," says Greenpeace.

7   Now, however, the relative peace ushered in under the government of President Joseph Kabila means the country has stabilized enough for multinationals to begin extraction and wholesale clearance of one of the oldest and most important areas of natural rainforest in the world. According to a World Bank–led forestry sector analysis earlier this year, industrial timber has a particularly poor track record

in Africa. Over the past 60 years, there is little evidence that industrial timber has lifted rural populations out of poverty or contributed in other meaningful and sustainable ways to local and national development. Similarly, a United Nations Security Group of Experts stated that urgent intervention against all forms of illegal natural resource exploitation is required. Figures estimate timber smuggling is so rife that export levels are as much as seven times higher than official figures.

8   Following the suspension of new logging titles and the renewal or extension of existing ones in May 2002, 163 noncompliant contracts—in areas deemed as dormant and not being logged and which covered 25.5 million hectares of rainforests—were cancelled. Yet since then, few new areas have been granted or afforded any special status protecting them in the future. At the same time, since April of last year, the then transitional government signed 156 new contracts with companies covering over 15 million hectares of rainforest.

9   Greenpeace alleges that many of these contracts have been "approved under the guise of remapping, exchange, adjustments, and relocations of old titles, as well as out-and-out new allocations." It further charges that in the context of corruption and poor governance in DRCongo, "the World Bank's attempts to reform the forestry sector are currently failing to control the expansion of logging." Behind the granting of logging concessions is the idea that companies pay relevant taxes, which will be used to develop forest communities through the construction of schools, health centers, and improved public services. Even the World Bank admits that in the last three years, none of the forest area taxes paid by companies have reached forest communities.

10   The 156 contracts signed over the last five years cover areas inhabited by forest-dependent communities, two thirds of which are also populated by pygmy hunter-gatherer communities. As stipulated in the 2002 Forestry Code, companies negotiate directly with communities and agree on the services they will provide in exchange for logging in their area. "These

contracts are a shameful relic of colonial times. Millions of hectares of the Congo rainforest have been traded away by local communities to the logging industry for gifts like salt, machetes, and crates of beer while logging companies and their taxes do next to nothing for local development," concluded Greenpeace's van Praet. [. . .]

11   Like the logging industry, Congo's mining sector offers some of the highest concentrations of strategic minerals in the world. One-tenth of the world's copper reserves and a profusion of diamonds, gold, tin, cobalt, and coltan (today's miracle mineral used widely in electronic gadgets), are all found in abundance. With recent stability in the country, multi-national mining companies and many smaller ventures have been scrambling to invest billions of dollars in the extractive sector.

12   According to the *Bretton Woods Project (BWP)*, a watchdog and critical think-tank on the World Bank and IMF [International Monetary Fund], "a confidential World Bank memo dated September 2005 and leaked to the *Financial Times* [of London] in November 2006 finds that three of the Congo's biggest mining contracts over which the World Bank had oversight were approved with 'a complete lack of transparency.'"[4]

13   Patrick Alley, director of Global Witness, says the government needs to ensure the highest standards of transparency and independence if the process is to be credible and restore public trust. "This review is a unique opportunity to halt the systematic looting of Congo's resources and to set a precedent for responsible investment practices, in accordance with national and international laws and standards," says Alley.

Editor's notes:

1. NST Group is an international holding company headquartered in Liechtenstein; Sodefor is a Portuguese-owned timber company. A holding company holds or owns controlling amounts of stock in other companies.

2. The World Bank is a group of five institutions formed in 1944 to reduce poverty. Although not technically a bank it provides "low-interest loans, interest-free credit and grants to developing countries for education, health, infrastructure, communications, and many other purposes" (http://www.worldbank.org/).

3. A hectare is a unit of measurement commonly used for measuring land; one hectare equals 10,000 square meters or 2.47 acres.

4. The IMF (International Monetary Fund, also formed in 1944) was established to oversee currency valuation and sustainable macroeconomic growth in impoverished countries.

669

BEFORE YOU READ: In the "Economy versus Environment" debate, proponents of protecting rare and endangered species are often accused of anthropomorphizing animals—that is, treating them as if they were human. Can you think of ways in which our culture and media contribute to the sense that animals are "almost human"?

ETHICS AND THE SPOTTED OWL CONTROVERSY*

Claire Andre and Manuel Velasquez

Claire Andre is associate director of the Markula Center for Applied Ethics at Santa Clara University; Manuel Velasquez is Dirksen Professor of Business Ethics at Santa Clara University and former director of the Markula Center.

1   For hundreds of years, a handsome, dark-brown owl with white spots has made its home in the lush, "old-growth" forests of the Pacific Northwest. Under the multilayered

---

*Claire Andre and Manuel Valasquez, "Ethics and the Spotted Owl Controversy," *Issues in Ethics* 4.1 (Spring 1991), online at Santa Cruz University, Markula Center for Applied Ethics, http://www.scu.edu/ethics/publications/iie/v4n1/homepage.html (accessed June 28, 2008).

canopies of these 200-year-old forests, the owl, known as the northern spotted owl, has fed off the rich plant and invertebrate life created by decaying timber and has nested in the cavities of old trunks. But the towering cedars, firs, hemlocks, and spruces which have served as the owl's habitat, also have become a primary source of timber for a multibillion dollar logging industry. Over the last 150 years, as a result of heavy logging, these ancient forests have dwindled. Only about 10% of the forests remain, most on federally owned lands. And as the forests have dwindled, so too has the number of spotted owls. Biologists estimate that only 2,000 pairs survive today.

2   In 1986, a worried environmentalist group petitioned the U.S. Fish and Wildlife Service to list the owl as an "endangered species," a move that would bar the timber industry from clearing these lands. In June 1990, after years of heated negotiation and litigation between the government, environmentalists, and the timber industry, the northern spotted owl was declared a threatened species. Under this provision, timber companies are required to leave at least 40% of the old-growth forests intact within a 1.3 mile radius of any spotted owl nest or activity site, a provision that is vehemently opposed by the timber industry. Industry representatives claim that the measure will leave thousands of Northwest loggers and mill workers jobless, and insist that such protectionist policies thoughtlessly fail to take into account the dire economic consequences of preservation. Environmentalists, on the other hand, argue that society has a fundamental obligation to preserve this rare species and the wilderness it inhabits.

3   The controversy over the northern spotted owl follows on the heels of debates over dolphins, whales, snail darters, and desert tortoises, each raising questions concerning society's obligation to protect animals threatened by extinction. In the case of the spotted owl, we must ask whether and to what extent preserving endangered species and the wilderness they inhabit should take precedence over other considerations, such as major economic dislocations.

WEIGHING THE COSTS AND BENEFITS

4   From the environmentalists' perspective, the benefits of preserving the northern spotted owl and its habitat far outweigh any of the costs. First, saving the spotted owl will save an entire ecosystem on which plants, other animals, and humans depend. The spotted owl is considered an indicator species—a gauge of the health of the ecosystem that provides its habitat. The steady decline of this species signals the demise of other species, such as elk and flying squirrel, that inhabit these forests, and the disruption of the productive forces of nature that sustain human life. The ancient forests and the life they harbor form a complex web of interdependent relationships that play a critical role in preventing soil erosion, floods, and landslides, providing clean water for agriculture and cities, enhancing the productivity of salmon fisheries, enriching the soil with vital nutrients, and ameliorating the greenhouse effect. No amount of reforestation can replace this highly developed and diverse system which has taken millennia to evolve.

5   Second, society ought to preserve this species and the unique ecosystem it represents because of their aesthetic value. What kind of society would trade the magnificence of these virgin forests and the splendor of the life that inhabits them—owl, elk, bald eagles, and mountain goats—for paper cups and two-by-fours? To allow such a tradeoff is equivalent to destroying a great work of art that has taken centuries to create, and that will be a source of rich experience for generations of hikers, backpackers, bird-watchers, and millions of others seeking a natural world away from our teeming concrete cities.

6   Finally, the owl and its habitat are of immense scientific value, providing opportunities for inquiry and for increasing our understanding of this unique ecosystem and its role in our lives and in those of future generations. To date, little research has been done on these

forests. To allow their demise is to permanently foreclose the possibility of exploration and the benefits generated by new discoveries. Had the obscure organism known as penicillin become extinct before its discovery, millions of human lives would have been lost. Who knows what secrets these forests may hold?

7   Environmentalists admit that saving the owls' habitat could cost jobs. But, they argue, these jobs will vanish no matter what. For if cutting continues at its current rate of 125,000 acres a year, the old-growth forests will be gone within thirty years and the mills forced to close anyhow. Many of the jobs in the Pacific Northwest could be saved simply by restricting the export of raw timber, a practice driven by the higher profits made through sales outside of the U.S. In 1988, nearly 4 billion board feet of raw logs were exported from Washington and Oregon. Had those logs been processed in the U.S., thousands of jobs could have been generated.

8   The timber industry, on the other hand, maintains that the benefits of saving the spotted owl are negligible compared to the harm that will be done. Reduced logging in the old-growth forests will harm all Americans and be particularly devastating to communities in the Pacific Northwest. These forests are a primary source of timber for most independent lumber mills in the Northwest, which account for about 65% of Western wood. Many of the saw mills are entirely dependent on old-growth cuts because their equipment can only handle trees with large dimensions. According to one report, if the volume of old growth declines, up to 28,000 jobs could be lost, leading to "increased rates of domestic disputes, divorce, acts of violence, delinquency, vandalism, suicide, alcoholism, and other problems." Nationwide, consumer prices for wood products will rise substantially. And, lumber-poor nations, such as Japan, which depend on massive amounts of timber from the U.S., will suffer.

9   Second, timber industry officials state that cutting the old growth is essential if present

and future generations are to be provided with the wood and paper products they need. Once these trees have reached their maturity, most of their energy is spent simply maintaining themselves, rather than in new growth. It is in society's best interest to replace these static forests with healthy, young trees that will provide an adequate supply of timber.

10   The industry counters the environmentalists' claim that preservation measures ought to be supported because of the aesthetic, scientific, and ecological benefits that would result. Hundreds of thousands of acres of old-growth forests, they argue, have already been set aside as national parks and wilderness areas. Half of Oregon's three million acres of old growth is not being logged because it has been designated as wilderness or is unsuitable for logging. Also, logging sites are continually being reforested. Old-growth and second-growth forests provide ample opportunities for "aesthetic experiences," recreation, and biological exploration. Moreover, our desire for aesthetic experiences or the value we place on the pursuit of knowledge should not be allowed to override more basic needs of persons, such as the need for jobs or housing.

11   The timber industry disputes the environmentalists' call for the use of alternative sources of wood. Second-growth wood, they point out, is less strong, and is knotty and twisted. It can't be used to produce many products, such as fine furniture and musical instruments, requiring the high quality old-growth wood that is characterized by fine, straight lines and few knots. Until substitutes can be found, society has no choice but to rely on wood from old-growth forests.

ANIMAL RIGHTS

12   Preservationists also defend their case on the basis of animal rights. Every living creature, they argue, has a right to life. An owl, like any other animal, is the subject of a life that has intrinsic value. To deliberately destroy this animal's habitat violates its right to exist.

671

13 Those opposing protectionist policies claim that while humans may have a duty to prevent unnecessary harm to animals, they are not obliged to forego their own interests in order to protect the interests of animals. We slaughter cattle, pigs, and sheep to meet our needs. Why should an owl, whose habitat is a source of material needed for housing, be given special consideration?

A DUTY TO PRESERVE RARE SPECIES

14 Some environmentalists counter that we also have an obligation to preserve species. A species represents a vital, nonreproducible combination of genetic processes that has evolved over millions of years. It has an integrity and potentiality of its own, manifest in its unique stages of development and its intriguing adaptation to the environment around it. The rarity of some species, such as the regal spotted owl, only increases its value. We have a duty to protect such genetically unique species and to ensure their continued existence.

15 Opponents of protectionist policies reply that it makes no sense to say that we have a duty to preserve species because species is only a category invented by humans to group individual members. In reality, there are only individual animals that are members of a species. And, the interests of these individual animals must sometimes be overridden by the weightier interests of individual human beings.

16 Moreover, simply because something is rare doesn't mean it is more deserving of preservation. Leprosy is rare, but we don't value it. Rarity only intensifies the value of valuable things. Finally, it is argued, the extinction of species is a natural and normal event. A recent report on endangered species estimates that by the year 2000, 600,000 plants and animals will become extinct. Extinctions caused by the practices of humans, who are part of nature, are no more "unnatural" than extinctions caused by other predators.

17 As government officials, environmentalists, and industry representatives work out the details of implementing the new regulations designed to preserve the owl, we can expect the debate over the spotted owl to subside. But the ethical issues it raises will repeatedly appear as our natural resources dwindle. How we resolve these issues will depend on how we weigh the ecological, aesthetic, and scientific benefits of preservation, the rights of animals, and an obligation to preserve species, against economic interests and human needs.

BEFORE YOU READ: What careers did you imagine yourself pursuing when you were young and what careers can you now imagine yourself pursuing? What was the reasoning behind your choices?

FOR JOB MARKET, GREEN MEANS GROWTH*
Brian Wingfield

Brian Wingfield writes for the *New York Times*.

1 In 1999, as the dot-com boom reached new heights, environmental journalist Joel Makower launched an online publication covering business and environmental interests: two areas he believed would become more connected.

---

*Brian Wingfield, "For Job Market, Green Means Growth," *Forbes.com*, July 3, 2007, http://www.forbes.com/home/wireless/2007/07/02/environment-economy-jobs-biz_cx_bw_0703green_greenjobs.html (accessed June 30, 2008).

2   Smart bet. The tech bubble burst, but Makower's publication, *GreenBiz.com*, boomed. Providing news and analysis, it's the flagship publication for Greener World Media, a for-profit company he created last year with associate Pete May." As the greening of business expands, it is filtering into every aspect of business," from procurement to marketing to human resources, says Makower.

3   According to Kevin Doyle, president of Green Economy, a Boston-based firm that promotes an environmentally healthy workforce, the green industry in the United States in 2005 was about $265 billion employing 1.6 million people in an estimated 118,000 jobs. This information was adapted from the *Environmental Business Journal*, he says, and does not include the organic industry.

4   Green businesses have also been growing at a rate of about 5% annually during the last three years, Doyle says. Two particularly hot areas are global carbon credit trading, which doubled to $28 billion from 2005 to 2006, and construction and services associated with "green buildings" that meet industry standards set by the U.S. Green Building Council. Today, the green building industry is worth $12 billion; 10 years ago, it was unquantifiable.

5   The greening of industry is creating a constellation of new careers, and they're not your everyday forestry professions. Many of them are environmental twists on old professions, like law, or in Makower's case, journalism. Others are engineering careers tied to research in renewable technologies like wind energy and ethanol production. For instance:

▶ **Emissions brokers:** In a market economy, credits to emit greenhouse gases can be traded on an exchange, and brokers facilitate the deal. If the U.S. ever moves to a mandatory trading system, expect this field to boom.

▶ **Bio-mimicry engineers:** This new branch of science uses Mother Nature as a model for solving engineering problems. For example, Atlanta's Sto Corp. created a self-cleaning paint that repels dirt whenever it gets wet, just like the lotus leaf does.

▶ **Sustainability coordinators:** Corporations from AstraZeneca to Wal-Mart are now employing managers to oversee the economic and environmental components of company efforts.

▶ **Green architects:** With an increasing focus on energy-efficient buildings, a growing number of architects and developers are getting certified to become specialists in green design.

6   Corporations assume that at some point in the future, governments will put a price on waste, says Doyle. So it's better to invest now in clean technologies than to lose money if new regulations come into play. "People want to get ahead of the game," he says.

7   Conversely, companies see new revenue streams in green technologies and social responsibility. Goldman Sachs, for example, has invested heavily in the wind industry. Earlier this year, Tyson Foods and Conoco-Phillips jointly announced plans to make diesel fuel from chicken fat. And Silicon Valley venture capital firms, like Kleiner Perkins Caulfield & Byers, are shoveling money into the development of clean technologies.

8   Universities   particularly business schools—also see opportunity. Schools such as Stanford, the University of Michigan, the University of North Carolina and the University of Michigan offer joint M.B.A./environmental science masters degrees. Derrick Bolton, director of admissions at Stanford's Graduate School of Business, says many students are taking positions with corporations that have a commitment to the environment.

9   "They're what I call the 'and' generation," he says. "They don't want to make money or support the environment. They want to do both."

10   Students in Michigan's dual degree program are encouraged to intern with both a non-governmental organization and a business while in graduate school. "Students coming in are very aware of the sustainability program," says Rosina Bierbaum, dean of the School of Natural

Resources and Environment at Michigan. "It's really just a matter of time before we're going to start valuing carbon and valuing pollution."

11   Makower's advice to students pursuing a green job is to learn all they can about business. The most exciting things are happening in product design, research and development, manufacturing, and buildings and grounds. "If you go into the environmental part of a company, you become ghettoized," he says.

12   But what if you're no longer in school? Where do you find a green job?

13   The Web site of Business for Social Responsibility (bsr.org), a group that helps companies navigate sustainability issues, is a good place to start. GreenBiz.com also contains a job board. Others are ecojobs.com, which includes a broad array of positions from conservation to engineering to international opportunities. Greenjobs.com focuses on the renewable fuel industry.

14   Makower, who survived the dot-com implosion, says the green boom is no bubble. There's a proven market, government backing and corporate buy-in. His take: Expect green business to grow even more over the next decade, and a new generation of green careers to blossom with it.

Reading Images: Near-Zero Energy Home, Advertisement

674

Home, sweet hybrid home.

**Image 1:
An Environmentally Friendly Home.**

For Discussion: What green careers would have to be created to either remodel or build new homes that would meet the specifications of a hybrid home? What other types of green careers that could not be outsourced to other countries can you imagine being established in the United States?

For Writing: Compare the image of this hybrid home with the image of the beach house on page 28. Write a short essay in which you develop two or three ideas about human life and environmental change that occur to you as a result of viewing the two images.

Context: This home serves as an example of how a home could be remodeled to make it more energy efficient.

Questions to Help You Think and Write about Issues of the Environment

1. Imagine Al Gore and George Will in a debate about Americans' responsibility to protect the environment. On what points raised in their respective essays would they agree and disagree? How does each of these writers define civic responsibility with respect to environmental issues? Finally, which position do you think is better, or which position would you be able to support and why?

2. As you read the essays by Gore, Harris, and Easterbrook, consider not so much the content of their articles, but the argumentation strategies employed by each writer. What strategies do they have in common? Where do they differ? What claims do they make, and what evidence and warrants support those claims? Based on your analysis, which argument is most persuasive?

3. The economies of both China and Appalachia depend heavily on the mining and production of coal. From what you have viewed in "Reading Images" on pages 660–661 and read in the essay by Reece, what similarities do these disparate cultures share? Reece quotes a former teacher as saying, "Distance negates responsibility." Do similarities between the environmental problems of widely separated nations affect your understanding of your own responsibility to the environment, and if so, in what ways?

4. Using the method employed by Andre and Velasquez to discuss ethical issues at work in the spotted owl controversy, analyze the nature and extent of our obligations, as humans and as Americans, to the Arctic polar bear or another animal of your choosing. Are we responsible for the welfare of these creatures, to what extent, and how can we either respect their "rights" or act as responsible caretakers for animal species?

5. In describing the environmental situation in the Congo, including the disappearance of the rain forest and its causes, Stuart Price suggests that the struggle between the needs of the economy and the environment is a global one. In what ways are the social and economic causes of the environmental situation in the rainforests similar to those governing the controversies in the United States over the spotted owl and mountaintop removal? In what ways are these situations different from the others?

6. Think about how specific environmental problems could affect your own community. Using Brian Clark's blog posting on the butterfly effect, develop a plan for individually based conservation efforts that would help address a larger environmental problem in your community.

7. Brian Wingfield and the advertisement for the BASF Near-Zero Energy Home describe some "green" careers that will become available soon to college graduates. If you were advising a college president on how better to prepare students for a world in which green industries will become increasingly important, what recommendations for social and curriculur change in American education would you make?

8. As we have seen, when talking about the environment, pictures act as arguments and also can carry a powerful emotional charge. Choose one of the photographers featured in this section (e.g., Lee, Stockman, Butler) and analyze several images by the same artist. (The "Context" section under each of the images will lead you to other examples.) What claims does the photographer make about the environment she or he studies and what artistic methods are used to support that claim?

SECTION 6

Issues concerning Immigration

The Issues

A. How Should We Respond to the Global Problem of Illegal Immigration?

While the United States has always been a nation of immigrants and the problem of illegal immigration is by no means new, in recent years it has become a highly charged social and political issue. The first three essays address the economic dimensions of migration in a global context. Marc Cooper investigates the problems and dangers illegal immigrants from Mexico face when crossing the United States–Mexico border. Daniel Altman challenges the idea that the presence of illegal immigrants in the American economy hurts the employment opportunities for citizens, and Peter Wilby, who writes about the economics of immigration in England, defends the right of citizens from poor nations to sell their labor on the international market. "Migration, the Larger Picture," an editorial from *America: The National Catholic Weekly*, defines illegal immigration as a human rights problem rather than an economic issue and calls for humane, consistent global policies on immigration. See also "Undocumented, Indispensable" (pages 247–249), the "Price of Oranges" cartoon (page 170), and the "Get Out!" cartoon (page 306).

B. Do Good Fences Make Good Neighbors When Defining National Borders?

In 2007, in response to concerns about the economic and social impact of illegal immigration, Congress authorized the U.S. president to build a 700-mile wall on the border between the Southern United States and Mexico. Jonah

Goldberg, who analyzes the symbolic significance of such a wall, refers to Robert Frost's poem "Mending Wall" to suggest that while many people think that "good walls make good neighbors," there is something inherently divisive about the wall as a symbol of national boundaries. An article by Kevin Hall from the *Fort Worth Star-Telegram* outlines the success of a low-tech wall in slowing down the flow of drugs and illegal immigrants in Columbus, New Mexico, while a companion piece outlines the benefits such a wall provides to community members. By contrast, Miguel Bustillo describes the way in which long-standing Hispanic homeowners along the Rio Grande in Texas respond to the allocation of their familial lands to build the wall. See also "Mending Wall" (pages 492–493), and the images of fences used to wall out enemies, (page 132, page 215, and page 300).

C. What Is the Relationship between Immigration and Nationality?

The United States has always considered itself as a nation built of and by immigrants, but the relation between "immigrant" and "American" as categories is complicated and always changing. Arian Campo-Flores writes that while lawmakers and law enforcement tend to distinguish between legals and illegals, many families are a mix of citizens and undocumented relatives who are at risk. The American immigrant, family is a new kind of family. Writing in the blog *Antiracist Parent*, Jae Ran Kim revisits the myth of the "Great American Melting Pot" from her perspective as both an immigrant and an American mother. The final essay, by James Montague, shows how the English can have as much trouble assimilating to other languages and cultures as any other immigrant group.

Web Sites for Further Exploration and Research

Center for Immigration Studies	http://www.cis.org/
Migrants' Rights Network (U.K.)	http://www.migrantsrights.org.uk/
Global Commission on International Migration (GCIM)	http://www.gcim.org/en/
Compass (U.K.)	http://www.compassonline.org.uk/
Global Forum on Migration and Development	http://www.gfmd-fmmd.org/
Immigration Policy Center (IPC)	http://www.ailf.org/ipc/ipc_index.asp
Pew Hispanic Center	http://pewhispanic.org/
Immigration . . . (Library of Congress, slide show 1 and 2)	http://sp.loc.gov/learn/features/immig/slide1.html (click on slide show 2 link on the bottom of the page)

677

Films and Literature Related to Immigration

Films *Avalon*, 1990; *Crossing Arizona*, 2005; *Schoolhouse Rock! The Great American Melting Pot*, 1977; *The Immigrant* (Charlie Chaplin), 1917; *I Remember Mama*, 1948; *The Kite Runner*, 2007; *Mississippi Masala*, 1992; *The Namesake*, 2006; *A Day without a Mexican*, 2004; *Under the Same Moon*, 2008.

Literature nonfiction: *Enrique's Journey* by Sonia Nazario; novels: *Angela's Ashes* by Frank McCourt; *Interpreter of Maladies* by Jhumpa Lahiri; short stories: *The Middleman and Other Stories* by Bharati Mukherjee; "The Foreigner" by Sarah Orne Jewett; poems: "Mending Wall" by Robert Frost; "The New Colossus" by Emma Lazarus; "You, Whoever You Are" by Walt Whitman.

The Rhetorical Situation

The idea that America is a land founded and sustained by immigrants goes back a long way. As early as the late eighteenth century, J. Hector St. John de Crevecoeur identified Americans as a mix of different European nationalities, which "melt" into one another to create a new identity. While the English, Spaniards, and the French who colonized parts of the North American continent are at its core, the Africans who were brought here as slaves as well as the Native American peoples already on the continent have also had a major influence on the construction of American national character. The history of nineteenth and early twentieth century immigration to North America has generally been constructed as the story of European immigration: Irish, Scottish, German, Polish, Italian, Jewish peoples and others who arrived in New York at Ellis Island in the shadow of the Statue of Liberty and (or so the story goes) enthusiastically assimilated into their new home. Such a view ignores the experiences of many nonwhite immigrants, such as the Chinese people who worked on railroads in the Western United States during the Gold Rush of the mid-nineteenth century, not to mention the Hispanic peoples who were already long-standing residents of Texas and California. (California, having been colonized by Spain, was not only a Hispanic culture but also a part of Mexico, between 1821 and 1846.)

The highly charged debates about immigration in the United States during the last three decades frequently center around issues of assimilation and language; nativists (those who think that there is an essentially American culture that must be defended and preserved) complain that more recent immigrants have kept to themselves and have often failed to learn English. This last complaint led to the English Only and English First movements in the 1980s, which were efforts to lobby local, state, and national governments to make English the "official" language of the nation. In Europe, on the other hand, the situation is complicated by the formation of the European Union, which generally has allowed for freer movement of workers and students among nations in the Union. Many people from former Soviet-bloc states have moved to western European nations; England and

Ireland, for instance, have both experienced an upswing in Polish immigration. Some of the same criticisms made of immigrants to America—nonassimilation and language preference—have also been made of immigrants to the United Kingdom and Ireland. Migration in search of political asylum or economic improvement is, in the end, a global phenomenon; thus, while Africans currently are finding more barriers to their migration to England, China is welcoming African workers.

Furthermore, both North America and Europe have struggled specifically with the economic and social impact of illegal immigration. In the United States, most of the debate about illegal immigration has focused on traffic in illegal immigrants along the southwestern border from California to New Mexico. The notion that poor illegals take jobs from Americans by working for very low wages, by increasing the crime rate, and by overburdening schools and the health system are all arguments advanced by Americans who want to curb illegal immigration. Other political activists, scholars, and policy experts suggest that these generalizations are untrue. Solutions to the problem of illegal immigration that are being advanced by both liberal and conservative politicians and lawmakers range from deportation, imprisonment, and stiff fines to exclusion from schools and drivers' licenses to full amnesty for all illegals currently residing in the United States.

One of the most highly charged controversies in this debate is the proposal to fortify the United States–Mexico border with a 700-foot fence. The idea of such a fence is not limited to the United States, however. Although the Berlin Wall, which separated West Germany from communist East Germany, was demolished in 1990, there exist across the globe other structures designed to keep different groups either inside or outside a specific geographical area. Thailand has just announced its intention to build a long security fence on its border with Malaysia in the interest of thwarting terrorism; India has a nearly complete barrier along its 1,800-mile border with Pakistan; and the divide between North and South Korea by the Demilitarized Zone has been in place since the 1950s.

The proposed "Great Wall of America"[*] is part of a general legislative trend to deal with illegal immigration. In 2005–2006, the Senate introduced its Comprehensive Immigration Reform Act to the U.S. Congress, which proposed increased security along the southern border, a program of "guest workers" not unlike such plans in Europe, and citizenship for long-time illegal residents. Protests against the bill occurred across the nation, and both this and a bill originating in the House failed in 2007. Between 2004 and 2007, the Department of Homeland Security also stepped up its efforts to catch and swiftly deport illegal immigrants. The Secure Fence Act, passed by Congress in 2006, now authorizes physical barriers—the "Great Wall of America"—along 700 miles of the 1,900-mile United States–Mexico border; the fence is designed to stop drug trafficking, terrorists, and illegal immigrants. The fence will include enhanced lighting and increased border checkpoints, plus more high-tech features such as censors, satellites, and cameras to aid detection of border crossings. On the Arizona border a "virtual fence" that relies on radar and cameras to capture illegal immigrants is being planned. The effectiveness of these fences continues to be debated even as portions of it are being built.

*So named by *Time* magazine on its cover, June 30, 2008.

A. How Should We Respond to the Global Problem of Illegal Immigration?

> **BEFORE YOU READ:** Marc Cooper's essay has a biblical title that refers to the Israelites' escape from slavery in Egypt. Based on this allusion, what attitude do you expect the author to have toward the illegal immigrants he writes about?

EXODUS*

Marc Cooper

Marc Cooper is a contributing editor of *The Nation* and a senior fellow at the Institute for Justice and Journalism at the University of Southern California's Annenberg School for Communication. This essay originally appeared in *The Atlantic* magazine.

1   On January 6, celebrated as Three Kings Day in Mexico, the flow of border crossers heading north restarts its annual cycle. So when I arrive on the following Wednesday in the dusty, gritty Sonoran Desert town of Altar, two hours south of the border via a liver-jostling dirt road, the local merchants couldn't be more delighted. I have been to Altar before. And on this trip, I can readily agree with the local street entrepreneurs and hustlers that this year's crossing season, barely in its third day, looks to be as bountiful and profitable as ever—in spite of an also cyclical uproar, north of the border, over illegal immigration. Once an anonymous bus stop on Mexico's Route 2, Altar—a diesel-marinated ten-block grid of around 10,000 people—has become the primary staging area for Mexican migrants before they make their desperate bounce across the border. And the town's entire commercial life rests on this singular enterprise.

2   All around the central plaza that skirts the butternut-colored colonial-era church, small groups—mostly men, mostly young, mostly dressed in dark clothing and running shoes, though there are also some women with babies in their arms—await contact with the *coyote* or *pollero* who has promised to push them through a treacherous but in many ways invisible membrane from which they will emerge, almost magically, on the other side as our carpenters, gardeners, waiters, pickers, pluckers, and nannies. The going rate, door-to-door, from the fields of Veracruz or Oaxaca to the orange orchards of Florida or to a Brentwood kitchen: about $1,500. No need, even, to pay it all in advance: installments, with interest, will be drawn from future income.

3   On the streets adjoining the plaza, tiny, airless shops selling phone cards and converting currency are doing brisk business, as are the occasional youth gangs, who find few other places in Mexico where so many people are walking around with so much folding money in their pockets. Other Mexican migrants fleeing the impoverished south operate a warren of kiosks and stands,

*Marc Cooper, "Exodus," *Atlantic Monthly*, May 2006, http://www.theatlantic.com/doc/200605/mexican-border (accessed June 24, 2008).

offering up for sale everything needed to ease the perilous crossing ahead: plastic gallon jugs of water; plastic baggies of combs, toothbrushes, aspirin tablets, and lip balm; dark jeans; black windbreakers; hooded sweatshirts; athletic shoes; baseball caps; bandanas; backpacks; and the black woolen ski masks favored by the salaried guides who lead the walkers across the desert. Also for sale are black plastic trash bags—$3 each—to be wrapped around the body; they're said to foil the heat-seeking sensors that the U.S. Border Patrol and the Department of Home-land Security have stitched into the other side of *la linea*. One Oaxacan vendor shows off a black cap with an embroidered green cannabis leaf. "They buy this one a lot," he says. "I tell them I don't think it's the best one to wear."

4   A few yards away, the Red Cross has just opened its first-aid trailer for this year's sea-son, and its advice is also readily spurned. "I tell them that they run a great risk," says uniformed paramedic Amado Arellano. He even shows them a colorful but macabre wall map—provided by the Tucson-based Humane Borders group—that marks every spot where a migrant has died in the desert. Hundreds of fatal red dots cluster just above the border. "We try to tell them not to go," he says. "But no one listens. The necessity is too great." . . . Approximately 40,000 migrants per month make this trip through and out of Altar.

5   Accompanied by Jorge Solchaga, a thirty-eight-year-old diplomat who works with the Mexican consulate in Phoenix, I walk through a nameless tortilla shop on a side street off the plaza, out its back door, and into a brick-and-cement courtyard teeming with people getting ready to cross. This is one of Altar's countless unregulated and ill-named "guest houses"—tenement flops that offer nothing except a body-sized patch of floor for $5 or $6 a night. On one side of the cramped courtyard, workmen plaster together an add-on to the tenement; its

owners clearly realize that they are part of a growth industry. A rickety iron staircase leads us to some second-floor lodgings, a bare twenty-by-twenty-foot room in which about fifty people have put down their sleeping mats and backpacks.

6   In the courtyard once more, Solchaga spots a dark-skinned girl with a nursing-age infant in her lap. She stares at the ground as Solchaga gently warns her that she is about to put her life and that of her child at risk. When he presses her on the dangers, she barely nods. Almost inaudibly she says that she's twenty, but she looks five years younger and somewhat terrified. However, the die is cast. She's given up everything back home and will be heading out into a new world within a few minutes. "Make sure your husband carries three extra gal-lons of water for you, you hear?" Solchaga says, nodding to the man sitting behind her. As we exit the flop, Solchaga tells me that the blank look in that girl's eyes will surely haunt him. One of his jobs at the consulate is to process the deaths of Mexicans in the United States. Three years ago in Altar, he tells me, he warned another nursing mother not to make the crossing, and less than a week later, when a call came in to his Ari-zona office requesting him to help identify a "fatality" that had been found in the desert, he recognized the same young woman. "This is my job, and I am used to it," he says. Last year he processed the deaths of 219 Mexicans in the Phoenix area; some were migrants who had wandered in the desert for eight or nine days before their souls and bodies burned out. "It's the young women I never forget," he says, shrugging his shoulders.

7   The night before my trip to Altar, I had dinner with the Tucson-based journalist Charles Bowden, author of more than fif-teen books, most of them set along the bor-der. In perhaps his most acclaimed work, *Down by the River*, certainly a must-read for anyone researching the border, Bowden

describes the poverty that swamps even the more prosperous Mexican border cities and that relentlessly churns the human flow northward. "Over there," he writes of Ciudad Juárez, just across from El Paso, Texas, "most of the streets are unpaved, two thirds of the houses lack any sewage connection. At least 200,000 people in the city live as squatters. . . . At least 35,000 more poor people descend on Juárez each year. Or sixty thousand, no one is sure. They take jobs at $3 to $5 a day that cannot sustain them."

8   When they realize that it's only the width of a river—or a twelve-foot wall, or three strands of cattle wire, or a three-day walk, for that matter—that separates them from a First World economy and some reasonable chance at a future, they push north. "The Mexican border is the only place," Bowden writes, "where the cyberspace world of a major economy rubs up against a world of raw sewage and mud huts. The world of mud is failing to sustain its people." [. . .]

9   With an estimated 11-to-1 manufacturing wage differential between the two countries (some experts put the agricultural wage gap at twice that), why is anyone shocked by what's happening? "You're looking at the biggest story of our lives," Bowden told me over dinner. "This is the largest cross-border human migration in history." Though rarely, if ever, posed in those terms, the staggering numbers tend to bolster Bowden's sweeping vision. Something like 15 million to 20 million migrants have crossed into the United States over the last two decades. An equal number are expected to do so in the next twenty years. "People aren't coming here as much as they are leaving a cratered economy," Bowden said. "The only way you'll stop Mexicans coming to the U.S. is if you lower American wages to the same level as Vietnam. Someone worth maybe $100 a month in Mexico who comes to the U.S. becomes a human ATM machine. McCain-Kennedy, Kyl-Cornyn?" he said, referring to the hodge-podge of current immigration-reform proposals. "It's all bullshit. What we're seeing is something right out of the Bible. This is an exodus."

BEFORE YOU READ: What jobs do you think of as low-level jobs? Which ones are high-level? Would it surprise you to discover that many illegal immigrants hold jobs that require significant skills and pay better than minimum wage?

SHATTERING STEREOTYPES ABOUT IMMIGRANT WORKERS[*]

Daniel Altman

Daniel Altman is an American author, journalist, and economist. He holds a doctorate in economics from Harvard University and writes columns on globalization and economic policy for the *International Herald Tribune* and the *New York Times*.

1   The debate about illegal immigrants' role in the economy has intensified. To some people, they represent a black-market work force that is lowering the wages of legal immigrants

*Daniel Altman, "Shattering Stereotypes about Immigrant Workers," *New York Times*, June 3, 2007, 4.

For Discussion: This is a straightforward journalistic photograph that does not try to be overtly artistic. Nevertheless, the visual composition of the scene is significant. What can you infer about the men from their posture? Why are they depicted only from the rear view? What is the effect of not being able to see their faces?

For Writing: What comment does the photograph make on the essay's title, "Shattering Stereotypes about Immigrant Workers"? Do you think that the photograph records or "shatters" such stereotypes?

Context: The caption reads: In Dallas, men gathered in hopes of being hired. Construction is attracting many illegal immigrants, but so is manufacturing. This photograph depicts men who are seeking work as day laborers with construction companies.

683

and native-born Americans. To others, they are an essential part of several big industries. What's the truth?

2   Getting the whole truth is not easy, because illegal immigrants are not always easy to find, interview, or otherwise include in government or private surveys. But some broad facts seem to be emerging, and they may shatter some preconceived notions: illegal immigrants do not just pick fruit, they do not just work off the books, they rarely earn less than the minimum wage, and they may even be raising employment without harming incomes.

3   For example, there are plenty of illegal immigrants who are not working on farms along the West Coast, gardening, or providing child care, according to figures from the Pew Hispanic Center, a research group in Washington. About 20 percent of illegal immigrants work in construction, 17 percent in leisure and hospitality industries, 14 percent in manufacturing, and 11 percent in wholesale and retail trade.

4   In addition, illegal immigrants represent a substantial share of overall employment in quite a few industries, some of which require extensive skills and training. They may make up at least 10 percent of the work force in construction, leisure and hospitality, and in agriculture and related industries, according to figures calculated by the Pew Hispanic Center. But in specific occupations like cooking, painting, washing cars, packaging by hand, and installation of carpets and floors, they may make up 20 percent or more.

5   A shortage of immigrant labor picking fruit on farms in the West has indeed made the news recently, but it disguises a much larger issue. Illegal immigrants also help big agribusinesses to keep prices low by working in processing and packaging, said Katherine A. Ozer, executive director of the National Family Farm Coalition, a lobbying group in Washington. Though family farms may depend on them to a lesser extent, she said, dairies and other operations do need

immigrant labor. Without them, she said, the structure of the industry would have to change.

6   In many cases, the jobs held by illegal immigrants are far from the minimum- or subminimum-wage stereotype, as well. Though the work itself is often unpleasant, the pay rates are commonly in the range of $10 to $20 an hour, said Jeffrey S. Passel, a senior research associate at the Pew center. "There are some indications that the majority of these workers, maybe 55 to 65 percent, are not in the underground economy," Mr. Passel said. "They're getting paid the same wage rates as everybody else is in those companies. It's written down, and if they work there long enough, they'll get health insurance and everything else."

7   The obvious question is how these immigrants' presence is affecting the overall labor market, especially in these midlevel occupations. Using Mr. Passel's figures, it seems likely that there are about eight million illegal immigrants with jobs right now. That is quite a bit more than the roughly 6.5 million unemployed people counted by the Census Bureau (some of whom might actually be illegal immigrants). Even if all illegal immigrants were deported overnight—the current bill would instead offer them a path to legal status—the rest of the work force might not be able to fill their jobs.

8   Indeed, the presence of illegal immigrants may actually be increasing overall employment, and at little cost to wages, suggested Robert J. LaLonde, a professor of public policy at the University of Chicago. He said that these immigrants increase the overall supply of labor. If demand remains the same, their presence raises the number of jobs in the economy but lowers wages for everyone. But Professor LaLonde said that demand for labor is likely to increase, too, as investment money follows immigrant workers into the country. "The evidence of the effect they have on labor markets in terms of depressing the wages of native-born Americans is quite unclear," he said. "Capital is a much more mobile factor than labor is, so if labor's moving in, you better believe that capital's not too far behind."

9   Professor LaLonde added that the presence of illegal immigrants in some service jobs makes it easier for Americans to participate in the labor force. The immigrants act as complements to higher-wage workers, who can then participate in greater numbers and become more productive. For instance, he said, "it's easier for women to work because you can hire more baby-sitters." Still, if illegal immigrants are often working side by side with native-born Americans and legal immigrants, it is worth asking whether they are reducing opportunities for others. Professor LaLonde dismissed that as unlikely, because in many cases an illegal immigrant may offer a combination of skills and cost that other workers simply cannot match.

10   Potential American competitors "would like these jobs, but they don't want to work at the lower price," Professor LaLonde said. "Mexican day labor doesn't get paid $5 an hour; they're getting paid $8 or $9 an hour. But if you're going to try to beat them at their own game, given that you're not as qualified as they are, you're going to have to undercut their price." If illegal immigrants weren't present at all, Professor LaLonde conceded, others might have more incentive to train for those occupations. "But over all, the U.S. would be poorer," he said. . . . Moreover, existing training programs have not necessarily resulted in a big influx of native-born Americans into immigrant-heavy industries. "The construction industry, at least, is viewed as an unattractive industry," Mr. Crew said. "Other industries are competing for those same people, so the wages in those industries are rising at the same time. It's a competition for people."

> **BEFORE YOU READ:** Do you think that people should be able to enter into work agreements without government regulation? What would be the benefits and drawbacks of a completely unregulated employment market?

THE RIGHT TO SELL LABOR*

Peter Wilby

Peter Wilby writes a weekly column for the *New Statesman*, a British current affairs magazine.

1   There is no longer, I think it is fair to say, a coherent left position on immigration. In principle, the left ought to favor it. Millions of people across the world—in Africa, eastern Europe, the Middle East, the Indian subcontinent—own nothing of marketable value except their labor. Why should they be prohibited from selling it freely?

2   No matter how much we give to Oxfam, the most effective way of helping poor people in developing countries is to welcome them here.[1] The life expectancy of a Ugandan baby who moves to London rises instantly by some 45 years. Remittances from migrant workers are worth far more to many developing countries than foreign aid or investment, with the bonus that the money reaches ordinary families rather than corrupt rulers. In Moldova, remittances account for 38 percent of the economy.

3   But what of social justice in our own country? Employers demanding cheap and pliable labor are the biggest beneficiaries of inward migration. As the Labor MP and former Blair aide Jon Cruddas puts it, migration has become "a key driver in tacitly de-regulating the labor market" and creating a "flexible," low-wage economy.[2] It's poor Britons who have to adjust to migrants, facing not only competition for jobs and houses but also pressure on public services, such as state schools, which are vital to disadvantaged families. All this has led to liberal fears, most cogently expressed by David Goodhart, editor of *Prospect*, that migration will damage the social solidarity and cohesion on which support for the welfare state depends.

4   The left pressure group Compass, with Migrants' Rights Network, has just published an attempt to grapple with these dilemmas (*Towards a Progressive Immigration Policy*, edited by Don Flynn and Zoe Williams). The contributors reach two broad conclusions. First, most attempts to restrict immigration lead only to further injustices. Second, most "problems" attributed to immigration are created by an anxious, insecure, unequal society. As Neal Lawson, the Compass chair, puts it, they will be cured "when we replace the market state with the social state."

5   The second point perhaps appears utopian; Cruddas's Dagenham constituents might observe they're not going to be living in a social state any time soon. The first point, however, is crucial. What no politician admits is that, in the 21st century, migration is nigh impossible to stop. It was difficult 20 years ago when east European states had armed guards and barbed wire to stop people leaving—and the west joyously welcomed asylum seekers as vindication for its way of life. Now there is too much legitimate movement of people and goods across borders for any state to have much hope of restricting what is deemed to be illegitimate. Poor people want work, rich employers want labor. One finds its way to the

*Peter Wilby, "The Right to Sell Labor," *New Statesman*, November 15, 2007, http://www.newstatesman.com/200711150019 (accessed June 24, 2008).

other as surely as the river finds its way to the sea. And if our welfare is the draw, why does America find it so hard to keep out Mexicans?

6   So trying to control borders leads to more illegal or undocumented migrants. They are unlikely to contact the authorities to complain about wages below the minimum, illegal working conditions, arbitrary dismissal or any of the things British workers wouldn't tolerate. They become a labor reserve that undercuts indigenous labor. Nor are they likely to pay taxes.

7   Controls and other measures to discourage immigration, far from protecting U.K. workers, compound the injustices done to them as well as to migrants themselves. As Bernard Ryan, a law lecturer at Kent University and a contributor to the Compass publication, points out, work permits inhibit a migrant's right to resign and seek alternative jobs while restrictions on access to social benefits leave migrants facing destitution if they don't accept whatever work is offered. No wonder employers prefer migrants to British workers.

8   Most proposals for controlling immigration are based on keeping out the riff-raff, but exempting those with valuable skills in, say,

medicine. This leaves poorer countries with the expense of educating professionals, but none of the benefits. According to the World Bank, Grenada has to train 22 doctors to keep just one. This policy, if successful, would trap the global poor in countries that would become more economically and socially impoverished than ever.

9   Regulated immigration—which nearly all politicians say they favor—is fine, as long as it doesn't mean heavily restricted immigration, which simply leads to more unregulated immigration. The best place for regulation is in the workplace. Migrants would not be so attractive to employers if minimum wages and conditions were enforced. Nor would migrants be so keen to come here if working conditions in their countries, often determined by multinationals and their suppliers, were improved. It is on those principles that the left should make its stand.

Editor's notes:

1. Oxfam is a multinational organization on three continents that seeks lasting solutions to poverty and injustice.
2. *M.P.* stands for "Member of Parliament."

BEFORE YOU READ: From your own experience, what is the best way to ensure that newcomers to any community (e.g, a nation, city, neighborhood, religious group) are treated properly?

MIGRATION, THE LARGER PICTURE[*]
Editorial, "Signs of the Times"

This editorial appeared in *America: The National Catholic Weekly*, which is one of the oldest and most respected Catholic magazines in the United States.

1   Amid the negative rhetoric of some . . . who seek to exploit the issue of undocumented immigrants, it is important to keep in mind a larger view of "people on the move." What is happening in the United States

represents just a small part of a worldwide phenomenon.

2   A major reason for migration lies in economics. Of special note is the extreme disparity in wages between countries in the

*Editorial, "Signs of the Times," *America: The National Catholic Weekly,* January 7, 2008, 6.

developing world and in the developed world. The Global Commission on International Migration, in its 2005 report, *Migration in an Interconnected World,* notes, for example, that people in sub-Saharan Africa earn less than a dollar a day.[1] Those who manage to move to higher income nations send remittances back to their home countries: an estimated $167 billion a year. Even though sub-Saharan Africa receives the lowest proportion of global remittances, the report observes that remittances amount to 50 percent of household income in Somalia, for example.

3   Almost half the world's migrants are women, according to the report. Some have received training in their home countries as teachers and nurses. Aware of the significant difference between what they can earn there and the much higher wages elsewhere, many choose to migrate to wealthier nations. The departure of such skilled workers, however, has had an adverse effect on their own countries, giving rise to a so-called brain drain. One long-term goal should therefore be to create adequately paying jobs in low-income countries to lessen the pressure on people to migrate for economic reasons.

4   Although migration may allow women to learn new skills and earn higher wages in destination countries, those with limited education are especially vulnerable to exploitation, and can easily be forced into prostitution. Their vulnerability is all the greater if they are unfamiliar with the language of the country to which they are brought. Children are also vulnerable to trafficking. The United Nations has called this the third largest criminal business in the world. Nor are men exempt from human trafficking. Lured to wealthy countries like the United States with promises of well-paying jobs, many have found on arrival that they are all but enslaved at work sites, with their passports taken from them.

5   Many migrants from Africa die at sea in desperate attempts to reach Europe. Hundreds of undocumented immigrants from Central and Latin America perish annually as they try to cross the southern border of the United States. Ironically, while wealthier countries create ever stricter barriers against undocumented migrants and asylum seekers, the parliament of the European Union has called for increased legal migration to offset the effects of aging populations. Some European officials point out that the possibilities now for legally entering European countries are so restrictive that in effect they encourage illegal immigration.

6   Advocates of a just approach to the world-wide migration challenge believe that it cannot be dealt with by individual countries, but must be addressed multilaterally. To that end Kofi Annan, before stepping down as secretary general of the United Nations, proposed a forum of the 191 member states to discuss best practices in international migration policy and the relation of immigration to global development. In making his recommendation, Mr. Annan said that "our focus in the international community should be on the quality and safety of the migration experience and on what can be done to maximize its development benefits." His proposal resulted in the creation of the Global Forum on Migration and Development, which held its first meeting July [2007] in Belgium.[2] For the forum to succeed, however, a level of generosity on the part of the U.N. member states will be required that has not always been in evidence. Ideally, women, men and children should be able to realize their potential in their home countries and not have to migrate.

7   In the meantime, nativists in the United States continue to press for a one-size-fits-all approach to undocumented immigrants. Some presidential candidates have urged that all 12 million be sent home as "illegal aliens." But as one advocate has said, "People themselves can't be illegal: the term is almost a slur against God." The Universal Declaration of Human Rights will celebrate its 60th anniversary next year.[3] With migrants ever more vulnerable at borders and in countries to which they move, 2008 is a fitting time for world leaders to remember that migration is a human rights issue.

687

Editor's notes:

1. This 2005 report can be read online at http://www.gcim.org/attachements/gcim-complete-report-2005.pdf.

2. July 9–11, 2007, was the first meeting of the Global Forum on Migration and Development, which was designed to start a new global process to use migration to enhance global development and to establish consistent global policies concerning migration.

3. The Universal Declaration of Human Rights was adopted by the United Nations in 1948. The Declaration can be found online at http://www.un.org/Overview/rights.html (accessed June 24, 2008).

B. Do Good Fences Make Good Neighbors When Defining National Borders?

> **BEFORE YOU READ:** One character in Robert Frost's poem "Mending Wall" says that "good fences make good neighbors." The other says, "Something there is that does not love a wall." From your own experience, do walls make for good or bad human relations? Can you give a specific example?

TO WALL OR NOT TO WALL[*]

Jonah Goldberg

Jonah Goldberg, editor at large for the *National Review Online*, is an American conservative commentator.

1   I'm torn between two symbolic arguments about the future of this country. Symbolism matters in politics, a lot. That's why political leaders show their respects to certain creeds and faiths by showing up at churches, synagogues, mosques, ashrams, AIDS clinics, NASCAR races, bratwurst eating contests, and the like. We build monuments and memorials for symbolic reasons. The fight over the confederate flag is a symbolic fight.

2   In short, I get it. Symbolism is important. But it ain't everything. If desecrating the America flag is the only way to stop a guy from setting off a bomb, then *hasta la vista*, Old Glory. And since we're speaking Spanish, I guess I should get to my point. On the one hand, I hate the symbolism of building a wall along our southern border. It would be both literally and figuratively ugly. It would change the narrative of this country in a significant way and send a terrible signal to the world of a fortress America. I don't think that's the only rational interpretation of such a wall, but few can dispute that's how it would be received by the rest of the planet (and our own media).

3   On the other hand, I think the symbolic significance of what's going on now is destructive and has the potential to poison our politics for a long time to come. Even grade-school textbooks make it clear that a country is defined by its borders. People instinctively understand that a nation that can't control its borders is a nation that lacks the confidence and will to stand up for its principles. It creates a culture of lawlessness, breeds contempt for lawmakers, and activates some of the baser instincts of the public. [. . .]

4   Working on the fairly reasonable—but not definite—assumption that a wall would actually work, one benefit would be that these emotional reactions would subside. But if every politician and movement in America that calls for taking illegal immigration seriously is reflexively denounced as "anti-immigration," never

*Jonah Goldberg, "To Wall or Not to Wall," *National Review Online*, August 25, 2005, http://www.nationalreview.com/goldberg/goldberg200508240813.asp (accessed June 24, 2008).

mind racist, then you won't get rid of those sentiments, you'll feed them. In other words, if you don't have a reasonable "anti" immigration movement, you will get an unreasonable one. That's what's happening in parts of Europe.

5   Opponents rightly say you don't need a wall if you simply enforce the laws we have now. O.K. But there's very little reason to believe that moment is just around the corner. They sound like the guys watching Noah load the ark, saying, "All that work will be unnecessary once the rain stops." And, whenever politicians suggest actually doing that, many of the same critics object to that symbolism as well. Indeed, enforcing the laws by placing thousands of armed men—troops, in effect—along the U.S. border isn't a great look, either. And, historically, troops on the border is a bigger provocation than concrete. [. . .]

6   It feels unserious to say this is ultimately all about symbolism, but that's where I come down. I think the economic arguments on both sides are usually unpersuasive. Paying busboys $10 an hour, one probable upshot of a complete halt to illegal immigration, isn't major progress in my book. And it's hard to take liberals seriously when they complain about the costs of a wall—estimates vary from $15 to $30 billion—when they regularly champion other grandiose public works projects. Clearly the cost isn't their real objection.

7   So here I am torn between two bad symbols. Everyone likes to quote Robert Frost's line that "good fences make good neighbors." But they leave out the opening line from the same poem, "Something there is that doesn't love a wall." That sums up my continental divide.

> **BEFORE YOU READ:** This essay and the one that follows discuss the ways in which very low-tech, easy to construct border fences are already showing good results in New Mexico. From your own experience, under what situations are fences most and least effective? When do they work and when don't they work?

LOW-TECH FENCE CUTS DOWN ON PROBLEMS*
Kevin G. Hall

Kevin G. Hall is a reporter for McClatchey News Service.

1   Columbus, N.M.—Taking the low-tech approach, the Border Patrol erected three miles of fencing this year around Columbus, where a 1916 raid by Pancho Villa killed 17 Americans and drew an American military force led by Gen. John J. "Black Jack" Pershing. The 15-foot-high metal fence extends west of town about 2.7 miles and east of town three-tenths of a mile. To the west of Columbus, a waist-high, concrete-filled metal vehicle barrier extends well beyond the fencing. Border Patrol officials wouldn't disclose how much of the vehicle barrier the National Guard has constructed.

2   But along James Johnson's ranch, which runs right to the Mexican border, the barriers have cut down on pickups freely crossing the common frontier with loads of drugs and illegal immigrants. "We don't get the very dangerous drive-through traffic that we used to . . . I like the fence," said Johnson, 32, whose family owns 157 square miles of farm and ranch land. "I think the fence is a very good idea. It will not work in all areas,

---

*Kevin G. Hall, "Low-Tech Fence Cuts Down on Problems," *Fort Worth Star-Telegram*, October 22, 2007, A2.

but there are very strategic areas where it will do a good job."

3 Border Patrol apprehensions for drugs and illegal immigration on this part of the border are down sharply for 2007. The success of such low-tech efforts stands out against the difficulties the Department of Homeland Security is having rolling out its high-tech "virtual fence." The department has given Boeing Integrated Defense Systems until the end of the year to fix the software problems that have prevented sensors, radars, cameras and mobile units from working together effectively.

4 Few politicians envision fencing the entire 2,000-mile U.S.–Mexico border. Plans call for 700 miles of fencing, and only 370 miles of that by the end of next year [2008]. But the low-tech hardware near the main official border crossings in New Mexico seems to discourage crossings along the state's 180-mile border with Mexico. "It's like the toothpaste effect. They were squeezing them in Arizona, and now we're pushing them," said Sharon Mitamura, a Luna County sheriff's deputy

and border veteran who's seen the flow of immigrants drop as they're forced to cross away from inhabited areas. "A lot of it is desolate desert, and we've had some fatalities; but as far as I can tell, it's made an impression. It's slowed it."

5 Statistics suggest as much. Border Patrol apprehensions in New Mexico in the last fiscal year, which ended Sept. 30, [2007] are down about 44 percent from fiscal 2006, when there were 73,518 apprehensions of illegal immigrants. Cocaine seizures by the Border Patrol have dropped from 1,175 pounds in 2006 to 408 pounds through Aug. 31 [2007]. All across the southern border, apprehensions of illegal immigrants are at their lowest level since 1999. In the first 11 months of fiscal 2007, through August, the Border Patrol made 809,056 apprehensions, about 80 percent of the number in the first 11 months of fiscal 2006. It's not clear, however, whether the declines are because of better enforcement or because more immigrants are eluding authorities.

MOST OF TOWN'S RESIDENTS SAY THEY SUPPORT SOLUTION*
McClatchy Newspapers Staff Writer

1 Outside Columbus, N.M.—James Johnson's family has farmed and ranched along the U.S.–Mexico border since 1918. He speaks fluent Spanish and says he's sympathetic to the plight of illegal immigrants and to growers in the interior of the United States who hire them. "But for those of us who have to sit on the front line and deal with these illegals coming across every night and the destruction they leave behind, it's a different story," Johnson said.

2 Illegal immigrants and drug traffickers trample on his onions and watermelons. His cattle are dying of thirst, afraid to go to water-

ing holes that have become makeshift campsites for immigrants making the 35-mile walk north through the desert to Interstate 10. Turning to his computer, Johnson calls up Google Earth, zooming in on a satellite image from last year that shows dozens of footpaths, which from space look like ant trails. Years of illegal immigrants crossing his property made the footpaths.

3 The Border Patrol erected a three-mile fence around Columbus. In the town, nearly everyone approached by McClatchy Newspapers said the fence and stepped-up enforcement are working. Anglos were

*McClatchy Newspapers Staff Writer, "Most of Town's Residents Say They Support Solution," *Fort Worth Star-Telegram*, October 22, 2007, A2.

mostly in favor of the fencing. Hispanic residents acknowledged its effectiveness, but some called the fence divisive. "I have family there in Mexico," said Ezequiel Osono, playing dominos with other elderly Hispanic men who said they were indifferent to the wall.

4   At the town's museum, historical interpreter W. Lee Robinson Jr. told the story of Pancho Villa's 1916 attack on Columbus. After the tour, Robinson confided that he's a Minuteman, part of a self-proclaimed border-protection group that Mexico considers a vigilante hate group. "Being a Minuteman in

New Mexico is getting pretty . . . boring," said Robinson, a Pennsylvania transplant. "There are no illegals here to be found." Across the border in Palomas, the story's the same. Merchants said the town of 10,000 has shrunk by half. Small businesses set up to sell food and drink to U.S.–bound Mexicans have disappeared.

5   At the Ignacio Zaragoza elementary school in Palomas, the new fence marks the end of a soccer field. Administrator Armando Villasana, 50, welcomes the fact that fewer people are trampling across school property at night.

Reading Images: What Is American?

Image 1:
American Gothic.

Context: Grant Wood's well-known painting of the American heartland and its citizens depicts the reigning idea of what it meant to be "American" in 1930 and pokes gentle fun at its subject. The term *American Gothic* refers primarily to the architectural style of the house in the background, but it is often applied to the farmer and the woman as well.

For Discussion: What draws you into this painting? What symbols are included? What is the effect?

For Writing: What items are placed in juxtaposition? What is the effect?

SOURCE: Grant Wood , American 1891-1942, "American Gothic," 1930. Oil on beaver board. 30 11/16" × 25 11/16" (78 × 65.3 cm). Unframed. Friends of American Art Collection. 1930.934. The Art Institute of Chicago. Photography © The Art Institute of Chicago. All Rights reserved by the Estate of Nan Wood Graham/Licensed by VAGA, New York, NY.

Reading Images: What Is American? cont.

Image 2:
Family Home.

For Discussion: What are some of basic elements this photograph has in common with the painting *American Gothic* on page 691? How are the photo and the painting relevant to the article that follows?

For Writing: Compare and contrast this photograph with the Wood painting. In what ways are the figures and the values they embody similar and different? What claim do you think the photographer is making about who is an American in the twenty-first century?

Context: The caption reads: Family Heirloom: Eddie and Gloria Garza's two-acre lot "has a senti-mental value that is worth more than any amount of money," Gloria says. The composition of this photograph, with a serious man and woman posed against a house, recalls in a subtle way Grant Wood's iconic image of American life and values.

692

BEFORE YOU READ: The article below discusses how building a portion of the "Great Wall of America" in Texas is creating a conflict between landowners' rights and the government's stated intention to protect the general public. In the abstract, which do you think is more important, the individual's property rights or the public's safety? Do you think that the wall described here will actually provide real protection for Americans?

TOWN AGAINST THE WALL[*]
Miguel Bustillo

Miguel Bustillo is a staff writer for the *Los Angeles Times*.

1   Granjeno, Texas—Gloria Garza doesn't have a whole lot. But what she has, she clings to with pride. She lives in a simple stucco house with a rustic wooden veranda and a well fashioned from odd stones her husband found around the state. Kittens stretch lazily in the sun beside her porch. Armadillos dart across her backyard. Her two-acre lot is her heirloom, her link to a legacy that dates to 1767, when Spain's King Carlos III gave her pioneer ances-tors a *porcion* of property that started at the Rio Grande and stretched inland for miles.

---

*Miguel Bustillo, "A Town Against the Wall," *Los Angeles Times*, December 17, 2007, http://www.latimes.com/news/nationworld/columnone/la-na-granjeno17dec17,1,4218804.story (accessed June 26, 2008).

2   So she is not going to be quiet while some bureaucrat in Washington tries to take it—to build a border fence. She doesn't want to become an unintended victim in a war against illegal immigration that she sees as misguided and wrong. "It would be heartbreaking," said Garza, 51, who teaches tots in a Head Start program. "For us, this place has a sentimental value that is worth more than any amount of money."

3   Granjeno is a frontier town of about 400 people, where everyone seemingly lives a door down from their uncle and descends from the same rancheros. It outlasted the rule of Spain, Mexico and the independent Republic of Texas. But it might not survive the U.S. government's plan to build 370 miles of steel fencing along the border with Mexico.

4   Blueprints show that about a third of Granjeno's house lots lie in the fence's path, even though the town sits more than a mile from the Rio Grande, the dividing line between the U.S. and Mexico. The fence would run alongside an earthen levee that passes just south of Granjeno, because federal officials fear that if it were built by the river it would be worn away by flooding. "I always thought, I'll serve my country, they'll pay me a little money and I'd build my house here and retire," said Mayor Alberto Magallan, 73, a 20-year Air Force veteran. "Now, a government man comes and tells me he's going to take my land? It's not right."

5   Granjeno weathered the racially charged land fights that shook the Rio Grande Valley after the Civil War, when Anglo newcomers acquired property through schemes that included using the Texas Rangers to intimidate the *Tejanos*, earlier Texans of Mexican or Spanish descent. Granjeno persevered again a decade ago, when it fought off Hidalgo County power brokers who decided that the path to prosperity after the North American Free Trade Agreement was a big bridge to Mexico that would run right over the town and consume much of it. But this fight may be the last for Granjeno, which is named for a thorny shrub with bright orange berries that is said to bloom more beautifully here than anywhere else.

6   Federal officials stress that the fence's location in Granjeno, just like the rest of the 70 miles of border walls being planned for the lower Rio Grande Valley, is subject to change. "No final decisions have been made in the construction of fencing in that area," said Michael Friel, a spokesman for U.S. Customs and Border Protection in Washington. "The input from the community will be a vital part of the process." Yet Border Patrol leaders have made it clear that they believe places like Granjeno—where drug smugglers and illegal immigrants can cross the river and slip into someone's house within minutes—are where physical barriers are needed most.

7   Wary locals note that government officials have already been knocking on doors, asking residents to sign release forms granting access to their properties so that surveyors can begin plotting where the fence will go. Many old-timers refused to sign, worried that if the properties are condemned, Granjeno will be too small to carry on. In response to similar resistance all along the border in Texas, Homeland Security Secretary Michael Chertoff said . . . that he would take landowners to court to seize property if needed, and also pledged that he would not pay more than market price for land.

8   Some in Granjeno argue that as descendants of the Spanish land grant families, they have property rights that the federal government cannot take away. A few attorneys think they may be right and recently offered to represent Granjeno's citizens *pro bono*. But in a post–Sept. 11 environment, legal experts said, there's virtually no chance of stopping a fence that's touted as a way to make the nation safer. "The way things look, nothing is going to be left," said Garza's uncle, Daniel Garza, 73. "Then two miles west, the fence is going to stop. Do they really think people won't go around?"

9   Similar complaints are heard from El Paso to Brownsville, in river towns only a football field away from sister cities in Mexico, where

the prevailing culture has long been bilingual and binational, and where everyone knows someone on the other side.

10   Many border residents still can't believe that a fence they ridiculed as a politician's pipe dream is about to become reality. They're stunned that the wild river that served as the playground of their youth will soon look like a military zone. But in Granjeno, the mood is especially melancholy. People feel like they are being fenced off from their heritage. Granjeno was once a rambling expanse of small ranchos that spanned thousands of acres of brushy country. The homesteads were owned by descendants of the land-grant families, the Munguias and the Bocanegras, and *Tejano* families such as the Garzas and Anzalduas that got parcels through business deals and marriages. Most existed well before the Treaty of Guadalupe Hidalgo, which recognized the Rio Grande as the border between Texas and Mexico in 1848.

11   "We didn't come to the United States," said Rey Anzaldua, 62. "The United States came to us."

12   Citrus farms, housing developments and flood-control projects chipped away at Granjeno over the last century, leaving little but some working-class families with historic last names. Now the town is just a city hall, a church, a cluster of small houses and one business—a bar with cinder-block walls named Cabrera's Place—all crammed into a third of a square mile. Crumbling plaster-coated buildings teeter next to sturdy brick homes. Ponies wander in fenced yards beside broken-down trucks.

13   Granjeno is so poor that until it recently installed solar-powered lamps, its streets went dark at night. The per-capita income is $9,022. Half of the population lives below the poverty line. It only got around to incorporating as a city in the last decade, when the border bridge threatened its existence. The town has little political clout in today's lower Rio Grande Valley, one of the nation's fastest-growing regions. "We have no voice in government," said Granjeno's unofficial historian, Yolanda Martinez, 61, who is Rey Anzaldua's sister. "Money talks, and we have none."

14   Though Granjeno is short on wealth, it is rich in tradition. Families that left years ago dutifully return to bury their dead in pastoral El Granjeno Cemetery. It was founded in 1872 by the heir to a sheep ranch named Don Juan Garza to inter his brother Antonio, who was killed in a gunfight across the river in Reynosa. Fresh flowers adorn family plots memorializing men who served in the Civil War, World War II and Vietnam. Among the marble and brick gravestones is a marker for Sgt. Luis Ramirez, who reportedly meant to sign up for the Confederacy like most Texans but mistakenly enlisted with the Union side instead.

15   Sotero Anzaldua, 39, who trims the trees and keeps the gravestones clean, thinks a border fence may do some good. "The government has a right to do what it wants," he said in Spanish. He blamed river-crossers for a burglary at his brother's house. But most here don't believe illegal immigration is becoming worse, or was ever bad. Gloria Garza fondly recalled that her mother used to leave aromatic plates of tacos on her porch at night— a token of *Tejano* hospitality for the migrants trudging north.

16   If anything, the clannish Granjeno folk— who shift easily between Spanish and English, often midsentence—seem more leery of newcomers such as the Border Patrol and the Minutemen than they are of illegal immigrants and drug-runners. Anyone not native to Granjeno is always going to be viewed with suspicion by some, no matter how long they've been around. "He's still on probation!" joked former Mayor Vicente Garza, 55, pointing to his 79-year-old neighbor. Felix de la Cruz, who fell in love with a Granjeno girl when Harry Truman was president, has lived in town since 1951.

17   Napoleon Garza wanted to show off a side of old Granjeno that was fast fading into memory. So the 31-year-old son of Vicente Garza, and nephew of Gloria Garza, hopped into his dilapidated car and headed beyond the earthen levee toward the Rio Grande. The government had condemned many acres in Granjeno to build the levee during the 1970s. But there were still a few isolated homesteads

to the south, including one with a perimeter of cactuses serving as a crude fence, and another that was inhabited by a man of scant words whom locals called "The Mexican Redneck." The redneck wasn't home, so Garza drove over a dead cottonmouth snake and kept going until he reached a *resaca*, or abandoned riverbed, where the Rio Grande ran decades ago before shifting course.

18   Then he headed for the river. "This is what I'm going to miss," he said as he stood by the banks, staring at the slowly moving water. For all his life he has hunted javelinas, pig-like critters, at this spot, he explained. Next he drove a few minutes west to the site of another massive public works project that was taking shape. Construction crews were lining up orderly rows of monolithic concrete pillars—the foundation for the international bridge Granjeno had successfully fought against a decade ago. It was being built just outside the town. Called the Anzalduas Bridge, it's expected to ease long wait times at the border when it opens in 2009. With the bridge and the border fence, Granjeno would

be walled off by manufactured structures on two sides.

19   Garza walked down to the slope where the 10-foot-tall Carrizo cane weeds had been cleared in preparation for the final pillars, and began chatting up a Mexican man who sat minding a fishing pole on the opposite bank, which was less than 50 yards away. "He's a lookout," Garza concluded, and drove back to town. Minutes earlier, Garza had pointed out that he was running over one of the electronic sensors the Border Patrol plants in the ground to detect movements. Soon, he predicted, he'd have company.

20   As he pulled into Granjeno, a white Border Patrol truck raced up. The agent quickly realized he was dealing with locals, not drug-runners, and sped away. But that did not stop a car full of neighborhood kids from pulling beside Garza and shouting "*Dame la maleta!*" ("Give me the suitcase!") to make fun of the border cop who mistook Garza for a smuggler. Garza ignored them. "Pretty soon, it will all be behind the wall," he said sadly. "I won't even be able to pick blackberries down there no more."

C. What is the Relationship between Immigration and Nationality?

BEFORE YOU READ: Many immigrants from different countries face the possibility of having their families separated. In your opinion, how important is it to keep families united?

AMERICA'S DIVIDE[*]

Arian Campo-Flores

Arian Campo-Flores has been the *Newsweek* Miami bureau chief since 2002. He covers stories in the southeastern United States, and he has also written about the war in Iraq. Most recently, Campo-Flores covered the war as an embedded reporter with the Third Infantry Division and, for a brief stint, with U.S. Special Forces. He wrote about the army's advance on Baghdad, Iraqi militia groups, and clandestine military operations. He was also one of the first *Newsweek* reporters to arrive at the World Trade Center on September 11, 2001.

1   Irma Palacios carries a faint remnant of her days as an undocumented fruit picker: a

scar on her right wrist left by the acidic secretion of citrus trees. It serves as a reminder of

---

*Arian Campo-Flores, "America's Divide," *Newsweek*, Oct 15, 2007, http://www.newsweek.com/id/45915 (accessed June 25, 2007).

how far she's come, from a frightened, forlorn little girl who crossed the border from Mexico nearly 20 years ago to a college-educated, hard-charging political organizer. As the Miami-based national field director for *Mi Familia Vota*—a Hispanic civic-engagement program of People for the American Way— she jets around the country, from Phoenix to Philadelphia, setting up grass-roots operations to register and empower Latino voters. [. . .]

2   Among the people whose cause she's championing: her undocumented brother-in-law Raymundo, who requested that his last name be withheld to avoid problems with authorities. While the immigration issue has galvanized Palacios, it has driven Raymundo deeper into hiding. He's more worried than ever about being deported—so much so that the skin under his chin sometimes breaks out in hives. When rumors circulate of immigration raids in Homestead, Fla., where he lives, he refuses to leave the house. At his handyman job in the Florida Keys, he monitors the radio constantly for reports of Cuban refugees washing up onshore, knowing the highways will soon be crawling with law enforcement. He's panicked about what to do when his driver's license expires; new rules require that he show proof of legal residency to renew it. "I try not to think about it all," says Raymundo, 28. But the feeling of vulnerability gnaws at him.

3   Raymundo's fear and Palacios's defiance show how diverse the immigrant experience can be—even within one family. The immigration debate is usually framed as though there were a clear demarcation between legal residents and illegal aliens who live "in the shadows." But reality is far messier. Palacios's clan—six siblings and their spouses and kids—includes Americans by birth, naturalized citizens, permanent residents and undocumented immigrants. Such "mixed status" families are no aberration. According to a recent Pew Hispanic Center study, 64 percent of the children of illegals are U.S.–born. Factor in those who hold one of countless tem-

porary work visas, and the shades of gray multiply even more. [. . .]

4   The immigration debate has divided the GOP [Republican Party]. While the business wing of the party clamors for a guest-worker program that will provide a steady supply of labor, social conservatives demand a crackdown on lawbreaking immigrants. The public appears just as split. According to a Pew poll, 53 percent of respondents say that people in the country illegally should be sent home, while 40 percent believe they should be granted some form of legal status. Another issue troubling Republicans: if they end up passing a law that alienates Hispanics, they risk squandering hard-fought gains among a constituency that's key to the party's future viability. But as political analyst Norm Ornstein reads the Republicans' thinking, concerns about "long-term dominance in presidential politics" may take a back seat— for now at least—to "short-term worry about alienating the populist, conservative, nativist base."

5   It would not be the first time in American history that nativist sentiment prevailed. When waves of immigrants from Southern and Eastern Europe arrived at the turn of the 20th century, doomsayers argued that the foreigners would never assimilate into Anglo culture. The result: a 1924 law establishing a quota system that sought to limit entry. More recently, the massive immigrant influx of the 1990s provoked a backlash personified by California Gov. Pete Wilson, who tried to deny education and health services to illegal aliens. Though that wave of both legal and illegal immigration has tapered a bit, the proportion of the undocumented has ballooned. According to studies by the Pew Hispanic Center, the illegal population living in the United States has grown from 5 million in 1996 to as many as 12 million today. Of the total, 78 percent came from Mexico and the rest from Latin America—the vast majority of whom were fleeing poverty.

6   That was certainly true of Irma Palacios's mother, María Hernández. Abandoned by her husband and left to raise six kids on her own in Reynosa, Mexico, Hernández struggled to make ends meet. So she set off alone one day in 1986 and illegally crossed the Rio Grande into Texas. The kids stayed behind, with the eldest caring for the little ones. When Hernández arrived in Homestead, Fla., where she had friends, she immediately got to work, picking tomatoes, squash and limes. After settling down and scraping together some savings, she began an arduous two-year process of bringing each of her children across the border. She secured false birth certificates for some, and arranged "coyotes"—guides who help migrants cross over—for others. Palacios made it across easily—fast asleep in the back seat of a car. Her brother Jorge, though, suffered a harrowing journey in which he nearly drowned, and was then caught and deported once he arrived in Texas (he succeeded on a second try). Eventually, all the kids joined their mother.

7   Soon thereafter, Hernández took advantage of the 1986 amnesty law. That allowed her to adjust the status of the three oldest siblings. But because of a paperwork error, Palacios and two of her sisters remained illegal. The results were heartbreaking for the family. Opportunities available to some of the kids were forbidden to others. Palacios vividly recalls one day when she and her sister Luz were preparing for work. Luz, who had a green card and could take legal jobs, slipped into a business suit to head to an air-conditioned office where she worked as a receptionist. Palacios, on the other hand, donned her flannel shirt and jeans to go toil in a sweltering vegetable-packing plant. Another sister, Sandra, who was also illegal, recalls with frustration how she couldn't qualify for financial aid at a community college. "I felt like I was handicapped," she says. "I had a lot of potential to be whatever I wanted to be, and I just couldn't."

8   In 1995, though, the younger sisters became legal with the help of an immigration attorney. Palacios remembers the giddiness at discovering her newfound freedom. That December, she told her mother that she needed to earn money to buy Christmas presents. When her mother suggested calling up the packing plant, Palacios agreed—then instantly caught herself. "Wait a minute," she said. "I have my papers. I can go work at Publix [supermarket]!" She put her legal status to good use, leveraging her 4.2 high-school GPA (11th out of a class of 500) into admission to Florida State University, where she got a bachelor's degree in Spanish in 1999. For her part, Sandra, now 32, has worked two jobs, 70 hours per week, over the last nine years to finance her education at Florida International University, where she'll earn her degree in public administration in December. Both are now applying for citizenship.

9   So, too, is the youngest sister, Isela, 26, who's married to Raymundo, the illegal immigrant. She's hoping that as a citizen, she'll be able to legalize his status. But the process is by no means automatic, and it's often arduous. Meanwhile, the family agonizes over his status. "He's going to get stopped sooner or later," says Isela, who shudders at the thought of his being wrested away from their daughter, Adriana. Over dinner one night last week, Palacios pointed to Raymundo's shaved head. "You look like a gang member," she said, concerned that he'd be a target of stepped-up gang sweeps by authorities. "Don't worry," he replied, assuring her that he wears his work cap whenever he goes out. Such is the wariness—bordering on paranoia—that illegal status breeds. The climate of fear "kills you psychologically," said Jorge, 37, the older brother, who recalls the feeling well.

10   Not all Latinos feel his pain. Past Pew Hispanic Center studies have shown that sizable minorities of Hispanics believe illegal immigrants hurt the economy by driving down wages and that migrant flows should either remain the same or be reduced. In

states like Arizona, significant numbers of Latinos have backed measures that curbed illegals' access to social services. But now, some of the more ambivalent Latinos may be rallying behind the undocumented in the face of what they consider excessive—and possibly racist—immigrant-bashing. A more recent poll of legal immigrants by Bendixen & Associates found that 76 percent of Latin American respondents believed that anti-immigrant sentiment was growing and 62 percent said it affected them and their families.

11   That noxious atmosphere has galvanized many Latinos. [. . .] Palacios's family has been energized as well. Isela, Raymundo's wife, plans to join the April 10 [2006] demonstration that Palacios is planning.

And Sandra, the Florida International University student, is plotting her own immigration rally and teach-in on campus. "Our family taught us to fight—*luchar*—for those who can't," says Palacios. She thinks her mother, who died four years ago, would be proud of what she and her siblings have accomplished: not just owning homes and developing careers, but offering succor to those striving illegal immigrants who have arrived in their wake. "I still see myself in that group," says Sandra. "I know how they're feeling—the desperation, the anguish." The strivers' best hope may well lie in what Sandra's planning: a campaign to remind America that it has always grown stronger, not weaker, when it opens its arms.

698

> **BEFORE YOU READ:** Before you read the essay, what generally does the metaphor of a "great American melting pot" mean to you?

THE GREAT AMERICAN MELTING POT?*

Jae Ran Kim

Jae Ran Kim, M.S.W., is a social worker, teacher, and writer. She was born in Taegu, South Korea, and was adopted and moved to Minnesota in 1971. She has written numerous articles and essays and, most recently, has work published in the anthology *Outsiders Within: Writings on Transracial Adoption*, from South End Press. Jae Ran's blog, *Harlow's Monkey*, can be accessed at http://harlowmonkey.typepad.com/.

1   Okay, I am totally showing my age here, but when I was a kid in the Midwest in the 1970's and 80's, my siblings and I spent every Saturday morning watching cartoons and it's safe to say that much of what I remember about the 3R's (reading, 'riting and 'rithmatic) came from the *Schoolhouse Rock* series that ran from 1973 to 1985.

2   Some of you might remember—Feeding on the commercial nostalgia and marketability, a few years back Disney put together a compilation of the 41 *Schoolhouse Rock* "episodes." I

---

*Jae Ran Kim, "The Great American Melting Pot?" *Anti-racist Parent* blog, http://www.antiracistparent.com/ (accessed June 26, 2008). Path: Authors; open Jae Ran Kim; scroll to title.

thought it would be a fun way to kick in the nostalgia-memory cells and show my kids how TV was done in the "olden" days. They were amazed at "Conjunction junction, what's your function?" and little, lonely "Bill" on Capital Hill. But then we came across the *America Rock* series.

3   In 1976, the *Schoolhouse Rock* creators began working on a series to celebrate and highlight the bicentennial that was titled *America Rock*. My favorite of the *America Rock* series was "The Great American Melting Pot" with the image of all these little kids jumping into a swimming pool "pot" shaped like the United States. Of course, as an internationally adopted kid, "The Great American Melting Pot" was a comforting notion. Heck, the United States is a country MADE of immigrants like myself! Right?

4   Uh, wrong. Looking back at TGAMP with fresh and adult eyes, here is what I learned: "America was founded by the English, German, French and Dutch." And the "immigrants" who came "in search of honest pay?" They were Russian and Italian. That's right—nary a Korean, Nigerian, Iranian, Japanese, Indian, or Kenyan. Not an Ethiopian, Somalian, Chinese or Guatemalan. According to the 1970s version of the United States, this country was only made up of Europeans and Eastern Europeans.

5   Nothing was mentioned about the people who were already on the land. Nothing about the slaves and indentured servants kidnapped and stolen and forced to "immigrate." In short, nothing but a happy, pastel rainbow version of how great all the "immigrants" have "melted" into a giant pot. My daughter, in her viewing of this clip, said outright, "That's racist!"

6   In the class I taught last semester, I used this clip in my lecture on the frameworks and messages we receive about race and differences in our childhoods, through media, and our culture. I think about how much more people of color are represented in the media

now, versus when I was a kid; yet mostly those representations are still founded on stereotypes.

7   None of the *America Rock* episodes address slavery or how the early colonists tried to wipe out the First Nations people who were living on the land they wanted to homestead—which in a way surprises me since this is after the Civil Rights movement and MLK [Martin Luther King], an era which I have always associated as a time of hippies, the feminist movement and 70s "Free to Be You and Me." To give you a comparison, the miniseries *Roots* was aired in 1977, the same year "The Great American Melting Pot" began its Saturday morning run.

8   In researching *America Rock*, I looked for some kind of critique of the biased representation of what "America" is (and of course, they say "America" but really mean the United States, not North or South America). I haven't come across one yet. Even when Disney re-issued these episodes, where was the review about how "old school" they are? That the idea of a pluralistic society back then was equated with a European-ethnic identity and not a truly global ethnic identity?

9   It's things like *America Rock* that contributed to my internalized racism and internal colonization. Despite the lack of people "like me" portrayed in these vehicles of education I completely bought into the melting pot mentality. It's bizarre that as an internationally adopted person who was raised by a family who embodied the perception of what "American" was I was raised to believe I had the same white privilege of my family and could not reconcile why other people did not "know this." Because duh—other people saw me as a racialized person. That's a humdinger of a concept to try and get.

10   In trying to negotiate the way people of color are portrayed in our society's cultural production, I've made a conscious decision not to prohibit my kids from watching these

shows and movies, but to watch them together and point out how people like ourselves and our friends are portrayed in entertainment. As a result, my daughter has honed a critical eye. When we went to a water park last spring, there was a "Tiki" theme to the park and my daughter was the first to notice the "mascot" was a buck-toothed, short and stout "Native Pacific Island" girl. When I was her age, I doubt I would have been able to articulate how I felt seeing someone like myself portrayed in such a stereotypical caricature—and although I was proud that my daughter is able to do so, it hurts to know that we're still facing these stereotypes at all.

THE GREAT AMERICAN MELTING POT

Music and lyrics by Lynn Ahrens

My grandmother came from Russia
A satchel on her knee,
My grandfather had his father's cap
He brought from Italy.
They'd heard about a country   5
Where life might let them win,
They paid the fare to America
And there they melted in.

Lovely Lady Liberty
With her book of recipes   10
And the finest one she's got
Is the great American melting pot
The great American melting pot.

America was founded by the English,
But also by the Germans, Dutch, and French.   15
The principle still sticks;
Our heritage is mixed.
So any kid could be the president.

You simply melt right in,
It doesn't matter what your skin,   20
It doesn't matter where you're from,
Or your religion, you jump right in
To the great American melting pot
The great American melting pot.

Ooh, what a stew, red, white, and blue.   25
America was the New World
And Europe was the Old.
America was the land of hope,
Or so the legend told.
On steamboats by the millions,   30
In search of honest pay,
Those nineteenth century immigrants sailed
To reach the U.S.A.

Reading Images: American Ideals

Context: In this image, European immigrants landing at Ellis Island are welcomed by the Statue of Liberty.

Image 1:
Illustration in *Frank Leslie's Illustrated* Newspaper, July 2, 1887.

For Discussion: From their dress and attitudes, where do you think that these passengers have come from, and what is their attitude toward arriving in the United States?

For Writing: Although the lyrics to "The Great American Melting Pot" (page 700) and this image of immigrants do not directly illustrate one another, they share a common set of values and beliefs about the relation of migrant cultures to America. Analyze the formal elements of both the sketch and the poem and describe how they define the process of immigration in a setting that considers the "melting pot" a cultural ideal.

Context: This cartoon image of immigrants arriving in America is part of the animation for *America Rock*, a part of the *Schoolhouse Rock* series seen on television in the 1970s and 1980s.

Image 2:
Immigrants Arriving in America.

For Discussion: What do you think is the significance of the idea of new immigrants "melting into" American culture? Is it an accurate metaphor? Why, or why not? Can you think of a better one?

For Writing: Compare this cartoon image with image 1. How are they the same, and how are they different? Consider these images as extensions of "The Great American Melting Pot" song lyrics on pages 700–702. How is the process of immigration depicted in these two images? What is the mood of the people and the Statue of Liberty? How accurate would you say these images and lyrics are for immigrants today?

Lovely Lady Liberty
With her book of recipes   35
And the finest one she's got
Is the great American melting pot
The great American melting pot.
What good ingredients,
Liberty and immigrants.   40

They brought the country's customs,
Their language and their ways.
They filled the factories, tilled the soil,
Helped build the U.S.A.
Go on and ask your grandma,   45
Hear what she has to tell
How great to be American
And something else as well.

Lovely Lady Liberty
With her book of recipes   50
And the finest one she's got
Is the great American melting pot
The great American melting pot.

The great American melting pot.
The great American melting pot.   55

> **BEFORE YOU READ:** The American tourist who never wants to leave his comfort zone and expects foreign countries to be just like home is a cultural cliché. This essay describes a British version of this stereotype, individuals who migrate to Spain but refuse to learn or speak Spanish. Why do you think people are resistant to learning new languages, even when that language is dominant in the culture where they live?

THEY JUST WON'T MIX*

James Montague

1 The class began badly. "*Como se llama*?" the teacher asked hopefully. I was stumped. I might have been living in Alcúdia, 20 miles south of Valencia, for ten months, but I'd managed to bumble through trips to the supermarket or post office with a shrug and a "*Sí, gracias.*" This time, I had come unstuck.

2 Mohammad, a Moroccan electrician, intervened. "She wants your name," he whispered helpfully. It was my first Spanish lesson for immigrants, under a government-subsidized scheme that gives migrant workers basic language skills. Moroccan butchers, Georgian gardeners and Romanian housewives fill the

---

*James Montague, "They Just Won't Mix," *New Statesman*, January 3, 2008.

seats in the strip-lit room, eager to learn. For 3 euros (£2.10) a year, you get four hours of evening classes a week in intermediate Spanish to help fill out forms, buy a stamp, or pick up some milk. It's a forward-thinking scheme that seems to benefit everyone. Except for one group: the British.

3   Despite there being between one and one and a half million of us living in Spain, I was the only Brit in the class. For the teachers, that was no surprise. "The English live apart, with their own jobs and own bars. They close themselves off," explained Juan, who has been teaching immigrants Spanish for 25 years at Alcúdia's Enric Valor college. "They just don't try to integrate with the Spanish." This year's course has been the most popular yet, he said, with 60 immigrants filling three classes. Another 25 are on the waiting list. "We have a few Scots in the advanced class, but that's the most British we have ever had."

4   According to the latest figures from the Office for National Statistics, 58,000 people left for Spain in 2004–2005 and the number is rising. More people emigrated from the UK [United Kingdom] in 2006 than has ever been recorded by the ONS. Yet, for the Spanish, this group of immigrants is proving problematic.

5   "There are even schools just for British children and they prefer that to mixing with Spanish children," said Ximo, another teacher at the college. "The Moroccans, Bulgarians— all of them try to live with us and try to integrate. The British don't."

6   Even some of the British immigrants in Spain agree. "The younger generation is learning Spanish, but the majority are retired, so they either can't or can't be bothered," says James Parkes, editor of the *Costa Blanca News*. "The central government is aiming [Spanish classes] at people outside of the EU [European Union], with a different culture. There's a bit of a 'stuck here with a load of North Africans' attitude." The irony in many of the Brits citing immigration and a loss of national identity as a big reason for upping sticks is not lost on Parkes. "The Spanish approach it differently because they emigrated in huge numbers themselves."

7   Maybe that is why Britain's current policy on English lessons for immigrants is in a mess. Everyone agrees it would be a good idea, but no one wants to pick up the tab. Private colleges charge huge fees for basic English lessons, putting them out of reach for low-wage migrants. A one-term English course at International House in London will set you back £435. Some further education colleges offer subsidised courses of English for speakers of other languages, but even these are expensive. A 15-week course at the North Essex Adult Community College in my home town of Witham would cost £99.

8   The Spanish see teaching their language to immigrants—even language-retarded Brits like me—as an investment. "The idea is to integrate, because it's better than to live apart," explains Ximo as he gathers his things for his next class. "Europe needs the immigrants for work. If we give them something, they give us something back."

703

Questions to Help You Think and Write about Immigration

1. Marc Cooper's "Exodus" and the essay entitled "Migration: The Larger Picture" both examine the situation of illegal immigrants from an ethical perspective. Based on what you have read about illegal immigration as a

global phenomenon, create a hypothetical scenario for such an immigrant (migrating from any country to any country) and analyze how that person's situation should be handled as a "human rights issue." What effect would particulars of this fictional person's life have on your response to his or her situation?

2. Make a list of stereotypes about immigrants that come to mind. Using the essays that you have read in part A of this section on immigration, argue the claim that these stereotypes are not supported by the available evidence.

3. Peter Wilby argues that labor is a personal possession that any individual should be able to capitalize on for themselves. Taking Wilby's argument to its logical conclusion, what kind of immigration policies might such a premise lead to or demand?

4. Part B of Section 6 is concerned with the ethics and practicality of walling off one nation from another. The "Great Wall of America" would not be the first barrier of this kind: recall the four imges of walls in Chapter 4, for example. What are the benefits and the drawbacks of defining the nation by such physical barriers? Can you still be an American if you live on the wrong side of the wall or if you lived in a foreign country? What defines national identity?

5. One thematic thread running throughout the essays by Goldberg, Hall (and its short companion piece), Bustillo, and Campo-Flores are the symbolic and practical importance of home, private property, and the family. Why are home, land, and family such powerful symbols of citizenship, belonging, and personal rights?

6. The essays in part C offer varied perspectives on the contemporary immigrant's experience of the United States. What do you think are the most difficult aspects of the immigrant experience, and what could the American government and people do to help migrants adjust to their new lives?

7. "The Great American Melting Pot" is a concept that goes back to the nineteenth century. What are the unspoken warrants that underlie such a claim? Do you agree or disagree with the social implications of the metaphor? If appropriate, offer and explain a metaphor that better suits your understanding of a healthy relationship of migrants to their old and new countries.

8. Assume, for the sake of argument, that you have moved to a new country, culture, or even planet and that you want very much to "fit in" to your new surroundings. What are the most important things a migrant must do to assimilate successfully to a different culture? For instance, consider characteristics like religion, language, clothing, customs, or other factors that might be crucial to this effort of fitting in culturally. When in your life have you been an outsider, and what did you do (or not do) to fit in or become an "insider"?

9. Compare any two images from the section on immigration as images engaged in a dialogue about what it means to be an American. What do these visual arguments suggest are the defining qualities of the "American" identity? What is omitted from these images, in your view?

Issues concerning War and Peace

The Issues

A. Is War Inevitable? How Does War Become Integral to Society?

In this section, three authors, one of whom is a major American philosopher, one a major figure in anthropology, and one a well-known war correspondent, provide competing perspectives on the inevitability of war. William James, a self-avowed pacifist, believes that people, and young men in particular, have a need for warfare and, given this view, offers a way to transfer their aggression to other, more productive outlets. James's essay is followed by images of war memorials that illustrate some of the virtues of the martial character alluded to in the James excerpt. Margaret Mead does not agree that the need to fight is a natural condition. Basing her work on research that shows some cultures do not understand the concept of war, Mead argues that war is neither a biological given nor a necessary condition, but is instead an invention. Chris Hedges has spent fifteen years of his life reporting from active war zones. He writes about the addictive qualities of war and why many people are drawn to it.

The final two essays explore the ways in which war becomes a part of society as a game. The first describes how the realities of their lives draw Iraqi children to war games, while the second discusses how the U.S. Army uses a video game to make armed service attractive to American boys. See also "The Gettysburg Address" (pages 274–275), "In the Shadow of Horror, SS Guardians Relax and Frolic" (pages 93–94), "War Casualty Total Jumps, But Is Revised after Article" (pages 207–208), "Forget Flag Burning" (pages 145–147) and excerpts from the graphic novel *Maus* (pages 499–509). See war images on pages 8, 92, 93, 146, 214, 274, 282, 284, 286, and 302.

B. How Do People Justify War?

The essays here focus on some ways in which individuals either justify war or try to come to terms with war. William Bennett explains the concept of a "just war," an idea that can be traced back to St. Augustine in the fourth century. Gerard Powers, although he opposed the war in Iraq, stresses that the U.S. has an ongoing moral duty to the Iraqi people, while Haim Watzman describes two situations in which a potentially immoral act is also the right one.

C. What Might Help Establish Peace?

The essays in this final section on war offer different perspectives on ways to achieve peace. Pulitzer Prize–winner Richard Rhodes discusses the continuing threat of nuclear arms and argues that the problem can only be solved by cooperation among nations. Robert Hirschfield, suggesting that individuals can make a difference in the quest for peace, writes about how exchanging war stories helped Israeli and Palestinian soldiers understand one another better. Susan Neiman reflects on a new lesson to be learned from the Holocaust, celebrating the valor of small, local, even passive acts of resistance to tyranny. Michael Walzer makes the case for U.S. military intervention in other nations for humanitarian reasons; paradoxically, sometimes force is necessary for a true and lasting peace. See also "We're Fighting Terror, But Killing Freedom" (pages 56–57), and "Never Again," (pages 309–310).

Web Sites for Further Exploration and Research

Images of War: Combat Photography 1918–1971	http://www.eyewitnesstohistory.com/cbpintro.htm
The Virtual Wall (Vietnam Veterans Memorial)	http://www.virtualwall.org/
Institute for War and Peace Reporting	http://iwpr.net/
America's Army: The Official Army Game	http://www.americasarmy.com/
U.S. Department of Homeland Security	http://www.dhs.gov/index.shtm
Nuclear Threat Initiative	www.nti.org/
Electronic Intifada	http://electronicintifada.net/
Combatants for Peace	http://www.combatantsforpeace.org/
Voice/Vision: Holocaust Survivor Oral History Archive	http://holocaust.umd.umich.edu/
War in Context	http://warincontext.org/
Carnegie Endowment for International Peace	http://www.carnegieendowment.org/

Films and Literature Related to War and Peace

Films *Apocalypse Now*, 1979; *Beaufort*, 2007; *Black Hawk Down*, 2002; *Full Metal Jacket*, 1987; *Grace Is Gone*, 2007; *Lions for Lambs*, 2007; *Mash*, 1970; *Munich*, 2005; *Operation Enduring Freedom*, 2002; *Pearl Harbor*, 2001;

Redacted, 2007; *Saving Private Ryan*, 1998; *Schindler's List*, 1993; *Valkyrie*, 2008; *Standard Operating Procedure*, 2008.

Literature novels: *A Farewell to Arms* by Ernest Hemingway; *Heart of Darkness* by Joseph Conrad; *Red Badge of Courage* by Stephen Crane; *Shorttimers* by Gustav Hasford; *War and Peace* by Leo Tolstoy; short stories: "Barbie and Ken Experience the War" by Diana Dell; "Stockings" by Tim O'Brien; poems: "Death of the Ball Turret Gunner" by Randall Jarrell; "The Diameter of the Bomb" and "Memorial Day for the War Dead" by Yehuda Amichai; "Tu Do Street" and "Starlight Scope Myopia" by Yusef Komanyakaa; "The Vietnam Wall" by Alberto Rios; "The War Works Hard" by Dunya Mikhail.

The Rhetorical Situation

Few issues are more controversial than whether or not a country should go to war. In the United States, nationalism and patriotism remained strong during World Wars I and II and almost all of the smaller wars in which this country has been engaged, but the war in Vietnam, like the American Civil War one hundred years earlier, tore the United States in half, changing the face of politics and conceptions of and responses to warfare.

More recently, the war in Iraq—beginning with the 2003 invasion through the 2005 Iraqi elections to the 2007 troop surge (increase)—has led to many deaths for both Americans and Iraqis and has been marked by continual problems of insurgency. While the Bush administration originally hoped to uncover Saddam Hussein's weapons of mass destruction (WMDs; chemical, biological, and/or nuclear weapons of large-scale destruction of life) and to liberate Iraq from tyranny and establish a democratic government, sectarian violence and anti-American sentiment continue to fuel further violence. Terrorism, too, continues to be a global problem.

At the same time, the proliferation of nuclear materials and the movement of both Iran and North Korea to develop nuclear weapons indicate that we may be reliving some of the tensions of the Cold War era, when the United States and Soviet Union were then superpowers poised in military and ideological opposition to one another. Complicating matters still further is the fact that as regimes such as the Soviet Union crumbled, their militaries lost track of these powerful weapons, and many are believed to have fallen into terrorist hands.

Wars, the problem of war itself, and its potential solutions lie in the constitution of human nature. Whether we think that war is innate or invented, war becomes almost an expected feature of life in afflicted nations, and the hostility and violence that characterize war as an event can be communicated and nurtured, both deliberately and accidentally, in activities as innocent as children's games. At the same time, education and conversation between individuals seem as important as national negotiations in reestablishing peace. Finally, lessons learned from wars of the past century ranging from wars for independence to the Holocaust, to the present century, with ongoing fighting in places ranging from Afghanistan to Africa, can help us deal more intelligently with war as a human problem. The lessons conveyed by history are various and even paradoxical: in some cases the past tells us that only force can bring a true and lasting peace and in other cases that the will to survive is itself an act of successful resistance.

The current state of national affairs and recent history will greatly affect the way you and others think about the nature of war. Answers to the questions posed by this section of "The Reader" may seem difficult to solve, but history shows that people persist in their efforts to solve the problem of war and violence and to restore a global peace. This is, as Richard Rhodes puts it, the good news.

A. Is War Inevitable? How Does War Become Integral to Society?

> **BEFORE YOU READ:** Do you think war is something we have in our "blood"? Or do you think that war is a way of resolving conflict people learn from culture and history? Do you know the source of your thinking about this issue?

THE MORAL EQUIVALENT OF WAR*

William James

The philosopher William James (1842–1910), brother of novelist Henry James, advanced pragmatic philosophy through his famous writings, *The Will to Believe and Other Essays in Popular Philosophy* (1897) and *The Varieties of Religious Experience* (1902). In the following essay, James claims that it is necessary to get the desire to fight out of men rather than going to war and proposes a solution. What is that solution? How pragmatic for civil life do you think his solution would be?

1 The war against war is going to be no holiday excursion or camping party. The military feelings are too deeply grounded to abdicate their place among our ideals until better substitutes are offered than the glory and shame that come to nations as well as to individuals from the ups and downs of politics and the vicissitudes of trade. There is something highly paradoxical in the modern man's relation to war. Ask all our millions, north and south, whether they would vote now (were such a thing possible) to have our war for the Union expunged from history, and the record of a peaceful transition to the present time substituted for that of its marches and battles, and probably hardly a handful of eccentrics would say yes. Those ancestors, those

*First Published by the Association for International Conciliation in 1910 and in *McClure's,* 1910. From *The Best American Essays of the Century,* Joyce Carol Oates, ed., and Robert Atwan, coed. (New York: Houghton Mifflin, 2000), 45–49, 52–55.

efforts, those memories and legends, are the most ideal part of what we now own together, a sacred spiritual possession worth more than all the blood poured out. Yet ask those same people whether they would be willing in cold blood to start another civil war now to gain another similar possession, and not one man or woman would vote for the proposition. In modern eyes, precious though wars may be, they must not be waged solely for the sake of the ideal harvest. Only when forced upon one, only when an enemy's injustice leaves us no alternative, is a war now thought permissible.

2   It was not thus in ancient times. The earlier men were hunting men, and to hunt a neighboring tribe, kill the males, loot the village and possess the females, was the most profitable, as well as the most exciting, way of living. Thus were the more martial tribes selected, and in chiefs and peoples a pure pugnacity and love of glory came to mingle with the more fundamental appetite for plunder.

3   Modern war is so expensive that we feel trade to be a better avenue to plunder; but modern man inherits all the innate pugnacity and all the love of glory of his ancestors. Showing war's irrationality and horror is of no effect upon him. The horrors make the fascination. War is the *strong* life; it is life *in extremis:* war-taxes are the only ones men never hesitate to pay, as the budgets of all nations show us.

4   History is a bath of blood. The *Iliad* is one long recital of how Diomedes and Ajax, Sarpedon and Hector *killed.* No detail of the wounds they made is spared us, and the Greek mind fed upon the story. Greek history is a panorama of jingoism and imperialism— war for war's sake, all the citizens being warriors. It is horrible reading, because of the irrationality of it all—save for the purpose of making "history"—and the history is that of the utter ruin of a civilization in intellectual respects perhaps the highest the earth has ever seen. [. . .]

5   Such was the gory nurse that trained societies to cohesiveness. We inherit the warlike type; and for most of the capacities of heroism that the human race is full of we have to thank this cruel history. Dead men tell no tales, and if there were any tribes of other type than this they have left no survivors. Our ancestors have bred pugnacity into our bone and marrow, and thousands of years of peace won't breed it out of us. The popular imagination fairly fattens on the thought of wars. Let public opinion once reach a certain fighting pitch, and no ruler can withstand it. In the Boer war both governments began with bluff, but couldn't stay there, the military tension was too much for them. In 1898 our people had read the word WAR in letters three inches high for three months in every newspaper. The pliant politician McKinley was swept away by their eagerness, and our squalid war with Spain became a necessity.

6   At the present day, civilized opinion is a curious mental mixture. The military instincts and ideals are as strong as ever, but are confronted by reflective criticisms which sorely curb their ancient freedom. Innumerable writers are showing up the bestial side of military service. Pure loot and mastery seem no longer morally avowable motives, and pretexts must be found for attributing them solely to the enemy. England and we, our army and navy authorities repeat without ceasing, arm solely for "peace," Germany and Japan it is who are bent on loot and glory. "Peace" in military mouths today is a synonym for "war expected." The word has become a pure provocative, and no government wishing peace sincerely should allow it ever to be printed in a newspaper. Every up-to-date Dictionary should say that "peace" and "war" mean the same thing, now *in posse,* now *in actu.* It may even reasonably be said that the intensely sharp competitive *preparation* for war by the nations *is the real war,* permanent, unceasing; and that the battles are only a sort of public

verification of the mastery gained during the "peace" interval. [. . .]

7   In my remarks, pacificist tho' I am, I will refuse to speak of the bestial side of the war-regime (already done justice to by many writers), and consider only the higher aspects of militaristic sentiment. Patriotism no one thinks discreditable; nor does any one deny that war is the romance of history. But inordinate ambitions are the soul of every patriotism, and the possibility of violent death the soul of all romance. The militarily patriotic and romantic-minded everywhere, and especially the professional military class, refuse to admit for a moment that war may be a transitory phenomenon in social evolution. The notion of a sheep's paradise like that revolts, they say, our higher imagination. Where then would be the steeps of life? If war had ever stopped, we should have to reinvent it, on this view, to redeem life from flat degeneration. [. . .]

8   Having said thus much in preparation, I will now confess my own utopia. I devoutly believe in the reign of peace and in the gradual advent of some sort of a socialistic equilibrium. The fatalistic view of the war-function is to me nonsense, for I know that war-making is due to definite motives and subject to prudential checks and reasonable criticisms, just like any other form of enter-prise. And when whole nations are the armies, and the science of destruction vies in intellectual refinement with the sciences of production, I see that war becomes absurd and impossible from its own monstrosity. [. . .]

9   All these beliefs of mine put me squarely into the anti-militarist party. But I do not believe that peace either ought to be or will be permanent on this globe unless the states pacifically organized preserve some of the old elements of army-discipline. A perma-nently successful peace-economy cannot be a simple pleasure-economy. In the more or less socialistic future towards which

mankind seems drifting we must still subject ourselves collectively to those severities which answer to our real position upon this only partly hospitable globe. We must make new energies and hardihoods continue the manliness to which the military mind so faithfully clings. Martial virtues must be the enduring cement; intrepidity, contempt of softness, surrender of private interest, obe-dience to command, must still remain the rock upon which states are built—unless, indeed, we wish for dangerous reactions against commonwealths fit only for con-tempt, and liable to invite attack whenever a centre of crystallization for military-minded enterprise gets formed anywhere in their neighborhood.

10   The war-party is assuredly right in affirming and reaffirming that the martial virtues, although originally gained by the race through war, are absolute and perma-nent human goods. Patriotic pride and ambition in their military form are, after all, only specifications of a more general competitive passion. They are its first form, but that is no reason for supposing them to be its last form. Men now are proud of belonging to a conquering nation, and without a murmur they lay down their per-sons and their wealth, if by so doing they may fend off subjection. But who can be sure that *other aspects of one's country* may not, with time and education and sugges-tion enough, come to be regarded with sim-ilarly effective feelings of pride and shame? Why should men not some day feel that it is worth a blood-tax to belong to a collec-tivity superior in *any* ideal respect? Why should they not blush with indignant shame if the community that owns them is vile in any way whatsoever? Individuals, daily more numerous, now feel this civic passion. It is only a question of blowing on the spark till the whole population gets incandescent, and on the ruins of the old morals of military honour, a stable system of morals of civic honour builds itself up.

What the whole community comes to believe in grasps the individual as in a vise. The war-function has graspt us so far; but constructive interests may some day seem no less imperative, and impose on the individual a hardly lighter burden.

11   Let me illustrate my idea more concretely. There is nothing to make one indignant in the mere fact that life is hard, that men should toil and suffer pain. The planetary conditions once for all are such, and we can stand it. But that so many men, by mere accidents of birth and opportunity, should have a life of *nothing else* but toil and pain and hardness and inferiority imposed upon them, should have *no* vacation, while others natively no more deserving never get any taste of this campaigning life at all,— *this* is capable of arousing indignation in reflective minds. It may end by seeming shameful to all of us that some of us have nothing but campaigning, and others nothing but unmanly ease. If now—and this is my idea—there were, instead of military conscription a conscription of the whole youthful population to form for a certain number of years a part of the army enlisted against *Nature*, the injustice would tend to be evened out, and numerous other goods to the commonwealth would follow. The military ideals of hardihood and discipline would be wrought into the growing fibre of the people; no one would remain blind as the luxurious classes now are blind, to man's real relations to the globe he lives on, and to the permanently sour and hard foundations of his higher life. To coal and iron mines, to freight trains, to fishing fleets in December, to dish-washing, clothes-washing, and window-washing, to road-building and tunnel-making, to foundries and stoke-holes, and to the frames of sky-scrapers, would our gilded youths be drafted off, according to their choice, to get the childishness knocked out of them, and to come back into society with healthier sympathies and soberer ideas. They would

have paid their blood-tax, done their own part in the immemorial human warfare against nature, they would tread the earth more proudly, the women would value them more highly, they would be better fathers and teachers of the following generation.

12   Such a conscription, with the state of public opinion that would have required it, and the many moral fruits it would bear, would preserve in the midst of a pacific civilization the manly virtues which the military party is so afraid of seeing disappear in peace. We should get toughness without callousness, authority with as little criminal cruelty as possible, and painful work done cheerily because the duty is temporary, and threatens not, as now, to degrade the whole remainder of one's life. I spoke of the "moral equivalent" of war. So far, war has been the only force that can discipline a whole community, and until an equivalent discipline is organized, I believe that war must have its way. But I have no serious doubt that the ordinary prides and shames of social man, once developed to a certain intensity, are capable of organizing such a moral equivalent as I have sketched, or some other just as effective for preserving manliness of type. It is but a question of time, of skillful propagandism, and of opinion-making men seizing historic opportunities.

13   The martial type of character can be bred without war. Strenuous honour and disinterestedness abound elsewhere. Priests and medical men are in a fashion educated to it, and we should all feel some degree of it imperative if we were conscious of our work as an obligatory service to the state. We should be *owned*, as soldiers are by the army, and our pride would rise accordingly. We could be poor, then, without humiliation, as army officers now are. The only thing needed henceforward is to inflame the civic temper as past history has inflamed the military temper.

711

Reading Images: War Memorials and Martial Character

Image 1:
Iwo Jima Monument (Marine Corp War Memorial), Washington, D.C.

For Discussion: Each of these monuments has a different *ethos* or concept of the dead men and women it honors. What values do these American monuments associate with the soldiers they commemorate?

For Writing: Consider these three war memorials as visual arguments about the nature of war and the nation's appropriate response to it. What claim does each monument make and how does its construction provide evidence in support of that claim? In what ways do the memorials offer a consistent idea of how to honor the war dead? In what ways do their arguments differ from one another?

Image 2:
Tomb of the Unknown Soldier, Arlington National Cemetery.

Image 3:
Vietnam Veterans Memorial.

Context: William James concludes the previous essay by stating that "the martial type of character can be bred without war." James wants to distinguish the civic virtues that military service cultivates from the violent act of war itself. The War Memorial is an important cultural symbol of the martial character and its virtues. Here we see three well-known American examples. The Marine Corps Monument (also known as the Iwo Jima Monument) near the Potomac River in Washington, D.C., was designed by Felix DeWeldon based on Joe Rosenthal's famous photograph of the flag being raised at Iwo Jima. Many nations have one or more tombs of the "Unknown Soldier." The Tomb of the Unknown Soldier in Arlington National Cemetery contains the remains of soldiers from World Wars I and II, the Korean Conflict, and the Vietnam War. The Monument's inscription reads: "Here Rests in Honored Glory an American Soldier, Known But to God." The Vietnam War Memorial on the Mall in Washington, D.C., has a very different character. Designed by sculptor and landscape artist Maya Lin, the Wall is made up of two black granite walls etched with the names of the dead. One wall points toward the Lincoln Memorial, the other toward the Washington Monument. Visitors search for names of friends and family and often leave tokens such as photos, flowers, or flags.

> **BEFORE YOU READ:** Can you imagine a world without war? What important social changes would characterize such a utopian world? Use your imagination!

WARFARE: AN INVENTION—NOT A BIOLOGICAL NECESSITY*

Margaret Mead

A leading cultural anthropologist, Margaret Mead (1901–1978) became a household name in the United States because of her best-selling work, *Coming of Age in Samoa* (1928), about her field research on sexuality among adolescents in Samoa. She went on to write forty-four books. In the following article, Mead argues against the traditional notion that warfare is a biological, not a cultural, drive. While you read, consider whether you think war and/or warring behavior is something we inherit from genetics or from society.

1   Is war a biological necessity, a sociological inevitability, or just a bad invention? Those who argue for the first view endow man with such pugnacious instincts that some outlet in aggressive behavior is necessary if man is to reach full human stature. It was this point of view which lay back of William James's famous essay, "The Moral Equivalent of War," in which he tried to retain the warlike virtues and channel them in new directions. A similar point of view has lain back of the Soviet Union's attempt to make competition between groups rather than between individuals. A basic, competitive, aggressive, warring human nature is assumed, and those who wish to outlaw war or outlaw competitiveness merely try to find new and less socially destructive ways in which these biologically given aspects of man's nature can find expression. Then there are those who take the second view: warfare is the inevitable concomitant of the development of the state, the struggle for land and natural resources of class societies springing, not from the nature of man, but from the nature of history. War is nevertheless inevitable unless we change our social system and outlaw classes, the struggle for power, and possessions; and in the event of our success

warfare would disappear, as a symptom vanishes when the disease is cured.

2   One may hold a compromise position between these two extremes; one may claim that all aggression springs from the frustration of man's biologically determined drives and that, since all forms of culture are frustrating, it is certain each new generation will be aggressive and the aggression will find its natural and inevitable expression in race war, class war, nationalistic war, and so on.

3   All three positions are very popular today among those who think seriously about the problems of war and its possible prevention, but I wish to urge another point of view, less defeatist perhaps than the first and third, and more accurate than the second: that is, that warfare, by which I mean organized conflict between two groups as *groups*, in which each group puts an army (even if the army is only fifteen Pygmies) into the field to fight and kill, if possible, some of the members of the army of the other group—that warfare of this sort is an invention like any other of the inventions in terms of which we order our lives, such as writing, marriage, cooking our food instead of eating it raw, trial by jury, or burial of the dead, and so on. Some of this list any one will grant are inventions: trial by jury is confined

Asia 40.8 (August 1940): 402–405.

713

to very limited portions of the globe; we know that there are tribes that do not bury their dead but instead expose or cremate them; and we know that only part of the human race has had a knowledge of writing as its cultural inheritance. But, whenever a way of doing things is found universally, such as the use of fire or the practice of some form of marriage, we tend to think at once that it is not an invention at all but an attribute of humanity itself. And yet even such universals as marriage and the use of fire are inventions like the rest, very basic ones, inventions which were perhaps necessary if human history was to take the turn it has taken, but nevertheless inventions. At some point in his social development man was undoubtedly without the institution of marriage or the knowledge of the use of fire.

4   The case for warfare is much clearer because there are peoples even today who have no warfare. Of these the Eskimo are perhaps the most conspicuous example, but the Lepchas of Sikkim are an equally good one. Neither of these peoples understands war, not even the defensive warfare. The idea of warfare is lacking, and this lack is as essential to carrying on war as an alphabet or a syllabary is to writing. But whereas the Lepchas are a gentle, unquarrelsome people, and the advocates of other points of view might argue that they are not full human beings or that they had never been frustrated and so had no aggression to expend in warfare, the Eskimo case gives no such possibility of interpretation. The Eskimo are not a mild and meek people; many of them are turbulent and troublesome. Fights, theft of wives, murder, cannibalism occur among them—all outbursts of passionate men goaded by desire or intolerable circumstance. Here are men faced with hunger, men faced with loss of their wives, men faced with the threat of extermination by other men, and here are orphan children, growing up miserably with no one to care for them, mocked and neglected by those about them. The personality necessary for war, the

circumstances necessary to goad men to desperation are present, but there is no war. When a traveling Eskimo entered a settlement he might have to fight the strongest man in the settlement to establish his position among them, but this was a test of strength and bravery, not war. The idea of warfare, of one *group* organizing against another *group* to maim and wound and kill them, was absent. And without that idea passions might rage but there was no war.

5   But, it may be argued, isn't this because the Eskimo have such a low and undeveloped form of social organization? They own no land, they move from place to place, camping, it is true, season after season on the same site, but this is not something to fight for as the modern nations of the world fight for land and raw materials. They have no permanent possessions that can be looted, no towns that can be burned. They have no social classes to produce stress and strains within the society which might force it to go to war outside. Doesn't the absence of war among the Eskimo, while disproving the biological necessity of war, just go to confirm the point that it is the state of development of the society which accounts for war, and nothing else?

6   We find the answer among the Pygmy peoples of the Andaman Islands in the Bay of Bengal. The Andamans also represent an exceedingly low level of society: they are a hunting and food-gathering people; they live in tiny hordes without any class stratification; their houses are simpler than the snow houses of the Eskimo. But they knew about warfare. The army might contain only fifteen determined Pygmies marching in a straight line, but it was the real thing none the less. Tiny army met tiny army in open battle, blows were exchanged, casualties suffered, and the state of warfare could only be concluded by a peacemaking ceremony.

7   Similarly, among the Australian aborigines, who built no permanent dwellings but wandered from water hole to water hole over their almost desert country, warfare—and

714

rules of "international law"—were highly developed. The student of social evolution will seek in vain for his obvious causes of war, struggle for lands, struggle for power of one group over another, expansion of population, need to divert the minds of a populace restive under tyranny, or even the ambition of a successful leader to enhance his own prestige. All are absent, but warfare as a practice remained, and men engaged in it and killed one another in the course of a war because killing is what is done in wars.

8   From instances like these it becomes apparent that an inquiry into the causes of war misses the fundamental point as completely as does an insistence upon the biological necessity of war. If a people have an idea of going to war and the idea that war is the way in which certain situations, defined within their society, are to be handled, they will sometimes go to war. If they are a mild and unaggressive people, like the Pueblo Indians, they may limit themselves to defensive warfare; but they will be forced to think in terms of war because there are peoples near them who have warfare as a pattern, and offensive, raiding, pillaging warfare at that. When the pattern of warfare is known, people like the Pueblo Indians will defend themselves, taking advantage of their natural defenses, the *mesa* village site, and people like the Lepchas, having no natural defenses and no idea of warfare, will merely submit to the invader. But the essential point remains the same. There is a way of behaving which is known to a given people and labeled as an appropriate form of behavior. A bold and warlike people like the Sioux or the Maori may label warfare as desirable as well as possible; a mild people like the Pueblo Indians may label warfare as undesirable; but to the minds of both peoples the possibility of warfare is present. Their thoughts, their hopes, their plans are oriented about this idea, that warfare may be selected as the way to meet some situation.

9   So simple peoples and civilized peoples, mild peoples and violent, assertive peoples, will all go to war if they have the invention, just as those peoples who have the custom of dueling will have duels and peoples who have the pattern of vendetta will indulge in vendetta. And, conversely, peoples who do not know of dueling will not fight duels, even though their wives are seduced and their daughters ravished; they may on occasion commit murder but they will not fight duels. Cultures which lack the idea of the vendetta will not meet every quarrel in this way. A people can use only the forms it has. So the Balinese have their special way of dealing with a quarrel between two individuals; if the two feel that the causes of quarrel are heavy, they may go and register their quarrel in the temple before the gods, and, making offerings, they may swear never to have anything to do with each other again. Under the Dutch government they registered such mutual "not-speaking" with the Dutch government officials. But in other societies, although individuals might feel as full of animosity and as unwilling to have any further contact as do the Balinese, they cannot register their quarrel with the gods and go on quietly about their business because registering quarrels with the gods is not an invention of which they know.

10   Yet, if it be granted that warfare is after all an invention, it may nevertheless be an invention that lends itself to certain types of personality, to the exigent needs of autocrats, to the expansionist desires of crowded peoples, to the desire for plunder and rape and loot which is engendered by a dull and frustrating life. What, then, can we say of this congruence between warfare and its uses? If it is a form which fits so well, is not this congruence the essential point? But even here the primitive material causes us to wonder, because there are tribes who go to war merely for glory, having no quarrel with the enemy, suffering from no tyrant within their boundaries, anxious neither for land nor loot nor women, but merely anxious to win prestige which within

715

that tribe has been declared obtainable only by war and without which no young man can hope to win his sweetheart's smile of approval. But if, as was the case with the Bush Negroes of Dutch Guiana, it is artistic ability which is necessary to win a girl's approval, the same young man would have to be carving rather than going out on a war party.

11   In many parts of the world, war is a game in which the individual can win counters—counters which bring him prestige in the eyes of his own sex or of the opposite sex; he plays for these counters as he might, in our society, strive for a tennis championship. Warfare is a frame for such prestige-seeking merely because it calls for the display of certain skills and certain virtues; all of these skills—riding straight, shooting straight, dodging the missiles of the enemy, and sending one's own straight to the mark—can be equally well exercised in some other framework and, equally, the virtues—endurance, bravery, loyalty, steadfastness—can be displayed in other contexts. The tie-up between proving oneself a man and proving this by a success in organized killing is due to a definition which many societies have made of manliness. And often, even in those societies which counted success in warfare a proof of human worth, strange turns were given to the idea, as when the Plains Indians gave their highest awards to the man who touched a live enemy rather than to the man who brought in a scalp—from a dead enemy—because killing a man was less risky. Warfare is just an invention known to the majority of human societies by which they permit their young men either to accumulate prestige or avenge their honor or acquire loot or wives or slaves or sago lands or cattle or appease the blood lust of their gods or the restless souls of the recently dead. It is just an invention, older and more widespread than the jury system, but none the less an invention.

12   But, once we have said this, have we said anything at all? Despite a few instances, dear to the hearts of controversialists, of the loss of the useful arts, once an invention is made which proves congruent with human needs or social forms, it tends to persist. Grant that war is an invention, that it is not a biological necessity nor the outcome of certain special types of social forms, still, once the invention is made, what are we to do about it? The Indian who had been subsisting on the buffalo for generations because with his primitive weapons he could slaughter only a limited number of buffalo did not return to his primitive weapons when he saw that the white man's more efficient weapons were exterminating the buffalo. A desire for the white man's cloth may mortgage the South Sea Islander to the white man's plantation, but he does not return to making bark cloth, which would have left him free. Once an invention is known and accepted, men do not easily relinquish it. The skilled workers may smash the first steam looms which they feel are to be their undoing, but they accept them in the end, and no movement which has insisted upon the mere abandonment of usable inventions has ever had much success. Warfare is here, as part of our thought; the deeds of warriors are immortalized in the words of our poets; the toys of our children are modeled upon the weapons of the soldier; the frame of reference within which our statesmen and our diplomats work always contains war. If we know that is it not inevitable, that it is due to historical accident that warfare is one of the ways in which we think of behaving, are we given any hope by that? What hope is there of persuading nations to abandon war, nations so thoroughly imbued with the idea that resort to war is, if not actually desirable and noble, at least inevitable whenever certain defined circumstances arise?

13   In answer to this question I think we might turn to the history of other social inventions, inventions which must once have seemed as firmly entrenched as warfare. Take the methods of trial which preceded the jury system: ordeal and trial by combat. Unfair, capricious, alien as they are to our feeling today, they were once the only methods open to individuals accused of some offense. The invention

716

of trial by jury gradually replaced these methods until only witches, and finally not even witches, had to resort to the ordeal. And for a long time the jury system seemed the one best and finest method of settling legal disputes, but today new inventions, trial before judges only or before commissions, are replacing the jury system. In each case the old method was replaced by a new social invention; the ordeal did not go out because people thought it unjust or wrong, it went out because a method more congruent with the institutions and feelings of the period was invented. And, if we despair over the way in which war seems such an ingrained habit of most of the human race, we can take comfort from the fact that a poor invention will usually give place to a better invention.

14   For this, two conditions at least are necessary. The people must recognize the defects of the old invention, and some one must make a new one. Propaganda against warfare, documentation of its terrible cost in human suffering and social waste, these prepare the ground by teaching people to feel that warfare is a defective social institution. There is further needed a belief that social invention is possible and the invention of new methods which will render warfare as out-of-date as the tractor is making the plow, or the motor car the horse and buggy. A form of behavior becomes out-of-date only when something else takes its place, and in order to invent forms of behavior which will make war obsolete, it is a first requirement to believe that an invention is possible.

> **BEFORE YOU READ:** Think of stories (real or fictional) that you have read or movies that you have seen about war. What can make war attractive to ordinary people?

WAR IS A FORCE THAT GIVES US MEANING[*]
Chris Hedges

The author has been a war correspondent for fifteen years. The following are excerpts from the introduction to his book *War Is a Force That Gives Us Meaning*. He draws his perspective on the inevitability of war by reflecting on his first-hand experiences.

1   War and conflict have marked most of my adult life. I began covering insurgencies in El Salvador, where I spent five years, then went on to Guatemala and Nicaragua and Colombia, through the first *intifada* in the West Bank and Gaza, the civil war in the Sudan and Yemen, the uprisings in Algeria and the Punjab, the fall of the Romanian dictator Nicolae Ceauşescu, the Gulf War, the Kurdish rebellion in southeast Turkey and northern Iraq, the war in Bosnia, and finally to Kosova. I have been in ambushes on desolate stretches of Central American roads, shot at in the marshes of southern Iraq, imprisoned in the Sudan, beaten by Saudi military police, deported from Libya and Iran, captured and held for a week by Iraqi Republican Guard during the Shiite rebellion following the Gulf War, strafed by Russian Mig-21s in Bosnia, fired upon by Serb snipers, and shelled for days in Sarajevo with deafening rounds of heavy

*Chris Hedges, *War Is a Force That Gives Us Meaning*. New York: Anchor, 2005, 2–14.

artillery that threw out thousands of deadly bits of iron fragments. I have seen too much of violent death. I have tasted too much of my own fear. I have painful memories that lie buried and untouched most of the time. It is never easy when they surface.

2   I learned early on that war forms its own culture. The rush of battle is a potent and often lethal addiction, for war is a drug, one I ingested for many years. It is peddled by mythmakers—historians, war correspondents, filmmakers, novelists, and the state—all of whom endow it with qualities it often does possess: excitement, exoticism, power, chances to rise above our small stations in life, and a bizarre and fantastic universe that has a grotesque and dark beauty. It dominates culture, distorts memory, corrupts language, and infects everything around it, even humor, which becomes preoccupied with the grim perversities of smut and death. Fundamental questions about the meaning, or meaninglessness, of our place on the planet are laid bare when we watch those around us sink to the lowest depths. War exposes the capacity for evil that lurks not far below the surface within all of us. And this is why for many war is so hard to discuss once it is over.

3   The enduring attraction of war is this: Even with its destruction and carnage it can give us what we long for in life. It can give us purpose, meaning, a reason for living. Only when we are in the midst of conflict does the shallowness and vapidness of much of our lives become apparent. Trivia dominates our conversations and increasingly our airwaves. And war is an enticing elixir. It gives us resolve, a cause. It allows us to be noble. And those who have the least meaning in their lives, the impoverished refugees in Gaza, the disenfranchised North African immigrants in France, even the legions of young who live in the splendid indolence and safety of the industrialized world, are all susceptible to war's appeal.

4   Those who make war do so for many reasons, although many of these motives are never acknowledged publicly.

5   The Palestinian uprising was not just about throwing the Israelis out of Gaza and the West Bank, but also about crushing the urban elite, the shop owners and businessmen, in East Jerusalem and Gaza City. The "strikes" organized by the *shabab*, the young men who fueled the uprising from the refugee camps, hurt the Palestinian community far more than they hurt the Israelis. In Bosnia it was the same, the anger turned against a Communist hierarchy that kept for itself the privileges and perks of power even as power slipped from their hands in the decaying state. There is little that angers the disenfranchised more than those who fail to exercise power yet reap powerful rewards. Despots can be understood, even tolerated, but parasites rarely last long.

6   War is a crusade. President George W. Bush [U.S. president when this was written] is not shy about warning other nations that they stand with the United States in the war on terrorism or will be counted with those that defy us. This too is *jihad*. Yet we Americans find ourselves in the dangerous position of going to war not against a state but against a phantom. The *jihad* we have embarked upon is targeting an elusive and protean enemy. The battle we have begun is neverending. But it may be too late to wind back the heady rhetoric. We have embarked on a campaign as quixotic as the one mounted to destroy us.

7   "We go forward," President Bush assures us, "to defend freedom and all that is good and just in the world."

8   The patriotic bunting and American flags that proliferated in the wake of the attacks on the World Trade Center and the Pentagon were our support for the war mounted against the "axis of evil." Elected officials, celebrities and news anchors lined up to be counted. On Friday, September 14, three days after the attacks, Congress granted the President the right to "use all necessary and appropriate force against those nations, organizations, or persons he determines planned, authorized, committed, or aided the

terrorist attacks." The resolution was passed unanimously by the Senate. There was in the House only one dissenting vote, from Barbara J. Lee, a Democrat from California, who warned that military action could not guarantee the safety of the country and that "as we act, let us not become the evil we deplore."

9   When we ingest the anodyne of war we feel what those we strive to destroy feel, including the Islamic fundamentalists who are painted as alien, barbaric, and uncivilized. It is the same narcotic. I partook of it for many years. And like every recovering addict there is a part of me that remains nostalgic for war's simplicity and high, even as I cope with the scars it has left behind, mourn the deaths of those I worked with, and struggle with the bestiality I would have been better off not witnessing. There is a part of me—maybe it is a part of many of us—that decided at certain moments that I would rather die like this than go back to the routine of life. The chance to exist for an intense and overpowering moment, even if it meant certain oblivion, seemed worth it in the midst of war—and very stupid once the war ended.

10   I covered the war in El Salvador from 1983 to 1988. By the end I had a nervous twitch in my face. I was evacuated three times by the U.S. embassy because of tips that the death squads planned to kill me. Yet each time I came back. I accepted with a grim fatalism that I would be killed in El Salvador. I could not articulate why I should accept my own destruction and cannot now. When I finally did leave, my last act was, in a frenzy of rage and anguish, to leap over the KLM counter in the airport in Costa Rica because of a perceived slight by a hapless airline clerk. I beat him to the floor as his bewildered colleagues locked themselves in the room behind the counter. Blood streamed down his face and mine. I refused to wipe the dried stains off my cheeks on the flight to Madrid, and I carry a scar on my face from where he thrust his pen into my cheek. War's sickness had become mine. [. . .]

11   As the battle against terrorism continues, as terrorist attacks intrude on our lives, as we feel less and less secure, the acceptance of all methods to lash out at real and perceived enemies will distort and deform our democracy. For even as war gives meaning to sterile lives, it also promotes killers and racists.

12   Organized killing is done best by a disciplined, professional army. But war also empowers those with a predilection for murder. Petty gangsters, reviled in pre-war Sarajevo, were transformed overnight at the start of the conflict into war heroes. What they did was no different. They still pillaged, looted, tortured, raped, and killed; only then they did it to Serbs, and with an ideological veneer. Slobodan Milošević went one further. He opened up the country's prisons and armed his criminal class to fight in Bosnia. Once we sign on for war's crusade, once we see ourselves on the side of the angels, once we embrace a theological or ideological belief system that defines itself as the embodiment of goodness and light, it is only a matter of how we will carry out murder.

13   The eruption of conflict instantly reduces the headache and trivia of daily life. The communal march against an enemy generates a warm, unfamiliar bond with our neighbors, our community, our nation, wiping out unsettling undercurrents of alienation and dislocation. War, in times of malaise and desperation, is a potent distraction. [. . .]

14   Patriotism, often a thinly veiled form of collective self-worship, celebrates our goodness, our ideals, our mercy and bemoans the perfidiousness of those who hate us. Never mind the murder and repression done in our name by bloody surrogates from the Shah of Iran to the Congolese dictator Joseph-Désiré Mobutu, who received from Washington well over a billion dollars in civilian and military aid during the three decades of his rule. And European states—especially France—gave Mobutu even more as he bled dry one of the richest countries in Africa. We define ourselves. All other definitions do not count.

719

15   War makes the world understandable, a black and white tableau of them and us. It suspends thought, especially self-critical thought. All bow before the supreme effort. We are one. Most of us willingly accept war as long as we can fold it into a belief system that paints the ensuing suffering as necessary for a higher good, for human beings seek not only happiness but also meaning. And tragically war is sometimes the most powerful way in human society to achieve meaning.

16   But war is a god, as the ancient Greeks and Romans knew, and its worship demands human sacrifice. We urge young men to war, making the slaughter they are asked to carry out a rite of passage. And this rite has changed little over the centuries, centuries in which there has almost continuously been a war raging somewhere on the planet. The historian Will Durant calculated that there have only been twenty-nine years in all of human history during which a war was not underway somewhere. We call on the warrior to exemplify the qualities necessary to prosecute war—courage, loyalty, and self-sacrifice. The soldier, neglected and even shunned during peacetime, is suddenly held up as the exemplar of our highest ideals, the savior of the state. The soldier is often whom we want to become, although secretly many of us, including most soldiers, know that we can never match the ideal held out before us. [. . .]

17   War exposes a side of human nature that is usually masked by the unacknowledged coercion and social constraints that glue us together. Our cultivated conventions and little lies of civility lull us into a refined and idealistic view of ourselves. But modern industrial warfare may well be leading us, with each technological advance, a step closer to our own annihilation. We too are strapping explosives around our waists. Do we also have a suicide pact?

18   Look just at the 1990s: 2 million dead in Afghanistan; 1.5 million dead in the Sudan; some 800,000 butchered in ninety days in Rwanda; a half-million dead in Angola; a quarter of a million dead in Bosnia; 200,000 dead in Guatemala; 150,000 dead in Liberia; a quarter of a million dead in Burundi; 75,000 dead in Algeria; and untold tens of thousands lost in the border conflict between Ethiopia and Eritrea, the fighting in Colombia, the Israeli-Palestinian conflict, Chechnya, Sri Lanka, southeastern Turkey, Sierra Leone, Northern Ireland, Kosova, and the Persian Gulf War (where perhaps as many as 35,000 Iraqi citizens were killed). In the wars of the twentieth century not less than 62 million civilians have perished, nearly 20 million more than the 43 million military personnel killed.

19   Civil war, brutality, ideological intolerance, conspiracy, and murderous repression are part of the human condition—indeed almost the daily fare for many but a privileged minority.

20   War is not a uniform experience or event. My time in the insurgencies in Central America, the Persian Gulf War—where two large armies clashed in the desert—and the Balkans, where warlords and gangsters tried to pass themselves off as professional soldiers, illustrated the wide differences that make up modern warfare. But war usually demands, by its very logic, the disabling of the enemy, often broadly defined to include civilians who may have little love for the Taliban or Saddam Hussein or Somali warlords. While we venerate and mourn our own dead we are curiously indifferent about those we kill. Thus killing is done in our name, killing that concerns us little, while those who kill our own are seen as having crawled out of the deepest recesses of the earth, lacking our own humanity and goodness. Our dead. Their dead. They are not the same. Our dead matter, theirs do not. Many Israelis defend the killing of Palestinian children whose only crime was to throw rocks at armored patrols, while many Palestinians applaud the murder of Israeli children by suicide bombers. [. . .]

21   And yet, despite all this, I am not a pacifist. I respect and admire the qualities of professional soldiers. Without the determination and leadership of soldiers like General Wesley

K. Clark we might not have intervened in Kosova or Bosnia. It was, in the end, a general, Ulysses S. Grant who saved the union. Even as I detest the pestilence that is war and fear its deadly addiction, even as I see it lead states and groups towards self-immolation, even as I concede that it is war that has left millions of dead and maimed across the planet, I, like most reporters in Sarajevo and Kosova, desperately hoped for armed intervention. The poison that is war does not free us from the ethics of responsibility. There are times when we must take this poison—just as a person with cancer accepts chemotherapy to live. We can not succumb to despair. Force is and I suspect always will be part of the human condition. There are times when the force wielded by one immoral faction must be countered by a faction that, while never moral, is perhaps less immoral.

BEFORE YOU READ: Remembering the games you and your friends played in childhood, can you think of ways in which those games responded to or helped to prepare you for the real world?

IRAQI KIDS PLAY MAKE-BELIEVE WAR GAMES[*]

Hamza Hendawi

Hamza Hendawi writes for the Associated Press.

721

For Discussion: To what extent does this children's game look familiar to you? When you read the description of the game in the following article, how does the specific context change your feeling about the game?

For Writing: Beginning with Mead's view that war is an invention, in what ways might these children's war games help them in their current situation? In what ways might the games be harmful?

Context: The caption reads: Children's war games in Iraq. Children play a war game in central Baghdad's Karradah neighborhood. Hundreds, possibly thousands, of the nation's children have been killed or wounded in the nearly four years of war and sectarian strife.

[*]Hamza Hendawi, *Washington Post*, February 24, 2007, http://www.washingtonpost.com/wp-dyn/content/article/2007/02/24/AR2007022400215.html (accessed June 28, 2008).

1   Baghdad, Iraq (AP)—Toting menacing looking toy guns, young boys swarm around an abandoned car, chanting battle cries of a Shiite militia and pointing their play weapons at the "terrorist" in the driver's seat. Outnumbered, the boy playing a would-be suicide bomber surrenders.

2   On Baghdad's dusty streets, Iraqi children are playing make-believe war games inspired by the Shiite-Sunni conflict, a development that shows the depth of the city's rapid and violent break-up along sectarian lines.

3   Some adults try to discourage such games, fearing they only contribute to sectarian hatred. Others believe there is little they can do to stop it—given the horror that children in Baghdad experience nearly every day.

4   "Playing such games is normal," said Rabab Qassim, a school teacher and mother of three from Hurriyah, where Shiite militiamen drove out hundreds of Sunni families last year. "It has become part of the kids' lives. It is not a figment of their imagination. It is in front of them everywhere and they live it every day."

5   Iraq's children have not escaped the ravages of nearly four years of war and sectarian strife, which escalated during the past year. Hundreds, possibly thousands, of them have been killed or wounded in the violence. Images of parents weeping over the dead or mangled bodies of their children define the brutality of the conflict. "You coward! I will kill you," shouted 6-year-old Haidar Faraj, who played a Shiite militiaman from the Shiite Mahdi Army militia on a recent afternoon in Hurriyah. His younger brother Abbas was the Sunni "terrorist."

6   Abu Ali, 40, who sells toys in Baghdad's Shorja market, said most of the children who visit his store are looking for the "biggest and most harmful toy guns." "About 95 percent of the toys I sell are guns," said Abu Ali, who refused to give his full name for security reasons.

7   So many toy guns—some of which look real at first glance—are circulating in the city that Trade Minister Abed Falah al-Sudani is considering banning them. Kids who can't afford toy weapons simply use their imagination. Take a wooden stick, tie on an empty water bottle with a black sock and presto—a rocket-propelled grenade launcher. Boys dart behind parked cars or sprawl on the ground and pretend to fire them.

8   The names of the games vary depending on the neighborhood. In Sadr City, the Baghdad stronghold of the Mahdi Army, the "bad guys" are "Wahabbis," or Sunni religious extremists. Sometimes the game becomes "Sadr City vs Azamiyah," referring to a nearby Sunni neighborhood. In New Baghdad, a mixed area where Shiites are most numerous, kids play "police and terrorists." Some of the children even dress up in black shirts that resemble Mahdi Army attire. Those playing the cops put on black ski masks, often used by Baghdad police to hide their identity. "These kids are not only mimicking what they see on TV, but also some of the real violence they see," said Sabah Mohammed Ali, a Shiite policeman whose two sons—Mohammed, 11, and Mustapha, 8—are avid players of such games. "I try to discourage them from playing and I talk to them about Shiites and Sunnis living in peace, but they keep going back to the same game," said Ali, 44, who comes from Sadr City.

9   Some Iraqis worry that the war games are contributing to an increase in aggressive behavior among children, many of whom are losing interest in their schoolwork. It's hard to tell whether war games—or the general state of life in Baghdad—are to blame. "They challenge teachers and even threaten them," said biology teacher Abu Ali. "They are so frustrated and do not care about their work because they think they may end up displaced or killed, so why should they bother to study."

722

Reading Images: Seeking Shelter Where He Can Find It

Context: The caption to this photograph reads: An Iraqi boy hid behind a U.S. soldier yesterday (May 28, 2007) as gunshots rang out after a car bombing in central Baghdad that killed 24 people."

Image 1:
Iraqi Boy and American Soldier.

For Discussion: Think about the composition of this photograph, which despite the fact that it is an action shot, is very expressive. What does the alignment of soldier and boy set against the background of fleeing people suggest about them as individuals and about their relationship?

For Writing: Some critics have suggested that this photograph is paradoxical and open to various interpretations. (For instance, is the boy trusting the soldier or just seeking protection because of his bulk, weapon, and body armor?) Building on your understanding of this photograph, discuss the ambiguities that leave its claim uncertain. After articulating several possible claims that the photo might make, choose the one you think is most accurate and explain why.

723

> **BEFORE YOU READ:** What is your general opinion about video games? Are they harmful or harmless? Can they be used to teach socially desirable qualities and behaviors?

ARMY'S WAR GAME RECRUITS KIDS[*]
Joan Ryan

Joan Ryan writes for the *San Francisco Chronicle*.

1 Your kids can download the "America's Army" video game for free. Well, it is free for them. You have already paid for it with your tax dollars. In the game, kids get to kill

---

*Joan Ryan, "Army's War Game Recruits Kids," *San Francisco Chronicle*, September 23, 2004, B1.

Context: The caption reads: "America's Army" game. Here you see the front page of the Web site where you can download the game, find out how to enter a tournament, and read about "Real Heroes" in the U.S. Army. It is available online at http://www.americasarmy.com.

people with cool weapons that look and respond like the real things. They get to ambush terrorists and, when caught in a firefight, they can hear bullets whistle past their ears and even hear the shell casings from their M-16s clatter onto the concrete floor.

2   The only thing better would be an actual war with actual weapons! Which is pretty much how the Army hopes your kids will respond.

3   "America's Army" is one of the U.S. Army's most popular and effective recruiting tools—conceived, designed, and distributed free to reach the 13- to 21-year-old crowd. It is a brilliant marketing tactic. Unlike 30-second TV ads, the game is what the ad industry calls "sticky" advertising: Consumers are engaged for much longer periods than with traditional commercials and ads.

4   The game and its upgrades have been downloaded more than 16 million times since the original version was released to strong acclaim in the gaming world two years ago. It comes bundled in gaming magazines. It is

given away at NASCAR events and state fairs. Since the game's release, players have completed 600 million missions during 60 million playing hours. There are more than 4 million current registered players, making it the No. 1 online action game.

5   So what's the problem? After all, the Army needs lots of recruits. The target for this year is to sign up 77,000 young men and women for active duty. Next year, according to an Army spokesman, the target is 80,000. Video games are the new frontier for marketing and advertising. McDonald's, Pepsi, Nike, and ESPN are among the many companies using games to attract customers and foster brand loyalty at young ages.

6   More recently, games have become the way to sell ideas, too, particularly to kids who are still trying to figure out who they are and what they believe. The Islamic group Hezbollah produced a game called "Special Force," which hit stores in the Middle East last year. In it, Palestinian good guys try to vanquish Israeli soldiers and

settlers. There's another lovely game called "Ethnic Cleansing," put out by a white supremacist group.

7   "Games are now a more important entry point into the consumer world than any other medium," said Curt Feldman, senior editor at Gamespot, a Bay Area–based Web site for gamers. "It has risen to the surface as the perfect way to reach very key demographic groups."

8   The Army was smart enough to recognize this marketing trend and use it effectively. But there are several troubling issues: Should the government be in the business of producing violent video games when research indicates a correlation to heightened aggression? Is it appropriate to depict war as a game at a time when real men, women, and children are being killed in Iraq?

9   And what are the ethics of using video games to feed propaganda to 13- and 14-year-olds, especially propaganda with such complex moral and life-and-death implications? Let's face it. The Army isn't trying to sell kids hamburgers. It's trying to sell kids on the notion that joining the Army would be a really cool thing to do when they grow up. Yes, they might get killed. They might get maimed. But just think of the awesome grenade launchers they'll learn to use!

10   "America's Army" taps into so many of the longings of a boy who is coming of age, says Diane Levin, author of *Remote Control Childhood* and a professor at Wheelock College in Boston. "[If they join the Army,] they'll be part of a group outside their parents," Levin said from Boston. "They'll feel powerful and important. They'll be masculine and attractive. The game is working to create an image that bypasses the mind and gets to the soul."

11   What the game does not capture of Army life is what it feels like to kill someone. Or what it feels like to see a buddy's leg shredded into a thousand pieces. It doesn't give kids a sense of the mind-numbing boredom and stomach-churning fear. In the real Army, you cannot press the escape button on your keyboard and come back to life.

12   Col. Casey Wardynski, who supervised the game's production, points out that only 41 percent of the game is simulated combat. The rest relates to adventure training such as parachuting, as well as medic training, weapons training, and team-building. The game, he said, depicts the Army's values of respect, discipline, and camaraderie.

13   And he says the difference between the Army's marketing to kids and, say, McDonald's, is that a kid can impulsively buy a hamburger as a result of targeted advertising, but because he's not old enough to enlist, he can't impulsively join the Army. But marketing to kids is important Wardynski says, because, "If you don't get in there and engage them early in life about what they're going to do with their lives, when it comes time for them to choose, you're in a fallback position."

14   Psychologist Susan Linn, author of the new book, *Consuming Children: Hostile Takeover of Childhood*, disagrees. "There should be different standards about marketing to kids," she said from her office in Boston. "The frontal cortex of the brain, where judgment sits, doesn't fully mature until the late teens or early 20s. [Kids] tend to be more swayed by emotion because of that."

15   Linn played "America's Army" during research for her book and said that it depicted war in the way teenage boys would want it to be: exciting and even attractive. "The fact that the Army needs to recruit doesn't mean it has the right to exploit children's vulnerabilities, and do it dishonestly by glamorizing violence and minimizing or ignoring the other, more complicated facets of war," she said.

16   Wardynski has heard all the criticisms before. "Kids aren't stupid," he said. "They know the Army is not a game. What the

game does is allow them to try it on for size and get more information about the many job opportunities." The Army, he said, put him through college all the way to his Ph.D. He loves the Army. It's a career choice he wants to share with all kids. His enthusiasm is not dampened by the fact that 30 percent of today's recruits will fight in Iraq.

17 America needs a standing army. So the army needs to recruit. But not at all costs. The army will have time enough to grab our boys for war when they turn 18. In the meantime, maybe it can let our kids be kids for just a while longer.

B. How Do People Justify War?

> **BEFORE YOU READ:** Just-war theory has very specific criteria that must be followed in order for a particular war to be considered "just." However, we all have general guidelines for whether or not we think a war is right. Divide a piece of paper into two columns. On the left, write down a list of what conditions would, in your mind, justify a war; on the right, list the parallel conditions that do *not* warrant war.

WHY WE FIGHT*

William J. Bennett

These excerpts come from a chapter titled "The Morality of Anger" in William J. Bennett's book *Why We Fight: Moral Clarity and the War on Terrorism*. First Bennett explains the concept of a "just" war and describes its historical origins. Then he describes the problems he personally has with pacifism. What would you say is his final claim about conducting war?

1 Nowhere in the New Testament do we find force itself held up for explicit praise— that would be all but unthinkable. But neither are the Gospel writers so unworldly as to posit that the answer to every human conflict is to turn the other cheek; in certain circumstances and for certain purposes, force would seem to be forbidden, in other cases allowed (even if never encouraged for its own sake). Indeed, it was to elaborate the why and how and wherefore of the latter case that the Church, over the centuries, developed the doctrine of "just war," a theory that received its first extended treatment in the late fourth century at the hands of St. Augustine and was significantly modified nine centuries later by St. Thomas Aquinas.

2 "A great deal," Augustine wrote in *Contra Faustum*, "depends on the causes for which men undertake wars, and on the authority they have for doing so." Aquinas, specifying, named three main criteria for determining if one could initiate war. (This part of just-war doctrine was called by the medieval scholastics *jus ad bellum*, the right to go to war, as distinct from *jus in bello*, the proper conduct

526

*William J. Bennett, *Why We Fight: Moral Clarity and the War on Terrorism* (New York: Doubleday, 2002), 27–30, 39–43.

of war.) The three were: whether war is declared by a legitimate sovereign; whether it is for a just cause—that is, a cause that avenges wrongs or rights an injustice; and whether the belligerents "intend the advancement of good, or the avoidance of evil." To those who argued that Christians should always seek peace, Aquinas responded that those who wage war justly do, in fact, aim at true peace, being opposed only to an "evil peace." Indeed, Christians would be shirking their religious duty were they not to struggle against an unjust peace, including by taking up arms. [. . .]

3   Did American military action in the wake of September 11 satisfy these three criteria? That it was waged by a legitimate authority is patent: that authority being the duly elected and sworn president, acting with the virtually unanimous approval of the elected representatives of the American people. Likewise, it was clearly waged in a just cause, against terrorists who sought and still seek to destroy us, as well as to avoid future evil.

4   True, even when a war is waged by a legitimate authority, for a legitimate reason, and for a legitimate end, other factors must weigh heavily. Implicitly referring to the tradition of *jus in bello*, the letter of the U.S. Conference of Catholic Bishops to the president warned: "Any military response must be in accord with sound moral principles, . . . such as probability of success, civilian immunity, and proportionality." Although war is certainly hell (in the pithy observation of General William Sherman), our conduct of it must nevertheless be appropriate. We may be unable to avoid injuring innocent civilians in the course of fighting, but we must not target them. Likewise, we must not kill or mistreat prisoners of war. And we must always be wary of producing, even unintentionally, evils commensurate with those we are seeking to eliminate.

5   Obviously there is a fine moral line here. As the scholar Jean Bethke Elshtain has pointed out, Augustine, in developing the idea of the just war, struggled with the fact that the weight of Scripture challenges the use of force. But he recognized, as most Christians have, that there are times when *not* resorting to force leads to evils far greater than the one we oppose. And as for whether we have fought a war justly (in contrast to fighting a just war), any proper assessment requires careful analysis based on specific facts—and often on the outcome of the hostilities themselves. To quote the Anglican theologian Patrick Comerford, "It is only long after a war is over that we have the time and the luxury to determine whether all conditions [of a just war] have been met."

6   By all these standards, both the military campaign in Afghanistan and our conduct of that campaign qualify unreservedly as just. In light of its aims and its achievements, in consideration of our extraordinary sensitivity to the avoidance of civilian casualties, and in light of our vast efforts of humanitarian relief for the suffering people of Afghanistan, I would not be surprised if, in historical retrospect, . . . the Afghanistan campaign were to qualify as one of the most just wars ever fought.

7   Why has the critique of violence taken such hold among us, and why does it exercise such influence? The answer is paradoxical. Contrary to the myth of our nation as violence-prone, Americans are in fact a peaceful people, averse to conflict. That is the larger truth about us. Our habits are the habits of a commercial society, resting on rich deposits of social trust and on laws that regulate and protect transactions of every kind. Our outlook is the outlook of a democratic polity, guided by the spirit of accommodation and compromise, superintended by guarantees of due process and judicial review.

8   It is exactly these same habits and this same outlook, I believe, that make so many of us susceptible to arguments of the give-peace-a-chance kind. I don't mean that we necessarily buy those arguments, but something in them appeals to something good in our

nature, and though we may know they are wrong we often do not know quite how to answer them. That is precisely why I have been at such pains to take them seriously on their own terms. But I also want to be clear about where they come from.

9   It is theoretically true that one can espouse nonviolence *and* support the war effort. As Scott Simon reminds us, some genuine pacifists and conscientious objectors have done just that in past conflicts. The trouble with many of today's pacifists is that, in the name of the higher morality of nonviolence, they have not only declined to support the war effort but have actively tried to hamper it, loudly warning about cycles of violence, accusing us of an unseemly lust for vengeance, invoking the supposedly dark record of our past, sowing doubts about our intentions, impugning our right to defend ourselves.

10   In short, many in the "peace party" who cloak their arguments in moral objections to war are really expressing their hostility to America, and it does the cause of clarity no good to pretend otherwise. That hostility—in more than a few cases, hatred is a more accurate word—is many-sided and has a long history, and we shall be encountering facets of it in our discussion. But where armed conflict is concerned, the arguments of today's "peace party" are basically rooted in the period of the Vietnam war and its aftermath. It was then that the critique of the United States as an imperialist or "colonialist" power, wreaking its evil will on the hapless peoples of the third world, became a kind of slogan on the Left. This same critique would, in due course, find a home in certain precincts of the Democratic party and, in more diluted form, would inform the policy preferences of the Carter and Clinton administrations, and it is with us still.

11   It is especially prevalent in our institutions of higher learning. At a teach-in at the University of North Carolina immediately after the [September 11, 2001] attack, one speaker remarked that, were he the president of the United States, his first act would be not to

avenge the infamy but to apologize to "the widows and orphans, the tortured and impoverished, and all the millions of the other victims of American imperialism." For a professor at Rutgers, whatever the "proximate cause" of September 11, "its ultimate cause is the fascism of U.S. foreign policy over the past decades." Like the character in Molière's *Le Bourgeois Gentilhomme* who was astonished to learn that he had been speaking prose all his life, these two seemed unconscious of the fact that they were speaking clichés, and clichés with a certain identifiable provenance.

12   Allied to the political critique of America that developed in the 1960s and 1970s was a cultural and psychological critique. Not just imperial ambition but a sort of deranged, Wild West machismo was said to be driving our activities abroad, impelling us to drop bombs on innocent people and/or to force upon them our uniquely rapacious model of economic activity. At home, this same derangement was said to lie behind everything from our alleged obsession with guns to our alleged obsession with order and the perverse way in which we brought up our children, especially our boys. Out of this critique there arose the by-now standard counterwisdom that I have already discussed: that conflict is always a product of misunderstanding, and that violence is always wrong.

13   In the past decades, since Vietnam and especially since our defeat there, our culture has undergone a process that one observer has aptly termed *debellicization*. Military virtues have been devalued and shunned, and along with them the very idea that war solves anything or is ever justified. Generations of schoolchildren have been taught that conflict is something to be avoided. Parents and teachers have been cautioned by psychologists and feminists alike that male aggression is a wild and malignant force that needs to be repressed or medicated lest it burst out, as it is always on the verge of doing, in murderous behavior. The 1999 shooting spree by two teenagers at Columbine High School in Colorado is taken

to be all too horridly typical; in the meantime, the Boy Scouts of America, an irreplaceable institution that has always known how to channel the healthy impulses of male aggression, and to inspire male idealism, is derided as irrelevant, "patriarchal," and bigoted.

14   What you get in the end is that eleven-year-old schoolboy, dutifully repeating his mantra: "We learned that you should always find a peaceful way to solve your problems because you should never be violent." [. . .]

15   "You should never be violent." In this world, a world in which, to the best of my knowledge, the lion has yet to lie down with the lamb, teaching children this lesson does an unforgivable injury both to them and to the adult community of which they are about to become a part. It renders them vulnerable to abuse and injury, and leaves them without moral or intellectual recourse when abuse and injury are inflicted upon them. If no distinction is made among kinds of "peace," children are deprived of the tools they require to distinguish a just from an unjust peace, peace with honor from the peace of the grave. They are robbed of the oldest and most necessary wisdom of the race, which is that some things are worth fighting and dying for.

16   Are we to tell our children that, because "you should always find a peaceful way to solve your problems," the brave men who fought in the Revolutionary War, the Civil War, the two World Wars, and every other conflict in our history were acting immorally? That way lies a generation prepared only for accommodation, appeasement, and surrender. If, heaven forbid, they should ever be faced in their turn with the need to respond to aggression and evil, better by far for them to have learned, understood, and taken to heart the words of John Stuart Mill:

> War is an ugly thing, but not the ugliest of things. The decayed and degraded state of a moral and patriotic feeling which thinks that nothing is worth war is much worse. A man who has nothing for which he is willing to fight—nothing he cares about more than his own safety—is a miserable creature who has no chance of being free, unless made and kept so by the exertions of better men than himself.

17   What term shall we reserve for those who in the current instance have preached to us that, given who we are, and what we have done in the world, nothing of ours is worth fighting for? "Much of what is passing for pacifism," wrote the characteristically blunt columnist Michael Kelly, "is not pacifism at all but only the latest manifestation of a well-known pre-existing condition." That condition, that plague, is anti-Americanism.

BEFORE YOU READ: Based on your past experience, how would you define the limits of what Americans owe to other countries?

OUR MORAL DUTY IN IRAQ[*]

Gerard F. Powers

Gerard F. Powers is director of policy studies at the Joan B. Kroc Institute for International Peace Studies at the University of Notre Dame.

1   Last year, 14 Catholic Democrats sent a letter about Iraq to the U.S. Catholic bishops.

After citing church leaders' just war arguments against the original intervention, Tim

*Gerard F. Powers, "Our Moral Duty in Iraq," *America: The Weekly Catholic Magazine*, February 18, 2008, 13–16.

For Discussion: This photograph acts as a support for Powers's claim that the United States has a moral duty to stay in Iraq and support its people. What does the handshake symbolize to you?

For Writing: Powers's argument is a complicated one. In the essay he contrasts the "ethic of efficacy (Is U.S. intervention working?) over an ethic of responsibility (What do we owe Iraqis?)." Using the picture and essay as complementary parts of Powers's argument, define what you think he means by the "ethic of responsibility." What *do* we owe Iraqis?

Context: The caption reads: A handshake. U.S. soldiers express their condolences to an Iraqi politician who has lost two sons in Baghdad.

730

Ryan, Rosa DeLauro, Marcy Kaptur, and their colleagues concluded that it is time "to seek an end to this injustice." They urged the bishops to support their efforts to force a withdrawal of U.S. troops as a way to "bring an end to this war."

2   If it was immoral to intervene in Iraq in the first place, is it immoral to stay? . . . Clearly, the ethics of intervention and the ethics of exit are related. The widespread, and correct, belief that the original intervention as illegitimate, the lack of broad international support, and the failure to tie the toppling of a brutal regime in Iraq to a realistic and clear post-intervention plan have contributed to the debacle there. That said, as Bishop William Skylstad, then president of the U.S. Conference of Catholic Bishops, emphasized in November, the focus now should be "more on the ethics of exit than on the ethics of intervention," for the two, while related, are distinct. A just war can lead to an unjust peace; less often, an unjust war can lead to a just peace. Today's challenge in Iraq is to ensure that an unjust war does not lead to an unjust peace.

3   Many in the antiwar camp fail to acknowledge that the United States bears a moral burden to help Iraqis build a just peace, a burden made heavier precisely because the war is unjust. As an uninvited occupying power, the United States has assumed a whole set of moral obligations to promote the common good of the Iraqi people until Iraqis can take control of their own affairs.

4   Legally, the United States is no longer occupying Iraq, but by almost any measure Iraq is a failed state. Morally, therefore, the United States retains significant residual responsibilities to Iraqis. The Iraq intervention may have been an optional, immoral war; but given the U.S. government's shared responsibility for the ensuing crisis, its continued engagement is not an optional moral commitment.

WHAT MATTERS MORALLY?

5   Others calling for U.S. withdrawal acknowledge the ethics of exit, but give too much

weight to an ethic of efficacy (Is U.S. intervention working?) over an ethic of responsibility (What do we owe Iraqis?).

6 Efficacy must be part of any moral analysis of Iraq. At a forum sponsored by Fordham's Center on Religion, the ethicist Michael Walzer, a vocal opponent of the Iraq intervention, argued that "we are consequentialists for the moment. Neither staying on nor leaving Iraq is a categorical imperative." Unlike many in the debate, Walzer is clear about the breadth of moral obligations that exist in Iraq and thus the range of consequences that matter morally. According to Walzer, "We have to figure out a strategy that produces the least bad results for the Iraqi people, for other people in the Middle East, and for American soldiers."

7 Arguments for withdrawal tend to give most weight to what is good for U.S. soldiers (and, I would add, U.S. interests). It would be morally irresponsible not to take into account legitimate U.S. interests, not least our moral obligations to the small percentage of Americans who are helping to shoulder the burden in Iraq, and the moral costs of spending more than $2 billion per week on the war while other pressing needs go unmet.

8 Moral clarity about what we owe ourselves is often not matched by moral clarity about what we owe Iraqis. The Catholic Democrats and presidential candidates who rally antiwar support by equating a withdrawal of U.S. troops with "ending the war" in Iraq define the "ought" mostly without reference to the Iraqi people. Proposals to deauthorize and stop funding the war and to set strict timetables for redeployment might "end the war" for Americans. But would they end the war between Sunnis and Shiites? Would they end the insurgency, the Al Qaeda terrorist attacks, or the widespread criminality in Iraq?

9 The moral question, then, is not the one put by Senator John Warner to Gen. David Petraeus: What policies and strategies will best serve U.S. national security interests? Rather, it is: What policies and strategies will best serve the interests and well-being of the Iraqi people?

WHAT THE UNITED STATES OWES THE IRAQIS

10 When U.S. obligations to Iraqis are taken into account, they are often defined in a minimalist way, such as: combating terrorist groups in Iraq; training and equipping Iraqi security forces; providing reconstruction assistance; pressing Iraqis to meet benchmarks for political "reconciliation"; taking in more Iraqi refugees, including those who have supported U.S. efforts; protecting the Kurds; and deterring Iranian aggression or regional instability. These are legitimate goals, but they do not seem commensurate with the magnitude of the needs of the Iraqi people, especially for security. [. . .]

11 Despite the obvious difficulties involved, the original U.S. objectives of building an Iraq that is "peaceful, united, stable, democratic, and secure" are closer to what the United States owes Iraqis than are the minimalist alternatives. There are four [U.S. responsibilities]: (1) not to end all political violence, but to ensure that an Iraqi government can maintain a reasonable degree of security for the whole country and minimize the threat of chaos or civil war; (2) not to impose a Western-style democracy, but to facilitate establishment of a stable, fairly representative government that respects basic human rights, especially minority rights; (3) not to promote a U.S.–style capitalist economy, but to restore Iraq's infrastructure and a viable economy that serves Iraqi needs, not U.S. interests, especially not U.S. oil interests; and (4) not to stay without the consent of a legitimate Iraqi government, or, lacking that, the United Nations. [. . .]

THE BEST ANTIWAR ARGUMENT

12   The strongest argument against the Iraq intervention was that preventive wars are wars of aggression, which often become wars of occupation. And wars of occupation often degenerate into wars of repression, as the occupier resorts to indiscriminate and disproportionate force, emergency measures (even torture) and other heavy-handed tactics to pacify a resistant population. Wars of occupation, moreover, invariably involve a sustained, extremely difficult, long-term commitment to nation building that is at odds with U.S. political culture. . . . Given the fears generated by terrorism and the spread of weapons of mass destruction, such preventive wars will remain all too tempting and all too easy for the United States, if it is not required to bear the burden of what it has wrought.

13   The best antiwar argument must address two moral failures in Iraq, not just one: it was immoral to intervene; in the ensuing nation-building process, the United States has failed the Iraqi people by willing an end (a peaceful and prosperous Iraq) without willing the means to achieve it. A preoccupation with what is good for U.S. troops and U.S. interests, coupled with speculative, short-term assessments of success and necessity, could compound this double moral failure. Those who say that it is too late and too costly to fix what we have broken must not forget what we owe Iraqis, lest they too readily impose on Iraqis alone the risks of a serious humanitarian, security, and political crisis if the U.S. withdraws too soon. The antiwar position must find a better balance between an ethics of efficacy and an ethics of responsibility, between meeting U.S. needs and interests and Iraqi needs and interests. Some might still conclude that strict deadlines for withdrawal are called for. I doubt it. But at least then withdrawal would be pursued, not with self-righteous calls to "end" an immoral war, but with a deep sense of anguish, remorse, and foreboding over our nation's failure to live up to its obligations to the Iraqi people.

BEFORE YOU READ: Based on your experience or from reading and listening to the news, can you describe a case in which you would feel that you had to "shoot first"? Can you think of any examples of when someone shot first but was then held responsible for the act?

WHEN YOU HAVE TO SHOOT FIRST*

Haim Watzman

Haim Watzman is the author of *Company C: An American's Life as a Citizen-Soldier in Israel.*

1   Jerusalem in the summer of 1984, as we manned a hilltop observation post during my first stint of reserve duty in the Israel Defense Forces, I heard an awful story from a friend whom I'll call Eldad. Like the story of the police officer who killed an innocent man at the Stockwell subway station in London last week, this one had elements that got my liberal hackles up.

2   Western democracies are supposed to defend the individual against the power of the state. For this reason, democratic

---

*Haim Watzman, "When You Have to Shoot First," *New York Times*, July 28, 2005, http://www.nytimes.com/2005/07/28/opinion/28watzman.html (accessed June 30, 2008).

governments place strict limits on the use of force by their agents—executives, judges, members of the military, and law-enforcement officers. When someone dies at the hands of one of these agents, citizens are justified in asking: Did the killer abide by the law? Were his motives pure? Was death really the only choice? All too often, the answer to these questions is no.

3   Eldad's story took place in Lebanon, where he and I had both served for the bulk of our regular army service, before we graduated to the reserves. He was stationed at a roadblock in southern Beirut. A car pulled up to the roadblock and three men jumped out and started spraying bullets at him and his comrades. Within a split second the Israelis were returning fire and, before they had time to even think through what was going on, two of the assailants were shot dead. The third was also on the ground, badly wounded but conscious.

4   "I went up to him and raised my rifle and switched it to automatic," Eldad told me. "He put up his hands as if to fend me off, or maybe beg for mercy. But I just pulled the trigger and filled his body up with bullets." "But you killed a wounded and disabled man," I objected. "That's against orders. It's also immoral."

5   "He could still use his hands, and he might have had a grenade," Eldad said testily. "He was going to die anyway. And he deserved it." Eldad's last two arguments were specious. He had no way of knowing how badly the man was wounded, nor was he authorized to mete out judgment. "You would've done the same thing." He glared at me.

6   I didn't know whether I would have done the same thing. I half thought I wouldn't have. But what I realized at that moment was that, if I hadn't, I would have been wrong. The man had control of his hands and could have had a concealed and deadly weapon.

7   A terrible thing happened in London last Friday. On his way to work, Jean Charles de Menezes, a 27-year-old Brazilian electrician, was chased down by suspicious police officers. When he tripped and fell, the officers asked no questions and gave him no warning. One of them fired eight bullets point-blank into his head and shoulder and that was that. At first sight, it was an act much more severe than Eldad's, because Eldad had been under attack and shot a man he had good reason to think was armed. Mr. Menezes had hurt no one.

8   On the other hand, it was an easier call. The police saw a man wearing a long coat out of place on a hot summer day jumping over a turnstile and running for a crowded subway train. He did not stop when he had been ordered to do so.

9   Just two weeks before the killing, four suicide bombers had blown themselves up on subway trains and buses in London. Just days before, there were all the signs of another coordinated attack—and the police had reason to believe that bombers were still at large. The long coat on a summer day was just the sort of telltale clue that the police had been told to look out for. A number of suicide bombers in recent years have used such coats to conceal the belt of explosives strapped around their waists. What's more, the police acted under express orders to shoot in the head someone they thought was about to commit a suicide bombing.

10   Suicide charges are usually built to be set off with the flick of the bomber's finger. The terrorist can be disabled, flat on the ground, and surrounded by heavily armed men and still blow up everything around him.

11   So the officer who killed Mr. Menezes did a horrible thing. But he also did the right thing. One of the tragedies of this age of suicide bombers—indeed of any war—is that the right thing to do is sometimes a horrible thing. Remember: there's an essential distinction between us and the suicide bombers. The suicide bombers perpetrate gratuitous horrors. We do terrible things only when it is necessary to prevent something even worse from happening.

733

C. What Might Estabish Peace?

LIVING WITH THE BOMB*
Richard Rhodes

Richard Rhodes is the author of twenty books, including *The Making of the Atomic Bomb,* which won the Pulitzer Prize, the National Book Award, and the National Book Critics Circle Award.

LIVING WITH THE
BOMB

EXPLODING INTO VIEW 60 YEARS AGO,
NUCLEAR WEAPONS REMAIN WITH US.
SO DOES THE POSSIBILITY
THEY MIGHT BE
USED AGAIN.

For Discussion: Consider the rhetorical relationship between the image and the title from this essay by Richard Rhodes. How does the image help to explain the paradox behind "living" with the bomb?

For Writing: In the early days of atom bomb testing, observers unwisely watched the bombs explode up close. From the image before you, what do you think was the attraction for onlookers? You might also want to see a video of this explosion at http://ngm.nationalgeographic.com/ngm/0508/feature6/multimedia.html.

Context: The caption reads: Mushroom cloud. A mushroom cloud storms over unmanned ships during the test of an atomic bomb in 1946. Exploded by the United States at Bikini Atoll in the Pacific, the 21-kiloton bomb was similar in size to those dropped on Japanese cities Hiroshima and Nagasaki in August 1945.

1   Sixty years ago, on a stormy night in 1945 the charismatic American physicist Robert Oppenheimer mounted the stage of a movie theater in the secret city of Los Alamos, New Mexico. Lean and intense, he was there to address hundreds of scientists—the men and women who built the first atomic bombs under his direction. Exploded over the Japanese cities of Hiroshima and Nagasaki on August 6 and 9, 1945, those bombs had just ended the most destructive war in human history—and changed the face of war forever.

*Richard Rhodes, "Living with the Bomb," *National Geographic,* August 2005, 98–113.

2   The world would soon learn what they already knew, Oppenheimer warned: Nuclear weapons were surprisingly cheap and easy to make, once you understood how. Soon, he said, other countries would be making them, too. Their power of destruction—"already incomparably greater than that of any other weapon"—will grow, he declared. Despite these unsettling predictions, Oppenheimer found positive benefit in the breakthrough, calling nuclear weapons "not only a great peril, but a great hope."

3   What was Oppenheimer thinking? The peril was obvious: Hiroshima and Nagasaki lay in ruins, with tens of thousands killed and thousands more seriously injured. What "great hope" nuclear weapons might offer was hard to imagine, even in victory. Sixty years later, it still is.

4   Today eight countries brandish known nuclear arsenals, while approximately 20 others possess the technology and materials to go nuclear within a year or so if they choose. And nations are only part of the story. The breakup of the Soviet Union put a vast array of nuclear weapons and materials at risk of theft or clandestine sale to nonstate actors, either terrorist groups or criminal networks. Expertise, too, is in demand. The so-called father of the Pakistani bomb, Abdul Qadeer Khan, is reported to have passed nuclear secrets, weapons production technology, and bomb designs to Libya, North Korea, and Iran; some fear his network may have passed secrets to others as well. Since the mid-1990s, Osama bin Laden and his followers have dreamed of acquiring nuclear devices to use in devastating attacks on the United States. No one knows whether terrorists are closing in on a radiological dirty bomb or even a nuclear weapon.

5   Oppenheimer's hope grew out of discussions with the brilliant Danish physicist Niels Bohr, who had escaped his Nazi-occupied homeland and found his way to Los Alamos late in 1943. The spread of nuclear knowledge, Bohr told Oppenheimer, would eventu-ally make nuclear weapons a common danger to all humankind, like a disease spreading to a global pandemic. When nations finally recognized the threat, Bohr and Oppenheimer agreed, the world would come together as never before—to limit the spread of nuclear weapons out of practical self-interest. And in forging those agreements through open nego-tiations and mutual understanding, nations would reduce the danger and ultimately ban-ish war.

6   In the decades that followed, as one nation after another scrambled to acquire the bomb, the two scientists' vision of an open, safer world must have seemed naive. But despite this rush to arms, the dream of Bohr and Oppenheimer began to be realized in the 1960s, when, after a harrowing brush with nuclear war during the Cuban missile crisis, the U.S. and Soviet Union began to back away from the abyss. The world followed, and the result was the 1968 Nuclear Nonpro-liferation Treaty (NPT). In exchange for for-going a nuclear arsenal, nonnuclear weapons nations that sign the NPT (183 countries today, plus the five major nuclear powers) are promised that the major powers will work toward disarmament, won't transfer nuclear weapons to states that don't have them, and will share nuclear technology for civilian purposes. Subsequent test ban treaties further restricted the spread of nuclear weapons.

7   Despite their limitations, such agreements succeeded in reducing the threat from nuclear arms during the 1970s and '80s. They also confirmed that nations do not inevitably develop weapons when they acquire the means to do so. Going nuclear is a political decision, driven mainly by national security concerns, and those concerns often can be managed.

8   And then came 1991, when a geopolitical earthquake—the end of the Cold War and the fall of the Soviet Union—shook the architec-ture of agreements, loosening alliances and destabilizing the world anew. What had been

one nuclear power, the U.S.S.R., fractured into a crowd of nuclear-armed countries. All battlefield nukes were returned to Russia in 1992, but three newly independent nations—Belarus, Ukraine, and Kazakhstan—retained thousands of warheads for intercontinental ballistic missiles (ICBMs).

9   Pressured by the U.S. and other countries, Belarus and Kazakhstan soon agreed to return their arsenals to Russia. "We had 81 mobile missiles, sufficient to eradicate Europe and the United States," Stanislav Shushkevich, the first head of state of Belarus, told me. "But who were we defending from? So I thought that the sooner they were out of the country, the happier we would be."

10   Ukraine took a different view. It insisted on keeping its 1,240 strategic nuclear warheads to deter Russian aggression and to bargain for Western security guarantees and financial incentives. Under international pressure, Ukraine finally agreed to return the weapons to Russia in 1993 and sign the NPT. Today only Russia has nuclear weapons.

11   By most standards, the world is a safer place now than it was during the Cold War. As a result of various initiatives and arms control agreements, the U.S. and Russia have withdrawn thousands of "battlefield" nukes and long-range weapons from active deployment.

12   The U.S. nuclear arsenal today counts about 10,000 warheads, the Russian about 16,000, down from 32,000 and 45,000, respectively, during the Cold War. The Moscow treaty that Presidents George W. Bush and Vladimir Putin signed in May 2002 restricts the two countries to no more than 2,200 deployed strategic warheads, each by the end of 2012.

13   France and Britain have cut their arsenals; China is modernizing its weapons, but has tightened control on nuclear exports after reportedly providing Pakistan with the design information it needed to go nuclear. Israel's formidable nuclear arsenal remains undeclared. Libya recently rolled up its program under pressure from Europe and the U.S.; Iraq's more advanced program was dismantled by International Atomic Energy Agency (IAEA) inspectors in the years after the Persian Gulf war. India and Pakistan confirmed their status as nuclear powers with a series of underground weapons tests in May 1998, but neither nation has yet accumulated as many as a hundred nuclear weapons, and their recent nuclear saber rattling seems to have stimulated sober second thoughts.

14   That's the good news.

15   The bad news begins with two nations, North Korea, which may possess a small nuclear arsenal, and Iran, which is suspected of working to develop one. The U.S. considered going to war with North Korea in 1993 when the Koreans, already suspected of having one or two nuclear weapons, threatened to withdraw from the NPT and seemed ready to extract additional plutonium for weapons from spent reactor fuel.

16   Negotiations led to a compromise: North Korea shut down the reactor in question and allowed the fuel rods to be monitored by IAEA inspectors, in exchange for the promise of two nuclear power reactors, U.S. shipments of heavy oil for power generation, and better U.S.–North Korea relations.

17   The agreement held until 2002, when the Bush Administration accused North Korea of secretly working to produce highly enriched uranium (HEU) for weapons. The U.S. suspended the vital oil shipments and moved to void the 1994 deal.

18   In retaliation, North Korea expelled the IAEA inspectors, removed the fuel rods from storage, and said it would begin extracting plutonium. Enough had been bred in the rods to make four to six atomic bombs, and North Korea has since claimed to possess a small nuclear arsenal. Yet it

surely knows that launching a nuclear attack on any of its neighbors, or the U.S., would invite a devastating response. "We are not in a position to blackmail the U.S.— the only superpower," a North Korean official told a U.S. congressional delegation visiting Pyongyang in June 2003. "Our purpose in having a deterrent is related to the war in Iraq. This is also related to statements by the hawks within the U.S. administration. If we don't have a nuclear deterrent, we cannot defend ourselves."

19   Iran is an even more complicated case. For decades, it has worked secretly to build the capacity to enrich uranium using centrifuges, in violation of its IAEA obligation to disclose all nuclear activities. When exposed, it claimed it was developing a complete nuclear fuel cycle to support a planned nuclear power program. . . . If Iran continues to develop its industry, even short of making bombs, it may become a "virtual" nuclear power, capable of fielding nuclear weapons within a year of starting a dedicated effort. And because Iran's theocracy is openly hostile toward Israel, such a capability may be militarily unacceptable to Israel and its ally, the U.S.

20   The most frightening prospect, however, involves not nations but terrorists—and the theft or sale of weapons-grade material from the countries of the former Soviet Union, or from rogue states like North Korea.

21   During the Cold War, the U.S.S.R. used a system of "guns, guards, and gulags" to protect its external borders and ensure domestic security, so that the nuclear materials dispersed throughout its far-flung network of weapons complexes and research centers were inherently secure, if not particularly well guarded or documented. When the U.S.S.R. dissolved and its zealously guarded perimeter opened, the Russian government faced (and failed at first to appreciate) a host of new challenges—ranging from an army of suddenly unemployed nuclear scientists to

the monumental task of keeping up with its nuclear material and preventing it from being stolen and smuggled to outside groups or states.

22   The U.S., with its more porous borders, had long ago learned to track and account for nuclear materials and offered its expertise to Russia. While scientists on both sides urged cooperation, mistrust lingering from the Cold War delayed agreement between the two countries well into the 1990s, and even then the joint effort was underfunded and hobbled by suspicion.

23   Since 1991 the U.S.'s Nunn-Lugar Cooperative Threat Reduction program has supported efforts to secure and eliminate these weapons and materials, but former Senator Sam Nunn, co-sponsor of the legislation with Senator Richard Lugar, estimated at the beginning of [2005] that the job of securing Russia's nuclear materials was only "between 25 and 50 percent" complete. "Increasingly," Nunn says, "we are being warned that an act of nuclear terrorism is inevitable. I am not willing to concede that point. But I do believe that unless we greatly elevate our effort [to secure nuclear materials] and the speed of our response, we could face disaster." [. . .]

24   Niels Bohr and Robert Oppenheimer would recognize our dilemma: What to do with the double-edged sword they handed us, forged from exotic metals by a nuclear reaction that science stumbled across one day in 1938 while going about its business of discovering how the world works. Their advice, I think, still holds: Only cooperation among nations can secure the deadly metals from which nuclear weapons are made. Only negotiated reductions in arsenals and limitations on weapons development can diminish the long-term risk to us all. That's what Bohr and Oppenheimer fervently believed, and what Oppenheimer told the scientists of Los Alamos that rainy night 60 years ago.

737

> **BEFORE YOU READ:** Under what conditions do you think formal conversations between people and groups opposed to one another work best? Can you describe an example from your own experience?

BATTLE STORIES BRING FORMER ENEMIES TOGETHER*
Robert Hirschfield

Robert Hirschfield is a freelance writer in New York.

1 In the winter of 2005, Elik Elhanan and a group of soldier refusers found themselves riding the back roads used by the settlers, on their way to Bethlehem. The group had been invited to dialogue with former fighters from Fatah at the home of Suleiman Al-Himri, but it is forbidden for Israelis to travel to Palestinian cities.

2 "We had to wait in an olive grove in the dark for cars to pick us up," Elhanan recalled. "We were afraid. I remember thinking we were doing something that was just incredibly stupid. We were not at all sure we would come back alive. I later learned the Palestinians were also afraid the meeting was a trap, and they would be arrested or killed."

3 Inside Al-Himri's house, the two groups struggled at first with their antipathy. Then the Palestinians began to tell their battle stories, and Israelis began to tell theirs. Able to recognize parts of themselves in the stories of the other, everyone listened, and out of their listening came an opening. At the end of the evening, no one was arrested, and no one was betrayed.

4 "We continued to meet every two or three weeks." Al-Himri said. "We grew little by little. We decided to name our group Combatants for Peace. We are completely committed to working for peace together."

5 The group has grown to more than 200 members. They protest the demolition of Palestinian houses. They protest the wall at Bil'in. Recently, they protested the building of a new settler road at Beit Umar, whose mayor is from Hamas. They stood alongside the Israeli-Palestinian bereavement group, Family Forum, and the Israeli-Palestinian peace group Ta'ayush to bear witness against a planned road that will be forbidden to Palestinian drivers on Palestinian soil.

6 Invited to New York by Brit Tzedek v'Shalom (the Jewish Alliance for Peace and Justice), a liberal Zionist group opposed to the occupation, Elhanan and Al-Himri told their stories to Jews at two synagogues on January 10 and 11, [2007]. Elhanan grew up in Jerusalem, on the edge of the West Bank. Despite its proximity, he said, "The West Bank was a distant country. I had no idea there was an occupation. I knew nothing about the Palestinians. I had no idea we were doing something wrong." Al-Himri smiled ironically at his young friend. He is 40, and graying. Elhanan is a boyish 29. Such illusions weren't possible on Al-Himri's side of the Green Line.[1] When he stood in his doorway as a boy, he saw Jewish settlements and Jewish soldiers. "A Palestinian kid like myself could tell you everything about the Israeli

---

*Robert Hirschfield, "Battle Stories Bring Former Enemies Together," *National Catholic Reporter*, February 2, 2007, 8.

soldiers. We could describe their uniforms, their appearance, their behavior. We saw everything."

7   In his teens, Al-Himri became a Fatah street fighter, throwing stones at soldiers and tanks.[2] At 16, he was imprisoned for a year and a half in Hebron. Six years later, he was placed under administrative detention and held at Ketziot Prison in the Negev for three years without trial. He estimates that he and his brothers have logged 25 years in Israeli jails. His father, also a Fatah member, was imprisoned for nine years for throwing a grenade at a jeep in Jerusalem. "My whole family agrees with what I am doing. They have suffered a lot. They are pro-peace. Like myself, they don't want to see that same suffering brought to the next generation of Palestinians."

8   Al-Himri reaches out within Fatah, especially to fighters and former fighters. Elhanan talks to any soldier willing to talk to him. The Combatants for Peace logo shows a fighter from each side stepping toward the other, throwing away their guns. Al-Himri has invited members of Hamas to meetings, but they have not accepted the offer. The two men also go to Israeli and Palestinian schools and community centers to speak. "We will speak to even three people in a room if they want to hear us," Elhanan said.

9   Elhanan served three years with an elite unit in Southern Lebanon in the mid-1990s fighting Hezbollah. He did shorter tours of duty on the West Bank fighting Palestinians. A student, like many Israeli soldiers, of the absurdist wisdom of *Catch-22*, he applied Joseph Heller's logic to his situation in Lebanon. "I am in Lebanon fighting Hezbollah because they shoot at us. They shoot at us because we are in Lebanon. Take us out of there, and they will have no one to shoot at." He observed that Hezbollah did not shoot at Israeli civilians unless the Israelis shot at Lebanese civilians.

10   It took two suicide bombers from Nablus on a morning in early September 1997, to detonate the last of his illusions. His 14-year-old sister, Semadar, had wandered too close to one of the suicide bombers on a downtown Jerusalem street and was killed instantly. "The attack that killed my sister did not promote in any way Palestinian interests. The violent actions I committed as a soldier did not promote in any way the security of Israel. Seeing that brought about a change in me."

11   Like Al-Himri, Elhanan has the support of his family. His parents participate in Combatants for Peace actions, and his brother is a group member. "It's not hostility I encounter, but indifference, which I find harder to deal with. What many Israelis object to, even some friends of mine, is that I am doing something. It's fine if I resist the occupation, but why do I have to do it so loudly? Why bother the neighbors?"

12   The incident that transformed Al-Himri happened in 1993 at Ketziot: Prime Minister Yitzhak Rabin came for a visit and told Fatah prisoners that he regarded them as the "real leadership" of the Palestinians, and he wanted to negotiate peace with them. "Rabin was known for his violence against Palestinians during the first *intifada*, which was nonviolent.[3] I saw then that it was possible for an Israeli leader to change. It made me think that another way out of the conflict was possible, that dialogue with the Israelis was possible."

13   A law was passed recently that turns the screw tighter on such dialogue: Israelis are forbidden from taking Palestinians into their cars on the West Bank. It was announced as a security measure. "The Israeli government," said Elhanan, "sees dialogue between Israelis and Palestinians as a menace, as something to be prevented. They want to make Israeli-Palestinian joint resistance to the occupation as difficult as possible. Our members have their phones tapped. We are harassed at the checkpoints. Whenever we have a joint meeting, the area is declared a closed military zone."

14   It all makes him feel a bit like an outlaw—a role he was not trained for, and a role Al-Himri was born into.

Editor's notes:

1. The "Green Line" was established in 1949, after the Arab-Israeli War, to separate Israel from the Arab nations on its borders. "The other side of the green line" includes the contested territories of the West Bank and Gaza Strip.

2. Founded in 1959, Fatah is an acronym for Harakat Al-Tahrir Al-Watani Al-Filastini, the Movement for the National Liberation of Palestine.

3. Literally a "shaking off," the word *intifada* refers to an uprising, resistance, or rebellion.

BEFORE YOU READ: Think of a story you know about an ordinary person or people who stood up to a oppressive power. What made this hero or heroes succeed where others had failed?

TO RESIST HITLER AND SURVIVE*

Susan Neiman

Susan Neiman, the director of the Einstein Forum, is the author most recently of *Moral Clarity: A Guide for Grown-Up Idealists* (2008).

1   Berlin—Walking to work on Tuesday I was startled to see three large wreaths of flowers tossed on the rainy sidewalk like the dead Christmas trees the garbage trucks just reclaimed. Recalling that the building on that sidewalk housed the tiny office of Potsdam's Jewish community, and that this week was the 75th anniversary of Hitler's seizure of power, I turned to look closer. The carnations and zinnias were mismatched and garish, the cheapest arrangements on the market in a budget-cutting age.

2   That said, Germany has spent millions of dollars commemorating the Holocaust with monuments, museums and educational initiatives that show no sign of letting up. The effort and expense is impressive and is a model for other countries dealing with their darkest pasts. Indeed, artists and intellectuals at the Center for Cultural Decontamination in Belgrade turn to their German colleagues for advice about coming to terms with the Milosevic era. Historians in Moscow debate whether to take lessons from their once-mortal enemy when examining their country's Stalinist terror.

3   What attracts international attention are Germany's largest initiatives. It was no small signal to set a Holocaust monument that's larger than a football field next to Brandenburg Gate, Berlin's equivalent of London's Big Ben. It takes more time to discover the smaller memorials: the wreaths commemorating one of the many annual dates marking

---

*Susan Neiman, "To Resist Hitler and Survive," *New York Times*, February 3, 2008, http://www.nytimes.com/2008/02/03/opinion/03neiman.html (accessed July 1, 2008).

For Discussion: Andrea Dezsö created this black-and-white paper cutout silhouette as an illustration for Neiman's essay in the *New York Times*. It is possible to see the image as representing the story of heroic resistance described in Neiman's article, but there also seems to be more narrative and more symbolism here. Which parts of the image seem most directly related to the story of the Rosenstrasse wives? What might be the significance of those images that do not seem to relate directly to their story?

For Writing: The narrative of Dezsö's illustration seems to start at the bottom right, with the image of a man and woman, and to move left and upward until it ends, at the top, with the image of birds holding an olive branch that surrounds a surreal sky of disembodied eyes. This is a highly symbolic image that will frustrate any effort to pin down its meaning exactly, but construct your own account of the narrative and explain why you read the image as you do. What is the image's claim about the significance of "resisting Hitler"? What is the final result?

741

Context: The caption reads: *To Resist Hitler,* by Andrea Dezsö. Andrea Dezsö, a Romanian artist and writer, is also assistant professor of media design at Parsons, the New School for Design in New York City. She creates artistic works through paper cutouts, silhouettes, and embroidery and creates pop-up books, among other things. Samples of her work and more information can be found at her Web site, http://a.parsons.edu/~andi/index.html. A useful introduction to the art of Andrea Dezsö is Roja Heydarpour, "Art Is a Bitter Pill, Coated with Sweetener," *New York Times,* June 5, 2007, http://www.nytimes.com/2007/06/05/nyregion/05ink.html?ex=1338782400&en=b5069154b694ca1f&ei=5124&partner=permalink&exprod=permalink (accessed July 1, 2008).

the steps to the Holocaust or the small brass plaques a German artist placed in front of apartment buildings listing the name of a Jew who had once lived there, along with the camp to which he or she was deported. There are no plaques outside my apartment, but the architect who renovated the building three years ago chiseled a long quotation from the playwright Heiner Müller reminding ordinary Germans of their responsibility for the Nazi regime and left a large swathe of facade unrenovated to remind tenants daily of the mortar holes left by the war.

4   The effort to find new ways to remember is prodigious, and it can still produce emotion among people who think they've seen it all. The German newsweekly *Der Spiegel* published a special issue commemorating the 75th anniversary filled with photos that turn your stomach today. But is nausea—or grief or guilt—what we want to induce to prevent racism and genocide? [. . .]

5   Germany is not alone in its quest for the right sort of memory, and it has done a better job than most. But the 75th anniversary of Hitler's rise to power should be an occasion to reflect on how historical crimes are remembered. I propose we restrain our attention to the suffering of the victims of those crimes and turn to the courage of those who worked to stop the criminals. This would return us to an older model, where claims to legitimacy are focused on what you've done to the world, not what the world did to you. It wouldn't ignore the victims, but it would return the heroes to center stage.

6   Which heroes we choose would be crucial. Here too Germany serves as a model from which we all could learn. It has chosen its resistance heroes, and it has chosen them wrong. Every child here knows the names of Hans and Sophie Scholl, college students who were guillotined for distributing anti-Nazi pamphlets. Most German cities have streets or schools named after them. Tom Cruise has added his fame to a new film about Claus Schenk von Stauffenberg, the oft-sung leader of a group of officers hanged for their failed attempt on Hitler's life.[1]

7   The courage of such people should not be forgotten, but the message their stories convey is grim: their deeds cost them their lives, and accomplished nothing. It's a message that comforts the millions of Germans who didn't try to oppose the regime.

8   By contrast, one of the most successful acts of resistance in the Third Reich is not well known. In 1943, when the Nazis were undecided about whether to deport and murder Jewish spouses of non-Jews, they tested the waters by rounding up nearly 2,000 Jewish men whose non-Jewish wives had already withstood considerable government pressure to divorce them. These wives spontaneously gathered in front of the building in the Rosenstrasse where their husbands were being held. For one long week they refused to leave the little square in central Berlin, despite the Gestapo machine guns trained upon them.

9   It's often said that nonviolent resistance worked for Gandhi and Martin Luther King because their oppressors were civilized; the governments of Britain and the United States could be bested by the moral courage of their opponents, while totalitarian regimes simply shoot them. This not only underestimates the evils of racism, but also our possibilities of combating them.

10   For in Berlin's Rosenstrasse, the police backed down. The men were released. They and their families survived. And in a country that devotes so much time and energy to commemorating the victims, these brave women remain anonymous; all that really marks their story is a small clay-colored memorial in a park that few Berliners know. Seeing it moves many to tears. But what's tragic are not these heroes, but the fact that there were not more. Others were deterred less by the Nazi terror than by a much older message: heroic action is futile, and mostly ends in death, besides.

11   After all these years, isn't it time to send a message to Germany's children—and everyone else's—that will help them to stand up against present evils as well as mourning past ones?

Editor's note:

1. The film referred to is *Valkyrie* (2008).

BEFORE YOU READ: This essay discusses when and under what aegis one nation should intervene in another nation's politics for humanitarian reasons. Consider the same question on a personal level. When do you think a responsible individual should intervene in a situation between two other people?

THE POLITICS OF RESCUE*

Michael Walzer

Michael Walzer is professor emeritus at the Institute of Advanced Study at Princeton University. He edits *Dissent*, a liberal journal about politics and culture, and has published extensively on the topic of "just wars."

1   To intervene or not?—this should always be a hard question. Even in the case of a brutal civil war or a politically induced famine or the massacre of a local minority, the use of force in other people's countries should always generate hesitation and anxiety. So it does today among small groups of people, some of whom end up supporting, some resisting, interventionist policies. But many governments and many more politicians seem increasingly inclined to find the question easy: the answer is *not*!

2   I am going to focus on the arguments for and against "humanitarian intervention," for this is what is at issue in the former Yugoslavia, the Caucasus, parts of Asia, much of Africa. Massacre, rape, ethnic cleansing, state terrorism, contemporary versions of "bastard feudalism," complete with ruthless warlords and lawless bands of armed men: Those are the acts that invite us, or require us, to override the presumption against moving armies across borders and using force inside countries that have not threatened or attacked their neighbors. [. . .]

3   No one really wants the United States to become the world's policeman, even of-last-resort, as we would quickly see were we to undertake this role. Morally and politically, a division of labor is better, and the best use of American power will often be to press other countries to do their share of the work. Still, we will, and we should be, more widely involved than other countries with fewer resources. Sometimes, the United States should take the initiative; sometimes we should help pay for and even add soldiers to an intervention initiated by someone else. In many cases, nothing at all will be done unless we are prepared to play one or the other of these parts—either the political lead or a combination of financial backer and supporting player. Old and well-earned suspicions of American power must give way now to a wary recognition of its necessity.

4   Many people . . . will long for a time when this necessary American role is made unnecessary by the creation of an international military force. But this time, though it will obviously come before the much heralded leap from the realm of necessity to the realm of freedom, it is still a long way off. Nor would a U.N. army with its own officers, capable of acting independently in the field, always find itself in the right fields (that is, the killing fields). Its presence or absence would depend on decisions of a Security Council likely to be as divided and uncertain

*Michael Walzer, "The Politics of Rescue," in *Arguing about War* (New Haven and London: Yale University Press, 2004), 67–81,

as it is today, still subject to a great-power veto and severe budgetary constraints. The useful role played by the U.N. in Cambodia suggests the importance of strengthening its hand. But it wasn't the U.N. that overthrew Pol Pot and stopped the Khmer Rouge massacres.[1] And so long as we can't be sure of its ability and readiness to do that, we will still have to look for and live with unilateral interventions. It is a good thing, again, when these are undertaken by local powers like Vietnam; most often, however, they will depend on global powers like the United States and (we can hope) the European Community.

5   Despite all that I have said so far, I don't mean to abandon the principle of nonintervention—only to honor its exceptions. It is true that right now there are a lot of exceptions. One reads the newspapers these days shaking. The vast number of murdered peoples; the men, women, and children dying of disease and famine willfully caused or easily preventable; the masses of desperate refugees—none of these are served by reciting

high-minded principles. Yes, the norm is not to intervene in other people's countries; the norm is self-determination. But not for *these* peoples, the victims of tyranny, ideological zeal, ethnic hatred, who are not determining anything for themselves, who urgently need help from outside. And it isn't enough to wait until the tyrants, the zealots, and the bigots have done their filthy work and then rush food and medicine to the ragged survivors. Whenever the filthy work can be stopped, it should be stopped. And if not by us, the supposedly decent people of this world, then by whom?

Editor's note:

1. Pol Pot, the leader of the Communist movement known as the Khmer Rouge, was prime minister of Cambodia from 1976 to 1979. His program of "agrarian relocation" resulted in the death of between 750,000 and 1.7 million people. An invasion of Cambodia by Vietnam led to the collapse of the Khmer Rouge and its regime.

Questions to Help You Think and Write about War and Peace

1. James calls for rethinking military service for young men. He claims that young men required to do civic rather than military duty will get the desire to fight out of their systems. As a result, young men will become more contemplative and less aggressive after their training. Do you agree or disagree with James's claim? Identify the reasons for your answer. What are the benefits of adopting James's plan? What are the drawbacks? In your opinion, is there a "moral equivalent of war"?

2. What is your response to Hedges's idea that war is addictive and to his conclusion that human beings may never give it up? Give examples from this section of "The Reader" and/or elsewhere of war being glorified or presented in a positive way. Provide other examples of the negative effects of war. Which position on war would you say is more persuasive to the greater number of people? Which is more attractive to you? Why?

3. After reading Mead's essay, explain how she justifies her position that war is an invention. How do you respond to her justification? Consider as well the

two essays on war as a game by Hendawi and Ryan. How do they support or undermine Mead's concept that war is cultural rather than biological?

4. Compare and contrast the photograph of Iraqi boys playing war games with the front page of the video game America's Army. What are the values attached to and realities of war represented by each image?

5. Compare James's "A Moral Equivalent of War" with Mead's essay. If these two authors were having a conversation on the "nature" of war, what do you imagine that they would say to one another? In pairs, have one person play the role of Mead and the other of James. Using the essays for support, attempt to persuade the other person of the nature of war. Whose arguments are more convincing? Why?

6. Analyze Khalid Mohammed's photograph *Seeking Shelter Where He Can Find It* as either supporting or contradicting Bennett's arguments about what constitutes a "just war." How did you arrive at your conclusion? What claim does the Mohammed photograph make and what details in the image support that claim?

7. Imagine Powers in conversation with James, Mead, or Bennett. What would he say to each about the morality of war? Which author's perspective would be most congenial to Powers in his efforts to articulate a correct U.S. policy for Iraq?

8. Consider together the essays by Hirschfield and Neiman. What does each author think that we can learn from past wars? In what ways do they agree or disagree with one another about the ways to use lessons from the past to make life better for people in the present and future?

9. After reading Rhodes's essay, do you think that the nuclear bomb provides a way of promoting international peace as well as the potential for global destruction? Why or why not?

10. Using the three American war memorials represented in this section (page 712), make a claim about our cultural attitudes toward soldiers as well as toward war. What is the *ethos* of an ideal military person? Analyze the memorials themselves as cultural artifacts to find evidence in support of your claim.

Credits

Text Credits

Abby Ellin, "The Laptop Ate My Attention Span." *The New York Times* (April 16, 2000, B15).

Audrey Rock-Richardson, "Pay Your Own Way! (Then Thank Mom)." *Newsweek* (September 11, 2000 p. 12). All rights reserved. Reprinted by permission.

Calvin and Hobbes. © by Waterson. Reprinted with permission of Universal Syndicate Press. All rights reserved.

American Indian College Fund. *Harper's Magazine* (October, 2007, p. 121). Reprinted by permission.

American Red Cross from *Wired* (March 2007, p. 183). Reprinted by permission.

Celtel ad "Embrace. One Network." Appeared in *New African* (October, 2007, p. 84). Reprinted by permission.

Citi Mobile ad from *Fashion Rocks* supplement to *Wired* (2007, pp. 23–24.) Reprinted by permission.

Chevy SUV Hybrid Ad from *Fashion Rocks* supplement to *Wired* (2007, pp. 53–54.)

www.Hewitt.com from *New York Times Magazine* (Sept. 9, 2007, p. 97). Reprinted by permission.

Ernest Martinez, "Giving People a Second Chance." *Hispanic* (June 1996, p. 64). Copyright © 1996 by Hispanic Magazine. Reprinted by permission of the publishers.

Judy Brady, "Why I Want a Wife." Reprinted by permission of the author.

Suzette Brewer, "One of Our Own: Training Native Teachers for the 21st Century." *Native Peoples* (March–April 2002, pp. 52–53).

Chang-Lin Tien, "A View from Berkeley." *New York Times* (March 31, 1996, Special Education Section, p. 30). Copyright © 1996 by The New York Times Company. Reprinted with permission. All rights reserved.

Randall Hamud, "We're Fighting Terror, but Killing Freedom," *Newsweek* (September 1, 2003, p. 11). Reprinted by permission.

Reiko Hatsumi., "A Simple Hai Won't Do," *The New York Times* (April 15, 1992, p. A12).Copyright © 1993 by Reiko Hatsumi.

Shirlee Taylor Haizlip, "We Knew What Glory Was." *The New York Times* (June 23, 1996, p. A13). Copyright © 1996 by Shirlee Taylor Haizlip. Reprinted by permission of the author.

Cartoonbank, "Because this family isn't ready to hold democratic elections—that's why!" from *The New Yorker* (April 19 & 26, 2004, p. 14).

Chris Piper, "'A' Is for Absent," *Shorthorn,* October 21, 2003, p. 3.

Brent Staples, "Driving Down the Highway, Mourning the Death of American Radio." *The New York Times* (June 8, 2003, p. A12). Copyright © 2003 by The New York Times Company. Reprinted with permission. All rights reserved.

Neil A. Lews, "In the Shadow of Horror, SS Guardians Relax and Frolic." *The New York Times* (September 19, 2007, B1 and B6). Copyright © 2007 by The New York Times Company, Reprinted with permission. All rights reserved.

Peter Applebome, "The Man behind Rosa Parks." *The New York Times* (December 7, 2005, A1 and A33). Copyright © 2005 by The New York Times Company. Reprinted with permission. All rights reserved.

Gina Kolata, "Psst! Ask for Donor 1913." *The New York Times* (February 18, 2007, p. 5). © 2005 The New York Times Company. Reprinted by permission. All rights reserved.

Jerry Adler, excerpt from "The Race for Survival." *Newsweek* (June 9, 2008, p. 42). Reprinted by permission.

Lance Morrow, "The Year That Changed Everything." *Time* (March 21, 2005, p. 90). © 2005 Time Inc. Reprinted by permission.

Major General Robert Scales, "Forget Flag Burning." *Time* (July 3, 2006, p. 100). Reprinted by permission.

Jeff D. Opdyke, "Kids and Chores: All Work and No Pay?" *Wall Street Journal*, Eastern Edition. Copyright © 2004 by Dow Jones & Co. Inc. Reproduced with permission of Dow Jones & Co. Inc. in the format Textbook via Copyright Clearance Center.

Figure 4.1: Designed by Eric West, Patricia Pulido, Ruby Chan and Sharon Young. Used with permission.

Figure 5.1: Adapted from Stephen Toulmin, *The Uses of Argument* (Cambridge: Cambridge University Press, 1958), p. 104.

Daryl Cagle, "So, How Has High School Prepared You for This Job?" MSNBC.com. Source: *Fort Worth Star-Telegram* (August 26, 2007, p. 2E).

Virginia Hefferman, "Calling Blue: And on That Farm He Had a Cellphone." *New York Times* (January 26, 2007, p. B33). © 2007 by The New York Times Company. Reprinted by permission. All rights reserved.

Richard D. Rieke and Malcolm O. Sillars, "American Value Systems," from A*rgumentation and the Decision Making Process*, 2/e. Published by Allyn and Bacon, Boston, MA. Copyright © 1984 by Pearson Education. Reprinted by permission of the publisher.

Stahler, "Oranges Hand Picked by U.S. Worker 3 for $20" © 2006 Stahler - The Columbus Dispatch. Appeared in *Newsweek*, April 10, 2006, p. 27.

Sense of Community Ad, *New Yorker* (January 26, 2004, p. 33)

Barry Schwartz, "When It's All Too Much." First appeared in *Parade* Magazine (January 4, 2005). © 2005 Barry Schwartz. All rights reserved.

"Brother Can You Spare a Word?" *New York Times* (November 20, 2006, pp. A26). © 2006 The New York Times Company. Reprinted by permission. All rights reserved.

Denise Grady, "War Casualty Total Jumps, but Is Revised after Article." *New York Times* (January 30, 2007, p. A17). © 2007 The New York Times Company. Reprinted by permission. All rights reserved.

Ian Urbina, "No Need to Stew: A Few Tips to Cope with Life's Annoyances." *New York Times* (March 15, 2005, pp. A1, A24). Copyright © 2005 by The New York Times Company. Reprinted with permission. All rights reserved.

James Holt, "Unintelligent Design." *New York Times Magazine* (February 20, 2005, pp. 15–16). © 2005 The New York Times Company. Reprinted by permission. All rights reserved.

Nicholas Bakalar, "Nicotine Addiction Is Quick in Youths." *New York Times* (July

Credits

748

Photo Credits

Figure 1-1: Paula Bronstein/Getty Images; **Figure 1-2:** Flip Nicklin/Minden Pictures; **Figure 1-5:** Tyler Hicks/The New York Times/Redux Pictures; **P. 28, Image 1:** "Blessed Art Thou," © 2006, Kate Kretz, 88 × 60, acrylic & oil on linen; **P. 28, Image 2:** (c) Gary Braasch; **Figure 2-1:** (c) Lawrence Jackson/CNP/CORBIS All Rights Reserved; **Figure 2-2:** Corbis RF; **Figure 3-1:** (c)The New Yorker Collection 2004 Lee Lorenz from cartoonbank.com. All Rights Reserved; **Figure 3-2:** Spencer Platt/Getty Images; **P. 90:** Courtesy of the Library of Congress; **P. 92:** David Silverman/Getty Images; **P. 93:** United States Holocaust Memorial Museum; **Figure 4-2:** Stephen Crowley/The New York Times/Redux Pictures; **P. 132, Image 1:** Chang W. Lee/The New York Times/Redux Pictures; **P. 132, Image 2:** Ernst Haas/Getty Images; **P. 132, Image 3:** (c) Jim Hollander/CORBIS All Rights Reserved; **P. 132, Image 4:** (c) Ali Haider/epa/CORBIS All Rights Reserved; **P. 134:** Lou Beach; **P. 146 left:** (c) CORBIS; **P. 146 center:** New York Daily News; **P. 146 right:** Andrew Lichtenstein/Getty Images; **P. 214, Image 1:** Ben Sklar/Getty Images; **P. 215, Image 2:** David Maung/AP Wide World Photos; **P. 215, Image 3:** Dominic Buettner/Aurora Photos, Inc.; **P. 217:** Ann Cutting/Getty Images; **P. 250:** Nicholas Roberts/AFP/Getty Images/Newscom; **P. 252:** Kevin Carter/Megan Patricia Carter Trust/Corbis/Sygma; **P. 253:** (c) Kim Ludbrook/epa/CORBIS All Rights Reserved; **P. 274, Image 4:** Courtesy National Archives, photo no. (NWDNS-111B-4975); **P. 274, Image 5:** Andre Jenny/Digital Railroad Marketplace; **Figure 9-1:** Eddie Adams/AP Wide World Photos; **Figure 9-2:** © Bettmann/CORBIS; **Figure 9-3:** Jamal A. Wilson/Landov LLC; **Figure 9-4:** Bernie Boston; **Figure 9-5:** (c) CORBIS; **Figure 9-6:** Douglas Kent Hall; **Figure 9-7:** Paula Bronstein/Getty Images; **Figure 9-8:** John Macdougall/AFP/Getty Images; **Figure 9-9:** Roman Genn; **Figure 9-10:** Todd Heisler/The New York Times/Redux Pictures; **Figure 9-11:** (c) Tribune Media Services, Inc. All Rights Reserved. Reprinted with permission; **Figure 9-16a:** WinMcNamee/Corbis/Reuters America LLC; **Figure 9-16b:** David Scull; **Figure 9-17:** Peter K. Rearden; **Page 300:** Goran Tomasevic/Corbis/Reuters America LLC; **Page 301 (top):** Yannis Kontos/Polaris Images; **Page 301 (bottom):** Shawn Thew/CORBIS-NY; **Page 302, Image 3:** Spencer Platt/Getty Images, Inc; **Page 302, Image 4:** Tom Stoddart/Getty Images; **Page 303, Image 5:** John W. McDonough/Sports Illustrated/Getty Images; **Page 303, Image 6:** Sam Abell/Getty–National Geographic Society; **Page 304:** Sistine Chapel, Vatican/Canali Photobank Milan/Superstock; **Page 305, Image 2:** Michael Langenstein, " Play Ball" 1982, Collection of Mr. and Mrs. Samuel A. Ramirez/Photographer Robert Rubic.; **Page 305, Image 3:** Yariv Katz-Yedioth Aharonot/Getty Images, Inc.– Agence France Presse; **Page 305, Image 4:** Mike Wells/Aspect Picture Library; **Page 309 (top):** Used with permission from Elisabeth Elsberg; **Page 309 (bottom):** Karen Hernandez; **Page 311:** Debbie Brian; **Page 327, Image 1:** Chuck Carlton/Photolibrary.com; **Page 327, Image 2:** Douglas Pulsipher/Acclaim Images; **Page 327, Image 3:** Sam Ward/USA Today; **Page 344:** From Life in the 60's. ed. Doris C. O'Niel. New York : Little Brown & Co. 1989. P. 3. (c) 1989 by the Time Inc. Magazine Company; **Figure 12-1:** Pearson Education/PH College; **Page 401:** Berton Chang for Wired, May 2007; **Page 449:** Carlos Osorio/AP Wide World Photos; **Page 451:** Reed Saxon/AP Wide World Photos; **Page 469:** Shutterstock; **Pages 500–508:** From MAUS II: A SURVIVOR'S TALE/AND HERE MY TROUBLE BEGAN by Art Spiegelman. Used by permission of Pantheon Books, a division of Random House Inc. **Page 531:** Megan Kelso; **Page 533:** Chris Mueller/Redux Pictures; **Page 538:** Edwina White/Kate Larkworthy Artist Representation; **Page 540:** Universal Pictures/ Photofest, ©Sony Pictures Photographer: Bill Kaye/Photofest, Picture Desk, Inc./Kobal Collection, Universal/Wing Nut Films/Picture Desk, Inc./Kobal Collection, Paramount/Picture Desk, Inc./Kobal Collection; **Page 541:** Edgardo Contreras/Getty Images; **Page 545:** Laub Gillian; **Page 562:** *Wikipedia*, The Free Encyclopedia; **Page 563:** Getty Images; **Page 564:** Tribune Media Services TMS Reprints; **Page 568:** Pearson Education/PH College; **Page 571 (clockwise from bottom):** The Granger Collection, New York, (c) Gareth Brown/CORBIS All Rights Reserved, Aaron Goodman Studios Inc.; **Page 584:** Balint Zsako; **Page 595:** Andrew Nelson, The Christian Science Monitor /Philomath Films; **Page 598:** Alex Garcia/The Chicago Tribune; **Page 600:** Scala/Art Resource, NY. Museo del Prado, Madrid, Spain; **Page 601:** Richard Carson/Reuters Limited; **Page 603:** AP Wide World Photos; **Page 625 (top):** Everett Collection; **Page 625 (bottom):** Carol Rosegg/Lauren Beyea/Shakespeare Theatre Company; **Page 628:** AP Wide World Photos; **Page 642:** A. Ramey/PhotoEdit Inc.; **Page 660:** Chang W. Lee/The New York Times/ Redux Pictures; **Page 661:** Photo by Vivian Stockman/ www.ohvec.org <http://www.ohvec.org>. Flyover courtesy SouthWings.org; **Page 665 (top):** Cagan H. Sekercioglu, Ph.D.; **Page 665 (bottom):** Rhett A. Butler; **Page 666 (top):** Rhett A. Butler; **Page 666 (bottom):** Rhett A. Butler; **Page 667:** Edward Parker/Alamy Images; **Page 674:** "Home, Sweet Hybrid Home." Courtesy of BASF; **Page 683:** LM Otero/AP Wide World Photos; **Page 691:** Grant Wood, American 1891–1942, *American Gothic*, 1930. Oil on beaver board. 30 11/16 "× 25 11/16" (78 × 65.3 cm). Unframed. Friends of American Art Collection. 1930.934. The Art Institute of Chicago. Photography (c) The Art Institute of Chicago. All Rights reserved by the Estate of Nan Wood Graham/Licensed by VAGA, New York, NY; **Page 692:** J. Michael Short; **Page 699:** Disney/ABC Television Group; **Page 701:** The Granger Collection; **Page 712 (top):** Henryk T. Kaiser/Stock Connection; **Page 712 (bottom left):** Susan Walsh/AP Wide World Photos; **Page 712 (bottom right):** (c) Alan Schein Photography, Inc/CORBIS; **Page 721:** Samir Mizban/AP Wide World Photos; **Page 723:** Khalid Mohammed/AP Wide World Photos; **Page 724:** Official Photograph, U.S. Army Air Corps; **Page 730:** Faleh Kheiber/Reuters Limited; **Page 734:** National Geographic Image Collection; **Page 741:** Andrea Dezso.

Index

TOPIC

AUTHOR-TITLE